WE ARE, WE CAN, WE WILL:

THE 1992 WORLD CHAMPION TORONTO BLUE JAYS

EDITED BY ADRIAN FUNG AND BILL NOWLIN
ASSOCIATE EDITORS LEN LEVIN AND CARL RIECHERS
FOREWORD BY DAVE WINFIELD
INTRODUCTION BY BUCK MARTINEZ

Society for American Baseball Research, Inc.
Phoenix, AZ

We Are, We Can, We Will: The 1992 World Champion Toronto Blue Jays
Edited by Adrian Fung and Bill Nowlin
Associate editors Len Levin and Carl Riechers
Foreword by Dave Winfield
Introduction by Buck Martinez

Copyright © 2022 Society for American Baseball Research, Inc.
All rights reserved. Reproduction in whole or in part without permission is prohibited.
ISBN 978-1-970159-83-7 ebook
ISBN 978-1-970159-84-4 paperback
Library of Congress Control Number: 2022913074
Design: Rachael Sullivan
All photographs throughout the book courtesy of the Toronto Blue Jays unless otherwise noted. Special thanks to Rod Hiemstra and Simon Wells.
Front cover photograph: Toronto Blue Jays Joe Carter, arm raised, is mobbed by teammates after recording the final out in the World Series in Atlanta, October 24, 1992. The Blue Jays beat the Braves 4-3 to win the series. (AP Images/Rusty Kennedy)

Copyright © 2022 Society for American Baseball Research, Inc.
All rights reserved. Reproduction in whole or in part without permission is prohibited.
Cronkite School at ASU
555 N. Central Ave. #416
Phoenix, AZ 85004
Phone: (602) 496-1460
Web: www.sabr.org
Facebook: Society for American Baseball Research
Twitter: @SABR

CONTENTS

BALLPARK

GENERAL MANAGER

MANAGER

COACHING STAFF

THE BROADCASTERS

POSTLUDE

SELECTED GAMES

INTRODUCTION

By Buck Martinez

When I was designated for assignment in Anaheim on April 30, 1981, I thought I was headed to the New York Yankees. I was the fourth-string catcher on the Milwaukee Brewers and hadn't even played in a game that season. I didn't catch an inning nor hit any baseballs outside of batting practice.

Ted Simmons, Charlie Moore, Ned Yost, and Buck Martinez. That was our catching lineup for the 1981 Milwaukee Brewers. Manager Buck Rodgers called me into the office, told me I was DFA'd and that was that. I made a quick call to the team hotel to tell my wife Arlene "stay put, I'm coming home." We had sold our house in Kansas City in the offseason planning to relocate after the season. Well, that wasn't such a good idea! Now, since we were in California, the next stop was my parents' house in Sacramento. There, we would wait the 10-day DFA period and see what was next!

In an attempt to stay in shape, I went out running. When I came home, my wife had a bottle of champagne sitting on the table with a blue bow around it. "We are going to Toronto!" Really, not the Yankees? Well, at least we were going somewhere.

The night I arrived in Toronto at Pearson International Airport, it was early May on a cold and rainy night. Rick Amos from the front office picked me up and drove me to the "Ex" (the Blue Jays' home ballpark, Exhibition Stadium). There I met Pat Gillick, the general manager, who told me I was there to help the young pitchers get better. I thought I would finish out the season with the Jays and head off into the sunset! After all, I had come from Kansas City through Milwaukee and Toronto wasn't exactly the way I saw my career ending. Little did I know this would be the best move of my career. Here we are, beginning the 2022 season and I am still here in Toronto with the Jays. What a great ride it has been.

The 1981 season, of course, was interrupted by the strike for 50 days. I was heavily involved in the Players Association so once the strike hit, I was off traveling around to meetings in New York City and beyond. My wife Arlene and son Casey were "stuck" in Toronto without a car. Normally, the team annually arranges Hondas for all the players but once the work stoppage hit, the cars were gone!

After the strike, as we were getting ready to resume the season, I remember team president Peter Bavasi meeting with the players in the outfield at Exhibition Stadium with a pep talk about how the season was now spilt into two halves and "we could make the playoffs." We players knew we weren't very good and wondered if he was talking about us.

Well of course we didn't win the second half nor get to the playoffs, but that offseason Bobby Cox was brought in to manage the Jays going forward. My first spring training with the Jays I was amazed how many good young players were in camp. Tony Fernandez, Damaso Garcia, Alfredo Griffin, Dave Stieb, Jim Clancy, Luis Leal, Jim Gott, Jesse Barfield, George Bell, and Lloyd Moseby. The organization was loaded. We had a great manager, some of the best coaches I have ever worked with, a team of scouts that stood above the rest and a GM that had a vision for long lasting success, Pat Gillick. This reminded me so much of my early years with the Royals. George Brett, Frank White, Hal McRae, Steve Busby, Paul Splittorff. This Jays team was going to win, win soon, and win for a long time! Well, they won the AL East Division for the first time in 1985 setting a franchise record that stands today, 99 wins, in a division that had the reigning world champion Tigers, up and coming Brewers, the Yankees, the Red Sox, and the Cleveland then-"Indians."

I broke my leg in 1985 so I was out for the best part of the season but it was fun watching the guys bring home the division title to Canada. The 1985 season began a run of success that would set the tone for the organization for the next several years. Bobby Cox left to be the GM of the Braves, and 1986 was a disappointment, 1987 was a collapse losing the final seven games of the year going from up 3 1/2 games to losing by two to the Tigers again. But the bar had been raised with the 1985 division championship so anything less than the playoffs going forward was unacceptable.

WE ARE, WE CAN, WE WILL

In 1989, John Olerud was drafted in June, signed in August, joined the team in September, and never played a day in the minors. He would become a big part of the 1992 team and win a batting title in 1993.

The team in 1992 reflected Pat Gillick's GM style. Pat didn't have one method of building a team. He was open to anything. He had been talked out of signing Bo Jackson by his baseball staff and never forgot that. He was sure about Olerud when he was in college at Washington State. Gillick sent one of his trusted scouts, Moose Johnson, to watch Olerud in a tournament in Hawaii. Johnson followed Olerud everywhere. They ate breakfast together, talked family, baseball, and life. Johnson was one of the best. Watching the games, the scout counted all of Olerud's swings. Fifty-four total, no misses. Olerud swung at 54 pitches and never missed. Johnson was sold. Gillick knew then he would take him in the draft and put him right in the big leagues.

The Jays in 1992 were a mixture of youth, veterans, stars, and role players. Guys on the way up and guys near the end. It was the perfect mix. Pat Borders, the catcher, was a sixth-round third baseman who was ticketed to be released in the minors, when he suggested he try catching. At one point, he was farmed out to another organization because he wasn't on the radar with the Jays. He became the MVP of the World Series in 1992.

Joe Carter and Robbie Alomar were acquired from San Diego for two of the most popular Jays, Fred McGriff and Tony Fernandez. Everyone thought Gillick had lost his mind. Alomar became a Hall of Famer and Carter a World Series hero.

Jack Morris pitched one of the best games in World Series history: Game Seven, 1991. Morris and the Twins against John Smoltz and the Braves. A 10-inning, seven-hit shutout in a 1-0 win. He could have signed anywhere as a free agent and named his price. He chose the Blue Jays because, "I wanted to play with the guys I couldn't beat." Pat Hentgen told me, much later, the impact the Morris signing had on the team. "When Morris walked into the clubhouse the first time, we knew we had our swagger." Morris won 21 games.

Dave Winfield signed as a free agent and quickly became the hammer that drove the nails. Big hits in big situations, none bigger than the game-winning double in the top of the 11th in Atlanta to wrap up the championship. David Cone, the star pitcher from the Mets, was acquired near the end of August to fortify the rotation. The first night he was on the bench, the Brewers pounded the Jays 22-2 in front of 50,408. He must have thought "what have I gotten myself into?" The next day, the Brew Crew touched him up for seven runs in 6 2/3 innings but he delivered a 4-2 record in September, beat Oakland in Game Two of the ALCS, and started the clinching Game Six in Atlanta. Another subtle move by Gillick.

When you take a look back at the 1992 champs, you get a tremendous appreciation for how free-wheeling "Trader Pat" was. His catcher Borders was nearly released in the minors but worked hard and ended up the MVP of the Series. John Olerud was 23 and would become a batting champ at first base. Alomar, in his second of five years with the Jays was just beginning to write his Hall of Fame speech. Shortstop Manny Lee was a Rule 5 player who joined the team in 1985 at 19. Kelly Gruber at third base was the best pure athlete to wear the Jays' uniform. Ed Sprague was a role player who hit a first-pitch ninth-inning home run off Braves closer Jeff Reardon in Game Two to turn a 4-3 loss into a 5-4 win. Mike Timlin who had one save during the regular season retired the only batter he faced in the bottom of the 11th of Game Six, Otis Nixon, to clinch the victory when he flipped the ball to Joe Carter at first.

Cito Gaston was the manager of this wonderful team. He was the perfect man to guide this eclectic group of ballplayers. He had a good career as a player and knew if you let the good players play, things would take care of themselves. Cito was a San Diego Padre when Winfield made his big-league debut in 1973. Cito got the best out of Devon White by putting him in the leadoff spot. "Just be yourself." It worked magic. He handled the bullpen well and Tom Henke delivered. Cito wasn't afraid to use any of his players and they all had their fingerprints on the trophy.

This was a great roster that featured three Hall of Famers, multiple all-stars, and Gold Glove winners. A Hall of Fame GM. A future batting champ and a future Cy Young Award winner. This book will tell you more about the people, the players and the staff that rocked the baseball world by winning the World Series for Canada.

I had a front row seat for the entire ride. I know this book will give you an inside look at what a special season 1992 was. Enjoy.

— May 2022

FOREWORD

By Dave Winfield

I have my own inside perspective of the historic 1992 Blue Jays season: the players, their individual contributions, the highs and lows, injuries and health, personal interactions with other players, and the eventual outcome.

For me, the year started with unprecedented optimism. I departed the California Angels for the Blue Jays, who'd been on the cusp of winning for a few years. Just as important, I was called to a team with a manager who I'd known for almost 20 years from my days in San Diego. As hard as I played for nearly two decades and three other teams, I hadn't reached the mountaintop … This, I felt, was my chance. It could be fun, energizing, and the biggest baseball opportunity I'd had in a decade.

My arrival was met with enthusiasm by the team, management, and media. However, it was second perhaps to the arrival of Jack Morris from Minnesota, who'd come off some legendary pitching over his career and more recently in World Series play.

To me, other than the 162-game regular season, three dominant elements emerged from this first World Championship. For the Toronto Blue Jays and the entire country of Canada, this dream came true because of a confluence of elements: veteran leadership, team chemistry, and the insatiable urge and contributions by the populace and fans to finally get that first World Championship. After coming so close for years, the fan support extended far beyond the city limits and the province of Ontario. It was an entire country that we played for, became connected with, and were supported by.

We opened the season with a bang, winning from start to finish. We were girded by both visible and tangible layers of experience and confidence. Notable contributions came from rookies, journeymen, veterans, and a few future Hall of Famers. The mission to go all the way was palpable from the start.

From day one, I was in the lineup as the DH. Cito Gaston allowed me to play almost every day. I ended up playing 156 games at age 40, with 26 of those in the outfield. I felt very comfortable and involved with the mix, as we contemplated readiness for postseason play. Those additional starts in the outfield proved beneficial because it helped me with production and my relationship with all of the players; being able to exert and demonstrate leadership not only on offense, but defense as well.

That year was the most fun I ever had as a player. The team camaraderie, the sold-out stadium every game, rain or shine, dome open or closed. The 4,000,000 plus fans in 1992 set an all-time record for attendance by a major-league club at the time.

"Winfield Wants Noise" became the motto as we entered postseason play, developed after an interview I'd given. I pointed out that to get a home-field advantage, our fans would have to make noise to make it happen and do it not only after action was initiated or achievement attained. The public and media jumped on that, and we immediately, arguably, became the loudest home field in the playoffs and World Series. We saw placards with "Winfield for Prime Minister" as a result, dotting the outfield seats. Man, I got a kick out of that. What an environment! What fans! What a culture and what a city! World class in all the aforementioned areas.

Being born on October 3, 1951, when the Shot Heard 'Round the World was hit ("The Giants win the Pennant … The Giants win the Pennant,") or having the name "Win-Field," hadn't taken me across the finish line yet.

It took 19 years of play for me to get to that mountaintop. I played with all kinds of combinations of players and managers. I ended up playing for six teams, in both leagues, on both coasts and in both countries. There were a number of years we hoped we could win it all, but we didn't.

In conclusion, Toronto brought me the highest honor of my professional career at the time, a World Championship. I had achieved individual goals to that point, but that team win stands above all of those. My ring is proof that hard work, commitment, and never giving up on one's goals pays off. I completed a trifecta, if you will; I'd now won at every level during my sports career. Not many people can say that.

Upon retirement and selection to the National Baseball Hall of Fame, I have always felt 1992 cinched a complete career for me. That's what Toronto, Canada and the Blue Jays organization mean to me. When I reflect on this prestigious achievement, this was the first ever World Championship outside of hockey for Canadians. It cemented the belief that baseball belongs and thrives north of the border. I kid my family and colleagues, "I don't need a passport to go North."

This one year was a huge part of my 22 years of professional play and a commitment to excellence to being the best player, contributor, and teammate I could be. The 1992 Blue Jays journey was one I'll never forget. That team will go down as winners and champions in the annals of not only Canadian sports history, but for all of major-league baseball.

— January 2022

3 FOR 3 IN '92

By Adrian Fung

The 1992 Toronto Blue Jays' season opened with guarded optimism. Despite the team's winning the first six games of the season for the first time ever, avid fans who had followed the team for most of its recent history knew that enthusiasm and lofty expectations for the Blue Jays in April were often cruelly rebuked by underachievement and disappointment in October.

In 1985 Toronto won a club-record 99 games to win its first American League East Division title. The Blue Jays took a 3-games-to-1 lead in the American League Championship Series only to lose three straight games to Kansas City, dashing their hopes of winning the pennant.

Two years later, the Blue Jays appeared even stronger, winners of 96 games with seven remaining and a 3½-game lead in the division. Yet the unthinkable happened: seven straight losses, including three one-run defeats in Tiger Stadium on the final weekend of the season to hand the East crown to Detroit.

Then, in both 1989 and 1991, Toronto lost in five games in the ALCS to Oakland and Minnesota respectively, leading many to wonder if the Blue Jays could ever come through under the pressure of postseason play.

So it is understandable why fans watched the 1992 season unfold with a degree of trepidation. However, if Blue Jays fans lacked confidence in the team's October prospects, its players were assured that this campaign would finish differently. To remind themselves of their present identity and their attainable future identity, the team developed a simple series of slogans that were printed on T-shirts worn by the players.

On the front: **3 FOR 3 IN '92.**

On the back: **We Are. We Can. We Will.**

We are the East Division champions. We can win the American League pennant. We will win the World Series.

Utility player Pat Tabler and outfielder Joe Carter are credited with creating the team slogans and the Blue Jays affirmed the first part of the trifecta when they clinched their second straight East crown – auspiciously – on the birthday of clubhouse leader Dave Winfield.

It seemed everyone in Toronto and across Canada held their breath as the postseason began with a loss to Oakland but watched with wonderment as Toronto reeled off three straight wins, including the wild and pivotal Game Four victory, which some consider the most significant game in Blue Jays history.

Suddenly, Toronto needed only one more win to secure their first pennant and a berth in the World Series. I can remember the atmosphere of anticipation at 13 years old, living in Waterdown, Ontario, a small town 40 miles west of Toronto, and, like millions across Canada, eagerly hoping that the Blue Jays would not let this opportunity slip away as they had

Toronto Blue Jays players celebrate on the field after the last out of the 1992 World Series.

Catcher Pat Borders holds the 1992 World Series Most Valuable Player trophy.

in the past. I had just started high school that autumn and on the morning of ALCS Game Six, the digital message board in the school cafeteria read, "Three down, Juan to go," a perfect and simple reference to Toronto pitcher Juan Guzman getting the start that afternoon with the chance to clinch. Guzman and his teammates came through, just as the players' T-shirts said they would; Toronto won its first pennant and was off to the World Series.

The excitement of the 1992 fall classic is often overlooked, perhaps due to being overshadowed by the unforgettable 1991 World Series. Yet Toronto and Atlanta played six entertaining games in late October 1992: four one-run contests, three of which were decided in the final inning, with crisp pitching from both sides. Young infielder Ed Sprague hit a game-changing home run early in the Series. Gold Glove center fielder Devon White made a catch for the ages. Mike Timlin lobbed the ball to Carter for the final out in Game Six to give Toronto, and Canada, its first World Series championship.

"*We Are, We Can, We Will: The 1992 World Champion Toronto Blue Jays*" is the first SABR book

about the Blue Jays. Co-editor Bill Nowlin emailed me, ironically, on the night Atlanta played Game Two of the 2021 World Series, wanting to know if I would be interested in helping to produce a SABR book commemorating the 30th anniversary of the 1992 Blue Jays championship season. I ruminated on the idea for a few days and knew this was an opportunity I could not decline.

As described above, I thought back to all the disappointments of seasons prior, and how finally, the 1992 Blue Jays winning the World Series occurred at the perfect time, fulfilling every Toronto baseball fan's dreams and without hyperbole, truly brought Canadians together. In a year when Canadians should have happily celebrated the nation's 125th anniversary, the news instead was filled with dread: high unemployment, economic recession, and endless governmental bickering over constitutional reform. The Blue Jays pushed those headlines – for a time – off the front pages and captured the imagination of the country.

This book exhaustively tells the story of the personnel and significant games from that season. We present biographies of all 40 players who appeared in either a regular-season or postseason game for the

First baseman Joe Carter leaps in celebration after catching the final out in Game Six to give Toronto its first World Series victory.

1992 Blue Jays. Many of them need no introduction, such as Hall of Famers Dave Winfield, Jack Morris, and Roberto Alomar. Meanwhile, some young players on the 1992 roster like Jeff Kent and Derek Bell started their careers as Blue Jays but went on to be more known in other clubs' uniforms. Pat Tabler and Rance Mulliniks retired after the season in storybook fashion – as World Series winners. There are biographies for Cito Gaston, the first Black manager to win the World Series, the coaches, Hall of Fame general manager Pat Gillick, and prominent team broadcasters.

Ten memorable 1992 Blue Jays games are recounted in this book, including the final six victories of the postseason. The game stories trace Toronto's magical season from Opening Day in Detroit – when Winfield drove in Alomar with the first run of the season – to the World Series-clinching night in Atlanta – when Winfield drove in Alomar with the final run of the season. One of the four regular-season game stories captures the spirit of John Fogerty's "a moment in the sun" (from his baseball ballad "Centerfield"), when

Jack Morris, a three-time World Series winner, celebrates with Dave Winfield, a first-time winner after 19 major-league seasons.

the unheralded rookie Doug Linton may have saved Toronto's season with a masterful spot start in August to turn back a division rival from pulling even atop the standings.

The book concludes with a profile of the Blue Jays' home stadium, the SkyDome, sold out night after night in 1992 plus an epilogue on the team's double celebration receptions – at the White House with the president of the United States and in Ottawa with the prime minister of Canada.

It was an honor to work with Bill Nowlin as co-editor, exchanging daily emails to bring the initial idea about the 1992 Blue Jays from concept to book. Thank you to Len Levin and Carl Riechers, associate editors, for their tireless copy-editing and fact-checking work, plus all 53 contributors of biographies and game stories, many from the Hanlan's Point (Toronto) SABR Chapter. Thank you to everyone who worked so hard at research, writing, and revising their respective articles. We would also like to thank the Toronto Blue Jays for providing photographs used throughout this book. Special thanks to Rod Hiemstra and Simon Wells.

Finally, special thanks to Dave Winfield for authoring the book's Foreword, Buck Martinez for his Introduction, and all the players, off-field personnel, and broadcasters who granted time to be interviewed for their biographies.

Champagne-soaked pitcher Duane Ward celebrates with fellow reliever Mike Timlin who saved the final game of the World Series.

THE PLAYERS

ROBERTO ALOMAR

By Chris Jones

The son of a longtime major leaguer and the younger brother of another, Roberto Alomar was immersed in the world of baseball from an early age.

Roberto's father, Sandy Alomar, spent 15 years as a major-league infielder, and Roberto and his brother, also Sandy, spent most summers in major-league locker rooms. It was during these times that the brothers learned the intricacies of the game from the best players in the world – Nolan Ryan taught 4-year-old Roberto how to pitch while Ryan was a teammate of Sandy, Sr.'s on the Angels.[1] Perhaps just as important, they also learned how to handle themselves like major-league ballplayers. The offseason brought with it the Puerto Rican Winter League (in which his father and three of his uncles all starred) and the annual Caribbean World Series.[2] Roberto frequently made the trek to games with his father, sometimes completing his homework in the dugout.[3]

Roberto Alomar was born on February 5, 1968, in Ponce, on Puerto Rico's south coast, to Santos (Sandy) and Maria (Velasquez) Alomar. He had an older brother, Santos Jr. (Sandy), and a sister, Sandia. They grew up in Salinas, 20 miles from Ponce. Roberto's baseball ability and instincts were evident even as a boy. When he was 6 a scout reportedly saw him playing pepper and inquired of his father (presumably tongue in cheek) if he could sign him.[4] By the age of 7, Roberto was selected as an all-star for the Salinas little league, but was declared ineligible when it was discovered that he was too young to play in the league.[5] The time for Roberto to sign his first professional contract came soon enough. When he was 16 he signed with Caguas in the Puerto Rican Winter League, where he was managed by Felipe Alou.[6] Alou later said that Roberto "was the best I had ever seen. He was a natural and definitely had the instincts that you just don't teach."[7]

On February 16, 1985, shortly after he turned 17, Roberto signed with the San Diego Padres – the same club for which his father was a coach and with which Sandy Jr. had signed two years earlier. While other teams (most notably Toronto) had expressed interest in the middle infielder and made higher offers than the

approximately $50,000 Roberto received, Sandy Sr. had given his word to family friend and Padres scout Luis Rosa that Roberto would sign with the Padres.[8]

Unlike many newly signed minor leaguers, Roberto did not have to adjust to living on his own for the first time. He was assigned to the same team, Class-A Charleston in the South Atlantic League, for which his father was a coach and to which Sandy Jr. was also assigned. His mother also made the trip and the family lived together and provided a stable foundation as Roberto's professional career began to flourish.[9] Roberto hit .293 and stole 36 bases for Charleston, and his manager Jim Skaalen recalled that "He was tearing up the league against older college players."[10]

Skaalen moved up along with Roberto the next season to Reno in the Class-A California League.[11] His brother and father, however, did not. Sandy Jr. was ticketed for Double-A Wichita (Texas League) and Sandy Sr. was promoted to coach with the Padres. Roberto later recounted the challenges of his time in Reno: "In the minor leagues everything is different.

I was making $700 a month. I had to pay for rent, utilities, food, clubhouse dues. All I had in the house I rented was a mattress on the floor, not even a table. I had no car and had to walk everywhere."[12]

Skaalen, though, saw him maturing on and off the field: "He seemed more relaxed away from his dad and brother. He got stronger and seemed to be enjoying every day. He was far ahead of the rest of the talent at that level, and I began to see the good, solid major-league player he was going to become."[13] Whatever the challenges off the field, Alomar's play certainly did not suffer. He led the league after 90 games with a .346 average and 123 hits, earning him a promotion to Double-A Wichita (and a reunion with Sandy Jr.).[14] Sharing a one-bedroom apartment with his brother, Roberto continued his torrid pace and finished the season hitting .319 with 12 home runs and 43 stolen bases.[15]

Roberto's minor-league success provided real hope going into the spring of 1988 that he could break camp with the Padres. His performance did nothing to dampen that enthusiasm, as he hit .360 and put together a 10-game hitting streak.[16] Padres manager Larry Bowa noted that "this kid is a finished product. All he has to do is go out there and play. He has all the tools; just turn him loose."[17] The Padres, though, had been burned each of the prior two seasons when they tried to promote second basemen (Bip Roberts and Joey Cora) from Double A to the big leagues, and Bowa was directed to give Roberto the bad news that his season would begin at Triple-A Las Vegas, not San Diego.[18] The 20-year-old Roberto took the news hard, tearfully retreating to the training room, where he was consoled by his father along with several teammates.

For his part, Bowa had no explanation for the sentence he was ordered to deliver: "I told him he did everything I asked," said Bowa. "I just told him to keep his head up, that it's a long season. The chances of Robbie coming to the big leagues in 1988 are pretty good."[19] They were pretty good indeed, as Roberto made quick work of the Pacific Coast League and was leading the league with 14 runs batted in when he was called up to San Diego 2½ weeks into the season.[20]

On April 22, 1988, Roberto stepped into the batter's box as a major leaguer for the first time. On the mound was none other than Nolan Ryan – the same Nolan Ryan who had helped teach him to pitch as a toddler. Unfazed, he beat out an infield single in his first major league at-bat.[21] Roberto finished the season with 145 hits, a .266 batting average, and 24 stolen bases, finishing fifth in the National League Rookie of the Year

voting. He was even stronger the next season, his first full year in the big leagues, batting .295 with 42 stolen bases in 158 games.

Continuing his ascent onto the national radar, Roberto was selected for his first All-Star Game in 1990. What made the honor even more special was that Sandy Jr. (who had been traded to Cleveland), was also selected. The two became the first pair of brothers to be selected for an All-Star Game since Jim and Gaylord Perry in 1970.[22] Sandy Sr. reflected on the accomplishments of his two sons: "People have to realize I'm very proud of my kids for the way they act as persons. And they have talent and know how to display that talent."[23]

While it appeared that Roberto had established himself as a core piece of the Padres' future, the Padres had other ideas. After the 1990 season the Padres and Blue Jays struck a blockbuster deal that sent Alomar and outfielder Joe Carter to Toronto in exchange for Fred McGriff and Gold Glove shortstop Tony Fernandez.[24] Along with Alomar and Carter, Blue Jays general manager Pat Gillick had also added center fielder Devon White days earlier as Toronto worked to position itself in the competitive American League East.[25] Padres' general manager Joe McIlvaine said, "We just felt it was something we wanted to give a shot to. It was kind of a gutsy trade on both ends."[26] Roberto was shocked: "I didn't expect it; I didn't understand it," he later recalled.[27]

Surprised or not, Roberto joined a collection of talented players in Toronto and paid immediate dividends north of the border, putting together an early six-game hitting streak as the Blue Jays streaked to the top of the American League East.[28] In May, however, Roberto once again ran into the task of facing Nolan Ryan – now pitching for the Texas Rangers. With two outs in the top of the ninth, the 44-year-old Ryan was one out away from his seventh no-hitter when Roberto strode to the plate. As the *Fort Worth Star Telegram* put it 25 years later, "[T]he kid he'd once coached stood between Ryan and history."[29] Ryan had the last laugh; he struck out Alomar on a 2-and-2 fastball to end the game.[30]

Later in the season, Roberto was once again elected to the All-Star Game, this time as an American League teammate of Sandy Jr. The long ovation he received from the Toronto crowd served as confirmation of how the city had taken to him: "When I was introduced they gave me such a long, loud ovation, I never expected it," Roberto said.[31]

As the season wore on, Alomar kept hitting and the Blue Jays kept winning, clinching the American League East. In his first postseason, Alomar's .474 batting average could not keep Toronto from being eliminated in five games by the Minnesota Twins. Alomar won his first Gold Glove, and it was clear that the Blue Jays were set to contend in the years to come. The off-season brought with it new riches as well: a three-year, $14 million contract that was the highest at the time on three fronts – for a second baseman, for a player 24 or younger, and for a player with four years or less in the major leagues.[32] The average annual value of $4,666,667 made Alomar the ninth-highest paid player in the game.[33]

Bolstered by the acquisition of Dave Winfield in the offseason and David Cone in August, the Blue Jays again clinched the American League East in 1992. At midseason Alomar returned to San Diego for the first time since being traded and participated in the All-Star Game – once again with Sandy Jr. as a teammate.[34]

Alomar was named the most valuable player in the ALCS, with the most memorable moment being his game-tying two run home run off A's closer Dennis Eckersley in the ninth inning of Game Four. He relished the opportunity to be part of the first Blue Jays team to reach the World Series: "I wasn't here when they didn't win in the past. … I just want to be here in the present when we win the big one, so we won't have to hear anymore about the past.[35] Alomar continued his clutch hitting and superb defense in the World Series, and helped the Blue Jays defeat Atlanta for their first championship. Alomar's contributions led Dave Winfield to comment that "You're one of the best players I've ever seen."[36] Manager Cito Gaston agreed: "I could talk about Robbie for an hour," he said.[37]

After a slow start in 1993, the Blue Jays took off yet again and Alomar had career highs in numerous categories, including 55 stolen bases and 17 home runs. In the ALCS against the Chicago White Sox, he stole four bases as the Blue Jays won, four games to two. In the World Series, against the Philadelphia Phillies, Alomar hit .480 and drove in six runs as the Blue Jays, on Joe Carter's game-winning home run in Game Six, won the World Series for the second year in a row.[38]

With two World Series titles in his back pocket, it was hard to imagine things ever going wrong for Alomar in Toronto. But go wrong they did. After a strike-shortened 1994 season, the Blue Jays began to take a step back in 1995 and look toward the future. This included trading veteran David Cone in July – a

move that Alomar protested by sitting out the next game.[39] Alomar was also removed from a game in early July when a fan, Tricia Miller, walked into the Skydome hotel where he lived and told employees that she planned to kill him.[40] Alomar said, "I wasn't shaken by it. I never knew that person. I never really knew what was happening. Cito told me in the dugout. They took me out of the game, but they had caught her by then, so I don't know why."[41]

By the end of the season, with rumors swirling about his future, Alomar was unhappy with what he felt was unfair treatment by the Toronto front office and local media:

> "I never said that I want to be traded. … They made it sound like I said, 'Trade me now, I want out of here.' And the fans believed what they read in the papers. When I stood out on the field in Toronto and heard them booing me, I knew they didn't understand or know what the truth was. I hadn't said anything like what the writers wrote. But I could do nothing about it, and I learned how the media is."[42]

With no offer from the Blue Jays, Alomar was ready to hit free agency: "If [the Blue Jays] had offered me something before the All-Star break, then maybe I

Alomar was a 12-time All-Star and four-time Silver Slugger.

Alomar won 10 Gold Gloves - the most ever for a second baseman, including all five seasons when he played in Toronto.

would've thought about it and gone for it. Now you're in the last week of the season. … Now maybe it's time for me to try the market."[43]

At 27 years old and already a six-time All-Star, Alomar inked a three-year, $18 million contract with the Baltimore Orioles in December 1995.[44] He was thrilled to team up with fellow All-Star Cal Ripken Jr.: "I never expected to play alongside one of the legends of baseball. … It's going to be like a dream come true for me."[45]

Alomar carried his winter-ball success (he led the league in hitting) over to Baltimore, going on a tear to begin the season, hitting .410 in the beginning part of June.[46] Former teammate Tony Gwynn heaped praise on the player Alomar had become, saying, "He has the ability to hit a home run, or work the count and hit a double down the opposite line and do whatever he wants to do. He's probably the best all-around player in the game."[47] Alomar went on to make his seventh consecutive All-Star Game, collect his sixth consecutive Gold Glove and set numerous career highs as the Orioles clinched the American League wild-card playoff spot.[48]

Perhaps the most memorable moment of the season, however, occurred during a late-September game in Toronto. After being called out on strikes in the top of the first, Alomar argued with home-plate umpire John Hirschbeck on his way back to the dugout. When Hirschbeck threw him out of the game, Alomar returned to the field. During the course of the argument, Alomar took offense to being called a derogatory name, and spit in Hirschbeck's face.[49]

Alomar apologized and donated $50,000 toward research into Lou Gehrig's disease, which Hirschbeck's son had.[50] This did nothing to prevent his being relentlessly booed for the remainder of the season and the playoffs, or from receiving a five-game suspension to be served at the start of the 1997 season.[51]

Alomar delivered a game-tying two-out single in the deciding Game Four of the Division Series against Cleveland, and then hit the game-winning home run in the 12th inning.[52] Brother and Indians catcher Sandy Alomar Jr. said, "He's my brother and with all the things that happened with this incident, I felt kind of sorry for him."[53] Roberto was ready to turn the page on the incident: "I've been going through a tough time. … Human beings make mistakes. I apologized to the umpire, his family, and all of baseball. It's time to move on."[54] The Orioles did move on to the ALCS, but were eliminated in five games by the New York Yankees on their way to the World Series title.

The fact that Alomar was even allowed to play in the playoffs did not sit well with many, including major-league umpires. When it was announced that his suspension would be delayed until the next season, the umpires voted to not work the playoffs unless the suspension was changed to apply to the first round.[55] The boycott was abandoned, however, when an agreement was worked out in a Philadelphia federal court.[56]

After he served his five-game suspension to start the 1997 season, Alomar helped the Orioles to 98 wins and the American League East crown. He also took the first step toward putting the spitting incident behind him, publicly shaking hands with Hirschbeck near first base in April before the first Orioles game Hirschbeck called since the incident.[57] Several nagging injuries pestered Alomar throughout the season, including a nagging groin injury in late July that made him miss close to a month of playing time. Alomar said the injury "made me grow up. I now knew what it was like to be hurt and what you had to do to come back."[58] After defeating the Mariners in the Division Series, the Orioles came up short of the World Series yet again, this time losing to Sandy and the Cleveland Indians in six games.

The Orioles were nowhere near contention in 1998. The season was not without its highlights though, as Roberto collected three hits (one of them a home run) and the All-Star Game MVP award in Denver, making the Alomar brothers back-to-back winners of the award since Sandy had won the year before. As his three-year contract with the Orioles came to a close, Roberto once again found himself on the free-agent market.

It did not take long for Roberto to find a new home. He signed a four-year contract with the Indians, reuniting with Sandy.[59] "It means a lot to be beside my brother, not only to me but to my family," Roberto said.[60] Indians general manager John Hart stated the obvious: "We are elated to have the Alomar brothers in the Indians family."[61] In addition to Sandy, the move to Cleveland also allowed Roberto to team with shortstop Omar Vizquel, who along with Roberto had also won six Gold Gloves. "It would be worth the price of a ticket just to watch Omar and Robbie turn a double play," said Hart.[62]

Free from the injuries that plagued him in 1998, Alomar made an immediate impact on the Indians. "Robbie is one of the few players in the game that can make everybody around him better," Indians manager Mike Hargrove said.[63] The Indians had compiled an enviable offense that exploded out of the gates,

and Alomar ended the year with what proved to be a career high 24 home runs. He finished third in the MVP voting (the highest he would ever finish). His hot hitting continued in the playoffs; he went 5-for-8 while the Indians surged to a 2-0 series lead over the Red Sox in the ALDS.[64] The Tribe would not win again, however, and fell in five games.[65]

Although things did not turn out as hoped in October, a late-season meeting helped Alomar to finally turn the page on the spitting incident, which had continued to follow him through the jeers of fans around the country. On September 5, during a rain delay at Camden Yards, John Hirschbeck and family came knocking on the visitor's clubhouse door, asking for Roberto. Hirschbeck's 13-year-old son was a fan, and wanted to meet Roberto. The moment together allowed both families to heal. "I don't see why he should be booed," Hirschbeck said afterward. "If he and I can forgive and forget, why not everyone else?"[66]

The next two seasons also ended in disappointment for the Indians. In 2000 they missed the playoffs altogether despite winning 90 games. They charged back to the playoffs in 2001, but fell in five games in the ALDS to the Seattle Mariners. Alomar won Gold Gloves and was an All-Star in both seasons, and stole a combined 69 bases. He still looked to be in his prime with one year left on his contract. But another change of scenery was in store.

On December 11, 2001, the Indians traded Alomar, pitcher Mike Bacsik, and first baseman Danny Peoples to the New York Mets in exchange for outfielders Matt Lawton and Alex Escobar, relief pitcher Jerrod Riggan, and two players to be named later.[67] While the move was designed to clear payroll and acquire younger talent, Indians general manager Mark Shapiro knew that the deal would not sit well with all fans. "I think I'll need a flak jacket when I get off the plane [from the winter meetings], probably," he said.[68] Alomar said he was "kind of disappointed … I was real happy in Cleveland and thought I did a great job."[69] Mets General Manager Steve Phillips was elated: "We sit up in that room and all we do is dream all day about different scenarios," he said, adding that "I have to admit that I thought this was a long shot."[70]

But what had seemed like a dream scenario for Phillips at the Winter Meetings would soon turn into a nightmare. The Mets came nowhere near meeting expectations, finishing in last place in the National League East, 26½ games out of first place. Alomar also began to show the first sign of decline, hitting .266 and snapping his 12-year streak of appearances in the

All-Star Game. The 2003 season began much the same way, with Alomar hitting .262 on July 1 when the Mets shipped him to the White Sox for three prospects.[71]

All told, Alomar played only 222 games for the Mets, and for his part understood that he did not perform at the high level that the Mets, and he himself, had expected. "Sometimes, you put too much pressure on yourself in New York, and maybe I did that," he said.[72] Along with providing a change of scenery, joining the White Sox allowed him to reunite again with Sandy.[73] But Roberto hit only .253 down the stretch and the White Sox finished in second place in the American League Central, missing the playoffs.

A free agent once again, Alomar signed a one-year deal in the offseason with the Arizona Diamondbacks in the hopes of rejuvenating his career. "If I can get in good shape, I think I can play the way I used to play," he said.[74] Despite missing 56 games with a broken right hand suffered when he was hit by a pitch in late April, he did indeed experience a resurgence of sorts in his limited time on the field with Arizona, carrying a .309 batting average into early August.[75] With the Diamondbacks hopelessly out of contention, Alomar was once again an attractive commodity for teams looking to add a veteran presence for the stretch run. So it was that the White Sox acquired him for the second consecutive season. Alomar struggled mightily in sporadic action, though, batting only .180 in 65 plate appearances as the White Sox once again missed the playoffs.

After multiple seasons of declining performance, Alomar made one last run at extending his career, this time with Tampa Bay, signing a one-year, $600,000 contract in January.[76] When he committed multiple errors in one inning of a spring training game, however, he decided it was time to walk away. "I played a lot of games and I said I would never embarrass myself on the field," he said, adding, "I had a long career, but I can't play at the level I want to play, so it's time to retire. I just can't go anymore. My back, legs and eyes aren't the same."[77] Alomar concluded his 17-year career with a .300 batting average, 2,724 hits, 210 home runs, and 474 stolen bases to go along with 12 All-Star Game selections and 10 Gold Glove awards.

There was no question that Cooperstown would be the final stop of Alomar's career. With some Hall voters still holding the Hirschbeck incident against him, though, he came up eight votes short of admission in his first year of eligibility, in 2010. "I feel disappointed, but next year hopefully I make it in," he said, adding that "at least I was close."[78] Some sportswriters were not as gracious in their assessment of the snub. The *Chicago Tribune's* Phil Rogers wrote, "If anybody didn't vote for Robbie because of the spitting incident, then shame on them."[79]

Whatever the concerns some Hall voters had in Alomar's first year of eligibility, resistance to his election was all but nonexistent the next year. He was named on 90 percent of the ballots, far over the 75 percent needed for induction into the Hall of Fame.[80] Even Alomar was surprised by the drastic increase in support from the previous year. "I didn't expect to get that many votes," he said.[81]

Alomar, who went into the Hall wearing a Blue Jays cap, opened his induction speech in Spanish and spoke fondly of his father's and brother's impact on his life and career.[82] Sandy Jr. recounted the brothers' year-long wager as teammates/roommates for Class-A Charleston: "We said whoever had the best game, would get the bed. I slept on the couch the whole year."[83] He added, "We didn't win a championship together but we won this together. And this is a big one. In my heart, you are a Hall of Famer."[84]

Statistics aside, it is the way Alomar's former teammates describe him that truly tells the story of the player that he was. Toronto teammate Pat Hentgen, asked how he described Alomar to present-day players, said, "I tell them Robbie was a career .300 hitter, a clutch hitter, a guy who could hit for power, a great baserunner and basestealer … and (pause) his best asset of all was his glove."[85] The Orioles' B.J. Surhoff perhaps best summed up Alomar's baseball career: "Robbie could beat you with the bunt, with the extra base, with the homer. He could beat you with a stolen base. He could beat you by going from first to third, a baserunning move. He could beat you by making plays in the field. Robbie's a baseball player. And a damn good one at that."[86]

Alomar continued to be involved in baseball after his retirement. In January of 2016, he and his wife, Kim, launched Foundation 12, a Canadian charitable organization serving youth baseball players, though the organization does not appear to be currently active as of 2022. In 2021, Alomar was placed on the ineligible list by Major League Baseball following an investigation into a 2014 sexual assault allegation.[87] Alomar stated that he was "disappointed, surprised, and upset" with the decision, and that he would "continue to spend my time helping kids pursue their baseball dreams."[88]

NOTES

1   "25 Years Later, Nolan Ryan Remembers His Seventh No-Hitter," *Fort Worth Star-Telegram*, April 30, 2016, star-telegram. com/sports/mlb/texas-rangers/article74925477.html.

2   Norman L. Macht, *Roberto Alomar* (Childs, Maryland: Mitchell Lane Publishers, Inc., 1999), 9-11.

3   Macht, 3.

4   Macht, 10.

5   "Like Father Like Son?: Padres Think Roberto Alomar Is a Bit More Than a Chip Off the Old Block," *Los Angeles Times*, April 22, 1988, articles.latimes.com/1988-04-22/sports/sp-2096_1_roberto-alomar.

6   Macht, 15.

7   Macht, 15.

8   Macht, 16.

9   Macht, 16.

10 Macht, 17.

11 Macht, 18.

12 Macht, 18.

13 Macht, 19.

14 Macht, 19

15 Macht, 21.

16 "Padre Notebook: Few Except Feeney Appear Satisfied as Roberto Alomar Is Sent Down," *Los Angeles Times*, March 26, 1988, articles.latimes.com/1988-03-26/sports/sp-354_1_roberto-alomar.

17 Macht, 23.

18 "Padre Notebook."

19 "Padre Notebook."

20 "Like Father Like Son?"

21 Macht, 25-26.

22 "Alomars an All-Star Family: Padres: Roberto Alomar, Along With Teammate Tony Gywnn, Is Named an NL Reserve. Brother Sandy Had Already Been Selected as The Starting AL Catcher for Tuesday's Game," *Los Angeles Times*, July 6, 1990, articles. latimes.com/1990-07-06/sports/sp-113_1_sandy-alomar-jr.

23 "Alomars an All-Star Family."

24 "Blue Jays Land Carter, Alomar From Padres San Diego Gets Fernandez and McGriff in Deal," *Baltimore Sun*, December 5, 1990, articles.baltimoresun. com/1990-12-06/sports/1990340005_1_blue-jays-fred-mcgriff-tony-fernandez.

25 "Blue Jays Land Carter, Alomar From Padres San Diego Gets Fernandez and McGriff in Deal."

26 "Blue Jays Land Carter, Alomar From Padres San Diego Gets Fernandez and McGriff in Deal."

27 Macht, 31.

28 "Padres Winning December Deal Looks Like Tie With Blue Jays in April," *Baltimore Sun*, April 21, 1991, articles.baltimoresun. com/1991-04-21/sports/1991111135_1_blue-jays-roberto-alomar-deal.

29 "25 Years Later."

30 "25 Years Later."

31 Macht, 33.

32 "Cadaret and 8 Others Settle Contract," *New York Times*, February 8, 1992, nytimes.com/1992/02/08/sports/base-ball-cadaret-and-8-others-settle-contracts.html.

33 "Cadaret and 8 Others Settle Contract,"

34 Macht, 35.

35 "Blue Jays Eck Out a 7-6 Victory in 11: AL Game 4: Alomar's Two-Run Homer Off Eckersley Ties It in Ninth as A's Blow 6-1 Lead," *Los Angeles Times*, October 12, 1992, articles. latimes.com/1992-10-12/sports/sp-138_1_blue-jays.

36 Macht, 37.

37 "Alomar's MVP Play Points to New Star," *Baltimore Sun*, October 15, 1992, articles.baltimoresun.com/1992-10-15/ sports/1992289072_1_alomar-blue-jays-toronto.

38 Macht, 42.

39 Macht, 43-44.

40 "Orioles' Multitalented Alomar Is Second to None," *Washington Post*, March 31, 1996, washingtonpost.com/archive/sports/1996/03/31/ orioles-multitalented-alomar-is-second-to-none/b8cd697d-9630-464e-bcd9-84d6ba8db8cf/?utm_term=.9d34bd1c1107.

41 "Orioles' Multitalented Alomar Is Second to None."

42 Macht, 44.

43 "Jays' Alomar in No Rush to Decide '96 Destination He, Molitor Express Interest in Joining Ripken," *Baltimore Sun*, September 27, 1995, articles.baltimoresun.com/1995-09-27/ sports/1995270116_1_alomar-blue-jays-second-baseman.

44 "O's Wave Money Wand Building Winner: Signing Six-Time All-Star Roberto Alomar Adds Exclamation Mark to New General Manager's Swift Revamping of Orioles," *Baltimore Sun*, December 22, 1995, articles. baltimoresun.com/1995-12-22/news/1995356066_1_gillick-orioles-rober-to-alomar. New manager Davey Johnson was informed of the signing in the dentist's chair when he answered a call from General Manager Pat Gillick who said, "Well, you've got yourself an All-Star second base-man." Johnson claimed to not feel any pain for the remainder of the day. "Alomar finds O's 2nd to none Six-time All-Star signs, three-year, $18 million deal," *Baltimore Sun*, December 22, 1995, articles.baltimoresun. com/1995-12-22/sports/1995356093_1_roberto-alomar-cone-orioles.

45 Macht, 47.

46 Macht, 46, 51-52.

47 "Alomar Hitting His Prime at Plate," *Los Angeles Times*, May 28, 1996, articles.latimes.com/1996-05-28/sports/sp-9201_1_alomar-hitting.

48 Macht, 51-52.

49 Macht, 52-53.

50 Macht, 54.

51 Macht, 54.

52 "Alomar Shows Some Spit and Polish," *Los Angeles Times*, October 6, 1996, articles.latimes.com/1996-10-06/sports/sp-51279_1_sandy-alomar.

53 "Alomar Shows Some Spit and Polish."

54 "Alomar Shows Some Spit and Polish."

55 "Umpires Vote to Boycott Over Alomar," *New York Times*, October 1, 1996, nytimes.com/1996/10/01/sports/umpires-vote-to-boycott-over-alomar.html.

56 "Umpires Abandon Boycott," *Los Angeles Times*, October 2, 1996, articles. latimes.com/1996-10-02/sports/sp-49681_1_umpires-working-game.

57 Macht, 57.

58 Macht, 59.

59 Macht, 62.

60   "Cleveland Lures Roberto Alomar," CBS News, November 23, 1998, cbsnews.com/news/cleveland-lures-roberto-alomar/.

61   "Cleveland Lures Roberto Alomar."

62   "Cleveland Lures Roberto Alomar."

63   "Alomar: Villain Turned Hero in Cleveland," *Los Angeles Times*, June 27, 1999, articles.latimes.com/1999/jun/27/sports/sp-50609.

64   "Baines Goes Deep as Indians Move One Game From Sweep," *Baltimore Sun*, October 8, 1999, articles.baltimoresun.com/1999-10-08/sports/9910080129_1_roberto-alomar-baines-cleveland.

65   "Red Sox Ace Out Indians," *Los Angeles Times*, October 12, 1999, articles.latimes.com/1999/oct/12/sports/sp-22770/2.

66   "Score One for Friendship," *Baltimore Sun*, October 27, 1999, articles.baltimoresun.com/1999-10-27/news/9910270108_1_roberto-alomar-john-hirschbeck-holy-water/3.

67   "Indians Trade Alomar to Mets," *Southeast Missourian* (Cape Girardeau, Missouri), December 12, 2001, semissourian.com/story/54375.html.

68   "Indians Trade Alomar to Mets," CBC Sports, December 11, 2001, cbc.ca/sports/baseball/indians-trade-alomar-to-mets-1.257404.

69   "Indians Trade Alomar to Mets," CBC Sports.

70   "Indians trade Alomar to Mets," *Southeast Missourian*, December 12, 2001, www.semissourian.com/story/54375.html.

71   "Mets Trade Roberto Alomar to White Sox," *New York Times*, July 1, 2003, nytimes.com/2003/07/01/sports/baseball/mets-trade-roberto-alomar-to-white-sox.html.

72   "Mets Trade Roberto Alomar to White Sox."

73   Sandy Alomar signed with Chicago prior to the 2003 season.

74   "Alomar Jr. Joins Diamondbacks, CBC Sports, January 7, 2004, cbc.ca/sports/baseball/alomar-jr-joins-diamondbacks-1.516620.

75   "Diamondbacks Trade Alomar to White Sox," *Orlando Sentinel*, August 6, 2004, articles.orlandosentinel.com/2004-08-06/sports/0408060185_1_dominican-republic-clemens-white-sox.

76   "Notebook: Roberto Alomar: "It's Time to Retire," *Seattle Times*, March 20, 2005, seattletimes.com/sports/notebook-roberto-alomar-its-time-to-retire/.

77   "Notebook: Roberto Alomar: "It's Time to Retire."

78   "Hall Passes: Alomar 8 Short," *Baltimore Sun*, January 7, 2010, articles.baltimoresun.com/2010-01-07/sports/1001060140_1_hall-s-veterans-committee-john-hirschbeck-roberto-alomar.

79   "Hall Passes: Alomar 8 Short."

80   "Alomar, Blyleven Elected to Hall of Fame," *Baltimore Sun*, January 5, 2011, articles.baltimoresun.com/2011-01-05/sports/bs-sp-hallo-fame-01-20110105_1_sandy-alomar-sr-pitcher-bert-blyleven-induction.

81   "Alomar, Blyleven Elected to Hall of Fame."

82   "Alomar, Blyleven and Gillick Enter Baseball Hall of Fame," *USA Today*, July 24, 2011, usatoday30.usatoday.com/sports/baseball/hallfame/2011-07-24-hall-of-fame-alomar-blyleven_n.htm.

83   "Alomar, Blyleven and Gillick Enter Baseball Hall of Fame."

84   "Alomar, Blyleven and Gillick Enter Baseball Hall of Fame."

85   "Robbie Was Best of the Best," *Toronto Sun*, July 16, 2011, torontosun.com/2011/07/16/robbie-was-best-of-the-best.

86   "Alomar Falls Just Short in First Bid for Hall of Fame," *Baltimore Sun*, January 7, 2010, articles.baltimoresun.com/2010-01-07/sports/bal-sp.alomar07jan07_1_roberto-alomar-greatest-second-basemen-ballot/2.

87   Keegan Matheson, "MLB Puts Roberto Alomar on Ineligible List," MLB.com, April 30, 2021. https://www.mlb.com/news/mlb-puts-roberto-alomar-on-ineligible-list

88   "MLB puts Roberto Alomar on Ineligible List."

DEREK BELL

By Joseph Thompson

It doesn't take long to make a lasting impression that sticks with someone throughout his professional baseball career. Some of the things Derek Bell said over the course of his career surprised many and outraged others. This did not seem to faze Bell in the slightest. "What can I say?" Bell would ask. "I just have to go out there and be Derek, and Derek's a pretty easygoing guy. I'm not going to let anybody intimidate me."[1] Bell's childhood hero Dwight Gooden perhaps understood Derek the most. "Derek wants to be liked by everybody. He's an easygoing guy, easy to get along with, but he's very sensitive. He needs to know the team is behind him all the way. He's one of those guys that needs to hear it constantly, especially when he's struggling."[2]

Derek Nathaniel Bell was born in Tampa, Florida, on December 11, 1968. He grew up with his mother, Chestine Bell, in Tampa and never really knew much about his biological father, Jimmie Lee Jackson. His father met Chestine while she was a freshman at Bethune-Cookman College in Daytona Beach, Florida. Jimmie had been a quarterback in high school and Derek's mother once said that she had caught a pass from him. "Derek was that pass," she said.[3] She moved back to Tampa after her freshman year to live with her parents.

On April 24, 1976, Jackson was found dead in his Manhattan apartment with two gunshot wounds to the head. Chestine found out about Jimmie's death seven months after his funeral when she contacted the family to inquire why Jimmie had not sent toys for Derek's Christmas. She kept the news of Jimmie's death from Derek until he was 14, when Jimmie's sister, Lillie Golden, told him what happened. "He was in college so I didn't get a chance to see him," Bell said. "Being that young, I know I had (a father) and I knew he was in college. Then they said 'No, he passed away' and then I was without a dad."[4] Bell never looked for anyone to take the place of the father he never really knew. "My mom's my mom and my dad; she's two people in one."[5] It would be his mother, who worked as a medical records technician, as much as anyone,

who gave Bell the support he needed once he started playing baseball.

Bell's interest in baseball started in a section of Tampa that produced over 35 African American major leaguers. The Belmont Heights Little League was where Chestine wanted Derek to play. Chestine used her mother's address in the College Hill Projects to make sure that Derek qualified to play in the league. "We never lived in Belmont Heights," Chestine said in response to reports that Bell had lived there, "but his grandmother did, and she was my sole babysitter."[6] Bell joined the league when he was 9. It was there that he met his best friend, Gary Sheffield. Bell grew to a height of 5-feet-9 over the next three years and into what the boys in the league called a monster "because that is what boys call boys who look like grownups."

Bell's coach had to carry his birth certificate around to prove that he was a kid.[7]

Sixty-four boys who have played in the Little League World Series have gone on to play in the major leagues. Bell is one of 14 to play in both the Little League World Series and the major-league World Series.[8] Bell and Sheffield were teammates on the 1980 Little League World Series team that lost to Taiwan's Hualien County in the championship game, 4-3. A year later, Bell became the first two-time Little League World Series player who would become a major leaguer when he played on the 1981 Little League World Series team from Tampa. Bell struck out nine in five innings, but his Tampa team lost 4-2 to Taichung, Taiwan.[9] Bell commented after being drafted by the Blue Jays in 1987 how important his time in Little League was in making him good enough to be a professional player. "My time playing for Belmont Heights was very important," said Bell. "That's where I started when I was 9, and if it wasn't for them, I wouldn't be where I'm at now."[10]

A few years after Bell's Little League career ended, University of Miami baseball coach Ron Fraser showed up at baseball tryouts at C. Leon King High School in Tampa to watch Bell take batting practice. Bell took two swings and then Fraser introduced himself to Bell, and told Bell's coach, Jim Macaluso, that he would give four guys off his roster for this one guy. Macaluso later said that Fraser told him "[h]e had only seen one other high school player with a better swing and that was Dave Winfield. He told me back then that this kid would make the big leagues."[11] Bell played center field his senior season at King, and he led the team in hitting with a .440 average and set a school record with 30 RBIs.[12]

The June 1987 amateur draft started with the Seattle Mariners picking Ken Griffey Jr. In the second round the Toronto Blue Jays selected Bell, by now a 6-foot-2, 190-pound senior center fielder at King High School. Bell signed a contract and was assigned to St. Catharines of the short-season Class-A New York-Penn League. "It feels great," said Bell. "I just want to play baseball, be successful, and get to pro ball."[13] He batted .264 for St. Catharines with 10 home runs and 42 RBIs his first season. Bobby Mattick, coordinator of Blue Jays minor-league development, when asked about Bell's progress as a hitter after his first season in the minors said, "He was hitting .240 for a while there, but (manager Joe) Lonett was saying it was the hardest .240 he's ever seen. This kid's right out of high school and he was hitting breaking balls in that

league – the better of the two rookie leagues we're in. It's really something. The boy's got a chance to be an outstanding hitter."[14] *Baseball America* ranked Bell the seventh-best major-league prospect in the league.[15] Bell continued to impress over the next few years, winning the Most Valuable Player Award in 1988 while playing for Myrtle Beach of the South Atlantic League, and the International League MVP Award in 1991 while with the Syracuse Chiefs. He was named the *Baseball America* Minor League Player of the Year in 1991, when he hit .346 in 119 games for the Chiefs.[16] (He also played in 18 games in two short stints with the Blue Jays and batted .143.)

During his first trip to the majors (June 28 to July 14), Bell went 1-for-17, a .059 average, reflecting that he was used only sparingly and that most of his at-bats were against Randy Johnson and David West. To Bell, he was not given a fair chance to prove himself. When the Blue Jays sent him back to the minors, Bell did not mince words when he told the press that he was not happy about being sent down. "I was shocked and upset when Cito Gaston called me into his office to tell me I was going down again," he said. "I didn't think I'd be sent down anymore. I thought it was too soon to give up on me. They've given a lot of other guys a lot more chance to prove themselves."[17] During his second call-up, at the end of the season, Bell went 3-for-11 with no extra-base hits. His first season in the majors was one from which Bell wanted to move on.

Bell arrived at Blue Jays spring training in Dunedin, Florida, in 1992 and made quite the impression. He sported a clean-shaven head and spent time talking trash with his teammates. He gave the impression, by one reporter's account, of being "the most merry fellow at the Toronto Blue Jay camp."[18] The reporter, Rosie DiManno of the *Toronto Star,* went on to say that Bell did not act like some rookies who come to camp "all shy and reticent, minding their manners and keeping their distance. Bell is in your face, in everyone's face, and yapping up a garrulous storm."[19]

Bell won the left field job out of spring training in '92 but his first season in the majors almost ended as soon as it began. In the second inning of the second game of the season, Bell fractured his hamate bone when he fouled off a pitch from Tigers starter Frank Tanana. He returned to the club from the disabled list on May 9 where he started in left field and went 1-for-4 with an infield single against the California Angels in Anaheim.[20] He struggled a bit when he returned but he hit .310 in his final 71 at-bats at the end of the season. General manager Pat Gillick praised Bell for his maturity during the playoffs in key moments that helped the Blue Jays win the World Series.[21]

Bell was on the receiving end of one of the major leagues' most famous practical jokes. On October 4, 1992, during Fan Appreciation Day, Joe Carter and Dave Winfield drove Bell's Jeep out onto the field and it was announced that the car was to be given away to a fan in the stands. "In Toronto, they gave us cars. Honda was a sponsor, so everyone had the same car. But Derek decided to drive his car. And he loved his Jeep. And he talked about his sound system – the sound system cost more than the car itself!" Carter said.[22] Bell got his car back, but the prank became one of the funniest moments in baseball history.

Bell did play a role in helping the Blue Jays win the World Series. He drew critical walks that led to the winning run scored in Game Four of the American League Championship Series against the Oakland Athletics and the tying run in Game Two of the World Series against the Atlanta Braves. Those moments and his batting average of .310 after the All-Star break did not prevent his time with the club soon coming to an end. Bell's over-the-top demeanor in 1992 and into 1993 became somewhat tiresome for management and some of his teammates. Bell did not see the problem. "I've always been this way, smiling and talking trash. Sliding into home plate, gee, I used to do that when we won games in Little League. Why should I change? Everybody around here likes my enthusiasm. Isn't that better than if I were mean all the time and never smiled at anybody?"[23]

GM Gillick told the press that Bell needed to learn how to control his enthusiasm a bit, saying: "He's a good kid. And I don't want to stifle his enthusiasm. But I think he's starting to learn that there are situations where you have to control yourself, where you have to concentrate on the job you're supposed to be doing. It's just a matter of channeling that enthusiasm."[24]

The final straw may have come during a 1993 spring-training game against the Tigers when manager Gaston publicly criticized Bell for letting a lazy fly ball fall in front of him for a hit and getting doubled off second base on a routine popup. "Maybe you can get away with that kind of play in Triple A somewhere," Gaston said. "That's just being careless. Everybody likes the kid, and I know he wants to do well, but I think he gets caught up in trying to look good rather than play good."[25] Bell was traded to the San Diego Padres less than 48 hours later.

Bell had two solid seasons with the Padres, coming into his own offensively. In 1993 he hit .262 with

21 home runs, 72 RBIs, and 26 stolen bases. In the strike-shortened 1994 season, in 108 games he hit .311 with 14 home runs and 54 RBIs, with 24 steals. Despite the offensive outburst, he was traded at the end of 1994 to the Houston Astros in a cost-cutting move by the Astros. Houston manager Terry Collins liked the idea of adding Bell's bat to his potent lineup. He dismissed the label that Bell was a good player who came with a lot of baggage. "Players can get tags put on them. People say, 'This guy is going to be a good player' or 'He has a chance to be a good player.' I think Derek Bell has proven he's a good player. He's a complete player," Collins said.[26]

Bell also dismissed the baggage label. "I'm living for today and the future," he said. "I don't even have a clue (how the label) got started. I've never heard any of my past teammates or managers say I didn't run the ball out, didn't hustle or give 100 percent all the time. I guess when you get rid of a guy, you have to have some excuse."[27] While in Houston, Bell met Tom McCraw, the Astros hitting coach, whom Bell described as the closest thing to a father-figure he ever had. McCraw acknowledged that he treated Bell "just like my son. I told him 'I'm going to tell you what's going wrong. I'm going to tell you how to do it.' He'd huff and he'd puff, then he'd do it." Bell once made a baserunning mistake and McCraw reprimanded him in the dugout. Bell cringed. "He said, 'Don't holler at me, I'm sensitive,'" McCraw recalled. "I realized I went past the line and backed it up."[28]

While with the Astros, Bell became one of the most lethal of the Astros "Killer B's" alongside Jeff Bagwell, Sean Berry, and Craig Biggio. He was an MVP candidate his first year with the team in 1995, and in 1998 he had arguably his best season as a major leaguer when he hit .314 with 22 homers, 108 RBIs, and 111 runs scored. Despite his successes on the field, Bell could not help but get himself in trouble. On July 15, 1999, the day Astros manager Larry Dierker returned to managerial duties after brain surgery, Bell complained because he was batting sixth, not second. This soured Bell's relationship with the club and the fans and was a contributing factor in his eventual trade to the New York Mets at the end of the season. Bell claimed the whole situation was misunderstood. "I'm a team player, and I felt that I couldn't hit-and-run and do the things I'm capable of doing from the six slot," he said. "That's the only thing I was upset about. Is that selfish? I want to win so badly. The only way I thought we could do that was with me batting second, making things go."[29]

Bell's salary jumped dramatically in Houston. He made $385,000 while with the Padres in 1994. His salary climbed to $1.45 million his first year with the Astros. By the time he left for the Mets in 2000, his salary was $4.5 million annually. This helped feed Bell's desire to live a flashy lifestyle.

Bell had a pretty good season in his one campaign with the Mets and it was the second and final time he made it to the World Series as a player, but it was his lifestyle that all the media in New York wanted to hear about. Bell purchased a yacht named "Bell 14" (for his number when he played with the Astros) and took it with him when he moved to New York. He lived in it while playing for the Mets because the cost of living was high in the city. Bell said he had more important things to spend his money on like his auto detailing business in Tampa called DB 14.[30] *Sports Illustrated,* in a piece about Bell's lifestyle, wrote that he had over 2,000 hip-hop CDs, 100 DVDs, games for his Sony PlayStation and Sega Dreamcast, and over 100 pairs of alligator shoes. He also owned a gold-and-diamond baseball pendant and sparkling diamond studs, one for each ear. Also included was a six-bedroom house in Tampa, a four-bedroom house in a Tampa suburb for his mother, a 2000 Mercedes-Benz S500, a 1999 Ford Expedition, and a $50,000 diamond ring. "Bell also gave his 22-year-old half-brother Marlon a '99 Mercedes," the magazine wrote. Finally, a 2000 Bentley Azure. "The Rolls is fresh," said Bell. "Florida State maroon, with a sweet interior, yo."[31]

Todd Zeile was a teammate of Bell's with the Mets during the 2000 season. Zeile said that Bell would have custom suits made for him on road trips. "The suits were orange, green, purple, white and black and they all had matching belts and shoes to go with them. The key to this was that he would only wear them once. Every time he wore a suit, that would be it. He would discard it. He would give it away."[32]

A free agent after the 2000 season, Bell signed a two-year, $9.75 million deal with the Pirates. He played in only 46 games in an injury-plagued 2001, where he had 27 hits and a .173 batting average, and was demoted to Triple-A Nashville. During spring training in 2002, Pirates GM Dave Littlefield wanted Bell to compete for the starting right field position with Armando Rios, Craig Wilson, and Rob Mackowiak. Bell responded by making a comment to the press that essentially ended his professional career. "Nobody told me I was in competition," he said. "If there is competition, somebody better let me know. If there is competition, they better eliminate me out of the race

and go ahead and do what they're going to do with me. I ain't never hit in spring training and I never will. Ask Littlefield and ask [manager Lloyd McClendon] if I'm in competition. If it ain't settled with me out there, then they can trade me. I ain't going out there to hurt myself in spring training battling for a job. If it is [a competition], then I'm going into 'Operation Shutdown.' Tell them exactly what I said. I haven't competed for a job since 1991. If I don't [start], then I guess I'll be out of here."[33]

Bell left the team on March 29 and was released two days later. The Associated Press reported that "[w]hen a Pirates spokesman saw Bell leaving the clubhouse, he asked him if he had any message to pass on. Bell said only, 'I got onto my yacht and rode off into the sunset.'"[34] Bell's yacht at the time was docked at the Twin Dolphin Marina on the Manatee River near Bradenton, Florida. The Pirates paid him over $4 million after he left the team. Mark Madden of the *Pittsburgh Post-Gazette* commented, "Derek Bell becomes the ultimate Pirate: lives on a boat and steals money."[35]

In a 2020 interview with the *Pittsburgh Post-Gazette*, Bell contended that the "Operation Shutdown" quote was a hip-hop term and he wished that the reporter, Robert Dvorchak, had asked him to clarify what he meant. "I worded it wrong, but I've always been that way," Bell said. "I say what's on my mind."[36] In the interview, Bell did apologize to Pittsburgh fans for not living up to the terms of his contract. "I do want to apologize and let Pirates fans know that I'm very, very sorry that I didn't live up to that contract. They expected me to do more, and I didn't get a chance to do more. It haunts me to this day that I didn't get a chance to show 'em because Pittsburgh is a great city. It's a steel town. They love their sports. They love their players. They just want you to do well."[37]

Bell largely avoided off-field issues throughout his career. When something went wrong either in his personal life or on the field, he often retreated to his home or his hotel room and played video games. It was his routine. Dwight Gooden and Gary Sheffield credited his mother for raising him that way. "For a long time, he was an only child, and I kept him shielded," said Chestine Bell. "Just go to school, play baseball, and come home. You've got to try and keep him on the straight and narrow."[38]

The straight and narrow path seemed to abandon Bell a bit after his playing career. Bell sold the Bell 14 yacht because it became too much for him to handle.

"It got old."[39] Bell also fell victim to a few drug issues in 2006 and 2008. "Things happen," he said. "I was retired. Sometimes, when you retire, you want to have fun. I never got in trouble when I played ball. I never did drugs when I played ball. I ran into a little rut. You do the wrong thing, and things happen. I've moved past that. Lesson learned. I'm moving on way beyond that."[40]

Bell's health took a hit as well, but he didn't stop engaging with fans. He regularly does autograph shows and is often asked to write "Operation Shutdown" on hats and balls. "I'm a fan-friendly person."[41] He had to quit helping his good friend, Ty Griffin, coach baseball at King High School and Tampa Catholic High School because of cataracts and the demands on his arms and legs. As of 2020, Bell's fiancée had to help him get around because of his cataracts.

Bell never made an All-Star team but his play on the field is not something that people will remember him for. Brash, showy, and full of enthusiasm, Bell's magnetism and energy in the clubhouse kept his teammates loose. In a YouTube video titled *The MLB Player Who Lived on a Yacht During His Career,* the narrator, "Mike," describes Bell as "possibly the most unique off-the-field presence in baseball history." The 9½-minute video details some of the stories that the narrator feels makes Bell's career unique. He ends the video by saying that Bell's story should inspire others because Bell came from nothing and had a prosperous and successful major-league baseball career. "But that is not what he is gonna be remembered for," Mike says. "In this story, talking about the players analytics isn't the most important thing about them. The important thing is what made them unique as a human being and highlighting that. Sometimes baseball fans don't do enough of that. They really don't make them like Derek Bell anymore."[42]

SOURCES

In addition to the sources cited in the Notes, the author also consulted Baseball-Reference.com and *Sports Illustrated*.

NOTES

1   Rosie DiManno, "Derek Bell Can Sure Talk a Good Game," *Toronto Star*, March 4, 1992: C1.

2   Tyler Kepner, "Still Room to Grow: For Mets' Bell, Numbers Haven't Matched His Power," *New York Times*, March 12, 2000: SP7.

3   Thomas Hill, "Bringing Up Derek: Bell Never Bothered by Life with No Father," *New York Daily News*, May 21, 2000.

4   Hill.

5   Hill.

6   Hill.

7   Kepner.

8   Three of the 14 (Ed Vosberg, Jason Varitek, and Michael Conforto) have played in the Little League World Series, the College World Series, and the Major League World Series. See "Current and Former Major Leaguers Who Have Played in the Little League Baseball World Series," *Little League*, accessed April 27, 2022. https://www.littleleague.org/who-we-are/alumni/major-leaguers-played-llbws/.

9   Jane Gross, "Tampa Team in Final of Little League Series," *New York Times*, August 28, 1981: A15. "Taiwan Nine Retains Title," *New York Times*, August 30, 1981: 204.

10   Brian Landman, "Put Me in, Coach // Life Lessons Are First on Baseball Diamond," *St. Petersburg Times*, June 14, 1987: 22.

11   Erik Erlendsson, "Derek Bell Still Has That Swing," *Tampa Tribune*, October 10, 1999.

12   Brian Landman, "Despite Disappointing Loss, King Had a Great Season," *St. Petersburg Times*, May 3, 1987: 9.

13   "King's Bell Signs Contract with Blue Jays," *St. Petersburg Times*, June 12, 1987: 5.

14   Allan Ryan, "Blue Jays Stars of the Future," *Toronto Star*, September 13, 1987: E28.

15   Neil MacCarl, "Blue Jays' Other Bell Awaiting His Chance to Play in the Big Leagues," *Toronto Star*, February 28, 1988: G8.

16   Allan Ryan, "Blue Jays Chase Seattle Reliever," *Toronto Star*, December 11, 1991: C6; Dave Perkins, "Is Derek Bell the Solution to Jays' Woes?" *Toronto Star*, December 9, 1991: D1.

17   Marty York, "Derek Bell Assails Demotion to Farm // 'Wasn't Given Fair Shot,' Says .059 Hitter After Being Sent Back to Syracuse," *Globe and Mail* (Toronto), July 19, 1991: C13.

18   Rosie DiManno, "Derek Bell Can Sure Talk a Good Game."

19   Rosie DiManno.

20   Tom Slater, "Jays Lose Tough Duel," *Toronto Star*, May 10, 1992: G1.

21   Brian Landman, "Jays' Bell Hustles Back Into Action After Injury," *St. Petersburg Times*, May 3, 1992: 5C; Rosie DiManno, "Bell Bubbles with Enthusiasm // Blue Jays' Young Outfielder Makes No Apologies for Antics," *Toronto Star*, March 4, 1993: D4.

22   Larry Brown, "Joe Carter Shares Story Behind Epic Derek Bell Car Prank," *Larry Brown Sports*, December 17, 2019. https://larrybrownsports.com/baseball/joe-carter-story-epic-derek-bell-car-prank/528745.

23   Rosie DiManno, "Bell Bubbles with Enthusiasm."

24   Rosie DiManno, "Bell Bubbles with Enthusiasm."

25   Jeff Pearlman, "Yo Ho Ho! Thrown Overboard by the Astros, the Mets' Hot-Hittin', Hip-Hoppin' Derek Bell Has Been Cruisin' Since He Docked In New York," *Sports Illustrated*, May 22, 2000. https://vault.si.com/vault/2000/05/22/yo-ho-ho-thrown-overboard-by-the-astros-the-mets-hot-hittin-hip-hoppin-derek-bell-has-been-cruisin-since-he-docked-in-new-york; Ronald Blum, "Mets Hope Hampton Is the Answer: New York Acquires 22-Game Winner, Along with Derek Bell from the Houston Astros," *Vancouver* (British Columbia) *Sun*, December 24, 1999: H12.

26   Bill Chastain, "Present perfect; Others May Have Doubted Derek Bell in the Past, but His Manager Calls the Astros' Outfielder a 'Complete Player,'" *Tampa Tribune*, August 15, 1995.

27   Chastain.

28   Hill.

29   Pearlman.

30   Hill.

31   Pearlman.

32   SNY, "Todd Zeile Shares Great Derek Bell Stories from the 2000 Mets," YouTube, May 11, 2018. https://youtu.be/WCML9LmwTbc.

33   Robert Dvorchak, "Pirates Finally part with Bell," Pittsburgh Post-Gazette.com Sports, March 30, 2002. https://old.post-gazette.com/pirates/20020330bucs3.asp; Craig Calcaterra, "Happy Anniversary to 'Operation Shutdown,'" NBC Sports, March 19, 2014. https://mlb.nbcsports.com/2014/03/19/happy-anniversary-to-operation-shutdown/; Jason Mackey, "It Haunts Me to This Day," *Pittsburgh Post-Gazette*, May 15, 2020: C1.

34   Associated Press, "Bell Packs His Bags and Leaves the Pirates," *New York Times*, March 31, 2002: G8.

35   Mark Madden, "Baker's Son Gives Us a Series Moment," Pittsburgh Post-Gazette.com, October 26, 2002. https://old.post-gazette.com/sports/columnists/20021026madden1026p1.asp.

36   Mackey, "It Haunts Me to This Day."

37   Mackey, "It Haunts Me to This Day."

38   Kepner, "Still Room to Grow."

39   Mackey, "It Haunts Me to This Day."

40   Larry Brown, "Derek Bell Has One Classic Mug Shot," Larry Brown Sports, December 2, 2008. https://larrybrownsports.com/darwin-nominations/derek-bell-mug-shot-d089. Jason Mackey, "It Haunts Me to This Day."

41   Mackey, "It Haunts Me to This Day."

42   Stark Raving Sports, "The MLB Player Who Lived on a Yacht During His Career," YouTube, April 17, 2021. https://youtu.be/RqRMLrShHnQ.

PAT BORDERS

By Malcolm Allen

The first American to win both a World Series ring and an Olympic gold medal, Pat Borders played parts of 17 major league seasons (1988-2005) for nine different teams.[1] When the Blue Jays won consecutive championships in 1992 and 1993, he caught more innings than any American Leaguer both years and earned 1992 World Series MVP honors.

Patrick Lance Borders was born on May 14, 1963, in Columbus, Ohio. His parents, Mike and Donna (Holbrook) Borders, taught social studies and math, respectively, and later had another child, Todd. Mike played softball into his 60s, and competed against his sons in basketball, Wiffle Ball, and baseball. "He was the biggest influence on me for learning the game," Borders said.[2] Pat attended his first big-league game at Cincinnati's Riverfront Stadium and saw his favorite player, Reds star Pete Rose.[3]

When Pat was 9, his family moved to Lake Wales, Florida, about 60 miles east of Tampa.[4] He often attended weekend ballgames at a local park, though he said, "I was more interested in chasing after the foul balls and then practicing with them afterward."[5] With his father pitching to him nearly every day, Borders developed his aggressive batting style. "I'd swing at every pitch because there wasn't any backstop, and if I didn't swing at it and hit it, I'd have to go chase it."[6]

At Lake Wales High School, Borders was an all-state quarterback and football defensive end.[7] He also played basketball for the Highlanders before baseball season. Initially, Pat was a designated hitter, as coach Don Bridges recalled that he had "hands of stone." Following a teammate's injury, however, Borders switched to third base as a sophomore.[8] "He practiced until it was dark. He could never get enough," Bridges said. Borders also worked hard off the field, describing his early occupations as "[a] lot of shovel work. Digging footers for houses, setting rebar, working a lot of construction jobs and agricultural jobs."[9]

As a senior, Borders drove in 36 runs in 25 games and batted .513 with 10 home runs.[10] His 29 career homers tied Glenn Davis's state high-school record.[11] Borders played in the 1982 Florida Athletic Coaches

Association North-South All-Star Game, where three of his teammates, Dwight Gooden, Ron Karkovice, and Rich Monteleone, became first-round picks in the June amateur draft.[12] Borders, on the other hand, planned to attend Mississippi State on a football scholarship.[13] That changed after he ripped a series of line drives in front of a Blue Jays scout that spring. Tim Wilken was in Kissimmee only because Toronto had other scouts at the first contest he'd visited in Tampa.[14] On Wilken's recommendation, the Blue Jays drafted Borders in the sixth round.

Borders signed quickly and joined Toronto's rookie-level Pioneer League club in Medicine Hat, Alberta. He batted .304 with 5 homers in 61 games to help them win the championship. In 1983 he advanced to the Florence (South Carolina) Blue Jays of the Class-A South Atlantic League and rapped 31 doubles to tie for second in the circuit while hitting

Borders was 1992 World Series MVP.

Borders batted .321 in 30 career postseason games for Toronto.

.274 in 131 contests. Back at Florence in 1984, Borders increased his home-run output from 5 to 12, tied for the SAL lead with 85 RBIs, and was named MVP of the league's All-Star Game.[15] He received the R. Howard Webster trophy, awarded to the top prospect at each Toronto affiliate.[16] Realistically, however, Borders's .864 fielding percentage through three seasons at the hot corner clouded his future. "It became apparent to us he would be a defensive liability at third base in the big leagues," said Blue Jays GM Pat Gillick.[17] Borders wasn't much better in the outfield and finished 1984 playing first base.

Although Borders led the Kinston (North Carolina) Blue Jays with 60 RBIs in the Class-A Carolina League in 1985, his .261 batting average, 10 homers, and 116 strikeouts in 127 games didn't impress, considering the Toronto organization's talented collection of first baseman. "I didn't think I could compete with Cecil Fielder, Fred McGriff, and Willie Upshaw in home runs," Borders conceded.[18] "I never thought I'd make it to the majors, to tell you the truth."[19] Gillick acknowledged, "We were going to release him. It was (Blue Jays VP Bobby) Mattick who suggested that

…we might try him behind the plate."[20] Mattick said Borders "called me in the winter of '86 and said he would like to try it."[21]

That offseason Borders asked former Dodgers and Senators backstop Doug Camilli for assistance. "He had the talent, and he had the desire," Camilli recalled "Here was a complete athlete who was willing to do whatever it took to get to the majors."[22] Borders said, "The position itself didn't hold any allure for me, especially getting beat up like catchers do. Once I got into it, I had more fun than any position I ever played."[23] Borders began the 1986 season in Florence but was promoted to the Double-A Southern League in mid-May. In six weeks with the Knoxville Blue Jays, he didn't play much, and he returned to the Carolina League on June 22 to finish the year with Kinston, now a co-op team featuring players from different organizations. Between three clubs, he hit a combined .339 with 11 homers in 77 games. Borders had caught in only 18 contests prior to joining Kinston, but manager Dave Trembley deployed him behind the plate 27 times and had him block countless balls in the dirt during drills.[24]

Borders gained more experience in the Florida Instructional League before beginning a fifth straight season at Class A in 1987.[25] After only three games with the Dunedin Blue Jays in the Florida State League, however, he returned to Knoxville to replace Jeff DeWillis, who'd been summoned to the majors because of Matt Stark's injury.[26] In 94 Double-A games, Borders hit .292 with 11 home runs and caught 77 times as he learned to call pitches and discern hitters' weaknesses.[27] "The whole thing was a lot more complex than I thought," he admitted.[28] The Blue Jays added him to their 40-man roster and sent him to the Dominican Republic for winter ball, where he batted .290 in 56 contests for the Caimanes del Sur.[29]

In spring training 1988, Borders and four other catchers competed for the chance to back up veteran Ernie Whitt. While Stark and Greg Myers had already tasted the majors, Borders, Francisco Cabrera, and Carlos Diaz were in big-league camp for their first "Class for Catchers" with Blue Jays coach John Sullivan. "[Borders] has impressed me," Sullivan said. "He receives well, has a strong arm, and has been good in the throwing drills." Hitting coach Cito Gaston reported, "Bobby Mattick had the catchers working on fielding bunts and he said Borders was the best of the young ones."[30] In Grapefruit League play, Borders hit .373 and gunned down nine of 17 opposing basestealers to win the job as Whitt's platoon partner.[31]

Borders debuted on April 6, 1988, at Royals Stadium, and lined a two-run triple to right-center off Kansas City southpaw Charlie Leibrandt in his first at-bat. Although he was charged with a throwing error and a passed ball, he also cut down speedster Willie Wilson trying to steal third and went 3-for-4 with five RBIs in Toronto's 11-4 victory. "[Borders] definitely has the attitude to be a good one for a long time," remarked winning pitcher Mike Flanagan.[32] On April 14 Borders hit his first homer, a solo shot off the Yankees' Al Leiter.

"I suppose my one big shock about the big leagues was how quickly the opposition picks up on your weaknesses," Borders said.[33] Nevertheless, he did a solid job, batting .276 with five homers in 41 games before pulling a rib-cage muscle prior to a July 7 exhibition.[34] After healing, he spent more than a month on a rehab assignment with the Syracuse Chiefs in the Triple-A International League before rejoining the Blue Jays in September.

Next, Borders joined the Cardenales de Lara for winter ball in Venezuela, explaining, "I wanted to work on picking off runners, being more selective at the plate, and improving things like blocking the plate." In one game, he picked off three runners – one at each base.[35] After hitting .283 with 7 home runs in 60 games, he returned to the United States and worked out with his brother Todd, who'd been drafted as a catcher by the Cubs.[36]

In 1989 the Blue Jays fired manager Jimy Williams after falling 12 games below .500 by mid-May. During the skipper's final series in Minnesota, Borders made throwing errors in consecutive losses and deepened a slump that grew to 4-for-46. "That affected my catching, or maybe my catching affected my hitting." he said. "I was pretty much a wreck mentally."[37] He temporarily lost his platoon job under new manager Cito Gaston, and Toronto still had a losing record when Borders blasted a game-winning eighth-inning grand slam off Willie Hernández on July 7 in Detroit. He finished with a .257 batting average and 3 homers in 94 games as the Blue Jays rallied to win the AL East. In Borders' only postseason at-bat, he stroked an RBI single, but Toronto lost the ALCS to the Athletics in five games. Four weeks later, Pat married Kathy Sellers, a former college softball and basketball recruit whom he'd first met at a Knoxville Pizza Hut. "Kathy understood me and understood sport," he said.[38]

The Blue Jays traded Whitt before the 1990 season. "I like Ernie; he helped me a lot, personally," Borders said.[39] Third baseman Kelly Gruber said Borders

deserved to start: "There's no question in my mind that Pat can play every day."[40] Gaston, however, planned for the lefty-hitting Myers to take over the busier side of the catching platoon. "Greg and I are friends and it's fine with me," Borders insisted.[41] Borders enjoyed his only career four-hit game on April 30 and started 20 consecutive contests when Myers went on the disabled list in May. On September 2 in Cleveland, he caught Dave Stieb's no-hitter. By season's end Borders had started more than half of Toronto's games and batted .286 in 125 contests. His 15 home runs were his most ever as a professional.

"[Borders] is getting to where he's an above-average catcher," remarked Sullivan. "He's one of the best throwing catchers in the league."[42] Through his first three seasons, Borders had nabbed 41.2 percent of attempted basestealers and gained confidence handling pitchers. "We came up at the same time and we roomed together, so Pat never had a problem coming to me and saying do this or do that," observed Todd Stottlemyre. "But I think it took a little longer for him to go to [veterans] Jimmy Key or Dave Stieb and tell them what they should be doing."[43] In 1991, however, Borders began the season 0-for-21 at the plate and cost Toronto a game on April 17 with a 10th-inning throwing error and passed ball. He also missed time after being steamrolled by Robin Ventura in a home-plate collision and entered the All-Star break batting .213 without a home run.[44] Borders rebounded to finish at .244 in 105 games and claimed the full-time job with a strong second half. Four of his five homers came in the final month, including a three-run shot off California's Jim Abbott to snap a scoreless tie in the 10th inning on September 24. The Blue Jays won their division and Borders started all five games of their ALCS loss to the Twins.

Borders made his first Opening Day start in 1992 and went deep in Detroit. In Toronto's home opener, he blasted a game-tying homer off Baltimore closer Gregg Olson in the bottom of the ninth. Nevertheless, for the second straight season, his name was mentioned in trade rumors involving the Padres Gold Glove catcher Benito Santiago. "Last year, it bothered me a lot," Borders confessed in the summer of '92. "But this year, it kind of helped me, knowing that someone else might want me. I learned not to let that stuff bother me."[45] In 138 games, he batted .242 with 13 homers and 53 RBIs as the Blue Jays repeated as division champs.

In October Borders caught every postseason inning for Toronto. He hit .318 in the six-game ALCS as the

Blue Jays bested the Athletics to claim the franchise's first pennant. With the pivotal Game Three tied, 2-2, in the fourth inning, Borders leaped to corral right fielder Joe Carter's throw and complete a momentum-shifting double play by holding onto the ball when 6-foot-5 Mark McGwire crashed into him attempting to score. "That was really the difference in the ballgame," Carter said.[46] In the World Series against the Braves, Borders batted .450 (9-for-20), including a homer off Tom Glavine in Toronto's 2-1 victory in Game Four, and a game-tying RBI double against John Smoltz in Game Five. Although Atlanta baserunners swiped 15 bases in 18 tries, Borders cut down pinch-runner Brian Hunter with Game Three deadlocked in the ninth inning and threw out the fleet Otis Nixon with Toronto protecting a one-run advantage in Game Six. Borders was voted the Most Valuable Player after the Blue Jays prevailed in six games.

Lake Wales erected "Home of Pat Borders" signs around town, but the catcher nixed the idea of a welcome-home parade in his honor, agreeing to a ceremony to have a youth field named after him instead. "He hasn't changed a bit," remarked Bridges, his high-school coach. "He's a very soft-spoken and withdrawn type."[47] Borders lived next to his parents and drove the same 1980 Ford Bronco that he'd owned since high school. He donated the van that he received for his MVP performance to his local YMCA.[48] "Winning the MVP goes way beyond anything I ever thought I'd accomplish," he said.[49] In January the Blue Jays rewarded him with a two-year contract for $5 million.[50]

By appearing in 138 games, Borders was the AL's busiest catcher for the second straight season in 1993, and he hit .254 with career highs in RBIs (55) and doubles (30). In the ALCS against the White Sox, he extended his record postseason hitting streak for catchers to 16 games.[51] The Blue Jays repeated as champions, with Borders batting .304 (7-for-23) in six World Series games against the Phillies. "The best thing about Pat is that when you have a runner on third and the score tied in the ninth inning, he will call for a pitch in the dirt, because he has confidence he can block it," Stottlemyre observed. "A catcher like that gives a pitcher confidence that he can throw any pitch at any time."[52] Borders insisted, "I'm average. If I don't block pitches, they'll find someone else who can. It's more like I'd better do it."[53]

Toronto had younger, cheaper options available – including power-hitting backup Randy Knorr, lefty slugger Carlos Delgado, and defensive specialist Sandy Martínez – and assistant GM Gord Ash acknowledged, "We believe that catching is a position we can trade."[54] Borders retained his job in 1994, but the Blue Jays finished under .500 for the first time in a dozen years. He was batting .247 with 3 homers in 85 games when the season ended prematurely in August because of a players strike. That offseason, although it meant they would not receive any compensation when Borders left, Toronto declined to offer him a contract because, Ash explained, they knew he would accept anything to remain with the Blue Jays. "I was very happy here," Borders confirmed.[55]

When the strike was finally settled in April 1995, Borders signed a one-year, $310,000 deal with the Royals on the first day that camps opened to returning regulars to platoon with lefty-hitting Brent Mayne.[56] In 52 games for a poor Kansas City club, he hit .231 with four homers before he was traded to the contending Astros on August 11. With Houston, Borders hit .114 in 35 at-bats, but he appeared only once in the last 23 contests after lefty-hitting Rick Wilkins joined the team in September.

A free agent again, Borders signed with the Cardinals for 1996 and started on Opening Day. He'd slipped to third string behind Tom Pagnozzi and Danny Sheaffer by June 15, however, when he was traded to the Angels. On June 29 Borders enjoyed his only two-homer game in the majors, but he was traded again on July 27 – to the White Sox to replace injured catcher Chad Kreuter. Overall, Borders appeared in 76 games for three teams in '96 and batted .277 with 5 home runs. He said that his bat speed and arm strength had finally recovered from his heavy workload of 1992 and 1993. As for playing for five teams in two years, he remarked, "It's educational. You learn a lot. It helps you as a player."[57]

Borders joined the Indians in 1997, a strong club that already had All-Star backstop Sandy Alomar. "I knew what my role was going to be," Borders said. "I'll take anything I can get."[58] Cleveland advanced to the seventh game of the World Series before falling to the Marlins, but Borders didn't see any postseason action after batting .296 with 4 homers in 55 regular-season contests.

He returned to Cleveland in 1998 and appeared in 54 more games, including both ends of a July 21 doubleheader when Alomar was hurting. "I don't think it even crossed his mind that he would be playing 18 innings, but that's his mentality," observed Indians second baseman Jeff Branson.[59] Cleveland made the playoffs again, but Borders was left off the postseason roster in favor of rookie Einar Díaz. When manager

Mike Hargrove asked him to remain with the team anyway, Borders agreed.[60]

Once a devoted weightlifter, Borders stopped in his mid-30s. "It was starting to hurt me," he explained. "I think it was slowing me down, slowing down my arm and my swing."[61] To extend his career, Borders retuned to the minors for the first time in 11 years, spending most of 1999 with the Buffalo Bisons of the Triple-A International League, other than a half-dozen July appearances for the Indians. After he was released on August 31, he signed with the Blue Jays and started at DH the following night in Toronto. Borders homered off the Twins' Eric Milton in the seventh inning, prompting the fans at SkyDome to demand a curtain call. "It's really not my style," he said after tipping his cap. "I'm embarrassed about it." In six games for the Blue Jays, he went 3-for-14.[62]

Borders considered retirement, but his family encouraged him to keep playing. "It's a game you can never master or conquer," he reflected. "Every situation presents a different challenge. You're always making adjustments either as a hitter or calling a game as a catcher. That's what makes it so interesting." Although he didn't appear in the majors for the first time in 13 years in 2000, the 81 games he caught for Tampa Bay's Triple-A Durham Bulls affiliate were his most since his first stint with Toronto. Bulls outfielder Jim Buccheri observed, "He's 37 going on 19."[63] Devil Rays minor-league director Tom Foley said, "Having Pat Borders is like having an extra coach."[64]

When Borders was invited to try out for the United States Olympic baseball team that summer, he recalled, "I wasn't gonna go, but Kathy kicked my butt and said I should just go do it. And she was right."[65] Professionals were allowed to play in the Summer Games in Sydney, Australia, but with the big-league season ongoing, clubs were reluctant to send stars or top prospects. Other than manager Tom Lasorda, Borders was one of the United States' more recognizable names. In the Americans' only loss, to the favored Cubans, Borders was hammered in a thunderous home plate collision.[66] He batted .429 (6-for-14) in the Olympics, including 2-for-3 with a double and an RBI in the Gold Medal game, when the USA defeated Cuba, 4-0.[67] "I've never had more fun than that time," Borders said. "It really was not like anything else I had ever been a part of."[68]

Borders could have retired to his farm home with orange groves, 200 cattle, and 100 acres of strawberries and vegetables.[69] He and Kathy already had five children: Lindsay, Levi, Luke, Laura Beth, and Leah.

(By 2021, their brood would grow to nine with the additions of Lance, Lily, Livia, and Landy Kate).[70] Every winter the family voted whether or not Pat should keep playing, and every year the consensus was yes. He spent most of 2001 in Durham but was sold to the Mariners on August 27 and appeared in five games for Seattle in September. From 2002 to 2004, Borders mostly played for Seattle's Tacoma Rainiers affiliate in the Triple-A Pacific Coast League. He could still hit, as evidenced by a 6-for-6 performance against the Colorado Springs Sky Sox on May 8, 2003.[71] Occasionally the Mariners summoned him to the majors: four games in 2002, a dozen the next year and 19 in 2004. On August 31, 2004, Borders was dealt to the Twins at the trading deadline. In 19 September contests, he batted .286 to help Minnesota win the AL Central. He went 0-for-2 in the Twins four-game ALDS loss to the Yankees to finish his 32-game postseason career with a .315 average.

Borders led AL backstops in games caught in 1992 and 1993.

Borders began 2005 with the Brewers' PCL Nashville Sounds affiliate but the Mariners purchased his contract on May 19 – five days after his 42nd birthday – after losing former All-Star catcher Dan Wilson to a torn ACL and backup Wiki González to a hamstring injury. Mariners skipper Mike Hargrove had managed Borders in Cleveland and was happy to have him back. "Pat just absolutely loves the game, that's what I think is cool about him," said Hargrove. "You get someone like him, with such a positive attitude, and he's so willing to teach. You talk to him, and he's willing to give all the information he has. He's a great presence to have around."[72]

When Borders caught Jamie Moyer on May 25 in Baltimore, it marked the first time in major-league history that a team started a battery of 42-year-olds. It would not be the last. Seattle went 8-3 when the ancient Mariners teamed up. In a little more than two months with the team, Borders started 37 games, though Hargrove insisted, "He can't and won't play every day. That's from me. Pat would go out there every day on bloody stumps."[73] On July 27 Borders played his 1,099th and final big-league contest, catching Moyer's 9-3 victory over the Tigers at Safeco Field. He was released two days later when González returned from the DL. Borders finished his career with a .253 batting average and 69 home runs, and threw out 35 percent of opposing basestealers. "Had it not been for catching, I'd have never made it as far as Double A," he reflected.[74]

The Dodgers invited Borders to spring training in 2006, but when he didn't want to leave home, he realized that he no longer had the desire to play.[75] At Los Angeles's request, he filled in for a few weeks: 20 games with Vero Beach in the Class-A Florida State League and six with the Triple-A PCL's Las Vegas 51s before retiring on May 26.

Borders assumed full-time father duties, including coaching the baseball team at Lake Wales High School during his son Luke's senior season. He was inducted into the Florida Sports Hall of Fame in 2010. In 2015 Borders became the manager of the Phillies' Williamsport (Pennsylvania) Crosscutters affiliate in the short-season New York-Pennsylvania League. He led the Crosscutters to 186 victories over the next five seasons, more than any other skipper in team history. When Borders announced that he would leave to manage the full-season Class-A Clearwater Threshers in 2020, Williamsport surprised him by retiring his number 10. "I'm speechless," he said.[76] Clearwater, merely 85 miles west of Lake Wales, was

a welcome destination for Borders, but the Threshers' 2020 season was canceled due to the coronavirus pandemic. In 2021, Borders was part of the inaugural Highlander Athletic Hall of Fame induction class organized by the community of Lake Wales. That fall, he left the Phillies' organization after serving as the bench coach for Philadelphia's Triple-A Lehigh Valley (Pennsylvania) IronPigs farm club for one season.

SOURCES

In addition to sources cited in the Notes, the author consulted www.ancestry.com, www.baseball-reference.com, and www.retrosheet.org.

NOTES

1   Baseball was a demonstration sport at both the 1984 and 1988 Summer Olympics, so official medals were not awarded. As of 2021, Doug Mientkiewicz (2000 Olympics; 2004 Red Sox) is the only other American to win both an Olympic gold medal and a World Series ring. Three Cubans --Orlando Hernández (1992 Olympics; 1998-2000 Yankees), José Contreras (1996 Olympics; 2005 White Sox) and Yuli Gurriel (2004 Olympics; 2017 Astros) – have also achieved the feat.

2   Godfrey Jordan, "Thanks, Dad," *Toronto Star*, June 19, 1993: F1.

3   Pat Borders, 1993 Donruss Studio Baseball Card.

4   Russ White, "Borders Avoids Celebrity Status," *Orlando Sentinel*, January 24, 1993: C10.

5   Jordan, "Thanks, Dad."

6   "Borders Has Proven He's Jays' Top Catcher," *Toronto Star*, March 27, 1991: C4.

7   Russ White, "Rising Star: Pat Borders," *Orlando Sentinel*, April 2, 1989: C9.

8   Gare Joyce, "The Lifer," August 2018, https://www.sportsnet.ca/baseball/mlb/pat-borders-blue-jays-williams-port-crosscutters-profile/ (last accessed March 5, 2021).

9   Tom Weir, "Borders, Nearly 42, Awaits Another Big-League Shot," *USA Today*, April 12, 2005: C6.

10 Pat Borders, 1988 Topps Traded Baseball Card.

11 In 1986 St. Cloud's Bruce Kiser hit 34 home runs to establish a new mark. Paula J. Finocchio, "St. Cloud's Kiser Smashes HR Mark," *Orlando Sentinel*, March 25, 1986: B4.

12 Mel Antonen, "Catchers Give GM Hart Coaching Flashback," *USA Today*, February 16, 1998: 6C.

13 Joyce, "The Lifer."

14 Brian Schmitz, "Borders Is Crossing from Obscure to Hero," *Orlando Sentinel*, October 24, 1992: B1.

15 "Reds Say Goodnight to Day," *The Sporting News*, July 30, 1984: 38.

16 Paul Patton, "Losing Record with Syracuse Prompts Firing," *Globe and Mail* (Toronto), September 6, 1984: M10.

17 Milt Dunnell, "Catching Switch Saved Borders from Early Firing," *Toronto Star*, August 11, 1990: B3.

18 Larry Millson, "Borders Relaxed More with Each At-Bat," *Globe and Mail*, April 8, 1988: A18.

19 Schmitz, "Borders Is Crossing from Obscure to Hero."

20 Dunnell, "Catching Switch Saved Borders from Early Firing."

21 Neil MacCarl, "Switch to Catcher Could Put Borders on Fringes of Jays," *Toronto Star*, February 16, 1988: B10.

22 White, "Borders Avoids Celebrity Status."

23 John Lott, "Mariners' Crash Davis," *National Post* (Don Mills, Ontario), August 29, 2001: B13.

24 Bob Elliott, "An Unforgettable Journey," *Toronto Sun*, March 22, 2012: S10.

25 Millson, "Borders Relaxed More with Each At-Bat."

26 "Young Hurler Making Headlines," *Toronto Star*, April 21, 1987: F4.

27 Larry Millson, "Borders Bids for Backup Job," *Globe and Mail*, February 22, 1988: E8.

28 Campbell, "In Only Three Seasons, Pat Borders Has Progressed."

29 Pat Borders' Dominican League Statistics from https://stats.winterballdata.com/players?key=436 (Subscription service. Last accessed March 17, 2021).

30 Neil MacCarl, "Jays Need Major Graduate from Class for Catcher," *Toronto Star*, March 2,1988: B2.

31 Neil MacCarl, "Big Test Tonight for Pat Borders," *Toronto Star*, April 6, 1988: G2.

32 Millson, "Borders Relaxed More with Each At-Bat."

33 Frank Orr, "Pat Borders Proves He Belongs in the Big Leagues," *Toronto Star*, June 23, 1988: C1.

34 Larry Millson, "Borders Adjusted to Stint in Minors," *Globe and Mail*, September 7, 1988: A18.

35 Neil MacCarl, "Winter Ball Helps Jays' Pat Borders," *Toronto Star*, January 24, 1989: C4.

36 Pat Borders' Venezuelan Statistics from http://www.pelotabinaria.com.ve/beisbol/mostrar.php?ID=bordpat001 (last accessed March 17, 2021).

37 Dave Perkins, "Borders is Armed with All the Tools Except Confidence," *Toronto Star*, June 8, 1989: B3.

38 Joyce, "The Lifer."

39 Neil MacCarl, "Blue Jays' Borders Looks Out for No. 1," *Toronto Star*, January 4, 1990: B4.

40 Marty York, "New Looks for Jays Tailored to Skydome's Vast Expanse," *Globe and Mail*, March 26, 1990: C1.

41 Larry Millson, "Jays Crush Birds for Best Season Start," *Globe and Mail*, April 18, 1990: A13.

42 Neil A. Campbell, "In Only Three Seasons, Pat Borders Has Progressed," *Globe and Mail*, March 5, 1991: D10.

43 Campbell, "In Only Three Seasons, Pat Borders Has Progressed."

44 Dave Perkins, "Cheap Shot Adds to Jays' Injury Woes," *Toronto Star*, May 21, 1991: D1.

45 "Blue Jays' Borders Emerges as Majors' Ironman Catcher," *Ottawa Citizen*, September 5, 1992: H6.

46 Larry Millson, "Borders Helps the Jays Hold On," *Globe and Mail*, October 12, 1992: D4.

47 Marc Topkin, "Blue Jays' Borderline Hero," *Ottawa Citizen*, April 1, 1993: D2.

48 Bob Elliott, "An Unforgettable Journey," *Toronto Sun*, March 22, 2012: S10.

49 Pat Borders, 1993 Stadium Club Murphy Baseball Card.

50 "Borders Gets $5 Million," *Globe and Mail*, January 20, 1993: C8.

51 Allan Ryan, "Borders Huge Hit in Series Showdown and Gets MVP Nod," *Toronto Star*, October 25, 1992: E5.

52 Bill Jauss, "Borders' Hit String Cut Short," *Chicago Tribune*, October 9, 1993: 5.

53 Jack Curry, "Borders' Bat Is Doing the Talking," *New York Times*, October 25, 1992: S3.

54 "Borders is Expendable, Blue Jays Say," *Kitchener-Waterloo* (Ontario) *Record,* December 2, 1993: C6.

55 Steve Milton, "Borders Says He's Ready to Adapt to a Life After the Blue Jays," *Hamilton* (Ontario) *Spectator,* January 16, 1995: C3.

56 Ben Walker, "Borders Goes to KC in Major Scramble," *Globe and Mail*, April 8, 1995: A19.

57 Larry Millson, "Borders' Crossings Take Him to Cleveland," *Globe and Mail*, March 18, 1997: D13.

58 "Borders Fills In, Indians Roll On," *Washington Post*, July 6, 1997: D6.

59 Liz Robbins, "Borders Steps Up to Double Duty," *Cleveland Plain Dealer*, July 22, 1998: 5D.

60 Paul Hoynes, "Borders Will Stay for Postseason," *Cleveland Plain Dealer*, September 24, 1998: 2D.

61 Tom Weir, "Borders, Nearly 42, Awaits Another Big-League Shot," *USA Today*, April 12, 2005: C6.

62 Geoff Baker, "New and Old Lead Way," *Toronto Star*, September 2, 1999: 1.

63 Tom Casey, "Having a Blast: Borders Shows How Game Is Played," *Ottawa Citizen*, May 24, 2000: C6.

64 Rodney Page, "Coaching May Be in the Future for Borders," *St. Petersburg* (Florida) *Times*, May 31, 2000: 5C.

65 Joyce, "The Lifer."

66 Bill Glauber, "Cubans Snap Back at Lasorda, US, 6-1," *Baltimore Sun*, September 2, 2000: 22D.

67 Mel Antonen, "Play's Still the Thing for Borders," *USA Today*, May 30, 2001: C8.

68 Joyce, "The Lifer."

69 Lott, "Mariners' Crash Davis."

70 Vinnie Portell, "A Bond Between Brothers," *Oracle* (University of South Florida), April 27, 2017, http://www.usforacle.com/2017/04/27/a-bond-between-brothers/ (last accessed March 5, 2021).

71 "Borders Perfect in Rainiers' Win," *Seattle Times*, May 9, 2003: D7.

72 Nick Daschel, "Catcher Knows No Borders," *Vancouver* (Washington) *Columbian,* May 24, 2005: C5.

73 Phil Rogers, "Borders, Moyer: Battery for the Aged," *Chicago Tribune*, May 29, 2005: 3-2.

74 Campbell, "In Only Three Seasons, Pat Borders Has Progressed."

75 Lisa Coffey, "Lake Wales, Family Now Borders for Ex-Catcher," *Lakeland* (Florida) *Ledger,* April 30, 2007, https://www.theledger.com/article/LK/20070430/News/608141511/LL (last accessed March 5, 2021).

76 "Cutters Manager Borders Has Jersey Retired," *Williamsport* (Pennsylvania) *Sun-Gazette*, January 16, 2020, https://www.sungazette.com/sports/local-sports/2020/01/cutters-manager-borders-has-jersey-retired/ (last accessed March 18, 2021).

JOE CARTER

By Joseph Wancho

The scene has been played out in every backyard, schoolyard, and makeshift ball diamond across the country. If not on a ball field, then the scene certainly unfolded in a child's dreams. Hit a game-winning home run in the World Series. Better yet, make it Game Seven, bases loaded, full count, a packed stadium. Then go yard. We have all been there, albeit metaphorically. Joe Carter was no exception to these fantasies as a young boy in his native Oklahoma City. But he had a different twist in this imagery. He stepped to the plate with his team down a run or two, and he was the last hope of the team, the fans, and the city.

On October 23, 1993, Joe Carter lived his dream. The Toronto Blue Jays were trailing the Philadelphia Phillies 6-5 in Game Six of the World Series. Toronto held the advantage, winning three games to two at that

point in the series. But Lenny Dykstra's fourth home run of the series, a three-run shot, lifted the Phils to a five-run frame in the top of the seventh inning.

Phillies manager Jim Fregosi brought in his closer, Mitch Williams, to face the Jays in the bottom of the ninth inning. Williams, who registered 43 saves during the regular season, was having an up and down series. The veteran left-hander earned a save in Game Two, but also gave up three runs in a 15-14 loss in Game Four.

Carter stepped to the plate, base runners on first and second and one out. Carter was known to be a low-ball hitter. Williams knew it full well, too, and realized he made a mistake. The count was 2-2 when he threw a down-and-in fastball toward the plate. Carter made him pay, driving the ball deep into the left-field bleachers of SkyDome. The crowd of 52,195 erupted into euphoria, as Joe rounded the bases, arms stretched, fists clenched, leaping as he loped towards home plate. The Toronto Blue Jays were World Champions for the second straight year!

Unfortunately, it was Williams who garnered most of the attention. Many viewed the winning homer as a result of a bad pitch from the lefty, rather than Carter blasting a mammoth home run. "The pitch was not a bad pitch, it had to be down and in, and it was going further down and further in. So it wasn't like a hanging fastball or a hanging breaking ball that was left out over the plate; this was a pitch that was down there right at my knees. Why not give Joe some credit and say that he hit a great pitch, instead of saying 'Mitch made a bad pitch.'"[1]

Williams had just blown a slider past Carter to even the count. When catcher Darren Daulton flashed the sign for the breaking ball again, Williams shook him off and went with the fastball. Williams knew it was a mistake as soon as he let go of the pitch. "I knew that if I had gone with my full leg kick and actually rushed because I know how to elevate a fastball, and throw a fastball up and away, he either swings through it or hits a fly-ball out," said Williams. "Almost as soon as it left my hands, I knew it was a mistake."[2]

Carter admitted that had he been looking for a fast-ball, in all likelihood he would have swung and missed or fouled the pitch away. "The only reason I kept it fair was that I was looking breaking ball the whole time."[3]

Joe felt that it was a shame that it took a game-winning home run in the World Series to bring him some recognition. It was something that he felt he should have earned by now in his major-league career.

Joseph Chris Carter was born on March 7, 1960, in Oklahoma City, Oklahoma. He was one of 11 children born to Joseph and Athelene Carter. The elder Carter owned a Conoco gas station in downtown Oklahoma City, the first in the city owned by a Black person. He later drove oil trucks for the company. Athelene worked nights at Western Electric.

Joe Carter was a four-sport star at Millwood High School. On the gridiron, he was the Knights' quarter-back and he possessed a strong arm. "He was probably the best all-around athlete to ever come out of this neighborhood," recalled head football coach Leodies Robinson. "He has a rifle for an arm. In football, his teammates would run 40 yards down the field before looking back to catch one of his passes."[4] He played shortstop on the baseball team. His home runs some-times found their way to the trailer park adjacent to Millwood, some 375 feet from home plate.

After high school, Carter enrolled at Wichita State with the intention of being a dual sport student-ath-lete in football and baseball. Even though he was ticketed to be the eventual starting quarterback for the Shockers, Carter gave up football and channeled his energy to the baseball diamond. Coach Gene Stephenson molded Carter into a solid outfielder, working on the accuracy of his strong arm. In 1980 and 1981 Carter was selected to the *Sporting News* NCAA All-American first team. Carter was honored as the *Sporting News* college player of the year in 1981 after setting a then collegiate record of 120 RBIs in a season, to go with a .411 batting average and 24 home runs. "I knew he was a player the first time I saw him," said Stephenson. "When you see a guy of his speed, with that size, it's only a matter of time. He was very raw in high school, but anyone who saw him play could tell he had the tools. The physical talent was there. It just needed direction."[5] Carter was inducted into the Wichita State Hall of Fame in 1988. He was only the second baseball player in Shocker history to be so honored.

While at Wichita State, Joe met the former Diana Tinch. The couple wed on January 3, 1981. They had three children, Kia, Ebony, and Jordan.

The Chicago Cubs drafted Carter in the first round with the second overall pick in the June Amateur Draft. Carter reported to AA Midland of the Texas League in 1981 and returned in 1982. His 25 home runs, 98 RBIs, and .319 batting average in 1982 earned him a promo-tion to AAA Iowa of the American Association the next season. He continued his assault on minor-league pitching, hitting .307, 22 homers, 83 RBIs, and he stole 40 bases. He made his major-league debut on July 30, 1983, as a pinch-runner for Cubs third base-man Ron Cey at Veterans Stadium.

Carter began the 1984 season in Iowa. Chicago broke from the gate early to lead the National League's Eastern Division. The team was in first place when they acquired pitcher Dennis Eckersley from Boston. But general manager Dallas Green knew that he needed another proven starter to stabilize the rotation. He dealt Carter, outfielder Mel Hall, pitch-er Don Schulze, and minor leaguer Darryl Banks to Cleveland on June 13 for pitchers Rick Sutcliffe and George Frazier and catcher Ron Hassey.

For Cleveland, it seemed the same old story of selling off a proven commodity for prospects with potential. Many suspected that the deal was about Cleveland dumping salary. General manager Phil Seghi disagreed. "Money had nothing to do with this," said Seghi. "The trade follows the pattern we began in the winter. We want to get the best young players we can and see what they can do. Hall and Carter are outfielders with some pop. Carter is a good prospect and Hall hit 17 homers for the Cubs. He (Carter) hits for power and average. Carter and Hall can also run."[6]

Seghi was correct; the Indians were a young club. Brook Jacoby, Brett Butler, Julio Franco, Pat Tabler, Carter, and Hall were all counted on to form a solid nucleus. But like all young teams, they had many ups and downs. Even though he played in only 66 games for the Indians in 1984, Carter hit 13 home runs, second on the team to Andre Thornton's 33 round-trippers. Two of Carter's homers came on August 12, 1984, against the New York Yankees. Carter victimized Ron Guidry twice, one home run being a grand slam. He drove in all the runs in the 6-0 Tribe victory. "I wish it was me," commented Tabler. "He has a lot of talent. I'll tell you he has a heckuva lot of talent-and he is still learning. Those two balls were crushed."[7]

Carter led the American League, and the majors, in RBIs in 1986 with 121. He had five hits in three separate games that year, his career high. He also enjoyed a 21-game hitting streak from May 17-June 8. The Indians finished above the .500 mark and it looked as if they were on the rise. *Sports Illustrated* predicted big things for the Indians in 1987, putting Joe and teammate Cory Snyder on the cover of their April 6 baseball issue. Instead the Indians lost more than 100 games, the second time in three years they achieved futility. However, Carter hit 32 home runs and stole 31 bases to become the first 30-30 man in Indians history. He also showed his versatility in the field. Carter moved to first base, allowing Snyder to start in right field and Hall to roam left field. "The man's an RBI machine," said Butler. "He's unbelievable. Every time you looked up, it seemed he was knockin' someone in. He cranks out RBI like no one I've ever seen, game after game. Like a machine."[8]

Although Carter was making a name for himself as an offensive force around the league, there were holes in his swing. In his career, Carter never walked more than 50 times, and neared or exceeded 100 strikeouts most seasons he was a regular. He was a free swinger, to be sure.

Like many struggling franchises, Cleveland could not afford to pay high salaries. Like many rising stars, Carter felt that he was underpaid and was waiting to be paid market value. The Indians made an offer, but

Carter drove in 100+ runs in 10 different seasons.

Carter refused, instead taking the team to arbitration prior to the 1989 season. He was awarded a $1.63 million dollar contract, making him the highest-paid professional player in Cleveland, no matter the sport. He clubbed 35 home runs and drove in 105 runs, but hit .243 for the season. The front office knew that Carter would leave when he became a free agent after the 1990 season, and made no secret that their star player was on the trading block.

A deal was struck with San Diego on December 6, 1989, sending Carter to the Padres for catcher Sandy Alomar Jr., third baseman Carlos Baerga, and outfielder Chris James. In order for the deal to be completed, Carter had to agree to a contract with San Diego, which he did, a three-year pact.

The Padres had finished three games behind division-winner San Francisco in 1989. Naturally, the acquisition of Carter was thought to put them over the top. At least that was the opinion of manager Jack McKeon. One of the highlights for Joe was a career-high seven RBIs (including a grand slam) against the Giants on April 23. Carter's 24 homers were second only to Jack Clark's 25, and his 115 RBIs easily led the team. No other Padre drove in more than 72 runs. McKeon was fired in the middle of the year as the Padres finished tied for fourth place in the division with a disappointing record of 75-87.

Padres general manager Joe McIlvaine went to the winter meetings needing a first baseman to replace the soon to be departing Clark and a shortstop to replace aging Garry Templeton. The Toronto Blue Jays could part with Fred McGriff, as John Olerud was ready to take over at first base, and offered shortstop Tony Fernandez. In return, the Padres sent second baseman Roberto Alomar and Carter up north. "It was a good old-fashioned baseball deal, value for value, a gutsy move by both sides," said McIlvaine.[9] The day before, the Jays acquired Devon White from California. Their new outfield was substantially upgraded.

The blockbuster deal catapulted Toronto back to the top of the American League's Eastern Division, a position they held for three straight seasons from 1991-1993. The pitching staffs were a blend of youngsters (Juan Guzman and Pat Hentgen) and veterans (Jack Morris, Jimmy Key, and Dave Stewart) and were supported in the back end by ace reliever Tom Henke.

Toronto's offense was led by Olerud, Alomar, and veterans Dave Winfield, Paul Molitor, Pat Tabler, Mookie Wilson, and the return of Fernandez in 1993. Winfield and Molitor each drove in more than 100 runs (Winfield 108 in 1992, Molitor 111 in 1993) as designated hitters and provided leadership in the postseason.

For Carter, the 1991 season was the first of five that he was selected to the All-Star Game. He averaged 33 homers and 116 RBIs from 1991-1993. On October 3, 1993, he became the first Toronto player to hit two home runs in one inning. He accomplished the feat in the second inning, victimizing Oriole starter Ben McDonald twice. Carter totaled four home runs and 11 RBIs in their back-to-back World Series victories over Atlanta (1992) and Philadelphia (1993). "From a pitching standpoint, if you make a mistake he hits it," said Orioles pitcher Mark Williamson. "When there's men on base, he sees the ball and swings at it. If it's a mistake, he swings harder. And it seems like he comes up with men on base three out of four times a game."[10] Indeed, Williamson's words proved prophetic in Game Six of the 1993 World Series.

Over the next four seasons, Carter knocked in 100 runs three times, including 1994, when he drove in 103 runs in 111 games despite a shortened season due to the season-ending players strike on August 11. The Blue Jays got a look at the other end of the spectrum, finishing in last place of the American League's Eastern Division in 1995 and 1997. They did not return to the postseason until 2015.

Carter signed on with Baltimore for the 1998 season. He was dealt to San Francisco in mid-year. He retired after the season. Carter batted a career .259, totaled 396 home runs and drove in 1,445 runs. He smacked 432 doubles and stole 231 bases. His 10 seasons of 100 or more RBIs ranks him among the highest in major-league history.

Joe Carter turned to a career in broadcasting after his playing days. He served as a color commentator for both Toronto (CTV Sportsnet) and the Cubs (WGN), as well as a studio guest for ESPN. In 2003, he was elected to the Canadian Baseball Hall of Fame.

When Rick Sutcliffe was traded to Chicago in 1984, he was miffed that the Indians would trade him. He was also puzzled about what they received in return. "It is a really bad trade for Cleveland," said Sutcliffe. "The Indians sent Ron Hassey, George Frazier and me to the Cubs and they got Mel Hall and three minor-leaguers in return. That's not much. It would seem that the Indians would get more than Hall, who was platooning in the outfield. I'd have thought they get some other regular players."[11]

They received much more, Rick. Much more.

SOURCES

In addition to the sources cited in the Notes, the author consulted Joe Carter's player file from the National Baseball Hall of Fame Library, *Cleveland Indians 1989 Media Guide*, Baseball-reference.com, GoShockers.com, Retrosheet.org, and SABR.org.

NOTES

1   Mark Newman, "Average Joe," *The Sporting News*, October 31, 1994: 47-50. The quotation is Carter speaking about himself.

2   Marc Narducci, "Bittersweet Memories," *Philadelphia Inquirer*, February 5, 2011: E1.

3   Narducci.

4   Tim Wendel, "Mimd OverMatter," *USA Today, Baseball Weekly*, March 31-April 6, 1993: 4-6.

5   Wendel.

6   Terry Pluto, "Sutcliffe Is traded to Cubs," *Cleveland Plain Dealer*, June 14, 1984: 1-G.

7   Bob Dolgan, "Rookie Joe Carter Takes Center Stage," *Cleveland Plain Dealer*, August 13, 1984: 8-C.

8   Rick Weinberg, "Super Joe," *Sport*, June 1992, 29.

9   Dave Nightingale, "Are Jays Best By Trade?," *The Sporting News*, December 17, 1990: 33.

10   Jim Henneman "Joe Carter of the Jays: He Swings a Productive Bat," *Baseball Digest*, September 1993: 23.

11   Terry Pluto, "Sutcliffe Questions Trade," *Cleveland Plain Dealer*, June 14, 1984: 6-G

DAVID CONE

By Tara Krieger

*I like to think of the world's greatest athlete
coming up to bat against me – Tiger Woods,
Wayne Gretzky, I don't care who it is – and I'm
looking at him thinking, you have no chance.*[1]

There was a moment in the third game of the 1996
World Series that felt eerily familiar for David Cone.
Bases loaded, no gas in the tank. He had been burned
in that situation a year before.

Game Five, American League Division Series,
Seattle, 1995: On his 147th pitch, Cone had walked
pinch-hitter Doug Strange in the eighth inning to allow
the tying run in the Yankees' eventual 11th-inning postseason exit.

*David Cone won four games after he was traded to Toronto, the
same amount by which the Blue Jays finished atop the AL East.*

No doubt he had replayed that moment all season.
But 1996 had brought its own trials – a life-threatening
aneurysm that had sidelined him for four months, so
that now his stamina was the equivalent of coming out
of spring training.[2] The defending champion Atlanta
Braves had embarrassed the Yankees at home in the
first two World Series games, and now 24 million pairs
of eyes were on Cone in Atlanta.[3]

On the winning side of a 2-0 duel against future
Hall of Famer Tom Glavine, a tiring Cone had loaded
the bases with one out in the sixth and cleanup hitter
Fred McGriff at bat. Yankees manager Joe Torre
jogged to the mound.

"David," said Torre, his face inches away from his
star right-hander's. "This is really important; I need to
know the truth. Are you okay?"

"I'm fine," Cone said, "I can get McGriff."

Torre asked if he was sure.

"I'm losing my splitter a bit, but it's more mechanical than anything."

"I wanted to hear him say it," Torre said afterward.
"If he had hesitated, I would have taken him out. But
he didn't."[4]

"I lied," Cone said. "But I had to make him believe
my lie."[5]

McGriff popped up to short, and Cone eventually
escaped with a one-run lead. The Yankees ultimately
took Game Three, and the next three games, for their
first championship in 18 years.

Typical Cone to believe the improbable – he was
often at his best when the odds were stacked against
him. Despite developing a reputation as a free spirit in
his early years with the Mets, and then in midcareer as
a hired gun after jumping multiple teams in time for
their playoff push, Cone's candor facing the New York
media had turned him into a sort of elder spokesman.
He was a player representative when team owners
threatened to shut the MLB Players Association down.
When his fastball began to slow as he hit his 30s, he
became, as he often said, "a finesse pitcher without
the finesse," adopting new arm angles and sometimes

inventing pitches on the spot to compensate for any flaws in his abilities.[6]

In some ways, David Cone's place among the pitching elite seems improbable – he doesn't look like a prototypical athlete. His baseball cards claim he is 6-feet-1 and 180 pounds,[7] but standing next to teammates he often resembled the runt younger brother, what with his slight hunch and a face that sportswriters ad nauseam likened to a "choirboy."[8] And his high school didn't have a baseball team.

In fact, ask a teenage Cone where he saw himself as an adult, and he figured he'd follow his fictional hero, Oscar Madison of *The Odd Couple*, into journalism, complete with the greasy, wrinkled sweatshirt and half-eaten bologna sandwich behind the couch. That was as good a dream as any for a kid growing up in the blue-collar Northeast district of Kansas City.

And yet, in other ways, the youngest of four children – a girl followed by three boys – born to Joan Sylvia Curran, a secretary and travel agent, and Edwin Mack Cone seemed intended to be an athlete from his birth on January 2, 1963. He was almost named Theodore Samuel Cone; Theodore after Ted Williams, Samuel after New York Giants linebacker Sam Huff.[9] Instead, he was David Brian Cone.

Ed Cone once had professional dreams as a side-armer, or perhaps going into business like his father and namesake, who managed a hotel chain and knew the local political bosses. Instead, Ed Cone worked as a mechanic, first at a steel plant, then at a meat-packing factory. He rose long before the sun to repair large hunks of metal for over 60 hours a week, often in rooms kept at freezing temperatures.

"There was never a suggestion that my success in sports, if it came along, would be some kind of avenue to financial success for him," David Cone said. "He wasn't proving anything through me. With him, sports was an avenue for his kids to get a better education. We were sports-crazy in my family, but the real obsession was always school. You might say it didn't work out that way with me."[10]

Fierce Wiffle-Ball games would take place in the Cones' backyard under the floodlights Ed and Joan Cone had installed for evening baseball. The family affectionately called it Conedlestick Park or Coneway Park. Pitching came naturally as soon as David realized the Wiffle Ball could bend and dive depending on his grip.[11] Ed Cone helped him fine-tune his mechanics.

Frequently playing alongside boys his older brothers' ages, David got used to fighting for what was his. He was cut from his first little league team at age 7,

because he was too small. He made it the next year, with Ed Cone as the new coach. David was also the star shooting guard on Ed Cone's junior-high basketball team.[12] Friends recalled the legendary squabbles between father and son – at least one particular temper tantrum ended with David being sent home.[13]

"He commanded respect, but there was a fear factor, too," David said of his father's coaching style.[14]

Cone described his parents as "tough, hard-nosed, blue-collar people. They went by the sort of kick-the-bird-out-of-the-nest type of theory. You had to fly or fall to the ground. In some ways, I really appreciate that. In other ways, maybe we both regret that we haven't fostered that close, affectionate relationship that some families have. Part of my resiliency and so-called toughness, emotionally, is due to that background. Part of the problems I have emotionally, too, are due to that background."[15]

However, the tight-knit Cone clan knew family first. When David's older brother Danny got into a fist-fight with a neighbor on their front porch, Joan Cone wrestled her son away from the larger man's blows. The neighbor's ire escalated into weapon-wielding[16] death threats, so Ed Cone grabbed a .22 and shot him. (The wound was superficial.) David, 14, learned that day not to "be bullied by anybody. The worst thing you could be called in this world is someone who didn't stand up for his family."[17]

Such attitude translated to sports. He played basketball with such intensity that he once struck an opponent who had caused him to foul out with a metal protector he had been wearing over an injured finger.[18] Another opponent who violently slammed a ball at his chest received it back in the face.[19]

This isn't to paint Cone as the belligerent sort – he just hated getting beat. At Rockhurst High School,[20] the all-boys Jesuit prep he attended as an alternative to the subpar Kansas City public-education system, he was generally an above-average student, charming and well-liked. His senior year, he led the football team, as its starting quarterback, and the basketball team, as a guard, to the district finals.

Rockhurst had no baseball team. His junior year, Cone, also a sportswriter for the school newspaper, had gathered over 700 signatures on a petition, as well as a potential field and coaching staff, but it was a no-go.[21] Instead, Cone played summer ball in the Ban Johnson League, a gangly adolescent mowing down college-age men interested in going pro.

At 16, he was called to an invitation-only tryout with his hometown Royals, where the scouts gave him a second look from among a couple of hundred talents.[22] He also pitched in an open tryout with the Cardinals. At 17, he hit 88 mph on the radar gun[23] and was telling his parents – much to his mother's concern – that he wanted to forgo college for the major leagues.[24]

Cone was considering a partial scholarship at the University of Missouri (in baseball, with a chance to walk on to the football team). But on June 8, 1981, a Western Union wire announced that the Kansas City Royals selected him in the third round of the free-agent draft.[25] It helped that his father and Royals scout Carl Blando had known each other since childhood.

Having grown up idolizing the likes of Dennis Leonard and George Brett, Cone was all too eager to sign on the dotted line for $17,500. Similar draftees were receiving $30,000, but Cone had never seen so much money in his life. He wouldn't be so cavalier about his worth in future negotiations.

Cone immediately reported to Sarasota for rookie ball, where he had a 2.55 ERA in 67 innings pitched, second most on the team. The next year, 1982, Cone split between Class-A Charleston and Fort Myers, going 16-3 with a 2.08 ERA, including seven complete games.

Then, in an exhibition game against the Pirates in March 1983, he tore the ACL in his left knee in a collision at home plate. If the hip-length cast from surgery didn't say it emphatically enough, Cone's season was done. Between the countless hours he spent on an exercise bike rebuilding his strength, he took a minimum-wage job at a conveyor belt company. For four months, he cut and bonded strips of rubber, frequently slicing his hands as an occupational casualty – not the smartest idea for a pitcher. The uncertainty of a comeback plagued him with visions of a future in manual labor, just like his father.[26]

Cone struggled with his control in 1984 at Double-A Memphis (110 strikeouts, 114 walks), and in 1985 at Triple-A Omaha (115 strikeouts, 93 walks). Such prolonged mediocrity may have prevented a September call-up with the big-league club, which won its first World Series title that fall.

Nor could he manage his money, as notices from the Internal Revenue Service went ignored. His first paycheck in 1985 was for $83; Uncle Sam had taken around 90 percent.[27]

Moved to the Omaha bullpen to start 1986, Cone rediscovered the strike zone, fanning 63 and walking 25 in 71 innings. The Royals were noticing. On June 8 – five years to the day after his draft – Cone replaced a concussion-suffering Mark Gubicza on the big-league roster. He relieved Bret Saberhagen in the top of the ninth against Minnesota and allowed three singles and a run. Three days later, he was summoned for mop-up work against Seattle (4⅔ innings, five earned runs, four strikeouts). After two more brief, scoreless relief appearances, he was returned to Triple A.

Rejoining the parent club as a September call-up, Cone appeared seven times from the bullpen, including four shutout innings with five strikeouts on September 20. His final line in his first major-league season: no decisions, a 5.56 ERA, 21 strikeouts, and 13 walks in 22⅔ innings.

"David had a fastball and a slider back then," said Jamie Quirk, an Omaha teammate. "He was almost there but he kept trying to strike everybody out. I wanted to persuade him to be in the strike zone more and set the batters up – let them hit the ball now and then but where you wanted them to hit it. He got the idea some days."[28]

Were there any doubts Cone was ready for "The Show," he spent the offseason helping the Ponce Leones capture the Puerto Rican Winter League pennant and the Caguas Criollos the Caribbean World Series championship.[29] Cone went 6-2 in 70 2/3 innings for Ponce, including two shutouts, tied for the league lead in wins, and was second in ERA (2.42) and strikeouts (45).

Cone headed to Royals spring training in 1987 energized with two pitches that would become signatures: a side-arm slider (the "Laredo"), which he learned from Gaylord Perry, and a split-finger fastball. A day after being told he made the team – March 27 – he was traded to the Mets.

Apparently the Royals needed a catcher, and they eyed Ed Hearn. Throw in pitching never-really-weres Rick Anderson and Mauro Gozzo, and Cone was headed to New York with outfield prospect Chris Jelic. Hearn would play a total of 13 more games in his major-league career. It may be the worst trade in Royals history.[30]

For Cone, the news that he was being ripped from his hometown and sent to some unfamiliar city hit him like a sucker punch to the gut. He had a spot in the Royals rotation, and now he was concerned about starting the season in Triple A if the Mets, the reigning world champions, could not fit him on their roster.

Cone needed not worry about his place in New York. During his first session at the Mets' spring training facility, his pitches moved so much that catcher Barry Lyons could barely hold onto them – Cone said pitching coach Mel Stottlemyre's jaw was "literally dropping."[31] Cone would start the season at Shea Stadium.

And players – a roster oozing with as much zany debauchery as raw talent – took swiftly to his congenial, slightly goofy nature. Lyons was lockered next to Cone when he first arrived. "We hit it off," Lyons said.[32] And first baseman Keith Hernandez, according to Cone, "made me feel more welcome in one day than the Royals had in six years."[33]

"[T]he Mets were a perfect fit for me," Cone said. "I'd do anything in the world to fit in with that wild group of guys."[34]

Injuries (and Dwight Gooden checking into rehab) forced Cone into the rotation. His first start in blue-and-orange, on April 27, was mortification – 10 runs (7 earned) in five innings. Undeterred, two starts later, on May 12, he went the distance for his first big-league win.

Just as Cone's place in the rotation seemed secure, a fastball by the Giants' Atlee Hammaker fractured his pinky as he squared for a bunt on May 27.[35] Surgery followed, and Cone would not return until the middle of August, the pinky permanently, grossly misshapen.

Cone finished 5-6 with a 3.71 ERA in 99⅓ innings, as the injury-ravaged Mets, despite the second-best record in the National League, missed the playoffs.

Injuries worked to his advantage – Cone exploded into the rotation permanently in 1988 after Rick Aguilera's elbow went bad. His first start, on May 3, was a complete-game shutout against Atlanta. Two weeks later, he struck out 12 in seven innings of a 1-0 win at San Diego. In fact, Cone won every one of his starts in May, as well as his final eight starts of the season. He recorded double-digit strikeouts seven times that season, averaging almost 7⅔ innings per start, including eight complete games (four shutouts), and another two he went 10 innings. Former President Nixon was waiting in the Shea Stadium dugout to shake Cone's hand upon his 20th win.

Cone's line included a league-best .870 winning percentage (20-3), a 2.22 ERA, 213 strikeouts (both second-best in the NL), a NL All-Star team selection, and third place, behind winner Orel Hershiser and runner-up Danny Jackson, in the NL Cy Young Award voting.

It wasn't hard to be a David Cone fan in the late 1980s.[36] A friend of his, Andrew Levy, with a bunch of college pals, started the "Coneheads" (after the *Saturday Night Live* sketch),[37] who wore pointy rubber head coverings and occupied "Cone's Co'ner" in the left-field upper deck. For every strikeout, they'd string orange construction cones from the rafters.

"I can tell you that the Coneheads were a motivating factor whenever I took the mound," Cone said in hindsight. "I didn't want to let them down."[38]

Candid, articulate, and slightly idiosyncratic, Cone embraced the New York media. He chatted with the writers regularly, sometimes showed up at their pickup basketball games,[39] and was one of the few starters who didn't mind being interviewed the day of his turn in the rotation. Reporters lapped up his clubhouse antics, such as when leaving tickets for *Wheel of Fortune* host Vanna White (a "Total ruse. Just for fun," he said) became an ongoing spoof.[40] When the Dodgers' Pedro Guerrero hurled his bat at Cone and charged the mound after Cone's slow curve hit him near his head, Cone was readily available after the game to claim the offending pitch was unintentional.

"If I'm going to hit somebody," Cone said, "it'll be a 90 mile-per-hour fastball."[41]

Another time, after Phillies broadcaster Chris Wheeler lightly criticized his batting average, Cone appeared in the booth in full uniform. "It's a hard .143," he defended himself on air.[42]

The 1988 Mets won the division by 15 games and were the overwhelming favorite against the Los Angeles Dodgers in the NLCS. Enter Bob Klapisch, writer for the *Daily News*. Under the guise of Cone realizing his other childhood dream of becoming a sportswriter, Klapisch agreed to turn daily clubhouse interviews into a ghostwritten column.

After the Mets had won the opener with a ninth-inning rally off reliever Jay Howell, Klapisch-as-Cone wrote that Dodgers starter Hershiser "was lucky for eight innings," and that the Mets knew they'd win when he came out: "Seeing Howell and his curveball reminded us of a high school pitcher."[43]

"Bob Klapisch just kind of asked me some questions in the clubhouse, and things got a little crazy in the aftermath of a big win in Game One of the playoffs," Cone said, "and I never got a chance to read it before it went out, and I got credit for the byline. To this day, I still can't believe I allowed that to happen, that I wouldn't at least see the final copy before I put my name on it."[44]

The Dodgers passed out copies and pinned it to their bulletin board. And lit up Cone for five runs in two innings that night. He'd only allowed five earned runs once, and he'd never been knocked out of a start before the fourth inning all season.

"It definitely affected how I pitched," Cone said. "It was the first time I felt physically inhibited by nerves. My legs felt heavy from being so nervous."[45]

Cone apologized to Howell the next day and dropped the column soon afterward. In its final iteration – which Cone wrote himself – the contrite righty admitted he'd said every word, a "feeble attempt at humor" which he was "naïve" to think wouldn't make print.[46]

"I had a choice to make, either stand up and be honest, or run away and hide," Cone said, "so that was an early hard lesson to learn."[47] Klapisch later praised Cone for owning his mistake, when he just as easily could have said he'd been misquoted.[48]

Cone recovered with a perfect ninth inning in relief in the Mets' Game Three win, and a complete-game victory in Game Six to stave off elimination. But the Mets lost in seven games, and some baseball insiders still believe that Cone's column cost the Mets the pennant.[49]

Cone wasn't as overpowering in 1989, but still tallied formidable numbers, with 190 strikeouts (fourth in the NL) and a 3.52 ERA. A third-year player ineligible for arbitration, he was a bargain at $332,500. But after that year he commanded $1.3 million in front of the arbitrator – and won.

Cone immediately flew to Kansas City and told his father, whose long hours at the plant had hastened arthritis, to quit his job.

"Nothing I've done in my life has meant more than that moment," Cone said.[50] A year later, when his salary nearly doubled to $2.35 million, he bought a condominium for his parents in Florida. Another arbitration win in 1992 yielded a $4.25 million salary.

Armed with the splitter, which teammate Ron Darling helped him perfect,[51] and the Laredo, which came from the side and broke six inches off the plate,[52] in addition to his usual four-seam fastball and curve, Cone topped the NL in strikeouts in both 1990 (233) and 1991 (241). He averaged more than a strikeout per inning both years, and had mastered pitch control, with a league-high 3.585 strikeout-to-walk ratio in 1990, and a second-best 3.301 in 1991. If sabermetrics were general parlance in 1991, Cone would have been ninth in WAR for pitchers (4.4), and would have led the league in Fielding Independent Pitching (2.52).

"My agent, Steve Fehr, was very progressive with numbers, the early sabermetrics movement," Cone said. "We used some of those numbers in arbitration cases against the Mets in the early '90s, and we actually won those cases. … A lot of it was based on numbers, trying to look inside the numbers, past won-loss record, and trying to get a better look at what the pitcher really did. So I was an early believer, really."[53]

Perhaps the Mets' sinking fortunes were partially to blame for Cone's underwhelming 14-8, 14-10, and 14-14 records between 1989 and 1991. Frustrated by a 20-22 start in 1990, general manager Frank Cashen replaced manager Davey Johnson with third-base coach Bud Harrelson. The Mets battled back to first place in early September, but couldn't stay ahead of the division-winning Pirates. In 1991 the team finished fifth, and Harrelson was dismissed. By late 1992, the Mets, with one of the game's highest payrolls, were hovering dangerously close to last place. The wild egos that had previously held the team together had given way to infighting, and age and injury had slowly sapped the team of its talent. Daily appearances on Page Six were not as easily ignored.

Cone still loved New York, but was slowly falling from favor with the Mets organization. There were on-field embarrassments, such as on April 30, 1990, when he allowed two Atlanta runs to score while he argued with the umpire over whether he had stepped on first base for the force out. Or on June 4, 1991, when Cone shook off a pitchout from bench coach Doc Edwards, and he and Harrelson erupted in a shouting and poking match in the dugout. The altercation overshadowed a 13-strikeout win in which Cone did not allow an earned run.

Even after these humiliations, Cone was at his locker, answering questions. Fittingly, in 1991 Cone switched his number from 44 to 17, to honor Keith Hernandez, the Mets' previous press point-man.

Still, his off-the-field behavior was a delicate dance. Cone never had the addiction problems of some of his teammates, but he often ran with them – carousing, staying out late, and frequently not going to bed alone.

In September 1991, three women sued Cone and the Mets for $8.1 million, claiming he had made death threats. According to Cone, at least one had been harassing Sid Fernandez's wife in the stands, and although he'd "dropped 90,000 F-bombs," he never threatened their life. "It was a farce of a lawsuit, to get publicity," he said.[54]

Three weeks later, the phone rang early in the morning in Cone's hotel room in Philadelphia, where he was scheduled to pitch that day. It was the final day of the season, and Cone had staggered in at 6:30 A.M. after another all-nighter with his Mets teammates.

Cashen broke the news: A woman who had been with Cone the night before was accusing him of rape, and police were investigating. He could skip his start if he wanted. Cone refused, despite near-hallucinations of a cop interrupting play at Veterans Stadium to arrest him.[55]

"If anything, it made me stronger," he says. "It gave me a cause. Either fold or get mentally strong, that's how I was thinking. I chose to get strong."[56]

Cone was at his best – three hits, one walk, no runs, 19 strikeouts (18 of which were swinging). The last tied an NL record, with Tom Seaver and Steve Carlton.[57] Within three days, police had concluded the allegations were "unfounded."[58]

In February 1992, another woman alleged she was Cone's girlfriend and she had been gang-raped by teammates Dwight Gooden, Daryl Boston, and Vince Coleman. Cone admitted he had been with the woman a few times, but wasn't currently seeing her. The police would drop the investigation.[59]

Not a month went by when perhaps the juiciest scandal hit the tabloids: WEIRD SEX ACT IN THE BULLPEN, famously howled the *New York Post* back page on March 26, 1992. The three women from the previous fall had amended their lawsuit to add other lurid claims, including that Cone had masturbated in front of them in the Shea Stadium bullpen in 1989. There was nothing to it – the suit never reached trial[60] – but the baseless gossip has become part of Cone lore. Angry fans would taunt, "Masturbation!" or make rude gestures from the stands during the season.

"Even though both cases were cleared up, my name was completely cleared, the damage had been done," Cone reflected years afterward. "I've had to live with that. There was part of me that said, at some point, 'Be more careful, cover your ass a little better, but you can still live, you can still have fun.' I thought there was a lot of reckless journalism, but I sort of came full circle and said, 'Now, wait a minute – you did put yourself in a position to be taken advantage of a couple of times.'"[61]

A few days later, Cone, fed up with the nosy tabloids, initiated a petition to ban all reporters from the clubhouse; his teammates were happy to oblige.[62] The Mets' media boycott lasted until they headed north on April 3.[63]

"I look back at that, I think we as players probably overreacted during that time," Cone said. "We should've handled that situation better. But we did feel like for the first time we were under attack, and we thought a lot of the stuff that was coming our way was not truthful, it was kind of reckless at times. We all collectively did it, realized we couldn't go on once

we got into it, and looking back, probably would've played it differently back then."[64]

Eventually, Cone had to take it. He fielded lewd questions from Don Imus and Howard Stern on air. He invited cartoonists who'd depicted his "weird act" to send him autographed copies.

However, as the Mets spiraled, even Cone's personality couldn't save him. On August 27, 1992, the Mets, mindful Cone was facing free agency that fall, traded him to Toronto for Jeff Kent and Ryan Thompson. At the time Cone was 13-7 with a 2.88 ERA, and leading the NL in shutouts (5) and strikeouts (214). Had he not been traded to the AL, the Mets' only All-Star Game representative that year would've won his third straight NL strikeout title, as the Braves' John Smoltz only passed him by one (215) in his final start. Cone's season strikeout total was 261.

"The trade was a wake-up call for me," Cone said. "It was time to take a hard look at myself –what am I doing wrong here? Or at least, what are the perceptions of what I'm doing wrong? You're getting a reputation as a kid with great stuff, some of the best stuff in the big leagues as far as pitching goes, and also one of the biggest flakes. I kind of looked at that and said, 'Is this how I want to be remembered?' Not that I had any great revelations or made any great changes in my life, but I certainly looked at it and tried to address it."[65]

"Excited" was what he told the press. The Blue Jays were hurtling toward a division title. Cone's four wins sealed the deal,[66] and Toronto beat the Braves in the World Series to bring a championship to Canada for the first time.

"It was like I was hitchhiking on the side of the road and got a ride to the World Series –unbelievable," Cone told cheering fans at the victory parade.[67]

It was Cone's first ring, but he felt "rented, like I was hired long enough to ensure the win."[68]

Toronto wasn't home – rather than find an apartment, Cone stayed in the SkyDome Hotel. This impermanence was further emphasized when mere days after the parade, Cone was back in New York, hosting a charity auction and appearing on the David Letterman TV show.

Cone could have returned to New York the next year – he made clear he was interested in signing with the Yankees,[69] and he'd maintained his New York apartment. But Cone became disillusioned with the Yankees' disorganized negotiating tactics – which he later learned were because their first choice had been Greg Maddux. When the Royals stepped in with an "unbelievable" three-year, $18 million offer, including a $9 million bonus, the choice was clear. Cone was going home to Kansas City as baseball's highest-paid pitcher.[70]

According to Cone, Ewing Kauffman, the Royals owner, who was dying of bone cancer, "made the offer with the caveat of, not 'take it or leave it,' but 'you need to decide pretty soon,' especially considering the uneven structure of the contract, the way he presented it. It was, 'Take a little bit of time, but not too much. Make your decision.' He was a good salesman."[71]

In 1993 Cone finished in the top 10 in the AL in ERA (3.33), strikeouts (191), innings pitched (254), complete games (6), and hits allowed per nine innings (7.264). What stands out is that he went 11-14 – the Royals' weak offense[72] barely supported Cone, with 2.93 runs per start.[73]

The next year, Kansas City gave him the support (5.11 runs per start), and Cone went 16-5 with a 2.94 ERA – including three consecutive shutouts in May – and a selection to the AL All-Star team. The Baseball Writers Association of America bestowed upon him the AL Cy Young Award that fall.

Outside events overshadowed those accolades. The MLB Players Association went on strike August 12, the World Series canceled for the first time since 1904. Cone, encouraged by Steve Fehr, union executive director Donald Fehr's brother, was involved as a player representative with the Mets, but his role grew that fall when players chose him as the AL representative. Cone attributed his leadership role in union negotiations to "timing."

"Sometimes, it's by default," he said. "I was one of the more established pitchers at that time. Some of the players, they get involved, they're worried about angering the owners, or losing their job, or getting labeled. Most of the guys back then, especially, that served on the Players Association boards, they had to be prominent guys or had to be the type of players that felt secure to be able to represent their teams without feeling like they were going to lose their jobs or feeling like there would be repercussions for their involvement."[74]

Part of Cone's role was to boost morale of those concerned players, so that they would not feel pressure to cross picket lines. At his most grandstanding during a rally, he bent over with his rear end to the crowd to remind players that "the owners are trying to stick it up your ass without Vaseline. That's what this strike is about. This is about your rights, not your money."[75]

Baseball's antiquated antitrust exemption had opened the door for owner collusion to suppress player salaries in recent collective-bargaining agreements. At the height of the strike, the owners unilaterally imposed a salary cap and made plans to bring in replacement players to start the 1995 season if the MLBPA didn't concede. It threatened the union's existence. Cone spent the winter in Washington, tirelessly lobbying senators and representatives to repeal the antitrust exemption.[76]

His efforts ultimately resulted in the Curt Flood Act of 1998, a partial repeal, so that players could bring antitrust lawsuits "involving conduct that directly relates to or affects" their employment.[77]

Cone also was among those urging the National Labor Relations Board to seek an injunction against the owners beginning the season with replacement players. On March 30, 1995, Federal Judge Sonia Sotomayor granted the injunction, and the players returned to work. Cone returned the favor in 2009 when he testified in favor of now-Justice Sotomayor's nomination to the US Supreme Court.[78]

Cone took at least one day off from his strike activities, November 12, 1994, to marry Lynn DiGioia, an interior designer from Connecticut. They met in Puerto Rico in 1987 and had dated on and off since.

The strike had been over but a week when the Royals traded Cone back to the Blue Jays for rookie Chris Stynes and minor leaguers Tony Medrano and Dave Sinnes.

"I don't blame my union activities for them trading me, but I know it didn't help," Cone said, noting that the $5 million price tag in the last year of his contract probably had something to do with it.[79]

Cone's second turn in Toronto didn't last much longer than the first. The last-place Blue Jays sent him to the Yankees near the trade deadline, July 28, for prospects Marty Janzen, Jason Jarvis, and Mike Gordon. The Yankees were languishing in mediocrity, but general manager Gene Michael ardently believed Cone was the missing piece to send them to the postseason for the first time since 1981.[80] Which he did, going 9-2 as the Yankees captured the AL wild card. It was the textbook definition of a "hired gun."

Cone had now mastered the art of appearing both straightforward and rehearsed with the press. During his first homestand in pinstripes, he reviewed his new team's media guide in full view of reporters, knowing the story would play better than if he had done it privately.[81] He also gently alerted a grateful in-game broadcasting team that the clubhouse could hear their between-inning banter, and that they should exercise some discretion before they embarrass themselves.[82]

Wearing number 36 in honor of Robin Roberts,[83] a still-durable Cone led the league with 229 ⅓ innings pitched. He threw 135 pitches in the ALDS opener victory against Seattle. But he blew a 4-2 lead in the eighth inning of Game Five, the tying blow coming on the aforementioned walk to Doug Strange on pitch 147. He still patiently answered reporters' questions afterward, albeit teary-eyed.

A free agent again, Cone almost didn't re-sign after the Yankees retracted their initial offer. He and Fehr had all but reached a deal with Baltimore[84] when Yankees owner George Steinbrenner allegedly jumped in from a pay phone and reinstated the bid – a three-year, $18 million deal with an additional $1.5 million in options.[85] Cone signed.

Now a seasoned New Yorker, Cone embraced his role as a leader by welcoming newer players. When Joe Girardi's early struggles led to frequent taunting on sports talk radio, Cone advised the first-year Yankees catcher that his critics would "lay off" if Girardi interacted with them rather than hiding from the press.[86] Girardi rebounded.

Cone pitched seven shutout innings in the Yankees' Opening Day victory in Cleveland, but coldness, numbness, and blueness persisted in his pitching hand for weeks after he'd left the 38-degree weather. An angiogram showed blood clots, and Cone was prescribed blood thinners. But a second angiogram on May 7 revealed a potentially life-threatening diagnosis: an aneurysm – the weakening and ballooning of an artery – in his right shoulder.

"I didn't even know what it was or what it meant," Cone said. "It was very scary. I just wanted to know if my career was over at that point."[87]

Vein-graft surgery was scheduled three days later, as doctors replaced the offending section of artery with a piece from Cone's left thigh. How long he would be out was anyone's guess.

The procedure had not left structural damage to his shoulder, and once the graft healed, Cone could throw again. After two rehab starts at Double-A Norwich, Cone boarded a plane to rejoin the Yankees in Oakland on Labor Day.

He walked two batters in the first. Then, no hits for seven innings. But he was being held to a strict pitch count, so manager Joe Torre replaced him with Mariano Rivera after pitch number 85.[88]

"If they had left the decision up to David, they would have needed a tractor to get him out of there," said Ed Cone, who had watched the game from behind the first-base dugout at the Oakland Coliseum.[89]

Cone would pick up two more wins and a loss, finishing 7-2 with a 2.88 ERA in 11 starts. He was shelled for six runs against Texas in the ALDS, and he was wild (five walks, six innings, 133 pitches) against the Orioles in the ALCS. But his gritty performance in the third game of the World Series jump-started the Yankees' march to their first championship since 1978.

He was no longer a hired gun.

In the first half of 1997, Cone showed the devastating promise the Yankees had hoped for when they re-signed him. Named to the AL All-Star team, he had 12 wins and a 2.68 ERA by early August. He'd hit double digits in strikeouts in six games, including June 23, when he fanned 16 Tigers, and averaged over 10 strikeouts per nine innings. Then he spent most of September on the disabled list for right-shoulder tendonitis and inflammation. He was chased from his one postseason start in the fourth inning, allowing six Cleveland runs in the ALDS.

The problem was a bone spur that required off-season arthroscopic shoulder surgery. It wasn't even clear that Cone would be ready to join the Opening Day roster in 1998, but again he flouted expectation. Despite a rocky first two starts, Cone quietly built up his record.

Now 35, Cone was learning to adjust to his own vulnerabilities – in terms of when he could throw (warmer weather suited him), how much he could throw, and the types of pitches he could throw.

"A lot of wear and tear just took its toll and I lost some velocity," Cone said of his later years, when he relied more on finesse, "so I had to adjust, get more creative, probably throw more breaking stuff, less fastballs, change angles a bit more."[90]

He skipped a start in early June when his mother's Jack Russell terrier, Veronica, nipped at his index finger. It paved the way for Orlando "El Duque" Hernandez, a Cuban defector with a peculiar high leg kick, to make his major-league debut. Cone, who joked about being "Wally Pipped,"[91] wasn't slowed in the slightest, striking out 14 Marlins five days later.

A pair of Adidas commercials airing around that time showcased Cone's self-deprecating humor. In one, the advice that he "rest that arm" led a fan entourage to embarrassingly baby him.[92] The other, depicting fans at a club doing "The El Duque," ended with Cone awkwardly grinding in the men's room in response to Luis Sojo's suggestion, "Hey, Coney, why don't you have a dance?"[93]

Cone was also the only player bold enough to sidle up to teammate and drinking buddy David Wells as he was in the middle of throwing a perfect game on May 17. "I think it's time to break out the knuckleball," he said.[94] Wells laughed. Tension released.

Despite arm fatigue toward September, Cone won his 20th game in his final start – the decade gap between 20-win seasons still a major-league record. He chugged through the postseason, winning the rubber games of both the ALDS and the ALCS, and starting Game Three of the World Series in San Diego (a cortisone shot to the shoulder helped), as the Yankees capped their incredible 114-48 season with Cone's third ring.

On July 18, 1999, against the Montreal Expos, Cone accomplished what only 15 other pitchers had done in major-league history – he threw a perfect game.[95] Cone had come close before – aside from the aneurysm comeback game, he'd also taken a no-hitter into the eighth in 1991 – but this was his first no-hitter. The timing almost seemed contrived: The Yankees honored Yogi Berra prior to the game,[96] and Don Larsen, the only man with a World Series perfecto, had thrown out the first pitch and watched the feat unfold at Yankee Stadium.

"It makes you stop and think about the Yankee magic and the mystique of this ballpark," Cone said afterward.[97]

An All-Star again in 1999, Cone was 10-4 with a 2.65 ERA, averaging 6⅔ innings per start the day he was perfect. Afterward, he was anything but – 2-5 with a 4.82 ERA, averaging 5.46 innings.[98] Although he insisted he felt better physically in 1999 than he did the previous season,[99] his velocity was down – his fastball topping off in the mid-80s. Nonetheless, Cone's big-game mentality kicked in with two October victories – he struck out nine Red Sox in the ALCS and allowed one Braves hit in seven innings in Game Two of the World Series – as the Yankees won their third championship in four years.

Before 1999, Cone had leveraged his option into a one-year, $8 million salary. Now, the Yankees, concerned about Cone's age, 37, and his tired second half, refused to accommodate his request for a two-year contract before 2000. Instead, the parties agreed to a one-year, $12 million deal.

Then Cone, in his words, "fell on my face,"[100] going 4-14 with a 6.91 ERA – or, as fans derided him, $3 million per win. In a Twilight Zonesque twist, the entire debacle was chronicled in Roger Angell's book, *A Pitcher's Story*, on which Cone had agreed to cooperate before his season went south.[101]

By early August Cone was 1-10.[102] After extended mechanical work at the Yankees' training facility, he won three of five starts. But on September 5, in front of family and friends in Kansas City, he dislocated his left shoulder fielding a bunt. As the injury wasn't to his pitching arm, Cone returned to the rotation after missing one turn, with disastrous results (23 earned runs, 14⅔ innings) in his final four starts.

Perhaps as a nod to Cone's team history, Torre put Cone on the postseason roster. With the Yankees clinging to a 3-2 lead in Game Four of the Subway Series against the Mets, Cone was summoned to face Mike Piazza with two outs in the fifth.[103] He popped up the future Hall of Famer on five pitches, and the Yankees won their fourth title in five years the following night.

The Yankees couldn't guarantee Cone a spot in the 2001 rotation, so they parted ways – Cone likened the split to a "divorce."

"I want to go where I'm needed, and there isn't a great need for me here with the Yankees," Cone said then.[104]

Cone discovered where he was needed when Red Sox pitching coach Joe Kerrigan visited him that off-season and diagnosed flaws in Cone's motion.[105] Cone signed with Boston for $1 million, with another million in deferred payments.

New York newspapers called him a traitor – the Yankees' $12 million liability had taken the money and run to their bitter rivals.

Cone shrugged it off. "It's better to be booed than forgotten," he said.[106]

A sore shoulder delayed Cone's Boston debut until May, but the season was somewhat redemptive – 9-7, 4.31 ERA, in spite of him being kept to low pitch counts and often given an extra day of rest. On September 2 the old Cone resurfaced, as he dueled Mike Mussina, his replacement in the Yankees rotation, over eight scoreless innings. He lost on an unearned run in the ninth – as Mussina came within one strike of a perfect game.[107]

The Red Sox didn't re-sign him, and Cone spent 2002 as a spectator. He led the Yankee Stadium Bleacher Creatures in their first-inning roll call of the starting lineup on Opening Day ("I've always wanted to watch a game from out here."[108]) and was pulled into the broadcast booth of the upstart YES Network for a few games.

He claimed he didn't really throw that year,[109] though news outlets kept hinting at a comeback. Before the 2003 season, John Franco and Al Leiter talked him into going to spring training. Cone made the Mets as the fourth starter, at age 40.

And for one "magical" night (his word),[110] the Coneheads returned to Shea. Wearing Dwight Gooden's old number 16, Cone pitched five shutout innings for his 194th career win. Then reality set in.

Cone said he "gave it a good shot, but just physically couldn't do it anymore. And it wasn't really my arm at that point, it was more my hip. My hip just gave me a bunch of problems that year. All those years of landing on my left hip, as a right-handed pitcher, kind of took its toll."[111]

He announced his retirement on May 30, six wins shy of 200. His 2,668 strikeouts ranked 18th all-time, then.[112] When he became eligible for the Hall of Fame in 2009, only 3.9 percent of the BBWAA voted for him – a player needs 5 percent to remain on the ballot.[113]

"I think one of the problems for me was the way I finished my career," Cone said. "I didn't finish off my career and get my numbers up there from a quantitative career perspective, just kind of fell a little short." The Hall of Fame Braves trio of Greg Maddux, Tom Glavine, and John Smoltz, for instance, "got started a little younger, and they lasted a little longer," and "they stayed healthy the whole time."[114]

After spending his entire adult life gripping a baseball, Cone's transition game wasn't seamless. He has always had his charities. His own David Cone Foundation has supported several not-for-profit organizations, including the Ban Johnson League that made him, Joe Torre's Safe at Home Foundation (domestic violence), and various medical causes, in particular the ALS Association and cancer research. He guest-bartended at Foley's New York Pub to raise funds for Hurricane Sandy victims.[115] He took a pie to the face to promote gastroparesis awareness.[116]

But finding his career niche took time. Coaching was always in the back of his mind, but "the window closes for opportunities for pitching coaches. To go back on the road full-time would be a big commitment; you have to be ready for that."[117]

Cone has two sons now. Brian was born in 2006, though David and Lynn divorced in 2011. Cone and his fiancée, Taja Abitbol, a restaurateur and real estate agent from Queens, have a son, Sammy, born in December 2011. As of 2022, he splits his time between Manhattan and Florida.

Would Cone encourage his boys to follow in his footsteps? "Absolutely – I wouldn't discourage it," Cone said. "Certainly if they showed the interest and the promise and that's what they wanted to try to pursue, I would try to help them in any way I could." But, he cautioned, "It was something I was always worried about as a father. I didn't want to push them or have them feel like they had to compete with their father or feel like they had to be as good as their father. I was always more protective in that regard."[118]

For a would-be sportswriter-turned-athlete, Cone's second career should have seemed obvious –media. In 2008 he became a part-time color commentator for the YES Network, among a rotating team of announcers providing in-game and studio analysis. His remarks have not always been the most filtered – asides have included recitations of song lyrics ("Rapper's Delight," "Call Me Maybe"), unintentional innuendos (a pitcher asked to warm up but not called upon got "jerked off" in the bullpen), or poking fun at his broadcast colleagues. ("It is high, it is far, it is off my forehead!" he said in John Sterling's voice when a pop foul got too close for comfort in the adjacent radio booth.). Yet Cone has won praise as a perceptive student of sabermetrics, with observations ranging from complicated statistics to a technical examination of how the ball spins across the plate – attention to detail not often found in an ex-ballplayer behind the microphone.

His analytical aptitude has opened more opportunities. In the fall of 2021, he was recruited by two baseball broadcasters with Yankees connections to co-host *Toeing the Slab*, a new podcast about (what else?) pitching. In January 2022, ESPN announced Cone would be part of their three-man *Sunday Night Baseball* broadcast team, alongside Karl Ravech and Eduardo Perez.

"Every year it's become a little easier, knowing what the job entails, when to use sabremetrics and when not to," said Cone. "I try to be an easy listen. I try to tell you something you don't know."[119]

The easy way out would've been to rest on his laurels and regale in tall tales about his days in uniform, as so many ex-players have done. But Cone has always been at his best when challenged to defy conventional expectation.

SOURCES

Statistics, unless otherwise noted, are from Baseball-Reference.com or Retrosheet.org. Special thanks to Andrew Levy for putting me in touch with David Cone, and to Thomas Van Hyning for information on the Puerto Rican Winter League.

WE ARE, WE CAN, WE WILL

NOTES

1   Roger Angell, *A Pitcher's Story* (New York: Warner Books, 2001), 29.

2   Announcer Tim McCarver made such an observation in the World Series Game Three broadcast on Fox, October 22, 1996.

3   The attendance at Fulton County Stadium that night was 51,843; another 23.99 million viewers watched the game on television, according to Nielsen ratings. Cone had lost Game One of the ALDS against Texas; he pitched better in Game Two of the ALCS against the Orioles, which the Yankees also eventually lost.

4   John Harper & Bob Klapisch, *Champions! The Saga of the 1996 New York Yankees* (New York: Villard Books, 1996), 197-98.

5   Angell, 45. Cone has suggested more recently that he was only joking at the time about having "lied" about his ability to finish the inning, but admits that he was "exhausted" and drained from the "pressure of the moment," and that it never really occurred to him that he might not be able to pitch out of the inning. Podcast, "30 With Murti: David Cone and the 1996 Yankees," May 5, 2016, newyork.cbslocal.com/2016/05/05/remembering-the-1996-yankees-david-cone-30-with-murti/.

6   Torre once dubbed Cone "Thomas Edison every day." Craig Wolff, "Uptown Local: David Cone is the toast of New York, but he's still a backyard K.C. boy in a pinch," *ESPN the Magazine*, October 5, 1998, espn.com/espn/magazine/archives/news/story?page=magazine-19981005-article25.

7   Cone is probably closer to 5-feet-11; he himself has admitted being under 6 feet tall. See, e.g., Bob Klapisch, "Klapisch: Q-and-A with David Cone," *North Jersey.com*, February 25, 2017, north-jersey.com/story/sports/columnists/bob-klapisch/2017/02/25/klapisch-a-q-and-a-with-david-cone/98423578/.

8   See, e.g., Ian O'Connor, "A Pair of Aces Jack, Cone hold Yank Cards," *New York Daily News*, August 3, 1995, nydailynews.com/archives/sports/pair-aces-jack-cone-hold-yank-cards-article-1.696298; Jennifer Frey, "A Grown-Up David Cone Takes to Life as a Leader," *Washington Post*, March 24, 1996, washingtonpost.com/archive/sports/1996/03/24/a-grown-up-david-cone-takes-to-life-as-a-leader/20719712-5429-4492-bbbc-dc6f5cdb0a7b/?utm_term=.d476711dd8ff; Chris Smith, "Wild Pitcher," *New York Magazine*, October 18, 1999, nymag.com/nymetro/news/sports/features/2138/; Angell, 14.

9   Angell, 76.

10   Angell, 80.

11   "I was 12 years old, in 1975, when Luis Tiant was in the World Series with the Red Sox," Cone said. "I just kind of fell in love with him, started copying him in the backyard. He had that kind of style." Interview with author, February 24, 2017.

12   Angell, 79.

13   John Ed Bradley, "The Headliner," *Sports Illustrated,* April 5, 1993, si.com/vault/1993/04/05/128316/the-headliner-strikeout-king-david-cone-hopes-the-news-he-makes-as-a-kansas-city-royal-will-be-about-baseball-not-off-the-field-shenanigans.

14   Angell, 78.

15   Chris Smith, "Wild Pitcher."

16   The Cones saw the neighbor brandishing something shiny, which could have been a gun. It turned out to be a knife.

17   John Ed Bradley.

18   Angell, 79.

19   John Ed Bradley.

20   Until 2016, Cone might have been Rockhurst's most famous graduate – if not for a suddenly prominent politician from Virginia named Tim Kaine.

21   Angell, 116. Rockhurst restored its baseball program in 1989, and a few years later Cone made a large donation toward the school's athletic programs.

22   Angell, 118-19.

23   John Ed Bradley.

24   Angell, 119.

25   Interestingly, four members of the Mets' 1990 rotation were chosen during that draft: Cone's future roommate Sid Fernandez (73rd overall pick) was chosen immediately ahead of Cone (74th) by the Dodgers; Ron Darling (9th) was selected by the Rangers in the first round; and Frank Viola (37th) was chosen by the Twins in the second round. Longtime Mets closer John Franco was also part of the 1981 draft, selected by the Dodgers in the fifth round.

26   See Angell, 124.

27   John Ed Bradley.

28   Angell, 147.

29   Ponce had the best record in the regular season. However, Caguas won the playoff round-robin to represent Puerto Rico in the Caribbean World Series, taking along several top Puerto Rican League players with it, regardless of whether they played for Caguas during the regular season. According to Thomas VanHyning, this practice of "reinforcement" was common. Other such reinforcements for Caguas in that Series included Bobby Bonilla, Juan Nieves, Luis DeLeon, and Candy Maldonado. *See also* Thomas Van Hyning, "Caguas Criollos: Five Caribbean Series Crowns and Cooperstown Connections," *SABR Baseball Research Journal,* Spring 2018, https://sabr.org/journal/article/caguas-criollos-five-caribbean-series-crowns-and-cooperstown-connections/.

30   See, e.g., Peter Botte, "Ed Hearn, known for Mets trade that got David Cone, flopped with Royals but finds success in life," *New York Daily News*, October 27, 2015, nydailynews.com/sports/baseball/mets/ed-hearn-finds-success-royals-flop-mets-cone-article-1.2412564.

31   Angell, 153.

32   Robert David Jaffee, "Former NY Mets Catche\r Barry Lyons Roars Back From Depression," *Huffington Post*, January 28, 2014, huffingtonpost.com/robert-david-jaffee/former-ny-mets-catcher-ba_b_4681263.html. Years later, after Hurricane Katrina had destroyed Lyons' home, Cone and friend Andrew Levy helped bring Lyons out of a spiral of depression and addiction.

33   Angell, 154.

34   Angell, 149.

35   Cone, a left-handed batter, described the pitch hitting "the bottom hand around the [k]nob of the bat. Like cracking a walnut." Twitter, June 25, 2013, https://twitter.com/dcone36/status/349595470978498560.

36   Dashing initial hopes of many New Yorkers, Cone is not Jewish. His last name originates from the Irish "McCone," not "Cohen."

37   Cone hasn't appeared on *SNL* in a Conehead, but he did show up twice on the late-night sketch comedy. The first time was among a group of players upstaging host Ben Stiller after the Yankees won the World Series in 1998. The second was in drag with pal David Wells and host Derek Jeter in 2001 – he played a "skank" in a leopard-print halter top and metallic black miniskirt who pulled underwear from his bra.

38   Vincent M. Mallozzi, "Live From New York, It's a Conehead," *New York Times*, October 29, 2006, nytimes.com/2006/10/29/sports/baseball/29cheer.html.

39   John Feinstein, *Play Ball: The Life and Troubled Times of Major League Baseball* (New York: Villard, 1993). Excerpt available at Google Books.

40   Correspondence with author, March 3, 2017.

41   Sam McManis, "HIT, THROW AND RUN: Guerrero Throws Bat at Pitcher; Dodgers Lose, 5-2," *Los Angeles Times,* May 23, 1988, articles.latimes.com/1988-05-23/sports/sp-2199_1_dodgers-lose.

42   Paul Hagen, "Now There's No Way Phils Can Lose 100," *Philadelphia Daily News,* September 28, 1988. Cone batted .234 in 1989, the highest average for any pitcher with more than 35 at-bats.

43   David Cone, "It was justice – not luck," *New York Daily News*, October 5, 1988.

44   Interview with author, February 24, 2017.

45   Interview with author, February 24, 2017.

46   Sam McManis, "BASEBALL PLAYOFFS: Cone Winds Up Eating His Words: Met Pitcher Apologizes; Career as a Columnist Is Over," *Los Angeles Times*, October 8, 1988, articles.latimes.com/1988-10-08/sports/sp-3095_1_david-cone; Robbie Andreu, "Cone Writes His Wrong. He Quits," *Sun-Sentinel*, October 8, 1988, articles.sun-sentinel.com/1988-10-08/sports/8802280502_1_bob-klapisch-column-gag-order (excerpts from column quoted).

47   Interview with author, February 24, 2017.

48   Gerard Cosloy, "Klapisch Recalls Controversial Cone Column," *Can't Stop the Bleeding*, September 11, 2006, cantstopthebleeding.com/klapisch-re-calls-controversial-cone-column (excerpted from the *Bergen Record*).

49   See, e.g., Murray Chass, "ON BASEBALL: Yankees Must Beware Fate of the 1988 Mets," *New York Times*, June 25, 1996, nytimes.com/1996/06/25/sports/on-baseball-yankees-must-beware-fate-of-the-1988-mets.html (Joe McIlvaine claimed the column "absolutely" contributed to the Mets' NLCS loss.); Buster Olney, *The Last Night of the Yankee Dynasty* (New York: HarperCollins, 2004), 166. (Mets manager Davey Johnson "would say his greatest regret of that season was 'David Cone's literary career.'")

50   Angell, 90.

51   David Laurila, "Q&A: David Cone, Stat-head All-Star," *FanGraphs*, November 20, 2012, fangraphs.com/blogs/qa-david-cone-stat-head-all-star.

52   Joe Sexton, "BASEBALL: Dawson Slaps Laredo Slider and Mets Go South," *New York Times*, August 10, 1991, nytimes.com/1991/08/10/sports/baseball-dawson-slaps-laredo-slider-and-mets-go-south.html.

53   Interview with author, February 24, 2017.

54   John Ed Bradley.

55   Angell, 175; John Ed Bradley.

56   John Ed Bradley.

57   Kerry Wood (1998) and Max Scherzer (2016) have since surpassed that record, with 20 K's.

58   Allen Barra, "The New Whitey Ford," *The Village Voice,* October 12, 1999, villagevoice.com/news/the-new-whitey-ford-6420696.

59   Barra; Michael Marriott, "BASEBALL; State Attorney Says 3 Mets Will Not Face Criminal Charges," *New York Times,* April 10, 1992, nytimes.com/1992/04/10/sports/baseball-state-attorney-says-3-mets-will-not-face-criminal-charges.html.

60   Two of the women dropped out of the suit, and the third woman settled privately over words that were exchanged – the worst thing Cone had apparently done was call her a "groupie." See Angell, 176-77.

61   Chris Smith, "Wild Pitcher."

62   Eric Pooley, "Why Are These Guys Laughing?" *New York Magazine,* April 13, 1992, 58, 60.

63   Bruce Kauffman, "Battered Mets Banish the Messenger," *AJR*, May 1992, ajrarchive.org/Article.asp?id=2061.

64   Interview with author, February 24, 2017.

65   Chris Smith, "Wild Pitcher."

66   The Blue Jays won the AL East over Milwaukee by four games.

67   Archived news footage from 1992 Blue Jays victory parade, available at youtube.com/watch?v=F5jxknTz7tl&t=682s (last visited March 11, 2017).

68   Allen Barra, "The New Whitey Ford."

69   Joe Sexton, "BASEBALL; Royals Make Cone Game's Highest-Paid Pitcher," *New York Times*, December 9, 1992, nytimes.com/1992/12/09/sports/baseball-royals-make-cone-game-s-highest-paid-pitcher.html.

70   Cone clarified that the "highest-paid" label was only "the highest average annual value" – the contract was actually "back-loaded," in that after the bonus, he was to make $2 million the first two years, and $5 million the third year. At least Greg Maddux, when he signed with the Braves a day after Cone did, was making more from a salary standpoint. Interview with author, February 24, 2017.

71   Interview with author, February 24, 2017.

72   Kansas City's offense was last in the AL in runs scored (675) and team on-base percentage (.320).

73   By comparison, the White Sox' Jack McDowell, who won the AL Cy Young Award, had similar numbers to Cone – except that he went 22-10.

74   Interview with author, February 24, 2017.

75   Angell, 247. Former MLBPA head Marvin Miller praised Cone as "one of the most articulate spokesmen for players' rights I've ever seen." Allen Barra, "The New Whitey Ford."

76   Before the Senate Judiciary Subcommittee, Cone forcefully testified that the negotiation process with the owners was "such a joke." See "Kansas City Royals Pitcher David Cone on baseball strike – 1995 Senate Judiciary Subcmte Hearing," *C-SPAN*.org, February 15, 1995, c-span.org/video/?c4510189/kansas-city-royals-pitcher-david-cone-baseball-strike. Cone has often been asked whether he would consider going into politics. He generally demurs –"too many skeletons."

77   S.53—Curt Flood Act of 1998, 105th Cong., congress.gov/bill/105th-congress/senate-bill/53.

78   See "Sotomayor Confirmation Hearing, Day 4, Legal Issues Panel," *C-SPAN*.org, c-span.org/video/?c1446191/clip-soto-mayor-confirmation-hearing-day-4-legal-issues-panel.

79   Interview with author, February 24, 2017.

80   Andrew Mearns, "This Day in Yankees History: David Cone, Hired Gun – July 28, 1995," *Pinstripe Alley*, July 28, 2012, pinstripealley.com/2012/7/28/3198562/this-day-in-yankees-history-david-cone-hired-gun-july-28-1995.

81   See Ian O'Connor, "A Pair of Aces Jack, Cone Hold Yank, Cards," *New York Daily News*, August 3, 1995, nydailynews.com/archives/sports/pair-aces-jack-cone-hold-yank-cards-article-1.696298.

82   George Vecsey, "Sports of the Times; Cone Faces Unfinished Business," *New York Times*, December 22, 1995, nytimes.com/1995/12/22/sports/sports-of-the-times-cone-faces-unfinished-business.html.

83   Roberts, a Hall of Fame pitcher, had also been active in the early days of the MLBPA, helping persuade the players to hire Marvin Miller as union head.

84   The Orioles attracted Cone, in part, because he'd worked with new general manager Pat Gillick (with the Blue Jays) and new manager Davey Johnson (Mets) before, and he respected owner Peter Angelos for not hiring replacement players during the strike. Harper & Klapisch, 14-15.

85   The Mets also made a last-minute offer, but the money wasn't there.

86   Podcast, "30 With Murti: David Cone and the 1996 Yankees."

87   Podcast, "30 With Murti: David Cone and the 1996 Yankees."

88   Only a controversial ninth-inning single stood between Rivera completing a combined no-hitter.

WE ARE, WE CAN, WE WILL

89   Jack Curry, "Sensational Comeback for Cone: Seven Innings, No Runs, No Hits," *New York Times*, September 3, 1996, nytimes.com/1996/09/03/sports/sensational-comeback-for-cone-seven-innings-no-runs-no-hits.html.

90   Interview with author, February 24, 2017.

91   Pipp was the Yankees first baseman whose injury contributed to the rise of his replacement, Lou Gehrig.

92   The commercial was one of a series featuring the "ANSKY" boys – five shirtless men wearing the letters Y, A, N, K, and S. https://www.youtube.com/watch?v=mi7dt4gZu64.

93   https://www.youtube.com/watch?v=v9gGWqVoxvU

94   Buster Olney, "BASEBALL; Rarest Gem for Yankees' Wells: A Perfect Game," *New York Times*, May 18, 1998, nytimes.com/1998/05/18/sports/baseball-rarest-gem-for-yankees-wells-a-perfect-game.html.

95   As of March 2022, 23 pitchers had thrown perfect games – seven since Cone.

96   Berra's number 8 was emblazoned behind home plate throughout the game, and Cone threw 88 pitches.

97   Murray Chass, "BASEBALL; On Day Made for Legends, Cone Pitches Perfect Game," *New York Times*, July 19, 1999, nytimes.com/1999/07/19/sports/baseball-on-day-made-for-legends-cone-pitches-perfect-game.html?ref=davidcone.

98   Cone still finished with the second-lowest ERA in the AL, at 3.44.

99   Jack Curry, "Baseball: Cone's Velocity Returns, Showing His Arm Is Sound," *New York Times*, August 17, 1999, nytimes.com/1999/08/17/sports/baseball-cone-s-velocity-returns-showing-his-arm-is-sound.html.

100   Joe DiLessio, "David Cone on Advanced Stats, the End of His Playing Career, and Riding on David Wells's Motorcycle," *New York Magazine*, May 26, 2011, nymag.com/daily/sports/2011/05/david_cone_on_advanced_stats_t.html. As perceptive triviaheads have indicated, "David Cone" anagrams to "Odd Cave-In."

101   Before his struggles dominated the narrative, Cone had envisioned Angell's book would cover "technical things about what pitchers do and how they take care of themselves, and who owns the pitcher's arm." Angell, 255. Eighteen years later, Cone got a chance to release such a book himself, collaborating with Jack Curry on *Full Count; The Education of a Pitcher* (New York: Grand Central Publishing, 2019).

102   Cone lasted once beyond the seventh inning all season, in a no-decision on May 9.

103   Cone had pitched a perfect inning of relief against Seattle in the ALCS, and Torre considered starting him in Game Four instead of the struggling Denny Neagle. Cone encouraged Torre to start Neagle over him, because, Cone claimed, he had gotten comfortable coming from the bullpen.

104   Angell, 283.

105   The Mets, Rangers, and Royals (as a closer) also expressed mild interest in Cone that offseason.

106   Joel Sherman, "Cone-Tamination; Is Complete," *New York Post*, February 19, 2001, nypost.com/2001/02/19/cone-tamination-is-complete/.

107   Cone is also the answer to the trivia question of who threw the final pitch to Cal Ripken, Jr. The Orioles Iron Man went 0-for-3 as Cone hurled another eight innings without allowing an earned run on October 6.

108   Jack Curry, "ON BASEBALL; That Face In a Crowd Is Cone's," *New York Times*, April 6, 2002, nytimes.com/2002/04/06/sports/on-baseball-that-face-in-a-crowd-is-cone-s.html.

109   News outlets in 2002 claimed that Cone was still throwing regularly. When the author asked Cone if he had been throwing throughout 2002, he replied, "No, not really. I just kind of took the year off." Interview with author, February 24, 2017.

110   "David Cone Announces Retirement," UPI Wire, May 30, 2003, upi.com/David-Cone-announces-retirement/76971054333945/.

111   Interview with author, February 24, 2017.

112   By the end of the 2021 season, Cone had slipped to 27th all-time, surpassed by Pedro Martinez, Curt Schilling, John Smoltz, Mike Mussina, CC Sabathia, Max Scherzer, Justin Verlander, Zack Greinke, and Clayton Kershaw.

113   Cone's career pitching Wins Above Replacement, at 61.6, ranks (after the 2021 season) right between Hall of Famers Juan Marichal and Don Drysdale—57th all-time.

114   Interview with author, February 24, 2017.

115   David G. Palacio, "After Sandy: Baseball's David Cone Serves Beer To Help Victims," *The Midtown Gazette*, November 17, 2012, themidtowngazette.com/2012/11/after-sandy-local-ball-player-serves-beer-to-help-hurricane-victims/.

116   The video was posted to social media: https://www.facebook.com/gastroparesispiefacechallenge/videos/466237433765594/

117   Interview with author, February 24, 2017.

118   Interview with author, February 24, 2017.

119   Bob Klapisch, "Klapisch: Q-and-A with David Cone," *North Jersey.com*, February 25, 2017, northjersey.com/story/sports/columnists/bob-klapisch/2017/02/25/klapisch-a-q-and-a-with-david-cone/98423578/.

ROB DUCEY

By Mark Davis

During orientation week of Rob Ducey's Grade 12 summer school English class, the teacher went around the room asking students what profession they wanted to pursue upon graduation. Some replied doctors, while others answered lawyers and dentists. When it was Ducey's turn to speak, he said, "I want to be a major-league baseball player." His response was greeted with a roar of laughter from his teacher and classmates.[1] Simply put, playing professional baseball was not considered a realistic option for young Canadian boys in the early 1980s. That moment ignited a spark inside Ducey and led to a 40-year professional baseball career that saw him play 13 major-league seasons, earn a World Series ring, represent Team Canada at the Olympics, and coach in five countries at both the professional and amateur levels.

Robert Thomas Ducey was born May 24, 1965 in Toronto. His biological parents placed him for adoption, and he was soon adopted by Leo and Anita Ducey of Toronto. Rob was the youngest and only son of the couple's five children. Leo left the family before Rob was 5 years old, leaving Anita as a single mother.[2] To support Rob and her four daughters, Anita worked as an administrative assistant in the Duceys' hometown of Cambridge, Ontario.[3] Rob's birth mother was English and his birth father Trinidadian, which led Anita to emphasize to Rob the importance of hard work. "She didn't want me just to settle for anything, because of the fact that she knew I would be a non-Caucasian in a Caucasian world, I had to do better than average."[4]

As a young boy Ducey's favorite sport was fast-pitch softball and he dreamed of one day playing for the Cambridge Gores of the local men's softball league.[5] He excelled in sports, especially wrestling, during his youth in Cambridge.[6] A representative from the Cambridge Terriers of the Junior Intercounty Baseball League took notice of the 15-year-old Ducey and invited him to a tryout. He soon made the team and played his first summer of organized baseball, in addition to his first love, softball.[7] Ducey initially found baseball boring compared to softball and considered not returning to the Terriers the next season.

Convinced of his potential, Terriers general manager Ed Heather encouraged him to give baseball a fair chance. Ducey proceeded to serve as the catcher for the Terriers' 15-16-year-old team, the center fielder for the 17-21-year-old squad, and the backup catcher for the 21 and over team. "It was a crash course in baseball," he said. "I played with my age group and playing with the older players helped speed up the process."[8]

Ducey's pursuit of baseball also led Ed Heather to meet Ducey's mother, Anita. The couple were married when Ducey was 17.[9] Known as "Mr. Baseball" throughout Cambridge, Heather was highly regarded for identifying baseball talent.[10] One of his many

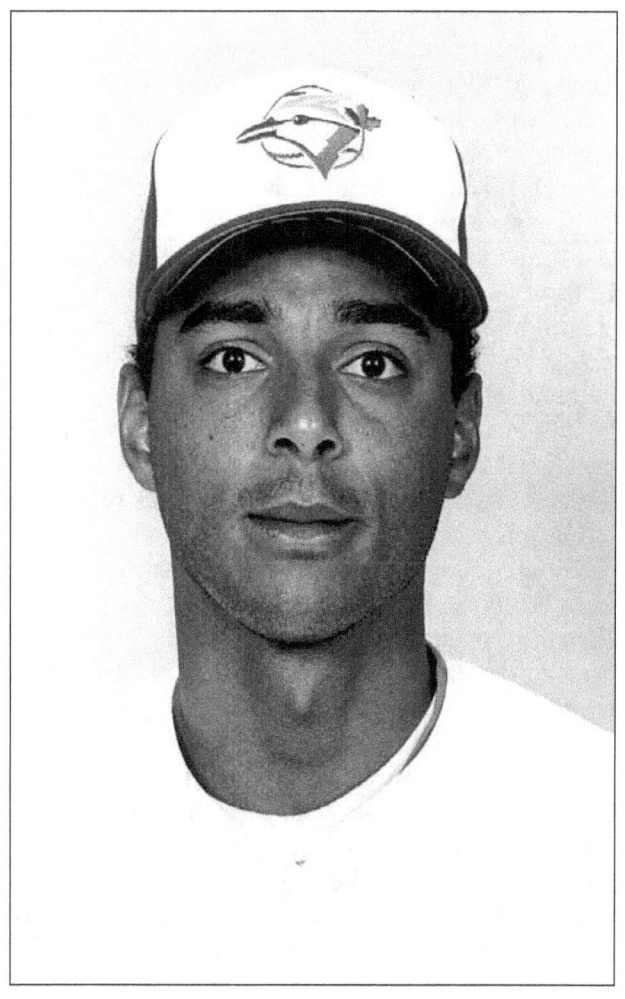

baseball roles included serving as a scout for the Toronto Blue Jays between 1992 and 2003, for which he was recognized as the organization's Canadian scout of the year in 1997.[11] Of his stepson, Heather commented, "Rob had natural ability. He liked to play, and worked hard at it. He had great instincts for the game, something that can't be taught."[12]

As Canadian players were not yet eligible for the major-league draft, after finishing high school Ducey left Cambridge on a baseball scholarship to Seminole Community College in Florida. The increased scouting exposure led Ducey to receive serious interest from three major-league teams, the Blue Jays, the Pittsburgh Pirates, and the Chicago Cubs.[13] He signed with the Blue Jays as an undrafted free agent in May 1984 and soon made his professional debut with the Medicine Hat Blue Jays of the Rookie Pioneer League. He played 63 games for Medicine Hat, batting .302 with 12 home runs and 49 RBIs, good enough to receive the team's MVP award.[14]

Ducey's strong play continued the next year in Class A with the Florence Blue Jays, where he had 13 home runs and 86 RBIs in 134 games. This prompted the Blue Jays to invite Ducey to their instructional league in September 1985.[15] His stay at instructional camp was short-lived, however, as minor-league director Bobby Mattick sent Ducey home early after his wrestling skills unintentionally injured fellow prospect Greg David during some clubhouse horseplay.[16]

Ducey continued to ascend the minor-league ladder and began the 1986 season with the Ventura County Gulls of the Class-A California League, where he hit .337 with 12 home runs and 38 RBIs in 47 games. His hot start earned him the Blue Jays minor-league player of the month for April.[17] In June he was promoted to Double-A Knoxville and continued his strong play, leading GM Pat Gillick to comment, "I'd say he's got the best chance of all our rookies to make the [big league] club."[18]

Ducey's dominance during the 1986 season also led to his receiving the annual James "Tip" O'Neill Award from the Canadian Baseball Hall of Fame. The award, named in honor of one of Canada's first baseball stars, is presented to "the Canadian player judged to have excelled in individual achievement and team contribution while adhering to baseball's highest ideals."[19]

Ducey's family baseball connections further deepened when he met his future wife, Yanitza, while playing winter ball in Venezuela in 1986. As pageant queen of the local baseball team, Yanitza was attending the league's all-star banquet and met Ducey while breaking up an argument between him and her mother over Ducey not making a play in the field the previous game.[20] Ducey and Yanitza married in 1987 and have two sons, Thomas and Aaron, and a daughter, Jenaka.

Ducey arrived at his first big-league spring training in 1987 and quickly received praise from the Blue Jays coaching staff. Hitting coach Cito Gaston commented, "He reminds me a lot of Lou Whitaker. … He's a gamer and an all-round player right now. I guess the big thing is just how much playing time can [manager] Jimy [Williams] give him?"[21] Gaston was referring to a possible outfield logjam due to the Blue Jays incumbent outfield trio of George Bell, Lloyd Moseby, and Jesse Barfield, who together formed "the best outfield in Blue Jays history."[22] In what would become a familiar pattern, the Blue Jays believed Ducey was best suited playing every day and assigned him to the Triple-A Syracuse Chiefs on the last day of spring training.[23]

After spending April in Syracuse, Ducey was called up to the Blue Jays and made his major-league debut on May 1 at home against the Texas Rangers. As circumstances had it, Ducey was already in Toronto to receive his Tip O'Neill Award when news came of his promotion.[24] He was the starting left fielder and batted eighth for the Blue Jays in a 3-2 win. He received three standing ovations from the Exhibition Stadium crowd during the game. The first occurred in the third inning when he flied out to center field, and the second and third ovations took place after his RBI single and stolen base in the fifth inning.[25] Despite the memorable start to his major-league career, Ducey had only 36 plate appearances in May and was soon sent back to Triple A. He returned to the Blue Jays in September and became part of major-league history by hitting his first big-league home run in an 18-3 rout at home against the Baltimore Orioles on September 14. Ducey's seventh-inning pinch-hit homer was the eighth of a record 10 home runs for the Blue Jays in the game. He was using a bat borrowed from teammate Jesse Barfield, which was sent to the Canadian Baseball Hall of Fame.[26]

The Blue Jays' 1988 spring training brought a new outfield dynamic and the potential for Ducey to secure a big-league starting job. Shortly before players and catchers reported to camp, GM Gillick announced that George Bell would play the majority of games that season as the designated hitter, with Lloyd Moseby moving from center field to left.[27] For the first time in five seasons, the Blue Jays' Opening Day starting lineup would not feature Bell, Moseby, and Barfield patrolling the outfield. Competition for the starting center-field role was primarily between Ducey and fellow outfield prospect Sil Campusano. Both players performed well in March but Campusano posted better offensive numbers and was named the starting center fielder, while Ducey was sent outright to Syracuse.[28]

Disappointed with not making the Blue Jays, Ducey initially struggled in Triple A. Further compounding his troubles was instruction from the Blue Jays coaching staff to change his uppercut batting style to one more conducive to making contact.[29] In June Blue Jays vice president Bobby Mattick visited Syracuse and informed Ducey that he could return to his former swing.[30] His production improved and he went on to bat .256 with 7 home runs and 42 RBIs with the Chiefs before being called up on August 2. He made 63 plate appearances in 27 games for Toronto down the stretch.

Ducey's development continued to evolve as he posted the best offensive numbers of all Blue Jays outfielders during spring training in 1989.[31] His Grapefruit League performance was perhaps best summarized in the *Toronto Star*: "SUPER DUCEY: He Hits. He Runs. He Fields. He Makes Things Happen. He Should Play Every Day."[32] For the first time in his career, Ducey went north with the team for Opening Day. But he played in only 41 games for the Blue Jays during the season, in large part due to a freak injury he suffered while shagging fly balls in batting practice on June 9 at the newly opened SkyDome. Unbeknownst to Ducey, the door to the right-field visitors' bullpen was closed but not latched. While leaping against the wall to make a catch, he flew through the bullpen door and landed awkwardly on the concrete floor, hyperextending his right knee, partially tearing a ligament.[33] Ducey was placed on the disabled list and was not reactivated until September 2.[34] The injury proved to be the turning point of his career, because his knee never recovered to 100 percent. "It was a very, very serious injury. I don't think people realized what that did to me because I kept quiet about it," he said. "But it basically turned me into a player with a lot of upside into a journeyman kind of player."[35] Ducey sued the Blue Jays and SkyDome for negligence as a result of the incident and the parties reached an out-of-court settlement in 1997.[36]

The 1990 major-league lockout resulted in an abbreviated spring training that featured competition for the right-field job between Ducey, Junior Felix, and Glenallen Hill.[37] In the end Ducey was the odd man out and was again assigned to Syracuse. He initially met the news with frustration: "Possibly, if I'd got a whole spring in – and there was competition – I might've made it."[38] Ducey spent nearly the entire season in Triple A but was called up to the Blue Jays in September. He made 62 plate appearances in 19 games, batting .302 with 16 hits and 7 RBIs as the Jays finished two games behind the Boston Red Sox for the East Division title.

The offseason acquisitions of All-Star outfielders Joe Carter and Devon White, combined with a growing list of promising outfield prospects meant that Ducey, about to turn 26, was destined to start the 1991 season in Triple A once again. He was called up to the Jays on June 29 and remained for the rest of the season, appearing in 39 games in a supporting role.[39]

The 1992 spring training began Ducey's sixth season with the Blue Jays. He was out of minor-league options, and the Blue Jays had to risk exposing Ducey to waivers should they send him to Syracuse.[40] Ducey made the 25-man roster but saw limited game action until his first start on May 27 versus the Milwaukee Brewers. Ducey kept loose between playing time by serving as one of the Jays' bullpen catchers and also saw game action as the catcher during a May exhibition game in Winnipeg.[41] He appeared in only 23 games for the Jays before being traded with Greg Myers to the California Angels on July 30 for reliever Mark Eichhorn. He played in 31 games for the Angels down the stretch, but did not see as much game action as anticipated. "The problem I have here is the same I had in Toronto, which is that they have guys they want to play ahead of me, and I'm caught in the middle again," he complained.[42] In recognition of his efforts with Toronto, the Blue Jays awarded Ducey a World Series ring and his former teammates voted him a percentage of their postseason playoff bonus.[43]

Now a free agent, Ducey signed a minor-league contract with the Texas Rangers in 1993 and was assigned to the Pacific Coast League Oklahoma City 89ers at the end of spring training. He batted .303 in 105 games and was named to the Triple-A All-Star Game in Albuquerque. He was called up to the Rangers on August 29 and continued his strong play for the remainder of the season. Ducey re-signed with the Rangers on a one-year contract and made the Opening Day roster in 1994. However, following a 5-11 start to the season, the Rangers demoted Ducey and teammate James Hurst to Oklahoma City in what manager Kevin Kennedy conceded was an effort to send a message to his struggling team.[44] Ducey made the most of the opportunity to play every day at Triple A, hitting 17 home runs with 65 RBIs for the 89ers, and

Ducey was the first player born in Toronto to play for the Blue Jays.

was named to his second consecutive All-Star Game. The strike-shortened major-league season meant that Ducey did not receive what would likely have been a September call-up with the Rangers. General manager Tom Grieve, however, decided to promote Ducey and teammate David Hulse to the big-league club after the strike began, as this meant Ducey – now on a major-league contract – was not paid the remainder of his salary.[45] The Players Association filed a default notice with the league on behalf of Ducey and 17 other players over the move. The owners responded by paying nine players and waiving the remaining ones, including Ducey, which made him a free agent.[46]

Disappointed with the situation in Texas and determined to seek an opportunity to play every day, Ducey signed a two-year contract with the Nippon Ham Fighters of the Japan Pacific League. He hit a combined 51 home runs and 120 RBIs in 1995 and 1996, in what were the best offensive seasons of his professional career. Ducey hit eight leadoff home runs during the 1996 season, tying the league record.[47] He continued to play the game hard and made Canadian sports headlines in 1995 when he was fined after a game against the Fukuoka Daiei Hawks for crashing

into the catcher while trying to score, and then punching the catcher after being hit by a pitch in his next at-bat.[48]

Ducey returned to North America and spent the 1997 and 1998 seasons as a reserve outfielder with the Seattle Mariners. He batted a combined .258 with 10 home runs and 33 RBIs in 401 plate appearances over the two-year span. The local media took an interest in Ducey's strong reserve play, at one point referring to him as "[Ken] Griffey's stunt double"[49] and declared him the 1997 Mariners' Unsung Player of the Year.[50] He received praise from his manager, Lou Piniella, who commented, "I like what Rob Ducey brings to the party."[51]

After his successful stint with Seattle, Ducey signed a one-year contract with the Philadelphia Phillies. He played well in 1999 as the fourth outfielder, batting .261 and posting a career-best 8 home runs and 33 RBIs. Ducey also delivered many clutch hits while pinch-hitting late in games, earning the approval of manager Terry Francona.[52] The Phillies rewarded Ducey with a two-year extension, the first multiyear contract of his major-league career.[53]

The 2000 season could be described as one of the most tumultuous of Ducey's career. On July 2 at home against the Pirates, he had a career-high five RBIs and two home runs in a 9-1 win. Three weeks later, the Phillies traded Ducey to the Blue Jays to make room on the roster for newcomers they received in the trade of Curt Schilling to the Arizona Diamondbacks.[54] Ducey's return to Toronto was short-lived, however; he played just five games with the Blue Jays before being traded back to the Phillies to complete an earlier trade with Toronto for Mickey Morandini. Manager Jim Fregosi lamented losing Ducey's versatility off the bench, but explained that a hand injury to second baseman Homer Bush meant that Toronto was forced to look for additional help to support its playoff push.[55]

Ducey played his final major-league season in 2001. He batted .222 with one home run and four RBIs in 30 games for the Phillies before being released in early June.[56] A few days later, he signed as a free agent with the Montreal Expos. Ducey quickly made a positive impression on Expos manager Jeff Torborg: "I didn't realize he had that kind of power. ... We thought of him as a pinch-hitter and part-time outfielder. He's been outstanding."[57] Despite the strong start as an Expo, Ducey's season came to an end on July 22 in Atlanta when he attempted to scale the left-field wall at Turner Field to catch a fly off the bat of Brian Jordan. The ball carried over the fence and Ducey's right spike lodged into the wall's padding as he went for the catch, fully rupturing his Achilles tendon.[58]

In 2002 Ducey reported to spring training with the St. Louis Cardinals with his Achilles only 80 percent healed.[59] He was cut midway through March and accepted an invitation from longtime friend and former Blue Jays prospect Kash Beauchamp to play independent baseball and serve as hitting coach with the Adirondack Lumberjacks of the Northern League. Ducey played 16 games with the Lumberjacks before knee issues and complications from his Achilles injury led him to retire as a player from professional baseball.[60]

With his playing career now over, Ducey continued his passion for the game through coaching and scouting. He has coached in three major-league organizations (New York Yankees, Montreal Expos, Philadelphia Phillies), the Mexican League (Delfines de Ciudad Del Carmen), the Chinese Professional Baseball League (Fubon Guardians), and the Dominican Republic (SFX Academy). He was also a scout for the Blue Jays and Tampa Bay Rays. As of 2022 Ducey was head of the baseball program at Bishop McLaughlin High School in Spring Hill, Florida.

Since retiring from the majors, Ducey has been an active contributor to the growth of amateur baseball in Canada. He briefly came out of retirement to play for Team Canada in the 2004 Olympics, and also coached for the senior men's teams at the 2006 World Baseball Classic, the 2008 Olympics, and the inaugural Premier 12 tournament.[61] He has also worked extensively with the junior national men's team at its instructional facility in Dunedin, Florida.[62]

On June 29, 2013 – 32 years after he took his stepfather's advice to give baseball a chance – Ducey was inducted into the Canadian Baseball Hall of Fame along with fellow players George Bell and Tim Raines, former Blue Jays broadcaster Tom Cheek, and former minor-league owner Nat Bailey.[63] Reflecting upon his career on induction day, Ducey spoke of his decision to remain in baseball. "I do think about it, the 'what ifs.' I have to believe that if I would have hung it up, I wouldn't be … in this position that I am in now."[64]

ACKNOWLEDGMENT

The author would like to thank Rob Ducey for taking the time to discuss his career and respond to the author's questions during telephone conversations on January 6 and February 5, 2022.

SOURCES

In addition to the sources cited in the Notes, the author consulted Baseball Reference, Retrosheet, and the Rob Ducey National Baseball Hall of Fame media file.

NOTES

1   Canadian Baseball Network Podcast, "Episode 17 - Rob Ducey," https://open.spotify.com/episode/0FS9NInUHxHXf0a0ScvcHK?si=Qn8ZaO7KQY-6jVq_sFv2a-Q&utm_source=copy-link&nd=1 (accessed January 16, 2022).

2   George Gamester, "Cookie Lover 'Hollow Leg' Hot-Dogged It into Baseball," *Toronto Star*, May 7, 1987: A2.

3   Gamester.

4   Ken Berger (Associated Press), "While His Mother Fights for Her Life, Rob Ducey Fights to Make the Phillies," *Hazleton* (Pennsylvania) *Standard-Speaker*, March 5, 1999: 27.

5   Canadian Baseball Network Podcast, "Episode 17 – Rob Ducey."

6   Author's telephone conversation with Rob Ducey, February 5, 2022.

7   Canadian Baseball Network Podcast, "Episode 17 – Rob Ducey."

8   Tony Reid, "Card Back Q&A: Rob Ducey Talks Playing Softball, High School Wrestling and Beauty Pageant Wife," https://www.sportscollectorsdaily.com/card-back-qa-rob-ducey-talks-playing-softball-high-school-wrestling-and-beauty-pageant-wife/ (accessed January 12, 2022).

9   Greg Mercer, "As a Canadian, Ducey Had a Snowball's Chance of Making It in Baseball," *Waterloo Region* (Ontario) *Record*, June 18, 2013, https://www.therecord.com/sports/2013/06/28/as-a-canadian-ducey-had-a-snowball-s-chance-of-making-it-in-baseball.html (accessed January 25, 2022).

10   Cambridge Sports Hall of Fame, "Ed Heather," http://cambridgeshf.com/inductee/ed-heather/ (accessed January 24, 2022).

11   Terriers Baseball, "Staff – Ed Heather," https://terriersbaseball.com/Pages/1076/Staff_Ed_Heather/ (accessed January 25, 2022).

12   Cambridge Sports Hall of Fame, "Rob Ducey," http://cambridgeshf.com/inductee/rob-ducey/ (accessed January 24, 2022).

13   Rob Ducey telephone conversation, January 6, 2022.

14   Cambridge Sports Hall of Fame, "Rob Ducey."

15   Garth Woolsey, "Lavelle Gets Tips on Screwball from Tiger Master," *Toronto Star*, September 12, 1985: H3.

16   Larry Millson, "Ducey's Attitude Impresses Jay Bosses," *Globe and Mail* (Toronto), March 28, 1987: C1.

17   Allan Ryan, "Ducey, Young Stars of April," *Toronto Star*, May 6, 1986: B3.

18   John Robertson, "Jays Going to Break Up That Old Gang," *Toronto Star*, November 20, 1986: H1.

19   Canadian Baseball Hall of Fame, "The James 'Tip' O'Neill Award," https://baseballhalloffame.ca/james-tip-oneill-award/ (accessed January 14, 2022).

20   Tony Reid, "Card Back Q&A: Rob Ducey Talks Playing Softball, High School Wrestling and Beauty Pageant Wife."

21   Allan Ryan, "Confident Ducey Makes Strong Bid as Fifth Outfielder," *Toronto Star*, March 22, 1987: G4.

22   Daneil Venn, "Blue Jays Bashers Back Together," https://www.milb.com/news/blue-jays-bashers-back-together-269801772 (accessed January 14, 2022).

23   Larry Millson, "Best outfield Still Intact; Ducey Gone," *Globe and Mail*, April 1, 1987: D2.

24   Larry Millson, "Blue Jays Promote Homebrew Ducey," *Globe and Mail*, April 30, 1987: C10.

25   Canadian Baseball Network Podcast, "Episode 17 – Rob Ducey."

26   Allan Ryan, "Two Blue Jay 'Home Run' Bats Going to Baseball Hall of Fame," *Toronto Star*, September 16, 1987: B3.

27   Neil MacCarl, "Bell Move May Be Break Rob Ducey Needs," *Toronto Star*, February 27, 1988: B9.

28   Allan Ryan, "Ducey Lost in Shuffle as Jays Slash Roster," *Toronto Star*, March 31, 1988: C1.

29   Marty York, "Jays Charged with Error in Ducey's Case," *Globe and Mail*, June 3, 1988.

30   York, "Jays Charged with Error in Ducey's Case."

31   John Robertson, "Hustling Ducey Deserves a Spot in Daily Lineup," *Toronto Star*, March 31, 1989: C2.

32   Robertson, "Hustling Ducey Deserves a Spot in Daily Lineup."

33   Allan Ryan, "Ducey Hits The Skids and Ends Up DL," *Toronto Star*, June 10, 1989: B3.

34   "Ducey rejoins Jays Gimpy Knee and All," *Toronto Star*, September 3, 1989: G2.

35   Marty York, "Ducey Settles Lawsuit Against Jays, SkyDome," *Globe and Mail*, March 3, 1998: S2.

36   York, "Ducey Settles Lawsuit Against Jays, SkyDome."

37   Tom Slater, "Ducey Making Case for Roster Spot," *Toronto Star*, March 29, 1990: D6.

38   Allan Ryan, "Ducey Gets Chop as Jays Cut Four," *Toronto Star*, April 4, 1990: F1.

39   Neil Campbell, "Deal Leaves Jay Outfield with a Familiar Ring to It; Candiotti Makes Debut; Bell, Ducey Get Call from Syracuse," *Globe and Mail*, June 29, 1991: A16.

40   Rosie DiManno, "Three Canadian Boys Trying to Live All-American Dream," *Toronto Star*, March 6, 1992: B4.

41   Neil Campbell, "Gaston Shuffles Blue Jay Lineup/Alomar, Winfield Rest; Ducey Makes First Start of Season," *Globe and Mail*, May 28, 1992: C8.

42   "Ball Clubs Trim Expenses by Cutting Minor Budgets," *Toronto Star*, September 23, 1992: D2.

43   Rob Ducey telephone conversation, January 6, 2022.

44   Simon Gonzalez, "Rangers Deliver Message," *Fort Worth Star-Telegram*, April 26, 1994: 29.

45   T.R. Sullivan, "Rangers Recall Outfielders Ducey, Hulse from 89ers," *Fort Worth Star-Telegram*, September 2, 1994: 53.

46   "Baseball talks Expected to Resume: Royals Hire Boone," *Fort Worth Star-Telegram*: October 8, 1994: 62.

47   Cambridge Sports Hall of Fame, "Rob Ducey."

48   Canadian Press, "Baseball – Rob Ducey Fined," *Globe and Mail*, September 19, 1995: C6.

49   Mike Digiovanna (*Los Angeles Times*), "No Griffey Proves No Problem for M's," *Bellingham* (Washington) *Herald*, June 17, 1997: 13.

50   Cambridge Sports Hall of Fame, "Rob Ducey."

51   Larry LaRue, "Spring Training Report," *Tacoma News Tribune*, March 12, 1998: 28.

52   Jim Salisbury, "Topps Deals Bad Hand to Card-Less Ducey," *National Post* (Toronto), March 22, 2000: 40.

53   Jim Salisbury, "Arm Is Tired, but Byrd Says He Won't Quit," *Philadelphia Inquirer*, September 21, 1999: 35.

54   Bob Brookover, "In 4-for-1 Swap, Schilling Is Sent West to Arizona," *Philadelphia Inquirer*, July 27, 2000: 43.

55   Allan Ryan, "Ducey Aced Out by Blue Jays; Outfielder Goes Back to Philadelphia in Deal for Morandini," *Toronto Star*, August 8, 2000: C2.

56   Bob Brookover, "Vallant Called Up; Ducey Let Go," *Philadelphia Inquirer*, June 7, 2001: 57.

57   Stephanie Myles, "Expos Story," *Montreal Gazette*, June 27, 2001: 11.

58   Stephanie Myles, "Ducey's Done for Season," *Montreal Gazette*, July 23, 2011: 31.

59   Jim Seip, "Lumberjacks Sign Major League Veteran," *Glens Falls* (New York) *Post-Star*, April 4, 2002: 13.

60   Seip.

61   Baseball Canada, "Baseball Canada Announces Roster for Inaugural Premier12," https://baseball.ca/baseball-canada-announces-roster-for-inaugural-premier12 (accessed January 26, 2022).

62   Baseball Canada, "Baseball Canada Announces Fall Instructional Camp Invitees," https://baseball.ca/baseball-canada-announces-fall-instructional-camp-invitees (accessed January 26, 2022).

63   "Ducey Makes Canadian Baseball Hall of Fame," *Waterloo Region* (Ontario) *Record* https://www.therecord.com/sports/baseball/2013/02/07/ducey-makes-canadian-baseball-hall-of-fame.html (accessed January 26, 2022).

64   Canadian Baseball Network Podcast, "Episode 17 – Rob Ducey."

MARK EICHHORN

By Tim Sitar

Drafted as a shortstop, Mark Eichhorn was initially a starting pitcher in the minors, but an injured arm led to the development of a submarine style that featured a release point so low to the ground that it became a nightmare for right-handed batters. His new delivery would lead to him becoming the set-up man for Tom Henke from 1986 to 1988, and two World Series rings over an 11-year major-league career.

Mark Anthony Eichhorn was born on November 21, 1960, in San Jose, California. His father, Bob, and his mother, Rita (née Firebaugh), made their home south of San Jose in the Santa Cruz County coastal city of Watsonville. Bob served in the famed 101st Airborne during World War II[1] and had a 30-year career with the US Postal Service. Rita had a long career as a nurse.[2]

During his early baseball life Mark was the classic youth baseball combination of a shortstop with a powerful arm who could also dominate when on the mound. At Watsonville High School, he was told he could do only one or the other, and Eichhorn wanted to play every day. So he became a star shortstop for the Wildcatz. He still pitched in the summer for youth teams, and during his senior season in high school was allowed to pitch occasionally.[3] Eichhorn stood 6-feet-3 at the time and was also the tallest member of the basketball team. A point guard, he earned honorable mention All-Santa Cruz County honors his senior year.[4]

It was Eichhorn's prowess at shortstop that first got the attention of scouts when the Wildcatz met North Salinas High School in a key game played before a crowd that included several big-league scouts. The scouts weren't there to see Eichhorn. They were there to study the star pitcher of the opposition, Steve Raine.[5]

On May 16, 1978, the two prep stars dueled each other during an eight-inning, 1-0 North Salinas win. Eichhorn matched Raine on the mound that day and accounted for three of the Wildcatz' five hits.[6] One of the scouts there that day represented the Blue Jays. Raine was drafted first by the Giants, and later by the Royals, and pitched for three seasons in the Royals chain.

Eichhorn ended his senior year as an All-Monterey Bay League and All-County selection, hitting .369 and sporting a 0.39 ERA on the mound.[7]

That summer he played on a Monterey Babe Ruth team with Raine and a future 10-year major leaguer, Mike Aldrete.[8]

In the January 1979 supplemental draft, Toronto chose Eichhorn as a shortstop as a second-round pick, 30th overall. He was the first Watsonville High player ever selected in a major-league draft and the highest pick of any player out of Santa Cruz County at the time.[9]

Instead of signing, Eichhorn ended up starting at shortstop for his local community college, Cabrillo, that spring. At Cabrillo College, he never took to the

mound. In June, he received a phone call. He was told to come to Watsonville High School with a catcher and take some bullpen. He showed up at the school with his high-school catcher and his bat, just in case.[10]

Eichhorn took to the hill in front of Jays scouts Bobby Mattick and Wayne Morgan. Three hours later, they signed him to a contract.[11]

Eichhorn's first professional stop was the Blue Jays Rookie-level team in Medicine Hat, Alberta, where laborious 12-hour bus rides to cities like Idaho Falls were the norm. At the time, the right-hander was the ace of the staff, but still saw himself as a shortstop. "In my heart, I was a shortstop," he said. "I would upset the coaches because I would take infield. Our shortstop was Fred Manrique, I thought I was as good as him."[12]

In the Florida Instructional League that fall, Eichhorn decided to show his coaches that he could hit, too, by taking some batting practice. "And they yelled at me to get out (of) there," Eichhorn told the *Santa Cruz Sentinel* on March 2, 1980. "I keep telling them I can hit," he said.[13]

The 1980 season was spent in the Class-A Carolina League at Kinston in what Eichhorn termed a break-out year. He was 14-10 with a 3.54 ERA. Also that season Eichhorn realized he probably wasn't a professional shortstop after all. Watching a slick-fielding 18-year-old named Tony Fernandez perform changed his mind. But the season brought a promotion to Double-A Knoxville (Southern League), where Eichhorn went 10-14 with a 3.98 ERA. "I had a bad first half, but I managed to turn it around in the second," he said.[14]

In 1982 Eichhorn started the season with Triple-A Syracuse, and after going 10-11 with a 4.54 ERA, he was called up to the Blue Jays in August after Jim Gott was lost thanks to a blister.[15]

It may have seemed like a dream come true for Eichhorn, but there was a problem. His arm was ailing. "I already felt my arm was on the way down. I knew something was wrong, but I didn't say anything," he said.[16]

He made his major-league debut on August 30, 1982, against the Baltimore Orioles at Exhibition Stadium. It was his first of seven starts for the Blue Jays. He took the loss, pitching 4⅔ innings and giving up five runs in the Blue Jays' 6-3 loss. He gave up six hits, including a third-inning home run by John Lowenstein.

Eichhorn was "roughed up"[17] in his third start, before a large group of family and friends at the Oakland Coliseum. He gave up five hits and three runs in two innings and his Santa Cruz County fans gave him a standing ovation as he walked to the dugout after being pulled from the game.[18] The Blue Jays rallied to win the game.

Eichhorn was throwing in the bullpen at the Seattle Kingdome prepping for his sixth start, when pitching coach Al Widmar asked, "Is your arm okay?"[19]

Eichhorn told Widmar everything was fine, took the mound, and proceeded to take a perfect game into the seventh. "I had it that day," Eichhorn said. "I had a low-90s fastball, and on that day it was probably just high-80s. My arm was cranky, but it worked well for me that day."[20] Eichhorn left with the game tied, 2-2, but the Mariners touched reliever Dale Murray for a run in the ninth to win the game, 3-2.

Eichhorn finished his first big-league stint with a record of 0-3, with a 5.45 ERA. He struggled over the next two seasons, in 1983 in Syracuse and splitting time between Knoxville and Syracuse in 1984. By August of 1984, there was talk of Eichhorn having a future in the Blue Jays organization – as a coach. "I thought it could be the end of my career, but I knew I wasn't done," Eichhorn remembered.[21]

Eichhorn was sleeping in on a Sunday at a Howard Johnson's in Pawtucket, Rhode Island, when the phone rang at 9 A.M. It was pitching coach Larry Hardy. As Eichhorn recalled, "He said, 'Hey, Eich, do you have a glove in your room?' I said yes, and he asked me to meet him in the back lawn area of the hotel. So, here we are on the back lawn of a Howard Johnson's with the backup catcher and Hardy says, 'Your arm has been shot, but you were drafted as a shortstop and threw at different angles, he mentioned [Dan] Quisenberry. He asked me to drop down and throw and asked how it felt. I told him I didn't feel anything.

"That night, we were losing 8-0, and I was warming up, I was called in and he signaled me to lower my arm. Well, I faced three hitters: groundball to third base, groundball to shortstop, groundball to third. When I got to the dugout the guys were yelling and high-fiving. I said, 'That's the first time in, I don't know, two years that I got three guys out in a row!'"[22]

It didn't take long for Eichhorn to learn that the Blue Jays were liking what they were hearing about his new pitching style. "They asked me what I thought about going to instructional league, and I said it was fine," he said.[23]

"At this point the Twins were interested in signing me to a minor-league deal. I let Toronto know, and they said, 'We will do you one better and invite you to spring training.' I was basically the last guy on the roster, but I didn't give up any runs that spring," said Eichhorn.[24]

Eichhorn's new arsenal now featured an extremely slow changeup, a slider, and his out pitch – a huge splitter. After more seasoning in the minors, Eichhorn was back in the big leagues in 1986. The season was his finest. He had a career-high 14 wins with six losses. Eichhorn also had career bests of 157 innings pitched and 166 strikeouts, yielded just 105 hits, and gave up just 45 walks. Right-handed batters hit only .135/.186/.165 against him.

There was one further career best, an ERA of 1.72. Eichhorn often pitched as many as three innings, including six in one game. Manager Jimy Williams offered him the chance to start one of the season's final games to get the six or so innings needed to become eligible for the ERA title.

"When we fell out of the race, I was the story. The reporters were showing up at my locker after games, asking about my ERA. I was really self-conscious about it. I really didn't want the attention. That whole last month of the season, it was the last thing I wanted to talk about. Jimy did come to me and ask if I wanted to start, but I said no. To me, it felt selfish to do that," he said.[25]

Had Eichhorn not spent some time on the disabled list that season, he might have won the ERA title after all. Still, 1986 was a very good year for him. *The Sporting News* named him the 1986 Rookie Pitcher of the Year. He finished sixth in the Cy Young Award voting and third in the Rookie of the Year Award voting, just behind Jose Canseco and Wally Joyner.

The following season was solid, too. Eichhorn pitched in a career-high and AL-leading 89 games, going 10-6 with a 3.17 ERA. His strikeouts were down to 96 and he walked 52 while giving up 110 hits in 127⅔ innings. In 1988 he was sent to Syracuse after the All-Star break along with David Wells. It was apparently a move by Jimy Williams to shake up the Blue Jays staff.[26]

In March 1989 Eichhorn's contract was purchased by Atlanta. He had been assigned to Syracuse after spring training. The Braves were looking for bullpen help and paid a $50,000 waiver fee for his services.[27] Again, he split time between Triple A with Richmond and the majors. He was brilliant in Richmond, going 1-0 with a 1.32 ERA and 19 saves. With the Braves he was 5-5 with a 4.35 ERA over 45 games. He was released by Atlanta and signed a free-agent deal with the California Angels in December.

Eichhorn's first stint with the Angels was a successful one. He said, "I credit pitching coach Marcel Lachemann with reviving my career. He asked me, 'What made you successful in '86?' I answered the slider and mostly the splitter, and he told me to work on the splitter."[28]

Eichhorn achieved a career-high 13 saves during the 1990 season, going 2-5 with a 3.08 ERA. In 1991 he was 3-3 with a 1.98 ERA and one save in 70 appearances. In 1992 things were going well in Anaheim again. By late July, Eichhorn had made 42 appearances for the Angels, going 2-4 with a 2.38 ERA.

It was just one day before the trade deadline and Eichhorn was on an airplane when he learned he would be returning to Canada. "We were on the plane, heading to Texas," Eichhorn said. "I was playing cards, when interim manager John Wathan (Buck Rodgers had injured his leg in a bus accident and did not travel with the team) came up and said, 'Whitey [Herzog] (the club's director of player personnel at

Eichhorn, a shortstop in his youth, had a career fielding percentage of .992.

the time) wants to talk to you.' That's how I learned I was traded." The Angels got outfielder Rob Ducey and catcher Greg Myers in the deal.[29]

When he returned to the card game, his teammates were curious. "They asked, 'Where are you going?' They guessed just about all the teams, but Toronto," laughed Eichhorn.[30]

The idea of returning to Toronto was exciting to Eichhorn. First there was the city itself, "I loved Toronto. It was an exciting city. My favorite city. The people are so nice. When you walked around the city, people knew who you were, and treated you so well," Eichhorn recalled.[31]

Then there was the club that the Blue Jays brain trust had assembled. At the time of the trade the Jays were tied with the Athletics with the best record in baseball at 60-41. Said Eichhorn: "I came to the team late in the season, but wow. It was the most talented team I had ever been a part of. You had a Hall of Famer at leadoff, a Hall of Famer batting second, Hall of Famers all over. And I had been on some talented teams. But you gotta have chemistry. You don't win the whole thing without chemistry.

"And Cito [manager Cito Gaston] just knew how to handle players. He trusted his players. He was soft-spoken, quiet, proud, careful with what he said, and when he did speak, you listened. The players wanted to win for each other, for Toronto, and they wanted to win for him."[32]

Down the stretch of the 1992 season, Eichhorn made 23 appearances for the Jays, going 2-0.

In the postseason, he pitched in the ninth inning of Game Five of the ALCS, a 6-2 loss to Oakland. He threw 11 pitches and faced three batters. He again took the mound in Game Five of the World Series loss to the Braves, facing three batters, and striking out one on 14 pitches.

Two days after the Jays' World Series victory, Eichhorn was interviewed by his hometown *Santa Cruz Sentinel*. He had just attended the victory parade in Toronto in front of over 250,000 fans. "As I'm talking right now, I'm still that high. It really hasn't sunk in yet; the feeling is indescribable. It was a first-class parade. The reaction is unbelievable. There had to be a half a million people. This is a big day for Canada."[33]

In 1993 Eichhorn enjoyed a full season with the defending champions, going 3-1 in 54 appearances. His ERA was 2.72. He struck out 47, while allowing 22 walks.

Once again the Blue Jays won the World Series and once again Eichhorn pitched some postseason innings. In Game Three of the ALCS, a 6-1 loss to the White Sox, he entered the game in the seventh inning. He faced eight hitters in two innings of work, surrendering one hit while walking one and striking out one.

In the Blue Jays' Game Two World Series loss to the Phillies, he pitched a third of an inning, giving up a hit and a walk. For him it was a memorable effort, but it was lost on some. "In 1994 I was with the Orioles. I see Cito. We shake hands and he says, 'You know I regret not getting you into that second series,'" laughed Eichhorn. "He hadn't remembered it, but I was touched that he thought to say that to me. That too was a special team."[34]

Eichhorn had signed a free-agent deal with Baltimore in December 1993. With the Orioles he was 6-5 with one save in 43 games. Rotator cuff surgery on February 5, 1995, led to his missing the entire season. The rest of the year was spent rehabbing his pitching arm.

Eichhorn started working out with fellow Santa Cruz County major leaguers Glenallen Hill and Tom Urbani in early 1996.[35] The work led to tryouts with the Blue Jays and Giants, where he threw for 15 or 20 minutes as manager Dusty Baker looked on.[36] Finally, on February 6, 1996, Eichhorn signed with the Angels. He went 1-2 with 24 appearances for Anaheim with a 5.04 ERA.

Eichhorn left the game – well, the American game anyway. He was coaching and conducting clinics in the Santa Cruz area in 1997 when he learned of a chance to return to the mound in Taiwan. The overseas adventure was short-lived; he missed his family, and a line drive to the head ended his two months in Taiwan.[37] Eichhorn again spent time coaching and conducting clinics. He even played shortstop again in a 35-and-over league,[38] but at the age of 37, he attempted a return to the major leagues, signing with Tampa Bay. He was 5-3 with 3.88 ERA and 18 saves for Triple-A Durham. "I was healthy again. With side-armers it can come and go, but I had it in Durham," said Eichhorn.[39] Then tendinitis in the elbow forced him to walk away from the game again.[40]

Still he wasn't done. After a failed December 1999 tryout with the Dodgers, Eichhorn was back in the Blue Jays family again following a tryout in June 2000.[41] He made a total of 22 appearances with Dunedin and Syracuse. "At that point it was a struggle to be on the road," he said "In August I was hearing that I would be a September call-up, but I decided to retire. I had three kids at the time, my wife was pregnant with number four. I had been there, done that."[42]

In all, Mark and his wife Mariann, whom he met during spring training in 1987,[43] have five children – four sons and a daughter: Kevin born in 1990, Brian (1991), Steven (1995), Sarah (1999), and David (2001). Kevin was drafted by the Arizona Diamondbacks. Despite arm issues, he pitched for seven seasons in the minors, 2008-2014.

In 2002 Mark was an assistant coach on the Aptos Little League squad that featured Kevin. The team went to the Little League World Series and was the subject of the documentary film *Small Ball*.

Mark's younger brother Dave was drafted three times by the Blue Jays and pitched in the Dodgers and Astros systems from 1983 to 1990. "I always thought [Dave] was with the wrong organization," said Eichhorn. "He had a great three-quarter delivery and a strong sinker, but the Dodgers were all about speed, velocity."[44]

Even when he was an active player, Eichhorn would conduct clinics in the Santa Cruz area during the offseason. He also had two stints as an assistant coach at Aptos High School, while his boys were in school.

He was elected to the Watsonville High School Hall of Fame in December 2000 along with former NFL defensive back Sherman Cocroft, former San Diego Padre John Sipin, and NBA standout Kenny Sears.[45]

As of early 2022, Eichhorn still resided in Aptos and provided baseball hopefuls with private coaching sessions. He said, "It is beautiful here, the ocean, the weather, it's where my roots are."[46]

SOURCES

Unless otherwise noted, statistics have been taken from Baseball-Reference.com. In addition to the sources cited in the Notes, the author consulted the following:

Blair, Jeff. *Full Count: Four Decades of Blue Jays Baseball* (Toronto: Vintage Canada, 2013).

NOTES

1   Obituary for Robert Eichhorn, *Santa Cruz* (California) *Sentinel*, April 23, 2004: 10.

2   Mark Eichhorn, phone interview with author, March 10, 2022.

3   Eichhorn interview.

4   "The Sentinel's 1978 All-County Basketball Team," *Santa Cruz Sentinel*, February 2, 1978: 49.

5   Eichhorn interview.

6   Garson Mattasoff. "North Salinas Clinches Baseball Title," *Salinas Californian*, May 17, 1978: 29.

7   "The Sentinel's 1978 All-County Baseball Team," *Santa Cruz Sentinel*, May 21, 1978: 51.

8   "Monterey in Ruth Tourney Finals," *Salinas Californian*, July 22, 1978: 16.

9   "Watsonville Shortstop No. 2 Draft," *Santa Cruz Sentinel*. January 10, 1979: 15. The other Watsonville player selected directly out of high school was pitcher Ken Swank, drafted by the Kansas City Royals in the 10th round of the June 1980 draft.

10   Eichhorn interview.

11   Eichhorn interview.

12   Eichhorn interview.

13   Ed Vyeda, "County Baseball Products Making Their Way Through Minors," *Santa Cruz Sentinel*, March 2, 1980: 55.

14   Eichhorn interview.

15   Eichhorn interview.

16   Eichhorn interview.

17   Eichhorn interview.

18   Ed Vyeda, "Eichhorn at 'Home' in Majors," *Santa Cruz Sentinel*, September 9, 1982: 29.

19   Eichhorn interview.

20   Eichhorn interview.

21   Eichhorn interview.

22   Eichhorn interview.

23   Eichhorn interview.

24   Eichhorn interview.

25   Eichhorn interview.

26   Brent Ainsworth, "Eichhorn Sent to Minors," *Santa Cruz Sentinel*, July 11, 1988: 15.

27   "Braves Deal for Eichhorn," *Santa Cruz Sentinel*, March 30, 1989: 13.

28   Eichhorn interview.

29   Eichhorn interview.

30   Eichhorn interview.

31   Eichhorn interview.

32   Eichhorn interview.

33   Brent Ainsworth, "Eichhorn Floating on Air," *Santa Cruz Sentinel*, October 27, 1992: 13.

34   Eichhorn interview.

35   Ed Vyeda, "Free Agent," *Santa Cruz Sentinel*, January 7, 1996: 13-14.

36   Ed Vyeda, "Eichhorn Starting Over, May End Up in Minors," *Santa Cruz Sentinel*, January 20, 1996: 13.

37   Dan Fitch, "Return of the Sidewinder," *Santa Cruz Sentinel*, May 2, 1997: 13, 15.

38   Dan Fitch, "No What If's for Eichhorn," *Santa Cruz Sentinel*, September 20, 1998: 15.

39   Eichhorn interview.

40   Josh Nagel, "Pitcher Has Designs on Another Comeback." *Santa Cruz Sentinel*, December 26, 1999: 21.

41   "Blue Jays Sign Pitcher Mark Eichhorn," *Santa Cruz Sentinel*, June 20, 2000: 24.

42   Eichhorn interview.

43   Nagel.

44   Eichhorn interview.

45   "Watsonville High Quintet Ready for Immortality, Hall of Fame," *Santa Cruz Sentinel*, December 29, 2000: 37.

46   Eichhorn interview.

ALFREDO GRIFFIN

By Justin Krueger

Alfredo Claudino Griffin was a professional baseball player for 20 years, 18 of which were in the major leagues. He was a fan favorite for his outgoing personality and sure-handed glove in the middle infield. And he's the answer to two great trivia questions: (1) Who was on deck when Joe Carter hit the ninth-inning Game Six home run off Mitch Williams of the Philadelphia Phillies to win the 1993 World Series? (2) Who was the first player to have played on the losing end of three perfect games (Len Barker in 1981, Tom Browning in 1988, and Dennis Martinez in 1991)?

Griffin was born on October 6, 1957, in Santo Domingo, Dominican Republic. He was the youngest of three brothers. His father, Alberto Reed, in order to financially support the family worked on the docks of Santo Domingo during the day and at night was

a musician at local clubs. Young Alfredo developed a love of music from his father and would often be found playing the conga at parties and fiestas as he grew older.[1] With civil unrest and the resulting turf wars arising from a coup d'etat in 1965, Alfredo's mother made the decision to take him and his two brothers away from the capital city and back to her family. His father stayed in Santo Domingo.[2]

Upon moving back to Consuelo at age 8, Alfredo eventually made his way to playing baseball for the local sugar mill, Ingenio Consuelo, at the behest of his uncle Clemente Hart who was a cricket player later-turned baseball player. Hart played baseball locally for the Estrella Orientales, a Dominican Winter League team. The Consuelo sugar-mill team had several other future major leaguers on its roster, including Rafael Santana, Nelson Norman, Rafael Ramirez, and Julio Franco. Major-league scouts were plentiful at its games.[3] Griffin was signed as a 15-year-old non-drafted free agent by the Cleveland Indians on August 22, 1973, by Cuban scout Reggie Otero. At the time, Griffin played second base. Otero believed that he possessed excellent range on the field, and suggested a move to shortstop.[4] With the signing Griffin became one of the growing number of players to sign professional contracts from San Pedro de Macoris, a port city on the country's southern coast. That area of the Dominican Republic in the late 1970s and early '80s became known as the City of Shortstops with the major-league success of players like Griffin, Pepe Frias, Rafael Ramirez, Julio Franco, and Tony Fernandez.[5]

Not long after Griffin signed with the Indians he was in A-ball. He was batting exclusively right-handed. In 1975, upon the request of San Jose player-coach Gomer Hodge who "told me to take the next at-bat left-handed. I slapped the ball and almost beat it out."[6] It turned out his early season batting struggles that had seen his average dip to around .080 had opened a path to becoming a switch-hitter.[7] Over the next few years he continued to work on his switch-hitting with Indians minor-league instructor Tommy McCraw. McCraw told him to keep at it, hit the ball on the ground, and take advantage of his speed. Griffin ended his major-league career with 1,688 hits in 6,780 at-bats. While none of his offensive statistics are eye-popping, they are reflective of a player known mostly for his glove who played the field with enough consistency to enjoy a major-league career for nearly two decades.

His minor-league career started in 1974 with stops in rookie ball with the Gulf Coast League Indians and the High-A Reno Silver Sox. Griffin spent the entire 1975 season with the High-A San Jose Bees. Through his first three seasons in the minors he racked up 43 steals. Highlighting his penchant for aggressiveness on the basepaths, he was also caught stealing 25 times. Griffin took a significant step forward in 1976. While starting the season again at San Jose, he earned a call-up to Williamsport of the Double-A Eastern League. After spending about 60 games at San Jose and Williamsport he played in 22 games with the Triple-A Toledo Mud Hens before getting his first major-league call-up.

Upon his first major-league call-up Griffin noted, "No, I am not excited, I am not nervous, but I am very happy."[8] Griffin made his major-league debut on September 4, 1976, as a late-inning substitution. His first hit came on September 7. Upon entering the game in the sixth inning, Griffin hit a single to left field on the very first pitch he saw from Milwaukee Brewers starting pitcher Gary Beare. Beare happened to be making his major-league debut in what turned out to be a nine-inning complete-game 17-4 victory over the Cleveland Indians. He was 18 years old. Between then and his last major-league appearance, in October 1993 as a member of the World Series-winning Toronto Blue Jays, Griffin strung together an 18-year career. Thirteen of those seasons were as an everyday starter for the Indians, Oakland Athletics, Los Angeles Dodgers, and two stints with the Blue Jays.

After a few short stints in the majors with the Indians from 1976-1978 in which he appeared in 31 games total, Griffin was eventually traded to the Blue Jays along with Phil Lunsford in exchange for pitcher Victor Cruz prior to the start of the 1979 season. It was as a Blue Jay that Griffin cemented his status as a major-league shortstop. Jerry Howarth, longtime Blue Jays broadcaster, said, "The Jays couldn't have asked for a better player or role model. He was at the leading edge of an influx of talented Dominican Republic players for the shore of Lake Ontario. ... Alfredo was a big part of the success story of the Blue Jays."[9]

At 5-feet-11 and 165 pounds, Griffin was known more for his defensive ability than anything he had to offer offensively. His best offensive season was his 1979 American League Rookie of the Year campaign. He batted .287, had 179 hits, hit 10 triples, and scored 81 runs. He shared the award with Minnesota Twins third baseman John Castino. He had been named the AL Player of the Month for September after batting .347 with six doubles, four triples, six RBIs, and five stolen bases. That season Griffin turned 124 double plays, a Blue Jays team record that he surpassed the next season with 126 double plays. He also made a league-leading 36 errors. In 1979 Griffin was called a bright spot in the otherwise unremarkable three-year history of the Toronto Blue Jays.[10]

Griffin's early success in the major leagues was neither immediate nor without growing pains. Recalling his early struggles, he said:

> "It was 1979. I was hitting about .170 after the first month. My confidence was shot. Our hitting coach [1986 Hall of Fame inductee] Bobby Doerr said, 'I'll help you, but you're about down to your last chance to stay in the majors.' So before our game in Texas that night, he worked with me on choking up on the bat, and relaxing a bit. Only trouble was, I did not speak English very well then. Or understand it. So he drew some pictures, and asked Rico Carty – one of our veteran Blue Jay players – to help out. Al Oliver, of the Rangers, was also with us. All three of them were very encouraging. ... I really appreciated their help. They not only improved my batting; they also built up my confidence."[11]

Griffin's value beyond his glove work was as a positive influence in the clubhouse. It was common for people to comment that Griffin was a positive influence on his teammates. A sentiment further echoed by A's front office adviser Bill Rigney, who said of Griffin: "His character? Top of the line."[12] This is high praise for a player who ended his career with a total WAR (wins above replacement) of 3.0, ranging from a career high of 3.4 in 1986 to a career low of -2.3 in 1990. By these analytical measures Griffin would be considered a replacement-level player. Not bad at all for a player able to carve out an 18-year major-league career.

During his first stint as a Blue Jay, Griffin played home games in the oft-windy and outdoor confines of Exhibition Stadium in Toronto. Recalling his early days in Toronto, Griffin said:

"Everybody said it was a bad place to play baseball. But I was a happy man to become a major-leaguer in Toronto playing at Exhibition Stadium every day. It gave me my future. It secured the future for my family. I made my living out of the place, so I've got nothing bad to say about the old place."[13]

Regardless of the playing conditions, Griffin had more than a few accomplishments during his first stint with the Blue Jays. He tied Willie Wilson of the Kansas City Royals for the American League lead in triples in 1980 with 15. He finished in the top 10 in the category four other times. It was also here that Griffin played in a personal best 414 consecutive games. Griffin played in all 162 regular-season games four times during his career. In 1984, he was an odd selection for the American League All-Star team. John Feinstein of the *Washington Post* explained:

"Major league baseball pays the expenses for each player here and for one guest. In most cases, players bring wives or girlfriends. Damaso Garcia, the Toronto Blue Jays' second baseman, brought his shortstop, Alfredo Griffin. When the Tigers' Alan Trammell hurt his arm and could not play tonight, Manager Joe Altobelli named Griffin to the team, partly because he's a fine player, but mostly because he was here."[14]

Garcia's wife had decided not to attend, and so Griffin came as his guest. It seemed like a good idea. The Blue Jays were slated to start the second half of the season in Oakland right across the bay from where the All-Star Game was being played in San Francisco. Griffin entered the game as a replacement for Cal Ripken in the sixth inning. He had no at-bats; Don Mattingly pinch-hit for him in the ninth inning. It was Griffin's only All-Star Game appearance.

Even though Griffin was popular in the clubhouse and with Blue Jays fans, his days as the full-time shortstop for the Blue Jays were numbered. In 1983 he began to split time at shortstop with the up-and-coming wunderkind and fellow Dominican Tony Fernandez. After two seasons, Fernandez took over as the full-time shortstop. Griffin was on this way out.

In December 1984 Griffin was traded to the Oakland Athletics with Dave Collins and cash for relief pitcher Bill Caudill. Griffin starred with the Athletics for three seasons (1985-1987). Athletics GM Sandy Alderson touted him as "the glue that held us together."[15] In his

first season, he won his only Gold Glove. In his first two seasons he played in all 162 regular-season games. But by 1987, with the Athletics looking for playing time for Walt Weiss, their up-and-coming shortstop, Griffin was again on his way to another team. He was traded to the Los Angeles Dodgers in December 1987. He went to the Dodgers along with pitcher Jay Howell in a three-team trade that also involved the New York Mets. Hoping that Griffin would be a positive influence on Dominican infielders in the organization, Dodgers GM Fred Claire cited Griffin's character as a needed positive. Dodgers manager Tommy Lasorda commented, "I haven't seen him that much but I hear he's a hell of a player. I looked over at his record and he's played all 162 four times and more than 140 the other two. That's something we haven't had."[16]

As luck would have it, Griffin's ability to avoid injury and be a stabilizing presence on the field did not initially work out well for the Dodgers. On May 21, less than two months into his first season with the Dodgers, Griffin was hit by a Dwight Gooden fastball and broke his right hand.[17] He missed the next 59 games. For the season, he ended up batting .199 in 95 games. With on-base and slugging percentages in the .250s he was a serious offensive liability. Still, Griffin played an integral role in the Dodgers' World Series victory over the Athletics as he started all five games at shortstop. He batted .188 with three singles. In an interview published in 2001, Griffin called the World series victory "the most special moment in my career."[18]

Even with the injury and offensive struggles of the previous year, Griffin signed a three-year contract extension with the Dodgers in January 1989, a signing that included the highest salary of his career: $1 million, in both 1989 and 1990.

A free agent after the 1991 season, Griffin returned to the Blue Jays for what were his last two major-league seasons. No longer a full-time shortstop, and quite possibly a greater offensive liability than ever, he nevertheless enjoyed enormous team success. Playing in only 109 games over the two years, Griffin tallied zero home runs, 10 doubles, and no triples over 245 at-bats. With only 13 RBIs to go along with an average barely above .220, Griffin was used sparingly. The Blue Jays won the World Series both seasons; Griffin appeared as a defensive replacement in both Series.

Griffin hit 24 major-league home runs; in eight seasons he had none. He hit a career-best four homers in three seasons. He hit 245 doubles and 78 triples. He drove in 527 runs with a career high of 64 in 1985. As a light-hitting infielder, Griffin never cracked a slugging percentage of .400 during a full season. His highest slugging percentage was .364 in 1979 and 1986. With a career slugging average of .319, he was never much of an offensive threat, a notion substantiated when considering his career batting average of .249 and on-base percentage of .285. Griffin struck out 664 times. His season high was 65. He drew 338 walks, with a high of 40 in 1979 and a low of 4 in 1984 (in 442 plate appearances).

Griffin made baserunning an adventurous endeavor. Having decent speed and a penchant for over-aggressive running on the basepaths led to plenty of good and bad decisions alike. A game in 1991 provides a clear illustration: Griffin walked and kept going after reaching first base. It did not work. He explained, "Man, I'm just playing baseball, trying to get something started."[19] Manager Tommy Lasorda commented, "It's a great play if you make it, even though I don't think I've ever seen anybody try it before."[20] In 1980 Griffin had 18 steals and was caught stealing 23 times. In three seasons he had stolen-base results under 50 percent. He had 192 stolen bases in the major leagues. But in a nod to his over-aggressiveness on the basepaths, he was caught stealing 134 times. Still, Griffin had decent speed. In eight seasons, he stole at least 10 bases, and in three others swiped at least 20. He had a career-high 33 stolen bases with the run-happy Oakland Athletics in 1986. His three seasons with the Athletics (1985-1987) resulted in his three highest single-season steal totals (24 in 1985, 33 in 1986, and 26 in 1987).

Griffin's fielding statistics are more impressive. He had a fielding percentage of .961 with 348 career errors, 340 of which were made when he was playing shortstop. Early on, he led the American League for four straight seasons (1979-1982) in errors by a short-stop with 36, 37, 31, and 26. He also led the National League as a member of the Dodgers in 1990 when he had 26 errors. Prone to off-balance and errant throws, especially at the start of his career, Griffin recalled, "Using two hands gave me problems, I'd put my right hand too close to the glove and sometime the ball would hit my bare hand. So, in my third year I switched to one hand (pickups)."[21]

With his playing career over, Griffin did not stay away from ballfields for long. In 2018 he completed his 19th season on the Los Angeles Angels coaching staff. He has served as both the first base coach (for 18 seasons) and infield coach (for one season). He worked as a roving minor-league instructor for the Blue Jays in 1995, and as their first-base coach in 1996 and 1997. He was a coach for the Dominican Republic team that won the 2013 World Baseball Classic. and was the general manager of the Estrellas Orientales (Eastern Stars) in the Dominican Republic Winter League, for whom he played for 12 major-league off seasons. The club has retired his number 4 jersey. Griffin was elected to the Dominican Sports Hall of Fame in 2002.

SOURCES

In addition to the sources cited in the Notes, the author consulted Griffin's clippings file from the National Baseball Hall of Fame, baseball-almanac.com, baseball-reference.com, retrosheet.org, and thebaseballcube.com.

NOTES

1   Mark Kurlansky, *The Eastern Stars: How Baseball Changed the Dominican Town of San Pedro de Macoris* (New York: Riverhead Books, 2010), 99.

2   Kurlansky, 99.

3   Kurlanksy, 99.

4   Kurlansky, 100.

5   Kurlansky, 97.

6   Associated Press, "Switch Hitting Takes a Special Skill," *Daily News Online* (Longview, Washington), June 2, 2018. Retrieved from tdn.com/sports/switch-hitting-takes-a-special-skill/article_c18ab4df-e8f4-55fa-a87b-3c918c90cf89.html.

7   "Switch Hitting Takes a Special Skill."

8   Russell Schneider, "Quick-Grower Griffin Brightens Indian Summer," *The Sporting News*, September 25, 1976: 12.

9   Jim Prime, *Tales from the Toronto Blue Jays Dugout: A Collection of the Greatest Blue Jays Stories Ever Told* (New York: Sports Publishing, 2014), 117.

10   United Press International, "Co-winners for AL Rookie Honors," *Salina Journal*, November 27, 1979.

11   Bob Bloss, *Rookies of the Year* (Philadelphia: Temple University Press, 2005), 135.

12   Ross Newhan, "Dodgers Pay a Big Price (Welch) to Improve: They Get a Shortstop and Two Relief Pitchers," *Los Angeles Times*, December 12, 1987. Retrieved from articles.latimes.com/1987-12-12/sports/sp-6647_1_relief-pitcher.

13   Richard Griffin, "Alfredo Griffin Takes a Trip Down Memory Lane," Toronto *Star*, June 3, 2009. Retrieved from thestar.com/life/travel/2009/06/03/alfredo_griffin_takes_a_trip_down_memory_lane.html.

14   John Feinstein, "Making the All-Star Team the Hard Way," *Washington Post*, July 10, 1984. Retrieved from espn.com/espn/page2/story?page=list/worstallstars.

15   Newhan.

16   Newhan.

17   Sam McManis, "Hit, Throw and Run: Guerrero Throws Bat at Pitcher; Dodgers Lose 5-2," *Los Angeles Times*, May 23, 1988. Retrieved from articles.latimes.com/1988-05-23/sports/sp-2199_1_dodgers-lose.

18   Rich Marazzi, "Alfredo Griffin: Dominican Dandy," *Sports Collectors Digest*, January 26, 2001: 70.

19   Bill Plaschke, "Baseball: Daily Report: Dodgers: Griffin Explains His Baserunning Ploy," *Los Angeles Times*, August 1, 1991. Retrieved from articles.latimes.com/1991-08-01/sports/sp-231_1_alfredo-griffin.

20   Plaschke.

21   Glenn Schwarz, "A's Expect Griffin to Cement the Infield," *San Francisco Examiner*, March 4, 1985: D1.

KELLY GRUBER

By Mark Davis

Gruber plays baseball the way paying customers expect to see a guy play baseball – at full speed. He runs hard. He crashes into things. He never met a takeout slide he didn't like. He dives for balls, spending a measurable portion of each game at third base down on the ground. If he isn't dirty by the fourth inning, he thinks he's not earning his money.[1]

Kelly Wayne Gruber was born on February 26, 1962, in Houston, Texas. His family name at birth was King, for his biological father was Claude King, a professional football player during the 1960s. His mother, Gloria (Hunt) King, won the 1957 Miss Texas pageant[2] and was part of a singing trio whose accomplishments included performing opening acts for Elvis Presley.[3] Soon after Kelly was born, Claude abandoned the family, leaving Gloria to care for Kelly and his older sister, Claudia. Gloria found work as an administrative assistant. She later married real estate executive David Gruber, who adopted Claudia and Kelly in October 1966.[4] Gloria and David welcomed a third child, David Jr., born in 1967.[5]

As a child, Gruber had a very close relationship with his maternal grandparents, Vita and Archie Hunt. While they played an important emotional role during Kelly's early years, their lack of discipline meant that he was ill prepared for the strict domestic structure that arose once David Sr. entered his life. David frequently chose whipping as the form of punishment, which he later regretted.[6] For his part, Kelly acknowledged that at times he never met his stepfather halfway where behavior was concerned. "I wasn't the son I should have been, because I thought [David Sr.] might leave me, too," he said. "I rebelled because of it. I think that's why I was so close to my grandparents. I was sure of them. I knew they would never leave me."[7]

Gruber was a gifted varsity athlete, playing football, baseball, basketball, and athletics at Westlake High School in Austin. His baseball coach, Howard Bushong, observed that Gruber performed best at baseball and never lacked self-confidence, telling a

sportswriter, "He was a go-getter, but backed up that attitude."[8] Gruber played three seasons as the starting shortstop for the Westlake Chapparals, where he earned All-American honors and won the state championship in 1980.[9]

Gruber's final year of high school proved to be the turning point of his athletic career. Not only was he offered a four-year scholarship from the University of Texas for either baseball or football,[10] the Cleveland Indians selected him 10th overall in the June amateur draft, the day before the state semifinals. This led to confusing emotions for Gruber. "For a young buck my age, it wasn't easy keeping my mind straight," he said.[11] In the end he decided to forgo college and signed with Cleveland for a $100,000 bonus paid in two installments.[12] In later years Gruber expressed no regrets with his decision: "I didn't care much about baseball. … But I picked [it]; it had the better

opportunity for a long career. And the bonus money was real good."[13]

Soon after signing his first professional contract, Gruber reported to Batavia of the New York-Pennsylvania League, Cleveland's short-season Class-A affiliate. Confident in his talent and abilities, he initially expected a short stay. "It wasn't necessary as far as I was concerned," he told his biographer.[14] His play, however, did not match his confidence. In 61 games he batted .217 and made 21 errors at shortstop. Despite the lackluster debut, his fielding coach, Luis Isaac, noticed that Gruber might not have been playing the most optimal position for his skill set. "The errors he was making, it was because he was too quick to the ball," Isaac said. "… In my reports to the big club, I would put that he was more suited to be at third."[15]

Gruber showed promise the next year with the Waterloo Indians of the Class-A Midwest League, making 500 plate appearances, the most of his minor-league career. He hit .290 with 14 home runs and 59 RBIs. In the field, however, Gruber's defense continued to waver; he made 56 errors at shortstop and had a .910 fielding percentage.

After a stint of winter ball in Venezuela, Gruber began the 1982 season with Chattanooga of the Double-A Southern League. It was here that Gruber's confidence and defensive performance reached an all-time low. On April 15 vs. the Birmingham Barons, he made five errors in a game, a league record at shortstop. "I wanted to dig a hole at shortstop and crawl into it. … I should've accepted what happened and put it behind me. … Instead, I let it bother me for the rest of the season," he told his biographer.[16] His offensive numbers declined in nearly all categories from the previous season.

Gruber continued in Double A in 1983, as a member of the Buffalo Bisons. The change of scenery did not improve his caliber of play. Further complicating matters was a sour relationship between Gruber and his manager, Al Gallagher. Gallagher moved Gruber from shortstop to third base after the fifth game of the season, finally carrying out a move first advocated by Luis Isaac in Batavia three years earlier. However, convinced that Gruber would never reach his full potential, Gallagher informed Cleveland's front office that it was time to move on from the Gruber experiment.[17]

After a disappointing season in Buffalo, Gruber headed to Colombia for another season of winter ball. Meanwhile, events were transpiring that would lead to his departure from the Cleveland organization.

In November, Indians general manager Phil Seghi phoned his counterpart in Toronto, Pat Gillick, to ask if Gillick wouldn't mind reviewing the scouting reports on Gruber. Coincidentally, Gillick received a call a few days later from Duane Larson, the Blue Jays' scout in Colombia, informing him of Gruber's impressive performance. Recognizing that an opportunity might be in the works, Gillick sent two senior scouts, Bobby Mattick and Al LaMacchia, to Colombia to watch Gruber. They agreed with Larson's assessment, prompting Gillick to select Gruber in the subsequent Rule 5 draft.[18]

Colombia winter ball was not the first time the Blue Jays took notice of Gruber, however. In 1979 Al LaMacchia had gone to Austin to scout one of Gruber's teammates, pitcher Calvin Schiraldi. It didn't take long for Gruber to make an impression on the veteran scout.[19] LaMacchia returned the next summer for a private workout with Gruber, which only helped to reinforce his belief in the young Texan. Despite a strong interest, the Jays chose infielder Gary Harris, who would toil in the minors for three years before retiring from baseball. This selection left Gruber available for Cleveland, which selected him with its first pick. Years later LaMacchia lamented the Jays' decision to select Harris over Gruber by concluding, "We made a tremendous mistake."[20]

Gruber made the Blue Jays' Opening Day roster in 1984, primarily because his Rule 5 status meant the Blue Jays would have to keep him on the major-league roster or return him to Cleveland.[21] He made his major-league debut on April 20, 1984, as a defensive replacement in the 12th inning at Exhibition Stadium against the California Angels, recording one assist in a 10-6 loss. Gruber saw little game action and in May was sent to Triple-A Syracuse for regular playing time. (In exchange for not returning Gruber to the Indians, Toronto sent Cleveland catching prospect Geno Petralli.) The season ended on a memorable note for Gruber: After he returned to the Blue Jays as a September call-up, his first hit was a two-run, pinch-hit home run in the ninth inning of a blowout loss to the Red Sox on September 25. He received a standing ovation from the Fenway Park faithful, along with chants of "Groo-bah! Groo-bah!," prompting teammates to shove Gruber to the top step of the dugout for his first big-league curtain call.[22]

Gruber played in only five games with the Blue Jays in 1985. He was maturing in his outlook and sought to take full advantage of an opportunity to play full time for Syracuse. "The Blue Jays told me they thought I had a shot (at making their 25-man regular-season roster). But, inside, I personally didn't think I was ready. I knew I needed another year at Syracuse."[23] He hit 21 home runs and had 69 RBIs in 121 games, and was named the International League's all-star third baseman.

Gruber spent the entire 1986 season with the Blue Jays, playing 87 games, 42 at third base, with the remaining appearances at second base, shortstop, and each outfield position. He received high praise from manager Jimy Williams: "We feel Gruber can do an excellent job at a number of positions. He can go in without weakening us in any way, shape or form."[24] He had 28 hits in 152 plate appearances, perhaps none more memorable than his only major-league inside-the-park home run, on June 12 against the Detroit Tigers. By the seventh inning of the night game, dense fog had crept in from Lake Ontario over Exhibition Stadium when Gruber stepped in the box to face reliever Bill Scherrer with two on and two out. He hit a "very catchable" fly ball that bounced about 30 feet to the left of the center fielder. Gruber scored easily on the play, breaking a 0-for-27 slump.[25]

Gruber entered the 1987 season with high expectations. "I know 20 home runs is possible, and, for sure, I want to bag as many stolen bases," he told a sportswriter. "… I like the first pitch a lot. I don't want to go up there surveying balls and strikes; I want to be hacking."[26] His intense style of play made him injury prone, leading to missed games as a result of rib, ankle, and foot issues. His aggressiveness and frequent injuries led to criticism from some of his teammates, much to Gruber's ire. "Some guys on the team have even had the nerve to tell me to stop diving for balls. But that's not my game," he said. "I play hard, aggressive; that's the only way I know how to play."[27] This aggressive style of play and the injuries that followed, along with the ensuing criticism from teammates, media, and fans would return to beleaguer Gruber later in his career. He finished the season with 12 home runs and 12 stolen bases in 138 games.

The next year Gruber began to round into major-league form. He learned in spring training that he'd be the backup third baseman to Rance Mulliniks. These plans changed during the first inning of the home opener on April 11 against the Yankees, when Rickey Henderson slid head-first into Mulliniks's knee while stealing third base.[28] Gruber replaced Mulliniks and ended up starting at third for 148 of the Jays' remaining 155 games.[29] Aside from regular playing time, a major factor for his emerging success was the

tutelage from Blue Jays hitting coach Cito Gaston. Of his student, Gaston noted, "Kelly's got a better idea of what he wants to do up there now. … You can't just go up there and hack away; you've got to have a plan."[30] The 1988 campaign turned out to be one of Gruber's best offensive seasons, as he finished with a .278 batting average and a .328 on-base percentage, along with 16 home runs and 81 RBIs.

The 1989 season provided a snapshot of how potent a player Gruber could be when he stayed healthy. GM Pat Gillick proclaimed Gruber one of his "untouchable" players in spring training, stating, "He's got more talent and all-round ability than any guy we've got."[31] On April 16 at home vs. the Kansas City Royals, Gruber made history by becoming the first Blue Jay to hit for the cycle. Gruber's impressive performance continued, leading to him being selected for the All-Star Game by American League manager Tony LaRussa. While he did not see game action, the confidence Gruber gained helped to sustain his play for the rest of the season, resulting in the Elias Sports Bureau ranking him the top third baseman in the American League.[32] His popularity soared among Blue Jays fans, who voted him Toronto's favorite athlete in an annual survey of readers of the *Toronto Star*.[33]

After a disappointing loss to the Oakland Athletics in the 1989 ALCS, the Blue Jays envisaged greater things for 1990. Gruber did his part by remaining relatively healthy and posting the best numbers of his career. He batted .274 with 31 home runs and 118 RBIs, earning an AL Silver Slugger Award. In the field he won his only AL Gold Glove Award. Gruber again was chosen for the All-Star Game and stole two bases, tying Willie Mays for the most stolen bases in the midsummer classic. By the end of the regular season, he earned fourth place in voting for the AL MVP Award, and was the unanimous choice as player of the year by the Toronto chapter of the Baseball Writers Association of America.[34] Gruber's play could not help his team reach the playoffs: The Blue Jays finished two games behind the Red Sox for the AL East title.

In February 1991 the Blue Jays rewarded Gruber with a three-year, $11 million contract, which at the time made him the highest-paid Toronto sports athlete and major-league third baseman.[35]

Gruber's success was short-lived, however, as injuries led to a rapid fall from grace. He tore several ligaments and suffered a fracture of his right thumb while running the bases against the Texas Rangers on May 1, 1991.[36] The injury affected him for the rest of the season and limited him to 113 games. His inability

WE ARE, WE CAN, WE WILL

In Game Three of the 1992 World Series, Gruber hit a game-tying eighth-inning home run.

to return to action caused teammates to question his commitment, calling him "Mrs. Gruber" behind his back.[37] This proved to be a far cry from the applause and accolades Gruber had seen the previous two seasons. After a disappointing playoff exit at the hands of the Minnesota Twins, many fans and the media thought Gruber should be dealt. As he had for many years, GM Pat Gillick remained committed to his third baseman, saying, "Everybody's tradeable, but we're not going to trade Kelly Gruber."[38]

Gruber's hand injury healed in the offseason and he began the 1992 season with hopes of 100 or more RBIs.[39] But he soon suffered an injury that eventually ended his major-league career. In his first at-bat of a game on April 26 vs. Kansas City, he swung through a pitch and "felt something pop."[40] The injury turned out to be a bone spur embedded in his spinal cord,[41] and was not properly diagnosed until 1995.[42] Gruber continued to play through the pain but performed nowhere near expectations. He hit 11 home runs, drove in 43 runs, and batted .229. The man who was voted Toronto's favorite athlete two years earlier was now vilified as being lazy by an increasing number of the Blue Jays' fan base.

Despite his injuries and inconsistent play, Gruber displayed flashes of his former self during the 1992

postseason. In Game Two of the ALCS against Oakland, he hit a two-run homer in the bottom of the fifth inning to break a scoreless tie, helping the Blue Jays win 3-1.

Five years earlier, in spring training, Gruber had told of his desire to play in the World Series as a Blue Jay. "I got a chance of a lifetime here to go to a World Series. People talk about how someone like Tony Kubek got there seven times or something and that's fine but, hey, just give it to me once."[43] Gruber's wish would come true, and it was in Game Three that he had his best performance. In the top of the fourth inning, Devon White made an incredible catch against the center-field wall, leading to chaos on the basepaths. In the confusion, Terry Pendleton crossed Deion Sanders at second base, leading to the second out. The ball then found its way to Gruber, who ran a stranded Sanders back to second, where Gruber dived and tagged Sanders on his right heel for what should have been the third out and a triple play. The second-base umpire disagreed, calling Sanders safe. While diving to tag Sanders, however, Gruber tore his rotator cuff. Despite the injury, Gruber continued to play, and in the top of the eighth inning, he made an error when he couldn't hold on to a line drive off the bat of Otis Nixon, who later scored and gave Atlanta a 2-1 lead.

When Gruber led off the bottom of the inning, boos echoed through SkyDome. Despite feeling incredible pain and unable to hold up his bat with his left hand, he hit a changeup off Steve Avery for a home run to tie the game. The jeers quickly turned to cheers and Gruber was once again a hero. "It was the only pitch … I could get that bat around (on)," he said later "… Going around those bases, finally, it was like, 'Wow. Well, at least I could do one good thing this series.'"[44]

Gruber's time with the Blue Jays was over. Shortly after Toronto's first World Series championship, Gruber was traded to the California Angels for Luis Sojo. Toronto agreed to pay $1.5 million of Gruber's $4 million salary in 1993 as part of the agreement.[45] While undergoing his medical in early 1993, Gruber was officially diagnosed with a torn rotator cuff and underwent surgery. He did not play until June 4, prompting the Angels to complain to American League President Bobby Brown that the Blue Jays had knowingly dealt them an injured Gruber. Brown's investigation concluded that Toronto was unaware of the severity of Gruber's injury and declared the matter closed.[46] Gruber played in 18 games for the Angels before heading to the disabled list on July 4 with recurring neck issues. He was placed on waivers on September 7 and subsequently released.[47]

Neck issues continued to keep Gruber away from baseball, ultimately leading to surgery in August 1995 to fuse a bone from his hip into his neck.[48] After his recovery, he signed a minor-league deal in late 1996 with the Baltimore Orioles, who were now under the guidance of Pat Gillick. Gruber was the final cut at the end of spring training and began the 1997 season with the Triple-A Rochester Americans. He played in 38 games for Rochester before suffering a strained hip flexor. After his rehab failed to sufficiently allow him to return to game shape, he determined that his playing career was over and retired.[49]

Gruber has remained active within Canadian baseball circles in his retirement. He has appeared in numerous charity events for the Jays Care Foundation and participated in several Blue Jays alumni events. He also traveled extensively throughout Canada hosting his Kelly Gruber Silver Slugger baseball camps for children aged 9 to 17. He made headlines in 2018 for two alcohol-related incidents, the first of which included an arrest in April in Austin, Texas, for driving under the influence.[50] The second incident occurred in June during a fan event at the Canadian Baseball Hall of Fame's annual induction weekend, when he made inappropriate remarks toward host Ashley Docking and fellow guest Kevin Barker.[51] Organizers, suspecting Gruber was inebriated, quickly ended the panel, and Hall of Fame organizers disinvited him from the weekend's remaining events.[52]

Gruber married Toronto native Lynn Seguin in 1986. They have two children, Kody and Cassie. The couple divorced in 1993.[53] While playing with the Angels, he met his second wife, Tosca. They reside in Texas with their three children, Samantha (from Tosca's first marriage), Kyle, and Kolton.[54]

SOURCES

In addition to the sources cited in the Notes, the author consulted Baseball Reference, Retrosheet, and the Kelly Gruber Hall of Fame media file.

NOTES

1   Dave Perkins, "Blue Jays' Fearless Kelly Gruber Is an All-Star at Third Base, a Heartthrob in Toronto," *The Sporting News 1991 Baseball Yearbook*: 34.

2   Miss Texas USA, "Hall of Fame: Miss Texas USA," https://www.misstexasusa.com/halloffame-miss/, accessed December 3, 2021.

3   Barry Davis, "Kelly Gruber: Outta the Park with Barry Davis," January 17, 2020, https://soundcloud.com/user-250213153/otp-kelly-gruber-jan-17, (accessed December 3, 2021).

4   Kevin Boland and Kelly Gruber, *Kelly: At Home on Third* (Toronto: Viking, 1991), 4-5, 251.

5   Rick Cantu, "Westlake's State Championship Seasons Provide Special Memories for Gruber Brothers," *Austin American-Statesman*, June 12, 2013, https://www.statesman.com/story/news/2013/06/12/westlakes-state-championship-seasons-provide-special-memories-for-gruber-brothers/9989001007/, (accessed December 3, 2021).

6   Boland and Gruber, 5-6.

7   Boland and Gruber, 6.

8   Dick Clarke, "Jays Glad Gruber Did Not Choose Football," *Syracuse Herald Journal*, August 19, 1990: 10.

9   Thomas Jones, "50 Years of Westlake Athletics: The Chaps' All-Time Baseball Team," *Austin American-Statesman*, June 30, 2020, https://www.statesman.com/story/sports/high-school/2020/06/30/50-years-of-westlake-athletics-chaps-all-time-baseball-team/113718960/, (accessed December 3, 2021).

10 Boland and Gruber, 28.

11 Cantu, "Westlake's State Championship Seasons Provide Special Memories for Gruber Brothers."

12 Boland and Gruber, 38.

13 Clarke, "Jays Glad Gruber Did Not Choose Football."

14 Boland and Gruber, 42.

15 Boland and Gruber, 42.

16 Boland and Gruber, 48-49.

17 Boland and Gruber, 60.

18 Milt Dunnell, "Gillick Was Asked: 'Is Kelly Gruber Worth $100,000?," *Toronto Star*, February 17, 1991: G4; Kristina Rutherford, "The Interview: Kelly Gruber on Pablo Escobar, ADHD, and the '92 World Series," https://www.sportsnet.ca/baseball/mlb/interview-kelly-gruber-pablo-escobar-adhd-92-world-series/, (accessed November 18, 2021).

19   Boland and Gruber, 21.

20   Boland and Gruber, 25.

21   GruberBaseball.com, "About Kelly," https://web.archive.
      org/web/20111019201914/http://gruberbaseball.com/
      about-kelly/, (accessed December 3, 2021).

22   Paul Patton, "Stieb Roughed Up as Bosox Breeze to an Easy
      Victory," *Globe and Mail* (Toronto), September 26, 1984: S3.

23   Garth Woolsey, "Kelly Gruber Certain He's Made
      Jays," *Toronto Star*, April 1, 1986: E1.

24   Jim Proudfoot, "Gruber's Versatility Gives Jays Added
      Dimension," *Toronto Star*, March 21, 1986: F1.

25   Allan Ryan, "Game Called After Seven – Key Gets
      Shutout Win," *Toronto Star*, June 13, 1986: B1.

26   Allan Ryan, "Afternoon of Good News for Gruber,"
      Toronto Star, March 30, 1987: D4.

27   Dave Perkins, "Gruber Can't Shake Injuries,"
      Toronto Star, April 29, 1987: C2.

28   Dave Perkins, "Mulliniks Gets Word Today on
      Knee," *Toronto Star*, April 12, 1988: H2.

29   Jim Proudfoot, "Gruber Expects Hot Time at Hot
      Corner," *Toronto Star*, March 7, 1989: B1.

30   John Robertson, "New, Improved Kelly Gruber Is in
      a Groove," *Toronto Star*, April 24, 1988: G2.

31   Dave Perkins, "Gruber Makes Untouchable List/Jays
      Third Baseman Is Pleased but Sore Finger Remains a
      Worry," *Toronto Star*, February 26, 1989: G4.

32   Associated Press, "Gruber's First in AL at Position,"
      Toronto Star, October 25, 1989: F1.

33   Ken McKee, "Star Readers Are Keen on Kelly, Naming Gruber
      Favorite Athlete," *Toronto Star*, March 3, 1990: B1.

34   Neil MacCarl, "Toronto Writers Pick Gruber as Blue Jay Player
      of the Year," *Toronto Star*, November 28, 1990: C7.

35   "Gruber's Highest Paid in T.O. Sports History,"
      Toronto Star, February 13, 1991: A1.

36   Allan Ryan, "Outlook Grim for Gruber," *Toronto Star*, May 5, 1991: C1.

37   Dave Perkins, "Whispers Are Wrong, Hurt Gruber
      Says," *Toronto Star*, July 12, 1991: C3.

38   Allan Ryan, "Jays Not Trading Gruber: Gillick,"
      Toronto Star, November 15, 1991: C1.

39   Tom Slater, "Gruber Sets Sights on RBI Century
      Mark," *Toronto Star*, March 29, 1992: G5.

40   Kristina Rutherford, "The Interview: Kelly Gruber on
      Pablo Escobar, ADHD, and the '92 World Series."

41   GruberBaseball.com, "About Kelly."

42   GruberBaseball.com, "About Kelly."

43   Ryan, "Afternoon of Good News for Gruber."

44   TheScore.com, "World Series Memories: Kelly Gruber of the
      '92 Blue Jays on Playing Through Pain," https://www.thescore.
      com/mlb/news/829328, (accessed December 3, 2021).

45   Associated Press, "Gruber Surgery Reveals Injury,"
      Toronto Star, February 17, 1993: B1.

46   Canadian Press, "Jays Cleared in Probe of Gruber-
      Sojo Deal," *Toronto Star*, July 9, 1993: D3.

47   "Gruber Released!," *Toronto Star*, September 8, 1993: E1.

48   Mark Zwolinksi, "After Surgery, Gruber Hopes to Play Ball
      Again/'Every Time I Point a Finger There's Three Fingers
      Pointing Back," *Toronto Star*, December 11, 1995: B5.

49   GruberBaseball.com, "About Kelly."

50   Katie Hall, "Former Baseball Player Kelly Gruber Arrested on DWI
      Charge," *Austin-American Statesman*, April 24, 2018, https://www.statesman.
      com/story/news/local/2018/04/24/former-baseball-player-kelly-gruber-arrest-
      ed-in-austin-on-dwi-charge/10374722007/, (accessed December 3, 2021).

51   Gregory Strong, "Gruber Event Cut Short Over 'Inappropriate
      Behaviour,'" *National Post*, June 16, 2018: FP17.

52   "Gruber Event Cut Short."

53   Allan Ryan, "Gruber Set for 'Homecoming,'" *Toronto Star*, June 6, 1993: E3.

54   Mary Alice Piasecki, "Shining Star: Tosca Gruber Shines Brightly
      in Austin's Hot Real Estate Market," *Austin Business Journal*,
      February 27, 2000, https://www.bizjournals.com/austin/sto-
      ries/2000/02/28/focus1.html, (accessed January 5, 2022).

JUAN GUZMÁN

By Malcolm Allen

A right-handed starter with a wicked slider, Juan Guzmán pitched parts of 10 seasons (1991-2000) for the Blue Jays, Orioles, Reds and Devil Rays. During his first three big-league seasons, he compiled a record of 40-11 while helping Toronto to three straight playoff appearances, including two World Series titles. The Dominican Republic native posted a 5-1 post-season record, was an All-Star in 1992, and won the American League ERA title in 1996.

Juan Andres Guzmán Correa was born on October 28, 1966, in Santo Domingo to Daniel and Francis Guzmán, who had four other children: Daniel, Roberto, Raúl and Nancy.[1] The family lived in a home without indoor plumbing in Manoguayabo, a poor sector in the western part of the capital city.[2] The elder Daniel was a building contractor. Juan assisted his father with carpentry, leaving little time for baseball, so long-distance running was his first favorite sport.[3] When Juan did play baseball, he was initially an outfielder, but converted to pitching in his early teens because his local team was shorthanded. "Also, I couldn't hit anything," he joked. "But, yeah, we needed another pitcher."[4] The main hurler was his friend and fellow Liceo Las Américas student, Ramón Martínez. "When we used to play in the neighborhood every Saturday and Sunday, [Ramón] would always start the first game, and I'd start the second game," Guzmán recalled.[5] "Nobody can really teach you to be a pitcher. They can only help you to become a better pitcher. But that first time I picked up the ball, it felt . . . natural."[6]

In the early 1980's Guzmán attended a Toronto Blue Jays tryout camp organized by scout Epy Guerrero. "I was too young. I was 14 or 15 years old," Guzmán said. "I was throwing hard, 84-85 miles an hour. Epy told me I had a good arm and all that stuff but that I was too young to leave the island."[7] A few years later, Dodgers scout Ralph Avila was organizing two national teams of Dominican amateurs and asked for recommendations from a clubhouse worker with the Tigres del Licey winter league club. The clubbie named his neighborhood teammates, Martínez and Guzmán.

"Ramón was a really skinny kid and Juan was a husky kid," Avila recalled. Impressed by Martínez's control and breaking ball, Avila moved him to a club headed for the 1984 Summer Olympics in Los Angeles, where baseball was a demonstration sport, and signed him shortly afterwards. The rawer Guzmán joined the team bound for the youth championships in Kindersley, Saskatchewan, where he played for Alfredo Griffin's uncle alongside two of George Bell's brothers.[8] After returning home, Guzmán's work at the Dodgers camp in Campo Las Palmas convinced Los Angeles to sign him, too.[9] "My parents were worried. They wanted me to continue to go to school," he said. "Finally, they said, 'Do what you want to do.' I could sign this contract and I could try to have a career. I could always

Guzman led 1992 Blue Jays' pitchers in ERA and strikeouts.

75

go back to school, but maybe I could not go back to baseball."[10] Guzmán signed for a $4,000 bonus.[11]

Working primarily as relievers, Guzmán, 18, and Martínez, 17, combined for a 9-2 record for the Dodgers' sub-.500 Rookie-level Gulf Coast League affiliate in 1985. Though Guzmán led the club in wins (5) and saves (4) in 21 appearances (three starts), his 3.86 ERA was worse than league average and more than a run-per-game higher than his friend's. "Ramón was always the better pitcher, the more natural pitcher. I had to learn, make mistakes, get help," Guzmán said.[12] "He helped me to learn pitches."[13] In Guzmán's 42 innings, he uncorked 15 wild pitches to lead the circuit.

In 1986, Guzmán threw 16 more wild pitches to lead the Single-A Florida State League. Overall, he was 10-9 with a 3.49 ERA in 24 starts (26 games) and led the Vero Beach Dodgers in victories and strikeouts. Alejandro Peña, Guzman's childhood hero, joined Vero Beach in May and made four appearances on a rehab assignment.[14]

Guzmán spent 1987 with the Bakersfield Dodgers in the Single-A California League. He struck out 113 batters in 110 innings but walked 84 and finished 5-6 with a 4.75 ERA in 21 starts (plus one relief appearance). He was pitching in the Instructional League on September 22 when a coach told him that he'd been traded to Toronto for infielder Mike Sharperson. "We felt [Guzmán] was several years away and would have to acquire command, always an unknown," explained Los Angeles GM Fred Claire.[15] "The file on him was always 'good arm, good person.' There was never a negative report on him in any way."[16] Guzmán said, "I was surprised because the Dodgers told me that I was one of the best prospects that they had."[17]

Also surprised were the Blue Jays, who had believed they could pick between two prospects and intended to select shortstop José Offerman. "We wanted Offerman and thought we had the choice," Toronto GM Pat Gillick confirmed in 1991. "In the end, Fred insisted it was his choice and gave us Guzmán. I wasn't happy."[18] If Gillick wasn't pleased, Guzmán was, at least initially. "A lot of my friends were playing in the Blue Jay organization," he explained. "But I was disappointed when they told me I was going to be a reliever. That toned everything down."[19]

In 1988, Guzmán led the Knoxville Blue Jays with 46 appearances (two starts) and posted a 2.36 ERA in the Double-A Southern League. He walked 60 in 84 innings but permitted only 52 hits. In the Dominican League that winter, he started 11 of his 12

appearances for the Tigres del Licey. Although his record was only 3-5, he posted a solid 2.84 ERA and the manager, Dodgers' coach Joe Ferguson, told him, "Wow, I don't know how they let you go."[20] Guzmán joined the circuit champion Leones del Escogido for the Caribbean Series in Mazatlán, Mexico, where he earned the Dominican Republic's only victory and was clocked at 97-mph.[21]

The Blue Jays promoted him to the Triple-A International League in 1989 but continued to use him out of the bullpen. Appearing in 14 games for the Syracuse Chiefs, Guzmán walked 30 batters in 20 ⅓ innings. "He had two or three different release points," recalled pitching instructor Galen Cisco.[22] "He'd bounce pitches 10 feet in front of the plate. He'd sail two or three over the back screen and that was about 10 foot high."[23] Following a June demotion to Knoxville, Guzmán was 1-4 with a 6.23 ERA in 22 outings (eight starts), still averaging more than one walk per inning. "I needed innings to develop. As a reliever I was getting one inning, two innings, then I might not pitch for a week. I couldn't get my control going. I couldn't get my mechanics consistent," Guzmán explained.[24] He was dropped from Toronto's 40-man roster and later confessed, "There was a time when I thought I was going to quit baseball."[25]

That winter, Guzmán reached out to Avila, who told him he was opening his shoulder too soon and overthrowing. Back at Knoxville in 1990, pitching coach John Poloni encouraged him to speed up his deliberate tempo and develop better balance in his delivery. Guzmán appealed to Knoxville manager John Stearns, recalling, "I told him, 'I'm not a reliever. If there's any chance I can be a starter, please give me a chance'."[26] By year end, 21 of Guzmán's 37 appearances were starts and he went 11-9 with a 4.24 ERA. Despite leading the team in victories, he was left off the 40-man roster again after leading a third league in wild pitches. Any team could have drafted him for $50,000, but none did. "I was upset with everybody," he said. "They didn't think I was good enough to play in the big leagues."[27] For Licey, Guzmán went 7-1 with a 1.69 ERA in nine starts (10 games) to win Pitcher of the Year honors. In five playoff games, he was 3-0, 1.71, including a complete game win in the finals to help Licey win the championship. In February 1991, he helped the Dominican Republic win the Caribbean Series (called "Winterball 1" that year) in Miami.

Guzmán began 1991 in Triple-A Syracuse and impressed Chiefs' skipper Bob Bailor while starting 11 of his 12 appearances. "The guy is driven, and he just goes about his business," Bailor said.[28] Though Guzmán was only 4-5 with a 4.03 ERA, he was leading the International League with 67 strikeouts in 67 innings when the Blue Jays called him up to replace Dave Stieb, who'd gone onto the disabled list with back problems.[29]

On June 7, Guzmán started in Baltimore and struck out five Orioles --including Cal Ripken-- in the first three innings of his debut. But he was knocked out in the fifth and lost, 6-4. Eight days later in Toronto, the Orioles beat him again. On June 22, however, Guzmán earned his first big-league victory by hurling seven shutout innings of three-hit ball against the Indians, striking out six and walking two. Next time out, he pitched into the eighth to defeat the Twins, 1-0, He went on to win 10 straight decisions, breaking Stieb's Blue Jays record.[30] It was also the longest winning streak by a rookie in 28 years.[31] Five of Guzmán's wins came in September and, by the time he lost his last outing to finish 10-3 with a 2.99 ERA in 23 starts, Toronto had clinched the AL East. "I always thought I could make it, but never in my dreams did I think it would turn out like this," he confessed. "I think the Lord has been with me."[32]

"I've never seen [Guzmán] unnerved," said Blue Jays' catcher Pat Borders. "The guy's a rock that way."[33] In the ALCS against the Twins, Guzmán pitched Game Two in front of 54,816 at the Metrodome. "At least the fans weren't throwing anything at me like they do sometimes in the Dominican," he said.[34] He walked two of the first three hitters but settled down to earn Toronto's only victory in the best-of-seven series with 5 ⅔ innings of four-hit work. "He's effectively wild," observed Minnesota manager Tom Kelly. "Just wild enough to be real good."[35] Guzmán finished second to Twins' second baseman Chuck Knoblauch in AL Rookie of the Year voting and claimed *The Sporting News*' honor as the circuit's top freshman pitcher. "I just have good concentration. When you can control your mind, you can do anything. I wasn't always this way - gradually I found it out for myself," Guzmán said.[36] "I've always worked very, very hard. It's finally paying off."[37]

One key to Guzmán's success was the late-breaking slider he developed in 1990 after scrapping his curveball. "Juan Guzmán has the most unusual slider I've ever seen," remarked broadcaster and former pitcher Jim Kaat. "It goes down so sharply that I thought it was a split-finger." Guzmán held it like the curve with a finger across a seam. Throwing overhand, he would turn his wrist just before releasing the ball to achieve

an effect that he described as being between that of a cut fastball and slider. "I only throw it when I can get a strikeout. I really like to throw it out of the strike zone and try to get the hitter to swing," he said.[38] His repertoire also included a three-finger changeup.[39] His mid-90s fastball was there all along. The Blue Jays asked Guzmán to take it easy in winter ball, but sellout crowds turned out to see his lone regular-season start and three playoff outings for Licey.[40]

In 1992, Guzmán won 11 of his first 12 decisions and finished the first half 11-2 with an AL-leading 2.11 ERA and 122 strikeouts. At the All-Star Game in San Diego, he struck out the first two batters he faced --Ryne Sandberg and Benito Santiago-- and completed a scoreless inning by popping up Barry Bonds after loading the bases. Guzmán missed most of August because his shoulder felt sore when he threw sliders and changeups.[41] He returned and helped propel Toronto back to the postseason, completing a 16-5, 2.64 campaign by one-hitting the Tigers over eight shutout innings to earn the AL East clinching victory on the season's final day. In 180 ⅔ innings, Guzmán permitted only six home runs, the circuit's stingiest rate. "I think anyone will tell you, when he's healthy he's the best pitcher in the American League," remarked Detroit manager Sparky Anderson.[42]

Guzmán beat the Athletics twice in the ALCS, winning Game Three in Oakland and Game Six at SkyDome to secure the Blue Jays' first-ever pennant. With the World Series even after two contests in Atlanta, Guzmán dueled southpaw Steve Avery in Game Three and held the Braves to two runs (one earned) over eight innings before departing with the score tied, 2-2. He received a no-decision when Toronto prevailed in the bottom of the ninth. Guzmán's potential Game Seven start became unnecessary when the Blue Jays triumphed, four games to two.

In spring training 1993, a bout with the flu cost Guzmán precious preseason innings which affected his feel for the release point on his changeup throughout the season.[43] His ERA climbed to 3.99 and he threw 26 wild pitches to set an AL record.[44] Nevertheless, he tossed his first major-league shutout against the Royals on April 29 and notched the first of his four career 11-strikeout games against the Athletics on June 5. By season's end, Guzmán had worked a personal-best 221 innings and posted a 14-3 record to lead the American League with an .824 winning percentage as the Blue Jays won a third consecutive division title.

Toronto's rotation included veteran stars like Jack Morris and Dave Stewart, plus 19-game winner Pat

Hentgen, but manager Cito Gaston opted to pitch Guzmán --winner of his last seven decisions-- in the 1993 ALCS opener against the White Sox at Comiskey Park. "Juan has been our ace since he came to the big leagues," said second baseman Roberto Alomar.[45] Guzmán walked a career-worst eight, but defeated that season's Cy Young Award winner, Jack McDowell, 7-3. With the series deadlocked at two games apiece, he hurled seven innings of three-hit, one-run ball to beat McDowell again in Game Five. After the Blue Jays clinched another pennant, Guzmán faced the Phillies' Curt Schilling in the World Series opener. In five innings, he allowed four runs and received a no-decision in a contest that Toronto won, 8-5. With a chance to deliver the Blue Jays' second consecutive championship in Game Five at Veterans Stadium, Guzmán held Philadelphia to two runs (one earned) over seven innings but suffered his first-ever postseason loss as Schilling tossed a shutout to keep the home team alive. Toronto eventually prevailed in six games.

Guzmán was the Blue Jays' Opening Day pitcher in 1994 and defeated Chicago's McDowell. Although

Guzman was 45-12 (including postseason) for Toronto from 1991-1993.

his pitch counts were always high due to his lofty strikeout and walks totals, the issue became more problematic as he nibbled around the corners. "That doesn't drive me crazy, but it does make me worry for him and his career," remarked Gaston after a May 16 start in which the pitcher needed 105 pitches to labor through only 5 ⅓ innings.[46] Guzmán's 25 starts tied for the league lead, but he needed a 6-2 finish to complete the strike-shortened season with a 12-11 record. During a year in which the overall AL ERA climbed from 4.32 to 4.80, Guzmán's figure soared over 5.00 to stay in April and wound up at 5.32. "I just didn't have my good velocity. My changeup is my third pitch, my slider is my second, my fastball is my best pitch," he explained. "I didn't have my best pitch."[47]

While Guzmán had always been a fitness fanatic --running stadium steps for an hour every non-pitching day, for example-- he added more pounds and repetitions to his offseason weight workouts in an effort to gain strength.[48] Though Guzmán didn't pitch winter ball for the third straight year, Ramón Martínez told reporters about a star-studded softball team in Santo Domingo. "I play first base," Martinez said. "[Marlins' prospect Quilvio Veras] plays second, [Expos' outfielder] Moisés Alou plays center field, Juan Guzmán is the designated hitter and [Montreal pitcher] Pedro [Martínez] plays second or DH."[49]

Back on the mound in 1995, Guzmán endured a nightmarish season. His ERA was 9.78 in four starts when he was placed on the disabled list May 21 with a muscle imbalance in his throwing shoulder. He returned to the DL in August with soreness in his right armpit. His lost five consecutive starts upon returning to extend his personal losing streak to nine in a row, matching Jeff Byrd's 1977 Blue Jays' record for futility by a right-handed pitcher.[50] Despite winning in Boston and allowing only one earned run over 15 innings in his last two starts, Guzmán finished the season with an ugly 4-14 record and 6.32 ERA. Since Toronto couldn't slash his $2.8 million salary by more than 20-percent, it seemed unlikely that they would tender him a 1996 contract. However, in December, the club relented and guaranteed a one-year deal for $2.24 million. "We feel there's some unfinished business that Juan has as a Blue Jay," explained GM Gord Ash.[51]

For the first time in four winters, Guzmán pitched for Licey, making two regular-season starts. After posting a 0.50 ERA in 18 playoff innings, he joined the champion Águilas Cibaeñas for the Caribbean Series in Santo Domingo. The Dominican squad disappointed in front of their home fans, but Guzmán looked sharp in a seven-inning, three-hit no-decision against Mexico.[52] In spring training 1996, he changed his uniform number from 66 to 57. "I changed a lot of things, not only my number. I changed a lot of personal problems that I cannot explain to anybody," he said. "I'm going to be a new me this year."[53]

Guzmán looked like his old self in April, claiming AL Pitcher of the Month honors after going 3-1 with a 1.88 ERA. His record briefly slipped below .500 in mid-June following his return from a 15-day disabled list stint for a strained pectoral muscle, but he soon righted himself.[54] Heading into his scheduled September 7 start at Yankee Stadium, Guzmán was 11-8 and walking fewer batters than ever. His 3:1 strikeout-to-walk ratio led the American League, as did his 2.93 ERA, 1.124 WHIP and 7.6 hits allowed per-nine-innings. He was hospitalized that day after experiencing chest pains, however, and missed the remainder of the season following an emergency appendectomy.[55]

The Blue Jays rewarded Guzmán with a two-year contract worth $9.5 million, with a third-year vesting option based on innings pitched.[56] He made his final five appearances for Licey that winter, three in the playoffs. Over parts of eight seasons with the Tigres, he was 10-7 with a 2.57 ERA in 37 games (27 starts), plus 6-1, 1.73 in 16 playoff outings (15 starts).

In winning his first two starts of 1997, Guzmán looked strong, but he allowed a career-worst four home runs in Texas before April was over and left two May starts early with shoulder soreness and arm fatigue. Then he broke the thumb on his pitching hand fielding a grounder on May 28 and went on the disabled list for a month.[57] After Guzmán failed to survive five innings in three of four starts when he returned --including another four-homer debacle-- he returned to the DL on July 16 with a shoulder strain. He pitched a total of four innings in two August rehab starts in Single-A before undergoing season-ending surgery to remove bone spurs and repair a torn labrum.[58]

Guzmán's ERA was over 5.00 until after the All-Star Break in 1998 and he lost 12 of his first 16 decisions. He was healthy enough to make all his starts, however, and improved as the season progressed. On July 30, for example, he beat the Rangers by hurling the first eight innings of a 1-0 victory in what proved to be the last appearance of his Toronto career. After enduring four straight losing seasons, the once mighty Blue Jays were under .500 again and dealt Guzmán to the Orioles for fellow Dominican Nerio Rodríguez and minor-leaguer Shannon Carter the next day at the trading deadline.

Former Toronto second baseman Roberto Alomar helped Guzmán win his Baltimore debut with a lead-off home run and starting an inning-ending double play. "I'll keep saying it, Robbie's the best player I ever played with," Guzmán said. In 11 starts for the Orioles, Guzmán was 4-4 with a 4.24 ERA to finish 10-16 overall. While that record earned him a share of the AL lead in losses, he triggered the 1999 option on his contract by exceeding 200 innings pitched for the first time in five years.[59]

On June 12, 1999, during an interleague contest in Atlanta, Guzmán --a career .118 hitter-- stroked an RBI single off Kevin Millwood for his first big-league hit. Seven weeks later, he was dealt at the trade deadline for the second straight year. Guzmán was 5-9 with a 4.18 ERA in 21 starts when the sub-.500 Orioles swapped him to the Reds for future closer B.J. Ryan and minor-leaguer Jacobo Sequea. In a dozen National League appearances, Guzmán went 6-3 with a 3.03 ERA to help Cincinnati win 96 games --the franchise's best result in a 35-year span from 1977-2011. The Reds missed the playoffs, however. After finishing one game behind the Astros in the NL Central, Cincinnati lost a one-game tiebreaker to the Mets for the league's lone wild card spot.

That offseason, Guzmán became a free agent and signed a two-year, $12 million deal with the Tampa Bay Devil Rays in January.[60] His debut for his new team proved to be the last game of his major league career. After Guzmán surrendered eight runs in 1 ⅔ innings to the Cleveland Indians on April 7, 2000, he was placed on the disabled list with tendinitis. He worked a total of 20 innings over four rehab starts with three different Tampa Bay minor-league affiliates before undergoing rotator cuff surgery in July.[61] In 2001, Guzmán made a dozen minor-league starts before retiring. His 10-year major league career ended with a 91-79 record and 4.08 ERA in 240 starts, plus a 5-1, 2.44 mark in eight postseason games. In 2012, he was inducted into the Dominican Republic's Hall of Fame.[62]

By the mid-1990s, Guzmán had started baseball, softball, basketball and volleyball leagues in Santo Domingo, providing outlets for thousands of Dominican youngsters. His off-field life, however, largely remained a mystery even to his teammates. "I don't like to mix my personal life with baseball," Guzmán explained. "I can't tell you a lot except that he's a very private person," Cito Gaston once said. "If you find anything out, let me know."[63] Although the 1992 Blue Jays media guide listed Guzmán's wife name as Anita, the *Globe and Mail* reporter who asked about her wrote, "Guzmán says he's single and that baseball is his whole life."[64] According to a 1996 *Ottawa Citizen* article, Guzmán had two daughters.[65] The 1999 Orioles Media Guide listed three children: Juan, Jr., Joanny and Kristy.[66] In 2021, Guzmán's own Facebook page listed a daughter, Rohana, and son, Marvin.[67]

In 1999, Guzmán became a Christian minister, which he described as a turning point in his life.[68] Since at least 2004, he's been married to the former Ana Delia Martínez. Ana is the sister of Juan's long-time friends, former big-league pitchers Ramón and Pedro Martínez.[69] As of 2021 they lived in Miami and focused on the Juan Guzmán Foundation. In addition to constructing the Juan Guzmán Sports Complex in the Dominican Republic, the foundation sought to fight hunger and poverty throughout Latin America.[70]

ACKNOWLEDGMENTS

This biography was reviewed by Eric Vickrey and David Bilmes and fact-checked by Kevin Larkin.

SOURCES

In addition to sources cited in the Notes, the author also consulted www.base-ball-reference.com and www.retrosheet.org.

Dominican League statistics from https://stats.winterballdata.com/players?key=1738 (subscription service).

NOTES

1   Juan Guzmán, Player Publicity Questionnaire, November 1, 1985.

2   Rosie DiManno, "The Great Juan," *Toronto Star*, October 10, 1991: A1.

3   Larry Millson, "Guzmán Seeks Spot in Starting Rotation, But Still a Long Shot," *Globe and Mail* (Toronto), February 24, 1989: A19.

4   Allan Ryan, "The Heat is On Young Guzmán in Encore Year," *Toronto Star*, February 26, 1992: C1.

5   Joe Donnelly, "Worth Waiting For," *Newsday* (New York, New York), October 9, 1991: 157.

6   DiManno, "The Great Juan."

7   Neil MacCarl, "Juan Guzmán: From 'Good Arm, Good Person' to All-Star," *Globe and Mail*, July 11, 1992: A16.

8   MacCarl, "Juan Guzmán: From 'Good Arm, Good Person' to All-Star."

9   Steve Fainaru, "Guzmán Self-Made Overachiever," *Ottawa Citizen*, October 2, 1991: C3.

10 DiManno, "The Great Juan."

11 MacCarl, "Juan Guzmán: From 'Good Arm, Good Person' to All-Star."

12 Ross Newhan, "Guzmán: Another Dodger Who Got Away," *Los Angeles Times*, October 11, 1991: C6.

13 Millson, "Guzmán Seeks Spot in Starting Rotation, But Still a Long Shot."

14 Juan Guzmán, 1993 Donruss Studio Baseball Card.

15 Newhan, "Guzmán: Another Dodger Who Got Away."

16 MacCarl, "Juan Guzmán: From 'Good Arm, Good Person' to All-Star."

17 Millson, "Guzmán Seeks Spot in Starting Rotation, But Still a Long Shot."

18 Newhan, "Guzmán: Another Dodger Who Got Away."

19 MacCarl, "Juan Guzmán: From 'Good Arm, Good Person' to All-Star."

20 Millson, "Guzmán Seeks Spot in Starting Rotation, But Still a Long Shot."

21 Millson, "Guzmán Seeks Spot in Starting Rotation, But Still a Long Shot."

22 Bob Ryan, "Guzmán in Complete Control," *Boston Globe*, October 10, 1991: 59.

23 Ryan, "The Heat is On Young Guzmán in Encore Year."

24 MacCarl, "Juan Guzmán: From 'Good Arm, Good Person' to All-Star."

25 Larry Millson, "Well-Rested Guzmán Faces Bosox in Opener," *Globe and Mail*, August 4, 1995: C11.

26 MacCarl, "Juan Guzmán: From 'Good Arm, Good Person' to All-Star."

27 DiManno, "The Great Juan."

28 "Armed with a Work Ethic," *Windsor Star*, July 13, 1992: C1.

29 Juan Guzmán, 1992 Donruss Baseball Card.

30 Juan Guzmán, 1992 Donruss Baseball Card.

31 Juan Guzmán, 1992 Upper Deck Team Heroes Holograms Baseball Card.

32 Newhan, "Guzmán: Another Dodger Who Got Away."

33 Dave Perkins, "Bring Back Guzmán to Start in Fifth Game," *Toronto Star*, 10/10/91: D1.

34 Newhan, "Guzmán: Another Dodger Who Got Away."

35 DiManno, "The Great Juan."

36 Chris Young, "Juan Guzmán's Cool Under Fire," *Toronto Star*, October 11, 1991: F3.

37 MacCarl, "Juan Guzmán: From 'Good Arm, Good Person' to All-Star."

38 "Slider," *The Sporting News*, July 11, 1994: 15.

39 Larry Millson, "Guzmán's Pleased with Progress on Crucial Changeup," *Globe and Mail*, March 19, 1994: A19.

40 Ryan, "The Heat is On Young Guzmán in Encore Year."

41 "Sore-Shoulder Guzmán Put On DL," *Ottawa Citizen*, August 6, 1992: C10.

42 "Jays Soaked in Joe," *Calgary Herald*, October 4, 1992: E1.

43 Millson, "Guzmán's Pleased with Progress on Crucial Changeup."

44 *1999 Baltimore Orioles Media Guide*, 98.

45 Mike Downey, "Guzmán's No-Look Class in the Stuff of Pennants," *Los Angeles Times*, October 11, 1993: 1.

46 Steve Milton, "At Last, A Win; Even if it Only is Detroit," *Spectator* (Hamilton, Ontario), May 17,1994: D3.

47 Mark Zwolinski, "Guzmán's Fastball in Hopping Form in Exhibition Debut," *Toronto Star*, April 16, 1995: B4.

48 Zwolinski, "Guzmán's Fastball in Hopping Form in Exhibition Debut."

49 Earl Bloom, "Final Hurdle to Martinez's No-Hitter Wasn't a Stranger," *Orange County Register*, July 16, 1995: C12.

50 *1999 Baltimore Orioles Media Guide*, 98.

51 Mark Zwolinksi, "Guzmán Signs But 'Penalty' Cut to Cost $560,000," *Toronto Star*, December 21, 1995: D5.

52 Larry Millson, "Guzmán Gives Jays Reason for Optimism," *Globe and Mail*, February 9, 1996: C11.

53 Stephen Brunt, "New, Changed Guzmán Offers Jays Good News," *Globe and Mail*, March 4, 1996: C8.

54   *1999 Baltimore Orioles Media Guide*, 98.

55   "Guzmán Expected to Miss Rest of Season," *Los
      Angeles Times*, September 8, 1996: 11.

56   Rod Beaton, "Guzmán Re-signs with Jays For $9.5M,
      Two Years," *USA Today*, November 14, 1996: C5.

57   *1999 Baltimore Orioles Media Guide*, 98.

58   "Guzmán Has Surgery on Right Shoulder," *Standard* (St.
      Catharines, Ontario), September 12, 1997: C1.

59   Dave Buscema, "As O(s) Canada Refrain," *York*
      (Pennsylvania) *Daily Record*, August 6, 1998: B1.

60   "Guzmán Gets $12 Million," *Times-Colonist* (Victoria,
      British Columbia), January 9, 2000: D8.

61   "Guzmán to Have Surgery," *New York Times*, June 26, 2000: D3.

62   "Lanzador Juan Guzmán Irá a Salón de la Fama," *Listín Diario*
      (Dominican Republic), October 2, 2012, https://listíndiario.com/
      el-deporte/2012/10/02/249362/lanzador-juan-guzmán-ira-a-sa-
      lon-de-la-fama (last accessed March 8, 2021).

63   Jim Byers, "Guzmán is Juan Mysterious Guy,"
      Ottawa Citizen, August 24, 1996: G3.

64   MacCarl, "Juan Guzmán: From 'Good Arm, Good Person' to All-Star."

65   Byers, "Guzmán is Juan Mysterious Guy."

66   *1999 Baltimore Orioles Media Guide,* 98.

67   Juan Guzmán, https://www.facebook.com/juan.guzmán.58760608/
      about_family_and_relationships (last accessed March 8, 2021).

68   Yamell Rossi Jesni, "Juan Guzmán, Con la Misión de Dios de
      Ayudar al Prójimo," *Diario Libre*, November 18, 2017, https://www.
      diariolibre.com/deportes/beisbol/juan-guzmán-con-la-mision-de-dios-
      de-ayudar-al-projimo-YF8610735 (last accessed March 8, 2021).

69   Rose Marie Santana, "Pitcher Juan Guzmán: 'Es Una Grave
      Tragedia lo Occurido a Big Papi ed RD," *Diario Digital*
      (Dominican Republic), June 11, 2019, https://www.diariodigital.com.
      do/2019/06/11/pitcher-juan-guzmán-es-una-grave-tragedia-lo-ocur-
      rido-a-big-papi-en-rd.html (last accessed March 8, 2021).

70   "Juan Guzmán Foundation," https://www.juanguzmánfoun-
      dation.org/about-us/ (last accessed March 8, 2021).

TOM HENKE

By Eric Vickrey

"He's got that slow, easy delivery, and then – poof! – it's on you. It's very tough to hit. Very tough."
– Dave Winfield[1]

Winfield was far from the only hitter who found Tom Henke's lively fastball problematic. Henke, a 6-foot-5, 215-pound right-hander, was one of the most dominant closers of his era. He debuted with the Texas Rangers in 1982 and came to prominence with the Toronto Blue Jays in the mid-1980s. The bespectacled stopper struck out hitters at a record-setting clip while leading the Blue Jays to the franchise's first four playoff appearances, culminating with a World Series championship in 1992. He returned to the Rangers in 1993-94 and walked away from the game after an All-Star season

Tom Henke compiled a franchise record 217 saves for the Blue Jays between 1985 and 1992.

with the St. Louis Cardinals in 1995. Henke retired with 311 career saves and is perhaps one of the more underrated players of his time.

Thomas Anthony Henke was born on December 21, 1957, one of 11 children born to Fred and Mary Jane (Grothoff) Henke.[2] Fred had been a catcher in his younger days and piqued the interest of the St. Louis Cardinals before joining the Navy and serving during the Korean War.[3] After his military service, he worked as a supervisor at various manufacturing companies and then at the Jefferson City Correctional Center. Mary Jane worked at a daycare and played organ at St. Francis Xavier Catholic Church.

Henke was born in Kansas City, Missouri, and raised in Taos, a central Missouri town of less than 1,000 inhabitants. He grew up a fan of the Cardinals, specifically Bob Gibson and Orlando Cepeda, and had aspirations of playing for the team himself someday.[4] Henke attended Blair Oaks High School, where he played basketball and baseball. A starting pitcher with an overpowering fastball, he routinely recorded double-digit strikeouts during his prep days. He graduated in 1976 and played for Taos in the South Missouri River League that summer.

Henke was reluctant to leave his hometown but eventually enrolled at East Central College in Union, Missouri, at the encouragement of the school's baseball coach, Tim Dill. Henke studied building construction and excelled as a starting pitcher. One day while in Union, Henke ordered a Big Mac at McDonald's. His server was Kathy Swoboda, a 6-foot-1 volleyball and softball player and fellow East Central student. As Henke later described it, "I was finished. It [was] almost like that proverbial love at first sight."[5] A couple of months passed before the 6-foot-5 Henke would gather up the courage to ask her out, but the pair eventually married.

During the 1979 season with East Central, Henke threw a no-hitter vs. Mineral Area College and was quickly drawing interest from major-league scouts.[6] He had a tryout with the Cardinals at Busch Stadium, but the young fireballer let the team know he intended to finish college.[7] He was selected by the Seattle Mariners in the 20th round of the June 1979 amateur draft and then by the Chicago Cubs in the first round of the January 1980 draft-secondary phase. He declined to sign with either club, instead returning to East Central.[8] In one contest in the spring of 1980, Henke's fastball was clocked at 91 mph in the first inning and 93 in the eighth.[9] His college teammates aptly nicknamed him "The Hose."[10] In June 1980 he was selected by the Texas Rangers in the fourth round of the amateur draft, and scout Lee Anthony signed him to a contract.

Henke was assigned to the Rangers' rookie-level team in the Gulf Coast League to begin his professional career. After eight games, including four starts, he had thrown 38 innings and allowed only four runs for an ERA of 0.95. His early success earned him a promotion to the Asheville Tourists of the Class-A South Atlantic League. Henke was roughed up in his first go-round facing Sally League competition. In his five starts, he posted a 7.83 ERA and walked more batters than he struck out. He found his footing in 1981 when he returned to Asheville for a second season. Henke began the campaign as a starter and had a record of 5-2 when the organization decided to make him a reliever. "I was a one-pitch pitcher," Henke later recalled. "They told me, 'If you want to make it [to] the big leagues, you should go to the bullpen.'"[11] He initially felt that going to the bullpen was a demotion, but he came to realize how impactful a reliever could be and grew to like the role.[12] He compiled a record of 8-6 and a 2.93 ERA in 28 games (eight starts). Henke was moved up to the Double-A Tulsa Drillers of the Texas League in July and recorded an ERA of 3.94 in 15 relief appearances.

Henke was again assigned to Tulsa for the 1982 season. All but one of his 52 outings were in relief. The righty amassed a losing record of 3-6, but his ERA of 2.67 and strikeout rate of 10.3 per nine innings painted a more accurate picture of his effectiveness. His 14 saves led the Drillers, winners of the league championship. Henke got an unexpected call-up to the Rangers when major-league rosters expanded in September.

Henke's major-league debut came on September 10, 1982, against the Seattle Mariners in Arlington. If the 24-year-old rookie was nervous, it was not reflected in his performance. He pitched 2⅔ innings of scoreless relief and then threw four more shutout frames in his next two outings. He notched his first win on September 29 versus Oakland with 3⅔ innings of scoreless relief to close out the game. The game ended with back-to-back punchouts of Rickey Henderson and Dwayne Murphy. Henke could hardly have been better in his first taste of the show. In 15⅔ innings, he allowed only two earned runs.

Henke went to spring training in 1983 competing for a spot in the Texas bullpen. However, manager Doug Rader quickly developed doubts about the young hurler, questioning his "makeup" and whether he could handle the pressure of the big leagues.[13] During one Grapefruit League contest, Henke threw to the wrong base and Rader berated him during a visit to the mound.[14] Pitching coach Dick Such observed that Henke was difficult to read. "He never unravels, always at an even keel," Such assessed.[15] While Rader and Such looked at these traits as potential flaws, Henke later proved that his combination of skill and temperament were ideal for the high stakes of late-inning relief.

Henke was ultimately optioned to the Triple-A Oklahoma City 89ers at the end of camp. Used primarily in middle relief, he picked up nine wins and overpowered American Association batters, striking out 90 in 77⅔ innings. "Other than Bob James at Wichita, nobody throws as hard as Henke in this league," said 89ers manager Tom Burgess.[16] Henke was recalled by the Rangers in August when Danny Darwin split a fingernail on his pitching hand. Henke pitched effectively when given the chance, winning his only decision and picking up his first career save with three scoreless innings against the White Sox on August 20. However, his opportunities were sparse. After an outing on September 1, Henke didn't see action for another 29 days. In eight games, he had an ERA of 3.38.

In 1984 Henke broke camp with the Rangers but was sent back to Oklahoma City after issuing eight walks and accruing an ERA of 7.71 in five appearances. With the 89ers, he posted a 6-2 record, a 2.64 ERA, and seven saves in 39 outings. Henke was recalled twice more during the season, finishing with a lackluster 6.35 ERA in 28⅓ innings. That offseason, he worked on throwing his split-finger forkball more consistently for strikes while pitching for the Santurce Cangrejeros in the Puerto Rican Winter League. The Rangers' hot-stove transactions included the signing of designated hitter Cliff Johnson, who was coming off a career year with Toronto. Johnson was classified as a type-A free agent, which entitled the Blue Jays to a compensation draft pick.[17] Texas got to protect

24 players. At the insistence of scout Moose Johnson, Toronto chose the 25th man on the list: Tom Henke.[18]

The Blue Jays assigned Henke to the Syracuse Chiefs, their Triple-A affiliate in the International League, to begin the 1985 season. Manager Doug Ault was immediately impressed. "I sensed he was special the first time I brought him in," said Ault. "I remember saying, 'Gosh, Texas let this guy go!' That's probably the most amazing thing in baseball I've ever seen."[19]

With Syracuse, Henke was practically unhittable. In addition to his mid-90s fastball, he had developed a slider, and his forkball was effective against both righties and lefties. In 51⅓ innings, he allowed a measly 13 hits while striking out 60 and notching 18 saves. His ERA was a microscopic 0.88. Henke credited Toronto's pitching coach, Al Widmar, with shortening his delivery during spring training. "I have a little more control of my body, and it has helped with my breaking pitches," he said.[20] When Toronto placed Jim Clancy on the disabled list on July 27, Henke was summoned to take his spot on the roster.

Henke made his Blue Jays debut on July 29 at Baltimore. With the game tied 3-3 in the ninth inning, Toronto skipper Bobby Cox thrust his new hurler into the high-leverage situation. Henke swiftly retired the Orioles in order to send the game to extra innings. Damaso Garcia hit a solo home run in the top of the 10th inning to give the Jays a 4-3 lead. Henke shut the door on the O's in the bottom of the frame, retiring Cal Ripken Jr. on a fly ball to deep center field to seal the win for himself and his team. "He can definitely throw a fastball," said Ripken, "in the true sense of the word."[21] The win lifted Toronto's record to 63-37, good for first place in the American League East.

Two days later, Henke got another win with two more scoreless innings against Baltimore. When the Blue Jays returned home and Henke made his Exhibition Stadium debut, fans gave him a standing ovation. Years later, he estimated that the applause carried on for at least 10 minutes and called it "one of the most amazing sights I have ever seen in my life in baseball."[22]

Cox kept going to Henke in close games and save situations, and the big righty performed flawlessly. In his first 11 games, he pitched 17⅔ scoreless frames with a 3-0 record and six saves. The Blue Jays remained atop the division, but the surging Yankees had closed the gap to 2½ games when the two teams met for a key four-game series at Yankee Stadium September 12-15. The Yankees took the first game and had the Blue Jays on the ropes heading into the second game. Toronto

clung to a 3-2 lead when Henke entered the game with one out in the bottom of the eighth. In front of 53,303 raucous Yankees fans, Henke blocked out the noise and calmly struck out Winfield on three pitches. After a single by Ron Hassey, he fanned Don Baylor to end the threat. In the ninth, Henke retired the side in order to nail down the save. After Toronto took the third game, Henke closed out the finale by retiring Don Mattingly and Winfield to secure another victory for the Blue Jays. The series win propelled Toronto to the franchise's first division title with a record of 99-62. Henke finished the season with a 2.03 ERA in 28 appearances and converted 13 of 14 save opportunities.

Having quickly become a fan favorite in Toronto, Henke had a tribute song written about him called "The Ballad of Tom Henke" by a group dubbed the Section 15 Orchestra. He also had acquired a nickname, the Terminator, which was bestowed by teammate John Cerutti after the pair watched the blockbuster movie of the same name.[23]

Toronto faced the Kansas City Royals in the 1985 American League Championship Series. Henke was the winning pitcher in Games Two and Four as the Blue Jays built a commanding 3-1 series lead. The Royals stormed back to take the final three games and the series as Henke watched helplessly from the bullpen. "That could have been the best Blue Jay team I played on," he later reflected. "I have a deep faith, and I believe that God has a plan for everything. [Royals manager] Dick Howser passed away a couple years after that World Series, and sometimes I wonder if it just wasn't meant to be, just wasn't our time."[24]

In 1986 Henke was anointed the Blue Jays' closer by new manager Jimy Williams. In his 63 appearances, Henke logged 91⅓ innings while posting a 9-5 record and converting a franchise-record 27 saves. He struck out 118 while walking 32 for the fourth-place Blue Jays. His strikeouts-per-nine-inning ratio of 11.63, for pitchers with a minimum of 50 innings pitched, was the best in major-league history, surpassing Dwight Gooden's mark from 1984.

Henke earned $191,000 in 1986 and sought a raise commensurate with his performance heading into the 1987 season.[25] He and the Blue Jays became embroiled in a monthslong contract dispute that carried into spring training. The two sides ultimately agreed on a deal for $291,000.[26] Henke earned every penny of the deal. He did not allow an earned run until May 20, his 19th appearance. Proving to be a reliable workhorse, Henke pitched in 72 games while leading the league with 34 saves and earning his first All-Star Game nod.

In 94 innings he recorded 128 strikeouts while allowing only 62 hits and 25 walks. He struck out 12.26 batters per nine innings, eclipsing his own record from the year prior. His won-lost record was 0-6, but as Henke pointed out, "A lot of times, wins come from blown saves. I prefer saves."[27]

Henke's pitches on the baseball diamond had earned him a spot as pitchman for Aqua Velva. The 30-second commercial showed the closer in his Blue Jays uniform staring in for the sign through his wide-rimmed glasses and then recording a game-ending strikeout. The ad then cut to a shirtless Henke using the aftershave in the locker room. While Henke exited the ballpark, a female admirer said, "Nice game, Terminator."

The Terminator and the Blue Jays could not agree on a contract for the 1988 season, and so the case went to arbitration. The arbitrator sided with Toronto, leaving Henke with a salary of $725,000 and a sour taste from the process. "I didn't enjoy sitting in there and listening to the people I work for telling me I wasn't any good," he said afterward.[28] The 30-year-old stopper remained highly effective for Toronto but saw fewer opportunities. Duane Ward, a 24-year-old righty, emerged on the scene and was given a number of late-inning assignments, converting 15 of 18 save opportunities. Henke threw 68 innings and posted a 2.91 ERA with 25 saves in 29 chances. The Blue Jays made a late surge to the finish line, winning 22 of their final 29 games, but fell two games short of the division-winning Boston Red Sox.

Toronto lost 24 of 36 games to start the 1989 season. Henke was uncharacteristically wild and ineffective during this stretch. In his first 12 outings, Henke blew three saves, walked nine batters, and had an unsightly ERA of 7.84. Williams was fired on May 15 and replaced with hitting instructor Cito Gaston. The fortunes of both the team and Henke quickly turned. The pride of Taos, Missouri, won all seven decisions, saved 18 games, and had an astonishing strikeout/walk ratio of 108/16 the rest of the way. By September, the Blue Jays had scratched and clawed their way to first place in the AL East.

On September 30, the Jays hosted the second-place Orioles with a chance to clinch the division. Toronto plated three runs in the bottom of the eighth to take a 4-3 lead. Henke entered the game in the ninth as a frenzied SkyDome crowd of 49,553 waved towels and scarves.[29] He fanned Mickey Tettleton to start the inning and retired Joe Orsulak on a groundout to the third. After getting ahead with a 1-and-2 count, Henke blew a 95 mile-per-hour fastball by pinch-hitter Larry Sheets to seal the win and clinch an ALCS birth for Toronto.[30]

The Jays faced the powerful Oakland Athletics in the ALCS. Toronto fell behind, losing the first two games in the series before returning to SkyDome for Game Three on October 6. The Jays mounted a 7-3 lead, which Henke held with a scoreless ninth. Unbeknownst to the hurler, Kathy was in active labor during the game and gave birth to the couple's fourth child just hours after the game ended.[31] It was the only win of the series for the Blue Jays against the eventual World Series champion A's.

With the help of agent Craig Fenech, Henke inked a three-year, $7.5 million deal with the Blue Jays in February 1990.[32] He remained one of the game's elite closers, converting 32 of 38 save opportunities with a 2.17 ERA. Toronto hung around in the race for AL East until the bitter end. Ultimately, losses in six of their last eight games dashed Toronto's playoff hopes, and the club finished two games back of Boston.

Toronto shook up its roster that offseason, trading Tony Fernandez and Fred McGriff to the San Diego Padres for Roberto Alomar and Joe Carter. The blockbuster deal, along with the emergence of young pitchers like Todd Stottlemyre and Juan Guzmán, helped propel the Blue Jays back to the playoffs in 1991. Henke missed more than five weeks in April and May with a groin strain and then suffered from shoulder tendinitis that kept him out of action for two weeks in late September. Ward proved a more than capable replacement, closing 23 contests in Henke's absence. When healthy, Henke maintained his usual dominance, equaling his prior-year total of 32 saves with another stellar ERA of 2.32. Toronto faced the Minnesota Twins in the ALCS. Henke, having just returned from his shoulder ailment, was relegated to set-up man behind Ward. There would be only one save situation, however, as the Twins won the series four games to one.

Entering the 1992 campaign, the talent-laden Blue Jays were favorites to repeat as AL East champs. "But until we reach the World Series," said Henke in spring training, "people will say we can't win the big game."[33] Henke's career strikeout rate of 10.4 per nine innings at that point was the top mark in major-league history for pitchers with at least 500 innings.[34] The 34-year-old veteran's strikeout rate dropped off, but he remained highly effective nonetheless. In 57 games, the stalwart reliever tossed 55⅔ innings, struck out 46 and was credited with 34 saves. The well-rounded

Henke's record-setting strikeout rate earned him a fitting nickname: "The Terminator."

Blue Jays won 96 games and repeated as AL East champions.

The ALCS between Toronto and Oakland was a rematch of the 1989 series, one the dominant A's had won with relative ease. This time, however, the Blue Jays had the talent to match their AL West foes. The Athletics took Game One, but the Blue Jays won the next three, all close games closed out by Henke. The Jays won the series in six games. Henke pitched 4⅔ innings without allowing a run. Toronto was World Series-bound for the first time in franchise history.

Toronto's World Series opponent, the Atlanta Braves, had won a major-league-best 98 games and squeaked by the Pirates in a seven-game NLCS. The Blue Jays and Braves proved to be evenly matched, and as a result nearly every game of the Series was a close affair. The Braves took Game One on their home turf, but the Jays rebounded with a come-from-behind, 5-4 victory in Game Two. Henke hit a batter and allowed a walk but closed out the game unscathed by retiring Terry Pendleton for the final out. Toronto won a thrilling Game Three in walk-off fashion as Henke watched from the bullpen. When Jimmy Key outdueled Tom Glavine in Game Four, Henke was brought in to protect a 2-1 lead. He retired the Braves in order for his second save. The Blue Jays, one game away from the World Series title, lost Game Five as the Series shifted back to Atlanta.

In Game Six, the Blue Jays held a 2-1 lead heading into the ninth inning. Gaston handed the ball to Henke to close out the game. Jeff Blauser led off with a single and advanced to second on a sacrifice. Henke walked pinch-hitter Lonnie Smith, and two batters later Otis Nixon snuck a grounder through the left side of the infield to tie the game. Henke escaped without further damage, sending the game to extra innings. Toronto took the lead in the 11th on a two-run double by Winfield. Key started the bottom half of the frame but was relieved by Mike Timlin, owner of four career saves, who got the final out to secure Toronto's first World Series trophy.

The Blue Jays offered Henke a one-year contract to return, but he ultimately settled on a two-year deal for "about $8 million" with the Rangers.[35] Henke saved a franchise-record 40 games in 1993 while sporting a 2.91 ERA. In 1994 he got off to a slow start, blowing four of eight save opportunities, before missing a month with a bulging disc in his back. He had returned to form and lowered his ERA from a season-worst 5.51 to 3.79 when the players strike ended the season in August. Texas declined Henke's team option, making him a free agent heading into 1995. He signed a one-year contract with the Cardinals, fulfilling his boyhood dream. "I'll be honest with you, if it hadn't been with St. Louis, I probably would have retired," Henke told the *St. Louis Post-Dispatch*.[36] Pitching just two hours from his home, the 37-year-old stopper was utterly dominant. He converted 22 consecutive saves during one stretch and 36 of 38 for the season while posting 1.82 ERA. For the second time in his career, he was selected to the All-Star Game.

For his accomplishments with the Cardinals, Henke was honored by the local chapter of the Baseball Writers Association of America as St. Louis Baseball Man of Year. He also took home his first Rolaids Relief award and donated the $25,000 prize money to the Taos Parks and Recreation Board and St. Francis Xavier School.[37] Though Henke clearly had more gas in the tank, he was content on calling it a career and going out on top. "People don't understand that this game takes a lot away from your life. You're gone eight months a year," he said.[38]

Henke finished his 14-year career fifth on the all-time saves list. He compiled a career record of 41-42 with an ERA of 2.67. In 789⅔ innings he allowed only 607 hits while recording 861 strikeouts and issuing only 255 walks.

After retiring from baseball, Henke filled his time in Taos farming, volunteering with local youth baseball teams, and serving "as a taxi service" for his and Kathy's four children: Kimberly, Ryan, Amanda, and Linsay.[39] Amanda was born with Down syndrome, something Henke initially saw as "punishment" from God, but he would quickly realize what a blessing she was. "She's taught me so much about patience, about how it's not that bad to have a bad game. She kind of put life in perspective for me," said Henke in 2011.[40] As part of his charitable efforts, he organized the Tom Henke Charity Classic Golf Tournament, an event that celebrated its 27th year in 2021. Beneficiaries of the endeavor include the Special Learning Center in Jefferson City and diabetes research. The event has raised over $1.4 million since its inception.[41]

The fact that he did not step into the role of closer until age 28 and retired at 37 likely cost Henke a shot at the National Baseball Hall of Fame. In 2001, his first year on the ballot, he received six votes (1.2 percent of the total), less than the minimum 5 percent needed to be considered for future consideration. Though overlooked by Cooperstown, he was enshrined in the Missouri Sports Hall of Fame in 2000 and the Canadian Baseball Hall of Fame in 2011.

Henke spent eight seasons with the Blue Jays and, as of 2022, remained the franchise leader in a number of statistical categories, including saves (217), ERA (2.48), WHIP (1.025), hits per nine innings (6.57), and strikeouts per nine innings (10.295). In a 2021 interview, Henke described the special bond he shares with his Blue Jays teammates and the city of Toronto, which he refers to as his second home: "I was very fortunate to be able to play for the Toronto Blue Jays for eight years. I had people that believed in me and stayed with me and gave me that second chance if I had a bad game. I will always be indebted to the folks I played with and for and the Toronto fans all across Canada."[42]

SOURCES

In addition to the sources cited in the Notes, the author relied on Baseball-Reference.com and newspapers.com.

NOTES

1 Peter Gammons, "Henke Has Been a Pleasant Surprise," *Boston Globe*, September 17, 1985: 71.

2 Fred Henke's obituary is available at https://www.legacy.com/us/obituaries/therolladailynews/name/frederick-henke-obituary?id=20115240.

3 "In Taos, Henke's Talk of Town," *St. Louis Post-Dispatch*, October 14, 1985: 13.

4 Dan O'Neill, "Fast-Finishing Henke Still Eyes World Series," *St. Louis Post-Dispatch*, October 6, 1989: 14.

5 John Lott, "Family Man," *National Post* (Toronto), June 20, 2011: 18.

6 "No-Hitter by E. Central's Henke," *St. Louis Post-Dispatch*, April 23, 1979: 33.

7 Dan O'Neill, "Fast-Finishing Henke Still Eyes World Series."

8 Henke's college coach, Tim Dill, later surmised that Henke did not sign because he wanted to be close to Kathy.

9 Steve Wade, "East Central Team Has St. Charles Flavor," *St. Louis Post-Dispatch*, April 18, 1980: 67.

10 Bob Snyder, "Syracuse's Tom Henke – He's Too Good to Be True," *The Sporting News*, July 15, 1985: 44.

11 Tom Verducci, "What a Relief: Henke, Ward Are Difference for Jays So Far," *St. Louis Post-Dispatch*, October 25, 1992: 36.

12 Jim Reeves, "Rangers Fitting Henke for Super Task in Bullpen," *Fort Worth Star-Telegram*, March 14, 1983: 30.

13 Gammons, "Henke Has Been a Pleasant Surprise."

14 Gammons.

15 Reeves.

16 Bob Hersom, "Summoned by Many Names, 89er Bullpen Responds," *Oklahoma City Daily Oklahoman*, July 3, 1983: 43.

17 This was the final year of the compensation draft system.

18 Gammons; Paul Hagen, "Rangers' Foulup Bonanza for Jays," *Fort Worth Star-Telegram*, October 8, 1985: 38.

19 Snyder, "Syracuse's Tom Henke."

20 Neil MacCarl, "Henke Quickly Shows He Belongs," *The Sporting News*, August 12, 1985: 18.

21 Kevin Cowherd, "Relief-Rich Jays Enjoy a Luxury," *Baltimore Sun*, July 30, 1985: 37.

22 Richard Griffin, "Canadian Hall Makes Call to Bullpen for Terminator," *Toronto Sun*, January 24, 2011, https://www.thestar.com/sports/baseball/2011/01/24/griffin_canadian_hall_makes_call_to_bullpen_for_terminator.html, accessed December 7, 2021.

23 Griffin.

24 Mike Wilner, host. "Tom Henke, Alyson Footer of MLB.com, and We Talk World Series Simulations," *Deep Left Field* podcast, posted October 28, 2021. https://www.thestar.com/podcasts/deepleftfield/2021/10/28/tom-henke-alyson-footer-of-mlbcom-and-we-talk-world-series-simulations.html, accessed December 12, 2021.

25 "Contract Dispute Drives Tom Henke from Jays' Camp," *Edmonton Journal*, March 2, 1987: 24.

26 "Free Agents Have Spring Fever," *Whitehorse* (Yukon) *Daily Star*, March 5, 1987: 22.

27 Joe Donnelly, "Henke Lives for No-Win Situations," *Newsday* (Long Island, New York), September 18, 1987: 196.

28 "Henke Loses Salary Arbitration," *Saskatoon* (Saskatchewan) *Star-Phoenix*, February 10, 1988: 21.

29 "Jays Exorcize the Ghost of 1987," *Victoria* (British Columbia) *Times Colonist*, October 1, 1989: 13.

30 "Jays Exorcize the Ghost of 1987."

31 "Henke's Wife Works on Her Delivery," *Sacramento Bee*, October 8, 1989: 42.

32 "Big Deals for Canseco, Henke," *Ottawa Citizen*, February 13, 1990: 58.

33 Barry Jackson, "Underachieving Toronto Starting to Feel Pressure," *Miami Herald*, March 20, 1992: 202.

34   Mike Henry, "Henke-Ward Combination Spells Relief," *Tampa Tribune*, March 21, 1992: 231.

35   "Rangers Haul in Henke," *Austin American-Statesman*, December 16, 1992: 65.

36   Dan O'Neill, "On Second Try, Henke Makes a Deal with Cards," *St. Louis Post-Dispatch*, December 13, 1994: 17.

37   "Henke Honored as St. Louis' Top Baseball Man," *Carbondale* (Illinois) *Southern Illinoisan*, February 7, 1996: 14.

38   "Henke Wants to Go Out on Top," *Alexandria* (Louisiana) *Town Talk,* August 22, 1995: 7.

39   Scott Peryear, "Henke Enjoying Retirement," *Springfield* (Missouri) *News-Leader,* March 27, 1995: 29.

40   John Lott, "Family Man."

41   Tony Mullen, "Henke Golf Tournament Celebrates 27th Year," https://krcgtv.com/sports/content/henke-golf-tournament-celebrates-27th-year, accessed December 12, 2021.

42   Mike Wilner.

PAT HENTGEN

By John Kennedy

Forever known in Toronto Blue Jays lore as the team's first Cy Young Award winner, Pat Hentgen by his accomplishments on the mound has been anointed as one of the best pitchers in Blue Jays history. Standing at 6-feet-2 and 210 pounds, Hentgen was a high-command fastball/curveball pitcher who had a stretch of being one of the most dominant pitchers in the American League during the mid-1990s.[1] His repertoire evolved over the years to include a cut fastball and a changeup, turning him into a four-pitch starter.[2] He is a member of the elite company of Blue Jays pitchers to win 100 games throughout their careers and as of 2022 sat fifth all-time on the organization's wins list and ranked in the top five in games started (238), innings pitched (1,636), strikeouts (1,028), and shutouts (9).

Patrick George Hentgen was born on November 13, 1968, to Patrick William and Marcia Hentgen in Detroit. He played shortstop and pitched for Fraser High School in the Detroit metro area, and was captain of the baseball team. He also played high-school football for two years.

"Fraser was a great place to grow up," Hentgen said in an April 2022 interview. "My dad was in construction. He did it all. He would bid jobs. He would install insulation. He was in insulation and he got mesothelioma, installing asbestos. That's how he died [in January 2015.] That was one of those ugly 50-year cancers. He got it when he was 25. It's a long cancer. It gets in the lungs and it can take 50 years, but he had a good quality of life, active up until probably the last year and a half.

"I had an older sister, Kelly. She just recently retired after 35-plus years as a schoolteacher. She taught eighth-, ninth-, and 10th-grade math and science. Our mom – she had the most important job. She was great. She was a stay-at-home mom the whole time until I left, until me and my sister were both out of the house. Then she worked doing administrative stuff in a tool and die place in Detroit for about 15 years but it was only after I graduated from high school."[3]

Pat received early attention from scouts when his coach, Mario Borrocci, informed other schools of the talented Hentgen, who he believed could pitch for Division I schools.[4] Many scouts took interest in Hentgen as up to a dozen radar guns could be seen with regularity during his senior-season high-school games. This led to a scholarship offer from Western Michigan University, which Hentgen eventually passed up in hopes of joining the major leagues.[5] Hentgen was the first player to be drafted out of Fraser High School and the first to make it to the major leagues.

At just 17 years old, the Detroit native was drafted by the Blue Jays in the fifth round (133rd overall) of the June 1986 amateur draft. His signing is credited

to Don Welke. This was a star-studded class that included Kevin Brown, Gary Sheffield, Bo Jackson, Joe Girardi, and Hentgen's future Blue Jays teammates Paul Quantrill and John Olerud.[6] Just after being drafted, Hentgen was assigned to the St. Catharines Blue Jays of the short-season Class-A New York-Penn League.

In an interview reflecting on his first stint in the minors, Hentgen said, "I was young [he was 17], and had never been on an airplane until the Jays drafted me actually, and had never been in a taxicab. … I remember my first game, and when the game ended I remember leaving the locker room and thought how do I get back to the nursing dorm they housed us in? I remember Willie Blair and Bob Cavanaugh taking me under their wing, and saying, 'Are you okay kid?' I didn't have a car, and then I called my mom and dad and said, 'Do you think it's possible you can bring my vehicle here?' And then I was everybody's best friend because I was one of only four guys who had a car. So I was driving everyone around St. Catharines.'"[7] Despite St. Catharines' 1986 season ultimately ending in a league championship, Hentgen's first season in the system was relatively lackluster: a 0-4 record alongside a 6.08 ERA as a starter.[8]

The next season, Hentgen was moved up to the Myrtle Beach Blue Jays of the low Class-A South Atlantic League, where as an 18-year old starter he posted an 11-5 record with a 2.35 ERA and 1.09 WHIP in 188 innings pitched with two shutouts. This performance earned him a promotion to the high-A Dunedin Blue Jays in 1988, where he spent the next two minor-league seasons. Due to poor run support, Hentgen's initial season with Dunedin was not that impressive on the stats sheets – a 3-12 record in 30 starts (151⅓ innings pitched) with a 3.45 ERA. He was the starter in a May 10 no-hitter against Osceola, combined with Willie Blair and Enrique Burgos. He bounced back in his 1989 Dunedin season, with a 9-8 record in 28 starts (151⅓ innings pitched) and an improved ERA of 2.68. He also posted more strikeouts (148 – ranking second in the league), fewer home runs allowed (5), and fewer hits (123) in the same number of innings as his 1988 season.

After this improvement, Hentgen moved up to Knoxville Blue Jays of the Double-A Southern League for the 1990 season. He replicated much of the success he had in high-A Dunedin, going 9-5 in 26 starts and two relief appearances with a 3.05 ERA and 142 strikeouts in 153⅓ innings. Opponents hit just .218 against him. In 1991 he was promoted to the Syracuse Chiefs of the Triple-A International League. In 28 starts (and three relief appearances), Hentgen was 8-9 with a 4.47 ERA in 171 innings pitched. He led the league in strikeouts with 155, good enough to get him promoted to three games in the majors. He made his debut on September 3, 1991, at SkyDome, pitching the final innings in a game won by Baltimore, 8-4. Hentgen allowed one hit in two innings. He pitched in two more games, for a total of 7⅓ innings and a 2.45 ERA.

With his first few innings in the majors notched, Hentgen made the team in 1992 and started in the Toronto bullpen; he was sent back to Syracuse a few times when other roster spots were prioritized. After August 12 he spent most of the rest of the season on the disabled list, which caused him to miss Toronto's memorable postseason run that resulted in the first World Series championship in franchise history. Overall, Hentgen had two starts and relieved in 26 games, going 5-2 with a 5.36 ERA and 39 strikeouts in 50⅓ innings pitched.

The 1993 season was Hentgen's first full season in a Toronto uniform. Again he started the season in the bullpen but ended up joining the starting rotation due to injury.[9] He started 32 games, posting an impressive 19-9 record (second in the American League in wins) with a 3.87 ERA. Hentgen earned his first All-Star Game appearance with Blue Jays skipper Cito Gaston managing the team (although Hentgen was not used in the game).[10] He was sixth in the Cy Young Award voting.

Hentgen was a key piece of Toronto's starting rotation going into the 1993 postseason. He pitched Game Three of the American League Championship Series against the Chicago White Sox in a losing effort, allowing six earned runs in three innings. The Blue Jays won the ALCS in six games. Hentgen threw a Game Three gem in the World Series against the Philadelphia Phillies in which he allowed one earned run in six strong innings. He was scheduled to be the starting pitcher in Game Seven but Joe Carter's walk-off home run in Game Six won the Series for the Blue Jays.

The 24-year-old was expectedly nervous about being asked to take the mound for what would have been the close-out game. "As it came down toward the end of the game I thought, 'Oh gosh, we're really going to play Game 7' and I thought, 'What the heck is Cito thinking, man? I'm 24 years old, my second year in the big leagues and I'm going Game 7? We've got (Dave) Stewart and (Jack) Morris and all these other guys,'" said Hentgen.[11] His Game Three win was

Hentgen's last playoff appearance for the Blue Jays and his only World Series appearance.

Hentgen's success carried over to the strike-shortened 1994 season, which ended around 50 games early as the players went on strike after the games of August 11, 1994, leaving the Blue Jays unable to defend their back-to-back World Series championships and attempt the ambitious and difficult "three-peat." The 25-year-old started 24 games (again just one shy of Juan Guzman for the most on the team), with six complete games and three shutouts, in this shortened season to the tune of a 13-8 record in 174⅔ innings. Hentgen improved upon his ERA (3.40) from 1993 while striking out more batters (147) and posting the highest strikeouts per nine innings of his entire career. These improved numbers came while pitching about 40 fewer innings than in the previous season. Hentgen earned his second consecutive All-Star selection and placed seventh in ERA, fifth in win shares, sixth in innings pitched, and fourth in strikeouts. His most notable start came against the Kansas City Royals on May 3, 1994, when he struck out a then-club-record (and career-high) 14 batters while giving up the fewest hits (two) he ever allowed in a complete-game effort.

The strike led to a late start in 1995, resulting in a schedule reduced to 144 games. It was statistically Hentgen's worst season as a Blue Jay. He was 10-14 with a 5.11 ERA in 200⅔ innings pitched. He gave up a league-leading 114 earned runs and 236 hits while the Blue Jays finished last in the AL East, missing the postseason for the first time since 1990.

Hentgen returned in 1996 to have the best statistical season of his career. He was 20-10, only the second Blue Jays pitcher at the time to accomplish a 20-win season, with a 3.22 ERA and 177 strikeouts, both vast improvements from his 1995 numbers, in 35 starts. He ended the season leading the league in innings pitched (265⅔), complete games (10), and shutouts (3). He allowed the fewest home runs per nine innings (0.678) and had the lowest slugging average against (.355). Perhaps even more impressively, he posted these career-best and league-leading statistics while facing a league-high 1,100 batters. At season's end, Hentgen won an extremely close battle for the AL Cy Young Award against New York Yankees ace Andy Pettitte, becoming the first Blue Jay to ever win the league's top pitching award. He beat Pettitte 110 votes to 104, matching the second-closest vote gap in the AL Cy Young Award's history.[12] Hentgen said, "I feel honoured that my name's next to that award forever. To be honest, I definitely prepared myself to come in

second (behind Pettitte, who was 21-8 that season). I was a little shocked. I think I'm overwhelmed right now."[13] Interestingly, despite being crowned the American League's best pitcher of the 1996 season, Hentgen was not voted into the All-Star Game; he had a pedestrian 8-6 record at the season's halfway mark, and subsequently went 12-4 with a 2.58 ERA over the back half of the season.[14] Hentgen recalled, "Things just snowballed for me in the second half. … There was just a point where I knew I could go out and pitch a good game."[15]

Hentgen followed his Cy Young 1996 campaign with a suitable 1997 season when he started a league-leading 35 games and posted a 15-10 record with a slight uptick in his ERA to 3.68. Although teammate Roger Clemens won the Cy Young Award, this was Hentgen's second consecutive season leading the league in complete games (9), shutouts (3), innings pitched (264), and batters faced (1,085). He was named to his third All-Star squad, but the Blue Jays once again missed the postseason, finishing last in the AL East.

Hentgen's final two seasons with the Blue Jays were somewhat underwhelming by comparison. His 1998 season was marked by suffering from severe shoulder tendinitis for most of the season but he chose not to go on the disabled list until early September, when the likelihood of Toronto catching the division rival Boston Red Sox for the fourth seed and a spot in the American League Division Series seemed unlikely. He finished the 1998 season starting 29 games and going 12-11 with a 5.17 ERA in 177⅔ innings pitched with a career-low (in a starting role) 94 strikeouts. Hentgen's 1999 season was statistically similar: 34 starts, 11-12 with a 4.79 ERA in 199 innings. It was during this season, though, that Hentgen became just the fourth pitcher in Blue Jays history to total 100 wins.[16]

Just after the 1999 season closed with a New York Yankees World Series championship, Hentgen was traded to the St. Louis Cardinals in November along with fellow pitcher Paul Spoljaric for catcher Alberto Castillo and pitchers Matt DeWitt and Lance Painter. Commeting on the trade 15 years later, Hentgen said, "I saw the writing on the wall. I was told at the end of the season that a trade could happen and then was dealt during the GM meetings (that offseason). I wanted to stay a Jay and didn't want to be traded."[17]

In his first (and only) stint in the National League, Hentgen started 33 games for the Cardinals, going 15-12 with a 4.72 ERA in 194⅓ innings pitched. St. Louis won the NL Central Division and swept the

The 1996 AL Cy Young Award vote was the closest in 24 years. Hentgen won by just six ballot points.

Atlanta Braves in three games. They faced the New York Mets in the 2000 National League Championship Series, in which Hentgen got the last postseason start of his career in a series-deciding Game Five loss. He gave up six earned runs, seven hits, and five walks in 3⅔ innings pitched.

After the 2000 season, Hentgen became a free agent and signed with the Blue Jays' AL East rival Baltimore Orioles. In an interview with the *Detroit Free Press*, he admitted that he was hoping to sign with his hometown Tigers but it was the Orioles who showed interest in signing him.[18] Unfortunately for Hentgen, his 2001-2003 seasons in Baltimore were injury-plagued. He pitched a total of 245 innings in the three seasons.[19] In 2001 he started just nine games, posting a 2-3 record, before undergoing Tommy John surgery in August. Because of the long healing process, he had only four starts in 2002, going 0-4 with a 7.77 ERA in 22 innings after six rehab starts in the Orioles minor-league system. In his final season with the Orioles (2003), Hentgen produced closer to his consistent career numbers in a combination of starting and relief roles. He started 22 games and pitched six times in relief, going 7-8 with one save, with a 4.09

ERA in 160⅔ innings. It was the first time since his 1997 campaign that he averaged less than one hit per inning.

For the 2004 season, Hentgen returned to the place where it all started, opting to sign with the Blue Jays in free agency. It was an unceremonious return, however; he was 2-9 with a 6.95 ERA in 16 starts (with two relief appearances) and just 33 strikeouts in 80⅓ innings.

After a string of disappointing appearances, Hentgen announced his retirement on July 24. He said, "I always said when I played here that I'd like to retire as a Blue Jay, and lo and behold I did."

Hentgen finished his career having started 306 games with a record of 131-112 and a 4.32 ERA with 1,290 strikeouts and 34 complete games.[20]

Hentgen had a keen eye for keeping tabs on baserunners; not many tried to steal against him.[21] He said, "I think my biggest legacy [with the Blue Jays] would be that I was a pretty good competitor. I didn't go on the DL (disabled list) besides my rookie year with the Jays."[22] Hentgen named Cecil Fielder and Wade Boggs among his most feared hitters to face.[23] In terms of helping his progression toward a Cy Young Award, Hentgen named Jack Morris, Dave Stieb, and David Cone as the three pitchers who helped him develop early in his career.[24] Hentgen himself had a huge impact on future Blue Jays ace Roy Halladay and former Jays prospect and St. Louis Cardinals ace Chris Carpenter (both future Cy Young Award winners).[25]

According to Halladay, "To me, Pat Hentgen was the ultimate. He never preached to me. You saw what he did on the field, you saw what he did off the field, and you wanted to emulate him. He was never a mentor, he was never a teacher, he was a teammate. I felt that way the last two years with Toronto. That's all I wanted to do. Coming here was the same thing. I just wanted to be a good teammate with these guys and continue to do the stuff that I saw these great pitchers do when I came up."[26]

Hentgen joined the Blue Jays coaching staff in 2011 under manager John Farrell.[27] He served as the Blue Jays bullpen coach for the 2011 and 2013 seasons.[28] Due to family reasons, this role was reduced in 2014 but he returned in various special-assistant and scouting positions for eight seasons before his position was eliminated by downsizing because of COVID-19.[29] In 2016 Hentgen was selected for membership into the Canadian Baseball Hall of Fame, alongside fellow inductees Dennis Martinez, Wayne Norton, Tony Kubek, William Shuttleworth, and Howard Starkman.[30]

Outside of baseball, Hentgen and his wife, Darlene, have three daughters – Taylor (b.1995), Hannah (1997), and Madison (2000). "We got married in 1992. We've been together since we were 18. She worked as a waitress while we were in the minor leagues and during the offseason, but for the most part she stayed with me once we were serious. She'd come and stay and visit at A ball, Double A, and Triple A. But I didn't have enough money to pay my own bills at the time."[31]

In 2015 Hentgen said he still felt he could pitch out of the bullpen at age 35 but was hoping to spend more time with his family rather than endure another season's travel.[32] Upon retiring, he cited how incredible it was to be able to go to his daughter Taylor's sporting events.[33] He started an initiative called "Hentgen's Heroes" through which he would buy Blue Jays tickets for children who could not afford them.[34] He also hosted an annual hunting camp for two weeks every fall for 22 years, held at his cabin in Ontario.[35]

Who had helped him the most along the way? "My father was the number-one influence. He went to every game, went to all the spring-training games. He was a baseball junkie. There were two people in the Blue Jays organization who really helped me – Mel Queen and Bobby Mattick. Two guys who ran the minor leagues back when I was playing. I was a kid. I signed at 18 [Actually 17]. They taught me how to become a professional baseball player. They taught me how to be a man."[36]

SOURCES

In addition to the sources cited in the Notes, the author consulted baseballalmanac.com and Baseball-Reference.com. Thanks to Mal Allen, Scott Crawford, and Adrian Fung.

NOTES

1   Canadian Baseball Hall of Fame, "Pat Hentgen," https://baseballhall-offame.ca/hall-of-famer/pat-hentgen/, accessed February 5, 2022.

2   David Laurila, "Q&A: Pat Hentgen," FanGraphs, November 23, 2011. https://blogs.fangraphs.com/qa-pat-hentgen/.

3   Pat Hentgen interview with Bill Nowlin on April 25, 2022, hereafter referred to as Hentgen interview.

4   Vito Chirco, "Q&A: Shelby's Pat Hentgen Talks MLB, Tigers and More," *Detroit Free Press*, June 18, 2015. https://www.freep.com/story/sports/mlb/tigers/2015/06/18/pat-hentgen-mlb-detroit-tigers/28943599/.

5   Chirco.

6   Neither Quantrill nor Olerud signed after the June draft. Both were drafted again in June 1989 and both signed that year, Quantrill with the Red Sox and Olerud with the Blue Jays. Quantrill arrived in Toronto, via the Phillies, in December 1995.

7   Rod Mawhood, "Did You Know? Pat Hentgen's Baseball Career Started in St. Catharines as a 17-Year-Old," *Niagara Independent*,

November 24, 2020. https://niagaraindependent.ca/did-you-know-pat-hentgens-baseball-career-started-in-st-catharines-as-a-17-year-old/.

8   Mawhood.

9   Chirco.

10   Tom Dakers, "Top 50 All-Time Greatest Blue Jays: #11 Pat Hentgen," *Blue Jays Banter*, March 31, 2021. https://www.bluebirdbanter.com/2021/3/31/22359696/top-60-all-time-greatest-blue-jays-11-pat-hentgen, accessed February 5, 2022.

11   Brendan Kennedy, "Blue Jays: Pat Hentgen Looks Back on 1993 World Series Win," *Toronto Star*, March 22, 2013. In his April 2022 interview, Hentgen said, "I was scheduled to pitch Game Seven and Joe hit the home run. Thank God I didn't have to pitch that. I had pitched Game Three and I remember thinking, 'Wow, we're going to play 180 games and it's going to come down to one game and I'm pitching it.' We charted the game, believe it or not."

12   Baseball Almanac, "Pat Hentgen Stats." https://www.baseball-almanac.com/players/player.php?p=hentgpa01.

13   "Hentgen Pulls Cy Surprise," *Tampa Bay Times*, November 13, 1996. https://www.tampabay.com/archive/1996/11/13/hentgen-pulls-cy-surprise/.

14   Tom Dakers, "Top 50 All-Time Greatest Blue Jays: #11 Pat Hentgen."

15   Ronald Blum, "Blue Jays' Hentgen Wins AL Cy Young", *Washington Post*, November 13, 1996. https://www.washingtonpost.com/archive/sports/1996/11/13/blue-jays-hentgen-wins-al-cy-young/2faff412-33dd-40c2-b7b6-5f2f239cbb3c/.

16   Tom Dakers, "Top 50 All-Time Greatest Blue Jays: #11 Pat Hentgen."

17   Vito Chirco, "Q&A: Shelby's Pat Hentgen talks MLB, Tigers and More."

18   Vito Chirco, "Q&A: Shelby's Pat Hentgen talks MLB, Tigers and More."

19   Tom Dakers, "Top 50 All-Time Greatest Blue Jays: #11 Pat Hentgen."

20   CBC Sports, "Jays' Pat Hentgen Retires," July 24, 2004. https://www.cbc.ca/sports/baseball/jays-pat-hentgen-retires-1.473935.

21   Tom Dakers, "Top 50 All-Time Greatest Blue Jays: #11 Pat Hentgen."

22   Chirco.

23   Mawhood, "Did You Know? Pat Hentgen's Baseball Career Started in St. Catharines as a 17-Year-Old."

24   Tom Dakers, "Pat Hentgen Interview: Part One," *Blue Bird Banter*, October 25, 2010. https://www.bluebirdbanter.com/2010/10/25/1772952/pat-hentgen-interview-part-one, accessed February 5, 2022.

25   Tom Dakers, "Pat Hentgen Interview: Part One"; David Singh, "Hentgen's Blue Jays Legacy Ranges from Cy Young to Connective Tissue," *Toronto Star*, June 12, 2017.

26   Tom Dakers, "Pat Hentgen Interview: Part Two," *Blue Bird Banter*, October 27, 2010. https://www.bluebirdbanter.com/2010/10/27/1777413/pat-hentgen-interview-part-two, accessed February 5, 2022.

27   Mark Zwolinski, "Pat Hentgen, the First Blue Jay to Win Cy Young Award," *Toronto Star*, March 5, 2015.

28   Shi Davidi, "Blue Jays Cut Positions of Hentgen, Quantrill, Offer Them Part-Time Roles," Sportsnet.ca, September 24, 2020. https://www.sportsnet.ca/mlb/blue-jays-part-ways-staff-members-hentgen-quantrill-huckaby/#:~:text=Players-,Blue%20Jays%20cut%20positions%20of%20Hentgen%2C%20Quantrill,offer%20them%20part%2Dtime%20roles&text=The%20Toronto%20Blue%20Jays%20parted,according%20to%20Sportsnet's%20Shi%20Davidi.

29   Davidi.

30   Canadian Baseball Hall of Fame.

31   Hentgen interview.

32 Richard Griffin, "Ex-Jays Ace Hentgen, Late Dad Bonded Through Baseball: Griffin," *Toronto Star*, March 5, 2015.

33 Kevin Lozon, "Hannah Hentgen Feels 'Very Lucky' to Have Her Dad by Her side," MI Prep Zone, May 24, 2014. http://www.miprepzone.com/macomb/results.asp?ID=7319

34 Tom Dakers, "Top 50 All-Time Greatest Blue Jays: #11 Pat Hentgen."

35 Todd Zolecki, "The Last Words of Roy Halladay: 'I'm Sorry. I Should've Just Gone with You. Another Wasted Day,'" *Toronto Star*, May 10, 2020. This changed after the COVID-19 pandemic and Hentgen now has a cabin in his native Michigan.

36 Hentgen interview.

JEFF KENT

By J.P. Garrett

Say the name Jeff Kent to a baseball fan and you'll get a variety of responses, ranging from aloof to egotistical to downright nasty. One of the most polarizing players of the last 30 years, Kent won the 2000 MVP Award but not many fans along the way. While some appreciated his competitive, old-school approach, most were turned off by his what had been described as an arrogant demeanor.

"It's not arrogant; it's confident," Kent once said. "Some people might interpret it that way, but that's OK. If I put up the numbers, bring home my paycheck to my wife to support my family, and help the team win, then that's fine. There are a lot of guys I hate in the big leagues, but I respect them. And that's what is important."[1]

What was first important to Jeffrey Franklin Kent growing up was not baseball, but motocross. Born March 7, 1968 in Bellflower, Calif., a suburb of Los Angeles, he grew up in Huntington Beach. Although his father, Alan, took Jeff and his two younger brothers, Eric and Adam, to Dodger games, "I never watched baseball on TV," he said. "It's slow and boring. I'm not a fan. Never was."[2] Kent followed in the tire tracks of his father, a motorcycle cop, in motocross competitions across California. As Kent has recounted, his father was a demanding parent who had no time for foolishness and small talk.

"Being a perfectionist is an attribute," said Alan Kent. "I don't mind being labeled a perfectionist, and that's what I taught Jeff – do the job right the first time around."[3]

So the seeds of perfectionism were sown with Kent at a young age, whether motocross racing, surfing, or participating in Little League. By the time Kent graduated from Huntington Beach's Edison High School in 1986, that constant striving for perfection had established him as a powerful hitter as well as a dominating pitcher. But he was asked to leave the team during his senior season for what coach Ron LaRuffa called an "attitude problem." "It was a bad case of senioritis," said LaRuffa. "We just couldn't come to an agreement on what was expected of him

and what he expected."[4] With no opportunity for a baseball scholarship, Kent was accepted on academics by the University of California at Berkeley.

By the spring of Kent's freshman year, Cal's baseball coach, Bob Milano, offered him a spot on the team as a walk-on. Kent quickly picked up where he left off in high school, ending the season with a school-record 25 doubles. He earned a partial scholarship and helped Cal qualify for the College World Series in 1988, but the 1989 season was a disappointment and once again clashes with his coach caused tension in the clubhouse. Eligible for the major-league draft, Kent left the team and Cal when he was drafted in the 20th round, the 523rd overall pick, by the Toronto Blue Jays.

Kent began his professional career as a third baseman with the St. Catharines Blue Jays of the short

season Class-A New York-Pennsylvania League. In 73 games, Kent batted .224 with a league-leading 13 home runs and a team-leading 37 RBIs.

For the Class-A Dunedin Blue Jays in 1990, Kent shone on both offense and defense. In 132 games at second base, he batted .277 with 124 hits, 60 RBIs, 16 home runs, and 17 stolen bases, and led the Florida State League in assists (404) and putouts (261).

Moving up to the Double-A Knoxville Blue Jays in 1991, Kent hit .256 in 139 games and led the team in runs (68), hits (114), RBIs (61), stolen bases (25), and walks (80). He also led both the team and the Southern League in doubles with 34.

Invited to Blue Jays' spring training in 1992, Kent impressed the club with his desire to learn from the veterans, his ability to play all four infield positions, and his big-swinging bat. He started the season with Toronto and in his major-league debut, on April 12, 1992, his first big-league at-bat was a double to left-center in SkyDome. By August he was starting almost every day at third base. Then, on August 27, Kent and Ryan Thompson were traded to the New York Mets for popular pitcher David Cone. Toronto, of course, won the Fall Classic later that season. "Cone helped them win the World Series," Kent has said. "I got a World Series ring, but I wasn't there for it."[5]

Kent did little to endear himself to the notoriously tough New York fans. On the field, he batted .239 for the last five weeks of the season. In the clubhouse, his teammates decided to haze the rookie by replacing his clothes with those of Mets broadcaster Lindsey Nelson. The Mets learned that day that the rookie didn't see the need to be hazed again, having already endured it in Toronto, and they were introduced to his no-nonsense approach to baseball and to life. They were eventually forced to return Kent's clothes to him when he refused to play along.

In 1993, no longer a rookie, Kent won the starting job at second base coming out of spring training. But he was soon benched after he (and most of the team) got off to a slow start. When manager Jeff Torborg was fired after only 38 games, new manager Dallas Green returned Kent to the starting lineup. He proceeded to bat .270 and set team records for home runs (21) and RBIs (80) by a second baseman. However, he also committed 18 errors, more than any other second baseman that year.

In 1994 Kent saved his job at second base by turning up the heat with his bat. He started the season hitting .315 with 8 home runs and 26 RBIs in April, and finished the strike-shortened season at .292/14/68 but still made 14 errors in 107 games.

When the players reported back to work in 1995, Kent's batting average for that year improved to .278 and his home runs to 20, while his error count decreased to 10 over 122 games – all for naught as the Mets suffered yet another sub-.500 season.

But Kent's time in New York was coming to an end. Shifted to third base for the 1996 season, he was batting a respectable .290 but had only 9 home runs and 39 RBIs at the end of July when he and Jose Vizcaino were traded to the Cleveland Indians for Carlos Baerga. Hitting poorly and replaced at second base by Vizcaino, Kent played only 39 games in Cleveland but did get to experience postseason play, when the Indians lost to the Baltimore Orioles in the American League Divisional Series.[6]

In November Kent, Vizcaino, Joe Roa, and Julian Tavarez were traded to the San Francisco Giants for yet another fan favorite, this time Matt Williams. But with five years' experience in "The Show," Kent was now a proven veteran, and Giants manager Dusty Baker treated him as such, ensuring that he was the team's starting second baseman and giving him the prime lineup spot after Barry Bonds.

Kent took advantage of his batting position to start the 1997 season. He notched 15 RBIs in the first two weeks of April and, despite leaving a Sunday doubleheader on a stretcher after spraining his neck on a "horrific" headfirst slide into third base, came to the plate the next day to hit a two-run, game-winning homer. More importantly to Kent, the Giants were in first place in the NL West for the first time in two years.

The Giants ended up winning the division, but they were swept in the NLDS by the eventual champion Florida Marlins. In 155 games, the most in his career to date, Kent produced career numbers in home runs (29), RBIs (121), runs (90), hits (145), and doubles (38), while batting .250. He also committed 16 errors, but now no one was talking about his defense.

By May of 1998 the Giants were talking about a three-year contract extension. Kent proved his worth through early June, batting .301 with 49 RBIs and leading the team to a 41-24 record. He returned from the disabled list to be voted NL Player of the Month for August, and the team was good enough to contend for the wild card, only to lose to the Chicago Cubs in a one-game playoff. Kent finished the year batting .297 with 31 home runs and 128 RBIs, while establishing new personal highs in hits (156), runs (94), on-base percentage (.359), and slugging (.555).

The Giants didn't make the postseason, but Kent made a difference by creating – in conjunction with the University of California at Berkeley athletics department – Women Driven, a program promoting the benefits of athletics and academics and providing scholarships for female athletes at Cal. Instrumental in establishing Women Driven were Kent's wife, Dana, an elementary-school teacher, and Lauren, their 2-year-old daughter. "You could say she was a major influence in our decision to focus in this area because I want her to have all the benefits of anyone else," Kent said.[7] For every run Kent drove in that season, he donated $500 to Women Driven. Including the contributions of corporate sponsors, he raised almost $114,000 in 1998.

Kent tried to make a difference for the Giants in the 1999 season, as well. In May he became the first San Francisco player in eight years to hit for the cycle, going 5-for-5 with four RBIs. In July Kent was San Francisco's lone representative in the All-Star Game in Boston, his first appearance in the midsummer classic. But the Giants finished a distant second in the NL West to the Arizona Diamondbacks. Kent batted .290 for the 1999 season with 23 home runs and 101 RBIs, joining Barry Bonds, Willie McCovey, and Willie Mays as the only San Francisco players to get more than 100 RBIs for three years in a row. Though his numbers didn't quite reach 1998 levels, his performance in 1999 merely hinted at what he would accomplish in 2000.

The Giants began the season in the new Pacific Bell Park, eager to leave the swirling winds of Candlestick Park behind. Kent also left behind any doubts about his place on the team. At midseason he was voted as a starter in the All-Star Game, and by August had surpassed 100 RBIs, adding his name to the list of Giants – Bonds, Mays, Mel Ott, Bill Terry, Irish Meusel, and George "High Pockets" Kelly – to do so in four straight seasons.

San Francisco won the NL West crown, only to lose to the wild-card Mets in the NLDS. Kent had batted .375 in the playoffs and capped the season with career-high numbers. He batted .334, hit 33 homers, and batted in 125 runs, for a total of 475 RBIs over four years. This surpassed Rogers Hornsby's 75-year-old record for second basemen, and Kent was the only second baseman in 51 years to drive in 120 or more runs in one season, let alone three. He also reduced his error count that season to just 10.

Across the NL, Kent was fourth in RBIs (125), fifth in batting average (.334) and hits (196), sixth in on-base average (.424) and extra base hits (81), seventh in total bases (350) and triples (7), eighth in doubles (41) and runs (114), and 10th in slugging percentage (.596). Kent won the Silver Slugger Award and was voted the NL Most Valuable Player for 2000, receiving 22 of 32 first-place votes and a total of 392 points. He was the first second baseman to be named MVP since Ryne Sandberg in 1984, and just the eighth second baseman in either league to win, a list that includes Joe Morgan, Jackie Robinson, and Nellie Fox.

In the 2001 season, even though the reigning MVP again made the All-Star team, hit a career-high 49 doubles, and drove in more than 100 runs for the fifth straight season with 106 RBIs, he couldn't compete with the aftermath of 9/11 and, closer to home, Bonds' breaking of the single-season home-run record with 73. Kent's season average dipped to .298 and his home-run total to 22, though he did win his second consecutive Silver Slugger Award. The Giants finished two games out of first place in the NL West and watched the Arizona diamondbacks go on to win the first World Series to be played in November.

The Giants began the 2002 season hoping to be the next ones representing the National League in the World Series, and were immediately faced with the "Wheeliegate" controversy. during spring training in Scottsdale, Kent reported to the facility in early March claiming to have broken his wrist by falling off his truck while washing it. Yet mounting eyewitness evidence indicated that the former motocross racer fell off a motorcycle while popping wheelies, a clear contract violation. Kent never admitted the true cause of the injury and the Giants did not enact any penalties against him, but he did start the season on the 15-day disabled list.

By June Kent was back in the starting lineup, now batting ahead of Bonds. In the dugout in San diego, Bonds was seen shoving Kent in the chest. despite any team tension, the Giants maintained their race for the NL West, and by August Kent was leading the NL in hits and ranked in the Top 10 in batting, home runs, RBIs, and runs. The Giants finished the season on a 25-8 run to win the wild card, then beat Atlanta in the NLDS and St. Louis in the NLCS. At last, Kent and the Giants would appear in the World Series, against the AL wild-card winner Anaheim Angels.

The Edison High School grad began his first World Series on Edison Field in Anaheim. Though Kent had had another outstanding individual year, batting .313

with 37 home runs and 108 RBIs (his sixth straight season of 100-plus runs batted in) and winning his third straight Silver Slugger Award, the Giants lost the World Series to the Angels in seven games.

The loss was tough on Kent. "I'd love to be a champion," he later said. "Any athlete wants to be the best. The only way you can do that is having your team pulling on the same side and win." Kent dealt with the loss by "just letting it go and moving on."[8]

And move on he did. Two days after the Series ended, Kent was granted free agency, and by the end of the year he would no longer be a Giant. With Craig Biggio agreeing to move from second base to the outfield, Kent joined the Killer B's and signed a two-year, $18.2 million deal with the Houston Astros. "I had my best years [as a Giant]," said Kent. But when manager Dusty Baker's contract was not renewed after the Giants lost the World Series, "it just wasn't the same," he said. "It probably was the biggest determining factor why I didn't come back."[9]

Kent's time in Houston began well; he batted .300 in April with 4 homers and 16 RBIs, though by June he was out for three weeks with a wrist injury. In early August, he was suspended for two games after a

vigorous dispute of a check-swing call resulted in his being ejected.

By September the Astros weren't able to maintain their momentum in the NL Central and the Cubs won the division in the infamous Bartman year. The wild card was also out of reach and was captured by the eventual champion Florida Marlins.

Kent's numbers were solid but a decline from the year before; he finished 2003 with a .297 batting average, 22 home runs, and 93 RBIs, breaking his streak of consecutive 100-plus-RBI seasons. He hoped to start a new streak in 2004, and all signs pointed in that direction when the Astros signed free-agent pitcher Andy Pettitte, who persuaded Roger Clemens to sign as well.

Kent heated up in May, hitting .346 with 5 homers and 28 RBIs, and in July he joined teammates Lance Berkman and Clemens to represent the NL in the All-Star Game at home in Minute Maid Park. A few days later, Houston manager Jimy Williams was fired and was replaced by Phil Garner. Soon after, Kent was again suspended for three games for arguing a strike call with the umpire.

Upon his return, Kent was part of a triple play on August 19 against Philadelphia – Houston's first triple play in 13 years. On October 2 he hit his 288th home run, surpassing Ryne Sandberg as the career home-run leader for second basemen. Kent and the Astros finished the 2004 regular season as the NL wild-card winners.

Houston beat Atlanta three games to two in the NLDS, moving on to face the Cardinals in the NLCS in St. Louis. In Game Five, with the series tied 2-2 and the game tied 0-0 in the bottom of the ninth with two men on base, Kent came up to bat in a situation kids have been imagining for generations. And he delivered, hitting a three-run homer over the left-field fence at Minute Maid Park to bring the Astros within one win of the World Series. But back home in St. Louis, the Cardinals tied the series with a 12-inning win in Game Six, and in Game Seven the Cardinals rallied to win both the game and a place in the World Series.

Kent finished 2004 with a .289 batting average, 27 homers, and a team-leading 107 RBIs. But his veteran salary didn't make sense in Houston, and in December he signed with the Giants' archrivals, the Los Angeles Dodgers. The last ones to know were Kent's parents, whom he invited to the press conference but kept the reason why a surprise. "My mom and dad didn't know about this. … That's why I'm emotional," Kent said as he occasionally teared up. "More so, probably because

Kent impressed the Jays with his ability to play all four infield positions; by July he was starting almost every day at third base.

… this might be my last turn … and I'm happy to be part of the organization. I grew up here, my dad taking me to Dodger games. … It's special for me."[10]

Kent began the season batting .407, and as the season progressed, a variety of team injuries required him to play some games at first base as well as second. August saw an escalation of a season-long feud between Kent and teammate Milton Bradley. When Kent accused Bradley of not hustling around the bases, voices were raised and Bradley knocked over a chair in the clubhouse. Chimed in former Giants manager Dusty Baker, "If that's what you need, it's what you need. … A real leader doesn't really need to let everybody know he's the leader. He needs to do it when he thinks it's right, and that's how Jeff is."[11]

But Kent wasn't able to lead the Dodgers to the playoffs that season, though individually he notched another All-Star Game appearance and his fourth Silver Slugger Award, and became the first second baseman to hit 300 home runs. He batted .289 with 29 homers and 105 RBIs.

The 2006 team hoped to be better positioned to win, bringing in Ned Colletti from San Francisco as general manager and replacing manager Jim Tracy with Grady Little. Kent was on and off the DL with a sore back and strained abdominal muscles that year. But by October the Dodgers had won their final seven games and nine of their last 10, tying the Padres at the top of the NL West. Given their record against San Diego, they won the wild card, only to get swept by the Mets in the NLDS. Kent batted a strong .292, but had only 14 home runs and 68 RBIs for the year. He was 38, and many questioned whether he would return for the 2007 season.

That question was answered when Kent showed up to spring training, having spent much of the offseason strengthening the oblique muscle that gave him trouble in 2006. The 39-year-old Kent batted .447 in July and reached base safely in 38 straight games, both league bests. He came back from a strained hamstring that sidelined him for a few games in August to try to lead the young team back to the playoffs, but they finished fourth in the NL West and manager Little resigned. Kent batted over .300 for the first time since 2002 (.302) with a team-best 20 home runs and 79 RBIs. He returned for the 2008 season as a 40-year-old with a new manager, Joe Torre.

As the season progressed, the Dodgers would continue to win, but it would have to be without Kent. Hampered by a bad back all season and then forced to undergo arthroscopic knee surgery, he was on the disabled list most of September and then was activated briefly as a pinch-hitter as the Dodgers won the NL West, only to be benched by Torre for the postseason. The Dodgers finished the season losing the NLCS to the Phillies, and Kent finished the year batting .280 with 12 home runs and 59 RBIs.

His official retirement announcement came on January 22, 2009, when his tightly bottled emotions finally came to the surface. With regard to the fans, he said, "I've learned to love and appreciate the fans, and I've learned to love and appreciate the Jeff Kent haters out there, too. I'm thankful for those people even more than the fans who gave me a hug every day, because those people motivate you."[12]

One motivation for his retirement was his desire to remain home in Austin, Texas, with his wife, Dana, and their children, Lauren, Hunter, Colton, and Kaeden, and pursue his interests in cattle ranching and motorsports. As of 2022, he was the proprietor of the Diamond K Ranch, south of San Antonio, three motorcycle dealerships along the Interstate 35 corridor in south central Texas, and Hill Country Indoor, a 150,000-square-foot family sports complex in the Austin area.

He established the Jeff Kent Women Driven Scholarship Endowment for the University of California at Berkeley, his alma mater, an extension of his Women Driven initiative. Women Driven eventually raised more than $600,000 for scholarships for female walk-on athletes at Cal. Kent's donation of $531,000, plus $100,000 in matching funds, created a fully endowed scholarship for one female student-athlete each year. He also donated $100,000 to help reinstate the Golden Bear baseball program, after it was threatened with discontinuation due to financial constraints. "Having the opportunity to get an education at Cal can make a profound difference in life. I know how much I benefited," Kent said. "Everybody should have a shot, and this is my chance to ensure others have their shot."[13]

With retirement and a look back on his most successful years in San Francisco also came a renewed focus on the issue of steroid usage in baseball, considering that he played with one of the game's most renowned users, Barry Bonds, and with the publication of the Mitchell Report, the book *Game of Shadows*, and the BALCO controversy. "I leave this game proud that I have treated it with the utmost respect," Kent said. "I have tried to carry on a legacy of winning wherever I have gone. Any integrity that I have had in this game is something that I'm very, very proud of.

I believe I played this game right, and I believe I'm leaving this game right."[14]

After he left the game, in 2011, Kent joined the Giants for two weeks as spring-training batting instructor. He also spent some time in 2012 competing on the television reality show *Survivor.* "Going into the game, I didn't think I was going to be that great at the social skills, but I wanted to challenge myself," Kent said. "It was a great opportunity."[15]

Kent's career numbers include a .290 batting average, 377 home runs, and 1,518 RBIs. In addition to his MVP season and five All-Star Game appearances, Kent is one of just four second basemen to hit 30 or more homers three times, and the only second baseman to drive in 100 runs in eight seasons. Compared with other second basemen previously inducted into the Hall of Fame, Kent has more home runs, more RBIs, a higher batting average, and a higher slugging percentage than Joe Morgan, Ryne Sandberg, Bill Mazeroski, and Nellie Fox. Yet in 2022, he was selected on just 32.7% of Hall of Fame ballots.

SOURCES

Besides the sources cited in the Notes, the author also consulted the player file for Jeff Kent from the National Baseball Hall of Fame Library, Baseball-Reference.com,

NOTES

1   Jennifer Frey, "Offense Is the Best Defense for Mets' Kent," *New York Times*, March 2, 1994: B15.

2   Franz Lidz, "Cleaning Up," *Sports Illustrated*, February 15, 1999: 58.

3   Jennifer Frey, "Kent Accepts Nothing but Perfection," *New York Times*, April 22, 1994: B9.

4   "Jeff Kent Is Dropped From Edison Team," *Los Angeles Times*, April 15, 1986: OC-B8.

5   Jeff Call, "Jeff Kent's son Colton 'finding his own path' at BYU," *Deseret News*, June 16, 2018. https://www.deseret.com/2018/6/16/20647181/jeff-kent-s-son-colton-finding-his-own-path-at-byu

6   He had a double in Game One of the ALDS.

7   Claire Smith, "By Driving in Runs, Kent Raises Money for Female Athletes," *New York Times*, May 14, 1998: C3,

8   Murray Chass, "He Left His Loathing in San Francisco," *New York Times*, March 10, 2003: D3.

9   Andrew Baggarly, "Giants to Put Kent on Wall of Fame," *Monterey County Herald* August 25, 2009. https://www.montereyherald.com/2009/08/25/giants-to-put-kent-on-wall-of-fame/

10   John Shea, "Kent Signs Two-Year Deal With Dodgers," *San Francisco Chronicle*, December 10, 2004: C1.

11   Steve Henson, "Bicker Isn't Better," *Los Angeles Times*, August 24, 2005: D1.

12   Henson.

13   Bay Area News Group, "Jeff Kent Provides Women's Scholarship Endowment to Cal Athletics," *San Jose Mercury News*, September 22, 2014.`https://www.mercurynews.com/2014/09/22/jeff-kent-provides-womens-scholarship-endowment-to-cal-athletics/

14   John Shea, "Kent Goes Out Swinging Against Steroids," *San Francisco Chronicle*, January 23, 2009: D3.

15   Radio interview, "Toucher and Rich," *98.5 The Sports Hub in Boston*, September 20, 2012. https://sportsradiointerviews.com/2012/09/20/jeff-kent-barry-bonds-performance-enhancing-drugs-mlb-survivor/

JIMMY KEY

By Sean Addis

When you ask people to name Blue Jays starting pitchers of the 1980s and '90s, they might answer with Jack Morris, Dave Stieb, Roger Clemens, and David Cone. Big arms accompanied by prominent personalities, pitchers who threw hard and had secondary wipeout pitches. Pitchers who were expressive on the mound, often showed emotion and, in some cases, had a fiery personality. Those attributes described what we defined as "aces." However, one pitcher who won *The Sporting News* Pitcher of the Year twice (second only to Roger Clemens during that era) and won the final clinching game for two World Series champions, is frequently forgotten. Why? Maybe it was because his fastball wasn't very speedy, his backdoor slider was fine but not flashy, and he had a quiet presence, an unassuming personality instead of the big-name starters of that era. Whatever the reason, his name may be forgotten, but his performance over those two decades cannot be.

James Edward Key was born on April 22, 1961, in Huntsville, Alabama, to Carol and Ray Key. Carol was a secretary who worked 30 years for NASA, while Ray was an engineer for the US Army for 35 years. Jimmy had two brothers, Richard and Mark, and a sister, Linda.

Ray was both father and coach and helped Jimmy develop his skills in baseball. When Jimmy practiced baseball, his father did not permit him to play catch like other kids his age. He wouldn't be encouraged to throw it as hard as he could. If he tossed or pitched a ball, it had to be precisely located in the catcher's glove. Ray preached that no pitch should be wasted; you should precisely locate the pitch every time.[1]

The control Key learned from his father never waned and led to success in his senior season at S.R. Butler High School. He went 10-0 with nine shutouts and a 0.30 ERA. Jimmy was also good on the other side of the field, hitting .410 with 11 home runs and 35 RBIs. His performance captured the attention of the Chicago White Sox, who drafted him in the 10th round of the 1979 amateur draft.[2]

The White Sox scouts weren't the only ones to notice Key. Bill Wilhelm, head coach of the Clemson University Tigers, watched Key pitch in the state quarterfinal game, where he struck out 19 batters in 11 innings. "I was so impressed that I went up to him after the game and offered him a full scholarship," said Wilhelm. "Without any hesitation and ever seeing Clemson, he (Key) said, 'I'll take it.' He was certainly one of the easiest to recruit."[3]

Heading to Clemson University and turning down the White Sox was an excellent decision for Key. He pitched in the 1980 College World Series. In 1982 he became the first Clemson baseball player to be named first-team All Atlantic Coast Conference at two positions in the same season – pitcher and designated hitter. Key won a league-best nine games (seven complete games) in 116 innings while hitting .359 with a

school-record 21 doubles. In 1982 he was again drafted, by the Toronto Blue Jays, in the third round, and Key this time signed.[4]

At Clemson, Key majored in recreation and park administration. He met a young woman on a swimming scholarship, Cindy; who became his first wife and they had a daughter, Jordan.

Key's success continued once he reached pro ball. The 6-foot-1, 185-pound left-hander pitched (14 games) in 1982 for the rookie-level Medicine Hat Blue Jays and the Florence (South Carolina) Blue Jays in the low Class-A South Atlantic League. In 1983 he split the season between Double-A Knoxville and Triple-A Syracuse. Having pitched in only 44 minor-league games, he made the major-league team in spring training 1984 and made his debut with Toronto on April 6, 1984. The Blue Jays manager, Bobby Cox, frequently liked to have rookie pitchers start in the bullpen. Key pitched in 63 games and led the Blue Jays with 10 saves in 1984, tied with right-hander Roy Lee Jackson.

In 1984 *Baseball America* described Key as "having a good assortment of pitches[;] he has the knowledge of how to use them to set up hitters."[5] This potential was seen by the Blue Jays, who moved him to the starting rotation to start the 1985 season. Key was part of the dominant rotation that helped lead the team to its first playoff appearance, finishing the season with a 3.00 ERA, 1.119 WHIP, and 5.0 WAR, and made his first All-Star Game appearance.[6]

In 1985 Key started 32 of his 35 games and posted a record of 14-6. Over the next couple of years, he became known for his control, a good sinker and curve, ability to change speeds on pitches, durability, and an excellent pickoff move. He won 14 games again in 1986.

Al Widmar, his pitching coach in Toronto, described Key as a pitcher, not a thrower. In a *Baseball Digest* interview in 1988, Widmar said, "He also throws a cut fastball with good movement on it. And his control is outstanding."[7]

In 1987 Key took his performance to the next level and delivered what management saw when he was selected in the third round in the 1982 draft. With a record of 17-8, he led the American League in ERA (2.76), WHIP (1.057), and fewest hits per nine innings (7.2) by a starting pitcher. He won *The Sporting News* Pitcher of the Year honors and finished second to Boston Red Sox ace Roger Clemens for the American League Cy Young Award. Key's achievements were tremendous but were overshadowed by the devastating collapse of the Blue Jays during the final week of the

season. A seven-game losing streak to end the season cost the team the American League East title to the rival Detroit Tigers. Key pitched in the final game with the season on the line and was masterful, going eight innings and giving up three hits with eight strikeouts. The problem was that one of those hits was a home run by Tigers outfielder Larry Herndon to help beat the Blue Jays 1-0.[8]

From 1988 to 1990, Key continued to be an essential piece of the Blue Jays' starting rotation, but he began to battle injuries that required him to miss time. During the 1988 season, Dr. James Andrews performed surgery to remove bone chips. This cost him several months, and Key regularly pitched through injuries during the 1989 and 1990 seasons.

As the Blue Jays pushed for a playoff spot in 1991, ace Dave Stieb suffered a season-ending injury in May when a herniated disk was aggravated by a collision.[9] However, a fully healthy Key was able to step up and deliver a season that was more in line with his breakout 1987 season. He had 33 starts, 16 wins, and a 3.05 ERA and was selected to his second All-Star Game. The game was played in Toronto and Key got the win, pitching a scoreless top of the third inning after which his teammates scored three runs in a 4-2 victory. His success didn't translate into the Blue Jays winning the American League pennant. In Game Three of the Championship Series, with the Series tied at one win apiece, Key allowed two earned runs in six innings; however, the Twins won in extra innings, 3-2. The Jays lost the next two games and the Series, four games to one.

After another disappointing playoff performance, the Blue Jays used the offseason to acquire multiple pieces to solidify an already strong team. One of those acquisitions was 1991 World Series MVP Jack Morris, who had beat Toronto twice in the ALCS. The addition of Morris, the emergence of young right-hander Juan Guzman, and the late-season acquisition of New York Mets ace David Cone seemed to push Jimmy Key to the back end of the rotation. He started a full complement of 33 games, though, finishing 13-13. The Blue Jays repeated as American League East champions and faced the Oakland Athletics in the ALCS.

The Blue Jays exorcised past playoff demons and won the ALCS. However, the durable and most successful left-handed starting pitcher in Blue Jays history was not part of the rotation. Key provided three scoreless innings out of the bullpen. After Toronto clinched the ALCS, Key told TSN broadcaster and former teammate Buck Martinez, "You know me,

Buck, I want to be there; it is tough for me to watch, as I told them before, as long as we win, I don't care what we do. Never been to a World Series, and I would love to pitch; I hope they give me a chance."[10]

Key would get his wish. Manager Cito Gaston named Key his starter for Game Four of the World Series vs. the Atlanta Braves with the Blue Jays up 2-1 in the Series. Key faced Braves left-hander Tom Glavine. He would also face the team managed by his first manager, Bobby Cox. After giving up a leadoff single to Otis Nixon, Key showcased his excellent pickoff move that electrified the crowd and settled down the longtime pitcher. Key pitched his best playoff start as a Blue Jay, going 7⅔ innings and allowing five hits and one run, with six strikeouts. As he left the mound, Key tipped his cap to a sold-out SkyDome. "I didn't think much about it when I was pitching. But when I was walking off with the crowd cheering and stuff, that's why I tipped my hat, because it might be the last time I pitch here," he said.[11] The Blue Jays won this game and took a commanding 3-1 lead in the Series.

Key wasn't finished. He entered Game Six in relief with the game tied 2-2 in the bottom of the 10th. He induced two groundouts and got out of the inning. Dave Winfield doubled in two Blue Jays runs in the top of the 11th. Key gave up a leadoff single and saw the second batter reach on an error. With runners on first and third with nobody out, Rafael Belliard sacrificed to put two in scoring position. Brian Hunter pinch-hit for the opposing pitcher, grounding out to first base unassisted and one run scored. Mike Timlin took over for Key and secured the final out. Key was the winning pitcher for the World Series-clinching game. The longtime Blue Jay, who was part of the previous playoff collapses, said, "I've been through everything here. This is special. This meant a lot"[12]

Key entered the offseason as a free agent for the first time. Several highly regarded pitchers were free agents, including teammate David Cone, Greg Maddux, Doug Drabek, and Greg Swindell. Typically, Key wasn't the flashiest free agent and was overshadowed by the others. He remained interested in returning to the Blue Jays, but the club had a policy of not signing a pitcher beyond three years.

The New York Yankees, who were turned down by other top names, turned their attention to Key, who was a favorite of the Yankees owner, George Steinbrenner. "I think Key is a guy I would have wanted as much as anybody," Steinbrenner said.[13] New York offered a fourth year, but Key wanted to let Blue Jays general manager Pat Gillick have a final opportunity to negotiate the deal. However, Gillick never called back and, while on a cruise to Hawaii, Key decided to sign the agreement with the Yankees. His career with the Blue Jays was over.[14]

Key negotiated a four-year, $17 million deal with the Yankees (and four years later another contract with Baltimore Orioles). At the time, it was reported that his wife, Cindy, who had a business administration degree from Clemson, had helped negotiate the deal.[15] In 2022, Key said he had negotiated the deal himself but that Cindy had been on agent "on paper" in order to save on any agent fee.[16]

Key always wanted to play for the Yankees or Dodgers and had his opportunity with the Yankees for the next four years. Some people wondered how he would adjust to the pressure of New York. Cindy Key believed his makeup as a pitcher and person made the fit perfect: "Because he doesn't have an overpowering fastball and isn't intimidating in that way, he compensates with location. In order to have great location, he can't be overly excited, or he'll lose it. A long time ago, he learned the only way he'd make it

Key dominating on the mound at old Exhibition Stadium

to the major leagues is by control. That really made him into the player he is."[17] Key's even-keel approach on the mound and personality was a perfect fit for the stress and bright lights of the big city.

Key proved his wife right with his dominant performance over the 1993-1994 seasons. He won his second *Sporting News* Pitcher of the Year Award (1994), was selected to both All-Star squads (and was the starter in 1994), and finished in the top five in Cy Young Award voting each year and received MVP votes, placing 11th in 1993 and sixth in 1994. Key was enjoying some of the best seasons in his career. However, everything changed in 1995.

In May 1995 Key was placed on the disabled list with a bout of tendinitis that ultimately required season-ending left rotator cuff surgery. There was some concern about how he would bounce back the next season.[18] Key struggled to regain his form, going 2-6 with a 7.06 ERA in 10 starts to open the 1996 season. The Yankees sent him to Florida to rehab, and Key was placed on the disabled list again, this time with a strained calf. He returned from the disabled list and from June 26 to the end of the season he was 9-5 with a 3.67 ERA. Key pitched for the Yankees in the 1996 World Series, his first since leaving the Blue Jays. Again, he was tasked with facing the Atlanta Braves, a team he cheered for as a child,[19] and facing Greg Maddux in both his starts. After losing Game Two, 4-0, in six innings of work, Key was given the ball in Game Six, and his grittiness was on full display. He didn't dominate the Braves but pitched 5⅓ innings of one-run ball to help the Yankees win their first World Series in 18 years.

Just as he did after winning his first World Series with the Blue Jays, Key became a free agent again after the 1996 World Series, and signed a two-year deal with the Baltimore Orioles. He had a successful 1997, winning 16 games and helping the Orioles to an American League East title, but again experienced injuries and ineffectiveness in 1998. Key announced his retirement after the 1998 season.[20]

In 2009 Key was inducted into the Alabama Sports Hall of Fame, joining other former major-league players like Ozzie Smith, Hank Aaron, Don Sutton, Willie McCovey, and Willie Mays.[21] Having retired to Florida, he joined the amateur golfing circuit. During the PB Kennel Club County Amateur Championship in Palm Beach in July 2014, Key explained his transition to golf: "The nerves and stuff helps a little bit having pitched in big games with some big crowds. Golf is a different animal; you are out there by yourself, you have got nobody to help you if have bad shots, you just have to find it and go hit it again. A lot of it is just believing in yourself and knowing you can do it. Whether it is baseball or golf, you have to have that belief."[22]

Key played in amateur golf tournaments for 15 years. In April 2022 he said, "I have been spending family time with my wife of 15 years, Karin (second wife) and our two children, Jenna and James. With Karin's help, I have been focused on getting them started in their life's journey."[23]

Jimmy Key remains one of the most successful Blue Jays pitchers. He won between 12 and 17 games for the Blue Jays for eight consecutive years, from 1985 to 1992. His 3.42 ERA as a Blue Jay is tied with Dave Stieb for the best by a starter, and he – with 116 wins to his credit – is the winningest left-hander in Toronto history.

SOURCES

In addition to the sources cited in the Notes, the author used the following:

Mopupduty.com

Pinstripealley.com

Bluebirdbanter.com

Blue Jays 1986 Program Book

Bluejays.com

Cooperstownersincanada.com

NOTES

1	Jack Curry, "Jimmy Key: The Man in Control," *New York Times*, June 26, 1994: A12.

2	Brian Hennessy, "Nine Former Greats to Be Inducted into Clemson Hall of Fame," clemsontigers.com, September 10, 1999. https://clemsontigers.com/nine-former-greats-to-be-inducted-into-clemson-hall-of-fame-2/.

3	Hennessy.

4	Hennessy.

5	Baseball America, https://www.baseballamerica.com/players/19721/jimmy-key/.

6	He pitched a third of an inning, facing one batter in the top of the third – Graig Nettles – who fouled out to the third baseman.

7	Al Widmar, *Baseball Digest*, March 1988, Quoted at BaseballAlmanac.com, https://www.baseball-almanac.com/players/trades.php?p=keyji01.

8	Gare Joyce, "The Fall of '87," Sportsnet Big Reads, sportsnet.ca. https://www.sportsnet.ca/baseball/mlb/big-read-inside-biggest-collapse-toronto-blue-jays-history/.

9	Graham Womack, "Dave Stieb on Hall of Fame: 'I surely Did Not Deserve to Be Just Wiped Off the Map,'" *The Sporting News*, February 21, 2017. https://www.sportingnews.com/us/mlb/news/dave-stieb-stats-hall-of-fame-case-interview-toronto-blue-jays-jmlb/15lhsyein7hj116xw137h58urx.

10	Buck Martinez interview with Jimmy Key, "Classic TSN: Blue Jays Post Game 1992 ALCS," YouTube.com, https://www.youtube.com/watch?v=xPLqiGUGG-Q&t=307s.

11   Thomas Boswell, "The Key to Toronto,"
      Washington Post, October 22, 1992: D1.

12   Boswell.

13   Jack Curry, "Yankees Finally Get It Right and Land a
      Lefty," *New York Times*, December 11, 1992: B7.

14   Jack Curry, "Jimmy and Cindy Key Are Co-stars in 'Honey, I Blew
      Up Your Salary,'" *New York Times*, January 24, 1993: A4.

15   "Jimmy and Cindy Key Are Co-stars in 'Honey, I Blew Up Your Salary.'"

16   Jimmy Key email to Bill Nowlin, April 7, 2022.

17   Jon Heyman. "While Key Pitches, His Wife Controls Money
      in the Family," *Los Angeles Times*, August 4, 1993: 3.

18   Jack Curry, "Key Is Out for the Season, and Possibly
      Longer," *New York Times*, July 4, 1995: A39.

19   Jerry Felts, "Huntsville Native Gets Good News," *Huntsville* (Alabama)
      Times Daily, October 18, 1992: 6B. https://news.google.com/newspa-
      pers?id=4E4eAAAAIBAJ&sjid=TMcEAAAAIBAJ&pg=4377,2626345.

20   "Key Retires After 15 Seasons," CBSNews.com, January 29, 1999.
      https://www.cbsnews.com/news/key-retires-after-15-seasons/.

21   "James Edward 'Jimmy' Key," Alabama Sports Hall of
      Fame. https://www.ashof.org/inductees/jimmy-key/.

22   "Jimmy Key Mastering Game of Golf," WPTV News, July 12, 2014.
      YouTube.com. https://www.youtube.com/watch?v=P4yX07ziB9U.

23   Jimmy Key email to Bill Nowlin, April 7, 2022.

RANDY KNORR

By Bob LeMoine

Randy Knorr spent 11 seasons as a catcher in the major leagues from 1991 to 2001, and 19 years overall in professional baseball, mostly as a backup catcher. Knorr appeared in 253 regular-season games at the major-league level and one postseason game. He played one inning of Game Five of the 1993 World Series. Knorr never batted but received two World Series rings with the 1992-93 champion Toronto Blue Jays. Knorr finished his career with Montreal in 2001 and remained with the organization in several capacities after it relocated to Washington, where he won another World Series ring in 2019 with the champion

Nationals. No one can question Knorr's persistence and determination: he appeared in 1,170 minor-league games.

Randy Duane Knorr was born on November 12, 1968, in San Gabriel, California, to Carlos Ranson Knorr and Judith (Krumme) Knorr. After playing baseball for Baldwin Park High School, Randy was drafted by the Toronto Blue Jays in the 10th round of the June 1986 amateur draft. He attended his high-school graduation party at Disneyland and had no sleep by the time he stepped off the plane the next morning. He arrived at Medicine Hat, the Blue Jays' Rookie Pioneer League affiliate in Alberta. "That was basically my first plane trip ever," Knorr remembered. "They had to show me on a map where it was. I flew into Lethbridge and took a little prop into Medicine Hat, so I went from a nice comfortable ride to a knuckleball express."[1]

He arrived bleary-eyed at 10 A.M. that first day. "They're all waiting on me," he remembered. "I walk in and they said, 'Let's go, we got to go out and hit.' I said, 'What?' So, I go out and hit. They told me, 'Go back to the hotel, get some sleep. You're in the lineup tonight." Sleep was not easy as the music blared at the Silver Buckle Hotel. The 17-year-old was hungry and went looking for a sandwich. He went into the lounge. "There's this naked lady swinging down the pole. I go, 'What a country.' I just grabbed me a sandwich and sat right there in front. Watched her dance a little bit."[2] Knorr had two productive seasons at Medicine Hat, batting .277 with 14 home runs, but appeared in just 55 games his first season due to a dislocated shoulder.[3]

Perhaps the most important training Knorr received at Medicine Hat was his transition to catcher. Knorr spent his first season playing the familiar first base he had in high school. Blue Jays farm director Bobby Mattick had other ideas. During spring training in 1987, Knorr was asked to help warm up a pitcher. The next day, he found catcher's equipment in his locker, thinking it was a mistake. He discovered it was not. Mattick soon had Knorr on his knees blocking pitches in the dirt. "He didn't tell me how to do it," Knorr said.

Randy Knorr played 1,201 games behind the plate in his 19 years as a professional, including 47 with the 1992-1993 world champion Blue Jays.

"He just told me to get in front of the ball. The ball hit me in the ear and hit me in the chin. I took off all the equipment and threw it on the ground."[4]

"I'm not doing this!" he yelled.

"Well, you can just go back home, then," Mattick replied. By the time Knorr's long career finished, he had played 1,201 games behind the plate, logging 1,698 innings at the major-league level. But it sure wasn't easy in the beginning. "I was really horrible when I started," he admitted. "No one wanted to throw to me. Balls were going back to the screen the whole time." The toughest part, he said, was throwing to second base "because everything has to work so perfect." But the mental focus required for the position was also demanding. "You have to be on your toes," he said, "and it does wear and tear on you mentally after a while."[5]

In 1988 Knorr was at Class-A Myrtle Beach, where he batted .234 with 9 home runs. He remained at the "A" level with Dunedin in 1989, batting .262 with six home runs. Knorr was on the Toronto 40-man roster in the spring of 1990, third on the depth chart for catchers behind Pat Borders and Greg Myers. But Knorr wasn't called up that season because the Jays opted to give rookie Carlos Diaz a try. Knorr spent the entire year with Knoxville of the Double-A Southern League (.276, 13 home runs, 64 RBIs).[6]

Knorr spent three winters (1989-1991) playing for the Melbourne Monarchs and the Williamstown Wolves of the Australian Baseball League. "It was a great time," he said. "I stayed at Black Rock Beach. I'm right on the ocean, and I walk across the street, and there's a nude beach. Then, one year, we make the playoffs. It's February 2, and I get a phone call at 2:00 A.M. – it's Pat (Gillick, Toronto GM), and wants to know why I'm not in big-league camp. I was playing A ball, and they were inviting me to their camp."[7]

Knorr began 1991 with Knoxville, then was promoted to Triple-A Syracuse, batting a combined .245 for the two teams. He was called up to Toronto near the end of the season and made his major-league debut on September 5 when he entered the game defensively in Cleveland in the bottom of the ninth with Toronto ahead, 13-1. His first at-bat was in the last game of the season, when he struck out against Allan Anderson. Knorr played three games for the AL Division champion Blue Jays, who lost to the Twins in the ALCS.

The 1992 season was a magical one for the Blue Jays and all of Canada as they won their first World Series title. Knorr spent most of the season at Syracuse but was recalled on July 31. At the trading deadline, the Jays sent Myers and reserve outfielder Rob Ducey to the Angels for reliever Mark Eichhorn. Knorr played eight games as Borders' backup, starting five of them. Before he even unpacked his suitcase, Knorr was in the game on July 31, replacing Borders in a 13-2 rout over the Yankees. Knorr singled off Jerry Nielsen for his first major-league hit. On August 16 he smashed his first home run, off Cleveland's Dave Otto. A few days later, Knorr tore ligaments in his thumb making a tag at the plate in Milwaukee, forcing him to miss all of September. He returned in time to be on the postseason roster but didn't see any action in Toronto's championship run.[8]

It was a different story in 1993, as Toronto sought back-to-back World Series titles. Knorr was with the Blue Jays all season, serving as Borders' backup. He played in 39 games, starting 28 of them and batting .248. On July 19, the Jays were in a first-place tie with the Yankees, with the Orioles and Tigers each only a half-game back. Knorr had a career-best three hits and three RBIs with a three-run home run in a 15-7 rout of Chicago that day. Knorr batted .389 in 20 games (21-for-54) and had a .441 on-base percentage from that time on to the end of the season, helping the Jays win the AL East. On July 19 Knorr had a career-best three hits and three RBIs with a three-run home run in a 15-7 rout of Chicago. On September 1 he homered against Oakland in an 8-3 win that kept the Blue Jays 2½ games ahead of the Yankees. In the four final games of the regular season, September 28-October 1, Knorr was 7-for-14 and was just a home run away from the cycle on September 28. Toronto had all but wrapped up the division at that point. In nine starts since August 12, Knorr had 11 RBIs.

The Blue Jays defeated Chicago to return to the World Series against the Phillies. Knorr appeared in Game Five, his only postseason appearance, replacing Borders in a 2-0 loss. It was still memorable for Knorr. In the bottom of the eighth, his batterymate, Danny Cox, called time to chat with his catcher. "He tells me to settle down, look around where you are," Knorr remembered. "You may never be here (World Series) again. That was an incredible moment for me, as I looked around at the crowd."[9] Joe Carter's memorable walk-off home run in Game Six gave Toronto its second straight title.

Knorr revealed the managerial mindset he would use later in life by grilling pitcher Dave Stewart on what philosophy he used to get batters out. Or, just talking to anybody. "I talk to a lot of the guys as much as I can to be ready when I get to play," Knorr said.[10] "When I'm down there in the bullpen, I play games. I think of game situations, what to do with the hitters, trying to stay ready all the time."[11]

Rookie Carlos Delgado made his major-league debut at the end of 1993 and many felt he was the heir-apparent to Borders as the Jays number-one catcher. Where would that leave Knorr? No one knew, but Knorr took advantage of his opportunities in 1994, batting .368 (.400 OBP) with four home runs in a 7-for-19 month of June. Knorr had a career-best day on July 23 against Texas. The Blue Jays pounded starter Hector Fajardo for six runs in the bottom of the first, including a two-run single by Knorr. He was just getting warmed up, homering off Fajardo in the fourth and reliever Rick Honeycutt in the eighth. Knorr finished 3-for-3 with 4 RBIs with three runs scored in addition to the two blasts. "I want them to think about me," he said after the 9-1 victory. "I've been up for two years and I want them to say, 'Hey, let's give Randy a shot.' I want (manager Cito) Gaston to come in in the morning and say, 'I'm going to put Randy in there' and not be worried about losing."[12] Knorr had seven home runs in 97 at-bats through July 23. There weren't many opportunities left, however, as the players strike soon ended the season. Knorr batted .242 in 40 games that season.

Borders was a pending free agent after the 1994 season and Knorr made it known he felt he should be the starting catcher. "If they trade Pat and make Carlos (Delgado) No. 1," Knorr said, "I want to go somewhere else."[13] The plan seemed to be a platoon situation with Knorr and Delgado. In hindsight, Delgado's major-league debut in 1993 was the *only* game he would start behind the plate in the major leagues. He returned to the minors, learned to play first base, and his 336 home runs (of his 473 total in his 17-year career) rank first in Blue Jays history. Borders moved on, but Knorr was bumped from the top spot again. Just before Opening Day, the Blue Jays acquired 39-year-old veteran Lance Parrish from the Royals. Parrish was playing his 19th and final season.[14] Much like his interactions with Stewart, Knorr welcomed Parrish's insights on catching. "That man has played in the major leagues for 18 years. I'm going to milk him of everything he's got if he'll let me."[15]

Knorr struggled defensively early in the season, allowing 22 stolen bases while throwing out only four runners through the end of May. The Royals alone had three players swipe two bases each in a game on May 23. Knorr quickly fell into Gaston's doghouse, starting only seven games in June while Parrish started 16. Also in the mix was rookie Sandy Martinez, called up from Knoxville at the end of June. The problems continued for Knorr in June as he allowed 11 more stolen bases with just two caught stealing. "I've been struggling," Knorr said in June," but I've been around long enough that I know I can play. I just felt that rather than sitting around I'd like to be in there trying to get myself squared away." He fractured a finger at the end of June and spent July rehabbing. It allowed him time to look at his mechanics on video. "It was a minor mechanical thing that caused a major problem," Knorr realized. "I wasn't keeping my shoulder square to the bag when I threw. I wasn't using my legs, it was all arm and I just wasn't getting any velocity."[16]

Knorr returned in mid-August and showed improvement, allowing seven stolen bases while throwing out four in 16 games. He finished the season throwing out only 20 percent of basestealers (10/40), well below the league average of 31 percent. He batted just .212 with three home runs and the Blue Jays fell to fifth place (56-88). Martinez caught the bulk of Toronto's games from that time on.

Knorr was sent back to Syracuse to begin the 1996 season, then was purchased by the Houston Astros for cash. His defense improved with his 37 Houston games: 12 stolen bases allowed and nine caught stealing (43 percent), but he batted a woeful .195. Houston assigned him to its Triple-A affiliate in New Orleans for the 1997 season. He returned to Houston for four games in September. Knorr was a free agent at the end of the season and signed a minor-league deal with the World Series champion Florida Marlins, who were quickly being dismantled. Knorr didn't see much of Florida, anyway, since he was farmed out to Triple-A Charlotte. He finally returned to the Marlins for 15 games late in the season, batting .204.

Knorr returned to Houston for 1999 and was reassigned back to New Orleans, where he batted .352. He returned to Houston in early July and played in 13 games, batting .167. Knorr signed a minor-league contract with Pittsburgh in the offseason and played 13 games for its Triple-A affiliate in Nashville of the Pacific Coast League before being released. He signed with the Texas Rangers and was sent to Oklahoma, its Triple-A affiliate, where he spent most of the season. Knorr was granted free agency at the end of the season after appearing in 15 games with the Rangers, where he batted .294.

Knorr signed with the Montreal Expos for the 2001 season, and backed up 34 games for Michael Barrett. Manager Jeff Torborg, a backup catcher himself for 10 seasons, recognized where Knorr would one day be. "He hands me a lineup card, no names on it,"

Knorr remembered of a day late in the season. "Then (Torborg) tells me to mark down what I should do with the names I'm filling in. Jeff didn't second-guess me. I learned how to prepare a team, when to bunt, what to do in certain situations during a game."[17] Knorr played in his final major-league game on September 9, 2001.

From 2002 to 2004, Knorr finished his career with the Expos' Triple-A affiliates, Ottawa and Edmonton. Eleven of his 19 professional seasons were with Canadian teams, starting with Medicine Hat (1986-1987), then Toronto (1991-1995), and the Montreal system (2001-2004). This did not go unnoticed by baseball fans in the Great White North. He was declared an honorary Canadian by fans of the Edmonton Trappers in his final season, 2004. "I've never had a bad experience in Canada," he said, proudly. "I love it up here. It's just been wonderful."[18] Knorr responded in gratitude by going 3-for-3 with a two-run homer in a Trappers win on the day he was honored.[19]

The Expos were considering assigning Knorr to be the hitting coach for their Vermont farm team but decided they needed his experience as catching depth in case of emergencies. "I really don't know anything else," he admitted. "I'm probably a lifer. I enjoy it. I like being out on the field."[20]

Knorr began his coaching and executive career with the relocated Nationals' franchise in 2005 and has remained through 2022. He managed Savannah of the Class-A South Atlantic League in 2005. From 2006 to 2008 he managed Potomac of the High Class-A Carolina League, and they won the league championship in 2008. In 2009 Knorr returned to the majors as bullpen coach for the Nationals. In 2010 he managed Harrisburg of the Double-A Eastern League. That year he also managed the Scottsdale Scorpions of the Arizona Fall League. In 2011 and 2018, Knorr managed Triple-A Syracuse and between those years served as Washington's bench coach (2012-2015) and as a senior advisor for player development (2016-2017). In 2019 Knorr managed Fresno of the Triple-A Pacific Coast League. Through 2019, Knorr had managed 1,117 games in the minor leagues with a record of 546-571.

In 2020, when minor-league seasons were canceled because of the Covid pandemic, he ran the alternate site in Fredericksburg, Virginia. In 2021 Knorr was the Nationals' first-base coach and in 2022 was named catching coordinator.

"I love being on the field, and developing players," Knorr said in 2018. "What I look for in players, what I learned in the big leagues, how a player carries themselves away from the ballpark is equally important during evaluations."[21]

Knorr was married to Kimberly (née Hartwell) for two decades. She was also from the Los Angeles area. They moved to Tampa, Florida, in the early 1990s. Kim studied journalism at Cal State Fullerton and taught Randy how to handle reporters. He was faithful to call her after each game and she could be a sounding board for him.

Tragedy struck on June 23, 2015, when Kimberly died suddenly at the age of 45. "Just when you think you're getting over it, something comes up some days to make you think of her," Knorr said in 2017. Kimberly battled rheumatoid arthritis. "Her liver gave out on her," he said. "She had a lot of migraines because of the arthritis. Her body couldn't take it anymore. I wasn't prepared for it."[22] Kim founded the charity Wheelchairs4Kids, which provides equipment and organizes events for children with physical needs. The charity holds an annual golf tournament in her memory.[23]

The Nationals' baseball community, Knorr said, is responsible for getting him through this devastating

Knorr was declared an honorary Canadian by fans in Edmonton in 2004. "I love it up here," Knorr said. "It's just been wonderful."

time. Fellow coaches and players rallied for him, even displaying a number-53 jersey in the dugout while Knorr was away. "There was no way I could've been alone," Knorr said. "I couldn't talk for three days or hold a conversation without breaking down. Not even on the phone. They did all that stuff for me. It's so touching," he said of all the support. "Being around them, I love these guys. It's been great."[24]

As of 2022, Knorr still awaited his ultimate dream of managing in the major leagues. It seems he could be a perfect fit for the right team, being a "genuinely positive and authentic guy," wrote Anthony Oppermann of the *Galveston County Daily News.* "Knorr is an accessible man, the type of person who calls everyone by name, even the wait staff at restaurants. Even through the trials and tribulations of being in management and having to deal with difficult situations."[25]

SOURCES

In addition to the sources cited in the Notes, the author consulted Ancestry.com, Baseball-reference.com, Familysearch.org, Myheritage.com, Retrosheet.org, Wheelchairs4kids.org, and the following:

Dougherty, Jesse. "Back in the Majors, Base Coach Randy Knorr Cares a Lot About the 90 Feet From First to Second," *Washington Post,* June 29, 2021.

"Sam Narron, Randy Knorr, Bobby Henley Named Coordinators in Nationals' Player Development Shakeup," *Washington Post,* November 8, 2021.

"Knorr Named 11th Manager in Grizzlies History," *Hanford* (California) *Sentinel,* January 9, 2019: D1.

NOTES

1   Norm Cowley, "'Wow! What a Country!'" *Edmonton Journal,* July 1, 2004: D1.

2   Adam Kilgore, "Bench Coach Randy Knorr Has Been with the Nationals Over the Long Haul," *Washington Post,* March 30, 2012. Retrieved March 19, 2022, https://www.washingtonpost.com/sports/nationals/bench-coach-randy-knorr-has-been-with-the-nationals-over-the-long-haul/2012/03/30/gIQAvyvdlS_story.html. Robin Brownlee, "A Heroes Welcome," *Edmonton Journal,* June 7, 1994: F2.

3   "Around the Minors," *The Sporting News,* July 20, 1987: 42.

4   Norm Cowley, "Mattick Made Knorr a Catcher," *Edmonton Journal,* May 31, 2003: C4.

5   Cowley, "Mattick Made Knorr a Catcher."

6   "Notebook A.L. East," *The Sporting News,* January 22, 1990: 42.

7   Don Laible, "Knorr Knows Value of Chiefs to Nats," *Utica* (New York) *Observer-Dispatch,* April 20, 2018. Retrieved March 19, 2022. https://www.uticaod.com/story/news/columns/2018/04/21/knorr-knows-value-chiefs-to/12595833007/.

8   "Blue Jay Notes," *National Post* (Toronto), October 1, 1992: 47.

9   Laible.

10 Associated Press, "Jays Get Straight A's," *National Post,* September 2, 1993: 38.

11 Tom Slater, "Given a Chance, Knorr Shows He Can Produce for Blue Jays," *Ottawa Citizen,* September 7, 1993: E3.

12 "Jays Thriving With Knorr," *Victoria* (British Columbia) *Times Colonist,* July 24, 1994: C2.

13 Steve Milton, "Knorr Makes Demand," *The Sporting News,* March 21, 1994: 19.

14 Associated Press, "Parrish to Catch for Jays," *Hartford Courant,* April 26, 1995: C4.

15 Mike Rutsey, "Knorr Eager for Increased Work," *National Post,* April 25, 1995: 59.

16 Bill Lankhof, "Knorr Talks with Ash About Future with Team," *National Post,* July 8, 1995: 74.

17 Laible.

18 Cowley, "'Wow! What a Country!'"

19 "Trap Wrap," *Edmonton Journal,* July 2, 2004: D5.

20 Cowley, "Knorr Shows Expos He Can Still Play the Game," *Edmonton Journal,* April 30, 2004: D4.

21 Laible.

22 "From Heartbreak to Managerial Track for Former Montreal Expos, Toronto Blue Jays Catcher Randy Knorr," *National Post,* March 30, 2017. Retrieved March 21, 2022. nationalpost.com/sports/baseball/mlb/from-heartbreak-to-managerial-track-for-former-montreal-expos-toronto-blue-jays-catcher-randy-knorr.

23 Jeff Rosenfield, "Celebs Tee It Up for Wheelchairs 4 Kids," *Suncoast News* (Florida), February 9, 2021. Retrieved Mar 4, 2022. https://www.suncoastnews.com/news/celebs-tee-it-up-for-wheelchairs-4-kids/article_34c96c48-6645-11eb-8c6e-dfcf500f47cc.html

24 James Wagner, "Nationals Organization Rallies Around Randy Knorr After His Wife's Death," *Washington Post,* September 25, 2015. Retrieved March 21, 2022. washingtonpost.com/sports/nationals/nationals-organization-rallies-around-randy-knorr-after-his-wifes-death/2015/09/25/cde0db1e-6150-11e5-b38e-06883aacba64_story.html.

25 Anthony Oppermann, "Thinking About You, Randy Knorr," *Galveston County* (Texas) *Daily News,* July 6, 2015. Retrieved March 3, 2022. galvnews.com/sports/free/article_7f6bd0ca-2397-11e5-a142-7f8b760091e7.html.

MANUEL LEE

By Malcolm Allen

In a major-league career spanning all or parts of 11 seasons (1985-1995), switch-hitting middle infielder Manuel Lee spent his first six years playing mostly second base for the Toronto Blue Jays while he backed up fellow Dominican Republic native Tony Fernández at shortstop. After Fernández was traded, the strong-armed Lee started at shortstop for two straight AL East-champion Toronto teams, including the 1992 World Series winners. Lee then joined the Texas Rangers for two seasons before finishing his career with the St. Louis Cardinals.

Manuel Lora Lee was born on June 17, 1965, in San Pedro de Macorís. His father – named Lara Sanchez according to a *Toronto Star* article – was in his early 60s at the time, while his mother, Ana Carolina Lee, was in her mid-40s.[1] Lora was Manuel's paternal surname, but he became known as Lee in professional baseball because of a misunderstanding of Spanish naming customs.[2] (The Rojas Alou brothers – Felipe, Mateo and Jesús – similarly gained fame as the Alous.)

It is likely that Manuel's father worked in the sugar industry, the city's chief source of employment. In his 1989 history of baseball in the Dominican Republic, *The Tropic of Baseball*, Rob Ruck described Lee as a descendant of *cocolos* – what some Dominicans called emigrants from the mostly British-controlled neighboring islands who had come to cut sugar cane in the early twentieth century.[3] Ana Carolina, a domestic, was born in Cuba, but her parents were from Montserrat, a small island in the Lesser Antilles. The family hoped to return to Montserrat after her father died but, she explained, "We never had the money to leave."[4]

Manuel had at least three siblings – brothers Gribi and Cortes, and sister Buena Ventura.[5] In 1985, a reporter visited the small wooden house with a cement floor where Lee had been raised and found seven family members still living there.[6] Pedro Guerrero, a co-MVP of the 1981 World Series for the Dodgers, grew up on the same street.[7]

Lee did not play baseball for Liceo José Joaquín Pérez when he was a student, but he ascended through the Dominican equivalents of Little League and American Legion.[8] He did not own his first glove until 1980, when he was part of a strong amateur squad representing the Ingenio Porvenir sugar mill.[9] Lee admired a San Pedro de Macorís resident who earned a share of the 1979 American League Rookie of the Year Award, Blue Jays shortstop Alfredo Griffin.[10] "Alfredo was my boyhood hero," he said.[11]

Lee was small – listed at 5-foot-9, 161 pounds in the majors.[12] He fashioned barbells out of concrete to strengthen his wrists and upper body. In his back yard, he swung at a tire that he hung from a steel pole to improve his timing and batting eye. "I thought it was strange," his mother acknowledged.[13]

Lee started all 12 of the 1992 Blue Jays' postseason games at shortstop.

When Lee signed with the New York Mets for $2,000 through scout Eddy Toledo on May 10, 1982, his family's annual income – through his father's pension and his brothers' employment – was just over $1,600. "I thank the Lord that baseball has allowed Manuel to help us," said his mother.[14]

Lee was assigned to the Kingsport (Tennessee) Mets of the rookie-level Appalachian League in 1982. New York's fifth-round draft pick, Gerald Young, was the main shortstop. Lee made nine of his 16 appearances at second base and batted .222.

In 1983 Young shifted to the outfield, but Lee remained primarily a second baseman in a year that he split between two short-season clubs. In 32 games with the Mets' rookie-level Gulf Coast League affiliate in Sarasota, Florida, Lee batted .247. With the Little Falls (New York) Mets of the Class A New York-Pennsylvania League, he improved to .289 in 17 contests.

Lee blossomed into an All-Star shortstop in the Class-A South Atlantic League in 1984.[15] In 102 games for the Columbia (South Carolina) Mets, his .330 batting average topped the circuit, and his .424 on-base percentage, 84 runs scored, 60 walks, and 24 stolen bases remained his best marks as a professional. Meanwhile the major-league Mets were surprise contenders and, to bolster their playoff chances, they traded three players to be named later to the Houston Astros for former All-Star Ray Knight on August 28. Houston acquired Lee and Young on August 31, and Double-A pitcher Tim Cook in September. "When I told [Lee] he was one of the players traded, he started to cry because he did not want to leave the Mets," recalled Columbia manager Rich Miller.[16]

Despite Lee's lofty average, one scout observed, "Most of his hits were soft. He needs a lot of work with the bat."[17] The Astros left Lee exposed in the Rule 5 draft, confident that no big-league club would fill a roster spot with such an inexperienced player. On December 3, however, the Blue Jays selected Lee and Single-A outfielder Lou Thornton, both of whom spent the entire 1985 season in the majors. "We were a little surprised that [Houston] didn't protect Lee," said Toronto GM Pat Gillick. "We've had him as a definite prospect since '82."[18] Epy Guerrero, the Blue Jays' chief Dominican scout, had recommended him.[19]

"I can't figure Toronto out," remarked Astros GM Al Rosen. "Manny is a young, young player – several years, maybe three years away from being major-league caliber. Maybe we know less than they do about Manny, but I think Alfredo Griffin and Tony

Fernández are pretty good players and, for the life of me, I can't figure out why they'd want a 19-year-old shortstop, too."[20] Five days after Lee was drafted, Toronto traded Griffin to the Oakland A's to clear a starting job for Fernández. From 1985 to 1989, Griffin and Fernández won five straight AL Gold Glove Awards.

That winter, Lee joined the San Cristóbal-based Caimanes del Sur for the Dominican League playoffs and went 3-for-5 in three games.

In spring training, Toronto issued Lee uniform number 4 – Griffin's former digit. With Fernández and Dominican second baseman Damaso García entrenched as starters, Lee wouldn't play much, but Blue Jays manager Bobby Cox observed, "He's exceptional with the glove."[21] Lee was the only teenager in the majors when he debuted on April 10, 1985, as a pinch-runner at Royals Stadium. He got his first hit on June 2 – a single off Cleveland's Rick Behenna. Overall, he and started just four of his 64 appearances and batted .200 (8-for-40). The Blue Jays seized first place in May and won their first-ever AL East title.

Like Lee and Fernández, Toronto's RBI leader, George Bell, was from San Pedro de Macorís. In the postseason, the city was also represented by the Dodgers' Pedro Guerrero and Mariano Duncan, and Joaquín Andújar of the Cardinals. "All of Macorís is hoping for the Jays to win," Lee's father told the *Toronto Star*.[22] Lee pinch-ran and played the final inning of Toronto's Game One ALCS victory over the Royals. But after building a three-games-to-one lead, the Blue Jays lost three straight and the Series.

Toronto wanted Lee to play a full Dominican League season, but he was suspended by the Caimanes over a salary dispute. The circuit's commissioner, Papi Bisonó, ordered that the team's initial 1,200-peso offer (roughly $520) be increased to 3,000 pesos, but Lee wouldn't sign because that was still less than the typical minimum for big leaguers. "He thinks he's a major leaguer," Bisonó said. "I told him he'd be going back to the minor leagues this year and he'd be riding on buses, not planes."[23]

Lee began 1986 in the Triple-A International League with the Syracuse (New York) Chiefs. After batting .167 in 17 appearances, he was demoted to the Double-A Southern League. With the Knoxville (Tennessee) Blue Jays, he regrouped, hitting .272 in 41 games, and he returned to Syracuse after Chiefs shortstop Alexis Infante broke his collarbone.[24] In Triple A, Lee raised his batting average to .246 before August 11, when he was recalled by Toronto to replace the injured Rance Mulliniks. During the nine-game winning streak that lifted the Blue Jays back into contention entering September, Lee started six times and collected his first big-league homer and RBIs. "Last year I was too young, like a little baby," he said. "My feeling is very different."[25]

After his recall, Lee started more games at second base than any Toronto player.[26] "He reads the ball off the bat real well. He's got a good arm, and a lot of range," said first-year Blue Jays manager Jimy Williams.[27] Although Lee batted just .205 in 35 contests, hitting coach Cito Gaston said, "We've got him choking up a bit, and he's been working on swinging down on the ball… I don't think he's going to be an out man."[28]

That winter, Lee played second base for La Romana-based Azucareros del Este and earned Dominican League Rookie of the Year honors by hitting .319 in 33 games. He was even better in nine playoff contests, batting .410.

Toronto traded García, but 25-year-old rookie Mike Sharperson was the Blue Jays' Opening Day second baseman in 1987 while Lee returned to Syracuse. Before May was over, however, Lee and Sharperson switched places. Lee split second base with Garth Iorg in Toronto, but the veteran claimed the position full-time before the All-Star break. "I played shortstop in Syracuse and when they called me up I played second base," Lee recalled. "I never felt comfortable."[29] Despite batting .267 in 34 games, Lee was sent back to Syracuse on July 24. A switch-hitting Dominican supplanted Iorg in late August, but it was Nelson Liriano, a speedy rookie who hit righties better than Lee. "If Toronto calls me up again, I guess I'd have to go, but I don't want to," Lee said. "I just want to stay in the big leagues somewhere and stop going up and down."[30]

As it happened, Fernández sprained a knee ligament and Lee was recalled in September to spell him in the late innings.[31] Toronto was battling the Detroit Tigers for the AL East title. The Blue Jays led by a half-game with 10 to play when Fernández suffered a season-ending elbow injury on a hard slide by Detroit's Bill Madlock. That night, Lee earned a standing ovation by snaring a seventh-inning line drive with a leaping, backhanded grab to preserve Toronto's one-run lead. He scored the winning run in the ninth inning the following evening after tying the game with a two-run triple off the Tigers' Willie Hernández. "He can flat out play," raved manager Williams.[32]

Toronto's advantage was one game entering a final-weekend showdown at Tiger Stadium. In Friday night's series opener, Lee's three-run homer off the right-field upper deck facing drew first blood but Detroit rallied to win, 4-3, behind former Blue Jay Doyle Alexander. On Saturday afternoon, Lee's fifth-inning error led to an unearned run that evened the score. The teams remained deadlocked until the bottom of the 12th, when the Tigers prevailed on Alan Trammell's bases-loaded single – a sharp grounder that was ruled a hit even though it went between Lee's legs. Toronto was eliminated the next day, 1-0, despite Lee's triple off Frank Tanana.

That winter Lee compiled a .373 on-base percentage in 44 games for the Azucareros. He was late for spring training in 1988 as he sought a visa for his widowed mother to summer with him in Toronto. Tendinitis in Lee's throwing shoulder forced him to begin the season on the disabled list. In mid-May he returned to the DL after suffering a contusion in the same shoulder on a stolen-base attempt.[33]

When Lee was healthy, his ability to play second, short or third afforded Williams valuable flexibility.[34] But Lee believed that playing multiple positions prevented him from mastering any. By season's end, he had taken over as Toronto's primary second baseman. Overall, Lee appeared in 116 games in 1988 and batted .291, his major-league best. "If I play, I'm happy in Toronto," he said.[35]

However, during the latter stages of a Dominican League campaign in which he hit .294 for the Azucareros, Lee attempted to gain free agency on a technicality – claiming the Blue Jays had failed to tender his contract before the December 20 deadline. (A similar situation had allowed Carlton Fisk to leave the Boston Red Sox and sign a lucrative deal with the Chicago White Sox in the 1980-81 offseason.) In January the Major League Baseball Players Association determined that Toronto had mailed the contract in time. "Manny is very disappointed, to say the least," said Lee's agent, Jaime Torres.[36] Two weeks later, Torres responded to Toronto's $130,000 salary proposal for his client by saying, "They've insulted him with a laughable offer."[37] Lee signed for $160,000 in 1989.[38]

During spring training, Lee said, "I like Toronto, I like the people, I want to play there again this year."[39] The second-base job was his according to Williams, but Lee shifted to shortstop less than one week into the 1989 season after Fernández fractured his cheekbone. On April 29, though, Lee sprained his left ankle.[40] By the time he returned on June 9, the sixth-place Blue Jays' new manager, Gaston, planned to platoon him with Liriano. Lee requested a trade.[41] Overall, he batted .260 in 99 games as Toronto came back to overtake the Baltimore Orioles for the division title. In the ALCS, Lee started two of the five games, but the Blue Jays fell to Oakland.

That winter, Torres – Lee's agent and Liriano's friend – said, "The Jays have been greedy by keeping both.… They've also deprived these two players of the kinds of income they would be receiving if they weren't on the same team."[42] Although Lee more than doubled his salary to $380,000 in 1990, he understood that playing every day in Toronto remained unlikely.[43] "If I do get traded, the two guys I'd probably miss most around here are Tony [Fernández] and Nelson [Liriano]," he said. "We have a lot in common. We always talk with each other. Tony's the only guy on the club who I talk to about baseball.… If I talked to Nelson about baseball, I might say something to him that I shouldn't say."[44]

Prior to the All-Star break in 1990, Lee batted .271 with six homers – one fewer than his previous career total. Five came within 42 at-bats in May. Liriano was traded on July 27, while Lee went on to lead AL second basemen with a .993 fielding percentage. But the Blue Jays finished two games behind the Red Sox in second place. Lee batted .222 in the second half and heard frequent boos.[45] Fans and coaches were frustrated by his inability to bunt and reported unwillingness to learn. "I feel like I've been letting everyone down," Lee said. "They say I'm the second baseman who should have been traded, not Nelson. That hurts."[46]

In December, Toronto traded Fernández and slugger Fred McGriff to the San Diego Padres for Joe Carter and future Hall of Famer Roberto Alomar – creating an opening for Lee at shortstop. "I've got big shoes to fill," Lee said. "I haven't played regular shortstop in five years. It's going to be tough for me."[47] The day after Fernández was dealt, Bell signed with the Chicago Cubs as a free agent. Earlier that week, the Blue Jays had sent Dominican outfielder Junior Félix to the California Angels in a six-player swap that landed Gold Glove center fielder Devon White. Lee acknowledged that many of his countrymen interpreted the transactions as proof that the Toronto organization had become anti-Dominican. "But I don't believe that the Blue Jays are like that," he said. "It's business, that's all."[48]

Regarding Blue Jays fans, however, Lee lamented his belief during spring training that many of them would prefer 1989 first-round draft pick Eddie Zosky to start at shortstop. "Toronto is the first and only town that I've played in where the people don't like me," he said. "When a Dominican guy does something wrong, the fans in Toronto are all over him right away. When an American player does something wrong, they don't bother him."[49] Going forward, Lee said that he wanted to be called "Manuel," rather than the diminutive "Manny" that he had been tagged with when he entered professional baseball.[50]

Lee won the position battle, and the Blue Jays enjoyed a strong start in 1991. "I knew Manny Lee could play shortstop," remarked Gaston. "I tell people around the league that Manny is one of the best-kept secrets in baseball."[51] Hours before one contest at SkyDome, Lee and Alomar were spotted talking at length, practicing their timing and footwork on double plays.[52] Lee executed 10 sacrifice hits to match his previous career total, but his batting average dropped to .234, and he became the first major-leaguer in history to strike out at least 100 times (107) without hitting a home run.[53] "I just forgot about hitting. I just thought about playing defense," he said.[54] The Blue Jays won their division but fell to the Minnesota Twins in the ALCS.

Although Toronto recorded the majors' second-best Defensive Efficiency in 1991, Lee did not rate as well personally.[55] Of the 10 AL shortstops who played at least 1,000 innings, he posted the worst range factor per nine-innings, and his Defensive Wins Above Replacement ranked sixth. "The most impressive thing about his range is his vertical leap, not the amount of territory he covers to his left or right," observed the *Globe and Mail*'s Larry Millson. "This is a shortstop who appears timid in plays around the bag at second."[56] Consequently, Lee would battle Zosky – coming off an All-Star season at Syracuse – to retain his job in 1992. The one-year, $1 million contract that Lee signed that winter offered little security, as Toronto would owe him just one-sixth of that amount if they released him before March 20.[57] When the Blue Jays played an exhibition at SkyDome shortly before the deadline, Lee was the only Toronto player booed.[58]

Lee remained Toronto's shortstop in 1992, albeit with a new uniform number. Griffin rejoined the Blue Jays as a reserve, so Lee returned number 4 to him and switched to 2, explaining, "He's still my hero."[59] That season, none of Lee's seven errors occurred on muffed grounders, and his .987 fielding percentage trailed only Seattle's Omar Vizquel among AL shortstops.[60] As the Blue Jays closed in on their third straight AL East title, though, Lee missed most of the final month because of a hamstring strain just above his left knee. Despite two cortisone shots, he was still limping noticeably when he tried to start for the only time in a 25-day span on September 11.[61]

On the final weekend of the regular season, Lee returned. In 128 games, he wound up with 50 walks and a career-high .343 on-base percentage, hitting righties better than ever before. "[New Blue Jays hitting coach Larry Hisle] gave me confidence," he said.[62] Hisle explained, "His game now is line drives and hard ground balls and don't strike out. I couldn't be prouder of anyone on this team.… When there's runners on base and two out or one out, the players are confident he'll come through. I know I am."[63]

After Toronto split the first two ALCS games at home against the Athletics, Lee's two-run triple with two outs in the seventh inning helped the Blue Jays take Game Three in Oakland, 7-5. Lee also scored an insurance run after walking to lead off the ninth. "Today, Manny was the star," said Devon White.[64] Four days later, when Candy Maldonado caught the final out to clinch the first pennant in franchise history, Lee was the first one to hug him, in left field.

In the World Series, the Blue Jays defeated the Atlanta Braves in six games. Although Lee went just 2-for-19, he singled against future Hall of Famer John Smoltz in Toronto's Game Two victory. The Blue Jays closed out the series with an 11-inning victory on October 24. But Lee had been removed for a pinch-hitter in the 10th. When he threw down his helmet in frustration, it bounced up and hit a Toronto coach in the face.[65]

On November 4, 1992, Lee became a free agent. He signed a two-year contract with the Texas Rangers for $3.4 million on December 19.[66] The Rangers had just learned that their incumbent shortstop, Jeff Huson, would miss at least half of the upcoming season following rotator cuff surgery. "I thought Lee came into his own this year," said Texas GM Tom Grieve. "He was good enough to be the front-line shortstop on a champion team." Lee acknowledged that he would miss some friends, but said, "I'm not really that sad about leaving… I feel really comfortable going to Texas. I'm happy they wanted me."[67]

Lee's 1993 season was a disaster. Mistakenly believing that he was Puerto Rican, the Rangers left Lee's name off the list of players requiring visas that they provided to the U.S. consulate in Santo Domingo.[68] Lee arrived 18 days late for spring training after the error was corrected.[69] During his first week in camp, he pulled a left rib cage muscle in a basepath collision.[70]

Lee's two-run triple helped clinch Toronto's Game Three victory in the 1992 ALCS.

Lee debuted in Texas's ninth game, on April 16. A month later, he went back on the disabled list for 10 more weeks with a strained ligament in his left thumb. When Lee returned to the active roster in July, it was only because he refused to accept a minor-league rehabilitation assignment.[71] Texas manager Kevin Kennedy summoned him for a closed-door meeting in August after two incidents that beat writer T.R. Sullivan said, "left [Lee] in disfavor within the clubhouse." In addition to refusing to shake hands with his teammates after a victory over the Angels, Lee had argued with hitting coach Willie Upshaw during batting practice.[72]

On August 31 Lee was batting .168, but he finished at .220 in 73 games. "There was a time when he wasn't playing as hard as we would have liked him to, now he's playing hard," said Kennedy. "I think you're going to see a better Manny Lee next year than you did this year."[73] In the ninth inning of the season finale at Arlington Stadium, Lee allowed a bouncer up the middle hit by the Royals' George Brett to roll into center field unmolested. It was the final at-bat of the future Hall of Famer's career. "Before he make contact, I say, 'If he hit it to me, I not even going to try,'" Lee confessed. "He's my favorite player, always."[74]

That winter, Lee returned to Dominican League action for the first time in five years. He appeared in just three games – two in the playoffs – for the Azucareros del Este and finished his career in his native country with a .283 batting average in 106 regular-season games, and .442 in 14 playoff games.

"Manuel Lee has been healthy and in a great frame of mind this spring," said Grieve prior to the 1994 season. "There's no reason why he can't do the job for us."[75] To begin the year, Lee started 51 straight games – a career high – and batted .294. Overall, he appeared in 95 of the Rangers' 114 games around a stint on the disabled list stint for a strained right rib cage muscle and hit .278.[76] When the season ended prematurely because of the players strike, Texas held first-place in the AL West despite a 52-62 record. In October, the Rangers bought out the option year on Lee's contract rather than pay him $1.9 million for 1995.[77]

When the strike was settled the following spring, Lee scrambled to find a team. On April 18, 1995, he signed a minor-league deal with the St. Louis Cardinals for $200,000. "I just want to be here," he said. "This year is kind of tough for free agents."[78] Eight days later, Lee batted eighth in the Cardinals' Opening Day lineup – playing second base alongside 40-year-old shortstop Ozzie Smith. In the top of the third inning, Lee sprained an ankle on a play on which he was charged with an error.[79] In the bottom of the frame, he grounded a leadoff single off the Phillies' Curt Schilling and came around to score. Then he left the game and went on the disabled list. Lee played six rehabilitation games with Class-A St. Petersburg and six more with Triple A Louisville before St. Louis released him on June 22 – five days after his 30th birthday. Lee's professional baseball career was over. In the majors, he appeared in 922 games and batted .255.

Lee disengaged from baseball. In August 2004, he fatally shot a 28-year-old man who tried to rob his home in San Pedro de Macorís.[80] A 2009 *Toronto Star* retrospective on the 1992 World Series champions said only that Lee was "involved in several small business ventures" in the Dominican Republic.[81] Lee's first wife, Magdalan, was from Canada, and they had one daughter. As of 2022, he is married to Purita. When a mural commemorating 21 former big leaguers was dedicated in San Pedro de Macorís in October 2021, Lee was among those featured, but he did not attend the unveiling.[82]

SOURCES

In addition to sources cited in the Notes, the author consulted www.baseball-reference.com, www.retrosheet.org, and https://sabr.org/bioproject.

Manuel Lee's Dominican League statistics are from https://stats.winterballdata.com/players?key=2302 (Subscription service. Last accessed January 6, 2022).

NOTES

1   Tim Harper, "Manny Lee Took the Baseball Road Out of Poverty," *Toronto Star*, October 8, 1985: B19. The caption of a photo that accompanied the article identifies Lee's father as "Ismael" in the Toronto Star Photograph Archives. https://digitalarchive.tpl.ca/objects/324999/manny-lees-parents-on-door-of-their-kitchen-ana-carolina-a (last accessed April 2, 2022).

2   Marty York, "Rodgers in a New York state of Mind About Next Job," *Globe and Mail* (Toronto), June 19, 1991: C12.

3   Rob Ruck, *The Tropic of Baseball* (New York: Carroll & Graf Publishers, 1991), 138.

4   Harper, "Manny Lee Took the Baseball Road Out of Poverty."

5   Sibling information was gleaned from Lee's personal Facebook page. https://www.facebook.com/manuel.loralee (last accessed January 6, 2022).

6   Harper, "Manny Lee Took the Baseball Road Out of Poverty."

7   *Toronto Blue Jays Official Guide 1992*, 84.

8   *1994 Texas Rangers Media Guide*, 72.

9   Lee posted a photograph of the team on his personal Facebook page and tagged teammate Sergio Pérez, a Philadelphia Phillies' minor leaguer from 1983-1986. https://www.facebook.com/photo.php?fbid=428482357278974&set=pb.100003516415337.-2207520000..&type=3 (last accessed January 6, 2022).

10   Griffin was born in Santo Domingo but moved to San Pedro de Macorís with his mother when he was 8. Justin Krueger, "Alfredo Griffin," https://sabr.org/bioproj/person/alfredo-griffin/.

11   "Lee Shows Some Class," *Financial Post* (Toronto), March 11, 1992: 36.

12   These figures appear in both the 1992 Blue Jays and 1994 Rangers media guides. Baseball-Reference lists Lee at 5-feet-10, 145 pounds.

13   Harper, "Manny Lee Took the Baseball Road Out of Poverty."

14   Harper, "Manny Lee Took the Baseball Road Out of Poverty."

15   *1994 Texas Rangers Media Guide*, 72.

16   Rich Miller, electronic communication with Malcolm Allen, January 5, 2022.

17   Marty York, "Rivals Ruffled by Jay Picks in Player Draft," *Globe and Mail*, December 4, 1984: S1.

18   York, "Rivals Ruffled by Jay Picks in Player Draft."

19   Jim Proudfoot, "Don't Forget Trade if Epy Guerrero Suggests It," *Toronto Star*, September 29, 1987: H1.

20   York, "Rivals Ruffled by Jay Picks in Player Draft."

21   Larry Millson, "Jays Rookie Shows Stuff with Bats," *Globe and Mail*, March 14, 1985: M9.

22   Harper, "Manny Lee Took the Baseball Road Out of Poverty."

23   "Jays' Dominicans Have Bad Time in Winter Ball," *Citizen* (Ottawa, Ontario), December 19, 1985: D2.

24   "Infante Breaks His Collarbone," *Toronto Star*, June 19, 1986: D6.

25   Howard Sinker, "Weak-Hitting Manny Lee on a Spree Against Twins," *Minneapolis Star-Tribune*, August 31, 1986: 9C.

26   In Toronto's 49 games after August 11 in 1986, Lee made 20 starts at second base, versus 17 for García and 12 for Garth Iorg.

27 Neil MacCarl, "Lee Leads Jays to 7th Win in Row," *Toronto Star*, August 31, 1986: D1.

28 MacCarl, "Lee Leads Jays to 7th Win in Row."

29 Larry Millson, "Lee Simply Wants Fair Play and Pay," *Globe and Mail*, February 25, 1989: A19.

30 Marty York, "Lee 'Fed Up': Young Blue Jay Farmhand Angry About His 'Up and Down' Career," *Globe and Mail*, August 25, 1987: D1.

31 "Jays' Fernández Plays Despite Sprained Knee," *St. Petersburg* (Florida) *Times*, September 15, 1987: 4C.

32 Tom Hawthorn, "Lithe Lee Fits Jays' Needs Like a Glove," *Globe and Mail*, September 26, 1987: E1.

33 Neil MacCarl, "Manny Lee Again Ready to Play as Alexis Infante Sent to Chiefs," *Toronto Star*, June 22, 1988: C3.

34 Larry Millson, "Lee Shows Up in Camp Ready to Play," *Globe and Mail*, March 2, 1988: A14.

35 Larry Millson, "Jays' Lee Sparkles After Earning Steady Job," *Globe and Mail*, July 25, 1988: C5.

36 Marty York, "Jays Fulfilled Rule to Letter, Union Tells Lee," *Globe and Mail*, January 27, 1989: A16.

37 Marty York, "Infuriated Lee Breaks Serenity of Jay Land," *Globe and Mail*, February 11, 11989: A15.

38 Larry Millson, "Cerutti, Lee Avoid Arbitration, Sign One-Year Deals," *Globe and Mail*, February 12, 1990: C3.

39 Millson, "Lee Simply Wants Fair Play and Pay."

40 *1994 Texas Rangers Media Guide*, 70.

41 "Lee Wants to Fly Blue Jay Coop Now," *Edmonton* (Alberta, Canada) *Journal*, June 11, 1989: F1.

42 Marty York, "Friends Lee, Liriano Need to be Separated," *Globe and Mail*, January 5, 1990: 13.

43 Millson, "Cerutti, Lee Avoid Arbitration, Sign One-Year Deals."

44 Marty York, "Lee's Unhappiness Makes Him Sure Trade Bait," *Globe and Mail*, April 12, 1990: A17.

45 Tom McAllister, "Chance to Play Short Accepted Eager-Lee," *Ottawa* (Ontario, Canada) *Citizen*, March 9, 1991: E5.

46 Marty York, "Batting Woes in Recent Months Cutting into Lee's Sleep," *Globe and Mail*, September 26, 1990: C14.

47 Marty York, "Now That Bell is Gone, Lee Does all the Talking," *Globe and Mail*, December 29, 1990: A14.

48 York, "Now That Bell is Gone, Lee Does all the Talking."

49 Marty York, "Fearful Lee Claims 'The People in Toronto Just Want to Hurt Me,'" *Globe and Mail*, March 20, 1991: C10.

50 Allan Ryan, "Now Batting for Jays No. 4, Manuel Lee," *Toronto Star*, March 10, 1991: G4.

51 Neil A. Campbell, "Manuel Lee Has Developed into an Effective Shortstop," *Globe and Mail*, May 11, 1991: E14.

52 Dave Perkins, "Lee's Walking Tall at Short," *Toronto Star*, June 1, 1992: B2.

53 *1994 Texas Rangers Media Guide*: 72.

54 Larry Millson, "Sheepish Lee Admits He's in a Fight," *Globe and Mail*, March 2, 1992: C6.

55 As defined by Baseball-Reference, Defensive Efficiency estimates the percentage of balls put into play against a team that are converted into outs.

56 "Sheepish Lee Admits He's in a Fight."

57 Allan Ryan, "Lee Saunters into Camp Figuring He's Still No. 1," *Toronto Star*, March 1, 1992: G1.

58 Dave Perkins, "Lee's Spring Moxie Outshines Dull Zosky in Shortstop Battle," *Toronto Star*, March 18, 1992: F1.

59 "Lee Shows Some Class."

60 *1994 Texas Rangers Media Guide*, 72.

61 Neil MacCarl, "Fly on the Wall," *The Sporting News*, September 21, 1992: 31.

62 Rosie DiManno, "Now It's Jays Over A's," *Toronto Star*, October 11, 1992: A1.

63 Neil A. Campbell, "Time Running Out for 'Day to Day' Lee with Knee Still Sore," *Globe and Mail*, September 24, 1992: E7.

64 DiManno, "Now It's Jays Over A's."

65 Bob Elliott, "Unlike His Predecessors, Manager John Farrell Has Fallout to Put Up with When He Sends in a Pinch Hitter," *Edmonton Sun,* May 13, 2012: S22.

66 The contract included a $600,000 signing bonus and salaries of $1.6 million (for 1993) and $1 million (1994), plus a $200,000 buyout if an option year for $1.9 million was not exercised.

67 "Manny Lee Flees to Texas to Join Teammate Henke," *Vancouver* (British Columbia) *Sun*, December 21, 1992: D4.

68 "Team-by-Team Notebook," *Orlando Sentinel*, March 14, 1993: D10.

69 *1994 Texas Rangers Media Guide*, 72.

70 "Clemente Family's Wishes Are Obeyed," *Salt Lake* (Utah) *Tribune*, March 24, 1993: D3.

71 T.R. Sullivan, "A Glut at Shortstop," *The Sporting News*, August 2, 1993: 32.

72 T.R. Sullivan, "Kennedy, Lee Clear the Air," *The Sporting News*, August 23, 1993: 31.

73 T.R. Sullivan, "Lee Might Return," *The Sporting News*, September 20, 1993: 30.

74 Berry Tramel, "Ryan, Brett Give Stadium Sendoff," *Oklahoman* (Oklahoma City), October 4, 1993, https://www.oklahoman.com/article/2443941/ryan-brett-give-stadium-sendoff (last accessed December 31, 2021).

75 T.R. Sullivan, "Short Depth," *The Sporting News*, April 11, 1994: 25.

76 "Notable," *Baltimore Sun*, June 25, 1994: 6C.

77 "Reds Grab Brantley; Henke Bought Out," *Edmonton Journal*, October 28, 1994: F5.

78 Rick Hummel, "Lee Says He Is Ready to Play, but Not Second," *St. Louis Post-Dispatch*, April 19, 1995: 6D.

79 Kevin Horrigan, "Lately in St. Louis: Thar's a Whiner," *St. Louis Post-Dispatch*, June 24, 2001: B3.

80 "La PN Someterá Hoy a la Justicia a Manny Lee," *Diario Libre* (Dominican Republic), August 17, 2004, https://www.diariolibre.com/deportes/la-pn-someter-hoy-a-la-justicia-a-manny-lee-CDDL46260 (last accessed January 4, 2022).

81 "Nesting," *Toronto Star*, August 7, 2009: S5.

82 Manuel A. Vega, "Alcaldía de SPM Inaugura Mural de "Las Glorias del Béisbol Petromacorisano," *El Caribe* (Dominican Republic), October 16, 2021, https://www.elcaribe.com.do/destacado/alcaldia-de-spm-inaugura-mural-de-las-glorias-del-beis-bol-petromacorisano/ (last accessed February 26, 2022).

AL LEITER

By Thomas J. Brown Jr.

Al Leiter spent 18 years in the majors and enjoyed pitching success in both leagues. During his career, he managed to earn two World Series rings and play on three different teams in the fall classic. Although Leiter never became one of the star pitchers of his day, he made important contributions to his teams' success throughout his career. Leiter is also an excellent example of how a player can make significant contributions to the game both on and off the field. Leiter's charity works as well as his second career as a television commentator have earned him many awards well beyond his playing days.

Leiter's breakout year came in 1993 when the Blue Jays won their second World Series title.

Alois Terry Leiter was born on October 23, 1965 in Toms River, New Jersey. Leiter's parents were Alexander and Marie Leiter. His father was a merchant seaman who met Leiter's mother in Liverpool, England during his travels. Both of his parents lost their own mothers at an early age. This deeply affected Leiter's father who in many ways never got over this loss. As a result, Leiter and his father were never close. His parents divorced when Leiter was 14; his later comment about it was, "Frankly, it was a relief." Leiter never made up with his father and in many ways came to regret it; he found out after his father passed away that he had been coming to see him play without telling him.[1] Leiter grew up in a large family. Besides his parents, he had five brothers and two sisters. Every brother played baseball at some point although only two of them, Kurt and Mark, had any success at the game. Kurt pitched for a few years in the Orioles organization. Mark, like Leiter, became a Yankees prospect when he was in high school. Mark eventually spent 11 years in the major leagues pitching for the Yankees, Tigers, Giants, Expos, Phillies, Angels, and Mariners.

Leiter grew up in Bayville, New Jersey and attended Central Regional High School. He drew the attention of major league scouts during his high school career. He became a baseball All-American in his senior year. His most significant high school pitching triumph also came that year. He threw two consecutive no-hitters and followed that up by striking out 32 batters while pitching 13 innings on April 19, 1984. The latter was a game that he did not win.[2] This accomplishment earned him recognition in a *Sports Illustrated* "Faces in the Crowd" segment.[3]

After graduating high school, the left-handed Leiter was drafted by the Yankees on June 23, 1984. He went in the second round as the 50th overall pick in the regular draft. Yankee scout Joe DiCarlo who had watched him play during his high school years, signed him.[4] "I want to be another Tom Seaver," Leiter said. "I really think I'm going to do it, too."[5]

Upon signing with the Yankees, Leiter was sent to the Oneonta Yankees of the New York-Penn League.

During the half-season that he spent in Oneonta, Leiter compiled a 3-2 record with a 3.63 ERA. It was at this time that former Yankees' great Ron Guidry taught Leiter how to throw the cutter that he used for rest of his career.[6] In 1985, he split time between the Oneonta team and the Fort Lauderdale Yankees. Leiter struggled when he was moved up to the Fort Lauderdale team. His ERA rose to 6.48 and he finished that season with a 1-6 record during his time in Florida. This inauspicious start earned him another stint with the Fort Lauderdale team in 1986. Leiter improved to 4-8 in his second season there and lowered his ERA to 4.05. He also struck out 101 batters in the 117 innings that he pitched.

Leiter's improved 1986 performance earned him a promotion to the AA Albany/Colonie Yankees in 1987. He pitched well during the first half of the season as he continued to lower his ERA to 3.35. The Yankees promoted him to AAA Columbus for the second part of that season. After his arrival in Columbus, Leiter struggled and saw his ERA rise as he faced better hitters at this more competitive level. But clearly the Yankees saw some promise in the young player; they brought him up to the majors in September of that year. Leiter made his major-league debut as the starting pitcher for the Yankees on September 15, 1987, earning the win in a Yankees 4–3 victory over the Milwaukee Brewers at Yankee Stadium. During this brief September stretch with the Yankees, Leiter pitched in four games and earned a 2-2 record.

When the 1988 season began, Leiter returned to the Columbus Clippers. But his stay there was short-lived. He only pitched in four games for the Clippers before being called up to the majors for the rest of the season.

Leiter was, however, soon bitten by the injury bug. He was struck by a line drive off the bat of the A's Carney Lansford on the first pitch of a May game and left the game with a severely bruised left forearm.[7] Then he developed soreness in his left elbow, a blister on the middle finger of his left hand and eventually a strain below his left shoulder blade that kept him from pitching after September 16.[8] For the 1988 season, Leiter started only 14 games and ended up with a 4-4 record.

The 1989 season was no more productive for Leiter. He continued to struggle with several different injuries that kept him from playing. In April, Leiter threw 163 pitches over the course of nine innings as Yankees manager Dallas Green decided to "stretch out" Leiter that night. In the third and fourth innings, Leiter struggled, walking five hitters and allowing four Twins runs. By the end of the fourth inning, he had thrown over 90 pitches.[9] Today, Leiter would likely have been pulled, but Green kept Leiter in the game. He ended up striking out 10 batters and walking nine before being removed in the top of the ninth inning.[10]

Leiter's struggles eventually led the Yankees to give up on him and on April 30, 1989, they traded him to the Toronto Blue Jays for Jesse Barfield. Leiter expressed disappointment with the trade saying, "There's nothing that I would rather do than pull on pinstripes (tonight)." But he went on to say "I hope to go out and win 20 games and have a great career and it will be just another instance of where the Yankees gave up on a young guy."[11]

Leiter had arthroscopic surgery in September of that year to try to help him overcome his arm troubles.[12] He pitched in fewer than 20 innings with the Blue Jays from 1989–1992. Besides the arthroscopic surgery, he also suffered with a pinched nerve in his elbow, tendinitis, and eventually had a second arthroscopic surgery on his left shoulder. His statistics were not spectacular, notably his 5.17 ERA and 10 strikeouts in 15 2/3 innings pitched during those years. He also suffered blisters on his pitching hand but overcame them with a special liniment that he continued to use for the remainder of his career.

Even with all of these problems, Leiter was still considered a promising prospect and 1993 became the breakout year in Leiter's career. He pitched the entire season without any injuries. He appeared in 34 games and made 12 starts for the Blue Jays that season. He had a 4.11 ERA for the year with a 9-6 record. Leiter earned a lot of attention during the playoffs and World Series that year. He appeared in five postseason games and earned a win while pitching 2 2/3 innings in relief in Game One of the World Series. He also swatted a double in the 15-14 slugfest that was the fourth game. Toronto eventually won that game to claim their second straight world championship.

Leiter continued to pitch effectively for the next two seasons. He became one of the Blue Jays' regular starting pitchers during these years. His statistics improved each year. In 1995, he had the eighth-best ERA in the American League to go with 153 strikeouts. Leiter used these improvements as a selling point when he applied for free agency at the end of the 1995 season.

The Florida Marlins signed Leiter as a free agent during the offseason. The Marlins had joined the National League in 1993 as an expansion team and were trying to become competitive under the leadership of manager Rene Lachemann. Leiter joined a pitching staff that included Kevin Brown and John Burkett. At his signing, Leiter said, "I feel real good about what I've been doing the last three or four years. I feel like I'm right on the verge."[13]

In his first Marlin season, Leiter put up some of the best numbers of his career. He had a 16-12 won-loss record and his ERA of 2.93 was the lowest of his career to that point. While his 119 walks led the National League, he was also seventh in strikeouts with 200. The 1996 season included several "firsts" for Leiter's career.

Leiter threw his only no-hitter for the Marlins against the Colorado Rockies on May 11, 1996. The 11-0 lopsided victory was also the first-ever no-hitter by a Marlins pitcher. "It was a feeling of jubilation," he said after the game. "Jubilation and relief and exhaustion. The whole thing is incredible."[14]

Leiter was chosen to participate in the 1996 All-Star Game in Philadelphia, his first All-Star appearance.. He recorded the last out in the National League's 6-0 victory when he got Dan Wilson to fly out to center field.

Leiter continued his pitching success in 1997. He started 27 games and ended the season with an 11-9 record for the 92-70 Marlins. They made the playoffs for the first time in their existence and eventually reached the World Series. They won the championship in seven games against the Cleveland Indians. In the series, Leiter started Games Three and Seven. He did not earn a win in either game. He lasted 4 2/3 innings in Game Three, which the Marlins won 14-11. He did better in Game Seven when he pitched six innings and gave up the Indians only runs in the 3-2 Marlins victory. In a span of four years, Leiter had pitched for two World Series winners.

In the following offseason, the Marlins cleaned house and traded away all of the team's stars. Owner Wayne Huizenga dumped every one of his high-priced stars: Bobby Bonilla, Moises Alou, Gary Sheffield, Brown, and Leiter. Leiter was traded along with Ralph Milliard to the New York Mets for Rob Stratton, A.J. Burnett, and Jesus Sanchez on February 6, 1998. After getting rid of all of their star players, the Marlins lost 108 games in 1998.[15]

Leiter wanted to stay in Florida since his wife, Lori, was from there but the Marlins had other plans. At the time of his trade, he said "Initially the whole shock of what was going on was bad. We were all upset. But it's part of the game. The uncertainty of not knowing where I was going was the agonizing part of it. But I realized that no matter what uniform I'm in, I've got to be ready."[16]

His arrival in New York was a bit of a homecoming for him since he had grown up across the river in New Jersey. He made an immediate impact with the Mets who were becoming competitive once again under manager Bobby Valentine. In 1998, Leiter had a 17-6 record to go with a career-best ERA of 2.47.

Leiter's charity work also began to get noticed soon after his trade to the Mets. When Leiter signed a four-year, $32 million contract with the Mets after the 1998 season, he said that he would contribute $1 million over the life of the contract to Leiter's Landing, a charity formed by Leiter and his wife Lori.[17]

Leiter anchored a Mets pitching staff in 1999 that included Orel Hershiser, Kenny Rogers, and Rick Reed. He finished the season with a 13-12 record while accumulating 162 strikeouts. Leiter's importance to the team really became evident in the one-game playoff at Cinergy Field in Cincinnati. Leiter pitched a two-hit complete game shutout to earn the win in the Mets' 5–0 victory, which put the Mets in the playoffs for the first time in 11 seasons.

"I just forget about everything. I forget about all the things that are negative and I try to concern myself with a positive mindset. I think about who I'm facing and I prepare myself for that, mentally and physically. I think about making a pitch. If you do that aggressively, one pitch after another, chances are you are going to pitch a very good ballgame," Leiter said when asked about the win.[18]

Leiter was recognized for his work outside of baseball in the fall of 1999 when he was given the Branch Rickey Award. This award is presented annually to a major-league player for his local community service. Leiter earned the award for his work with Leiter's Landing Foundation. He and Lori used the foundation to raise funds for and awareness of children's education, health, social, and community service issues, especially in the New York City area.[19]

The Mets and Leiter continued to improve in 2000. Leiter posted more respectable statistics, finishing 16–8 with a 3.20 ERA while fanning 200 batters. He made the All-Star team again. He became the losing pitcher in that game after giving up a single to Derek Jeter in the fourth inning. Jeter's hit scored two runs to give the American League a lead that they did not relinquish. But this disappointment was a minor blip on a successful season for Leiter.

The Mets made the playoffs again in 2000. Leiter pitched two solid games during the playoffs. He pitched eight innings but without a decision against the Giants in the NL Divisional Series and then he pitched another seven innings, again without a decision, against the St. Louis Cardinals in the NL Championship Series. The Mets reached the World Series for the first time since 1986. Leiter was on his third different World Series team. This was the 2000 "Subway Series" against the Yankees and Leiter started the first and fifth games.

Leiter finished with a 2.87 ERA and had 16 strikeouts in 15 2/3 innings but the Mets lost both games that he started. They eventually lost the World Series to the Yankees in five games. His best performance in the series was Game Five when he pitched eight solid innings despite losing the game when he struggled in the ninth. "Al Leiter got into some kind of a zone and he was blowing people away. It was a great effort," said Yankees outfielder Bernie Williams who managed to get a home run off him in the game.[20]

At the end of the 2000 season, Leiter was honored again for his community work, this time receiving the Roberto Clemente Award. This award is arguably baseball's most important non-playing award. It goes to a player who combines good play on the field with strong work in his community. Although Leiter was primarily honored for his continuing work with Leiter's Landing, he also took other philanthropic actions that received notice. He gave his royalty from Microsoft's placement of his image on the cover of its computer baseball game to his charity. Leiter arranged for Microsoft to donate 25 computers to needy New York City schools. Additionally, Leiter gave the stipend that he received for his work with fashion design house Hugo Boss to a group that was feeding the elderly in Queens during the holidays. He also established a scholarship fund for the high school students who volunteered in that program.[21]

Leiter pitched in three World Series for three teams - Toronto, Florida, and the New York Mets.

Over the next three seasons, Leiter continued to be a vital part of the Mets pitching staff. In 2002, he became the first pitcher in history to notch a win against all 30 major-league teams. He did it by pitching seven solid innings against the Arizona Diamondbacks and earning the win in a 10-1 Mets victory. Astonishingly, Leiter had won at least one game against 29 of the 30 major-league teams in the process of earning his first 69 victories. It took him another four years and 51 wins to finally beat the 30th and final team.[22] During these three seasons, 2001-2003, Leiter averaged 30 starts and pitched well, maintaining a 3.50 ERA. But he didn't have the same success that he had during the Mets playoff runs. By the end of the 2004 season, he ranked high on several Mets all-time lists; he was sixth in wins with 95 and seventh in strikeouts with 1106 at the end of the 2004 season.

Unfortunately, the Mets chose not to reward his efforts. In the offseason, the team declined Leiter's $10 million option for 2005. This made him a free agent. Nevertheless, hoping to pitch one more year and finish his career in New York, Leiter tried to negotiate a new deal with Omar Minaya, the Mets general manager.[23] But he was rebuffed and, disappointed with the Mets management, left New York.

Leiter decided to return to Florida where he had his original success as a pitcher. His former team, the Marlins, signed him to a one-year, $8 million contract on December 8, 2004. Marlins general manager Larry Beinfest said that the team was excited to have Leiter return. "This thing has a good feel to it, right from the start. We really wanted Al."[24]

Leiter did not pitch well after returning to the Marlins. He walked more batters and gave up more hits than he had in the past. By midseason, he had made 16 starts and finished with a 3–7 record. He took much of the criticism for the Marlins' first-half struggles that year. At one point in late June he was even demoted to the bullpen but later returned to the rotation after an injury to Josh Beckett.

Due to his lackluster performance in the first half of the 2005 season, the Marlins designated Leiter for assignment.[25] The next day, he was acquired by the Yankees for a player to be named later. "When you think this is where I started in '87, and then 21 years ago when I was drafted by the Yankees, to come full circle like this, it's very exciting," he said at his signing.[26]

His first start as a Yankee since 1989 came on July 17, 2005. Leiter pitched against the division-leading Boston Red Sox and won the game. He pitched 6 1/3

innings, allowing one run and three hits while striking out eight. But after this initial strong performance, he had mixed success on the mound and eventually he was assigned to the Yankees bullpen. Leiter's last major-league appearance came on October 2, 2005. He pitched the final two-thirds of the ninth inning in a 10-1 Red Sox win on the final day of the season.

The Yankees granted Leiter his free agent status on November 4, 2005. On January 6, 2006, Leiter signed as a free agent with the Yankees but indicated his desire to retire after the World Baseball Classic in March.[27] Leiter never pitched in a game for the U.S. team and officially retired from baseball on March 19, 2006.

When he announced his retirement, Leiter said that he didn't want to be a hanger-on. "I love the game but when you've been a front-end starter that's the way you think of yourself. I think I can still get people out but my body tells me differently.[28]

While Leiter did not garner any major pitching awards during his 19-year career, he was a member of two World Series championship teams, the 1993 Blue Jays and 1997 Marlins. He also played in the World Series for the 2000 Mets.

Long before Leiter left baseball, he had started his second career as a commentator when he worked with ESPN as a studio analyst during their post season broadcasts in 1998 and 1999. He moved out of the studio and began to work in the television broadcast booth for the Fox MLB broadcasts during the 2003 NLCS and 2004 ALCS series. He provided in-depth analysis of the various pitchers. Since 2006, Leiter has worked as a color commentator and a studio analyst for the YES Network that covers the Yankees.[29]

Leiter won a New York Emmy in 2007 for his work on the "Manny game" in Boston. The game, which took place on May 24, 2006, culminated in a Yankees victory when they overcame two home runs by Manny Ramirez to win 8-6. The Yankees were first down 2-0 and then 5-4 but ended up scoring four runs in the fifth inning to take the lead for good.[30]

In 2009, Leiter was hired by MLB Network and appeared on the very first show they produced on January 1, 2009. He became a studio analyst for the MLB Network while continuing to work for the YES Network. In 2009, 2011, 2013, and 2015, Leiter was nominated for a National Sports Emmy Award for Best Studio Analyst. In 2012, 2014, and 2016, he won Sports Emmy awards for Outstanding Studio Show-Daily as an MLB Tonight Segment Producer. Leiter also started working as a color commentator for the Miami Marlins on Fox Sports Florida in 2016.[31]

As of 2021, Leiter continues to work for MLB network as a studio analyst. In September 2021, MLB Network announced that Leiter and John Smoltz would only work remotely for the network due to their refusal to get the coronavirus vaccine.[32]

Leiter's post-baseball career keeps him extremely busy. He has appeared on a variety of shows and he regularly appears on *Hot Stove*, *Diamond Demo*, and *Path to the Pennant* along with other special events coverage. He also continues to work in his community in a variety of ways. Over the years, Leiter's work has earned him numerous accolades such as the Good Guy Award from the New York Press Photographers Association in 2000. He was appointed to the board of directors of the Twin Towers Fund by Mayor Rudy Giuliani after 9/11 and played an important role in helping to allocate more than $280 million in donations.[33] Bud Selig picked him to serve on the Commissioner's Initiative to evaluate baseball heading into the twenty-first century. Mayor Michael Bloomberg put him on the board of NYC & Company, the city's tourism agency.[34]

Leiter was mentioned as a possibility to succeed Senator Frank Lautenberg (D-NJ) after the senator's death in 2013. Although he had never served in public office, he had worked for New Jersey Governor Chris Christie's transition team after Christie's election and served on the New Jersey Sports, Gaming and Entertainment Committee. "Who wouldn't be interested if the governor of your state for whatever reason of their due process thought [you were] worthy, in their opinion?," he said at the time. "So, yeah, I would be interested."[35]

Leiter returned to baseball in 2019 in a front office role. He became baseball operations advisor and will focus on scouting and player development at every level of the Mets organization. His work with players will emphasize mental preparation for pitchers. "I am thrilled to be reunited with the Mets organization, which I hold so near and dear to my heart," he said. "I grew up a fan of the team and then was fortunate enough to realize my childhood dream of pitching for the Mets. Now, thanks to the Wilpon family and to Brodie, I couldn't be more appreciative or more excited."[36]

Leiter and his wife, Lori, who is an attorney, continue to manage the Leiter's Landing foundation as well as raise their three children in Summit, New Jersey. The children are Lindsay Brooke, Carly Jayne, and Jack Thomas. As of 2021, it appears that Jack is planning to follow in his father's footsteps. With an 85-mph fastball, he has showed lots of promise as a member of his Delbarton High School team.[37] After graduating high school, he pitched on the Vanderbilt University team. As a sophomore, Jack went 11-4 with a 2.13 ERA and 179 strikeouts in 110 innings. The Texas Rangers chose him second in the 2021 amateur draft and he signed a contract with the team shortly after the draft.

Although his playing days are over, Leiter continues to make contributions to baseball and his community in his own personal way. He may offer advice to young pitchers like the Marlins Adam Conley who said after meeting Leiter, "I was totally caught off guard. He just came right up and said, 'Hey, I'm Al Leiter.' I wasn't expecting that at all. Didn't even know that was him. He introduced himself and had a lot of good things to say about what he thought of my abilities and my stuff."[38] Or he might spend time with military children such as when he went to McGuire Air Force Base and spoke to about 300 children of servicemen and women at a school just off the base. "I told the kids that because of my profession; sometimes people regard us as heroes. I just told them that in my mind, their mothers and fathers were the real heroes. We just play a simple game of baseball."[39]

Leiter's exemplary career, both on and off the field, shows how baseball can be a springboard for even more important work when the player's playing days come to a close.

SOURCES

In addition to the sources cited in the Notes, the author also utilized the Baseball-Reference.com and Retrosheet.org websites for box scores, player, team, and season pages, pitching and batting game logs, and other material pertinent to this biography.

NOTES

1   Jill Leiber, "Mets' Leiter delivers hope for others," *USA Today*, August 28, 2002.

2   Randy Miller, "Reliving Al Leiter setting N.J. prep record with 32 Ks in 13 innings," *NJ.com*, April 14, 2016.

3   "YES Announcers - Al Leiter, New York Yankees analyst," *YES Network.com*, accessed September 20, 2016.

4   Mark Feinsand, "Baseball loses an unsung hero," comment on Blogging the Bombers, *New York Daily News.com*, December 18, 2010.

5   "Central's Leiter Will Sign," *Daily Register* (Red Bank, New Jersey), June 22, 1984: 19.

6   http://mms.businesswire.com/bwapps/mediaserver/ViewMedia?mgid=80672&vid=1&download=1, accessed September 21, 2016.

WE ARE, WE CAN, WE WILL

7 Michael Martinez, "What a Relief, Allen Goes 9," *New York Times*, June 1, 1988.

8 http://mms.businesswire.com/bwapps/mediaserver/ViewMedia?mgid=80672&vid=1&download=1, accessed September 21, 2016.

9 Mark Ferenchick, "Recounting the time Al Leiter threw 163 pitches in one game," *SB Nation.com*, November 28, 2015

10 David Schoenfield, "The Pitchers Who Changed Baseball," comment on Sweet Spot blog, *ESPN.com*, July 28, 2009.

11 Michael Kay, "Yanks Trade for Now," *New York Daily News*, May 1, 1989: 42.

12 http://mms.businesswire.com/bwapps/mediaserver/ViewMedia?mgid=80672&vid=1&download=1, accessed September 21, 2016.

13 Ed Price and Scott Tolley, "Leiter and Marlins A Nice Fit," *Palm Beach Post*, December 15, 1995: 4D.

14 Greg Doyel, "No Runs, No Hits, One Hero," *Miami Herald*, May 12, 1996: D1.

15 Rob Neyer, "A brief and unhappy history of fire sales," *SB Nation.com*, accessed October 25, 2016.

16 Mike Phillips, "Marlins Trade Leiter to Mets," *Miami Herald*, February 7, 1998: 2D.

17 Jill Leiber, "Mets' Leiter delivers hope for others," *USA Today*, August 28, 2002.

18 Mark Hermann, "Leiter Lights Way," *Newsday* (New York), October 5, 1999: A72.

19 "Mets pitcher Al Leiter to dedicate Leiter's Landing Playroom," comment on *Science Blog.com*, February 2002.

20 Thomas Hill, "Yankees Reign," *New York Daily News*, October 27, 2000: 2.

21 Rafael Hermoso, "Leiter's Pitching Is Only Part of the Story," *New York Times*, April 1, 2002.

22 Chris Jaffe, "10th anniversary: first man to beat 30 franchises," *The Hardball Times*, accessed October 20, 2016.

23 Lee Jenkins, "Leiter Looks Back at the Mets and Feels a Sense of Betrayal," *New York Times*, December 9, 2004.

24 Ronald Blum, "Marlins Sign Leiter," *Star Gazette* (Elmira, New York), December 9, 2004: 5B.

25 Murray Chass, "Leiter Gets Save From Mets, and Another From the Yanks," *New York Times*, July 19, 2005

26 Ken Davidoff, "Leiter Adds to Patchwork Staff," *Newsday (New York)*, July 17, 2005: 74.

27 Barry Bloom, "Leiter likely to retire after Classic," *MLB.com*, accessed October 2, 2016.

28 Bill Maddon, "With One Last Out, That's It for Al," *New York Daily News*, March 20, 2006: 54.

29 "YES Announcers - Al Leiter, New York Yankees analyst," *YES Network.com*, accessed September 20, 2016.

30 Ben Masur, "Al Leiter: In The Booth, Politics, Charity & 3P Sports," *Diamond Nation magazine*, Summer 2010.

31 Barry Jackson, "Miami Marlins hire Al Leiter, Eduardo Perez, Preston Wilson to share TV analyst duties," *Miami Herald*, February 12, 2016.

32 Michael Shapiro, "John Smoltz, Al Leiter to Leave MLB Network Studios After COVID-19 Vaccine Refusal," Sports Illustrated.com, September 1, 2021. https://www.si.com/mlb/2021/09/01/john-smoltz-al-leiter-refuse-covid-19-vaccine-mlb-network

33 Ben Masur, "Al Leiter: In The Booth, Politics, Charity & 3P Sports," *Diamond Nation magazine*, Summer 2010.

34 Lee Jenkins, "Leiter Lives a Life of Many Interests Outside Baseball," *New York Times*, March 14, 2004.

35 Andrew Marchand, "Senator Leiter? Al Would Be Interested," ESPN.com, June 4, 2013. https://www.espn.com/blog/new-york/yankees/post/_/id/56552/senator-leiter-al-would-be-interested

36 "Al Leiter Joins Mets as Baseball Operations Advisor," MLB.com, March 4, 2019. https://www.mlb.com/press-release/al-leiter-joins-mets-as-advisor

37 Jeff Dahn, "Leiters light up Jr. National," *Perfect Game.org*, accessed November 22, 2016.

38 Craig Davis, "Marlins' Conley takes lesson from Leiter on pitching, talking good game," *South Florida Sun-Sentinel*, April 14, 2016.

39 http://mms.businesswire.com/bwapps/mediaserver/ViewMedia?mgid=80672&vid=1&download=1, accessed September 21, 2016.

DOUG LINTON

By Joel Rippel

Doug Linton's career as a professional baseball player spanned 18 seasons. He spent time with nine organizations and played for 12 minor-league teams and five major-league teams. He also spent one season in Taiwan and one in Korea.

But the major-league portion of the right-handed pitcher's nomadic career – which included parts of seven seasons – began and ended in the same place – Boston's Fenway Park.

Douglas Warren Linton was born in Santa Ana, California, on February 9, 1965. Linton, his older brother, Robert, were raised by their single mother, Carol, in Orange, California, before moving to nearby Anaheim Hills when Doug was 8 or 9 years old. Carol worked as a receptionist at U.C. Irvine Medical Center.

Linton attended Canyon High School, where he participated in baseball, football, track, and basketball – with his 6-foot-6 brother as a teammate – as a sophomore.

As a junior and senior, Doug concentrated on pitching.

As a senior, Linton was 9-3 and was named to the All-Century League team. After the season, he was selected to play in the annual Orange County North/South baseball game.

After high school, Linton enrolled at U.C. Irvine, where he lettered for three seasons for the Anteaters. After going 5-5 as a freshman in 1984 and 5-7 as a sophomore in 1985, Linton was used mostly out of the bullpen in 1986. He was 4-7 with three saves in 22 appearances (which included five starts).

After his junior season, Linton was selected by the Blue Jays in the 43rd round of the June 1986 amateur draft.

Linton spent the summer of 1986 pitching for the Alaska Goldpanners, based in Fairbanks, in the Alaska Baseball league. He had a successful summer, helping the Goldpanners to a first-place finish in the league's Pacific Division with a 26-16 record. After the season concluded on August 5, the Goldpanners and the Anchorage Pilots, who finished first in the Continental Division, competed in the National Baseball Congress Tournament in Wichita, Kansas.

The Goldpanners, who had an 11-game winning streak going into the tournament, won their first five games – Linton was the winning pitcher in two of the games – in the 34-team tournament. The Goldpanners ended up in fourth place in the tournament.

"I went up to Alaska expecting to return to UCI for my fourth year," said Linton. "At the beginning, Toronto wasn't going to offer (me) anything. I was very successful in Alaska. I was co-MVP of the team (the Goldpanners) that had (future first-round draft pick and major-leaguer) Mike Harkey. Once Toronto saw how I was doing up there, they boosted the money after I got back home. They offered more money than a 43rd-round pick normally would get. It was enough to make me sign."[1]

WE ARE, WE CAN, WE WILL

Linton credited his experience in Alaska with helping him refine his approach heading into his first season of professional baseball.

"Alaska turned me around as a pitcher," said Linton. "[Cal State Fullerton assistant coach] Larry Corrigan gave me some ideas that helped me realize what I need to do to be successful. The ideas helped me win and I carried it over into pro ball in 1987."[2]

Linton's rookie season in professional baseball was a revelation. He went 14-2 with a 1.55 ERA for the Blue Jays' Myrtle Beach (South Carolina) farm team in the Class-A South Atlantic League. He struck out 155 in 122 innings.

On July 24 he was promoted to Knoxville of the Double-A Southern League. In his debut, on July 28, he allowed three runs and five hits in three innings against Chattanooga. Knoxville rallied for a 9-4 victory.

"Doug Linton might be the South Atlantic League's best pitcher, but due partly to a tender arm, the young right-hander fell short of expectations in his Class AA debut," a Knoxville sportswriter commented.[3]

The initial plan to deal with Linton's sore arm was rest. "He won't throw for five days and then begin rehabilitation," Knoxville manager Glenn Ezell said.[4]

When Linton's soreness persisted, an examination revealed a torn rotator cuff. He had surgery on August 29; Linton was sidelined until late in the 1988 season.

"At times, I was just learning to throw again, and it was depressing," Linton said. "I was thinking maybe I should go back and get that college education. But then things slowly started to come back."[5]

Late in 1988, the 6-foot-1, 190-pounder made 12 relief appearances for Dunedin of the Class-A Florida State League, going 2-1 with two saves and a 1.63 ERA. He struck out 28 in 27⅔ innings.

He returned to Dunedin to start the 1989 season, going 1-2 with two saves and a 2.96 ERA before being promoted to Knoxville. With Knoxville, he was 5-4 with a 2.60 ERA. In 13 starts and 90 innings with Knoxville, he threw two shutouts and struck out 93.

"It was just nice to be back throwing," said Linton.[6]

After the 1989 season, Linton pitched for the Venezuelan team Leones del Caracas, which advanced to the Caribbean World Series. Linton threw a shutout in the World Series.

Linton was promoted to Triple-A Syracuse for the 1990 season. He went 10-10 with a 3.40 ERA in 26 starts. Among his eight complete games were three shutouts. He returned to Syracuse in 1991, going 10-12 with a 5.01 ERA.

Linton opened the 1992 season in Syracuse. Early in the season, he was a bright spot for the Chiefs. They won just three of their first 14 games, but Linton was the winning pitcher in two of them. In early May, Linton was 3-2 with a 3.77 ERA and 28 strikeouts in 31 innings.

In early August, Linton was recalled by the Blue Jays and he made his major-league debut on August 3, 1992. He allowed one earned run in 3⅔ innings of relief in the Blue Jays' 7-1 loss to the Red Sox at Fenway Park.

Two days later, he pitched 3⅓ innings of hitless relief as the Blue Jays rallied for a 5-4 victory over the host Red Sox.

On August 8 in Detroit, Linton relieved Dave Stieb in the fourth inning with the Tigers leading 5-2. After the Blue Jays scored three runs in the top of the sixth inning to tie the score, Tigers catcher Mickey Tettleton hit a solo home run in the bottom of the sixth to break the tie. It was the only run Linton allowed in three innings. The Tigers went on to defeat the Blue Jays 8-6, giving Linton his first major-league loss.

Five days later in Toronto, he made his first career start, in the finale of a four-game series with the second-place Baltimore Orioles. It was a crucial game for the Blue Jays.

Since being a half-game behind in the AL East standings on May 24, the Blue Jays had spent 80 consecutive days either tied for first or in sole possession of first place in the AL East. But the Blue Jays, who had a 4½-game lead on August 2, had lost five of six games going into Linton's start. After the Blue Jays won the series opener from the Orioles, Baltimore had won the next two games to pull within one game of the Blue Jays in the standings.

The Orioles scored a run in the second inning when Glenn Davis led off with a solo home run. Linton walked the next hitter, Randy Milligan, and retired 15 consecutive hitters before Cal Ripken Jr. led off the seventh with a double. After Davis grounded out to first with Ripken advancing to third, Milligan hit a sacrifice fly to center to score Ripken and tie the game, 2-2.

After the Blue Jays took the lead in the eighth inning, Tom Henke retired the Orioles in order in the ninth to save Linton's first major-league victory.

Linton said his teammates deserved the credit: "It's a great feeling. But if we don't score two runs in the eighth, I wouldn't be talking about my first win."[7]

Blue Jays manager Cito Gaston emphasized the importance of Linton's outing and the Blue Jays' victory.

"We were just hoping he'd get us through the fifth or sixth and get by," said Gaston. "He did a lot more than we expected. And he did it at the right time. The difference is that instead of being tied (for the AL East lead), we're two games up. That tells it all. That's the best start we've had in a long, long time."[8]

Gaston added, "Earlier in the year, [Syracuse pitching coach] John Poloni told me Linton would be starting for us soon, but with all the stars we had, I never thought much about it. It turns out he was right."[9]

Linton lost his next starts – in Milwaukee on August 19 and to the White Sox in Chicago on August 24. On August 28, he allowed six runs in a third of an inning in the Blue Jays' 22-2 loss to Milwaukee. The next night Linton pitched a scoreless inning in their 7-2 loss to the Brewers.

After that game, Linton was sent back to Syracuse for the final week of the International League season. On September 1 he allowed three earned runs in Syracuse's 4-0 loss at Rochester. On September 7, he allowed seven earned runs in five innings in Syracuse's 8-7 season-ending victory over Rochester. He was recalled by the Blue Jays the next day after Syracuse's season ended, but he did not appear in any games for the final three weeks of the regular season.

For the season, Linton was 1-3 with an 8.63 ERA in eight appearances for the Blue Jays. He was 12-10 with a 3.74 ERA in 25 starts for Syracuse, which was 60-83. Only two pitchers in the International League had more victories – Richmond's David Nied (14) and Pawtucket's Larry Shikles (13). Linton was fifth in the league in strikeouts (126). Nied led the league with 159 strikeouts.

In 1993 Linton was with the Blue Jays in spring training but was optioned to Syracuse on March 21. With several middle relievers among the 15 pitchers still in camp, he was expected to get more opportunities to pitch with Syracuse.

Linton was recalled by Toronto on May 7. After allowing seven earned runs in 7⅔ innings in two starts, he was returned to Syracuse on May 13. He rejoined Toronto and made two relief appearances before being placed on waivers. Linton, who was 0-1 with a 6.55 ERA in those four appearances, was claimed by the California Angels on June 17.

He made his first appearance with the Angels at home on June 20. In back-to-back relief outings on July 7 (against Boston) and July 11 (against the Yankees), he was the winning pitcher in each game.

In 19 appearances with the Angels – all in relief – Linton was 2-0 with a 7.71 ERA before being released by the Angels on September 14.

In December Linton signed with the New York Mets. He made the Mets' Opening Day roster in 1994. After beginning the season with two scoreless relief outings, he picked up his first NL victory by getting two outs in the Mets' 10-9 victory over the visiting Chicago Cubs on April 14.

Linton didn't allow a run in his first six NL outings. He allowed just five earned runs in his first 16 innings (15 appearances) and was 4-0. After allowing four earned runs in 1⅔ innings in an 8-3 loss to the Dodgers in Los Angeles on July 9, Linton was sent to Norfolk.

In three starts with Norfolk, he was 2-1 with a 2.00 ERA to earn a return to the Mets. He finished the season with the Mets, for whom he was 6-2 with a 4.47 ERA in 32 appearances (three starts).

Linton became a free agent after the season and signed with the Kansas City Royals. He split the 1995 season between the Royals and their Triple-A Omaha farm team.

In early May, Linton had memorable outings in back-to-back starts for the Royals. On May 5 in Chicago, he started and allowed one run and four hits in eight innings in the Royals' 3-1 victory in 12 innings over the White Sox.

Four days later in Cleveland, Linton started against Cleveland on three days' rest. The Indians, who were on their way to a 100-victory season (in 144 games), tied a major-league record by scoring eight runs before they made an out – something previously accomplished by the New York Yankees in 1960 and the Cleveland Indians in 1954.

The Indians hit three home runs in the inning -- which tied the Royals' record for the most allowed in one inning.

The Indians added two runs in the second to extend their lead to 10-0. Linton regrouped to retire 11 of the last 12 batters he faced in the five-inning outing.

Royals manager Bob Boone said he left Linton in the game to "to chew up some innings. The consolation was that he let me keep my bullpen intact."[10]

For the season, in seven appearances with the Royals, Linton was 0-1 with a 7.25 ERA. With Omaha, he was 7-7 with a 4.40 ERA in 18 starts.

Linton began the 1996 with Omaha. He went 1-1 in four starts with Omaha before being recalled by the Royals on April 30.

Linton tied a Royals record by striking out six consecutive hitters in a 7-5 victory over the White Sox on

July 20 in Chicago. He struck out eight in five innings to earn the victory and improve to 4-5 for the season.

On August 31 he allowed one run and three hits in 6⅓ innings in the Royals' 3-1 victory at Detroit. He struck out a career-high nine as he tied his career high with his sixth victory.

After allowing two runs in six innings while pitching the Royals to a 4-2 victory – his career-high seventh victory – over the Seattle Mariners on September 11 in Kansas City, Linton was sidelined by soreness in his elbow and did not pitch the rest of the season. With the Royals, he was 7-9 with a 5.02 ERA in 21 appearances (18 starts).

After the season, Linton was eligible for arbitration. "Going into arbitration," he said, "my agent told me that I was second – only to Greg Maddux – in strikeout-to-walk ratio in the big leagues in 1996."[11]

Linton, who had struck out 87 and walked 26 in 104 innings, and the Royals avoided arbitration when he agreed to a one-year deal for $500,000. He had asked for $620,000 and the Royals had offered $400,000.

At the beginning of the Royals' training camp of 1997, the soreness persisted in Linton's elbow. An MRI showed inflammation. Six to eight weeks of rest was initially recommended but then surgery was recommended. In early March, Linton had Tommy John surgery and he missed the 1997 season.

Linton signed with the New York Yankees on January 26, 1998, but was released during spring training.

In May of 1998, he joined the Minnesota Twins' Triple-A Salt Lake farm team. He was 0-3 with an 8.22 ERA in his first six starts for Salt Lake before throwing seven shutout innings in a 10-1 victory over Colorado Springs on July 27. For the season, he was 4-4 with a 5.99 ERA in 18 appearances (14 starts).

After the season, Linton was granted free agency and in December he signed with the Baltimore Orioles. He split the 1999 season between the Orioles (1-4 in 14 appearances) and Triple-A Rochester (7-5 in 18 starts). He was released by the Orioles and signed with the Colorado Rockies organization for the 2000 season. Linton spent the entire 2000 season with Triple-A Colorado Springs, going 10-13 in 28 starts. Among his six complete games were three shutouts.

In January of 2001, Linton signed with the Los Angeles Dodgers organization. In late March he was reassigned to the Dodgers' minor-league camp before being released on April 1. He signed with the New York Mets in early May and joined Norfolk. He went 7-3 with a 3.21 ERA in 12 starts before the Mets sold his contract to the LG Twins of the Korean Baseball League on July 25. In 12 starts in Korea, Linton was 4-4 with a 3.17 ERA.

Linton spent the 2002 season in the Atlanta Braves organization. He was 9-11 with a 2.53 ERA and a career-high (and International League-leading) 160 strikeouts in 174 innings for Triple-A Richmond.

After the season, Linton became a free agent and signed a minor-league contract with the Blue Jays. He was invited to the Blue Jays spring training camp "to build organizational depth."[12]

Linton made the Blue Jays' 2003 Opening Day roster. In his first major-league appearance since 1999, he pitched two shutout innings in the Blue Jays' 8-4 loss to the visiting New York Yankees on Opening Day.

His next three appearances were against the Minnesota Twins. In each of the first two, he threw a shutout inning. In the third, on April 13, he allowed two runs in 1⅔ innings in the Twins' 9-3 victory in Toronto. Linton followed with two scoreless outings against the Yankees in New York (one inning on April 14 and 1⅓ innings on April 17). On April 18 in Boston, pitching for the fifth time in seven days, he allowed one run – a solo home run by Doug Mirabelli – in the Blue Jays' 7-3 loss.

Linton was optioned to Syracuse the next day. With Syracuse, he was 2-10 with a 5.28 ERA in 32 appearances.

Linton spent the 2004 season with the Royals organization, starting the season with Triple-A Omaha, where he was 3-9 in 27 appearances. He also went 1-0 in one start for Double-A Wichita.

Linton's final season as a player was in 2005 – at the age of 40 – in Taiwan. He went 6-11 with a 3.64 ERA in 20 starts for Uni-President of the Chinese Professional Baseball League.

In seven major-league seasons, Linton had a 17-20 record and a 5.78 ERA in 112 appearances.

"The (1992) Blue Jays were a very talented club," said Linton. "The team came to the field every day knowing it was going to win. It was a great, winning atmosphere. The players hung around the clubhouse talking about the game."[13]

In 17 minor-league seasons, including parts of 14 seasons at the Triple-A level, Linton had a 109-111 record and 4.07 ERA in 339 appearances. In his two "foreign" seasons, he was 10-15 with a 3.46 ERA.

In 2006 Linton began his coaching career with the Colorado Rockies as a pitching coach for Tri-City in the short-season rookie Northwest League. After one season at Modesto and two at Colorado Springs, he became a roving pitching coordinator in 2012. In 2013 he became the Rockies pitching coordinator. The 2021 season was Linton's 16th with the Rockies organization.

"The game has changed," said Linton. "Especially on the analytical side. I like numbers, but the bottom line is you still have to pitch in a game. Analytics verify what your eyes are telling you."[14]

Linton and his wife, Lisa, reside in Surprise, Arizona. They have three children – Ryan, Austin, and Carter. Carter signed a minor-league contract with the Atlanta Braves in 2020. He pitched for Augusta of the Low-A East South Division in 2021.

SOURCES

In addition to the sources cited in the Notes, the author also consulted Baseball-Reference.com, Newspapers.com, and Retrosheet.org and conducted phone interviews with Doug Linton in December of 2021 and March of 2022.

NOTES

1   Joel Rippel, "Blue Jays' Linton Discovers That Time Indeed Helps Heal," *Orange County Register* (Anaheim, California), July 24, 1989: D6.

2   Rippel.

3   Nick Gates, "Knoxville Rallies Past Lookouts," *Knoxville News-Sentinel*, July 29, 1987: C1.

4   Gates, "Knoxville Is Hurting for Wins," *Knoxville News-Sentinel*, August 3, 1987: C1.

5   Steve Kresal, "Minor League Notebook," *Los Angeles Times*, June 18, 1990: C17.

6   Kresal.

7   Associated Press, "Blue Jays Rookie Brings Down Orioles, 4-2," *Los Angeles Times*, August 14, 1992: C6.

8   Bill Lankhof, "Linton Saves the Day," *National Post* (Toronto), August 14, 1992: 35.

9   Lankhof.

10 LaVelle E. Neal III, "Royals Worst in First," *Kansas City Star*, May 10, 1995: D1.

11 Doug Linton, interview with author.

12 Shi Davidi, "All Eyes on the Jays' Pitchers on the Eve of Spring Training," *National Post*, February 14, 2003: S3.

13 Doug Linton, interview with author.

14 Doug Linton, interview with author.

BOB MACDONALD

By Paul Sinclair

It has been said that "the left-handed are precious; they take places which are inconvenient for the rest."[1] Perhaps there is no place where the left-handed are more precious than in baseball. For baseball has long had a unique proclivity for the left-handed and particularly the left-handed pitcher. A recent study titled "The Southpaw Advantage" noted that "left-handed pitching has long been one of the most prized commodities in professional baseball. Teams strive to obtain lefty pitchers [who] make it to the big leagues about three times as frequently as righties."[2]

The left-handed pitcher has been analyzed, discussed, and debated from many perspectives – from talent procurement to roster building to optimal rotations to in-game strategy. While those efforts have utility in their own context, it is the individual stories

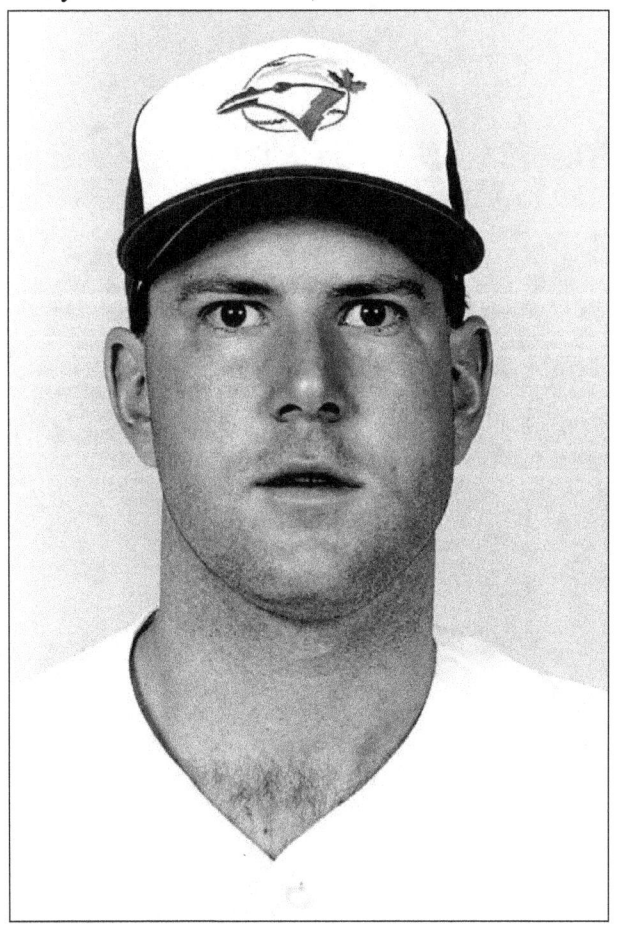

of the southpaws who played the game that garner the deepest appreciation of the left-handed pitcher in baseball.

This is one of those stories: the account of Bob MacDonald, left-handed relief specialist.

Robert Joseph MacDonald was born on April 27, 1965, in East Orange, New Jersey, a primarily residential suburb of Newark.

He was born with a genetic condition that impacts 10 percent of society: left-handedness.[3] MacDonald's ability and passion for baseball developed during his childhood and youth. Being left-handed, he had a potential competitive advantage over those who dreamed of reaching the big leagues.

MacDonald attended Point Pleasant Beach High School and was a multisport athlete, active in football, basketball, and baseball. Named to the All-Ocean County baseball team, he led the Garnet Gulls to a championship in his senior year.[4]

Upon graduation from high school in 1983, he stayed in New Jersey and attended Rutgers University. Skipping his freshman year, he played three seasons for the Scarlet Knights under head coach Fred Hill, who took over leadership of the Rutgers baseball program in 1984. Used primarily as a starter at Rutgers, he overcame a rough sophomore season to improve in both his junior and senior years.

In MacDonald's senior season, he ranked fourth among the Atlantic 10 Conference pitchers with an attractive ERA of 2.97.[5] This was a dramatic turn-around from his sophomore season's ERA of 7.74. Control improved throughout his collegiate career as average walks per nine innings declined from 7.38 (sophomore) to 4.78 (senior). Without an overpowering fastball, he had a modest strikeout rate of six per nine innings.

After MacDonald's senior season, in June 1987 he was selected in the 19th round of the amateur draft by the Blue Jays. Starting his professional career with the St. Catharines (Ontario) Blue Jays, a short-season A-level team in the New York-Penn League, he played in only one game. As the starter, he got a no-decision for four innings of work, giving up two runs on eight hits while striking out four and issuing no walks.

Reassigned to the Medicine Hat Blue Jays of the Rookie-level Pioneer League, MacDonald received the career-defining label of "left-handed reliever." He continued the strong performance of his senior year at Rutgers. MacDonald transitioned well to professional baseball and after just 13 games at Medicine Hat, he was promoted to the Myrtle Beach (South Carolina) Blue Jays of the Class-A South Atlantic League.

By the time MacDonald arrived in Myrtle Beach, he had thrown approximately 97 innings in 1987. This almost doubled his sophomore season's innings pitched, and the extra workload impacted his performance. Appearing in relief in 10 games, he gave up 13 earned runs in 20⅔ innings, an ERA of 5.66, and surrendered the first home run of his collegiate and professional career.

In 1988 the 23-year-old MacDonald returned to Myrtle Beach for another year of development at the A level. He spent the entire season with Myrtle Beach and, pitching solely in relief, he had an outstanding season. Sharing the closer role with right-hander Steve Wapnick, MacDonald led the team with 15 saves and an ERA of 1.69.

For the start of the 1989 season, MacDonald was promoted to the Knoxville Blue Jays of the Double-A Southern League. He was the main left-hander in the Knoxville bullpen. MacDonald excelled in his role as left-handed closer, posting an ERA of 3.29, a WHIP of 1.19, and a strikeout-to-walk ratio of 2.5. He did not surrender a home run.

MacDonald continued his rise in the Blue Jays' farm system, joining the Syracuse Chiefs of the Triple-A International League in late August 1989. The opportunity for MacDonald's promotion arose when the Toronto Blue Jays traded Tony Castillo, the main left-hander in the Chiefs bullpen, and catcher Francisco Cabrera to the Atlanta Braves for pitcher Jim Acker. Used solely in relief, MacDonald surrendered 10 runs in 16 innings.

For the 1990 season, MacDonald returned to the Knoxville Blue Jays and continued as the left-handed closer. He led the team with 15 saves. As in 1989, MacDonald was promoted to Syracuse and once again, he did not pitch well. Appearing in nine games, he walked nine batters in 8⅓ innings and surrendered five earned runs, but did earn two saves.

MacDonald's struggles at Syracuse did not matter to the Blue Jays. He was promoted to Toronto and made his major-league debut on August 14, 1990. In a blowout win against the Chicago White Sox, he faced three batters, walking one before inducing an inning-ending double play. He returned to Syracuse on August 30, but was recalled to Toronto as part of the Blue Jays' September roster expansion. He appeared in one game, against Cleveland, throwing one pitch to retire the side. Overall, he pitched 2⅓ innings of no-hit baseball for the Blue Jays in 1990.

In the 1990 offseason, the Blue Jays' free-agent signing of left-handed reliever Ken Dayley created competition for MacDonald to secure a roster spot. The 31-year-old Dayley had spent seven seasons with the St. Louis Cardinals, posting an ERA of 3.56 and two saves in 1990. The Blue Jays had a surplus of pitchers at the 1991 spring-training camp and would not commit to whether they would have one or two left-handers in the bullpen. Competing for a final roster spot with left-hander Al Leiter, MacDonald pitched well that spring, surrendering no runs in 11 innings. But he was included in the final cuts and started the season at Syracuse.

MacDonald's time in Syracuse was short. By the end of April, he had been recalled to Toronto, an opportunity that arose from injuries to bullpen pitchers Dayley and Tom Henke. Over the next month, he was used sparingly and in 6⅓ innings pitched, posted an ERA of 2.84.

His third game for Toronto in 1991, on May 1 against Texas, was memorable, though not particularly noteworthy careerwise for MacDonald. He pitched a scoreless seventh inning with Toronto losing 3-0. With two out in the top of the ninth inning, Texas starter Nolan Ryan threw a third strike past Roberto Alomar to record the final out of his major-league-record seventh no-hitter. To be part of a game so prominent in baseball history is one of MacDonald's fondest memories, despite being on the losing side.[6]

In late May Dayley, who had been suffering from vertigo, was activated from the disabled list and MacDonald was the odd man out and sent back to Syracuse. He was very frustrated with being returned to the minor leagues. He had pitched well, both in spring training and in the early season. But there was no room on the roster with the Blue Jays carrying only one left-hander in the bullpen and with Willie Fraser, a right-hander, holding down the long-relief role. Wanting a consistent role in the big leagues, MacDonald had started throwing a curveball which he had not attempted previously, and he expressed his willingness to pitch in long relief.[7]

WE ARE, WE CAN, WE WILL

Having just returned to Syracuse, in early June MacDonald was again recalled to Toronto. Starter Dave Stieb had gone on the disabled list with tendinitis. His frustration abated; MacDonald stayed in Toronto for the remainder of the 1991 season.

With the prospect of a consistent role, MacDonald was spectacular, with an 18-inning scoreless streak. His ERA was a remarkable 0.75 when he entered in the eighth inning on July 19 against the Texas Rangers. Allowing a run, he saw his shutout streak snapped. Amid concerns that the Blue Jays were burning out their bullpen, MacDonald struggled in that game and in his next seven.[8] In those eight games, he allowed eight earned runs in nine innings, surrendering 14 hits and walking 11.

After this slump, MacDonald pitched in 19 more games and finished the remainder of the season with an ERA of 3.05 over 20⅔ innings. A WHIP of 1.79 and 18 walks and only 11 strikeouts over the final 27 games suggest that he was allowing baserunners but was escaping innings without runs scored.

MacDonald made his first postseason appearance in the American League Championship Series, as the Blue Jays, winners of the American League East, played the Minnesota Twins. He faced five batters in his one inning in that series, giving up a hit, a walk, and an earned run. The Blue Jays lost to the eventual World Series champion Minnesota Twins in five games.

For MacDonald, the 1991 season, being up and down between Syracuse and Toronto before staying in Toronto from early June onward was a tale of two parts. In his first half of the season, he was excellent, but he slumped after the All-Star break. Of particular concern was that left-handed hitters hit .325 against him. Southpaw effectiveness against left-handed hitters is a prerequisite to maintain a lefty's competitive advantage. MacDonald would have to significantly improve against left-handed hitters if he wanted to secure a left-handed-reliever role in the Toronto bullpen.

As spring training 1992 commenced, the opportunity for MacDonald to make the Blue Jays' roster hinged on the misfortune of others. Injuries to Stieb (back), Dayley (elbow), and Leiter (blisters) eliminated most of his competition. Stieb's injury meant that left-hander David Wells would be moved from the bullpen to the starting rotation. With Dayley and Leiter headed for the disabled list, MacDonald competed with Graeme Lloyd, a 6-foot-8-inch Australian who had four years of professional experience, all at the A level except for two games at Double-A Knoxville.

To improve against left-handed hitters, MacDonald adjusted his positioning on the mound, starting from the first-base side of the pitching rubber rather than the third-base side.[9]

Defending their AL East title, the Blue Jays started the 1992 season in Detroit. For the first time in his career, Bob MacDonald left spring training on a major-league roster.

In the first two months of the season, MacDonald pitched extremely well. Appearing in 11 games, he had an ERA of 2.25 and a WHIP of 1.10, and did not surrender a home run in 20 innings. However, he was rarely used in May, playing only four games and often going eight days between appearances. This inactivity may have hurt him. As the calendar turned to June, he slumped badly. Relegated to pitching mainly in blowout games, he posted a 5.60 ERA in nine appearances in June. He pitched once in July before being sent down to Syracuse.

In mid-August, MacDonald was recalled after an injury to starter Pat Hentgen. Back in Toronto, he continued to pitch ineffectively, and was limited to appearing in four blowout losses. His ERA since returning was 5.87. His performance put him in the vulnerable position of being sent down again to Syracuse. In late August, the Blue Jays, in anticipation of a return to the ALCS, were making key roster moves. Roster spots were needed for their acquisition of pitcher David Cone and the activation of pitcher Juan Guzman from the disabled list. So for the second time that season, MacDonald was optioned to Syracuse. He returned to Toronto as part of the September roster expansion after the Chiefs' season ended. He was rarely used in September and faced only four batters in two games. MacDonald was not eligible to play for the Blue Jays in the postseason, a historic playoff run that culminated in the Blue Jays' first World Series championship.

With an ERA of 4.37 in Toronto and 4.63 in Syracuse, MacDonald's season, which had commenced so full of promise, fell short of expectations. On a positive note, he held left-handed hitters to an anemic batting average of .143. With that level of effectiveness, he may have been ideally suited to be a "lefty one-out guy" or "Loogy" who specializes in pitching to left-handed batters. Clearly, the Blue Jays were not rooted in that strategy as MacDonald averaged 1.74 innings per appearance.

As spring training approached for the 1993 season, MacDonald still sought a consistent role in the Blue

Jays bullpen. Appreciating that he was in the often difficult position of being a role player, he was looking for an opportunity to pitch every two to three days. There was much uncertainty as to whether there would be a role for him. The Blue Jays bullpen was crowded with Mike Timlin, Duane Ward, and Henke, all right-handers. In fact, when he was demoted to Syracuse the previous July, the Blue Jays went with an all-right-handed bullpen. In spring training 1993, MacDonald competed with Wells to be the sole left-hander in the bullpen. Given the number of times that he had been optioned to Syracuse, if he failed to make the major-league roster, he had the right to decline a minor-league assignment. He made it clear that if he was included in the roster cuts, he would become a free agent.[10]

MacDonald was used sparingly that spring, getting only seven innings of work. He allowed only one earned run, but was crowded out of a roster spot and by the end of spring training, MacDonald was sold to the Detroit Tigers for $20,000. He left Toronto hoping that Detroit's manager, Sparky Anderson, would be the one to finally give him a consistent role.

In Detroit MacDonald had an excellent start. On May 13, in a game against Toronto, he made his 16th appearance of the year in the eighth inning with an ERA of 2.16. The Blue Jays exacted some revenge against their former teammate. MacDonald was sent out to pitch the bottom of the ninth, his second inning of work, with Detroit leading 5-4. He walked lead-off hitter Darnell Coles and Alfredo Griffin sacrificed pinch-runner Willie Canate to second. After hitting Devon White with a pitch, MacDonald struck out Roberto Alomar. The save opportunity was blown when Paul Molitor drilled a fastball away to right field for a two-run double to give the Blue Jays a 6-5 win.

This game proved to be a pivotal point in MacDonald's season: He never regained his early-season form. With his effectiveness waning as the season went on, Detroit nonetheless stuck with him as Anderson continued to use MacDonald as a "Loogy." After the blown save in Toronto, he played in 53 more games and had an ERA of 6.43 and a WHIP of 1.63. Left-handed hitters hit .222 against him that season.

In his first and ultimately only full season in the major leagues, MacDonald got the consistent role that he desired. Ranked 10th in the American League with 68 appearances, he averaged 0.97 innings per appearance. His performance was not deemed good enough to be included in the Tigers' plans for 1994.

Detroit lost faith in MacDonald and released him in December 1993.

MacDonald remained unsigned until, on the eve of spring training, he signed a minor-league contract with the Houston Astros. In spring training, as a nonroster invitee, he did not pitch well and was released before the start of the season. Within a week, he signed with his fourth organization, the Seattle Mariners. Assigned to the Mariners' Triple-A affiliate in Calgary of the Pacific Coast League, he struggled. The Mariners were impatient, giving MacDonald no opportunity to turn around his season. After 25 games and an ERA of 7.55, he was released.

The demand for southpaws was strong so MacDonald's time away from the game lasted only two weeks. The Chicago White Sox signed him to a minor-league contract. With the hope of regaining his effectiveness, he was assigned to the Birmingham Barons of the Double-A Southern League. Other than two games with the Triple-A Nashville Sounds, he played the rest of the 1994 season at Birmingham and had an excellent season. But his ERA of 1.78 and a WHIP of 0.83 was not seen good enough to secure a spot on the White Sox' 40-man roster. For the fourth time, he was granted free agency.

In February 1995 with the players strike ongoing, MacDonald signed a minor-league contract with the New York Yankees. He started the season with the Triple-A Columbus Clippers and once again had an excellent start to his season, and was called up on May 11.

The Yankees went with two left-handers in their bullpen as MacDonald and Steve Howe split the left-handed relief role. His first month with the Yankees did not go well. He was used primarily in blowout games, and his ERA hit a high of 8.16 in mid-June after a disastrous outing against Detroit. He remained on the Yankees roster for the remainder of the season. After mid-June, he pitched effectively, posting an ERA of 3.38 to lower his season ERA to 4.86. He was less effective against left-handed hitters, who averaged .261. The Yankees did not primarily use him in a Loogy role; he averaged 1.4 innings per appearance.

New York finished the strike-shortened 1995 season with a record of 79-65 and qualified for the playoffs. MacDonald was left off the postseason roster for the Division Series, against Seattle. The Yankees decided to go with two left-handers in the bullpen. MacDonald was the odd man out as the Yankees put left-handed starter Sterling Hitchcock in the bullpen with Howe.

While cheering on his teammates, MacDonald watched a remarkable Game Two of the ALDS. With the score tied 4-4 in the 12th inning, Ken Griffey Jr. homered off John Wetteland to put the Mariners ahead 5-4. In the bottom of the 12th inning, with two out and Jorge Posada and Bernie Williams on second and first respectively, Ruben Sierra doubled, scoring Posada, but Williams was tagged out at the plate. Extra innings continued with the score tied 5-5. Finally, in the 15th inning at 1:22 A.M., Yankees catcher Jim Leyritz hit a 3-and-1 pitch for a two-run home run. The Yankees had won the marathon 7-5 and took a 2-0 lead in the ALDS. No adjective can adequately describe the atmosphere in Yankee Stadium throughout that game. For MacDonald, a nonparticipating Yankee, that game was a career favorite moment.[11]

In January 1996 MacDonald joined the crosstown New York Mets and made the major-league roster out of spring training. Averaging one inning per appearance, he pitched well in the first two months of the season. With the Mets struggling in early June, he was caught up in a roster overhaul and demoted to Norfolk, the Mets Triple-A affiliate. At Norfolk, he was playing close to his birthplace. His baseball journey had come full circle.

MacDonald made his last major-league appearance on June 7, 1996, an outing of 2⅔ innings in a lopsided 12-2 loss to Florida. After he entered the game in the seventh inning with the bases loaded, his first pitch to former Blue Jays teammate Devon White was hit into the left-field bleachers for a grand slam. In MacDonald's final game, the winning pitcher for Florida was Al Leiter, whose injury woes back in 1992 had opened the way for him to make the Blue Jays roster.

MacDonald pitched well for Norfolk for the remainder of the season. For the 31-year-old, his ERA of 3.13 in 31⅔ innings was good but not enough to avoid being released for the sixth time in his career at the end of the season.

Hoping to keep his professional career going, MacDonald signed with the Tigers. This time the team was not in Detroit. Traveling across the Pacific Ocean, he signed with the Hanshin Tigers of the Japan Central League. At Hanshin, former major leaguers Mike Greenwell, Darnell Coles, and Phil Hiatt were teammates. In his short stint with Hanshin, he pitched 7⅓ innings in nine appearances and gave up six earned runs.

His sojourn in Hanshin was the final chapter in MacDonald's baseball journey. Little is known about his travels since then. Attempts to learn about his life since leaving baseball in 1997 have proven fruitless; he is not registered with the MLB Players Alumni Association. Any additional information would be welcome.

As a 19th-round draft pick, MacDonald had a 1-in-10 chance of reaching the big leagues.[12] Despite such forbidding odds, he played six seasons in the majors and appeared in 197 games. He reached the major leagues because he was very effective in the minor leagues – an ERA of 3.27, a WHIP of 1.26, and 49 saves over nine seasons.

In the major leagues, MacDonald had periods of great promise. His career had a pattern that as a season progressed, his effectiveness waned. The consistent role afforded him in the minors was elusive in the major leagues. When released from an organization due to lack of overall effectiveness, the southpaw advantage prevailed as there was always another team willing to sign him. He had many opportunities to extend his career and played for seven organizations after being released six times in the 1994-1996 seasons.

What is to be learned from Bob MacDonald's career? The answer seems to be that for a lefty reliever, what gets you to the major leagues and keeps you there is consistent effectiveness, much more than the southpaw advantage. The southpaw advantage creates opportunities, but what truly matters most is what is achieved when those opportunities arise. Bob MacDonald had the answer.

SOURCES

In addition to the sources cited in the Notes, the author consulted Baseball-Reference.com, the baseballcube.com, *Toronto Star* archives, newspaperarchive.com for articles from the *Syracuse Herald Journal* and the *Post-Standard*, and PaperofRecord.com for *The Sporting News*

NOTES

1   Quote by Victor Hugo, quotefancy.com.

2   Guy Molyneux and Phil Birnbaum, "The Southpaw Advantage," fangraphs.com, September 8, 2020. https://blogs.fangraphs.com/the-southpaw-advantage/.

3   Katie Kerns Geer, "12 Little-Known Facts about Left-Handers," everydayhealth.com, August 13, 2015. https://www.everydayhealth.com/healthy-living-pictures/little-known-facts-about-lefthanders.aspx.

4   *Toronto Blue Jays Official Guide 1992*, 92.

5   Mark Rizzi, *1988 Rutgers University Baseball Media Guide*, Rutgers Division of Intercollegiate Athletics, 21.

6   lettersfromhomeplate.com, Bob MacDonald. https://lettersfromhomeplate.com/2021/03/03/bob-macdonald/

7   Tom Slater, "Jays Off to Take on the West," *Toronto Star*, April 30, 1991: D2.

8   Tom Slater, "Gaston Wants to Avoid Burning Out
    Bullpen," *Toronto Star,* April 30, 1991: D2.

9   Dave Perkins, "This MacDonald Shuns Farm and Hopes to
    Stick with Jays," *Toronto Star*, March 17, 1992: B4.

10 Tom Slater, "MacDonald Hopes Axe Will Fall,"
    Toronto Star, March 29, 1993: C4.

11 lettersfromhomeplate.com, Bob MacDonald.

12 Mike Rosenbaum, "Examining the Percentage of MLB Draft Picks
    Who Reach the Major Leagues," bleacherreport.com, June 12,
    2012. https://bleacherreport.com/articles/1219356-examining-the-
    percentage-of-mlb-draft-picks-that-reach-the-major-leagues.

MIKE MAKSUDIAN

By David Fuller

In nine years of professional baseball, Michael Bryant Maksudian played only parts of three seasons in the majors, but he managed to leave an impression with his teammates thanks to his offbeat personality – and a penchant for eating bugs that had an impact on the Toronto Blue Jays World Series campaign of 1992.

Maksudian was born on May 28, 1966, in Belleville, Illinois. His great-grandfather Gamsar was an Armenian from Van, Turkey, who emigrated to the United States before 1918.[1] His father, Gregory, a steel buyer, was transferred to Randolph, New Jersey, in 1979. Mike played his freshman year of high-school ball in Randolph, and when the family moved to Parsippany, New Jersey, in 1981, he attended Parsippany High School, where he became the team's star player as a power-hitting outfielder and helped the team win its first county tournament championship.

At 5-feet-11 and 200 pounds, he went undrafted after high school and continued his playing career at New Jersey's County College of Morris. Once again, he became a team leader and helped his team to within one game of winning the Junior College World Series. While at County College of Morris, Maksudian was selected twice in the amateur draft; in 1985 by the Detroit Tigers and in the June Draft-Secondary Phase 1986 by the Houston Astros. He signed neither time; in the winter of 1986 Maksudian accepted a baseball scholarship to the University of South Alabama, where he met his future wife, Betty Hancock.

Maksudian broke his left foot in a game against South Florida in the 1987 season, a year when he hit .407 with 14 home runs and 63 RBIs and was named Sunbelt Conference All-Tournament Team MVP. His team went to the NCAA Regional finals, and he homered in four consecutive games. "It was in late April and things were going really well," Maksudian said. "There was a ball hit deep to left field and I tried to jump as high as I could to get it. The ball went off the wall and I just came down on the foot wrong." The injury kept Maksudian out of the lineup for six weeks and a total of 25 games. "When I got back, I got right in the groove again," he said, "but the time out cost me. I lost about 100 to 125 at-bats. I think I could have been an All-American and I figured I would be drafted, but because of the injury, I wasn't."[2] He also played with the Falmouth Commodores of the summer Cape Cod League that year.[3]

Maksudian signed as a free agent with the Chicago White Sox on July 13, 1987, starting in rookie ball with the White Sox of the Gulf Coast League. In 1988 he was moved up to the White Sox' Class-A Midwest League affiliate in South Bend. By this time, he was playing first base and catcher – and had married Betty. Although he hit .303 in South Bend, he and Vince Harris[4] were traded to the New York Mets for pitcher Tom McCarthy and infielder Steve Springer on August 4. After struggling with the Mets' team in St. Lucie of the high Class-A Florida State League (he batted just .214), the club tried to send Maksudian to low-A ball.

He refused and was released on March 30, 1989. He was puzzled about why the Mets had traded for him only to seek to relegate him to low-A. "My career's been such a jumpy mess," he said. "Eventually, I'll get my break. Sometime, somewhere, someone's going to be impressed."[5]

The Mets' farm director at the time, Steve Schryver, explained that the transaction was more about McCarthy and Springer, who were about to become free agents. The team did not view Maksudian as a prospect, saying he was a bit weak defensively, but they thought he might develop into a pretty decent hitter.[6]

At 23 and disappointed with the course of his career, Maksudian, who took accounting and psychology in college, went home to Alabama and took a job in the front office of the Birmingham Barons, ready to settle into normal life. But it didn't take long before he decided he still wanted to play and he signed with the woeful Miami Miracle, a new independent team in the Florida State League.[7] He hit .313 with 9 home runs for a team that finished with a 43-91 record.

On December 5, 1989, the Toronto Blue Jays took Maksudian in the Rule 5 Double-A draft and assigned him to Knoxville, where he went on to hit .287 in 1990 and become a spark plug and team leader – but behind Randy Knorr and Ed Sprague on the Toronto catching depth chart. After starting him in Knoxville again for the 1991 season, the Blue Jays promoted him to Triple-A Syracuse by early May. He spent the rest of the season in Syracuse and again in 1992 until he was called up on August 30 as a utility player and – having hit four pinch-hit home runs – a left-handed bat off the bench. Most of the Blue Jays' other left-handed batters were injured.[8] When the August roster deadline passed the next day, Maksudian found himself still a Blue Jay and eligible for the postseason. As the team chased down a division championship and pennant in September, Maksudian had the only three pinch-hit at-bats he was to get as a Blue Jay. He went 0-for-3 and finished the season as the only one of 23 Jays players to make a plate appearance and not get a hit.[9] He was on the bench for the postseason and caught in the bullpen.

After the World Series Maksudian was voted half of a World Series share and received a championship ring.[10] But perhaps his biggest contribution to the team that fall was his talent for keeping his teammates loose – particularly Joe Carter, according to *Sportsnet Magazine*. "Mike Maksudian was a young guy who came up in [August] and had a fetish for eating bugs.

He ate a lot of bugs while he was with the team," Carter said. Tom Henke recalled the team organizing a pool to see him eat a locust in Kansas. "I caught a couple great big locusts out in the bullpen. We got a pool together: 700 bucks, still alive. He put a piece of spaghetti around one and chewed on it and swallowed. The bug was buzzing in his mouth. I thought Dave Winfield was gonna upchuck right there."[11] (Devon White also claimed to organize the locust snack, including the spaghetti.)[12]

The bug-eating antics became Maksudian's main claim to fame with the media, generating many headline puns and nicknames – "Orkin Man" was one, after the pest control company – that followed him wherever he went for the rest of his career. The real story, as Maksudian told it, is this: The bargaining for the stunt continued in the clubhouse after the bullpen cleared out and reached $1,400 and Maksudian ate the bug. It was supposed to be just a private team thing, but a reporter who was still in the clubhouse heard it all and wrote about it.[13] At the time, Maksudian needed the extra money, still making the league minimum, and the $1,400 was welcome, especially since his credit card had been pulled from the pile at a team dinner one night, leaving him on the hook for the entire bill. It turned out, however, that he didn't collect the full amount. His teammates fined him $400 in kangaroo court for "eating during a game."[14] A coach later told him he should knock off the stunts; he was up in the bigs to hit, not make jokes. Maksudian took the tip to heart and toned it down – until manager Cito Gaston called him into the office one day and said, "Sheik,[15] what's wrong?" When Maksudian told him what the coach had said, Gaston dismissed it and said, "Forget that, just go back to being you." When the Jays won the World Series, Maksudian vowed to fans that he would get a tattoo on his butt to commemorate the occasion.[16] He barely had time to have it done before he was selected off waivers by the Minnesota Twins with a strong chance of making the team, according to Blue Jays general manager Pat Gillick and assistant GM Gord Ash when they broke the news to him.[17]

Maksudian's 1993 season went south after he sustained a stress fracture in his arm in spring training and missed the early part of the season. On his return, he was sent to Triple-A Portland, where he batted well. He was called up to the Twins as an injury replacement on June 11 but played in only five games and went 2-for-12. His second series after the call-up was against Toronto, where he did not get an appearance. During the next series he got his first major-league

RBI on a sacrifice fly against Oakland on June 13. He recorded his first hit, an RBI double, against New York Yankees pitcher Mike Witt on June 17. After the short stint was over, he was sent back down to Portland to make room for Kent Hrbek, who had been activated from the injured list on June 23.

The Twins released Maksudian on October 15 and two months later he signed with the Chicago Cubs. He said he also had an offer from Montreal, but decided to play in Illinois, where he still had family. In hindsight, he said, it was probably a mistake as Montreal was leading both leagues in wins (74-40) when the players strike began on August 12, 1994.[18] His third trip to the majors began in Des Moines, Iowa, playing for the Cubs' Triple-A affiliate. Maksudian played in 58 games, batting .318 with 8 home runs before being called up to the Cubs in midseason after Ryne Sandberg announced his first retirement on June 13. There, Maksudian played in 26 games, batting .269, but was released on October 10, 1994.

Maksudian's major-league career was over at age 29, but his dream lived on. He joined the Oakland A's Edmonton Trappers of the Triple-A Pacific Coast League for the 1995 season and played in 100 games. But the season was a hard one. He had had rotator cuff/labrum surgery during the offseason and his comeback was not to be. He hit just .150 to start the year and only a second-half stretch of hitting over .300 raised his average to .265 by season's end with eight home runs. "It's been a battle since the day I walked back on the field," he said. "I keep trying to find that same old swing, but I've had to make some changes. Every day you come out and you think to yourself, 'This is the day I come out of it.' And every day you don't, you leave the yard upset with yourself. This is the worst I've ever hit in my life, but I'll get past it."[19]

Maksudian's time with the Trappers was also hampered by an incident after he hit his first home run of the year, on June 30. Maksudian went to a club in downtown Edmonton with roommate Jim Bowie to celebrate, but the two became involved in a fight when Bowie, who is Black, was taunted with racial remarks by other patrons, who happened to be members of a Vietnamese drug gang (although police denied it).[20] Maksudian hit one of them in the mouth as tempers flared and the bouncer advised him to leave quickly as he had just bloodied the lip of the gang's leader. As he and Bowie tried to exit the second-floor bar, a bunch of gang members appeared downstairs, blocking their exit, and things escalated. As he threw a punch,

Maksudian was stabbed in the chest. The knife just missed his aorta, nearly killing him. Maksudian said he moved his body just as he was being stabbed – a reaction that he believes saved his life.[21] He was noticeably absent from the clubhouse for several days afterward with no explanation. Then the team released a statement on July 3, calling his injury a "contusion of the ribs," implying that it was game-related. The true story came out days later. Bowie told reporter Robin Brownlee that he and Maksudian weren't looking for trouble. The outing was part of a bet the two had made that whoever hit a home run first would have his drinks paid for by the other. "I finally hit one out after the season I've been through and this happens," said Maksudian. "I was just starting to get my swing back too."[22] The wound was only three or four inches deep and hit no arteries or organs, so he was back playing within two weeks.

Although he finished the season at Edmonton with a hitting streak, Maksudian, then 29 and worn down from injuries, was at the end of his career. He was also about to become a father: His wife, Betty, was pregnant with their son Mason, so he hung up his spikes after the 1995 season. But he wasn't quite finished with baseball. He said he had always planned to go into business after his playing days were over and he was not as sorry to see his career end as some players are. By this time, he had accepted the fact that he was a minor leaguer who was playing out the string. He was looking forward to having a family and enjoying a home life.[23] By November, Maksudian was back in Montgomery, Alabama, holding baseball clinics for local youth and running camps.[24] The camps were part of an idea for a new computer recruiting system he was developing that he hoped would be a boon to team scouts and managers. They were designed as showcases for local players who would be tracked in a database. The software did not gain a big market and he shelved the project.[25]

Maksudian went on to enjoy a successful career as an IT sales professional/consultant who has sold hundreds of millions of dollars in enterprise-class IT products and services. He and Betty founded New Economy Technology Solutions IT (NETSIT) in 2009 and as of 2022 lived in Scottsdale, Arizona, where the company has its headquarters.[26] His company also has an office in Islamabad, Pakistan. The Maksudians have two children, Mason and Alex, and two grandchildren, and "Mak" said he loves golfing and traveling – and being a grandfather.

NOTES

1   Ancestry.com, U.S., World War I Draft Registration Cards, 1917-1918.

2   Ed Mills, "Maksudian, Vallorosi Bigger Hits in College," *Morristown* (New Jersey) *Daily Record,* July 6, 1987: 31.

3   "Major League Baseball Players From the Cape Cod League" (PDF) from archived page of capecodbaseball.org. https://www.google.com/url?sa=t&rct=j&q=&esrc=s&source=web&cd=&cad=r-ja&uact=8&ved=2ahUKEwiyu8DShu_2AhVTXMoKHd5KCxoQF-noECAIQAQ&url=https%3A%2F%2Fcapecodbaseball.org.ismmedia.com%2FISM3%2Fstd-content%2Frepos%2FTop%2F2012website%-2Farchives%2FCurrent%2520Year%2FAll_Time_MLB_CCBL_Alumni.pdf&usg=AOvVaw12xVRQAyN11fnOZ1OY1AeY, accessed March 30, 2022.

4   Vincent Edward Harris was a minor-league player for 10 years, playing mostly Class-A and Double-A ball. Baseball Reference, https://www.baseball-reference.com/register/player.fcgi?id=harris001vin.

5   Anthony Rieber, "Maksudian Still Chasing a Dream," *Morristown Daily Record,* August 20, 1989: C8.

6   Rieber, "Maksudian Still Chasing a Dream".

7   Baseball Prospectus.com, https://www.baseballprospectus.com/news/article/42338/defensive-indifference-the-strange-legend-ary-times-of-mike-maksudian/.

8   Allan Ryan, "Maksudian Lines Up with the Jays," *Toronto Star,* September 1, 1992: C3.

9   Baseball Prospectus; Ryan.

10 Author interview with Mike Maksudian, April 4, 2022.

11 "Memories of '92, *SportsNet Magazine,* https://www.sportsnet.ca/baseball/mlb/blue-jays-oral-history-memories-of-92-stretch-run/.

12 Jim Byers, "Jays Get Key Win," *Toronto Star,* September 9, 1992: D3.

13 Jim Byers, "Jays Bug Rookie Catcher the Day after the Locust," *Toronto Star,* September 10, 1992: D3.

14 Maksudian interview.

15 Maksudian interview. "Sheik" was his nick-name before the bug-eating incident.

16 500levelfan.com http://500levelfan.com/2010/05/14/blast-from-the-past-mike-maksudian/.

17 Maksudian interview.

18 Maksudian interview.

19 Robin Brownlee, "Trying to Find 'That Same Old Swing,'" *Edmonton Journal,* May 30, 1995: D6.

20 Ian Williams, Robin Brownlee, and Charles Rusnell, "Trappers' Catcher Knifed in a Fight," *Edmonton Journal,* July 13, 1995: A1, A11.

21 Maksudian interview.

22 Robin Brownlee, "Stabbing No Laughing Matter," *Edmonton Journal,* July 13, 1995: D3.

23 Maksudian interview.

24 Greg Klein, "Former World Series Winner to Hold Clinics," *Prattville* (Alabama) *Progress,* November 25, 1995: 9.

25 Maksudian interview.

26 NETSIT company website, http://www.netsit.com/teams.php.

CANDY MALDONADO

By Tom Hawthorn

Fred Merkle had his boner and Steve Bartman his bobbled foul ball. For Candy Maldonado, a momentary lapse and blinding lights contributed to a play less infamous but just as devastating for the unfortunate protagonist.

It was October 13, 1987, as Game Six of the National League Championship Series pitted Maldonado's San Francisco Giants (90-72) against the St. Louis Cardinals (95-67). The Giants needed just one more win to advance to the World Series for the first time in 25 years.

Tony Peña, leading off the bottom of the second inning for the hometown Cardinals, lined a Dave Dravecky pitch toward Maldonado in right field. The

Candy Maldonado: They called him the Candy Man.

fielder charged in before sinking to his knees on the artificial turf as the ball sailed over his head. By the time the ball was returned to the infield, Peña was standing on third base.

One out later, with the Giants infield playing in, batter Jose Oquendo sliced a soft fly toward Maldonado. "Fly ball to right field and pretty shallow," Vin Scully told television viewers. "Maldonado makes the catch and Peña's going to come! Here's the throw, the play, he is …"

Maldonado raced about 15 steps toward the seats, his momentum taking him across the foul line as he caught the ball before quickly pivoting to face home plate. He made a strong, one-hop throw to catcher Bob Melvin, the ball arriving about 10 feet up the line as Peña sidestepped his counterpart. "He is … safe!" Scully declared.[1]

The Cardinals nursed that lone run to victory. After the game, Maldonado was disconsolate. "I just lost the ball in the lights," he said. "I tried to protect my face. I got the glove up but fell and missed it." Nor did the outfielder ignore his lapse on the throw home. "If I make a good throw, the man is out. We might still be playing the game."[2] Newspapers the next day showed Maldonado on his back like an overturned turtle, glove helplessly up in the air, the ball bouncing away. The Cardinals went on to win Game Seven and the Giants' promising season seemed to have turned on an outfielder's misplay.

Nine months later, lingering tensions between the teams erupted when a hard slide led to a bench-clearing brawl. With Will Clark on first base, Maldonado hit a grounder fielded by Cardinals shortstop Ozzie Smith, who tossed underhand to José Oquendo as Clark barreled through and beyond second base. Oquendo's response was to knee or kick Clark (the video evidence is inconclusive), whose rise from the dirt led to a flurry of pushing and punching. Smith punched Clark from behind. Seeing his teammate ganged up on by four Cardinals, including Oquendo, a fellow Puerto Rican, Maldonado raced from first base to throw a desperate, diving haymaker punch at Smith, bloodying his lip.[3]

Those lowlights in a 15-season career were more than matched by highlights, including several breathtaking throws, spectacular catches, and timely hits, most notably during the 1992 World Series, when he helped the Toronto Blue Jays win the first championship by a team not based in the United States.

In his career, Maldonado went from being a touted (but surplus) prospect to a struggling (and self-doubting) newcomer to a valued (but mercenary) hitter. He patrolled the outfield for seven major-league teams – the Los Angeles Dodgers (1981-85), Giants (1986-89), Cleveland Indians (1990, 1993-94), Milwaukee Brewers (1991), Blue Jays (1991-92, 1995), Chicago Cubs (1993), and the Texas Rangers (1995).

Cándido Maldonado y Guadarrama was born in Humacao, Puerto Rico, on September 5, 1960. His father, Cándido Maldonado de León, worked as a heavy-machinery operator, while his mother, Irene Guardarrama de Jesús, worked in a factory, later establishing her own food business. The young athlete moved to Arecibo on the island's north shore to play Little League baseball. He would eventually drop out of junior high school to pursue a baseball career. As he played in his homeland, he attracted the attention of scouts representing six major-league teams, though none was prepared to make an offer.

"I was kind of disappointed," Maldonado later said, "but I kept playing hard."[4]

After a game, he was approached by Ralph Avila, a scout for the Dodgers best known for his work in the Dominican Republic. The interest after so much rejection left the player unimpressed. "I gave him my name and all the details, but I didn't care anymore. After all those others, I was tired of wasting my time."[5]

The Dodgers liked the youth's whip-like batting stroke and strong right arm. He was signed as a non-drafted free agent on June 17, 1978, soon establishing himself as an exciting, power-hitting prospect at age 17 with the Pioneer League team in Lethbridge, Alberta. After another season split between Lethbridge and the Dodgers farm team in Clinton, Iowa, Maldonado graduated to the Lodi Dodgers of the California League, where he smacked 25 home runs in his first 121 games in 1980. He was leading the circuit in home runs, runs batted in, and total bases when his season ended prematurely after he suffered a spiral fracture of the pinky on his left (catching) hand while diving for a line drive. Sportswriters and official scorers named him a league all-star, while he also shared most valuable player honors with Jamie Cocanower, a pitcher.[6]

Maldonado feasted on Triple-A pitching after being promoted to the Albuquerque Dukes of the Pacific Coast League for the 1981 season. The outfielder whacked two homers and knocked in six runs in a 15-9 win over Phoenix on April 22. He was only getting warmed up. On April 30, he hit two round-trippers in his final two at-bats against the Tucson Toros. He was plunked in his first plate appearance the following night, and responded by hitting a solo shot in the fourth and a two-run homer in the fifth to power his team to a 7-5 success. The homers on four consecutive at-bats tied a league mark set by Gus Zernial in 1948 and matched by Ted Beard five years after that.[7]

Maldonado didn't only do his slugging with a bat. On August 18, 1981, he was hit in the helmet by a pitch thrown by Rick Aponte of the Toros. Maldonado charged the mound, only to be tackled by trailing Toros catcher Tom Vessey. As both dugouts emptied, Maldonado's manager, Del Crandall, went after Aponte, who blocked a punch with his gloved hand. For his efforts, Crandall was punched in the nose by Toros first baseman Danny Heep. It was the fifth time in the season that Maldonado fought a pitcher.[8]

Maldonado and first baseman Mike Marshall gave the Dukes a mighty power duo and the pair received attention from *The Sporting News* and other newspapers as future stars. Both players were September call-ups, debuting in the majors at Dodger Stadium on September 7, 1981, two days after Maldonado's 21st birthday. The 6-foot, 180-pound outfielder replaced Dusty Baker in left field in the ninth inning of a 5-1 victory over the San Francisco Giants. The Candy Man, as he was called, went just 1-for-12 with five strikeouts in his first stint with the Dodgers.

After a stellar 1981 campaign with the Dukes (.335, 21, 104), he returned to Albuquerque for more seasoning in 1982, once again recording strong numbers (.301, 24, 96) and again joining the parent Dodgers in September.

Meanwhile, Maldonado continued to play in the Puerto Rico Winter League with the Arecibo Lobos (Wolves), who took the league title in 1982-83. The Lobos went on to win the Caribbean World Series in Caracas, Venezuela, posting a 5-1 record. Against Mexico, Maldonado hit a two-run single in the eighth inning for a 2-1 victory. He also hit a three-run homer and saved another game with a leaping, over-the-fence catch. The heroics cemented his reputation among Puerto Rican fans, and to no one's surprise Maldonado was named the tournament's all-star center fielder.

WE ARE, WE CAN, WE WILL

Scouts admired Maldonado's sweet batting stroke.

A month later, Maldonado reported to training camp at Dodgertown in Vero Beach, Florida. At 22, he had been in the organization five years, still without a spot on the parent club. The Dodgers already had five outfielders. "Where am I going to put him?" lamented manager Tommy Lasorda.[9] Maldonado was asked to try third base as a potential backup to Pedro Guerrero, another player who had chafed at a long internship.

With his options running out, Maldonado figured he might be traded to another team. "I've got to realize that a lot of ballplayers are going through the same thing," he said. "I guess what makes the difference between being a kid and a man is having a little more understanding of what's happening around you, why this may not be for you."[10]

Maldonado split the 1983 season between Albuquerque and the Dodgers, where he replaced Ron Roenicke as a fifth outfielder. Maldonado recorded just 12 hits, including his first big-league home run, in 62 at-bats (.194), as both Lasorda and batting instructor Manny Mota blamed impatient aggressiveness at the plate for the poor showing. He got his first taste of the postseason, going 0-for-2 as a pinch-hitter as the Dodgers lost the best-of-five National League Championship Series in four games to the Philadelphia Phillies.

Maldonado would become one of those players who seemed always to be in the playoffs even as he bounced from team to team, seeing postseason action in 1983, '85, '87, '89, '91, and '92.

Maldonado spent the next two seasons full-time with the Dodgers before he was traded to the Giants for Mexican-born catcher Alex Trevino in December 1985. The Giants at first used him as a pinch-hit specialist. In his first month in San Francisco, the new acquisition registered eight hits, including two homers, in 10 pinch-hit appearances, knocking in six runs. That earned him a full-time spot in the lineup at last, and Maldonado hit 18 and 20 home runs in successive seasons.

On May 4, 1987, Maldonado, batting cleanup, hit for the cycle in game against the Cardinals at Busch Stadium. Maldonado was left stranded after hitting a third-inning triple. By the time he came to bat in the seventh, he was 1-for-3 and his team was trailing by 7-2. Maldonado homered off starter Danny Cox, who lasted only one more batter. Maldonado then singled in the eighth and doubled in the ninth as the Giants came from behind for a 10-7 victory.

Following their collapse in the 1987 Championship Series, the Giants returned to the playoffs two years later, eliminating the Chicago Cubs before being swept in the Earthquake Series by the cross-bay rival Oakland A's. Before the Series, Maldonado lamented a season-long slump in which his swing seemed to have deserted him. "I went through a lot of things that probably could have destroyed me, because (baseball) is something that I love," he said. "It's frustrating when you know you're not doing the job you can do and you see the other guys doing it all and you want to be a part of it."[11] In the end, Maldonado struck out four times in 11 at-bats, his only safety a pinch-hit triple off reliever Rick Honeycutt in Game Four. The outfielder signed as a free agent with the Cleveland Indians the following month. He hit a career high 22 homers for the Tribe in 1990 before signing with the Milwaukee Brewers just before the start of the 1991 season. In August, the Blue Jays pried him from the Brewers in exchange for minor leaguer Bob Wishnevski and a player to be named later, who turned out to be minor leaguer William Suero. Maldonado responded by hitting .277 in 52 games with 7 homers and 28 RBIs, though he sagged with a 2-for-20 run in the postseason.

Maldonado hit .272 with 20 homers for the Blue Jays in 1992. He had timely hits in the World Series, the first coming in the bottom of the ninth inning of Game Three against the Atlanta Braves at Skydome in Toronto. A series of managerial chess moves pitting relief pitchers against pinch-hitters led to a situation with the bases loaded and one out in a 2-2 game. Jimy Williams, acting in place of manager Bobby Cox, who had been tossed for throwing a helmet onto the field, called on Jeff Reardon to face Maldonado, who had a woeful 2-for-13 career record with seven strikeouts against the right-hander. Maldonado swung and badly missed two curveballs from Reardon, who then threw a third. The Candy Man was waiting for it. "I figured after the first two made me look so bad, he wasn't going to change," Maldonado said later.[12] The batter drove the ball to deep center for a game-winning single in the first World Series game played in Canada.

Maldonado's second hit in the Series came against left-hander Steve Avery in Game Six, a solo homer to left field in Atlanta in the top of the fourth inning to give the Blue Jays a 2-1 lead. Maldonado and the Jays went on to win the game, 4-3, in 11 innings, and the World Series.

He spent the next three seasons wearing four different uniforms. Maldonado retired after the 1995 season with a .254 career average, 146 homers, and 618 RBIs in 1,410 major-league games.

Five years later, Maldonado joined the Spanish-language ESPN Deportes as an analyst and co-host of such shows as *Beisbol Esta Noche*. Among his contributions was a weekly online video, called *La Esquina de Candy* (Candy's Corner), in which he addressed newsworthy topics.

Maldonado, who was nicknamed the Candy Man during his playing days by broadcaster Chris Berman, maintains a presence on social media, notably on Twitter (@Candy_Baseball) and Instagram (@candymaldonado23). He lost his analyst's position in 2016 and now promotes his availability to deliver personal and corporate greetings for a fee on Cameo.

Maldonado has been inducted into the Salón de la Fama del Béisbol Profesional de Puerto Rico (Puerto Rican Baseball Hall of Fame) and the Pabellón de la Fama del Caribe (Caribbean Baseball Hall of Fame).

This biography is included in Puerto Rico and Baseball: 60 Biographies *(SABR, 2017), edited by Bill Nowlin and Edwin Fernández.*

SOURCES

In addition to the sources cited in the Notes, the author also consulted Baseball-Reference.com and Retrosheet.org. Thanks to Jorge Colon-Delgado and Candy Maldonado for helping with information for this biography

NOTES

1   "Tony Pena Scores on Candy Maldonado's Throw," YouTube.com. Retrieved January 17, 2017. youtube.com/watch?v=2q6tH9KNSag.

2   Steve Wilstein, "Maldonado: 'I Feel Real Down,'" *Star Press* (Muncie, Indiana), October 14, 1987.

3   "Will Smith Takes on Ozzie Smith and Jose Oquendo," YouTube.com. Retrieved March 13, 2017. https://youtube.com/watch?v=2hbxU20SkNQ.

4   Paul Scherr, "Maldonado, Marshall Climb Fast on Dodger Ladder," *The Sporting News*, July 25, 1981: 38.

5   Scherr.

6   "Season Ends Early for Maldonado," *The Sporting News*, September 13, 1980: 57.

7   "The Candy Man," *The Sporting News*, May 23, 1981: 41.

8   "Dukes Duke It Out," *The Sporting News*, September 12, 1981: 69.

9   Gordon Edes, "Maldonado: What He Wants Is a Chance," *Los Angeles Times*, March 7, 1983: III-8.

10 Edes.

11 "Giant Hopes Slump Is a Thing of the Past." *Press-Citizen* (Iowa City, Iowa), October 13, 1989.

12 "1992 World Series," YouTube.com. Retrieved April 3, 2017. https://youtube.com/watch?v=mDVND9PC8DQ.

DOMINGO MARTÍNEZ

By Richard Bogovich

"It is difficult to muster up much sympathy these days for the young men who make their livings in professional baseball, but I submit for your consideration a possible exception," Toronto sportswriter Marty York commented in 1993.[1] He was referring to Domingo Martínez. Players have complained for decades about lacking chances to prove their worth, but very few can point to tremendous productivity in their limited opportunities. Domingo Martínez had only 22 at-bats in the majors, but his productivity in such a low total was almost unmatched over close to 70 years. His nine hits during Toronto's back-to-back World Series years gave him a career .409 batting average. From the start of World War II through 2000, only Vic Rodriguez of the 1984 Orioles and 1989 Twins achieved a higher lifetime average (.429) with that many at-bats.[2] For Martínez, it wasn't a fluke. "For more than eight seasons, Martínez [had] toiled as a mostly impressive

farmhand while working his way up the ladder at every level of the Jays' organization," York wrote.[3]

Domingo Emilio Martínez y Lafontaine was born in Santo Domingo, the capital city of the Dominican Republic. Many sources, including baseball-reference. com, identify his date of birth as August 4, 1965, but during his second pro season he wrote the year as 1967 on a Spanish-language questionnaire he completed.[4] He is a cousin of Francisco Cordero, who pitched in the majors from 1999 through 2012 and said Martínez was "pretty much" his favorite player growing up. "I saw how proud my dad was that he made it to the major leagues," Cordero said just a few years into his own major-league career.[5]

Little has been made public about Martínez's childhood. However, he once commented that as he learned baseball then, field conditions in Santo Domingo required full concentration on defense. "The fields are brutal," he said, "so you've always got to keep your eye on the ball because you never know where it's going. Yes, I think that background helped me."[6]

A Blue Jays media guide reported that he attended La Isabela primary school in Santo Domingo's Pantoja neighborhood, and later the nearby Gustavo Adolfo Bécquer high school.[7] He attended the latter for two years, according to the aforementioned questionnaire. On it he also said he was signed on behalf of Toronto by Epy Guerrero, known as the Super Scout.[8] Martínez signed as an amateur, non-drafted free agent on August 23, 1984, shortly after his 19th birthday.[9]

Martínez made his professional, regular-season debut on June 21, 1985. He had been assigned to the Blue Jays of the rookie-level Gulf Coast League (in 2021 called the Florida Complex League). One week into his pro career, he was the offensive star in an 11-inning win over the Gulf Coast Royals with a homer and two singles. Through July 3 he played in all 12 of his team's games and led his team with a .327 batting average.[10] He played in 58 of 62 games and led the league's third basemen in chances and assists, and tied for the most putouts. Among all batters he was tied for second in total bases, and his .297 batting average was eighth-best. He was an all-star and won the R. Howard Webster Award as his team's most valuable player.

During his first pro season, Martínez experienced common problems due to unfamiliarity with English. He could speak just a little, and couldn't read any. One day the team bus stopped at a McDonald's, and after the teammate in line ahead of him ordered, Martínez stepped forward and simply said, "Same." He was hoping for a Big Mac or Quarter Pounder. He didn't open his bag until back on the bus and was disappointed to find only a Danish and a carton of milk.[11]

For 1986, Martínez was promoted to Ventura County of the Class-A California League. He was switched from third base to first, which was his predominant position for the rest of his time with US teams. From 1986 through 1990, he was his team's regular first baseman but in each of those five seasons his batting average was modest, always within nine points of .255. What had happened after his exciting debut season? "He ate a lot of junk food and ballooned to 230 pounds," noted Matt Michael of the *Syracuse Post-Standard*. That weight wasn't optimal, even though Martínez was 6-feet-2. Michael also reported that Martínez made frequent telephone calls to Santo Domingo, "seeking encouragement from his parents," but that his mother died in 1985 and his father in 1986. "With his support system shattered, Martinez lacked motivation to lose weight, and he played just well enough to keep the Jays interested," Michael concluded.[12]

For 1987, Martínez remained in Class A except with Dunedin in the Florida State League. He then spent 1988 through 1990 with Knoxville in the Double-A Southern League. Though he couldn't replicate his Gulf Coast League batting average, he did build power and productivity during his Class-A and Double-A years. In 1987 he led Florida State League batters with 32 doubles and topped his team with 65 RBIs. In 1988 he led the Southern League with 14 game-winning RBIs. After the 1990 season, Martínez's third with Knoxville, he was finally promoted to Triple A, after leading his club with 17 homers and 66 RBIs. He was also second in walks with 51.[13] He never played below the Triple-A level in the minors again.

Though Martínez had impressed enough to be the starting first baseman for the Triple-A Syracuse Chiefs, it's quite unlikely anyone considered him a hot prospect. "Nothing in Martinez's past foreshadowed the banner year he would enjoy in 1991," Matt Michael observed. "But never before had Martinez worked with Syracuse trainer Randy Holland, who made slimming Martinez down a pet project."[14] By getting Martínez down by 20 pounds, to 210, so much clicked: He was second in the league in total bases, tied for second with 83 RBIs, had the third-best slugging percentage at .465, tied for third in hits, and finished fourth in pursuit of the batting crown with a .313 average.[15]

In October 1991 Martínez was added to Toronto's 40-man roster, and on February 17, 1992, the Jays signed him to a one-year contract.[16] Then during spring training he had just one hit in 21 at-bats, and on March 23 he was demoted to Syracuse's camp. "It was my first time ever at the major-league camp and I wanted to play so much and I wanted to do everything good," Martínez said. "I put too much pressure on myself."[17]

Martínez played in 116 games with Syracuse. He batted .274 and led the team with 21 homers. Three came from June 22 to 28, along with six RBIs and an average of .322, for which he was named Toronto's minor-league player of the week.[18] He was recalled by the Blue Jays on September 8, after rosters expanded. He didn't ride the bench for long.

Martínez made his major-league debut on September 11, 1992, in the first game of a doubleheader in Texas, against the Rangers. He entered as a defensive substitution in the ninth inning, but had no fielding chances. The Blue Jays won, 7-5. He entered the nightcap in the bottom of the eighth inning with his team trailing. He again didn't touch a live ball, and still didn't get to bat.

Martínez had to wait a full week to play again and bat in the majors for the first time. On September 18, Toronto hosted Texas. The Blue Jays led 10-0 after the top of the sixth inning, so with two outs in the bottom half, Martínez pinch-hit for John Olerud. On a 1-and-1 count from reliever Brian Bohanon, Martínez lined a single to right field. A groundout then ended the inning. His defense for the remainder of the game was fine, and two of his three putouts completed inning-ending double plays. But Martínez saved his biggest splash for the bottom of the eighth. With two outs and a runner on first, he homered on the first pitch from Mike Jeffcoat, deep to right-center. He played in four more games through October 4 but batted in only two. He had hits in both contests, and by going 5-for-8 all told, he concluded his stint with Toronto with a .625 batting average.

Martínez wasn't eligible for the postseason, but was voted a 15 percent share ($18,000) of the team's World Series share. Later, in a vote of confidence by the front office, the club listed him among 15 players who couldn't be selected by the Colorado Rockies or Florida Marlins in the expansion draft.[19]

On March 4, 1993, the Blue Jays signed Martínez to another one-year contract. He was in Toronto's Opening Day lineup, on April 6 in Seattle. He batted sixth and played first base. He went 1-for-4 in an 8-1 loss. He played the next day as a ninth-inning defensive replacement in a 2-0 victory for the visitors. Though Matt Michael said Martínez had delivered "a monster spring training" for the Blue Jays, after a few days of inactivity he was sent back to Syracuse on April 13, reportedly because Toronto wanted him to relearn third base there.[20] That experiment ended quickly. He played just three games at third base for Syracuse, plus two in the outfield, yet logged 121 games at first base. His batting average was almost identical to a year earlier, .273 instead of .274, but he increased his slugging percentage to .488 from .468 and boosted his RBIs to 79 from 62.

As in 1992, Martínez got into a few games with Toronto in September and early October. He played briefly on September 7 and 10, and then waited 18 days for his next opportunity. At Milwaukee on September 28, he played his final full game in the majors, manning first base and batting cleanup. His highlight that night was a long homer in the second inning, off Teddy Higuera. Martínez pinch-hit the next night and drove in two runs with a single. On October 1 he played the final few innings of a game in Baltimore and was in Toronto's final regular-season game of 1993, on October 3. He played from the second inning through the seventh. Martínez went 1-for-3, with a single in the fourth inning. He struck out in his final plate appearance, in the top of the sixth. He didn't have any fielding chances after that, and thus concluded his short but impressive major-league career.

During the first half of March 1994, Steve Milton wrote for *The Sporting News* that Martínez "understandably wants to be traded" because he couldn't conceivably bump either Olerud or designated hitter Paul Molitor from Toronto's lineups often. What's more, "Martinez's chances of making the team as a bat off the bench depend on whether manager Cito Gaston goes with 11 or 10 pitchers," Milton wrote.[21] On March 29, 1994, the Jays traded him to the Chicago White Sox for outfielder Mike Huff.

Martínez might not have been encouraged by his new situation with Chicago. "Domingo Martinez just can't catch a break, wrote Mike Rutsey in the *Financial Post*. "Martinez was dealt to the White Sox yesterday where he'll be able to sit and watch last year's league MVP, Frank Thomas."[22] Predictably, Martínez spent all of 1994 with Chicago's Nashville team in the American Association. He had his fourth consecutive praiseworthy Triple-A season, with 22 homers, 81 RBIs, and a .270 average in 131 games.

Since the players strike ended the major-league season before mid-August, there were no White Sox games in September for which Martínez could have been promoted. Instead, he almost won Nashville the American Association championship series. On September 12 his homer was the only run against Indianapolis to tie the best-of-five series at one win apiece. In the finale two days later, he resisted elimination with a three-run homer in the eighth inning, but Nashville fell short and lost, 7-5.[23]

Martínez became a free agent, and signed with Louisville, the St. Louis Cardinals' affiliate in the American Association. That winter he was the Most Valuable Player of the Dominican League.[24] A hip injury kept him out of some of Louisville's games in late June and early July, but after 64 games his offensive stats hadn't slipped much from recent seasons. He was released on July 11, though the *Louisville Courier-Journal* didn't identify a reason.[25] He then disappeared from newspapers through September, suggesting that his hip injury had become persistent.

By mid-February 1996, Martínez was with the Reynosa Broncos of the Mexican League, which had Triple-A status.[26] He was productive at bat for Reynosa, and managed to be even more so when he joined Triple-A Rochester, a Baltimore affiliate, in early August. In 29 games he had a .362 batting average and a .603 slugging percentage. Those games were the last he played during a regular season in the United States.[27]

Except for part of the 1999 season, when Martínez played with the Mexico City Red Devils in the Mexican League, from 1997 through 2001 he played in Japan. In 1997 and 1998 he was with the Seibu Lions, and from 1999 to 2001 he was with the Yomiuri Giants. In the first four of his five seasons in Japan he hit between 16 and 31 homers and his batting average ranged from .283 to .324.

Early in 1999, Martínez attempted a return to pro ball in the United States. On January 5 he agreed to a minor-league contract with the Pittsburgh Pirates. He was among 20 nonroster invitees to spring training, but on March 11 he was reassigned to Pittsburgh's minor-league camp.[28] He instead switched to Tokyo's Yomiuri club. On a bigger stage little more than a year later, he demonstrated that he still "had it." On March

28, 2000, his two-run homer in a 9-5 game helped the Yomiuri Giants sweep a series from the New York Mets just before the Mets opened the season in Japan against the Chicago Cubs.[29]

During his final season, 2001, Martínez generated as much power as he had in 1998 and 2000 but his average was an uncharacteristic .237, and he played in fewer games than he had during his four other seasons in Japan. In February 2002 Martínez was in camp with the Orioles. "I enjoyed Japan," he said, "but I'm really happy to be back in the United States." But the Orioles made it clear his contract would probably be sold to a Japanese club again. Baltimore released him in mid-March when he wouldn't accept a minor-league assignment. He did have a last hurrah of sorts as a player in April 2003 when he was among more than 50 players named to the Dominican Republic's initial roster for the Pan American Games.[30]

As of early 2022, Martínez was the Caribbean scout for Japan's Chunichi Dragons. He had that role for them back in 2009, if not earlier.[31]

SOURCES

Except where otherwise noted, seasonal highlights through 1992 are from the *Toronto Blue Jays Official Guide 1993* (see Note 7). In general, the source for additional statistics, along with details from Toronto games, is baseball-reference.com.

NOTES

1   Marty York, "Jay Evokes Sympathy for Predicament," *Globe & Mail* (Toronto), May 7, 1993: C9. Thanks to Shelley (surname not provided) of the Toronto Public Library's Answerline Staff for providing the full citation for this article.

2   From https://www.statmuse.com/mlb/, where it is possible to generate a variety of lists of players, ranked, such as the highest batting averages or slugging percentages with a certain minimum number of at-bats or plate appearances with the most.

3   York.

4   The questionnaire was prepared by baseball historian William J. Weiss and is accessible via ancestry.com. See John Maffei, "New Baseball Collection at Central Library," *San Diego Union-Tribune*, February 13, 2014, at https://www.sandiegouniontribune.com/sports/mlb/sdut-baseball-collection-william-weiss-central-library-2014feb13-htmlstory.html. A respected source that identifies his birth year as 1967 is https://www.baseballamerica.com/players/21233/domingo-Martínez/. Martínez's Instagram post on August 4, 2021, shows him holding a birthday cake with the writing "Feliz 56 Domingo" on it.

5   Kathleen O'Brien, "Chat Room," *Fort Worth Star-Telegram*, September 19, 2002: 2D.

6   Tom Leo, "Martinez Makes the Plays, Hopes It Pays," *Syracuse Herald-Journal*, June 30, 1991: C8.

7   *Toronto Blue Jays Official Guide 1993* (Toronto: Dan Diamond and Associates, Inc., 1993), 91. The guide misspelled the names of both schools, as "La Lisabela" and "Gustabo Adolfo Beker." Like the aforementioned questionnaire, it identified his year of birth as 1967.

8   Weiss questionnaire.

9   See https://www.baseball-reference.com/leagues/majors/1984-transactions.shtml at August 23. Tom Leo, in "Martinez Makes the Plays, Hopes It Pays," specified that Martínez was "a non-drafted" signee.

10   "Baldwin's Triple Lifts GCL Astros," *Sarasota* (Florida) *Herald-Tribune*, June 29, 1985: 5C. "GCL Averages," *Sarasota Herald-Tribune*, July 18, 1985: 5C. The Gulf Coast Blue Jays had a record of 5-7 through July 3, according to "GCL Standings," *Bradenton* (Florida) *Herald*, July 4, 1985: D-2. At the time the GCL averages were published, with a lag of about two weeks, Martínez had played in 12 games, according to Peter Giannetti, "Life Below the Chiefs: Looking at the 5 Clubs," *Syracuse Herald-American*, July 21, 1985: D7.

11   Tom Leo, "Playing in America," *Syracuse Herald-Journal*, June 13, 1993: G1.

12   Matt Michael, "Weight Loss Gains Martinez Shot at Big Leagues," *Syracuse Post-Standard*, March 26, 1992: D-1. In fact, he weighed just 185 pounds entering his second pro season, according to "Ventura Gulls: 1986 Roster," *Los Angeles Times*, April 9, 1986: part III, page 10.

13   *Toronto Blue Jays Official Guide 1993*. The 1990 season was the only one in which Martínez was tried as a pitcher. He pitched in three games, and in three innings total. The only run he surrendered was on a homer. Before the 1990 season he played for the Dominican team in the Caribbean World Series, according to "Blue Jays," *The Sporting News*, February 19, 1990: 38. After the 1990 season, he played winter ball in the Dominican, for Escogido, according to the *Toronto Blue Jays Official Guide 1993*.

14   Michael.

15   Michael.

16   "Toronto Blue Jays," *The Sporting News*, October 28, 1991: 24. "Jays 'Last Man' Ward Signs Deal," *Financial Post* (Toronto), February 18, 1992: 39.

17   Michael, D-5.

18   Bill Lankhof, "Bell, Myers Spark Jays' Celebration," *Financial Post*, July 2, 1992: 27.

19   "Jays Divvy Up Loot from World Series," *Whitehorse* (Yukon) *Star*, October 30, 1992: 37. Bob Elliott, "Martinez on List, Morris, Gruber Out in Cold," *Financial Post*, November 10, 1992: 43. To put his World Series share in perspective, his baseball-reference.com entry identifies his salary from Toronto in 1993 as $109,000 and credits *USA Today* as the source.

20   "Sojo Complains of Sore Wrist," *Ottawa* (Ontario) *Citizen*, March 5, 1993: C5. Matt Michael, "Martinez to Try Third," *Syracuse Post-Standard*, April 16, 1993: C5.

21   Steve Milton, "Toronto Blue Jays," *The Sporting News*, March 14, 1994: 20.

22   Mike Rutsey, "Domingo's Curse," *Financial Post*, March 30, 1994: 43.

23   Kim Rogers, "Nashville Knots Series with Tribe," *Indianapolis News*, September 13, 1994: B-1. Jimmy Davy, "Indy Powers Past Sounds to Win Series," *Nashville Tennessean*, September 15, 1994: C1.

24   George Rorrer, "Redbirds Forecast Optimistic," *Louisville Courier-Journal*, February 4, 1995: B2.

25   George Rorrer, "Redbirds Look to Rebound at Home," *Louisville Courier-Journal*, June 27, 1995: D1-2. Mike Grant, "Righetti Stymies Birds on 1-Hitter," *Louisville Courier-Journal*, July 2, 1995: D1, D4. Oddly, Martínez appeared in a Louisville Redbirds box score a week after his release, because it documented the completion of a game suspended on June 11 due to rain. That was explained by Randy Weiler in "Redbirds Complete Rout of Sounds," *Louisville Courier-Journal*, July 18, 1995: D2.

26   Leonardo Andrade, "Broncos Open Preseason Workouts," *McAllen* (Texas) *Monitor*, February 16, 1996: 2B. As of 2022 baseball-reference.com has no stats for Reynosa in 1996, but in late June Martínez had a .299 batting average and led Reynosa with 14 homers and 73 RBIs, according to Roger Pinckney and Roy Hess, *Monitor*, June 30, 1996: 1D, 7D.

27   Martínez signed with Baltimore on August 6, 1996, according to "& Etc.," *Knoxville* (Tennessee) *News-Sentinel*, August 7, 1996: D2.

The Orioles inked him to a minor-league contract on October 12 and assigned him to Rochester, according to "Sports Etc.," *Orange County Register* (Anaheim, California), October 13, 1996: 18. Baltimore purchased his contract from Rochester on November 20, 1996, according to "Transactions," the *Memphis Commercial Appeal,* November 21, 1996: D4, but nothing substantial resulted from that decision.

28 "Transactions," *Syracuse Herald-Journal,* January 6, 1999: C2. "Pittsburgh Pirates," *Burlington* (Vermont) *Free Press,* February 21, 1999: 7C. "Transactions," *Clearfield* (Pennsylvania) *Progress,* March 12, 1999: 11.

29 "Essential Baseball," *National Post,* March 29, 2000: B16. The Cubs, meanwhile, had edged the Seibu Lions, his former team, 6-5.

30 Roch Kubatko, "Facing Long Odds Beats Long Trip for Japan League Vet Martinez," *Baltimore Sun,* February 22, 2002: D3. George Richards, "Red-Hot Orioles Win 7th Straight," *Miami Herald,* March 15, 2002: 9D. "Dominican Names Pan-Am Team," *Lansing* (Michigan) *State Journal,* April 26, 2003: 4C.

31 His Instagram account, @martinezd48, identifies this as his job in early 2022; similarly, see "Chunichi Signs Four out of The Dominican," December 11, 2009, at http://www.npbtracker.com/tag/domingo-martinez/.

JACK MORRIS

By Stew Thornley

With a competitive, sometimes combative, spirit and a devastating split-fingered fastball, Jack Morris became the pitcher of the 1980s and continued his dominance into the early 1990s. His 162 victories in the 1980s were 22 more than runner-up Dave Stieb of Toronto.

Four times he was a member of a world-championship team, including a one-year stint in his home state, pitching a 10-inning shutout in the final game of the 1991 World Series for the Minnesota Twins. He finished his career with more than 250 wins.

John Scott Morris was born May 16, 1955 in St. Paul, Minnesota, and grew up watching the Minnesota Twins at Metropolitan Stadium in suburban Bloomington. He also remembers a television being wheeled into his grade-school classroom so they could watch the 1965 World Series, which the Twins lost in seven games to the Los Angeles Dodgers.

Morris's dad, Arvid, was an electronic technician for Minnesota Mining and Manufacturing (which became 3M), and his mom, Dona, was a housewife. Arvid and Dona now live in Grand Rapids in northern Minnesota, after their son helped Arvid retire early from 3M "thanks to baseball." Morris has an older sister, Marsha, and a younger brother, Tom, a lefthanded pitcher who was a college teammate for one year and later spent two seasons in the minor leagues. (Tom was drafted by the Twins in 1978 but did not sign; he then pitched two years for Quad City in the Cubs organization.)

The family lived in several Twin Cities suburbs as Morris grew up before settling into the Highland Park neighborhood of St. Paul. In addition to baseball, Morris was a ski jumper for the St. Paul ski club when he was in junior high and played on the varsity basketball team for Highland Park High School. On the diamond, Morris was a third baseman and shortstop. With better control than his older brother, Tom was the top pitcher at Highland Park, and Jack's appearances on the mound in high school and on his American Legion team were relatively rare.[1]

"He could throw hard enough to knock down the backstop in high school," said Bill Lorenz, Morris's

baseball coach at Highland Park. "He just couldn't hit the backstop."[2]

However, because of his strong arm, he was recruited by coach Glen Tuckett and given a scholarship to pitch for Brigham Young University (BYU) in Provo, Utah. "When I saw that arm, I lit up like a pinball machine," said BYU athletic director and former baseball coach Glen Tuckett.[3]

Until his senior year, Morris had hoped to pitch for the Minnesota Gophers under longtime coach Dick Siebert. "All through high school that's [Minnesota] where I wanted to play," he said. However, the

Jack Morris tied for the major-league lead with 21 wins for the Blue Jays in 1992.

Gophers did not recruit Morris. In addition, Morris took a closer look at the Gophers' yearly schedules and realized how short it was. The Gophers at that time were making one southern trip a year, and, before the Hubert H. Humphrey Metrodome was built, the team could not start its home schedule until April, leaving barely two months to play.

"I wanted to play for a baseball school where they played in good weather and good teams," Morris explained. He applied and was accepted at Arizona, Arizona State, Florida State, but he would have been a walk-on. Then BYU offered a scholarship. They would play a schedule with Arizona, Arizona State, Cal State Fullerton, Hawaii. "The schedule was phenomenal. I knew I would get exposure. That's why I went there."[4]

Morris lettered with the Cougars in 1975 and 1976. His Brigham Young teammates included his brother (who, unlike Jack, made the team as a freshman) for two years; Cam Killebrew, son of future Hall of Famer Harmon Killebrew; and Vance Law, who went on to the major leagues and later came back to Brigham Young as its head baseball coach. Law's dad, Vernon Law, a 16-year major-league veteran who had won the Cy Young Award in 1960, worked with the Brigham Young pitchers in the 1970s. A 16-year major-league veteran who had won the Cy Young Award in 1960, Law helped transform Morris from a youngster with a strong but erratic arm into an accomplished pitcher who was drafted after his junior season in 1976 in the fifth round by the Detroit Tigers.[5]

Morris was assigned to the Tigers' Class-AA farm team in Montgomery in the Southern League, where he struggled with his control. Morris walked a batter an inning and had a 6.25 earned-run average (ERA) in 36 innings pitched in 1976. Nevertheless, he was promoted to the Triple-A level in 1977.

Pitching for Evansville in the American Association, Morris lowered his walks and upped his strikeouts (both on a per-inning basis) in 20 starts with the Triplets. Morris got the call to the big leagues when the Tigers put Mark Fidrych, who had won 19 games as a rookie in 1976 but had knee and arm problems in 1977, on the disabled list.

Morris made his debut in Chicago July 26, relieving Dave Roberts in the fourth inning with the Tigers behind, 6-2. He inherited a runner at first base with no out but got out of the inning without it scoring. Morris pitched four innings and allowed two runs as the Tigers lost, 8-3. Five days later, he got his first start, pitching against Bert Blyleven in Texas. Morris allowed two runs in the first inning but gave up only

three hits and no runs after that as he pitched nine innings, walking five batters and striking out 11. Both he and Blyleven went nine innings, and neither got a decision as the Rangers won in 10 innings.

Morris stayed in the starting rotation, winning one and losing one over the next month. However, he also had some arm problems. The Tigers, after the situation with Fidrych, had become protective of their young pitchers and, at the end of August, shut Morris down for the season. "He's too good a prospect to fool with," said Tigers manager Ralph Houk.[6]

Morris was back in 1978, but he was again limited by arm problems and finished the year with a won-lost record of 3-5. In 1979, he didn't even make the team out of spring training and was sent back to Evansville. However, he wasn't expected to stay long in the minors. "You better get a good look at him now," said Evansville Manager Jim Leyland, "because he won't be here in a month."[7]

Leyland's prediction was accurate because Morris was back in Detroit, this time for good, making his first start for the Tigers May 13. Despite the delayed arrival with the Tigers, Morris won 17 games and had an ERA of 3.28, fifth-best in the American League.

To this point, Morris had relied on a standard repertoire of a fastball, slider, and change-up. In the early 1980s, he began having some problems with his slider and was on the lookout for a new pitch. "My slider started flattening out. I couldn't get the big break anymore. I was having some inconsistency with my slider, hanging a few too many. I was looking for that 'out' pitch. My fastball was still good, change-up was still good, but I was looking for that 'strike three' pitch."

It was about that time he discovered the forkball, or split-fingered fastball. Although his pitching coach with the Tigers, Roger Craig, is often credited with teaching him the splitter, Morris says the credit belongs to his Tigers teammate, Milt Wilcox. In the Chicago Cubs organization in the mid-1970s, Wilcox had crossed paths with Bruce Sutter, who would make a Hall of Fame career out of the splitter. "He watched Sutter throw it," Morris said of Wilcox. "He [Wilcox] couldn't throw it himself because his fingers were too short." One day Morris was throwing in the bullpen when Wilcox asked if he'd like to try the forkball. "I threw about eight or nine pitches and nothing happened." Morris was ready to give up, but Wilcox suggested some adjustments with the grip and release. "I threw one and the bottom dropped out. I thought, 'I gotta work on this thing because this is ridiculously nasty.' And I threw about six more in a row that all worked the same way. . . . I saw what this thing could do, and I said, 'I've got to master this thing.'"

Morris said he started working on the pitch at the end of the 1982 season and started throwing it regularly in 1983, the first year he won 20 games. "In 1983 and 1984, I pretty much had it to myself in the American League. It was a total gift. It was like nobody knew it was coming. It was awesome. It was so much fun. And then everyone else started trying to learn how to pitch and then hitters started to adjust to it. My forkball was above average. I could almost tell guys it was coming, and they still couldn't hit it. . . . When I threw it right, nobody hit it."[8]

Led by Morris, the Tigers got off to a great start in 1984, winning their first nine games and 16 of their first 17. Morris had four of the team's wins in that opening run. He pitched the season opener in Minnesota, where he had never lost a game in the majors, and won, 8-1.

Four days later, on a cold and wet day in Chicago, Morris was unhittable. After eight innings, the Tigers had a 4-0 lead, and Morris hadn't allowed a hit. As he sat in the dugout in the top of the ninth, his teammates stayed away from him, following the superstitious tradition of not mentioning that a no-hitter was in progress. However, Morris broke the silence and declared, "I'm going to do it." On his way back to the mound, he turned toward a couple hecklers and said, "Just watch."[9]

He retired the first two White Sox batters and went to a 3-2 count on Greg Luzinski. The next pitch was close, but plate umpire Durwood Merrill called it a ball. Even many of the partisan Chicago fans, hoping to see a no-hitter, howled in protest. But Morris got ahead of the next batter, Ron Kittle, then came in with a splitter. The pitch was low, but Kittle bit, trying to hold up but going too far with his swing. Morris had his no-hitter, the first for the Tigers since Jim Bunning had no-hit the Boston Red Sox in 1958.

Morris won 10 of his first 11 decisions in 1984, and, for a time, all was well. However, he missed two starts in June with a sore elbow. He won his first game back but then lost three in a row, dropping his season record to 12-6.

Morris battled with umpires, sometimes blaming them for his problems, as well as with his teammates. He resigned as the team's player representative and quit talking to the press, which had already dubbed him "Mount Morris" for his sometimes explosive temper. Roger Craig publicly said Morris should "quit acting like a baby," and relations with his fellow players weren't much better.[10]

However, as Morris regained his form on the mound, he began talking with the press again and healed other rifts as the Tigers cruised to the American League East title and went on to win the World Series. Morris went the distance and won both his starts in the World Series as the Tigers beat the San Diego Padres, four games to one.

In 1986, Morris posted a 21-8 won-lost record with a 3.27 ERA in 267 innings. His 21 wins were second in the American League, behind Roger Clemens, and he led the league with six shutouts while finishing fifth in the voting for the Cy Young Award. Morris's contract with the Tigers was up after the season, making him one of the top free agents on the market.

Fans in Morris's home state were excited about the possibility of him pitching for the Twins as he came to Minnesota in late 1986 to talk with the team's owner, Carl Pohlad, and new general manager Andy MacPhail. However, Morris left without the parties reaching an agreement on a contract.

Morris and his agent, Dick Moss, had presented four proposals, including one for a two-year contract in which the salary would be determined by an arbitrator. MacPhail later decried the take-it-or-leave-it approach of Moss and Morris, who had also drawn some criticism for his opulent attire that day, a full-length fur coat.[11]

In reality, however, it was unlikely the Twins would have signed Morris, since major-league teams, operating in concert, had adopted a hands-off policy with regard to signing free agents from other teams for the purpose of keeping salaries down. (Arbitrators later determined that teams had conspired against free agents over the course of three off-seasons, and the owners had to agree to establish a $280 million fund to distribute to the players affected by the collusion.)[12]

"No, there was no chance of signing," Morris said of his negotiations with the Twins and the role of collusion. He said he had once been asked if he would ever write a book about his career and added, "If I ever did, it would be about the collusion years in baseball. Nobody has talked about it, it has been pushed under the table. I led the charge in that whole thing, and I understood it better than anyone else. I was the premier pitcher in baseball, and I couldn't get a nickel, couldn't get a penny.

"I had actually almost agreed to terms with Mr. Pohlad when Andy MacPhail stepped out of the room. My agent and I had a few minutes to talk alone with Carl, and Carl pretty much agreed to a contract. Andy came back and excused us and told Carl there was no

When the 1992 Blue Jays were beset by injuries in August, Morris led the way, going 5-1 with a 3.07 ERA.

way he could sign me. That in itself defines what was going on. Andy was on the phone with somebody, and somebody told him, 'Nobody gets signed.' And that's the end of that story."[13]

Morris re-signed with Detroit for the 1987 season and, with a record of 18-11, helped the Tigers win the East Division title with a record of 98-64. However, the Tigers lost in the playoffs to the Minnesota Twins. Morris lost his only start in the series, which was also the first time he had lost in Minnesota as a member of the Tigers. (Morris had been the losing pitcher for the American League in the 1985 All-Star Game at the Metrodome in Minneapolis.)

The Twins went on to win the World Series, and Morris noted that he could have been a member of that championship team if not for collusion. However, he got his chance to pitch for the Twins, and for the championship, a few years later.

In the meantime, he went through a couple of losing seasons. His 1989 season included elbow surgery for a stress fracture, and he finished with a record of 6-14. Despite four straight wins at the end of the year, he finished the 1990 season with a record of 15-18. However, he was second in the American League in

innings pitched (and tied for second in the majors) and demonstrated that he could still be counted on as a workhorse.

He could also still be Mount Morris, at least at times. A noted incident during the 1990 season was Morris's response to Jennifer Frey, a sportswriter intern of the *Detroit Free Press.* Even though Frey was a credentialed member of the Detroit chapter of the Baseball Writers Association of America, Morris did not appreciate her presence in the locker room and let her know it.[14]

Morris later said of the incident, "That was totally blown out of proportion. It was a situation where a woman was not supposed to be in the locker room. She was." [Note: The right of female reporters to have the same access to locker rooms as male reporters had been established in court cases as far back as the late 1970s.[15]]

"I reacted very poorly," Morris acknowledged.[16]

Morris was a free agent again after the 1990 season. With collusion by this time a thing of the past, Morris finally signed with the Minnesota Twins for 1991. He had turned down a three-year contract worth more than $9 million from the Tigers to sign for a guaranteed salary of $3 million a year with the Twins and the chance to earn more based on incentives. The contract he signed also allowed him the option to become a free agent after the end of each season.

Morris was emotional as he talked about how much it meant to sign with his hometown team. He even shed a few tears, an act that would be held against him by many local fans within a year.[17]

For the 1991 season, Morris was outstanding, posting an 18-12 won-lost record while leading the team with 246-2/3 innings pitched. The Twins, after having finished in last place in 1990, won the American League West title. Morris got the call for the opening game of the league playoffs. He won that game, as well as Game Four, and the Twins defeated the Toronto Blue Jays, four games to one, to advance to the World Series. Their opponents would be the Atlanta Braves, another team that had finished last the season before.

Morris won the series opener against the Braves, and did not get a decision in Game Four, which the Twins lost. The series went to a decisive seventh game, and Morris was on the mound again with John Smoltz pitching for Atlanta.

The aces matched shutout innings over the first half of the game, but Morris found himself in a jam in the fifth as the Braves put runners at first and third with one out. But Morris used his split-fingered fastball to get Terry Pendleton to pop out and then went to a full count on Ron Gant. Morris placed a fastball right where he wanted it, on the low-outside corner, freezing Gant with a called third strike to end the inning.

The game remained scoreless into the eighth, when the Braves mounted an even greater threat, putting runners at second and third with no out.

While Twins fans were sweating, Morris later said he was still calm. "I never had a negative thought," he maintained. "I'm such a positive thinker, I never really felt like I was in trouble. It was my will that carried me through the game."[18]

Morris needed every bit of his will, as well as his nasty splitter, as Gant stepped to the plate. Gant had stranded a pair of runners in each of his previous two at-bats, although this time, with no out, even an out could bring in a run. Minnesota responded by pulling in its infield. Gant popped the first pitch foul, then went after a splitter on the outside part of the plate, resulting in a feeble grounder down the first-base line. First-baseman Kent Hrbek fielded it and kept his eyes on Lonnie Smith, making sure he held at third, as he tagged Gant for the first out.

Getting Gant was the key to the inning as it now allowed the Twins to walk the dangerous David Justice to load the bases, set up a double-play, and bring Sid Bream to the plate. Bream pulled a 1-and-2 pitch to Hrbek, who fired home to start an inning-ending first-to-home-to-first double play.

Past the jam, Morris appeared stronger, putting down the Braves in order on eight pitches in the ninth. Manager Tom Kelly planned to send reliever Rick Aguilera out for the 10th inning, figuring Morris, with 118 pitches to that point, had had enough. But Morris told Kelly, "I'm not going anywhere. This is my game."[19]

Morris later said that, after getting out of the eighth inning, "I was getting stronger. I just felt like I could have gone another six, seven, eight more innings. I was getting stronger as the game went on."

Morris retired the Braves on eight pitches again in the 10th inning. In the bottom of the inning, the Twins finally scored to win the game, 1-0, and the World Series.

"I probably had the best mindset in that game that I've had in any game in my whole career, and that's because I didn't allow negative thoughts into my game," Morris said. "Even when I was in trouble, I didn't acknowledge trouble. I just said, 'Well, I'll get this next guy. We're going to win this game.' If I could bottle that, I'd be the richest man in the world.

If I could bottle it and sell it to athletes or sell it to businessmen or whatever, it would be a phenomenal thing. I can't hardly even describe it, but I can tell you it was something I had never experienced before and really never experienced again."[20]

Minnesota fans celebrated their second world championship in five seasons, but the man largely responsible for the title would not be back with the Twins. He exercised his option to become a free agent after the season and signed with the Toronto Blue Jays. Reaction from Minnesota media members and fans was sharp, and his tearful press conference when he had signed with the Twins less than a year before was held against him by many.[21]

Morris said the difference in contract offers by the Twins to retain him and the Blue Jays to acquire him "wasn't close." Morris said Carl Pohlad made it clear that the team was looking ahead to re-signing the team's star, Kirby Puckett, after the 1992 season and were conserving money for that purpose.

"I never wanted to leave here," Morris said. "I never wanted to leave Detroit [after the 1990 season]. Had Detroit taken care of me the way I felt I should have been taken care of in Detroit, I never would have left Detroit."[22]

In Toronto, Morris played on two more world championship teams. He was 21-6 in 1992, but arm troubles hampered his 1993 season. He didn't pitch in the World Series that year, and the Blue Jays released him at the end of the season. Morris signed with the Cleveland Indians for 1994 and had a 10-6 record before a players' strike ended the season.

Morris tried but failed to catch on with the Cincinnati Reds in 1995. Confident he could still pitch, Morris made a comeback in 1996 with the St. Paul Saints, a local team playing in an independent professional league. "The Twins needed pitching bad, and I wanted to come back and maybe finish my career right here again," said Morris. "But they didn't come across the street to even look at me. I guess they were still mad that I left. I don't know what happened there.

One of Morris's teammates on the Saints was another player looking to make it back to the majors, Darryl Strawberry, who ended up being signed off the St. Paul roster by the New York Yankees. "I had a chance to go to New York with Strawberry, and at the time I didn't want to play for the Yankees," Morris said. I regret that today. If I had one thing to go back and do again, I would have signed with the Yankees and probably put two or three more [championship] rings on my finger."[23]

Morris is now back with the Minnesota Twins organization, working as an analyst on the team's radio broadcasts. He and his wife, Jennifer, have a son, Miles. Morris also has two grown children, Austin and Erik, from a previous marriage.

"Life is good," he says. "I'm a very lucky person. I have my health, I have a very loving family and an organization I'm very happy to be working for. If there was any animosity between us [Morris and the Twins] for leaving . . . all those bridges have been mended, and I'm very happy to be here, and I think they're very happy to have me here, and I think it's a good relationship."[24]

SOURCES

A number of sources for basic statistical information were used, including *The Baseball Encyclopedia,* Tenth Edition, (New York: Macmillan Publishing Company, 1996), *Total Baseball,* Sixth Edition, edited by John Thorn, Pete Palmer, Michael Gershman, and David Pietrusza with Matthew Silverman and Sean Lahman (Kingston, New York: Total Sports, 1999) as well as from http://www. baseball-reference.com and annual guides published by *The Sporting News.*

Another source was Retrosheet with play-by-play being available from its web site (http://retrosheet.org) or directly from Retrosheet founder Dave Smith. The information used was obtained free of charge and is copyrighted by Retrosheet. Interested parties may contact Retrosheet at 20 Sunset Road, Newark, Delaware 19711.

NOTES

1   Interview with Jack Morris, Minneapolis, May 27, 2007.

2   Dennis Brackin. "Morris Good Pitcher, Better Competitor," *Minneapolis Star and Tribune,* May 24, 1987: 10C.

3   Brackin.

4   Interview, May 27, 2007.

5   Interview, May 27, 2007. Statistics and materials provided by the Athletic Communications Department of Brigham Young University, Provo, Utah.

6   "Tito, at 33, Truly a Tiger on Triples," Jim Hawkins, *The Sporting News,* October 1, 1977: 11.

7   "Momentary Morris," *The Sporting News,* May 12, 1979, p. 37.

8   Interview, May 27, 2007.

9   Interview, May 27, 2007; Tom Gage, "Morris' Masterpiece Silences White Sox," *The Sporting News,* April 16, 1984, p. 25.

10   "Sour Morris Buttons Lip" by Tom Gage, *The Sporting News,* August 6, 1984: 14; "Morris Finally Unbuttons Lip" by Tom Gage, *The Sporting News,* September 17, 1984: 12.

11   Howard Sinker, "Twins to Morris: Hit the Road, Jack," *Minneapolis Star and Tribune,* December 17, 1986: 1D.

12   1987 Speech by Andy MacPhail to the St. Paul Old Timers' Hot Stove League Banquet, January 28, 1987.

13   Interview, May 27, 2007.

14   "Women Not Welcome," *Sports Illustrated,* August 20, 1990: 15.

15   Email correspondence with Jennifer Frey, May 2007; Court case allowing women access to locker rooms: Melissa Ludtke and Time, Inc., Plaintiffs, v. Bowie Kuhn, Commissioner of Baseball, United States District Court, Southern District of New York, 461 F. Supp. 86, September 25, 1978; Ralph Ray, "Women Writers Win Access to Yank Clubhouse," *The Sporting News,* October 14, 1978: 36.

16   Interviews with Jack Morris, May 27 and June 10, 2007.

17   Dennis Brackin, "Comin' at Ya: Winning Is Everything for Ultra-competitive Morris," *Minneapolis Star and Tribune,* February 6, 1991: 1C.

18   Interview with Jack Morris, July 11, 2002 in Milwaukee following Major League Baseball's press conference to name the most memorable moments in history of the game.

19   Interview, May 27, 2007.

20   Interview, May 27, 2007.

21   Jon Roe, "Money Talks, Morris Walks: Toronto's $10 Million Offer Lands Righthander," *Minneapolis Star and Tribune,* December 19, 1991: 1C.

22   Interview, May 27, 2007.

23   Interview, May 27, 2007.

24   Interview, May 27, 2007.

RANCE MULLINIKS

By Paul Hofmann

Rance Mulliniks was a slightly built 6-foot, 160-pound left-handed-hitting infielder who played 16 major-league seasons with the California Angels, Kansas City Royals, and Toronto Blue Jays that culminated with a 1992 World Series championship for Toronto. The mustached and later glasses-wearing infielder from Central California developed into an excellent fielding third baseman who was also known for his keen batting eye, high on-base percentage, and clutch hitting.

Steven Rance Mulliniks was born on January 15, 1956, in Tulare, California, and grew up in nearby Woodville, a community of about 1,700 residents. He was one of three children of Harvey and Ganell Mulliniks. Harvey was a US Army veteran of the Korean War, serving from 1953 to 1955. He managed a finance company in Tulare for several years, and then was a real estate appraiser for the Tulare County Assessor's Office for 26 years before retiring in 1994.[1]

Harvey was a fine baseball player himself. He won the Giants Baseball Player of the Year Award at Sequoia College in 1956 and pitched two years with the Modesto Reds, a New York Yankees farm team in the Class-C California League. He finished his minor-league baseball career with a record of 0-2. Harvey undoubtedly passed along his love and passion for the game to Rance.

Rance was swinging a bat from the age of 3 and started playing organized baseball at the age of 7.[2] He played in the area's Little League, Babe Ruth, and Connie Mack leagues.[3] He remembered spending hours at the Little League field, where his father would throw batting practice to him, "working towards the goal of one day becoming a Major League baseball player."[4] Like many boys who grew up in California's Central Valley, his favorite team was the San Francisco Giants. His favorite player was Willie Mays.[5]

While baseball was his passion, Rance developed other interests off the diamond. He enjoyed hunting, fishing, reading, and playing all sports. An all-around athlete, Mulliniks earned varsity letters in baseball, football, and basketball at Monache High School in Porterville.[6] He was a standout performer in both basketball and baseball. In basketball he was a member of the East Yosemite League championship team his sophomore year. During his senior year he scored 628 points and averaged 24.2 points per game, which is believed to still be a single-season school record. He was the first boys player at Monache to score over 1,000 points and finished his high-school career with over 1,200 points. He was All-League his junior and senior years and league MVP his senior year.[7]

In baseball, Mulliniks was a member of two East Yosemite League championship teams and earned All-League honors in his sophomore, junior, and senior years.

Mulliniks graduated from MHS in 1974 and was a member of the inaugural class of athletes and coaches

Rance Mulliniks with his signature mustache and glasses.

inducted into the school's Athletic Hall of Fame in 2017.[8]

Mulliniks was drafted by the California Angels in the third round of the 1974 amateur draft. He was signed by Angels scout Satoshi "Fibber" Hirayama[9] for $32,500.[10] Mulliniks had earned full-ride scholarships in baseball to USC, Arizona State, and University of Arizona and in basketball to Pepperdine, Loyola Marymount, and Gonzaga.[11] However, he thought the signing bonus was enough that he could pursue his education later if baseball didn't work out.

He began his professional career with Idaho Falls of the Rookie-level Pioneer League. In 66 games with the Angels, Mulliniks hit .218 with 24 RBIs and 14 stolen bases. Reflecting back on his first professional season, Mulliniks commented on how homesick he felt. "I had never been away from home and that two and-a-half months seemed like an eternity," he said.[12]

Mulliniks started the 1975 season with the Quad City Angels of the low Class-A Midwest League. He was batting .269 with one home run and 21 RBIs when he was promoted to Salinas of the Class-A California League. In 59 games with the Packers, Mulliniks hit .258 with 10 RBIs.

Mulliniks continued to quickly progress through the Angels' minor-league system and played in 1976 with the El Paso Diablos of the Double-A Texas League. It was a breakout season of sorts for the 20-year-old shortstop. Despite missing the final six weeks of the season with a fractured left thumb, Mulliniks hit .315, eighth highest in the circuit, and was named to the Texas League all-star team.

Recovered from the broken thumb that sidelined him at the end of the previous season, Mulliniks started the 1977 season with the Salt Lake City Gulls of the Triple-A Pacific Coast League and picked up where he left off. He was hitting .309 with a team-leading 11 home runs and 51 RBIs at the time of his call-up on June 14. Looking back on hearing the news that he was going to join the Angels, Mulliniks said, "Suffice to say, I didn't get much sleep that night because I was so excited. … I remember thinking to myself, when I walked to the clubhouse for the first time and put that major league uniform on for the first time, no matter what happens from this point on I can at least always say I did play in the big leagues and that would be a childhood dream come true."[13]

Mulliniks made his major-league debut on June 18, 1977, against the Milwaukee Brewers in Milwaukee's County Stadium. He pinch-hit for second baseman Orlando Ramirez in the top of the seventh and grounded out to third. Mulliniks remained in the game and played shortstop. In the bottom of the seventh, Robin Yount, Don Money, and Sixto Lezcano all grounded out to short. In his second at-bat, Mulliniks drew a walk off rookie right-hander Sam Hinds.

Mulliniks collected his first major-league hit five days later at Comiskey Park in Chicago. In the top of the second inning, he lined a single to center off White Sox right-hander Francisco Barrios.

His first major-league home run came on July 4 at Anaheim Stadium. With the Angels leading the Oakland Athletics 2-1 in the bottom of the fourth, Mulliniks came to the plate with one on and no outs. Facing A's right-hander Rick Langford, Mulliniks homered to deep right field, scoring Dave Chalk ahead of him. The Angels went on to win the game, 4-2.

Mulliniks finished his rookie year with every reason to feel optimistic about the future. Serving as the Angels' regular shortstop for the second half of the season, he played in 78 games and hit .269 with 3 home runs and 21 RBIs.

Hampered by a bad back and a slow start at the plate, Mulliniks split time between the Angels and Triple A in 1978. He hit just .185 in 50 games with the Angels. In 34 games at Salt Lake City, he hit .307 with 3 home runs and 21 RBIs.

He started 1979 with the Angels, but once again struggled at the plate and was optioned to Salt Lake City. He was hitting just .148 when he was sent down. He played the balance of the Triple-A season with the Gulls, attempting to play himself back to where he was prior to the back injury. In 116 games with the Gulls, he hit .343 with 3 home runs, 59 RBIs, 21 stolen bases, and a .924 OPS. He was named to the Pacific Coast League and National Association Triple-A all-star teams.

He received a September call-up to the Angels but played in only three more games, going 1-for-7 to finish the season with a .147 average. Although he was only 23 years old, it was clear that the Angels questioned whether he would be able to hit at the major-league level.

On December 6, 1979, Mulliniks was traded, along with Willie Aikens, to the Kansas City Royals for Al Cowens, Todd Cruz, and Craig Eaton. He was excited about the opportunity to join the Royals, a veteran team coming off a second-place finish in the AL West after winning three consecutive Western Division titles from 1976 to '78. However, with Frank White at second base and U L Washington at shortstop,

Mulliniks was limited to a middle-infield utilityman role with the Royals.

Mulliniks played in only 36 games for the 1980 American League champion Royals. In 62 plate appearances, he hit .259 with 6 RBIs. He was left off the American League Championship Series and World Series rosters.

The strike-shortened 1981 season brought even less playing time for Mulliniks. In 24 games he hit .227 with 5 RBIs. Again he was left off the playoff roster when the Royals met the Oakland Athletics in the divisional round of the playoffs.

While he didn't play enough to develop as a player, Mulliniks said, he learned a lot about baseball during his time with the Royals. Hal McRae, the Royals' DH, had a lasting impact on the young Mulliniks. "I learned a lot about how to play from Hal McRae," he said.[14]

In the spring of 1982, it was clear to Mulliniks that he wouldn't have a chance to consistently play in Kansas City in a way to "have a chance to have a career at the major-league level."[15] Accordingly, he let the Royals know that he would be open to a trade if there was any way to move him.

On March 25 Mulliniks was traded to the Toronto Blue Jays for Phil Huffman. The right-handed Huffman, who lost 18 games for the Blue Jays in 1979, pitched at the Double-A and Triple-A level in the Royals farm system before being released a year later. Mulliniks, on the other hand, was about to embark on an 11-year career with the Blue Jays that culminated in a World Series title and being named to the all-time Blue Jays team in 2001.

Mulliniks joined a Blue Jays team that was in transition from the lowly club that occupied the AL East cellar to a team with a nucleus that was poised to begin contending. It was also a year of transition for Mulliniks. The Blue Jays didn't have an obvious choice to play third base, so manager Bobby Cox took the left-handed-hitting Mulliniks and right-handed-hitting backup second baseman Garth Iorg and turned them into a long-term, cost-effective platoon at third base.[16] In 112 games, Mulliniks hit .244 with 4 home runs and 35 RBIs.

The chance to play consistently sat well with Mulliniks. By 1983 he was seeing more time at third base and was a reliable left-handed bat off the bench. He played in a career-high 129 games (equaled in 1985), hit 10 home runs and drove in 49 runs while hitting .275. He also hit a team-leading 34 doubles, finished second among AL third basemen in fielding percentage (.971), collected 10 pinch hits and led all

AL pinch-hitters in slugging percentage (.652) and on-base percentage (.591).

Mulliniks continued to improve at the plate in 1984. In 125 games, he hit a career-high .324 with 3 home runs and 42 RBIs. He was particularly hot in the month of July, hitting .426. He cooled off very little in August, hitting .367, and collected eight consecutive hits and reached base safely 10 times in a row in a four-game series against the Minnesota Twins in late August. He led all AL third basemen with a .968 fielding percentage.

There was a great deal of optimism surrounding the Blue Jays as they entered the 1985 season. After winning 89 games and finishing in second place the year before, the team was poised to contend for the AL East title. Once again, Mulliniks was a steady presence at third base and proved to be a clutch performer off the bench. On April 14 he had the only four-hit game of his career, against the Baltimore Orioles at Memorial Stadium. On June 12, pinch-hitting for Iorg, he led off the top of the 10th inning with a tiebreaking home run off the Yankees' Rich Bordi at Yankee Stadium. Although it was only June, the home run played a significant role in the AL East pennant race. When the season was finished, the Blue Jays were 99-62, two games ahead of the second-place Yankees. Mulliniks finished the year hitting .295 with 10 home runs and a career-high 57 RBIs while leading all AL third basemen with a .971 fielding percentage.

As a testament to his off-the-field contributions and calming presence in the clubhouse, Mulliniks was the winner of the 1985 "Good Guy" Award given by Toronto's chapter of the Baseball Writers Association of America. He is credited with having mentored John Olerud and Jeff Kent as they came up through the Blue Jays system.

Mulliniks performed well in the 1985 American League Championship Series. He went 4-for-11 with a Game Three home run off Bret Saberhagen and two RBIs. Mulliniks pointed to Game Three as the one game the Blue Jays should have won and the game that ultimately came back to haunt them. Leading the series two games to none, the Jays scored five runs in the top of the fifth, fueled by Mulliniks' two-run homer, to take a 5-2 lead. The team appeared to be in a position to take a three-game lead in the series but the Blue Jays failed to hold the lead and, despite going up three games to one, lost the series. Had the Blue Jays won the series, Mulliniks certainly would have been in the conversation for the Championship Series MVP.

The left-handed hitting Mulliniks was known for his keen batting eye, high on-base percentage, and clutch hitting.

The 1986 season was the last for the Mulliniks-Iorg platoon. Mulliniks had an off year by the previous season's standards, partially due to a compressed nerve in his lower back that landed him on the disabled list for much of August. For the third consecutive year, he led AL third basemen in fielding percentage (.975). While his batting average dipped to .259, he hit 11 home runs (a career high to that point).

Not known for his power, Mulliniks had three multiple-home-run games in his career. The first was on July 3, 1986. In an 8-5 Jays victory over the Red Sox at Fenway Park, he hit a two-run homer to right field off Dennis "Oil Can" Boyd in the fifth and added a solo shot off Mike Brown in the seventh. He finished the game 3-for-4 with 4 RBIs.

He repeated the feat twice in 1987. On June 24 he took Tigers ace Jack Morris deep twice at Tiger Stadium to lead the Jays over Detroit, 5-3. On September 14 he hit home runs off left-hander Eric Bell and right-hander Ken Dixon in the Blue Jays' 18-3 drubbing of the Baltimore Orioles at Exhibition Stadium. The game was notable on three fronts: The Blue Jays hit 10 home runs off Orioles pitchers, Jays catcher Ernie Whitt hit three home runs, and Orioles manager Cal Ripken Sr. replaced Cal Ripken Jr. at

shortstop in the eighth inning, ending Junior's streak of consecutive innings played at 8,264.[17]

Mulliniks had a bounce-back year in 1987. He started the season as the team's designated hitter against right-handed pitchers. However, he found increasingly more playing time at third as Kelly Gruber went through the growing pains of becoming an everyday major-league third baseman. Mulliniks hit .310, in part due to a two-month stretch at the end of the season in which he hit .352 (51-for-145). He also matched his 11 home runs from the year before and drove in 44 runs during the first year he wore eyeglasses.[18]

The end of the 1987 season was the most heartbreaking in Mulliniks's baseball career. The Blue Jays were leading the AL East by 3½ games with just seven to play. The Jays ended the season with seven consecutive losses and finished second, two games behind the Tigers. "That was definitely a season that we should have gone to the postseason. We had a great club," Mulliniks lamented.[19]

In 1988 Gruber took over the third-base job full time, and Mulliniks platooned as DH with Cecil Fielder. Being the left-handed hitter in the platoon meant Mulliniks had the majority of the at-bats. He had perhaps the best offensive season of his career, hitting .300 and setting career highs with 12 homers and an OPS+ of 143.[20] He drove in 48 runs. However, the Blue Jays failed to recover from the late-season collapse of a year earlier and finished tied for third in a tightly contested AL East pennant race.[21]

Mulliniks saw his offensive production drop off in 1989 as the Blue Jays returned to the top of the AL East. Now 33 years old, Mulliniks finished the year with a .238 average, 3 home runs, and 29 RBIs. The personal highlight of his season came on May 2 when he hit his only career grand slam, off Oakland's Bob Welch in the bottom of the first at Exhibition Stadium in Toronto.

The Blue Jays faced the Oakland A's in the 1989 ALCS. Mulliniks made only one appearance in the series, a Game Four ninth-inning pinch-hitting assignment. He was struck out by A's closer Dennis Eckersley. Looking back on the A's five-game series victory, Mulliniks said, "That year I thought the Oakland A's were the best team in baseball. ... We lost to a better team that year."[22]

In 1990 his role on the team changed again. He became a pinch-hitter. Mulliniks went 8-for-22 (.364) with 7 RBIs as the team's left-handed bat off the bench. In 120 plate appearances over 57 games, Mulliniks hit .289 with 2 home runs and 16 RBIs.

In 1991 Mulliniks was back in the DH platoon role, this time with Pat Tabler. In 97 games he batted .250 with 2 home runs and 24 RBIs to help the Blue Jays win their third AL East Division title since 1985.

The Blue Jays faced the Minnesota Twins in the 1991 ALCS. Mulliniks played in all five games, going 1-for-8 with three walks. Once again, the Blue Jays came up short as the Twins won the series four games to one.

Early in spring training of 1992, Mulliniks had made the decision that it would be his last year. Struggling with the same back problem he had in 1978, he spent nearly the entire season on the disabled list. He had an eight-game rehabilitation stint with the Knoxville Blue Jays of the Double-A Southern League. Rejoining the Blue Jays in September, he made three pinch-hitting appearances, going 1-for-2. He was left off the roster for the ALCS but was added to the Jays' 25-man World Series roster. He did not play in the World Series, but in looking back, Mulliniks stated, "When I reflect back I think about how fortunate I was to have been a member of a world championship team."[23]

The end of the World Series brought an end to Mulliniks's 16-year playing career. He compiled a .272 batting average over 3,569 at-bats in 1,325 games, with 445 runs, 972 hits, 226 doubles, 17 triples, 73 home runs, 435 RBIs, and 460 walks. However, one needs to go beyond the numbers to truly appreciate Mulliniks's career. He was a member of five division-winning teams, two American League champions, and one World Series champion. He was also a clutch performer, holding the Blue Jays' record for career pinch hits (58) and a .287 career batting average with runners in scoring position.

After retiring as a player, Mulliniks has stayed active in the game. He coached at the professional level with the South Bend Silver Hawks (1996), Birmingham Barons (1997), and as a hitting instructor with the San Francisco Giants and Chicago White Sox. He later worked in the Canadian Broadcast Corporation's broadcast booth doing color commentary for the Blue Jays from 2006 to 2010. He opened the Mulliniks Baseball School in Visalia, California, and he participates in baseball camps run by the Blue Jays. Like his father, he has also had a career in the real estate industry. Mulliniks is a licensed real estate agent for Century 21 in Visalia.

Mulliniks has been married twice. He shares five children with his current spouse, Lori. The couple are also proud grandparents.

SOURCES AND ACKNOWLEDGMENT

In addition to the sources cited in the Notes, the author also relied on Baseball-Reference.com and Retrosheet.org.

A special acknowledgment goes to SABR member Mal Allen, who provided valuable research materials.

NOTES

1   Obituaries: Harvey Mulliniks. Retrieved from http://www.recorderonline.com/obituaries/article_eb05c02f-e4b2-5a77-88de-c40f51a6d160.html?msclkid=dc2bce6dafb311ecbd4496a06939a552.

2   Monache High School: 2017 Hall of Fame. Retrieved from onache.portervilleschools.org/apps/pages/index.jsp?u-REC_ID=283895&type=d&pREC_ID=1318231.

3   Player questionnaire completed for William J. Weiss, August 20, 1974. SABR, San Diego, California; *U.S. Baseball Questionnaires, 1945-2005*; Box Number: 555697.

4   "Clubhouse Conversation: Rance Mulliniks." Retrieved from clubhouseconversation.com/2015/11/rance-mulliniks/.

5   "Clubhouse Conversation: Rance Mulliniks."

6   Weiss questionnaire.

7   "MHS graduate Mulliniks Became a World Series Champion," *Porterville* (California) *Reporter*, March 10, 2017. Retrieved from http://www.recorderonline.com/sports/mhs-graduate-mulliniks-became-a-world-series-champion/article_5d272d06-0555-11e7-8a3a-cf231e06087b.html?msclkid=78355d9cb0b011ec9551fc992f7ee94e.

8   "MHS Graduate Mulliniks Became a World Series Champion."

9   Hiroyama is considered the best pound-for-pound wrestler in Fresno State history. After graduation he played one season with the Stockton Ports of the California League and later embarked on a 10-year baseball career in Japan for the Hiroshima Carp before returning to work as a school administrator in California's Central Valley.

10 Weiss questionnaire.

11 "MHS Graduate Mulliniks became a World Series Champion."

12 "Clubhouse Conversation: Rance Mulliniks."

13 "Clubhouse Conversation: Rance Mulliniks."

14 "Clubhouse Conversation: Rance Mulliniks."

15 "Clubhouse Conversation: Rance Mulliniks."

16 Tom Dakers, "Top 60 All-Time Blue Jays: #28 Rance Mulliniks," bluebirdbanter.com, February 25, 2021. Retrieved from http://www.bluebirdbanter.com/2021/2/25/22300397/top-60-all-time-blue-jays-29-rance-mulliniks?msclkid=62548866b0fd11ec961c4c3109e741b5.

17 Trent McCotter, "Ripken's Record for Consecutive Innings Played," *Baseball Research Journal* (SABR), Fall 2012, Volume 41 (2): 7-9.

18 *Toronto Blue Jays Official Guide 1992*, 96.

19 "Clubhouse Conversation: Rance Mulliniks."

20 Tom Dakers.

21 Five teams finished within 3½ games of each other, and the Red Sox won the division by one game over the Detroit Tigers.

22 "Clubhouse Conversation: Rance Mulliniks."

23 "Clubhouse Conversation: Rance Mulliniks."

GREG MYERS

By Bob Webster

Early in his career, just after the movie *Bull Durham* was released, Greg Myers was given the nickname "Crash" by fellow teammates after Kevin Costner's "Crash Davis" character in the movie. Little did they know at the time that Myers was going to have an 18-year major-league career that included 13 trips to the disabled list, mostly from plays at the plate when he was catching.

Gregory Richard Myers was born on April 14, 1966, in Riverside, California, to Dennis and Stephanie Myers. His father was a police officer who went on to law school, became a lawyer, and then a judge. His father also played a season as an outfielder in the Dodgers organization in Artesia, New Mexico. He has two older brothers, John and David, and a younger sister, Deanna.

Myers played at every level of youth baseball while growing up. He had a growth spurt during his sophomore year of high school and since he was fully grown, his high-school coach at Riverside Polytechnic High School, Rich Graves, appointed him a catcher.[1] Before graduating from high school in 1984, Myers was named All-Conference three times and led his team to a conference championship in 1982. Myers was scouted extensively by Larry Maxie and Wayne Morgan. In the June 1984 Amateur Draft, he was the Blue Jays' third-round pick.

Myers' brother David, one year older than Greg, was good at many sports, but really loved basketball. David played basketball at Riverside Polytechnic and was on a really good team. This team had been together for many years with David at one guard position and future NBA Hall of Famer Reggie Miller at the other guard spot. After seeing this basketball talent while growing up, Greg decided to focus on baseball.[2]

After signing a contract, Myers reported to the Medicine Hat Blue Jays of the Rookie-level Pioneer League, where he played in 38 games, batting .316. His next stop, in 1985, was to the Low-A Florence Blue Jays, where the 19-year-old played in 134 games. In 1986 it was on to the High-A Ventura County Gulls, batting .295 with 20 home runs and 79 RBIs in 124 games.

The Syracuse Chiefs of the Triple-A International League were the 21-year-old's team for 1987. In 107 games, Myers hit .246 with 10 home runs and 47 RBIs. He was called up to Toronto and made his major-league debut on September 12, 1987. Myers made seven appearances behind the plate, starting two games, to get his feet wet and began an 18-year major-league career. On Friday, October 2, he started at catcher and in his first major-league at-bat he singled in front of a crowd of 45,167 at Tiger Stadium and scored on a home run by Manny Lee off Doyle Alexander in the second inning.[3]

After starting the 1988 season in Syracuse, Myers tore his rotator cuff and played in only 34 games.[4] He hit .283 with 7 home runs and 21 RBIs in 128 plate appearances.

Myers started the 1989 season at Double-A Knoxville and his contract was purchased by Toronto on July 2. He appeared in 14 games before being optioned to Syracuse on August 2. On July 30 against the Yankees, Myers got his first major-league RBI. Lloyd Moseby tripled in the second inning and scored when Myers grounded out to second. Ernie Whitt was the Blue Jays catcher throughout the late '70s and all through the '80s along with Pat Borders in 1988 and 1989. Whitt was traded to the Atlanta Braves after the 1989 season, making room for Myers to get more major-league playing time.

On April 20, 1990, Myers hit his first major-league home run. After Fred McGriff opened the Blue Jays' sixth with a walk and John Olerud singled, Myers sent a deep drive into the seats in right-center field of Toronto's SkyDome, giving the Blue Jays a 15-4 lead, while raising his batting average for the season to .286. Myers had to leave the game against the Tigers on May 4, after a collision with Detroit's Lou Whitaker at home plate. He was placed on the 15-day disabled list with a small separation and bruised shoulder.[5] Back in action, Myers went 9-for-14 in a three-game period from June 9 to 12 against Milwaukee and Minnesota. He finished the season with a .236 batting average with 5 home runs and 22 RBIs in 87 games.

In his second full season with the Blue Jays, 1991, Myers' bat really started to come around. After a good start, his average dipped as low as .250 on June 12, but after a couple of good weeks, he was batting .291 by June 27 and finished the season with a .262 batting average with 8 home runs and 36 RBIs. The 25-year-old Myers played in 107 games that season, splitting time behind the plate with Borders. Myers was on the postseason roster but did not play in the ALCS against Minnesota.

Myers was a backup to Borders in 1992, appearing in 22 games and batting .230. On July 30, the trade deadline, he was sent to the California Angels with outfielder Rob Ducey for Mark Eichhorn, just hours after Eichhorn picked up the win for the Angels with a hitless inning in relief.[6] Myers appeared in eight games with the Angels before suffering a chip fracture in his right hand on August 26 against the Orioles.

In a phone interview, Myers said he was afraid to throw the ball to second with 100 percent effort after the rotator cuff tear in 1988, which is why the Blue Jays traded him in 1992. "Angels' coach Ken Macha told me that I have to start throwing hard to second to remain in the game," said Myers. "I threw hard and it felt good, so I continued to throw hard and never had any problems with it."[7]

The 27-year-old Myers handled most of the catching duties for the Angels in 1993, appearing in 108 games. Myers hit .255 for the season, with 7 homers and 40 RBIs. On September 17 against the Texas Rangers, he became Nolan Ryan's final career strikeout victim. During the offseason, he was flown to the Hard Rock Café in Houston to celebrate the future Hall of Famer's career, along with Ryan's first strikeout victim, Pat Jarvis. "My claim to fame," Myers said.[8]

On April 23, 18 games into the 1994 season with the Angels, Myers was involved in a collision at the plate with the Red Sox' Mike Greenwell. Myers suffered a torn cartilage in his left knee that kept him out of action until June 21. Mo Vaughn hit a fly ball to center fielder Chad Curtis. Greenwell tagged up from third, Curtis threw the ball home and the ball and Greenwell arrived at the plate at the same time. Greenwell lowered his shoulder and caught Myers in the face. Myers was knocked unconscious and when he came to, he noticed his knee injury. "I remember my neck snapping back and ringing in my head," Myers said, "but when I came to, that's when I felt my knee. It wasn't moving."[9] It was a tough day for the Angels, especially for the catchers. Mick Billmeyer, the Angels bullpen catcher, was warming up pitcher John Dopson. Billmeyer was expecting a slider, but instead, a fastball caught him on the left arm and shattered a bone.[10] For Myers, after missing two months with his knee injury, the season came to an end when the players went on strike on August 12. Myers said, "I've already had my two months off, I'd like to keep playing. I don't want to miss any more than I have to."[11]

Injuries plagued Myers in 1995. He started the season on the disabled list with a fractured right big toe, was back on the disabled list with a strained left quadriceps from June 5 to 21, and again on September 30 with a strained left rib cage. Even through the injuries that catchers are susceptible to, Myers managed to hit .260 with 9 home runs and 38 RBIs in 85 games.

Myers was granted free agency on November 3 and signed with the Minnesota Twins on December 8.

After hitting just .220 on April 22, 1996, Myers turned it on. He went 2-for-3 the next day and then on April 24 went 5-for-6 with five RBIs. They were the first five-hit game and the first five-RBI game of his career. He kept his hot bat going throughout the season. In a nine-game hit streak from June 4 to 15,

Myers went 13-for-37 (.351), including his first career two-home-run game on June 10 against the Seattle Mariners. He finished the season with career highs up to then in batting average (.286), at-bats (329), runs scored (37), hits (94), triples (3), and RBIs (47) in 97 games.

The 31-year-old Myers played in 62 games for the Twins in 1997, batting .267, before being traded to the Atlanta Braves for Steve Hacker on September 5. Added to the roster after the deadline, he was ineligible for postseason play. On October 27 Myers became a free agent and signed with the San Diego Padres on November 25.

Myers got off to a hot start with the Padres in 1998, batting .298 with 5 doubles and 7 RBIs in 16 games in April. He missed 44 games while on the disabled list from June 4 to July 24, with a chipped bone in his left hand as a result of making a tag at the plate. In 69 games for the season, Myers hit .246 with 4 home runs and 20 RBIs. Season highlights included his second five-RBI game, on April 3, against St. Louis and his bases-loaded pinch-hit single off the Phillies' Mark Leiter in the bottom of the ninth on May 16 that gave the Padres a 3-2 win. He also made his postseason debut. In Game Five of the NLCS, Myers hit a two-run

In 2003, Myers batted .307/.374/.502 with 15 home runs and 52 RBIs, all career-high statistics.

homer off Atlanta's Kerry Ligtenberg in the bottom of the ninth, but the Padres came up short, with the Braves prevailing, 7-6. He was 0-for-4 in two World Series games against the New York Yankees.

Myers played 50 games for the Padres to begin the 1999 campaign, hitting .289 with 3 home runs. He was on the disabled list from June 29 to July 26 with a strained right hamstring. When he came off the DL, he was reacquired by the Braves for minor-league pitcher Doug Dent after Atlanta catcher Javy Lopez went down with an injury. Myers played in 34 games the rest of the way and hit .222 with 2 home runs. In the postseason, he went 2-for-8 in six games against the Mets and Yankees. In his second World Series appearance, he was 2-for-6 against the Yankees, with an RBI in Game Two's 7-2 loss. On November 1 Myers was granted free agency and he signed with the Baltimore Orioles on December 17.

Myers aggravated his left hamstring circling the bases on a home run in the final exhibition game of 2000 spring training and wound up on the disabled list to start the regular season. After his return, with Charles Johnson and Brook Fordyce ahead of him, Myers split time between DH and catcher and hit .224 in 43 games and 134 plate appearances for the year.

Myers started the 2001 season on a hot streak, going 10-for-26 (.385) in April. In May he was 10-for-34 and finished the month with a .333 batting average. He went 0-for-14 in five games in June and the Orioles released him on June 14. Myers signed with the Oakland Athletics on June 23 and was sent to Triple-A Sacramento. After just two games he was recalled on June 26, and remained with Oakland for the rest of the season. He finished the season with a .224 batting average with 11 home runs and 31 RBIs. It was a career high in home runs. Once again, he made it to the postseason and appeared in three games against the Yankees, with one hit in seven plate appearances. On November 5 he was granted free agency but re-signed with Oakland 10 days later.

Myers had another hot start in the 2002 season, hitting .417 at the end of April, after appearing in 10 games. He cooled down after that and ended up batting .222 for the season in 65 games. He once again appeared in the postseason, against the Twins, and was 0-for-1 in two games. On October 29 he was granted free agency from Oakland and signed for a second stint with the Blue Jays on December 16.

The 37-year-old had a standout year with the Blue Jays in 2003. He played in a career-high 121 games and set career highs in hits (101), home runs (15), RBIs

(52), and walks (37). He batted .307 for the season, also a career high. He led the American League with a .486 OBP when leading off an inning. At the All-Star break he was hitting .343 with 10 home runs and 36 RBIs in 74 games.

Myers was back with the Blue Jays for the 2004 season, but after only eight games, he severely sprained his left ankle and was out for the season. The injury occurred in a game at Minnesota. As he rounded third on the FieldTurf, he rolled his ankle. "I turned it inside outside – I just remember feeling the grinding of the bone, it felt like I slammed it," he said. "That's a sick feeling. I've never felt that before, just the bone grinding and that's what I felt when I went down (and) I go, 'Oh my God, what was that?'"[12] Myers was going to retire after the 2004 season but did not want to go out like that. He was granted free agency by the Blue Jays on October 29 and re-signed with them on November 19. In a 2022 telephone interview, he said that this is an injury that he can still feel.[13]

The 39-year-old was valuable in the 2005 spring-training camp, helping all the young players. When camp broke, he was on the major-league roster, but in six games had only one base hit in 12 at-bats with one RBI. On April 26 he was optioned to Triple-A Syracuse, but instead of reporting to Triple A, he decided to test the free-agent market and retire if he couldn't get a deal.[14] No deal was forthcoming, so Myers retired.

"They don't come any better than Crash," Blue Jays manager John Gibbons said at the time. "He's had a wonderful career. Hopefully, if he still wants he can catch on with someone else. If not, he's done it right."[15]

After his playing days were over, Myers tried coaching at his old high school for a couple of years, but recurring pain from his ankle injury prevented him from continuing.

Myers married the former Angela Comstock in 1998. They have five children: Megan, Amanda, Randy, Summar, and Amy. After his baseball career was over, he has supported Angela as owner of a gas station and in the boutique clothing business.

SOURCES

The author used Retrosheet.org and Baseball-Reference.com for stats and game information, and had a phone conversation with Greg Myers.

NOTES

1   Telephone interview with Greg Myers March 23, 2022.

2   Myers interview.

3   The Baseball Cube, https://www.thebaseballcube.com/content/box/DET198710020~r/pbp/.

4   Susan Slusser, "Silence Is a Strength of Catcher / A's Myers Quietly Makes His Mark," April 30, 2002; https://www.sfgate.com/sports/article/Silence-is-a-strength-of-catcher-A-s-Myers-2844319.php.

5   Tom Cage, "Sparky Says There Was No Players-Only Meeting," *Detroit Free Press*, May 6, 1990: 189.

6   "Baseball Daily Report: Eichhorn Traded for Two Blue Jays," *Los Angeles Times*, July 31, 1992: 509.

7   Myers interview.

8   Slusser.

9   Bob Nightengale, "Angels Suffer Through a Catchers-22," *Los Angeles Times*, April 24, 1994: C1, C10.

10 Nightengale.

11 Dave Cunningham, "Though Hapless, Most Angels Would Rather Continue Playing," *Temecula Californian*, August 12, 1994: 18.

12 Jeremy Sandler, "Myers' Enthusiasm Mired Only by the Thought of Turf," *National Post* (Toronto), February 25, 2005: 33.

13 Myers interview.

14 "Toronto Blue Jays Catcher Greg Myers to Become Free Agent," *Alberni Valley* (British Columbia) *Times*, April 27, 2005: 7.

15 Shi Davidi (Canadian Press), "Blue Jays Call Up Huckaby; Myers Becomes Free Agent," *Brantford* (Ontario) *Expositor*, April 27, 2005: 16.

JOHN OLERUD

By Steve Sisto

To many fans, John Olerud was the player who wore his batting helmet while in the field. But to those who knew him best, he was a player with a gorgeous swing, a reliable glove, and a refusal to ever say anything remotely mean or controversial. After suffering a nearly fatal brain aneurysm in college (his reason for wearing his helmet in the field), Olerud went on to help win two World Series championships over a 17-year career with five teams.

John Garrett Olerud was born to John E. and Lynda (Daley) Olerud on August 5, 1968, in Seattle, Washington. John was later joined by his sister, Erica. As of 2021, the elder Olerud works as a dermatologist and professor of medicine at the University of Washington. He had also been a minor-league baseball player who saw his son's talent and love for the game develop at an early age.[1]

"I'd go to spring training and he was a little kid who really loved balls and to hit," Dr. Olerud said.[2] "I remember once in spring training I was with the Montreal Expos organization, and we were in West Palm Beach, he'd be down there with this little plastic bat. I'd be throwing balls and he'd be ripping the balls into the surf. People would stop and say, 'Wow, that little kid is good!'"

John G. Olerud played baseball and golf at Interlake High School in Bellevue, Washington, lettering for three years on both teams.[3] Baseball was his top passion, and as a junior he led his team to the Kingco Athletic Conference championship game. He batted .435 and had a pitching record of 9-2 with a 1.54 earned run average. During his senior season, he was named to the All-County and All-State teams, and was awarded Most Valuable Offensive Player of the All-State game.

Olerud was drafted out of high school by the New York Mets in the 27th round of the 1986 major-league draft, but decided instead to attend college at Washington State University.[4]

In his first year with the WSU Cougars, he earned All-American honors after he hit .414 with five home runs and 20 runs batted in. He also had an 8-2 pitching record with a 3.00 ERA.[5]

As a sophomore in 1988, he had arguably the best season all-time for a two-way college baseball player. As a pitcher, he went 15-0 with a 2.49 ERA over 122 2/3 innings. He recorded 113 strikeouts and just 39 walks. At the plate, he batted .464 with 23 home runs and 81 RBIs. He was the first player in college baseball history to win 15 games as a pitcher and hit 20 home runs in the same season. He broke or tied 12 school records, including: batting average (.464), hits (108), home runs (23), total bases (204), slugging percentage (.876), longest hitting streak (22 games), pitching victories (15), innings pitched (122 ⅔), and strikeouts (113).[6] He was also named College Player of the Year by *Baseball America*.[7]

A similar performance in 1989 would have easily made him a top draft pick after his junior year.

However, a severe health issue almost derailed his dream of playing professional baseball.

In December 1988, he suffered an intense headache while working out. It happened again another week later. He didn't think they were too worrisome and didn't tell anyone about them.[8] But things got worse on January 11, 1989, when he collapsed while jogging around the Washington State athletics complex.[9] He didn't wake up until an hour later. He stayed in the hospital for two weeks before returning to school in February, planning to resume baseball in March.[10]

His recovery process hit another snag on February 24 when he went to see Dr. Richard Winn, the head of neurosurgery at the University of Washington. Dr. Winn took several X-rays of Olerud's brain and found something potentially deadly: an aneurysm near the brain.[11]

"The guy brings out the X-ray, and I go, 'There it is,'" Olerud said. "You didn't have to be a brain surgeon to pick it out."[12]

John underwent six hours of extremely high-risk surgery. The operation was a success, but he still faced a multitude of challenges. Surgeons had to cut open his head to get to the aneurysm, which left an unprotected portion when they were finished. As a result, he began to wear a helmet on the baseball field at all times, a practice he continued his whole career.[13]

He made his season debut on April 15, less than two months after going under the knife. Over his entire junior season, he batted .359 with five home runs and 30 RBIs in 78 at-bats, and had a 3-2 pitching record with a 6.68 ERA.[14]

"I definitely feel a little more mortal because of what happened," Olerud said. "Being young and in good shape, I obviously had no idea anything like this could happen to me. I feel fortunate it turned out the way it did."[15]

Even after a solid post-surgery season, he decided to skip the 1989 major-league draft and return to Washington State for his senior year. He even went so far as to explicitly tell teams not to select him.[16]

The Toronto Blue Jays, however, didn't seem to listen and took him in the third round. Toronto made him an offer of $400,000, which would have been the highest bonus in baseball history. Olerud turned it down, but later that month signed a three-year deal for $800,000 that included a $250,000 bonus. It also guaranteed that he would start his career in the majors.[17]

"They made me an offer that was too good to pass up," Olerud said.[18] "I had an opportunity to be in a pennant race, and that's something a lot of great players never experience... I didn't think they could offer me enough to drive me away from Washington State, but what they came up with were things I couldn't have had after my senior year."[19]

Despite playing for only three years in college, Olerud left WSU as the school's record holder in batting average (.434), slugging percentage (.824), and wins for a pitcher (26).[20]

Olerud joined the Blue Jays in September 1989, becoming one of the rare players to skip the minor leagues and debut in the majors – other players in that group include Hall of Famers George Sisler, Frankie Frisch, Mel Ott, Bob Feller, Sandy Koufax, Jim "Catfish" Hunter, Dave Winfield, Eppa Rixey, and Ted Lyons.

Olerud went 3-for-8 with two runs in six games to close out the 1989 season. During the offseason, he and the Blue Jays decided that he would no longer be a two-way player and would solely be a hitter. "I knew sooner or later I'd have to give one of the two up," he said about no longer being a pitcher. "I was expecting it but hoping to postpone it as long as I could. I still dream about doing both every now and then, but Toronto said concentrate on one and become the best I can be."[21]

In 1990, Olerud's first full professional season, he was leading all major-league rookies in home runs (10), RBIs (33), walks (35), slugging percentage (.465), and on-base percentage (.375) at the All-Star break.[22] He platooned with Glenallen Hill as designated hitter and served as backup to Fred McGriff at first base.[23] He finished fourth in the American League Rookie of the Year voting behind Sandy Alomar Jr., Kevin Maas, and Kevin Appier.

"He has unbelievable ability," Blue Jays catcher Pat Borders said about Olerud. "It makes me mad, because I work so hard and I could never have a swing as nice as his. He reminds you of Wade Boggs – he has a super eye and a great swing. Everything is so compact, it's hard to make him look bad on any pitch."[24]

During his second full season, 1991, Olerud established himself as the team's main first baseman after Fred McGriff, who had averaged 35 home runs over the previous three seasons, was traded away. With McGriff gone, Olerud had 17 home runs and 68 RBIs. The Blue Jays lost the ALCS to the Minnesota Twins, four games to one. Olerud hit .158 but drove in three of the Blue Jays' 19 runs.

In 1992, he finished third on the Blue Jays in average (.284), on-base percentage (.375), and walks

(70). In the World Series, he started 0-for-7 with three strikeouts, but then went four for his next six, scoring twice. Toronto beat the Atlanta Braves in six games to win their first championship in franchise history. "I've had some bad stretches where I haven't hit the ball too well," Olerud said. "I've been hurt. But overall, I've done my share and made my contributions when I was asked. It's been a great season."[25]

It was a good year all around for Olerud; on November 28, 1992, he married Kelly Plaisted. They had known each other in high school and become a couple while in college.

The 1993 season was the best single year of Olerud's career. He had a 25-game hitting streak at one point and was batting above .400 into August. His incredible run even caught the eye of another legendary ballplayer – Ted Williams.

"John Olerud may just be the No. 1 subject on Ted's mind these days," said Bobby Doerr, Williams' former Red Sox teammate. "Ted's very impressed with him. He said he's never seen a youngster with as much discipline at the plate as John has. Ted really thinks John has a chance to become the first player since himself to hit .400... Ted and I agreed that, if any kid has the combination of ability and personality makeup to hit .400 nowadays, it's John."[26]

Olerud ended up falling short of .400, but he still led the majors in on-base percentage (.473) and doubles (54). He also led the American League in batting average (.363), OPS (1.072), and intentional walks (33).

"As it got closer and closer to the end of the season, I started to think I could do it," he said about his quest for .400. "And that's maybe when I started struggling a little bit. When you change your focus, that's usually not a good thing."[27]

Olerud finished third in MVP voting behind Frank Thomas and teammate Paul Molitor. He also earned his first selection to the All-Star game. He hit .300 in the playoffs on his way to collecting his second World Series ring, helping beat the White Sox in the ALCS and the Phillies in the 1993 World Series.

He was also awarded the Hutch Award, named after former pitcher and manager Fred Hutchinson, who died of cancer in 1964, and is given to a player who showed the kind of character and fighting spirit as Hutchinson. Olerud was honored for overcoming his brain aneurysm in college.[28]

During the following offseason, Olerud and the Blue Jays managed to avoid arbitration, and the reigning American League batting champion signed a three-year, $17 million contract that came with a $6.5 million option for the fourth year, well above the $1,562,500 he earned in 1993.[29]

Despite the new deal, his performance at the plate declined in 1994. He hit .297 with 12 home runs and 67 RBIs while playing in 108 of the team's 115-game strike-shortened season. It wasn't just Olerud who faltered; the Blue Jays finished 55-60, ending a streak of 11 consecutive years with a winning record.

The Blue Jays, like the rest of the major leagues, played a shortened schedule of 144 games in 1995, but they only won 56, tying the Twins for the worst record in the AL. Olerud also had the worst season of his career up to that point, falling under .200 at the start of May and going into the All-Star break at .246. He turned things around during the second half of the year, posting a .336 batting average the rest of the way, finishing at .291 with eight homers and 54 RBIs.

After the 1996 season, in which Olerud hit .274 (nearly 90 points lower than his .363 mark just three years prior), the Blue Jays traded him to the New York Mets for right-handed pitcher Robert Person, who went 4-5 with a 4.52 ERA that season. Toronto also gave New York $5 million, meaning the Mets would only have to pay Olerud $1.5 million for the upcoming year.

"It's been frustrating the last couple of years to not play as well as I feel I'm capable of playing," Olerud said. "I'm looking forward to the new opportunity, turning things around and having a good year."[30]

The newest Met quickly found himself among the millions of people looking for a place to live in the Big Apple. "New York is a big city; there are a lot of things to do," he said. "I want to make sure we're conveniently located to Shea Stadium. I definitely don't want to be stressed out about getting to the ballpark every afternoon. But we'd also like to see some things in the city and be somewhere safe."[31] He and Kelly ultimately decided to live in Manhattan, joining Derek Jeter and David Cone as the only New York ballplayers to live inside the city itself.[32]

When the 1997 season started, Olerud wasted no time making an impact on his new team. On Opening Day, he led off the third inning with an opposite-field single to left, and scored the Mets' first run of the season when he was driven in by a two-run homer off the bat of Todd Hundley. He walked to load the bases with two outs in the fourth, setting up a two-run single by Bernard Gilkey. He also doubled to left-center in the sixth and hit a sacrifice fly in the eighth.

Over the next two games, he recorded a home run, two doubles, a single, and two walks.

In September, Olerud hit for the cycle – the first of his career – and drove in five runs. His night included an RBI double in the first, a single in the third, a solo homer in the seventh, and a bases-loaded triple in the eighth. He became the seventh Met to hit for the cycle and the first to do it at Shea Stadium since Tommie Agee in 1970.[33]

Olerud's first year with the Mets saw a return to a high level of offensive production, a .294 batting average with 22 home runs and 102 RBIs. His performance took a dip during the middle of the year, but he picked it back up at the end. After the season, he signed a two-year deal with the Mets worth $8 million.

"What determines the salary is the previous few years," Olerud said about the new deal. "The pay cut is directly related to those years. I'm going with a two-year deal and look forward to having two solid years and getting the value up."[34]

Unlike previous years when Olerud's performance dropped in the summer months, 1998 was a different story. In July, he started a hitting streak that lasted 23 games, and he also took the lead in the NL batting race with a .349 average.

"I don't know if there is a better pure hitter there," Mets manager Bobby Valentine said about Olerud. "But as far as who I want up there for one hit or who hits the best, I'd have to vote for John. Maybe I'm prejudiced because he's my guy, but if I wanted to go out and watch a pure hitter in New York I'd have to buy a ticket to see John."[35]

In September 1998, Olerud left the Mets during a road trip to join his wife Kelly in New York after hearing she would soon be going into labor.[36] He was heading back to the hotel on the team bus after a game in Philadelphia when he received the call. He boarded the 12:37 A.M. train to New York, making it back home to bring Kelly to the hospital in the morning. That night around 9:00 Kelly gave birth a 9-pound, 4-ounce boy named Garrett.[37]

"Garrett takes after his father – very steady, calm, and laid back," Kelly said when their son was just nine days old.[38]

Olerud returned to the team with 14 games left in the season, and the birth of his son seemed to give him a boost. He hit .468 over those last two weeks, with 3 home runs, 10 runs batted in, and nine runs. He finished at .354, breaking the club record for a single season set by Cleon Jones in 1969 – Olerud's mark still stands.[39]

"There could be something to that," Olerud said about his impressive stats after becoming a father. "When you have your first child, you look at things from a different perspective. It seems like the ball slows down; I'm picking up the off-speed pitches sooner."[40]

Olerud started the 1999 season by reaching base safely in each of the first 30 games. He batted .330 over those 30 games with a 1.099 OPS, six home runs, and 17 RBIs.

"He's climbing rapidly," Mets catcher Mike Piazza said about Olerud. "He's so disciplined. You watch him every day and he just does not make mistakes with his at-bats."[41]

"I don't feel like I've got it all figured out just yet," Olerud said about himself. "But I feel like I've gotten better and more comfortable as the years go by at just knowing what I need to do to be successful and to help a team."[42]

He ended up playing in all 162 games of the 1999 season, enjoying his third straight season with an on-base percentage above .400.

Defensively, Olerud, along with second baseman Edgardo Alfonzo, shortstop Rey Ordonez, and third baseman Robin Ventura, were named the "greatest infield in baseball history" by *Sports Illustrated*. They committed just 24 errors all season (Olerud had eight), taking down the 1964 Baltimore Orioles as the best-fielding team in history.[43]

Olerud was eligible for free agency for the first time after the 1999 season, and after his years in New York, his market value was pretty good. The Detroit Tigers were reportedly willing to offer him around $8 million, while one agent said he could get a contract similar to Robin Ventura's from the year before, which was for four years and $32 million.[44]

Ultimately, Olerud decided to return to his home state of Washington, signing a three-year, $20 million deal with the Mariners.[45]

"This was a real difficult decision for me," Olerud said. "There were times where I was leaning towards the Mets, definitely. I came close, but never to the point where I said, 'Let's go for it.'"[46] "One of the big things was family considerations. It's definitely a tough decision. You look at the things you're going to miss with the Mets, but I think this is the right decision for me, the right decision for my family. I have a good feeling about it, a peaceful feeling about the decision."[47]

He finished the first year in his new uniform with his third triple-digit RBI total (103) to go with 45

Olerud has the highest on-base percentage (.395) in Blue Jays' history.

doubles, his second season with 40+ two-baggers. He also led all American League first basemen in fielding percentage, while winning his first career Gold Glove.[48]

On June 16, 2001, he became just the second player in major-league history to hit for the cycle in both the American and National Leagues, joining Bob Watson in that exclusive club.[49] His night included a double in the second inning, a triple in the third (the ball got caught under a bench in the Mariners' bullpen, helping Olerud, who was never known for his speed, reach third base), a single in the fifth, and a two-run home run in the ninth to complete the cycle.[50]

In June 2002, he became the 46th player in major-league history to record 400 doubles, 1,000 walks, and 1,000 RBIs. At the time, the only other active players in that club were Jeff Bagwell, Barry Bonds, Mark Grace, Rickey Henderson, Fred McGriff, Rafael Palmeiro, and Edgar Martinez.[51]

Olerud also won his second Gold Glove Award in 2002 after posting a .996 fielding percentage, with only five errors in 1,275 chances, as well as 101 assists.[52]

Over 2001 and 2002, he averaged .301 with 21 homers and 98 RBIs. Those stats helped him sign a two-year deal worth $15.4 million to stay with the Mariners.[53]

On June 16, 2003, he hit a two-run homer in the fourth inning against the Anaheim Angels, his 2,000th career hit.[54] It took him 1,933 games to reach that number.[55]

"That was nice, especially the ovation I got," he said about becoming the 224th player to join the 2,000-hit club. "I think it means I'm getting older. But it is a big milestone, a nice milestone to get to."[56]

That ended up being one of the lone high points of 2003 for Olerud. He finished the year with a .269 batting average, 28 points below his career average and his lowest in 12 years. His 83 RBIs were 16 fewer than his average over the previous six years. It was also the last season in which he played at least 150 games. He recorded 145 hits, breaking his streak of six consecutive 150+ hit seasons. He did, however, collect his third Gold Glove award thanks to his usual stellar play at first base.

Entering the 2004 season, the 35-year-old Olerud began seriously considering whether it was time to retire. "I've been thinking of retirement for some time, but it really entered my thoughts last year," he said. "The team would take a loss and you'd have a bad game, and you sit at your locker and think, 'Maybe the time is drawing near.' You can't help but think like that. No one wants to go through stuff that is no fun."[57]

When Opening Day 2004 came around, Olerud was still playing for the Mariners in the last year of his contract. On July 24, he was designated for assignment. But he wasn't out of a job long. Less than a month later, he was picked up by the New York Yankees to play first base while Jason Giambi was injured.[58]

"This is a place I've always admired, a team I've always admired because of the way they do things," Olerud said. "I think it's going to work out well around here."[59]

"He's a very good player. He's had a very good career. I think this is going to work out well for both of us, the team and for John," Yankees manager Joe Torre said.[60]

When Olerud joined the team, there was already a fan waiting for him in the clubhouse. "He's the best player I ever played with," said Alex Rodriguez, who played with Olerud in Seattle. "I'm very excited because I know what he can do for any team. He just completes our team."[61]

Olerud wasted no time making an impact for the Yankees, going 5-for-8 with four RBIs in his first two games in pinstripes. Over his final three weeks with the Mariners, he went just 4-for-37 with three RBIs.

He spent the 2004 offseason without a team to call home as he recovered from a torn ligament that occurred during Game Three of the ALCS against the Boston Red Sox when he hit his foot with his bat while running out of the batter's box.[62]

He eventually signed a contract with the Red Sox in May 2005 worth about $750,000. The deal meant more than just a new team for Olerud; it also meant the first time he would play in the minor leagues.[63]

He hadn't played baseball outside the major leagues since he played for the Alaska Summer League Palouse Cougars in 1989. But age 36, he found himself suiting up for the Pawtucket Red Sox.

"When I went to Pawtucket, other players called me up and said, 'You're doing things backwards,'" he said. "But I was hurt, and I needed to do a rehab assignment. It was just a normal thing to do. Everybody starts in the minors. Going down there was a good experience. I had a great time there."[64]

When he made it back to the major leagues, he showed that he could still contribute to an offense. He hit .294 with four doubles, six RBIs, and one home run in his first 22 games.

"When a young player doesn't play, he fears that people will forget about him," he said about his role on the Red Sox. "He thinks, 'If I stay backup too long, they'll look at it as if it's all I can do.' He's afraid that'll be his role instead of playing every day. For me, I'm established. I'm not trying to make a name for myself. Everybody likes to play every day. But my circumstances were that I was hurt, and the Red Sox picked me up after the season started. I understand the role that I have, and that makes it easier to accept. Still, there isn't anybody in here who wouldn't want to play every day if they could fill out the lineup."[65]

By season's end, he had appeared in 89 games and hit for a .289 average with 37 RBIs. He was 2-for-7 in three postseason games, as the Red Sox lost to the White Sox in the 2005 ALCS.

The 2005 season turned out to be Olerud's final year in the majors; he retired in December. In typical Olerud fashion, there was no big press conference for him to announce he was hanging up his cleats. In fact, most people in the baseball world didn't even know until the winter meetings when Boston was asked why Olerud's name wasn't listed among the unsigned free agents.

"He retired," assistant to the general manager Jed Hoyer said.[66]

Olerud finished his career with a .295 batting average, a .398 on-base percentage, 255 home runs, 1,230 RBIs, 2,239 hits, and 500 doubles. He never struck out more than 96 times in a season and had a career strikeout rate of 11%. He also had a .995 fielding percentage at first base, collecting three Gold Glove awards throughout his career.

In 2007, Olerud was inducted into the National College Baseball Hall of Fame. Three years later, the College Baseball Foundation created the John Olerud Two-Way Player of the Year Award, which is now given annually to the best dual hitter/pitcher at the collegiate level.[67]

"There have been a lot of great players in college baseball and for the College Baseball Foundation to name it after me, I am humbled and honored," he said about having the award named after him.[68]

In 2011, Olerud's first year on the Hall of Fame ballot, he received only four votes, eliminating him from future ballots.

In 2016, Olerud was selected as the Pac-12 Conference Player of the Century for his stellar play as both a hitter and pitcher, as well as for the way he returned to the field after overcoming his potentially life-threatening brain aneurysm.

After retiring from baseball, Olerud and his wife, Kelly, moved back to Washington with their three children: Garrett (b. 1999), Jordan (b. 2000), and Jessica (b. 2004).

Garrett and Jessica were both healthy children, but unfortunately, Jordan has had a much more difficult time. She was born with a condition known as "trisome 2p, 5p-," which meant she had an extra second chromosome and was missing part of her fifth chromosome. She spent the first years of her life eating through a tube, unable to walk or speak, save for the occasional "yes" or "no." She underwent close to a dozen surgeries and other medical procedures in her first five years of life. At the time of her diagnosis, she was the only person in the world known to have the condition.[69]

"You never expect something like that to happen," Olerud said about Jordan's diagnosis. "You figure you're going to have healthy kids. Just not knowing what to expect down the road, what sort of life our daughter is going to have. It's tough. It's still tough."[70]

In 2003, the Oleruds started the Jordan Fund to help other parents with special needs children pay for their treatments.[71]

"The thing that really hit us about having Jordan and a special needs child is that we had the financial means to get help and to get as good as care as we could get for her," Olerud said. "We have family and friends around to help us out and it's still really hard... We came up with the Jordan Fund, because that was our desire to help kids and families with special needs. If there were things we could do to help out families, we wanted to make sure that we could do that."[72]

Jordan passed away in 2020 at the age of 19.[73] Those who are interested in learning more about the organization can visit the Jordan Fund here.

In December 2014, Olerud, joined by his family, received the honor of raising the "12th Man Flag" at CenturyLink Field before a Seattle Seahawks NFL game. Talking about the highlights of his career, he said: "A lot of great times, great teams and teammates...it's hard to pick just one, but I would say probably the 1993 World Series, just because in '92 I was a nervous wreck the whole time during the World Series – in '93 I felt like I could relax more and contribute more to that team."[74]

Even in 1990, Olerud put his overall life in perspective well: "[Baseball is] hardly a life-and-death situation for me. I've had the chance to think about dying. I know what's really important... [That's to] live life to its fullest. Don't waste a moment. I plan to enjoy whatever life brings my way and be thankful I have a life to enjoy."[75]

ACKNOWLEDGMENTS

This biography was reviewed by Rory Costello and Jan Finkel, and fact-checked by Alan Cohen.

NOTES

1 He had been a catcher who put in seven seasons in the minors, including five at Triple A.

2 Larry Clark, "John E. Olerud '65 - Science Is A Lot Like Baseball," *Washington State Magazine*, April 26, 2012.

3 "John Olerud," *Washington Interscholastic Activities Association*. http://www.wiaa.com/ardisplay.aspx?ID=333

4 "Former Washington State, Seattle Mariners Standout John Olerud To Be Inducted Into Pac-12 Conference Hall Of Honor," *Spokesman-Review*, March 9, 2019.

5 Greg Johns, "John Olerud: The Ultimate Two-Way Player," *Seattle Post-Intelligencer*, February 18, 2010.

6 Tom Leo, "Not Invincible, But Still A Top Prospect," *Syracuse Herald American*, March 24, 1990.

7 Jim Callis, "Olerud Rebounds To Success After Near-Fatal Aneurysm," *Baseball America*, 1989.

8 Callis, "Olerud Rebounds To Success After Near-Fatal Aneurysm."

9 Callis, "Olerud Rebounds To Success After Near-Fatal Aneurysm."

10 Callis, "Olerud Rebounds To Success After Near-Fatal Aneurysm."

11 Callis, "Olerud Rebounds To Success After Near-Fatal Aneurysm."

12 Hank Hersch, "A Gentleman And A Slugger," *Sports Illustrated*, August 15, 1991.

13 Jim Callis, "Olerud Rebounds To Success After Near-Fatal Aneurysm."

14 Callis, "Olerud Rebounds To Success After Near-Fatal Aneurysm."

15 Anstine, "John Olerud."

16 Callis, "Olerud Rebounds To Success After Near-Fatal Aneurysm."

17 Callis, "Olerud Rebounds To Success After Near-Fatal Aneurysm."

18 Mike DiGiovanna, "Big Leagues No Big Deal To Him: Blue Jays," *Los Angeles Times*, May 24, 1990.

19 Tracy Ringolsby, "Draft Gambles Sometimes Hit Big," *Baseball America*, July 10, 1990.

20 "Timeline: John Olerud's Baseball Career," *Washington State Magazine*. https://magazine.wsu.edu/web-extra/timeline-john-oleruds-baseball-career/

21 Tom Leo, "Not Invincible, But Still A Top Prospect," *Syracuse Herald American*, March 24, 1990.

22 Jeff Redd, "Olerud Makes Smooth Move," *USA Today*, July 20, 1990.

23 Leo, "Not Invincible, But Still A Top Prospect."

24 DiGiovanna, "Big Leagues No Big Deal To Him: Blue Jays."

25 Larry Whiteside, "Olerud breathing easier at first," *Gazette* (Montreal), October 25, 1992: D1.

26 Marty York, "Williams Keeps Eyes On Olerud," *Toronto Globe And Mail*, June 19, 1993.

27 Jeff Bradley, "Olerud Knows Pressure Will Build Up On O'Neill," *New York Daily News*, May 25, 1994.

28 Hal Bodley, "Honors," *USA Today*, 1994.

29 "Blue Jays Sign Olerud For $17 Million," *USA Today*, February 4, 1994.

30 Chuck Johnson, "Mets Figure Timing Is Right To Acquire Olerud From Jays," *USA Today*, December 23, 1996.

31 Thomas Hill, "Heading For Home," *New York Daily News*, January 12, 1997.

32 Hill, "Heading For Home."

33 "Mets' Olerud Hits For Cycle," *Associated Press*, September 12, 1997.

34 David Waldstein, "Olerud Returns To Mets For 2 Years At $4M Per," *New York Post*, November 25, 1997.

35 David Waldstein, "Olerud Streaks Closer To Amazin' Record," *New York Post*, August 14, 1998.

36 Tom Keegan, "John Gets Wide Birth," *New York Post*, September 11, 1998.

37 Filip Bondy, "With Sleep, Pop's Ready To Do More Than Dream," *New York Daily News*, September 21, 1998.

38 Bondy, "With Sleep, Pop's Ready To Do More Than Dream."

39 Mike Piazza also hit .348 in 1998.

40 Bondy, "With Sleep, Pop's Ready To Do More Than Dream."

41 Joel Sherman, "Olerud Is Following O'Neill's Recipe For Success," *New York Post*, April 30, 1999.

42 Jason Diamos, "The Most Cosmopolitan Met," *New York Times*, May 7, 1999.

43 Tom Verducci, "Glove Affair," *Sports Illustrated*, September 6, 1999.

44 Rafael Hermoso, "Mets Take Stock Of Olerud Market," *New York Daily News*, October 31, 1999.

45 "Olerud Returns To Seattle Roots," *Associated Press*, December 7, 1999.

46 "Olerud Returns To Seattle Roots."

47 Murray Chass, "You Can Go Home Again: Olerud Joins Mariners," *New York Times,* December 8, 1999.

48 "American League Winners," *USA Today,* November 16, 2000.

49 "Season Of Accomplishments," *USA Today,* October 9, 2001.

50 "Olerud Hits For Cycle In Dramatic Seattle Win," *Associated Press,* June 17, 2001.

51 *New Jersey On-Line,* July 1, 2002.

52 "Molina Halts I-Rod's Streak, 3 M's Win AL Gold Gloves," *ESPN,* November 13, 2002.

53 "Baseball: Garciaparra, Hamm Engaged," *New York Post,* December 7, 2002.

54 Jim Street," Olerud Milestone Highlights Win," *MLB.com,* June 17, 2003.

55 Jim Cour, "John Olerud Homers For 2,000th Career Hit," *Midland Daily News,* June 15, 2003.

56 Street," Olerud Milestone Highlights Win."

57 Bob Finnigan, "Olerud On Fence, But Still In Ballpark," *Seattle Times,* March 15, 2004.

58 Anthony Reiber, "It's Olerud At First Soon," *Newsday,* August 2, 2004.

59 Mike Vaccaro, "Yanks & John A Perfect Match," *New York Post,* August 4, 2004.

60 Vaccaro, "Yanks & John A Perfect Match."

61 Jack Curry, "Olerud Will Be Satisfied Being Lost In The Mix," *New York Times,* August 6, 2004.

62 Dom Amore, "Olerud Out With Foot Injury," *Hartford Courant,* October 18, 2004.

63 Chris Snow, "Olerud Signed To Give First Aid," *Boston.com,* May 2, 2005.

64 Ron Indrisano, "Olerud Has Role Down Pat," *Boston Globe,* June 29, 2005.

65 Indrisano, "Olerud Has Role Down Pat."

66 John Blanchette, "Olerud Retired In Typical Way, With Quiet Class," *Spokesman-Review,* December 8, 2005.

67 Mark Zwolinski, "Old Blue Jays Rarely Fly Together," *Toronto Star,* August 7, 2009.

68 Zwolinski, "Old Blue Jays Rarely Fly Together."

69 Adam Kilgore, "Growing Family: Oleruds' Faith Helps Them Cope With Their Daughter's Illness," *Boston Globe,* June 24, 2005.

70 Kilgore, "Growing Family: Oleruds' Faith Helps Them Cope With Their Daughter's Illness."

71 Kilgore, "Growing Family: Oleruds' Faith Helps Them Cope With Their Daughter's Illness."

72 Jason Krump, "John Olerud '88: Faith, Hope, and Horses," *Washington State Magazine,* November 3, 2011.

73 Alyssa Newcomb, "John Olerud's daughter Jordan, born with a rare chromosome disorder, dies at 19," Today, March 1, 2020.

74 https://www.seahawks.com/video/12-flag-raiser-john-olerud-interview-104736

75 Leo, "Not Invincible, But Still A Top Prospect."

TOM QUINLAN

By Joel Rippel

After a stellar high school athletic career at Hill-Murray High School in Maplewood, Minnesota, Tom Quinlan had options.

In June 1986 Quinlan, who was named to All-State teams in baseball and hockey and had scholarship offers to play college baseball and hockey, was selected by the Toronto Blue Jays in the 27th round of baseball's amateur draft.

Later that month, Quinlan was selected by Calgary in the fourth round of the NHL Entry Draft. He was rated the number-26 overall prospect for the draft by the NHL Central Scouting Bureau.

Before the NHL draft, Glen Sonmor, the Minnesota North Stars' director of player personnel, said Quinlan would not be a first-round draft pick because the 21 NHL teams were wary that he would pursue a career in baseball instead of hockey.[1]

While mulling his options, Quinlan played for the North baseball team at the US Olympic Festival in Houston. On August 1 he signed a letter of intent to play baseball at the University of Minnesota.

Starting the next day, Quinlan and the US junior national team played in the World Friendship Junior Baseball Tournament in Windsor, Ontario. Playing shortstop, he batted over .300 as the US team earned a bronze medal.

In late September, Quinlan decided to forgo the scholarship offer and signed a contract with the Blue Jays.

"Toronto increased their offer two weeks ago," Quinlan said. "It was just a matter of me deciding what was the best way to go."[2]

The week after signing with the Blue Jays, Quinlan joined the Blue Jays instructional league team in Florida before embarking on his first professional season in 1987.

Thomas Raymond Quinlan, who went on to spend 16 seasons in professional baseball, was born on March 27, 1968, in St. Paul, Minnesota, to Thomas and Marilyn Ann Quinlan. The family, which also included brothers Robb and Craig, lived in Maplewood, about 10 miles east of the Twin Cities. The elder Thomas Quinlan managed a trucking company and Marilyn Ann cut hair and also worked as a banquet waitress.

Quinlan spent his rookie season with the Myrtle Beach (South Carolina) Blue Jays in the Class-A South Atlantic League. He got off to a good start, going 5-for-12 as Myrtle Beach opened the season with a four-game sweep of Savannah.

Myrtle Beach, managed by Barry Foote, finished first in the South Division with an 83-56 record and defeated the Asheville (North Carolina) Tourists, 3-2, in the league's championship series. The team had 14 players who would go on to play in the major leagues.

For the season, Quinlan batted .223 with 5 home runs and 51 RBIs in 132 games. Primarily a shortstop in high school, he played third base for Myrtle Beach and led South Atlantic League third sackers in double plays (29), putouts (96), and total chances (368).

Quinlan was promoted to Knoxville of the Double-A Southern League for 1988. After hitting his first home run of the season in Knoxville's 6-5 victory over Chattanooga on April 17, he hit a walk-off solo home run the next day to give Knoxville a 2-1 victory over Chattanooga.

On June 15 Quinlan was placed on the disabled list with an injury to his right foot. He returned to Knoxville's lineup on July 14. He finished the season hitting .218 with 8 home runs and 47 RBIs in 98 games.

Quinlan returned to Knoxville in 1989, hitting .210 with 16 home runs and 57 RBIs in 139 games. Defensively, he led Southern League third basemen in total chances (374) and assists (259).

Quinlan returned to Knoxville yet again in 1990 and received the Toronto organization's Webster Award as the MVP of the team. He batted .258 and was second on the team with a .426 slugging percentage, 15 home runs and 51 RBIs in 141 games. He was called up by the Blue Jays and made his major-league debut on September 4 in Detroit. Quinlan started at third base and batted ninth.

He was at the plate in the second inning, when the Blue Jays' Ken Williams was thrown out stealing. In the top of the third, in his first major-league at-bat, he struck out against Tigers starter Frank Tanana.

In the fifth inning, Williams led off with a double and Quinlan was hit by a pitch. The Blue Jays loaded the bases but didn't score. In the seventh inning, facing reliever Paul Gibson with one out, Quinlan singled to center.

It was his only appearance of the season with the Blue Jays, who finished second in the AL East with an 86-76 record.

Quinlan went to spring training with the Blue Jays in 1991, before being reassigned to the club's minor-league camp on March 22. He spent the entire 1991 season with Triple-A Syracuse. In 132 games with the Chiefs, he batted .240 with 10 home runs and 49 RBIs. He was second in the International League with 72 walks and had a .347 on-base percentage.

Quinlan returned to Syracuse for the 1992 season. In early July, when Blue Jays third baseman Kelly Gruber was placed on the disabled list with a sore knee, Quinlan was recalled. On July 1 he doubled in two runs in the ninth inning off Mark Eichhorn in the Blue Jays' 9-5 victory over the California Angels in Anaheim.

After making one more appearance, as a defensive replacement, Quinlan was returned to Syracuse on July 23, when Gruber was reactivated. He was recalled again on August 27 and spent the rest of the season with the Blue Jays. He played in seven games but didn't make his first start until the Blue Jays' 7-4 victory over the Tigers in Detroit on the final day of the regular season.

Quinlan was on the Blue Jays roster for the ALCS but did not play in any of the six games against Oakland. He was replaced by Rance Mulliniks on the Blue Jays roster for the World Series.

In his two stints with the Blue Jays in 1992, Quinlan played in 13 games, going 1-for-15 with a double and two RBIs. In 107 games with Syracuse, he batted .215 with 6 home runs and 36 RBIs. He was voted a 30 percent World Series share ($36,000) by the Blue Jays regulars.[3]

Quinlan spent the entire 1993 season with Syracuse. He hit .236 with 16 home runs and 53 RBIs and a team-best .340 on-base percentage. (He walked 56 times.) After the season he became a free agent and signed with the Philadelphia Phillies.

Quinlan was invited to the Phillies' 1994 spring training as a nonroster player but was reassigned to their minor-league camp on March 19.

He opened the season with Triple-A Scranton/Wilkes-Barre and got off to a good start offensively. He went 13-for-28 in his first seven games and was hitting .300 in early May when he was called up by the Phillies after infielder Kevin Stocker was placed on the disabled list with a wrist injury.

"I'm a little surprised. I didn't know anyone was hurt," Quinlan said. "I have to have a chance to show I can play. If you do a job, who knows? Maybe you can stay a while."[4]

Quinlan entered the Phillies' game on May 10 in Atlanta in the bottom of the seventh inning as a defensive replacement after the Phillies had scored five runs in the top of the inning to take an 8-1 lead. The Braves rallied with seven runs in the ninth to tie it and eventually won the game 9-8 in 15 innings. Quinlan grounded out in the ninth, then singled off Mike Stanton in the top of the 12th for his first NL hit.

He made eight more appearances, primarily as a defensive replacement, before going 2-for-2 with a double in the Phillies' 8-3 victory at home over the New York Mets on May 22. The next day he made the first of three consecutive starts at third base. After going 1-for-7 in the first two games in St. Louis, he was 2-for-5 with an RBI in the Phillies' 10-5 loss to the Cardinals.

On May 29 in Philadelphia, Quinlan hit a two-run homer off Houston's Doug Drabek in the second inning of the Phillies' 4-2 victory over the Astros. Over the next three weeks, he played in eight games (four starts). Quinlan, who was 7-for-24 in his first 16 games with the Phillies, went 0-for-11 in those eight and was returned to Scranton on June 25.

He spent the rest of the season with Scranton. He had two two-home-run games in August. In the Red Barons' 13-3 victory on August 6 in Ottawa, he hit two two-run home runs. On August 30 he hit a solo home run and a two-run homer in the Red Barons' 7-1 victory over the visiting Norfolk Tides.

With the Red Barons, Quinlan batted .241 with 9 home runs and 23 RBIs in 76 games. After the season he became a free agent and signed with the Minnesota Twins. He spent the entire 1995 season with the Twins' Triple-A Salt Lake farm team and put together his best professional season to date. During the regular season, he batted .279 with 17 home runs and 88 RBIs (third-best in the PCL), and led PCL third basemen in fielding percentage (.940).

Quinlan's season included many highlights. He hit three home runs and drove in four runs in Salt Lake's 12-2 victory over visiting Edmonton on July 28. In mid-August he put together a season-high 11-game hitting streak, going 19-for-48 with 2 home runs and 10 RBIs.

Salt Lake, 79-65 in the regular season, reached the PCL championship series (losing to Colorado Springs in five games). In eight postseason games, Quinlan batted .300 with 3 home runs and 6 RBIs.

After the season, Quinlan was added to the Twins' 40-man roster, but in early December he was designated for assignment to clear a spot on the roster.

He re-signed with the Twins and was invited to the 1996 big-league camp. In 24 exhibitions, he batted .340 with one home run and 7 RBIs, which earned him a spot on the Twins' Opening Day roster.

"I had my best season (in 1995)," Quinlan said. "After I got used to hitting this way (an open stance), my strikeouts were down. I had my best RBI year (88). My average was .279. I came here this spring with more confidence as a hitter than I've had in a long time."[5]

The Twins opened the season at home and Quinlan made four appearances (one start) during the initial homestand. He went 0-for-6 and did not make another appearance before being sent to Salt Lake on April 19.

He spent the rest of the season with Salt Lake, hitting .283 with 15 home runs and 81 RBIs in 121 games.

After the season, Quinlan became a free agent again and signed with the Colorado Rockies organization.

He spent the 1997 season with Triple-A Colorado Springs and hit .285 with 23 home runs and 113 RBIs (both career highs) in 134 games.

In 1998 he played for the Texas Rangers' Triple-A Oklahoma farm team, hitting .278 in 137 games with 16 home runs and 97 RBIs.

In 1999 he spent his fifth consecutive season in the Pacific Coast League, playing for the Chicago Cubs' Iowa farm team. He batted .250 with 17 home runs and 58 RBIs in 133 games.

Quinlan spent the final three seasons of his professional career in Korea.

He joined the Hyundai Unicorns of the KBO for the 2000 season. He helped the Unicorns win the KBO championship by hitting 37 home runs (third-best in the league) and driving in 91 runs (10th-best).

The Unicorns, who were 91-40-2 in the regular season, defeated the Doosan Bears, 4-3, in the league's championship series. Quinlan, who didn't miss a game during the regular season, was the MVP of the championship series.

Quinlan returned to the Unicorns in 2001, hitting 28 home runs and driving in 66 runs in 123 games. The Unicorns, who were 72-57-4 in the regular season, seven games behind the first-place Samsung Lions, lost in the first round of the playoffs.

In 2002 Quinlan joined the LG Twins. After going hitless in 13 games, he retired.

"I got off to a slow start and was dealing with some injuries," Quinlan said. "So, I retired. I really enjoyed my time in Korea. It was a wonderful experience and they treated me very well."[6]

In 16 professional seasons – 13 in Organized Baseball and three in Korea – Quinlan finished with 239 home runs and 966 RBIs and a .247 batting average in 1,932 games.

In parts of four seasons in the major leagues, he played in 42 games. He went 9-for-58 with three doubles, one home run and five RBIs.

"What I remember most is all the great relationships with teammates," Quinlan said. "We had a group of guys who came up together through the Blue Jays system. About 10 years ago, we got together at a reunion. We hadn't seen each other in a long time, and we didn't miss a beat. It was great."[7]

After retiring from baseball, Quinlan went to work in the mortgage business.

Tom and his wife, Daneen, live in suburban St. Paul. They have two children, son Cory and daughter Cali. Cory played baseball for his father's alma mater and college baseball at the University of St. Thomas.

Tom Quinlan spent about 10 years as an assistant baseball coach at his alma mater.

Tom's brother Craig, who is one year younger, was also selected in the MLB and NHL drafts and played one season in the Toronto Blue Jays organization. Brother Robb, who is nine years younger, spent parts of eight seasons in the big leagues, appearing in 458 games for the Angels from 2003 through 2010, with a career .276 batting average, 25 homers, and 121 runs batted in. He was 2-for-6 in postseason play, appearing briefly in 2005 and 2007 with a solo home run producing the only run in the Game Two ALCS loss to the White Sox in 2005.

As of early 2022, Tom and Robb were part of an ownership group for a proposed team in the Northwoods League, a summer collegiate, wood-bat league based in the Midwest. The team will be based in Hudson, Wisconsin.

SOURCES

In addition to the sources cited in the Notes, the author consulted the 1996 Minnesota Twins Media Guide, Baseball-Reference.com, Newspapers.com, and Retrosheet.org, and conducted a phone interview with Tom Quinlan in March 2022.

NOTES

1   Jerry Zgoda, "Best Field of Americans Comes in Off-Year for State," *Minneapolis Star and Tribune*, June 17, 1986: 1D.

2   John Gilbert, "Quinlan Joins Blue Jays, Skips Scholarship at 'U,'" *Minneapolis Star and Tribune*, September 25, 1986: 5D.

3   Marty York, "Dividing Up the World Series' Spoils," *Globe and Mail* (Toronto), October 30, 1992: C14.

4   Paul Hagen, "Stocker on DL for 2 Weeks, Maybe More," *Philadelphia Daily News*, May 4, 1994: 76.

5   Patrick Reusse, "Quinlan Not Yet Ready to Put His Game on Ice," *Minneapolis Star Tribune*, March 29, 1996: S2.

6   Quinlan interview.

7   Quinlan interview.

ED SPRAGUE JR.

By Bill Nowlin

There have been two Ed Spragues in major-league baseball, father and son. The Ed Sprague we focus on here is the son, a two-time World Series champion with the 1992 and 1993 Toronto Blue Jays. Primarily a third baseman, he played in more than 1,000 games – 888 of them for Toronto – over an 11-year stretch. He played for five other teams in his final four years, including two stints in one year for the San Diego Padres.

Most notably, Sprague is the only major leaguer to have been on two World Series-winning teams in the majors and also win the College World Series (twice, with Stanford in 1987 and 1988) and a Gold Medal in the Olympic Games (at Seoul, South Korea, in 1988).[1] His wife, Kristen Babb-Sprague, holds an Olympic

Gold Medal, too, in synchronized swimming at the 1992 Summer Olympics in Barcelona. The two married in February 1991.

His father, Edward Nelson Sprague Sr., was a right-handed pitcher who pitched in parts of eight seasons for four different ballclubs from 1968 to 1976. His career wrapped up a little more than a month before Ed Junior turned 9 years old. He had pitched in 198 games with a record of 17-23 (3.84 ERA).[2]

Ed Junior – who will simply be called Ed Sprague throughout this biography, except when necessary to distinguish him from his father – was born on July 25, 1967, in Castro Valley, California, about 15 miles from Oakland. His mother, Raelene, and father divorced when Ed was around 12 years old. Ed has a 15-year-younger brother, Dennis.

Around 1979 Ed Senior became a baseball magnate, part-owner and president of the Stockton Ports minor-league baseball team, and the family moved there. His wife – Ed Junior's stepmother, Michele – had a successful career in property development and owned the Lodi Crushers for a couple of years, a collegiate wood-bat team.[3]

Ed Junior was right-handed and grew to 6-feet-2, listed at 215 pounds. He attended St. Mary's High School in Stockton, some 60 miles from Castro Valley.

He grew up around baseball, and he started baseball early. "I was 4 years old. My father lied about my age and got me into a T-Ball league."[4] He added, "Of course, when you're that young, you just let kids play a little bit. But he coached me in Little League, following his playing career."[5]

He spent some of his earliest years in big-league clubhouses. "I've got a lot of fond memories of Pete Rose and Joe Morgan when he was with Cincinnati. Johnny Bench. And Robin Yount, when he was with Milwaukee."[6]

After moving to Stockton, Ed helped out at the ballpark. "I did a little bit of everything – I was batboy, clubhouse kid. I got the bullpens when I got a little older. I did a number of jobs there, but – yeah – I was a clubhouse rat."[7]

The Boston Red Sox selected Sprague out of St. Mary's in the June 1985 draft but he chose not to sign and to enroll at Stanford University. He excelled at Stanford, the team not only winning the CWS (Sprague drove in the final game-winning run in 1987) but also playing in tournaments such as the 1987 Pan-American Games. It was there that he met his future wife, Kristen Babb.[8]

Sprague was the first-round pick of the Blue Jays, the 25th overall selection in the June 1988 draft.

Wayne Morgan was the area scout who followed and recommended Sprague to the Blue Jays. It was GM Pat Gillick who secured the actual signature. "He actually signed me in the Chicago airport. I was in between flights."[9]

Sprague's pro career started in 1989 with a full season split between Class-A Dunedin (52 games, batting .219) and the Triple-A Syracuse Chiefs (86 games, batting .208). He played winter ball in Venezuela for the Cardenales de Lara.

He put in a full 142-game season at Syracuse in 1990, upping his batting average to .239 (.293 on-base percentage), with 20 homers and 75 runs batted in. Most of his games were at third base, though he worked nine games at first base and caught in six.

Sprague started 1991 with Syracuse as well, but after driving in 25 runs in 23 games, batting .364, he was elevated to the majors after third baseman Kelly Gruber was hurt. He debuted on May 7. He was 0-for-3 with a strikeout, and collected his first base hit four days later, a single between third and short. He came around to score, for his first time crossing the plate. On the 12th, also at SkyDome against the White Sox, he got his first RBIs, two of them, on singles in the second and fourth innings, both off Greg Hibbard. The Blue Jays won, 4-2. Sprague's first homer was off Hibbard, too, on May 18 at Comiskey Park, a two-run homer in a 7-2 Jays win. Through May 21, he was batting .522. That, of course, didn't last.

Ed Senior was on the scouting staff of the Baltimore Orioles at the time. When the O's called him for a report on his son, he says, he told them, "Throw him fastballs right down the middle. Big, fat fastballs."[10]

Ed Junior enjoyed a solid first season – 35 games at third base, 22 at first, with two stints catching, filling in for Kelly Gruber at third and John Olerud at first base. Sprague finished the season with a .275 average (.361 OBP) and 20 RBIs. The Blue Jays finished first in the AL East, but lost to the Twins in the ALCS, one win to Minnesota's four. Sprague was on the roster but did not play.[11] He returned to Venezuela, to Lara, to continue to work on converting to the role of catcher.[12]

The Blue Jays went all the way in 1992, winning the division, the ALCS over Oakland, and the World Series over the Atlanta Braves. Sprague spent most of the year with Triple-A Syracuse again, as in 1991 often being used as catcher, joining the team in the same utility role as of July 31. He drove in 50 runs in 100 games for the Chiefs. After joining the Blue Jays, he appeared in 22 of the remaining 61 games, more often than not as catcher (in 15 games). In early September, pitcher Todd Stottlemyre had won three games in a row and credited Sprague: "He's had as much to do with my last three wins as I have."[13] He hit .234 with seven RBIs, three of them on a home run off Mike Trombley that beat Minnesota, 4-2, on September 6, that bumped the Jays from a half-game lead in the division to 1½. They never dropped back.

Sprague pinch-hit five times in the postseason, 1-for-2 in both the ALCS and the World Series, with an intentional walk mixed in. Batting in the top of the ninth for reliever Duane Ward in Game Two of the World Series, at Atlanta-Fulton County Stadium, with the Blue Jays trailing 4-3, Sprague – "a reserve catcher pinch-hitting for the Blue Jays" – faced Jeff Reardon, who at the time held the record for the most saves in baseball history – and still does.[14] Sprague swung at the first pitch and homered into the left-field seats, winning the game, 5-4, after Tom Henke shut the door on the Braves in the bottom of the inning. Sprague said, "I've dreamed about it as a kid. Every kid dreams about it. But having it come true, that's a different story."[15]

It was only the third time in World Series history that a pinch-hit home run had given the batter's team a lead. The first was Dusty Rhodes, who hit a three-run homer in the bottom of the 10th inning in Game One of the 1954 World Series. Kirk Gibson's Game One home run the 1988 World Series was the second.

In the bottom of the ninth in Game Three, the score tied 2-2 and runners on second and third with one out, the Braves brought on left-hander Mike Stanton to relieve Mark Wohlers and pitch to left-handed batter John Olerud. Jays manager Cito Gaston countered by having Sprague pinch-hit. Stanton walked Sprague intentionally, loading the bases to pitch to Candy Maldonado, who singled deep to right-center to win the game. The Blue Jays won Game Four and then Game Six – both by one run – and thus the World Series.

After the season Kelly Gruber was traded to the Angels, opening up third base. Sprague played his first full major-league season in 1993 as the team's regular third baseman, appearing in 150 games.[16] His 73 RBIs ranked fifth on the team. He hit .260 (.310 OBP). The Blue Jays finished seven games ahead of the Yankees in the AL East, then won the ALCS in six games against the White Sox and repeated as world champions, beating the Philadelphia Phillies, four games to two. Sprague had four hits in Game One of the ALCS, including a triple, driving in two runs. He hit .286 in the ALCS with four RBIs, but had only one hit in the World Series. With no DH for the games in the National League park, Paul Molitor played third base for most of the three Philly games. Sprague drove in two runs, both with sacrifice flies, one in Game Three and one in Game Six.

The 1994 season was shortened by a strike, but Sprague played in 109 of the 115 games. It was a year he dipped a bit across the board. At one point he endured an 0-for-35 stretch, but then homered on June 1. He hit .240 with 44 RBIs, and 11 home runs. Sprague was player rep for the Blue Jays.

The 1995 season started late, with all teams playing 144 games. Sprague drove in two runs in the first game and five more – thanks to his first grand slam – in the second. He played in every game, batting .244. His 74 RBI total was second on the Blue Jays, just shy of Joe Carter's 76. The team finished in last place. A fair amount of trade talk mentioned Sprague but nothing came of it. Indeed, he signed a new three-year contract with the team in January.

The 1996 Blue Jays played a full 162-game schedule and Sprague appeared in all but three games. The Jays finished fourth. Sprague drove in 101 runs, only six behind Carter. He out-homered Carter, 36 to 30. He hit .247 (.325 OBP). The home-run and RBI totals were both career highs. In December the Blue Jays signed three-time Cy Young Award winner Roger Clemens to a contract. Clemens said, "Joe Carter and Ed Sprague have two championship rings here. I want to be part of one of those banners."[17]

Though Clemens led the majors in wins both in 1997 and 1998, Toronto finished last again in 1997. Sprague's offense dropped across the board in 1997: .228/14/44 in 138 games. His last game was September 3; coming off a 225-consecutive-games streak, an MRI revealed a torn labrum in his right shoulder. He had it surgically repaired.[18]

Looking back on Sprague's 1996 season, we see it was an outlier in home-run totals. He hit 18 homers in 1995, 36 in 1996, and 14 in 1997. One can understand that injuries hampered him badly in 1997, but why had his homers doubled the year before? Indeed, in that one season he hit almost 24 percent of his 152 career home runs. He says that major-league baseballs had been hardened in the wake of the 1994-95 work stoppage and that home-run totals in both leagues had increased.

Tim Johnson was the new manager for the Blue Jays in 1998. Sprague played steadily – in 105 of the team's first 111 games, his average at .238. He'd already exceeded his home-run and RBI totals from the year before, but Toronto was in fourth place, not far from third. Sprague was seen as underperforming, and with too many strikeouts. Knowing that he was to become a free agent after the season, and that they could cut payroll in the meantime, the team made a move with an eye toward the future. Sprague was traded on July 31 to the Oakland Athletics for right-handed relief pitcher Scott Rivette of the Double-A Southern League Huntsville Stars.[19] Sprague played most of August for the Athletics but only seven games in September. One report in late August noted that he had committed four errors in a five-game stretch and said he "just keeps looking like a man in a fog."[20] He hit just .149 in 87 at-bats. The Athletics declined to exercise their option for 1999.

Sprague signed with the Pittsburgh Pirates and had a good year in 1999. The Pirates were looking for someone to play third base for a year, until Aramis Ramirez was ready, and they got good production. One highlight came on May 5. The Giants were in Pittsburgh. Sprague homered to tie the game in the eighth inning, then won it in the 12th with an RBI single to center. After 938 regular-season games, he had his first walk-off hit. "I never did it before. I've had hits in the top of an inning, but never in the last at-bat when it ended a game."[21]

In 137 games, Sprague had his second-highest RBI total: 81. He hit .267 with 22 homers and was named to the 1999 National League All-Star team.[22] He had started the year strong on offense, hitting over .300 into early June, but suffering a spate of defensive errors, 11 in his first 29 games. Both reverted closer to his norm, but by season's end Sprague's .352 on-base percentage was his best of any full season in the majors. He led the National League in getting hit by pitchers – 17 times. Back in 1995, he had led the American League in the same statistic, being hit 15 times. His 1999 season ended on September 19 due to a left broken hand, hit by a Pete Harnisch pitch.

The year 2000 brought another trade and Sprague signed twice during the year as a free agent with the San Diego Padres. Before spring training, he signed with the Padres. In 53 games he hit .274, playing first base as a backup to Ryan Klesko more than any other position. He homered 10 times and drove in 25 runs. At the end of June, the Padres traded him to the Boston Red Sox for two prospects – infielder Cesar Saba and right-handed pitcher Dennis Tankersley.[23] The Red Sox needed a third baseman who would be more solid than a struggling Wilton Veras.

It didn't work out as well as both parties had hoped. In 33 games for Boston, Sprague played in July and the first half of August, hitting .216 with 9 runs batted in. His two-run homer in Oakland on July 28 won that game, 4-1. But on August 23, the Red Sox released him. Eight days later, he signed with the Padres again. Pinch-hitting most of the time, he got into 20 more games, batting .225 and driving in a couple more runs.

Sprague became a Seattle Mariner for 2001 and was used in 45 games, pinch-hitting (mostly against left-handed pitchers) and playing left field, third base, and first base, with three games starting as DH. He hit .298 with a .374 on-base percentage, both the highest figures of his career, but only in limited action.

There was one more season in Sprague's years as a player – in 2002 he signed a minor-league contract with the Texas Rangers and played in Triple A for the Oklahoma RedHawks (Pacific Coast League), batting .268 but never getting summoned to the majors.

Sprague then went into coaching and for the 12 years from 2004 through 2015, he was head coach for the University of the Pacific, based in Stockton, California, a Division I NCAA baseball team. That job ended, and Sprague found new work quickly. "I made one call – to Grady Fuson, who pretty much told me to call Billy Beane. They hired me and I kind of went from there."[24]

He returned to work in pro ball in February 2016, becoming the assistant director of player development and coordinator of on field analytics for the Oakland Athletics in 2018. In October 2019, he became director of player development.

Baseball still runs in the family. The Spragues have four children – Payton, Jed, Paris, and Johnny. Payton, Ed Junior's daughter, spent nearly five years, through most of 2021, working for the Oakland Athletics, becoming the team's partnership marketing manager. She then moved to New York City and a position as sports manager, rights holders for Nielsen Sports. Jed attended St. Mary's of Stockton, as had his father. A first

Ed Sprague's two-run homer won Game Two of the 1992 World Series.

baseman, he played under his father at the University of the Pacific and then transferred to the University of Nevada, Reno. He was drafted by the Chicago White Sox in the 37th round of the 2014 draft, but did not sign. He is a growth account executive with Twilio, a San Francisco-based cloud communication platform.

Sprague's position as director of player development is, quite obviously, an extremely important one. Asked to summarize the work for the Athletics, he explained, "I oversee all of our minor-league players – 180 domestically and 35 internationally. About 65-70 staff."[25] He doesn't travel with the big-league club, "but I travel throughout all our minor-league system."

How long might he continue? "I enjoy it right now. I like what's going on and I love the organization. We'll see what happens.

"I've been fortunate. Baseball's been pretty much my whole life. From the time I was born, and growing up in it. When I retired, I coached in college. Now I'm back in the pro game. I guess I've never really gotten out of baseball since the time I was born."[26]

SOURCES

In addition to the sources cited in the Notes, the author consulted Baseball-Reference.com, Retrosheet.org, and SABR.org.

NOTES

1   Baseball was deemed a "demonstration sport" in the 1988 Olympics.

2   He said of himself, "I was a journeyman. I was never very impressive in my big-league career. I really don't know how I stayed in the big leagues as long as I did. I guess I just tricked some people into letting me stick around." Marty York, "A Successful Outing for Jr. Would Make Father's Day," *Globe and Mail* (Toronto), June 15, 1991: A12. Of his father, Ed said, "He's been the main influence on my life, obviously. He never forced me to play ball, but he always was there when I need him."

3   When the team lost its major-league affiliation with the Chicago Cubs before the 1985 season, Michele Sprague sold the team. A story in the *Los Angeles Times* featured a photograph of her. Jerry Crowe, "The Town That Lost Its Team," *Los Angeles Times*, August 21, 1985: v_b1.

4   Paul Patton, "Jays' First Pick a Third Sacker," *Globe and Mail*, June 2, 1988: A22.

5   Author interview with Ed Sprague Jr. on January 13, 2022, hereafter "Sprague interview."

6   Sprague interview.

7   Sprague interview.

8   The two were housed in the same dormitory in Indianapolis. An article discussed their "gold-medal marriage"– see Tim Larimer, "His and Hers," *The Sporting News*, August 17, 1992: 15. Larimer says, "He invited her to a baseball game. She found it boring. She introduced him to synchronized swimming. He thought it silly." Sprague majored in economics, and completed three years of college before turning to professional baseball.

9   Sprague interview. He reportedly received a $100,000 signing bonus.

10   Marty York, "A Successful Outing for Jr. Would Make Father's Day."

11   Ed Sprague Sr. had been with the Cincinnati Reds in the 1972 World Series but was not used.

12   Neil MacCarl, "Toronto Blue Jays," *The Sporting News*, October 14, 1991: 26. The following spring, it was reported that "[t]he Blue Jays seem convinced that Ed Sprague is their catcher of the future." Peter Pascarelli, "Piniella Should 'Really Like This Club,'" *The Sporting News*, March 30, 1992: 13.

13   Tribune wires, "Blue Jays' 1-2 Punch KO's Twins," *Chicago Tribune*, September 7, 1992: 9.

14   The phrase was Mark Newman's. See "Ninth-Inning Homer Gives Toronto Home-Field Advantage," *The Sporting News*, October 26, 1992: 10. Reardon had 357 saves.

15   Newman. He said he hadn't seen the ball land. "I looked up right into the lights. All I saw was Deion's back and I knew it was gone." He was referring to left fielder Deion Sanders. Joey Reeves, "More Limelight for Spragues with Home Run," *Chicago Tribune*, October 19, 1992: A9. For further perspective on the perhaps-unlikely hero, see Jim Murray, "Another Masked Man Is Turned into a Hero," *Los Angeles Times*, October 1, 1992: OCC1.

16   He was, at times, challenged in fielding, not surprising in that the organization was inconsistent in its training him for catcher as well as third base, and occasionally first base. "The biggest thing you want is to separate your offence and your defence," Sprague said. "I'm going to make my mistakes in the field, no question. But Cito has talked to me about all this. He said, 'Whatever happens defensively, don't let it affect your offence.'" Marty York, "Sprague Lets Bat Do the Talking," *Globe and Mail*, April 10, 1993: A14.

17   Jeff Jacobs, "Two World Titles, and No Duquette," *Hartford Courant*, December 14, 1996: C1.

18   In a 2008 interview, he acknowledged having taken over-the-counter androstenedione in 1998 while rehabbing from his 1997 shoulder injury. CBC Sports, "Former Jay Ed Sprague Took Steroids: Report," CBC.ca. April 11, 2008. https://www.cbc.ca/sports/baseball/former-jay-ed-sprague-took-steroids-report-1.720564. Accessed December 6, 2021. See also Mark Zwolinski, "Glory Jay Admits to Steroid Use," *Toronto Star*, April 11, 2008: S1.

19   Rivette joined the Jays team in the Southern League. He never did make it to the majors.

20   Steve Kettmann, "Oakland," *The Sporting News*, August 24, 1998: 26.

21   Alan Robinson, "Giants Fall in 12 Innings to Pirates," *Santa Cruz* (California) *Sentinel*, May 6, 1999: 13. The walkoff hit won his 938th game.

22   In his lone at-bat, he grounded out.

23   Tankersley pitched in 25 games for San Diego, during parts of three seasons, 2002-2004, with a 1-10 record (7.61 ERA). Saba didn't make it to the majors.

24   Sprague interview.

25   Sprague interview.

26   Sprague interview.

DAVE STIEB

By Joe Cox

He won the second-most games of any pitcher in the 1980s, was a seven-time All-Star, and helped transform the Toronto Blue Jays from expansion basement-dwellers to world champions. But Dave Stieb may be best known for his terrible luck in attempting to close out no-hitters. Four times in five years, Stieb reached the ninth inning with no-hitters. Three times in 12 months, he actually reached the last out of a no-hitter. Each time he missed out on finishing the bid. Just when it looked as if Stieb would never join the no-hit club, on September 2, 1990, he successfully completed the game that, three decades later, remained the only no-hitter in Blue Jays history.

David Andrew Stieb was born on July 22, 1957, in Santa Ana, California. Stieb's father was a contractor. His older brother, Steve, was a catcher in the Atlanta Braves system for three seasons, batting .217 as a professional and never reaching above Double-A ball. Dave initially made a splash in baseball as an outfielder, rather than as a pitcher. He described himself as having "decent power and an exceptional arm," but noted that he "had never tossed a competitive pitch until I played for Southern Illinois University – and then only in emergencies."[1] In fact, Stieb hit .394 with 12 home runs and 48 RBIs in 1978 as a junior, and was named to *The Sporting News*'s All-American squad.[2] Stieb noted in his autobiography that he pitched a grand total of 17 innings that season.[3]

But when Toronto drafted Stieb in the fifth round of the 1978 major-league draft, they saw him as a pitcher. Stieb later recalled that Toronto asked him if he would mind pitching, and while he was initially reluctant, his attitude changed when Toronto officials told him, "The quickest way to make it would be pitching."[4] Stieb pitched a grand total of 128 innings in the minor leagues in 1978 and 1979 before Toronto called him to the big-league club, where he proceeded to grow up as a pitcher on baseball's biggest stage.

Stieb described his stuff in 1986 as featuring a tailing fastball, a regular fastball, a slow, straight overhand curve, a near side-arm hard curve, a batting-practice fastball, which Stieb called a "dead fish," and a slider, which quickly became Stieb's out pitch.[5]

In the early years of the Blue Jays, Stieb could be brilliant, but often still lose games. As a rookie in 1979, Stieb compiled an 8-8 record with a 4.31 ERA. The rest of the Blue Jays' staff went 45-101, and Stieb's eight victories were only one shy of the team lead. The Blue Jays finished in last place in 1980 and 1981, as well, and the struggles behind him gave Stieb a reputation for hard-fought competitiveness – and for not always accepting the mediocrity that surrounded him in those early seasons in Toronto. Withering glares might be shot at opponents, umpires, or even Blue Jays who made errors behind Stieb. In time he would learn to control such outbursts, but his reputation as a fierce competitor was made. Speaking of such behavior, Blue Jays catcher Ernie Whitt said of Stieb,

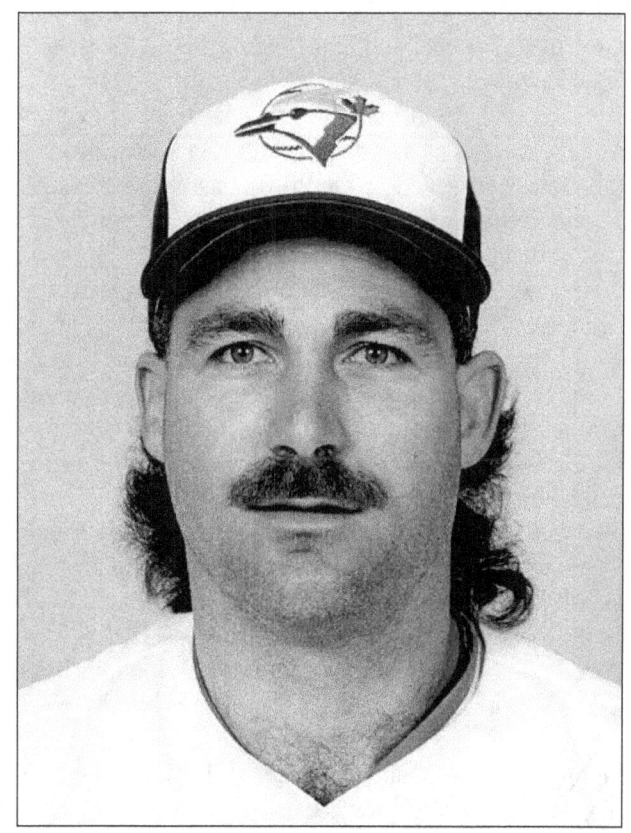

"That's just his makeup, the way he competes. He's like that on the golf course, playing cards, whatever."[6]

In 1980 Stieb made his first All-Star Game appearance. While he finished the season 12-15 with a 3.71 ERA, Stieb pitched 14 complete games and finished among the top seven or eight AL pitchers in pitching WAR. In a strike-shortened 1981 campaign, Stieb again was an All-Star, and his 11-10 mark (with a 3.19 ERA) marked the first time a Blue Jays pitcher had worked 150 innings and completed the season with a winning record.[7] Stieb was unhappy playing for such a poor team, and Toronto engaged in serious trade discussions in the offseason involving him, including one contemplated deal that would have moved him to Philadelphia for six players including Ryne Sandberg.[8]

Stieb was eventually considered too valuable to trade. The following season, 1982, saw Toronto approach respectability with the best season in the franchise's young history. The Jays won 78 games, led by Stieb, who tallied 17 victories, and 19 complete games, pitching 288⅓ innings and finishing fourth in AL Cy Young Award balloting. Stieb won the AL Pitcher of the Year award from *The Sporting News*.

Stieb's hard feelings about Toronto were largely smoothed over when he inked a six-year, $5 million contract before the 1983 season. At the end of May Stieb was 8-3 with a 1.66 ERA. He started and won the All-Star Game, and his 17 victories and 3.04 ERA helped Toronto to its first winning season.

Stieb won 16 more games in 1984 as Toronto finished second in its division to the World Series winner, the Detroit Tigers. For the third consecutive season, Stieb led the American League in WAR for pitchers. He again started the All-Star Game.

In 1985 Stieb led Toronto to its first postseason appearance. He was just 14-13, but led the league with a 2.48 ERA, and was again an All-Star. On August 24, 1985, Stieb completed eight hitless innings against the White Sox before Rudy Law led off the ninth inning with a home run to spoil the no-hit bid. Still, Stieb helped Toronto win the division. The LCS had changed formats to best four of seven, and when Stieb shut out Kansas City for eight innings to win Game One, Toronto was in good shape. In Game Four Stieb worked six innings of one-run baseball. When Toronto rallied to win in the ninth inning, the Jays held a 3-games-to-1 lead in the series. However, Toronto lost the last three games, and thus the series, with Stieb taking the loss in Game Seven. Still, Toronto extended his contract through 1995.

After winning at least 11 games for six seasons and posting an ERA of no higher than 3.71, Stieb had a miserable 1986 campaign. At the All-Star break, instead of starting the midsummer classic, he was stuck at home with a 2-9 record and a 5.80 ERA. One contemporary account blamed Stieb's poor performance on some lingering elbow issues, which had caused him to move away from his trademark slider.[9] Whatever the problem, Stieb did improve in the second half of the year, but finished just 7-12, with a 4.74 ERA. The Jays also struggled, finishing fourth in the AL East.

The 1987 season represented something of a return to form for Stieb. He started cold, but finished the year at 13-9, with a 4.09 ERA in 185 innings. The season ended in disaster for the Blue Jays, though, as they held a 3½-game lead for the AL East title with just seven games to play. Toronto lost all seven, and Detroit won the division outright with a 1-0 win over the Jays on the last day of the season. During that horrific stretch run, Stieb contributed a disappointing loss in which he was knocked out in the fifth inning. Manager Jimy Williams had bounced Stieb in and out of the starting rotation during the last month of the season.

During the offseason Toronto shopped Stieb extensively, but decided to keep him.[10] One columnist called Stieb "erratic" and opined that he "will likely never be as good as he was a few years ago."[11] In fact, after two straight difficult seasons, Stieb strung together three more excellent seasons from 1988 to 1990, nearly equaling his work from 1982 to 1984 as the peak performances of his career.

Stieb reached the 1988 All-Star break with a 10-5 record and a 2.93 ERA, which earned him his sixth All-Star Game selection of the 1980s. Stieb faltered a bit in midseason, but finished 1988 with a series of games that demonstrated both how good and how unlucky he could be.

Stieb gave up one run in seven innings to Detroit on September 13 to claim his 13th win of the season. On September 18 he shut out Cleveland on four hits for his 14th win. On September 24 Stieb faced the Indians again, this time in Cleveland, and nearly made baseball history. He completed 8⅔ hitless innings against Cleveland and had a 2-and-2 count on Julio Franco. Franco grounded the next pitch to second base, where the ball hit a divot left at the Stadium from a Cleveland Browns game and ricocheted over the head of second baseman Manuel Lee for a single, spoiling the no-hitter.[12] A disappointed Stieb then got the last out and completed his second straight shutout. After the game he told reporters, "I needed one ounce of luck right there and what did I get? Bad luck. Oh well."[13]

Unbelievably, in his next start, the last of the year, on September 30, Stieb again flirted with a no-hitter, retiring 26 Baltimore Orioles without yielding a base hit. Again, he was disappointed, as pinch-hitter Jim Traber blooped a 2-and-2 pitch into right field for a single. Stieb retired the next hitter to end the game. "It's a heartbreaker," he admitted after the game. "I'm just wrecked. You get through it all, the ball hits the bat, and you wait. Then it doesn't happen."[14]

Stieb's final line for 1988 featured a 16-8 mark and a 3.04 ERA, as well as a 31⅓-inning scoreless streak to end the year. In his last three starts of the 1988 season, he pitched three shutouts, allowing just six hits over the 27 innings and twice falling one pitch shy of no-hitters. Even Stieb's harshest critics had to admit that he had shown the ability to again dominate opposing hitters.

After he finished 1988 so well, Stieb and the Blue Jays both had a poor beginning to 1989. Manager Jimy Williams was fired on May 14, at which point Toronto was 12-24 and Stieb had a 4.84 ERA. Longtime Jays coach Cito Gaston succeeded Williams, and the team rallied to a 77-49 mark for the rest of the season, winning the AL East. The memorable season was also highlighted by the unveiling of the SkyDome, Toronto's state-of-the-art new stadium.

The year was memorable for other reasons for Stieb, who finished the season at 17-8 with a 3.35 ERA. He again suffered no-hit heartbreak when on August 4 he set down the first 26 Yankees he faced before Roberto Kelly broke up the perfect game with a double. Stieb struck out 11 batters, and held on to win the game, 2-1, but had yet again lost a no-hitter on the last batter. Stieb also lost both of his starts in the ALCS, as the Jays lost to Oakland in five games.

The 1990 season proved to be an odd one, both for Stieb and for the Blue Jays. Stieb was 11-3 at the All-Star break, and was chosen for his seventh (and final) All-Star squad. On September 2 he no-hit the Indians in Municipal Stadium, the Blue Jays first (and as of over three decades later, only) no-hitter.

In his next start, on September 8, Stieb won his 18th game of the year. He made five more starts, but did not win another game. The Blue Jays, who spent most of the season in second place, had a late-season surge, and led the AL East race by 1½ games with eight games to play. They lost six of the last eight, and on the last day of the season needed to beat Baltimore and have Boston lose to Chicago to force a tie for the

Stieb appeared in seven All-Star Games, a Toronto team record.

division crown. Stieb pitched well, working into the eighth inning, but the bullpen lost the lead around the same time that Boston edged out Chicago, and Toronto was knocked out of the playoffs.

Still, Stieb had begun the 1990s with an 18-6 season and a 2.93 ERA, good for fifth in the Cy Young Award voting. But the rest of his career included just 10 more major-league victories. Stieb was effective early in the 1991 season, going 4-3 with a 3.17 ERA, but shoulder tendinitis and a herniated disc in his back limited him to just nine starts, the last of which came on May 22.

In 1992 Toronto had finally formed the nucleus to win a championship. Unfortunately for Stieb, he was reduced to a bit player. He was 4-6 with a 5.04 ERA in 96⅓ innings for Toronto, and his last appearance of the year came on August 8. Accordingly, when the Blue Jays beat the Atlanta Braves in the World Series, Stieb savored the moment, but as an injured spectator instead of as a starting pitcher. "It was very bittersweet," Stieb admitted. He recalled that when the Series ended he "celebrated like I won the last game … but I don't look at it like somebody that played in it and won it."[15]

The Blue Jays did not renew Stieb's contract after the season, and he signed a free-agent deal with the Chicago White Sox for 1993. Stieb made only four starts with Chicago, going 1-3 with a 6.04 ERA, before he was released. Stieb signed a minor-league deal with the Kansas City Royals, but six weeks later was released again, and decided to retire from baseball.

This held until 1998, when Stieb was in spring training as a coach for Toronto. He had thrown on numerous occasions, and did not notice the old elbow soreness. Eventually he was talked into asking manager Tim Johnson for a shot to pitch.[16] Stieb went to the minors and worked his way back to the Blue Jays for one last hurrah. Stieb pitched 19 times, including just three starts, and went 1-2 with a 4.83 ERA. After the season, Toronto approached Stieb about continuing his career as a reliever, but he elected instead to again retire, this time for good.

Stieb continued to serve the Blue Jays as a coach for a few years, but gradually drifted back home to Nevada, where he was part of a construction company and spent much of his time with his family. As of 2022, Stieb remained Toronto's leader in many pitching categories, including wins (175), innings pitched (2,873), and strikeouts (1,658). Stieb threw five one-hit games in his career, but treasures the memories of the September 1990 day when he finally nailed down his no-hit masterpiece.

NOTES

1   Dave Stieb with Kevin Boland, *Tomorrow I'll Be Perfect* (Garden City, New York: Doubleday & Company, Inc., 1986), 14.

2   Lou Pavlovich, "Horner and Gibson Stand Out in Selections," *The Sporting News*, July 8, 1978.

3   Stieb with Boland, 31.

4   Murray Chass, "Switch Helps Stieb's Career," *New York Times*, June 3, 1982.

5   Stieb with Boland, 80-81.

6   "Stieb Cools Temper, Gets Hot," *St. Louis Post-Dispatch*, July 31, 1985.

7   Neil MacCarl, "Losing Took Toll on Jays' Mattick," *The Sporting News*, October 24, 1981.

8   Peter Gammons, "'82 Will Be Brighter for These 10 Players," *The Sporting News*, January 2, 1982.

9   Moss Klein, "Beneath 30-Year Malaise, Pulse Felt in Tribe," *The Sporting News*, May 12, 1986.

10   Neil MacCarl, "Blue Jays," *The Sporting News*, January 4, 1988.

11   Moss Klein, "Blue Jays at Critical Point; Next Is Critical List," *The Sporting News*, May 2, 1988.

12   "Perez: One-Legged No-Hitter," *The Sporting News*, October 3, 1988.

13   Associated Press, "Stieb Loses No-Hitter With Two Outs in 9th," *Chicago Tribune*, September 25, 1988.

14   Dan Hafner, "Baseball Roundup: Out Away, It's Oh, No for Stieb No-Hitter Again," *Los Angeles Times*, October 1, 1988.

15   Dave Stieb, telephone interview with author, January 23, 2016.

16   Stieb interview.

TODD STOTTLEMYRE

By Alan Cohen

Life has its defining moments. For many ballplayers, the remembered moments come from first appearances to championship wins and include everything in between. But the life of a ballplayer is often defined by moments off the playing field and away from the crowds. A defining moment in the life of young Todd Stottlemyre came when he was only 15 years old. It took place in a hospital room. The opposition that day was a lifelong enemy of the Stottlemyre family – leukemia. Todd gave his younger brother, Jason, a bone-marrow transplant. The procedure was painful for Todd. Jason was 11 years old and had been diagnosed in 1977, four years before the procedure. On March 3, 1981, within days of the procedure, Jason died.

"I suppose we expected it to happen, but I can't say we were prepared for it. Now I take him every day to the field with me. And if something bad happens to me out there, well, it doesn't mean so much."[1]

And fully coming to grips with the loss of his younger brother would take some time.

Todd Vernon Stottlemyre was born on May 20, 1965, in Sunnyside, Washington, a small city near Yakima in the south central part of the state. He was the second of three sons born to Mel and Jean Stottlemyre. His father was in his second season with the New York Yankees. His older brother, Mel Jr., had been born two years earlier. Jason came along in 1969.

Growing up, Todd was primarily an infielder. He took to the mound, for the first time since Little League, while playing American Legion baseball. In the summer between his junior and senior years, he enjoyed much success and hurled a two-hitter in shutting out Moorhead, Minnesota, in the semifinals of the regional tournament in Miles City, Montana.[2]

Todd graduated from Davis High School in Yakima, where in his senior year he started the season with an 8-0 record, a 0.53 ERA, and 87 strikeouts in 54 innings.[3] His record, and his being the son of an accomplished big-league pitcher and coach, attracted attention. Shortly after graduating from high school,

he was drafted by the Yankees in the fifth round of the June amateur draft in 1983 but did not sign.

He went on to the University of Nevada at Las Vegas. In his freshman year at UNLV, he went 10-4 with a 4.20 ERA and 91 strikeouts in 105 innings.[4] He hurled a one-hitter on March 19, 1984, to defeat Nebraska, 2-1. He was selected for Team USA's 43-man roster on May 3, 1984 but was not selected for the Olympic team. Todd and his brother Mel Jr. withdrew from UNLV after Todd's freshman year, as their father thought they were being overworked by the UNLV head coach. They were both eligible for the draft in January 1985.[5] Todd was made the overall number-one pick in the draft's secondary phase (for previously drafted players) and was selected by the Cardinals. Brother Mel Jr. was drafted third overall and was the first choice of the Astros.

Todd, while negotiating with the Cardinals, transferred to Yakima Community College, where he pitched in the spring of 1985. He was unable to come to terms with St. Louis, and Toronto in June 1985 staked its claim, making him their number-one pick in the draft. He signed with the Blue Jays on August 12, 1985.

Stottlemyre's first pitch as a professional was thrown in the Florida Instructional League in the autumn of 1985. He was assigned to the Class-A Ventura County Gulls of the California League at the beginning of the 1986 season. With Ventura he was 9-4 with a 2.43 ERA before being promoted in June to the Knoxville Blue Jays of the Double-A Southern League. In his best game with Knoxville, on June 30 he had a no-hitter against Jacksonville through seven innings but had thrown 100 pitches. His manager, Larry Hardy, pulled him from the game.[6] The win in that game brought Stottlemyre's early record with Knoxville to 3-0 (0.42 ERA). He wound up posting an 8-7 record (4.18 ERA) with Knoxville.

He went to spring training with Toronto in 1987 and was assigned to Triple-A Syracuse. He went 11-13 (4.44 ERA) in 34 starts with the Chiefs. He started the 1988 season with Toronto. In his fourth start, on May 3, he flirted with a no-hitter. He took a perfect game into the seventh inning. With one out in the bottom of the seventh, and the Blue Jays leading the game, 3-0, Stottlemyre hit Rey Quinones with a pitch. He recorded one more out that inning before losing the no-hitter and shutout on a double by Alvin Davis that scored Quinones. At that point, manager Jimy Williams removed him from the game. The Blue Jays pulled away in the late innings for a 9-2 win, and Stottlemyre had his first major-league victory.

However, through 23 appearances, Stottlemyre was 3-8 with a 5.36 ERA. He was sent back to Syracuse and in one month with the Chiefs, he was 5-0 (2.05 ERA). He rejoined the Blue Jays in September, and the 23-year-old right-hander finished his first big-league season with a 4-8 record in 28 appearances. The Blue Jays finished third in the AL East.

In 1989 Stottlemyre got off to a rocky start and was 0-3 (5.81 ERA) when he was once again dispatched to Syracuse. He was there from May 15 through the end of June, appearing in 10 games and going 3-2 (3.23 ERA). In July he returned to the major leagues to stay. The big difference in 1989 was that Stottlemyre had, during the offseason, developed a slider. By the time he returned to the Blue Jays, he was making good use of the pitch. During the balance of the 1989 season,

he was 7-4 with a 3.38 ERA as the Blue Jays finished first in the AL East. Stottlemyre got his first taste of postseason play. The Blue Jays lost the best-of-seven ALCS to Oakland in five games. Todd started Game Two and was charged with the loss as Toronto lost to the A's, 6-3.

"It was the most frustrating time of my career. I wondered if I would ever come back as a Jay, or somewhere else." – Todd Stottlemyre, in April 1990, reflecting on being sent down in 1989 and coming back to have success.[7]

While in the minors in 1989, Stottlemyre had been mentored by Syracuse pitching coach Galen Cisco, who joined him with Toronto in 1990. Cisco had told him, "You have to work on your concentration, your intensity, and controlling your emotions." The hard work, which included Todd being the first to report for spring training in 1990, paid off.[8]

Manager Cito Gaston, who had sent Stottlemyre to the minors in 1989, handed him the ball on Opening Day in 1990. Although he lost the opener to Texas, 4-2, he put together a string of four straight wins in the early going, topped off by his first complete game of the season, a 5-1 win over Detroit.

"This ballpark was my playground and backyard. It was my fantasyland." – Todd Stottlemyre discussing Yankee Stadium on June 15, 1990.[9]

On Father's Day 1989, Stottlemyre made his first career appearance at Yankee Stadium, where his father had hurled for the Yankees. He defeated the Yankees, 8-1, in his second complete-game win of the season and just missed a shutout when Matt Nokes homered with two outs in the ninth inning.

Toronto was in contention in 1990 and finished in second place. Stottlemyre, after beginning the season 9-7, was 13-17 with a 4.34 ERA. He led the Blue Jays staff with four complete games. The next season, he won his first five decisions, and was undefeated at home (6-0) until August 10. He wound up with a season's record of 15-8 and was the staff leader in innings pitched (219) as the Blue Jays won their second division title in three years. In the postseason, Toronto lost the League Championship Series to Minnesota in five games. Stottlemyre started Game Four and was on the short end of a 9-3 decision. The Twins had reached him for four fourth-inning runs, and he came out of the game with two outs in the inning, trailing 4-1.

In 1992, after knocking at the door for five seasons, Toronto earned the first World Series trophy in the 16-year history of the franchise. Stottlemyre was 12-11 with a less-than-stellar ERA of 4.50, but his season had more than its share of highlights. On April 29, pitching at home against the Angels, he had his first career shutout, scattering seven hits in a 1-0 win. His second shutout, on August 26 at Chicago, put Toronto up by two games as the season entered its last 30 contests. As often happened in 1992, the Toronto bats came through with Stottlemyre on the mound. The score on August 26 was 9-0.

In postseason play in 1992, Todd was moved to the bullpen and made five appearances. In Game Four of the ALCS against Oakland, he entered with one out in the bottom of the fourth inning. Starter Jack Morris had been ineffective, and the A's had built up a 5-1 lead. Runners were at the corners. Stottlemyre left the game after pitching the seventh inning. Toronto scored three runs in the top of the eighth to cut Oakland's lead to 6-4. Mike Timlin came on to pitch for Toronto in the bottom of the eighth. A homer by Roberto Alomar tied things up in the ninth inning, and Toronto won, 7-6, in 11 innings. The Blue Jays took a 3-1 series lead and won in six games.

In the 1992 World Series, Toronto faced Atlanta. Stottlemyre appeared in four games, pitching a total of 3⅔ innings of scoreless ball. His Game One entrance marked the second time that a father-son pitching combo had made World Series appearances. Jim Bagby (1920) and Jim Bagby Jr. (1946) had preceded Mel and Todd. In the Game Six win that clinched the championship for Toronto, Stottlemyre was called on at the beginning of the seventh inning. Toronto was leading 2-1. After striking out Mark Lemke and inducing Jeff Treadway to ground out, he allowed an infield hit to Otis Nixon. At that point, with left-hand-hitting Deion Sanders due up, manager Cito Gaston brought in David Wells to replace Stottlemyre. There was no scoring in the inning, but Atlanta tied the game in the ninth inning. Toronto went on to win the game, 4-3, in 11 innings.

In 1993, as the Blue Jays won their second consecutive World Series championship, Stottlemyre was 11-12 with a 4.84 ERA. The highlight of his season was a shutout of the Boston Red Sox on September 21. He struck out 10 and walked only one batter in the 5-0 win. The win extended Toronto's division lead to five games. The Blue Jays wound up winning the division by seven games. Although his team was successful during the postseason, Stottlemyre did not do well in either the ALCS or the World Series. In Game Four of the ALCS against the White Sox, he allowed five runs, including a monster homer by Frank Thomas, in six innings of work and was charged with the loss as

Toronto fell, 7-4. In Game Four of the World Series against the Phillies, he was pulled after allowing six runs in the first two innings of a slugfest that was ultimately won by Toronto, 15-14.

But at a time in his life when Stottlemyre should have felt fulfilled, the demons that had been with him since the death of his brother still haunted him. As a pitcher, despite an increasing repertoire of pitches, he still tried to overpower everyone. As a person, he could be temperamental. He saw himself as the "murderer" of his little brother, as he had been the transplant donor.[10]

Stottlemyre let his temper get the better of him after the World Series. During the Series, Mayor Ed Rendell of Philadelphia, remembering the long homer hit by Frank Thomas in the ACLS against Stottlemyre, said, "I'd like to hit against him." After the Blue Jays won the World Series, there was a parade followed by a rally at the Toronto SkyDome. Stottlemyre stepped to the microphone and said, "Well, I've got one message for the mayor of Philly, he can kiss my ass."[11] Stottlemyre's emotions had gotten the best of him, and he was noticeably out of control.

He sought guidance from Harvey Dorfman, a noted mental skills coach. Dorfman's training enabled Stottlemyre to cope with his guilt and to address his challenges. Dorfman advised Stottlemyre not to have a knee-jerk reaction when faced with a problem – to be less confrontational. He had not always been successful in handling confrontations, but he was now better equipped to deal with them.[12]

It was during spring training of 1994 that Stottlemyre was confronted with a challenge that tested the behavioral standards he had learned from Dorfman. He was with mentor and teammate Dave Stewart, a fellow pitcher. On February 19, they and a few guests had been out to dinner in Tampa to celebrate Stewart's 37th birthday. After dinner, as the clock passed midnight, the group went to the Masquerades Nightclub. Stottlemyre and several of the guests entered, but Stewart was detained by police officers. In short order, Stottlemyre was also detained. In the process, he was brutalized by the officers and thrown in the back of a police cruiser. He successfully resisted the urge to retaliate.

What provoked the incident? Stewart refused to pay a $3 cover fee and did not want to wear a wristband (indicating he was old enough to drink) when entering the bar. A security person named Steve Bell called the police, and the police, 14 in number, overreacted. Stewart and Stottlemyre were arrested and accused

On July 25, 1990, while George Brett hit for the cycle, Todd and brother Mel Stottlemyre Jr. also pitched in the same game.

of attacking the police. The local media portrayed Stottlemyre and Stewart as criminals. A trial date was set for after the season, and throughout the season there was a cloud over Stottlemyre. Throughout the ordeal, the players maintained their innocence.[13]

After the 1994 season, in which he was 7-7 with a 4.22 ERA before it ended with a player strike in August, Stottlemyre had his day in court. The trial took place in November. The testimony from the police, according to Stottlemyre, was fabricated and, per accounts of trial observers, inconsistent with accounts given in depositions during pretrial hearings and investigations.[14] On November 10 Stottlemyre testified and spoke of the abuse he suffered in February. At the end of the trial, the jury came to the realization that the police had been lying and found Stottlemyre and Stewart not guilty on all counts.[15] One week after the trial began, it had taken the jury 45 minutes to deliberate as to the outcome.[16]

It was then back to baseball. Stottlemyre had become a free agent and signed with the Oakland Athletics.

With the A's in 1995, Stottlemyre was 14-7 and finished second in the American League with 205 strikeouts. The good news was that he led the staff in wins. The bad news was that when the top pitcher on the staff wins only 14 games, you are in trouble. The A's were 67-77 for the strike-shortened season and finished in fourth (last) place. The pitching staff was in chaos: 23 men had pitched for the A's during the 1995 season. Seven of the pitchers were 30 or older. In the offseason, the A's went for youth and dealt the 30-year-old Stottlemyre to the St. Louis Cardinals for four unknown players.

With the Cardinals in 1996, Stottlemyre went 14-11 and brought his ERA down to 3.87 in a career-high 223⅓ innings. His turnaround was due in large part to the mentorship of Dave Duncan. Of course, he always had another mentor closer to home, his father.

On September 3 Stottlemyre was the winning pitcher as the Cardinals defeated Houston, 12-3. Over eight innings, he scattered four hits and struck out nine batters, bringing his record for the season to 12-10. The win put the Cardinals a half-game ahead of Houston. It also was Stottlemyre's 95th career win. That was significant: Combined with his father's 164 wins, it made Mel and Todd the winningest father-son pitching combo in major-league history. Their 259 wins eclipsed the record previously held by Dizzy and Steve Trout. (When Todd retired at the end of the 2002 season, their record mark stood at 302 wins.)

The win on September 3 was the fifth straight for the Cardinals. By the time that streak ended on September 8, they had won eight in a row. They extended their division lead down the stretch. After Stottlemyre earned his 14th win on September 23, St. Louis led the division by 5½ games. The magic number was one. They clinched the division the next night, and advanced to postseason play.

It was Stottlemyre's fifth postseason. In the opening game of the Division Series against the Padres, he earned his first postseason win. He pitched into the seventh inning, allowing only one run, a homer by Rickey Henderson. He struck out seven batters and left the game with a 3-1 lead, which wound up being the final score.

In the LCS against Atlanta, Stottlemyre was the winner in Game Two. He pitched six innings as the Cardinals won 8-3 to take a 2-0 lead in the series. Duncan noted after the game that Stottlemyre's new-found maturity was a key factor in the win. "The old Todd wouldn't have known himself well enough to back off (after issuing a two-run third-inning home run to Marquis Grissom that cut the Cardinals' lead to 3-2). His young mentality was to overpower everybody."[17]

Of Duncan, Stottlemyre said, "You lose focus, and he reminds you (to take it one pitch at a time). It sounds so simple but it's tough sometimes. He gives you a game plan. His preparation is unbelievable."[18]

The Braves came back and won the series in seven games. Stottlemyre absorbed the loss in Game Five when the Braves feasted on the offerings of five Cardinals pitchers in a 14-0 blowout. Todd lasted three batters into the second inning and was charged with seven runs. His final appearance in 1996 came in Game Six against Atlanta. He entered the game in the bottom of the eighth inning with the Cardinals trailing 2-1. He allowed Atlanta an additional run as the Braves won, 3-1, to even the series at three games apiece.

In 1997 Stottlemyre went 12-9 (3.88 ERA) in his second year with the Cardinals, tying for the team lead in wins, but St. Louis was out of the running early that season, finishing in fourth place with a 73-89 record. In 1998, with free agency looming, the Cardinals elected to trade Stottlemyre to the Texas Rangers on July 31 after he had gone 9-9 (3.51 ERA) in 23 appearances. He went to the Rangers with shortstop Royce Clayton for third baseman Fernando Tatis and pitcher Darren Oliver. With the Rangers, he was 5-4 (4.33 ERA) as his temporary employers finished first in the AL West. In the postseason opener, Stottlemyre pitched a complete game, but was the losing pitcher as the Yankees, with his pitching-coach father in the dugout, defeated the Rangers, 2-0, to go one up in the Division Series. New York swept the best-of-five series.

A free agent after the season, Stottlemyre signed a four-year contract with Arizona worth $32 million. In 1999, his first year with the pitching-rich Diamondbacks, he started 17 games and went 6-3. For the first time in his career, he spent a prolonged amount of time on the disabled list with a torn rotator cuff. He had come out of a May 17 contest at San Francisco after four innings. It was obvious to his manager, Buck Showalter, that something was wrong.

Generally, season-ending surgery is the prescription for a rotator cuff tear, but Stottlemyre opted to not throw for a month and to engage in an exercise program that would strengthen his arm and body. During his recuperation, he addressed problems with his delivery that had put undue stress on the shoulder. His hope was to return to action late in the season. With surgery, he would not have returned until the beginning of the 2001 season.

"Next thing I know, there was a team standing there with cameras and baseballs. I didn't know what was going on." – Todd Stottlemyre, August 5, 1999[19]

Stottlemyre made his first rehab start on August 4 with the Diamondbacks entry in the Arizona Rookie League. Before the game he was into his well-known pregame ritual. He did not communicate with anyone, bringing his intensity to a peak level, focusing total anger on his opponent, albeit a group of very young minor-league players. The team was known as the Mexican Stars. The team was unaffiliated, and its players interrupted Stottlemyre to hug him and take pictures – not quite the norm.

After the disruption, Stottlemyre took to the mound and threw 58 pitches in four shutout innings, yielding three hits and striking out five batters. His fastball was clocked at 91 mph. He had two more rehab appearances and returned to the Diamondbacks on August 20.

Down the stretch, Stottlemyre was 2-2. The Diamondbacks easily won the AL West, outdistancing second-place San Francisco by 14 games. Arizona faced the Mets in the Division Series and Stottlemyre started Game Two. In six innings, he allowed one run, and the Diamondbacks had a 5-1 lead. He came out of the game with one out in the seventh inning and the bullpen maintained the lead. Arizona won the game, 7-1, and evened the series at one game apiece. The Mets won the next two games and proceeded to the LCS.

In 2000 Stottlemyre once again spent a major part of the season on the DL. Suffering from tendinitis in his pitching elbow, he was shut down in late June after coming out of a game on June 25 when he hurled only one inning against the Rockies. The inflammation in his elbow had pushed against his ulnar nerve, causing discomfort through his forearm.[20] He did not pitch again until September 3.

Not only was the 2000 season fraught with physical challenges, but there were emotional challenges as well. Stottlemyre and his wife, Sheri, had been married for 10 years but were in the process of getting a divorce. They had one child, a daughter, Rachel, born in 1996.[21]

For the 2000 season, Stottlemyre went 9-6 with a 4.91 ERA. The Diamondbacks finished third in the NL West. In September, Stottlemyre had nerve-repositioning surgery on his elbow and missed the 2001 season.

On November 17, 2000, Stottlemyre received the Branch Rickey Award. The award, presented by the Rotary Club of Denver, cited Stottlemyre for his community service, including his longtime efforts to raise funds for leukemia research. Along with his father and brother, he had also hosted a golf tournament in Las Vegas to raise funds for the Make-a-Wish Foundation.[22]

Stottlemyre never was quite 100 percent again, experiencing pain in his shoulder and elbow. He was on the sidelines as the Diamondbacks won the 2001 World Series, and pitched in only five games in 2002, going 0-2.

Stottlemyre retired as a player after that season, having posted a 138-121 record in 372 games, 339 as a starter. His career ERA was 4.28. His 25 complete games included six shutouts.

Since retiring as a player, Stottlemyre has pursued a successful career as a financial adviser. In 1999 he had come to a crossroads in his life when his father was hospitalized with cancer. Mel Sr. survived that battle but ultimately succumbed to the disease in 2019. In recent years Stottlemyre has directed his energies to advising people on how to better live their lives and achieve not only financial but emotional fulfillment. He has authored two books, the first of which was *Relentless Success*, published in 2017. A novel, *The Observer*, was published late in 2020.

In 2021 Todd's brother Mel Jr. was diagnosed with prostate cancer two months after the second anniversary of the death of Mel Sr., and the family came together for another battle.

Stottlemyre has five children and in 2022 lived with his wife, Erica, and their family in Phoenix, Arizona.

SOURCES

In addition to the sources shown in the notes, the author used Baseball-Reference.com. and the following:

Blackwell, Mike. "Stottlemyres Put Pros on Hold, Form Heart of Rebel Pitching Staff," *Austin American-Statesman*, May 25, 1984: F6.

Lang, Jack. "Baseball Free-Agent Draft Is a Father & Son Affair," *The Sporting News*, January 21, 1985: 44.

MacCarl, Neil. "Stottlemyre Tries Again," *The Sporting News*, March 27, 1989: 30.

Packet, John. "Another Up-and-Coming Stottlemyre Passes Through," *Richmond Times-Dispatch*, April 12, 1987: D-5.

Pearlman, Jeff. "Against All Odds Diamondbacks Righthander Todd Stottlemyre Is Trying to do What No One Before Him Has Ever Done: Pitch Effectively with a Torn Rotator Cuff," *Sports Illustrated*, February 28, 2000.

Pepe, Phil. "Class, Courage Fit Stottlemyre," *New York Daily News*, March 16, 1981: 54.

Poliquin, Bud. "Stottlemyre Grows into His Fine Name," *Syracuse Herald American*, April 12, 1987: D1

NOTES

1   Peter Richmond, "Blue Jays' Stottlemyre Now Has 'The Look,'" *Seattle Times*, March 22, 1987: C3.

2   "Yakima Wins Miller Title," *Billings* (Montana) *Gazette*, July 13, 1982: 5-B.

3   Kevin Taylor, "On the Diamond, Area Teams Are Seeking a Gem," *Spokane Chronicle*, May 26, 1983: 33.

4   "Stottlemyre Brothers Picked 1st, 3rd in Free-Agent Draft," *Seattle Times*, January 9, 1985: F2.

5   Chris Mortensen, "Expos Show Interest in Benedict," *Atlanta Journal Constitution*, January 6, 1985: C-14.

6   "Stottlemyre Just Ran Out of Pitches," *Toronto Star*, July 3, 1986: F3.

7   "Stottlemyre Starts Opener for Jays," *The Sporting News,* April 16, 1990: 20-21.

8   "Stottlemyre Starts Opener for Jays."

9   "Jays Don't Feel at Home in the Dome," *The Sporting News*, July 2, 1990: 12-13.

10   Rick Hummel, "For a Long Time, Stottlemyre Felt He 'Was the Murderer of My Little Brother,'" *St. Louis Post-Dispatch*, November 23, 2020.

11   Joe Weinert, "Blue Jay Victory in World Series Brings Out Mob," *Atlantic City Press*, October 25, 1993: D1.

12   Hummel.

13   Rosie DiManno, "Baseball Stars and Tampa Police in Volatile Mix," *Toronto Star*, November 9, 1994: A5.

14   Rosie DiManno, "Bug-Ridden Jury Typical of Weird Trial of Two Jays," *Toronto Star*, November 10, 1994: A4.

15   Todd Stottlemyre, *Relentless Success: 9-Point System for Major League Achievement* (Issaquah, Washington: Made for Success Publishing; 2017).

16   DiManno, "Ex-Jay Pitchers Winners in Court: Stottlemyre and Stewart Acquitted in Just 45 Minutes," *Toronto Star*, November 16, 1994: A1.

17   Steve Marantz, "Arm in Arm: The Cardinals-Braves Series Featured Some Outstanding Pitching Because It Featured Some Outstanding Pitching Coaches," *The Sporting News*, October 21, 1996: 15-17.

18   Marantz: 17.

19   Ken Brazzle and Chris Walsh, "Stottlemyre Making Quick Recovery," *Tucson Citizen*, August 5, 1999: 7-D.

20   "With Stottlemyre Sidelined, Morgan, Daal Must Step Up," *The Sporting News*, July 10, 2000: 41.

21   Jack McGruder, "A Special Fan Watches Stottlemyre," *Arizona Daily Star* (Tucson), September 4, 2000: C5.

22   "Todd Stottlemyre Wins Branch Rickey Award," *BusinessWire*, September 9, 2000.

PAT TABLER

By Harry Schoger

On February 2, 1958, in Hamilton, Ohio, Mrs. Marian H. Tabler introduced newborn Patrick to his dad, siblings, and the world. Patrick was born into a family of German heritage on both paternal and maternal sides. Sometime after the families were connected, it was discovered that, in fact, both sides immigrated from Alsace-Lorraine, a predominantly German-speaking region that was incorporated into the new state of Germany in 1871. Marian was a nurse and her husband, William J. Tabler, an artist, having graduated from Central Academy of Art in Cincinnati. He worked as a commercial artist in retail at L.S. Ayres, a department store in downtown Cincinnati. Neither parent had prior links to sports and/or athletic endeavors. However, Patrick and his older brother, Greg, of their own determination and initiative got deeply involved in sports with total parental blessing. The boys had one older and two younger sisters, respectively Kimberly, Kateri, and Kristen.

Patrick's primary focus was basketball. He made varsity as a starter for McNicholas High School in his freshman year. His icon was Jerry West, arguably West Virginia's most notable basketballer. Pat adopted Jerry's number 44 for his own in both basketball and baseball. In his sophomore year he was a starter along with Greg. In one notable basketball game against favored Loveland High School, the Tabler boys spearheaded a victory that stopped a 45-game winning streak for nontournament games, which included a 30 home-game winning streak.[1] They also went to the final four of the state tournament but failed to win it all. In Pat's junior year he was named to the all-city team and selected as an honorable mention all-stater. In his senior year he was an Ohio Class AA first-team player for the Southwestern region and shared Player of the Year honors with another athlete. He averaged 25 points, 10 rebounds, and 6 assists per game as a guard. Pat established records at McNicholas that still stood in 2022. His number 44 has been ceremoniously retired by his school. It was no surprise that colleges wanted Pat to play basketball for them. He signed a national letter of intent with Virginia Tech.

Baseball was secondary for Pat. He did not go out for the team in his freshman year, nor did he play any summer ball. He thought summers were meant for honing one's basketball skills. He did go out the next year. Pat Quinn, his baseball coach, thought Pat was the best sophomore he ever had. In fact, he thought Pat had more potential in baseball than in basketball, despite mistakes he had made that Quinn attributed to lack of concentration. For the second summer in a row, he did not play baseball, but the omission was not evident in his play. He started with the team when it hit the gym for preseason workouts. Quinn started him in center field but moved him around to different positions as conditions warranted.[2] Pat adapted

Pat Tabler, Mr. Utility

seamlessly to the changes. The diversity became a hallmark of his professional career. He said the experience of playing several positions extended his playing time in the majors.[3] He helped McNicholas win city titles in both his junior and senior years. Pat led the city in batting (.487) his junior year. He got plenty of looks from major-league scouts during those last two years. Two prominent ones were Wayne Morgan and Dave Yokum of the Yankees.

A highlight of Pat's life was a personal invitation to work out with the Cincinnati Reds of Big Red Machine fame. It was a real ego boost to play ball and talk one-on-one with the likes of Pete Rose, Joe Morgan, and Johnny Bench. Manager Sparky Anderson told him the Reds would draft him in the first round if he was still available.[4] For a high-school teenager, it was surreal.

On June 8, 1976, Pat dropped by coach Quinn's small office to hang out for the start of baseball's amateur draft. There was hope that he might get a call in one of the early rounds. A reporter was also squeezed in the tiny office. McNicholas's catcher, Jeff Savage, had precariously perched his 210-pound frame on a tilted chair in the door frame. After 15 picks, the phone rang. Coach Quinn answered the phone. After some pleasantries, he handed it to Pat. On the other end was Yankees scout Wayne Morgan calling from a local hotel. The conversation lasted only moments. The Yankees had taken him in the first round, 16th overall. Pat, a low-keyed kid, was not sure what to think of it all but was inwardly awestruck. He would have liked to be a Cincinnati Red or a Los Angeles Dodger (his two favorites), but the tradition of the pinstripes was magnetic. Fifteen minutes later he left to get a physical exam requested by Virginia Tech and then drove to Hillsboro, Ohio, to play an evening doubleheader.[5]

It didn't take Tabler long to opt for the Yankees deal. In the long haul, baseball would be less demanding on his body. There are fewer spots available in professional basketball. He drove to Blacksburg, Virginia, to decline his Virginia Tech scholarship, before reporting to Oneonta, New York, for his first professional assignment. Oneonta has produced a score of notables, of whom the most famous baseball player was Jim Konstanty, a reliever for the Phillies in the 1940s and '50s and former MVP.

Tabler was a right-handed batter and fielder, 6-feet-3, and weighed 175 pounds. He toiled in the Yankees' farm system for the better part of five seasons. His first assignment was with Oneonta in the short-season, instructional Class-A New York-Penn League.

His manager was Eddie Napoleon, whom he credited as his all-time favorite. Napoleon was patient with him and taught him the ropes for surviving in professional baseball. Tabler cited Cito Gaston as the second most influential manager. Tabler's offensive production at Oneonta was unspectacular. He hit .231 with an OPS of .567.

In 1977 the Yankees moved Tabler up to Fort Lauderdale (Class-A Florida State League). Napoleon was his manager again. Tabler's offensive production was only slightly better: .238 batting average and .580 OPS. In 1978 he found himself in Fort Lauderdale again. To break up the tedium of travel around the state in a bus, Tabler became immersed in the soap opera *All My Children*.[6] His passion for the show was triggered by many of his teammates, who routinely watched their favorite soaps. He entertained his teammates with his $200 six-string acoustic guitar. He had taught himself to play back in Cincinnati, where he "jammed" with musical friends. His specialty was folk-country rock. Avowedly, Jethro Tull was one of his favorite artists. Besides his extracurricular pursuits he posted solid numbers at the plate in 1978. He had 455 at-bats, 124 hits, 19 for extra bases, 70 RBIs, and a .273 batting average.

Tabler started the 1979 campaign for the third season in a row with Fort Lauderdale. He seemed to be stuck. By mid-June he had played first base, second base, third base, designated hitter, and all three outfield positions. The versatility seemed to be holding him back even though it was a godsend for his manager. Regardless, it was the one-position players who were moving up. Tabler engaged manager Doug Holmquist on the subject and the latter admitted his grievance was valid.[7] After 75 games with Fort Lauderdale, he was elevated to the West Haven A's of the Double-A Eastern League to finish the season and reunite with Napoleon.

Tabler's disposition might be described as "straight arrow." One reporter said that Mother Teresa compared to Tabler "… would come across as exceedingly impolite. The Dalai Lama would be told to do something about his attitude. … Lassie is crankier than Pat Tabler."[8] He followed his manager's requests without grumbling. Tabler once said, "I'm not a guy that will cause problems."[9] He was not contentious, was even-keeled, and never exerted a negative influence, in fact, quite the opposite, never letting adversity get him down. He learned to adapt quickly to new settings. He was a positive in every locker room he found himself in. When he was traded to Kansas City, he was soon elected player representative.

On October 27, 1979, Patrick married Susan M. Butler of Cincinnati. They had been going steady since they were 10 years old.

Tabler spent the entire 1980 campaign with the Double-A Nashville Sounds (Southern League) and at a fixed position, second base. He put up impressive numbers. He produced 38 doubles, second in the league. He was fifth in total bases with 244, his .898 OPS was sixth-best, and his 83 RBIs seventh, with a respectable batting average of .297. The most notable future major leaguer in the league that season was Charlotte's Cal Ripken Jr.[10]

In 1981 the Yankees placed Tabler with the Triple-A Columbus Clippers (International League). He was determined to take advantage of the opportunity and posted solid numbers. By June 12, he had played in 52 games at both second base and third base with vitals of .296/.394/.592. June 12 was the day he was traded to the Chicago Cubs for players to be named later. The Cubs sent Bill Caudill to the Yankees on April 1, 1982, and Jay Howell on August 2, 1982, to complete the trade.[11]

At first Tabler was chagrined by the trade. The Yankees had told him they had plans for him. After some reflection, he decided he might have better odds getting a shot with the Cubs. Although the Cubs were eager to see Tabler in action, they could not on major-league turf. It was the first day of the 1981 players strike. He was assigned to Iowa of the Triple-A American Association, for whom he played 63 games over the balance of the season with some respectable numbers. Major-league play resumed with the All-Star Game on August 9. Tabler was brought up from Iowa and played his first major-league game on August 21.

In his major-league debut, at home against the San Francisco Giants, Tabler came to the plate against pitcher Tom Griffin in the bottom of the second with one out and Jody Davis on first with a walk. Tabler hit the ball to shortstop for a single. Shortstop Billy Smith threw wild trying to get Davis at third. Ken Reitz's double scored Davis and send Tabler to third, where he was stranded. He failed to hit in three other at-bats. Tabler started at second base in 31 games for the balance of the season and was the designated hitter in four. His hitting statistics were not impressive during that period: .188 with 5 RBIs.

Tabler spent most of the 1982 season at Triple-A Iowa. It was his minor-league high-water mark: career highs in runs (89), triples (11), homers (17), RBIs (105),

stolen bases (15), batting average (.342), OBP (.444), slugging (.581), and OPS (1.025). Iowa fans really took to the tall blond with an infectious smile.[12] The Cubs brought Tabler up at the end of the season. In 25 games, he batted .235 with 7 RBIs.

On January 25, 1983, Tabler became property of the Cubs' crosstown rivals, the White Sox. Tabler, Scott Fletcher, Randy Martz, and Dick Tidrow went to the White Sox in exchange for Warren Brusstar and Steve Trout. Eddie Napoleon came back into Tabler's life. He was now a Cleveland Indians coach. Cleveland manager Mike Ferraro had also coached Tabler in the minors. The White Sox coveted Jerry Dybzinski but could not dangle enough bait in front of the Indians during the winter meetings.[13] When the White Sox acquired Tabler, they dangled him in front of the Indians, who eagerly took the bait.[14] On April 1 Tabler was traded to the Indians for Dybzinski. In some quarters it was thought that defensive lapses are what got him traded by the White Sox.[15]

Tabler was placed in Triple A with the Charleston (West Virginia) Charlies but was called up after four games. The Indians' third baseman, Toby Harrah, had suffered a broken hand.

Tabler played his first game as an Indian on April 18, at third base, getting two hits in three at-bats as Cleveland fell to the Baltimore Orioles, 4-1. The Indians were not a competitive team during Tabler's five-plus years with them.[16]

Tabler's 1983 season was his first full one in the majors. He played in 124 games, 88 of them in the outfield. He led the team with a .291 batting average and was third in RBIs with 65. His on-base percentage of .370 was the best of his 12-year major-league career. He led the team in batting average with runners in scoring position with .386. At 25, Tabler was the sixth youngest player on the team. The Indians finished seventh (last) in the AL East Division, 28 games off the pace with a record of 70-92.

The 1984 season was nearly a cookie-cutter of 1983. Tabler hit .290 and drove in 68 runs, third-best on the team. His value as a utilityman was plain. He played first base (67 games), second base (1), third base (36), left field (43), and DH (1). To top it off, he pinch-hit eight times and pinch-ran four. The Indians improved to 75-87 and moved up to sixth place.

In 1985 Tabler played 92 of his 117 games at first-base. His time as first-sacker was at the expense of Mike Hargrove, who publicly voiced his objection to the situation because of his greater fielding prowess. Manager Pat Corrales replied that Hargrove would

WE ARE, WE CAN, WE WILL

Mr. Clutch, teeing off.

get little sympathy from anybody. Tabler's "amiability is hard to hate."[17] Tabler's hitting declined to .275 with 59 RBIs. Against the Seattle Mariners on June 8, he drove in six runs. His production for the year was curtailed by surgery to remove degenerative torn knee cartilage on September 5, causing him to miss the balance of the season. The Indians won just 60 games (60-102).

Both Tabler and the Indians bounced back in 1986. His .326 batting average led the team and was fourth in the league. The Indians had four hitters over .300. Tabler had a personal-best of 154 hits, a personal-high OBP of .368, and a career-high slugging percentage of .433. He played 107 games at first base and 18 as designated hitter. The Indians won 24 more games than the previous year, 84-78, climbing to fifth place.

The 1987 season was Tabler's pinnacle year on offense. He set or tied major-league career highs in most of the standard stats. He led the team in hits (170) and doubles (34) and was second in batting average (.307) and RBIs (86). He was selected as a reserve on the All-Star team at first base. His season, however, ended on a negative note – an 0-for-33 slump, a drought that ended with hits in his final two at-bats of the year. The Indians finished seventh with a record of 61-101, 37 games off the pace.

Tabler's woes at the plate continued to nag him in 1988. It was slow going. It was not long before he was relegated to DH duty. By early May his batting average since the prior September 9 was .177 (20-for-113). The next day, Tabler had a breakout game against the Angels. He got four hits, including a home run, three RBIs, and seven total bases.

Despite the Indians' perennial plight, Pat and Susan Tabler liked Cleveland. It was a great place to raise kids. Pat liked the team, the locker-room camaraderie, and the Indians organization. They both liked it so much that they bought a house.[18]

Feeling they needed a left-hander, on June 3, 1988, the Indians traded Tabler for Bud Black of the Kansas City Royals.[19]

During his tenure with the Indians, Tabler earned the title of Mr. Clutch. He was 29-for-54 with the bases loaded over five seasons with the team. People – including his wife – often asked him how he did it, and when he couldn't explain, they offered the obvious advice to pretend the bases were loaded at every at-bat. In 2001 the club celebrated its 100th anniversary. In commemoration of the event, a panel of veteran players, baseball historians, and journalists selected Tabler one of the team's 100 greatest players.

Kansas City gave Tabler a royal welcome. Bo Jackson was hurt and in need of a replacement. Tabler was given the assignment even though he had not played the outfield since 1984. He quickly earned the respect of his new teammates and they made him their player representative before the end of the season. When he arrived, he was batting .224. He still had plenty of work to do to shake the bad taste of the slump. As it turned out, the change in venues introduced him to Mike Lum, the Kansas City hitting coach. Lum made Tabler a special project. He was a good teacher and Tabler was a good learner.[20]

Lum's tutelage was a plus for Tabler, who rebounded solidly from the "slump." He compiled a .309 average during his 89 games with the Royals. He stroked 93 hits that produced 49 RBIs. He led the club with a .337 average against lefties. He certainly made things happen on the diamond. In his specialty, hitting with the bases loaded, he was 5-for-5 with a walk and 12 RBIs. He continued to carve out a niche as a utilityman, playing five positions during the season, with designated hitter being the most prevalent. He batted .322 as the DH, far and away the best on the team. The Royals finished third in the AL West, 19½ games behind Oakland.

Hit on his left knee by a pitch on September 18, Tabler soon realized that despite trying to play in three more games, he was dealing with a season-ending fracture and not a bruise.[21]

The 1989 season saw Tabler hit .259 in 123 games. The Royals made a good run for the pennant, coming in second to Oakland, seven games short.

Tabler had a one-year contract with Kansas City for 1990. He was suddenly the forgotten man. Manager John Wathan could not find productive roles for him in the lineup. In late June his work picked up when George Brett was hurt. Tabler did get into the lineup against left-handed pitchers, against whom he had the team's best batting average. He wound up batting .272, tied in team stats with Bo Jackson for fifth place and sixth best for OBP at .338. At age 32, though, he was dealt to the New York Mets on August 30 for 23-year-old right-handed pitcher Archie Corbin.

The Mets were absorbed with Tabler's "Mr. Clutch" legend as much as anybody. Tabler got his first hit with his new club on September 10, with the bases loaded, a pinch-hit single that drove in two runs in a 10-1 victory over the Cardinals. The Mets came in four games short of the division-leading Pittsburgh Pirates. Tabler hit a respectable .279 with one homer and 10 RBIs during his short stay.

After the season Tabler was a free agent. He negotiated a $1.6 million two-year deal with the Toronto Blue Jays. He wanted to quit playing for losing teams. The Blue Jays had finished second in 1990 and first in 1989. They had made some trades before the 1991 season that promised to keep them at the top of the heap. One of those acquisitions was his favorite player in baseball, Joe Carter, a former Indian.

On a personal level, the season did not go as well as Tabler probably wanted. He played only 21 games in the field and 56 as DH. He did get 33 pinch-hitting opportunities. He always seemed to hit better the more he played. It is probably not surprising that he had mediocre offensive stats. He batted only .216, the lowest he ever had in a full season. He had only 185 at-bats, hit one home run, and drove in 21 runs. Still, the Blue Jays won the AL East title. Tabler had two plate appearances in the ALCS, a walk and an out.

The 1992 season was Tabler's last as a player. He got even fewer appearances than in the previous year. (He did manage to raise his batting average to .252.) However, he did get to experience the thrill of being on a World Series championship team. He had two at-bats in the World Series; in Game One, he popped out to center pinch-hitting in the eighth, and in the top of the 10th in Game Six he lined out to the pitcher. The Blue Jays won that game – and the Series – in the 11th.

Released after the season, Tabler thought he could still contribute and considered several playing options. Some well-founded opportunities he rejected out of hand. One that he actively pursued with the Reds dried up. While he was in this state of flux, he found worthy pastimes. He was faithful to his alma mater McNicholas. He helped with fundraisers and coaching.[22] He also had more time to watch his own five kids play their sports. When one door shuts another opens, usually unexpectedly. In Tabler's case, it was about to happen.

The family took a vacation in the spring of 1993, their first since 1975. While they were away, the Blue Jays at their home opener handed out the players' World Series rings. Subsequently, the club invited him to come to Toronto to receive his ring.

At his hotel in Toronto, Tabler bumped into a baseball acquaintance, Tommy Hutton, an ex-major leaguer who was beginning a career as an announcer for the Blue Jays. Hutton invited Tabler to come to the announcer's booth for some on-air dialogue. An official of The Sports Network, which carried the Blue Jays' games, was impressed with Tabler's natural ease on the air.

Back home, Tabler had hardly unpacked when he got a call from TSN Baseball asking him to return for an interview and test for a job as a color commentator. The network was starting a pregame segment called *Baseball Tonight* and was eager to have him audition for a spot on the program. He repacked his bags and flew back to Toronto. He did an interview and underwent a voice test. The network hired him on the spot. That evening he was working his new job. In 2001 he became a full-time analyst in the broadcast booth with Buck Martinez and Dan Shulman. As of 2022, he has been in broadcasting for 29 years and is entering his 46th year working in professional baseball.

Tabler holds the major-league record for the highest batting average with the bases loaded. Over his career, he finished 43-for-88 (.489). He can also vie for the title of "Mr. Utility." During his career he played all the infield positions except shortstop, as well as left field and right field (but never center, his position in high school). He was also a designated hitter.

Pat Tabler played baseball at its highest level for a dozen years, a proven clutch hitter, and an All-Star who capped his career as a member of the World Champion 1992 Toronto Blue Jays.

SOURCES

In addition to the sources listed in Notes, the author used Baseball Reference.com, Ancestry.com, Retrosheet.org, and the following:

Video: https://www.youtube.com/watch?v=_QXFmaAWE1Q&t=2195s

Video: https://www.youtube.com/watch?v=CAWCGVAZBFI

Miami Valley Society. "Winklejohann-Tabler," *Dayton Daily News,* March 20, 1955.

"Pat Tabler valuable DH," *Coshocton* (Ohio) *Tribune,* March 6, 1988.

Associated Press. ""Two-run Single Gives Mets Fans Look at Clutch Hitting of Former Royal," *Kansas City Star,* September 12, 1990.

Hoynes, Paul. "Tabler Versatile Indian," *Mansfield* (Ohio) *News Journal,* February 26, 1984.

Luder, Bob. "Tabler Wants to Add Homers to Repertoire," *Kansas City Star,* August 30, 1988.

Melvin, Chuck. "Tabler Excelling as Starter," *Cincinnati Enquirer,* April 26, 1983.

Ocker, Sheldon. "Torn Knee Cartilage Ends Season for Tribe's Tabler," *Akron Beacon Journal,* September 5, 1985.

Sachare, Alex. "Basketball Wrap Up," *Lancaster* (Ohio) *Eagle Gazette,* March 10, 1976.

NOTES

1   J.P. Lyons, "McNicholas Guns Down Loveland's .45 in AA Showdown," *Cincinnati Enquirer,* November 23, 1974: 32.

2   Denny Dressman, "Tabler's Baseball Talents Hidden by Basketball," *Cincinnati Enquirer,* April 26, 1975: 32.

3   Author interview with Pat Tabler on January 19, 2022.

4   Lonnie Wheeler, "Be It Ever So Humble, Tabler Finds Place in Cleveland," *Cincinnati Enquirer,* February 9, 1984: 33.

5   Joe Quinn, "Pat, This Is the Yanks …,'" *Cincinnati Post,* June 9, 1976: 25.

6   Greg Cote, "Before the Game, He's a Soap Opera Addict," *Miami Herald,* August 25, 1978: 165.

7   Greg Cote, "Pat Tabler's Playing Everywhere, but It's Not Taking Him Anywhere," *Miami Herald,* June 14, 1979: 338.

8   Craig Daniels, "For Jays' Mr. Utility, Boring Is Just Fine," *National Post* (Toronto), March 1, 1991: 41.

9   Daniels.

10   On 10 offensive statistics, Ripken led in runs, hits, homers, and total bases. Tabler led in doubles, triples, RBIs, stolen bases, batting average, and OPS. He had 79 fewer at-bats.

11   As part of the overall deal, the Cubs had exchanged pitchers, sending veteran **Rick Reuschel** to the Yankees for **Doug Bird**. Associated Press, "Cubs Trade Reuschel to Yankees," *Vedetter Messenger* (Valparaiso, Indiana), June 13, 1981: 15; Marc Hansen, "Tabler Now Sees Trade as Break," *Des Moines Tribune,* July 24, 1981: 17.

12   In 1993 Iowa fans were asked to participate in a survey to select the best player at each position during the previous 25 years of American Association baseball in Des Moines. Tabler was elected number one at third base.

13   Paul Hoynes, "Indians Deal Dybzinski to White Sox," *Mansfield* (Ohio) *News Journal,* April 2, 1983: 13.

14   Chuck Melvin., "Tabler Excelling as Starter," *Cincinnati Enquirer,* April 26, 1983: 29.

15   Sheldon Ocker, "Tribe Spotlight on Tabler Now," *Akron Beacon Journal,* April 19, 1983: 44.

16   Cleveland hovered near last place most of his career with them. In only one season did they play above .500.

17   Mike Bass, "Tabler Finds Happiness in Cleveland," *Cincinnati Post,* April 10, 1985: 31.

18   Tabler interview.

19   The trade was made one day after the renovations on the Tablers' new home were completed. At the end of the day the Indians were 1½ games out of first. That lofty position did not last long. They finished the season in sixth place with a record of 78-84.

20   Bo Jackson was a special player to Tabler. They were friends. Tabler believed Jackson was the greatest baseball talent he had ever seen and the greatest athlete who ever lived. In one famous incident, Jackson nonchalantly broke a bat over his head. It was a great stunt. The truth was that the bat was already cracked, and he was wearing a helmet. One day at the end of batting practice, Tabler broke a bat over his own head as he left the batting cage and said for all to hear, "Bo Who?" Dick Kaegel, "Tabler Believes He Can Help When Given a Chance," *Kansas City Star,* June 28, 1990: 48.

21   Bob Nightengale, "Injury Will Keep Tabler Out for Season's Last Week," *Kansas City Times,* September 27, 1988: 5.

22   Dave Schutte, "McNick Baseball Gets Expert Help," *Cincinnati Enquirer,* April 11, 1993: 31.

MIKE TIMLIN

By Bill Nowlin

Right-handed reliever Mike Timlin pitched in more than 1,000 major-league games and has four World Championship rings. His 1,058 games rank him eighth all-time among pitchers. He played postseason baseball with 11 teams during his 18 years in the major leagues.[1] The World Series wins were with the Toronto Blue Jays in 1992 and 1993 and the Boston Red Sox in 2004 and 2007.

In a big-league career that ran from 1991 through 2008, Timlin started four games and relieved in 1,054, thus averaging more than 58 appearances per season and facing a total of 5,082 batters in 1,024⅓ innings. His career ERA was 3.63, with a won-lost record of 75-73.

Timlin's best pitches were described as "a sinking fastball that is regularly clocked at around 94 mph and a vicious, biting slider. … he keeps the ball low and induces groundouts."[2]

Michael August Timlin was born in Midland, Texas, on March 10, 1966, and graduated from Midland High School, moving on to Southwestern University in Georgetown, Texas.[3] After his junior year, he was a fifth-round selection of the Blue Jays in the June 1987 draft. Timlin was 6-feet-4 and listed at 205 pounds.

"Coming out of West Texas, all you know is oil fields and football," he said in 2000. "Baseball wasn't a real big thing. But it was a God-given ability for me to play baseball. I grew fast, but I grew skinny. I wasn't a football player. It wasn't for me."[4]

Timlin's parents were Jerome Francis Timlin Sr. and Nancy Sharon Beyer, known in the family as Sharon. "I never knew my father," Mike Timlin said in a December 2021 interview. "He was gone before I was born. My mom raised me and my three older sisters alone. Her mom and dad helped out. We lived on our own but they lived in the same town. Basically, my father was her father. His name was Sylvester August Beyer – 'Jake.'"[5]

Mike's sisters were Jeri, Tracy, and Sherri. As of 2022, two lived near Austin, Texas, and Sherri lived in Maine. Their mother, Sharon, "worked for Exxon for 27 years," Mike said. She worked in Midland, where

Exxon had a headquarters office overseeing the exploration and drilling work done in the region. "She worked in the operations file room. She had a high-school education, but she had precedence over every well or operation that was in that area. All you had to do was mention the name of an operation – exploration or drilling – and she could locate the file and tell you what was in it."

Jerome Timlin had been a truck driver. The first time Mike met him was when he was perhaps 11 or 12 years old, at a truck stop. There were two other times they met, once when Mike was in college and once when Mike was a major leaguer playing with the Red Sox in Texas.[6]

Of his mother, Mike said, "It wasn't real easy with four kids, but she did a hell of a job."[7]

Her parents, Jake and Opal Beyer, helped. After elementary school, Mike would walk over to their house until his mother returned home from work. His grandmother had a home sewing shop where she worked on alterations and clothing and made quilts. Grandfather Jake, interestingly, worked for a different oil company, Gulf Oil.

It was at Midland High School that Mike began to blossom at baseball. Most of the time he played outfield. But one day when he was on the junior varsity team, playing against the varsity, his coach beckoned him to the mound. Mike told the coach he didn't really want to pitch, but the coach – times were different – told him, quietly, "You'll pitch because I'll tell you to pitch. Otherwise, you can walk off the field." As he tells it, Mike said, "'OK,' and I turned around and pitched. And I turned out to be a pitcher."

When others were pitching, Timlin returned to center field, though he put in a bit of time as backup catcher and first baseman. His pitching earned him a half-scholarship to Southwestern University in Georgetown, Texas. Before beginning his freshman year, becoming an architect had appealed to him, but the school didn't offer appropriate programs. Instead, he majored in physical education. It was while pitching in college that he was spotted by pro scouts.

"The dream for most of the kids in Texas was to play for the University of Texas or A&M or a Division I school. At Southwestern, since we were just north of Austin, we played against University of Texas. The scouts were watching the games there. I pitched the first game of a doubleheader; I was facing off against Calvin Schiraldi. I lost that game, 1-0. I gave up three hits. He gave up one hit. I think that was the first time I was on somebody's radar."

Scout Jim Hughes contacted Timlin on behalf of the Toronto Blue Jays, leading to his being drafted, and ultimately came to Mike's house to sign him for what was in 1987 a significant bonus.[8]

Timlin's first assignment took him far from Texas – to Medicine Hat, Alberta, where he pitched in rookie ball in the Pioneer League. He started 12 of 13 games, and was 4-8 with a 5.14 ERA for the 26-43 Medicine Hat Blue Jays, who finished last in the North Division.

He showed far better in his first full season of pro ball, starting in 22 of his 35 appearances in the South Atlantic League's Single-A Myrtle Beach Blue Jays and producing a 1988 record of 10-6 with a strong 2.86 ERA.

Timlin was asked to put in another year at Single A, in 1989 for the Dunedin Blue Jays in the Florida State League, and to begin to work primarily in relief (26 of his 33 games). He was 5-8 (3.25).

Over those first three years, Timlin essentially been converted to become a reliever. Pitching coach Bill Monbouquette had counseled him at Myrtle Beach that he was "only a step or two away from the big leagues." Timlin didn't necessarily believe it at the time, but it essentially proved to be true.

The 1989 Dunedin team, though a Single-A team, had 15 players make it to the majors.

Most of 1990 was at Dunedin as well, working exclusively in relief. In 42 games, closing 40 of them, he recorded a 1.43 ERA. Timlin also got substantial work in Double A for the Knoxville Blue Jays (Southern League); after arriving in late July, he was 1-2 in 17 games with a 1.73 ERA. He played winter ball for Lara in Venezuela.

The next year, 1991, Timlin made the majors. He debuted on April 8 and after pitching a total of $5\frac{1}{3}$ innings, he was 2-0. His first two innings were at SkyDome against the visiting Red Sox. He faced six batters and didn't let the ball out of the infield, though he did walk two. His first win came two days later, also against Boston. Working the top of the eighth, he struck out the first two batters and got a groundout from the third, then saw teammate Pat Tabler hit a three-run homer to boost the Jays to a 5-3 lead they maintained as Tom Henke closed the game.

Two days after that, on April 12, Timlin faced the Brewers and pitched the 9th, 10th, and 11th innings, allowing just a single. The Jays tied the game in the bottom of the ninth and won it on Mark Whiten's leadoff homer in the 11th. Manager Cito Gaston was no doubt pleased. Pitching coach Galen Cisco was certainly pleased with Timlin's first start, in Cleveland on June 12. Timlin worked six innings, allowing one hit, a high bouncer that was the only ball to leave the infield.[9] "Impressive? He was nearly impeccable, and there's a word I've always wanted to use."[10] Timlin was OK with starting, but he really appreciated the value he could bring out of the bullpen. "'I don't mind starting because I'm all for the team concept and that overrules what I want,' Timlin said. He went on to suggest, though, that he sees himself as a stopper, saying 'I've had success at it.'"[11]

In a game on August 1, Timlin went on the disabled list with tendinitis in his right elbow. A very effective set-up man, Timlin was 11-6 (3.16) by season's end. His 63 appearances were topped only by Duane Ward's 81, but Timlin pitched one more inning than Ward.

During the last stretch of the season, he became less effective.[12]

Timlin appeared in four postseason games, the four games the Jays lost to the Minnesota Twins in the 1991 ALCS. His ERA was 3.18 but he bore the loss in Game Three, when pinch-hitter Mike Pagliarulo homered off him in the top of the 10th. "It was a horrible pitch," Timlin said afterward, "Right down the middle."[13] There was a reason he'd been less effective; after the season, he underwent arthroscopic surgery to remove a bone spur and a chip from his right elbow.

The next year, 1992, the Blue Jays went all the way and won the World Series. Timlin didn't join the team until June, as it took time to rebuild arm strength after the surgery.[14] He pitched in six games in Dunedin and then in seven games for Triple-A Syracuse as part of his rehab, a total of 21⅓ innings. His first game with Toronto was on June 13. Of the first 11 batters he faced after rejoining Toronto, only one got a hit, a single. He bore a loss on June 18, giving up four runs (two earned) in two innings against the Tigers. His only two decisions in 1992 were both losses, the other one coming on July 29. By the end of the year, Timlin had worked in 26 games for a total of 43⅔ innings, with an ERA of 4.12, just marginally above the team ERA of 3.91.

Timlin pitched in the ALCS, with a hold in Game Three against Oakland and a scoreless eighth inning in Game Four. In the World Series, against the Atlanta Braves, he pitched a perfect seventh inning in Game Five and then earned a save in the final, triumphant Game Six. With a 4-3 lead in the 11th inning, two outs, and a runner on third base, Timlin took over from Jimmy Key. The speedy Otis Nixon thought to perhaps take advantage of a reliever who had worked only one inning in the past 13 days. On an 0-and-1 count, Nixon laid down a squeeze bunt. Timlin "fielded it cleanly and then threw what [fellow pitcher and teammate David] Cone called 'an Olympic shot-put.' To Blue Jays fans, it was the longest throw in club history. But when it finally arrived, it was true."[15] Timlin hadn't been caught unaware. First baseman Joe Carter had advised Timlin, "This guy will lay it down. You got to bounce off the mound." Timlin said he was "surprised that he was able to remain calm. 'It's just a Single "A" game,' he said he told himself. 'Just relax and throw strikes.'" Fielding the bunt, he said, "I wanted to tag him but he was already past me. Then I wanted to make sure I didn't throw it over Joe's head."[16] The Blue Jays had won the World Series. During the clubhouse celebration, the Jays chanted,

"Pee-eff-pee! Pee-eff-pee!"[17] The initials p.f.p. stood for pitchers' fielding practice. Clearly, they appreciated Timlin's work.

The Jays became repeat champions, winning it all again in 1993, beating the White Sox in the ALCS and the Phillies in the World Series. With 71 appearances, closer Duane Ward ranked first but set-up men Mark Eichhorn and Timlin were tied for second-most with 54 apiece – and Timlin did close 27 games. Timlin's regular-season record was 4-2 with a 4.69 ERA, one of the higher ERAs in his career. It had been 5.64 as of August 12 and he was sent to Dunedin to work with coach Bill Monbouquette on his mechanics and control. That strategy seemed to work. He had a strong stretch-run drive in September, shaving off nearly a full run from his ERA. In the postseason, Timlin worked 2⅓ innings in the ALCS, allowing just one run, and 2⅓ scoreless innings in the World Series, appearing in Games Two and Four.

The Jays fell to third place in the strike-shortened 1994 season and fifth (last) in 1995, with the bullpen workload being spread more evenly among several. He missed 15 days in late May and early June with a right-shoulder issue. He wasn't used as much in pressure situations. Timlin's ERA climbed to 5.18 in '94, the highest of his career until his final season in 2008.[18]

Timlin very successfully brought the ERA down to a career-best 2.14 in 1995. Again there was a mixture of set-up and closing work, and a brief trip to the disabled list. The Blue Jays finished in last place, 30 games out. His own record was 4-3.

In 1996 Timlin became the Jays' closer, in 56 of his 59 appearances. His won-lost record was 1-6 but his ERA was good at 3.65, and he racked up 31 saves, including eight in September alone. After the season, the Jays signed him to a two-year contract – but he was swapped to Seattle on the last day of July 1997.

The season hadn't started well. The very first pitch Timlin threw was on Opening Day at SkyDome, with the Blue Jays holding a 5-4 lead heading into the top of the ninth. Norberto Martin homered to left-center. The game was tied. Dan Plesac coughed up the winning run to the White Sox in the 10th. Timlin pitched quite well after that, and as July ended he was 3-2, 2.87, closing 26 of 38 appearances. Toronto traded for Jose Cruz Jr., sending both Timlin and Paul Spoljaric to the Mariners for a player who was believed could be a budding star. Timlin worked as set-up man for closer Heathcliff Slocumb. Timlin's ERA was 3.86 (3-2).

Seattle won the AL West but lost the Division Series to Baltimore in four games. Timlin appeared just once, in Game One at Kingdome. The Orioles already had a 5-1 lead when he came in to pitch the sixth. Chris Hoiles hit a leadoff home run. Timlin was charged with three more runs, departing with just two outs.

Timlin worked the full 1998 season for Seattle. The team finished in the middle of the pack in the AL West. The closer's role was shared by four pitchers, though Timlin's 40 games finished ranked first, as did his overall 70 appearances. His 2.95 ERA was tops, better by more than two full runs than any other reliever on the staff. From May 26 to July 15, he allowed just one (inconsequential) earned run in 19 appearances. September was particularly strong, with seven saves and one win. He was an example of what a *Chicago Tribune* writer called an unsung workhorse.[19]

Entering free agency for the first time, Timlin signed a four-year deal with the Baltimore Orioles beginning in 1999. He was seen as a "proven closer," something the O's needed.[20] He truly looked forward to the role, saying, "Any relief pitcher prefers to pitch the ninth. It's nice to be out there to win the game and have everybody come out to shake your hand."[21] He was with them for a year and a half. The '99 team finished in fourth place, 20 games behind the Yankees. The season started roughly, with a 6.45 ERA through June 8. Through the All-Star break, Timlin had 10 blown saves or losses. He began to settle down and 10 of his 27 saves came in September as he finished strong again. Timlin's season record was 3-9, but with a solid 3.57 ERA that was more than a run better than the 4.77 team ERA.[22]

The Orioles, though, were less than satisfied and reportedly willing to eat a significant portion of Timlin's salary if there was a deal to be made. Beginning 2000 on the DL with an abdominal strain, he had a dismal start to the season but got progressively better as the weeks went on. He brought his ERA under 5.00 in late July, but was traded on the 29th to the St. Louis Cardinals for a minor leaguer, first baseman Chris Richard, and cash.[23] In the National League, the Cardinals used him less frequently to close games. He shaved a run and a half off his earned-run average, while working in 25 games.[24]

Timlin helped stabilize the bullpen and the Cardinals finished first in the NL Central. He worked in five more postseason games. The only one in which he surrendered an earned run (two of them) was in NLDS Game Two, which the Cardinals won, 10-4. They swept the Braves in the NLDS but lost the NLCS to the Mets, four games to one. Timlin bore the loss in Game Two in the ninth inning, 6-5, after his first baseman committed an error, followed by a sacrifice bunt and then a single.

In 2001 the Cards reached the postseason again, but lost out in the NLDS to Arizona. During the regular season, Timlin had worked in 67 games, closing 19, but the 67 games ranked him only tied for third in relief appearances by a frequently-used staff. He would have worked more but for arthroscopic surgery at the end of July to fix torn cartilage in his left knee. His 4.09 ERA was the highest among the five top relievers. His one appearance in the playoffs was in Game Three, when he got four groundouts, giving up just one single.

In 2002 Timlin was traded again at the end of July, this time to the last-place Phillies.[25] He'd pitched very well for St. Louis – with a 2.51 ERA in 42 games (closing 10). In the mix was one solitary start – on April 19 in Milwaukee. It was his first start since the three he had in 1991, and also the last of his career. It didn't go well; he gave up four runs in 4⅓ innings. For the Phillies, he was 3.79 in 30 games. The team improved and finished in third place. For the season as a whole, Timlin gave up 15 homers. Never before had he topped nine.

A free agent once more, Timlin signed in January 2003 with the Boston Red Sox. He was with them for the final six seasons of his career, a team that made the postseason in five of those six years.

The original idea was to have Alan Embree, Ramiro Mendoza, and Timlin constitute a "three-headed closer committee."[26] As spring training progressed, the idea transformed into a "committee in short relief."[27] As it turned out, Timlin's 72 appearances led the pitching staff, but only 13 of them were as closer. Byung-Hyun Kim and Brandon Lyon closed most of the games. Timlin was 6-4 (3.55) with 17 holds and two saves.[28] He had a very impressive 7.22 strikeout-to-walk ratio (65 K to 9 BB) in 83⅔ innings. It was by far his best year in that department; for his career, Timlin's K/BB ratio was 2.31.[29]

The 2003 Red Sox finished second to the Yankees in the AL East, beat Oakland in a five-game Division Series, and then lost to the Yankees in the 11th inning of Game Seven of the ALCS. Timlin pitched in eight of the 12 playoff games, a total of 9⅔ innings with an ERA of 1.38. In five of the eight games, he earned a hold. His longest stint was in Game Three of the ALDS, which ran to 11 innings, with Timlin working a perfect 8th through 10th. In Game Seven of the ALCS, when Boston manager Grady Little famously sent spent starter Pedro Martinez back out to pitch in the eighth – at which point Martinez coughed up three runs and brought New York into a 5-5 tie, Alan Embree faced one batter and got him out. Timlin finished that inning and pitched a scoreless ninth. Tim Wakefield took over and Aaron Boone homered off him to win the game, and the series, on his first pitch in the 11th. Had Little replaced Martinez after the seventh, it likely would have been Timlin who replaced him.[30]

In 2004 Timlin added 11 more postseason games to his growing total. He also earned another World Championship ring – despite a postseason ERA of 6.17. Terry Francona was Boston's new manager. Timlin was back under a new two-year deal. Curt Schilling (21-6) was the new ace. Timlin (5-4, 4.13) led the team in appearances with 76 (and a nearly-identical 76⅓ innings pitched). Though he finished 12 games, the closer was Keith Foulke with 61 (in 72 appearances).

The Red Sox swept the Division Series from the Angels in three games, surviving Vladimir Guerrero's grand slam off Timlin that tied the game 6-6. David Ortiz hit a two-run homer in the bottom of the 10th to win it. The grand slam was the only home run Timlin surrendered in 28 playoff games with Boston.[31]

In an understatement, Timlin said before the ALCS got underway, "The Red Sox have a long history of not quite getting there."[32] The Yankees got to him for two runs in Game One of the ALCS, and caused him to blow a save in Game Four – though the Red Sox famously won that game, kicking off an eight-game winning streak that catapulted them over the Yankees and into sweeping the World Series from St. Louis. Timlin pitched in Games One, Two, and Three of the World Series. The Red Sox had won it all for the first time in 86 years.

The year 2005 saw the Red Sox reach the Division Series but they were swept there by the ultimate World Series-winning Chicago White Sox. Timlin had led the entire American League in appearances, with 81 – exactly half of the 162-game schedule. He was 7-3 (his 13 saves were only two fewer than closer Foulke's) with a 2.24 ERA. He allowed only two home runs all year long, and had a 2.95 K/BB ratio (59-20). He appeared in the postseason, pitching the final top of the ninth in Game Three, giving up one run as the White Sox prevailed, 5-3. Red Sox fans voted him the "10th Player Award."

In the offseason, Timlin and catcher Jason Varitek were on the US team in the inaugural 2006 World Baseball Classic.

The 2006 season was an off-year for the Red Sox, who finished third. Timlin was back on a new contract,

Mike Timlin's first two of four World Championship rings were with the 1992 and 1993 Blue Jays.

one he negotiated himself without an agent, part of an ongoing series of one-year deals that took him through 2008. He was 6-6 in a club-leading 68 games, gave up seven homers, and had a 4.36 ERA. He struck out 30 and walked 16. He battled injury during the season, missing games between May 25 and June 13 with a strained right shoulder and another week in the latter half of September.

Though missing more than five weeks with tendinitis – including all of May after May 2 – Timlin still appeared in 50 games, and picked up his fourth World Series ring, in 2007. His regular-season record was a modest winning one (2-1). Jonathan Papelbon was the closer. Hideki Okajima had the most relief appearances (66). Javy Lopez worked in 61 games (for Papelbon it was 59), but Timlin's 55⅓ innings pitched were third on the bullpen staff, despite the long stretch on the DL. His 3.42 ERA was better than the team's 3.87.

The 2007 Red Sox finished first in the division, two games ahead of the Yankees. On August 31 Timlin made his 1,000th major-league appearance. The Red Sox swept the Division Series (against the Angels) and the World Series (against the Colorado Rockies), but the ALCS was a hard-fought seven games against

Cleveland – Boston winning the first one, then losing three in a row before coming back with the three wins necessary to prevail. Timlin wasn't used in the ALDS. He pitched in the first three games of the ALCS, without giving up a run and he pitched a perfect eighth inning in Game One of the World Series. In Game Three, he got the final two outs in the sixth, then gave up singles to the first two batters in the seventh. Okajima replaced him and Matt Holliday homered, narrowing Boston's lead to 6-5. The Red Sox added four more runs and won, Timlin credited with a hold. In Game Four, he struck out the only two batters he faced, to finish the seventh and earn another hold.[33] The Red Sox won the game, 4-3, and thus the Series.

Timlin's last season in the majors was in 2008. He was 42 years old, and when he and Tim Wakefield (41) combined on a shutout of the Tigers on May 6, it was said to be the first time in the modern era that two pitchers over 40 had done so.[34] Though the other four relievers each worked more games, Timlin still got into 47. Papelbon closed 62, but Timlin was second with 26. His season ERA was elevated – 5.66. There was one more run at the postseason, Boston beating the Angels three games to one in the Division Series. Timlin again sat out the ALDS but when playing Tampa Bay in the ALCS, he pitched in Games Two and Four. He was saddled with the loss in Game Two, coming into an 8-8 tie game to pitch the bottom of the 11th at Tropicana Field. After walking the first two batters, then seeing both runners advance on a groundout that went third to first, he intentionally walked the next batter, but lost the game on a sacrifice fly by B.J. Upton. In Game Four, he entered in the top of the eighth in a game the Rays were winning, 11-2. A walk, groundout, triple, and single added two more runs before he induced a 4-6-3 double play. He had thrown his last pitch in the majors.

Timlin's 46 postseason appearances place him sixth all-time, through the 2021 season.

Giving it one last shot, after something of a chance conversation with Colorado Rockies GM Dan O'Dowd early in the season, Timlin worked out for a month and then signed a minor-league deal in July 2009. He was sent to Casper, Wyoming, to pitch for the rookie-league Casper Ghosts – interestingly, a team in the same Pioneer League where he had first begun. He pitched well in two games there, and was promoted to the Triple-A Colorado Springs Sky Sox, for whom he worked 4⅔ innings in four games (six strikeouts, seven hits, two runs). When the Sky Sox

left for a road trip and his status has not been clarified, he chose to officially retire, leaving on his own terms.

After a lengthy career, Timlin was financially secure enough that he could pursue what interested him. He had married Dawn Wood in 1992 and the couple had two children – Jacob, born in 1996, and Mykayla, born in 2000. He became pitching coach for Valor Christian High School in Highlands Ranch, Colorado, and served in that role for nine years, until both children had graduated. "Luckily, we won three state championships while I was there. I worked with some awesome kids. It was a great time. As soon as my daughter graduated, we decided I'm going to stop there, we'll travel and go watch her play volleyball. She doesn't play anymore but that's what we do now. We just kind of travel and go and have fun."

While in Boston, Dawn Timlin was known for her charitable efforts and running the Boston Marathon, which she did five times. Husband Mike said, "She does a lot of charity work. We're involved with the Angel Fund there; we help Dr. Robert Brown at Mass General. We raise money for research for ALS. She does a lot of stuff helping raise money."

SOURCES

In addition to the sources cited in the Notes, the author consulted Baseball-Reference.com, Retrosheet.org, and SABR.org.

NOTES

1   It could have been 12, in that he started the 2002 season with a Cardinals team that made it to the NLCS, but in late July he had been traded to the Phillies, who were not a contender.

2   Richard Justice, "Orioles' Timlin Savors Closer Role," *Washington Post*, February 28, 1999: D8.

3   Mike Stanton was a teammate of Timlin's at both Midland High and Southwestern. Al Pickett, "Abilenian Pulls for Blue Jays, and Other Notes," *Abilene Reporter-News*, October 3, 1991: 21. Stanton enjoyed a 19-year major-league career. His 1,178 appearances rank second all-time, following only Jesse Orosco's 1,252. Timlin primarily played outfield at Midland High.

4   Mike Eisenbath, "Oft-traveled Timlin Is Relieved to Have Landed with the Cards," *St. Louis Post-Dispatch*, August 18, 2000: D1.

5   Author interview with Mike Timlin on December 10, 2021. Unless otherwise indicated, all direct quotations attributed to Timlin come from this interview.

6   His father had two sons with him that latter time. See Gordon Edes, "Timlin Stands Tall off and on Mound," *Boston Globe*, March 24, 2005: C1, C3.

7   Eisenbath.

8   It was only some years later, when visiting Midland and talking with his former high-school coach that the coach let Timlin know a letter of interest had come to the school from Stanford. "You got a letter from Stanford when you were in high school but I didn't give it to you because I didn't think you could make the grades." Interview December 10, 2021.

9   Associated Press, "Rookie Timlin acts like old pro," *Globe and Mail* (Toronto), June 13, 1991: D12.

10   Neil MacCarl, "Toronto Blue Jays, "*The Sporting News*, June 24, 1991: 19.

11   Neil A. Campbell, "Jays Rotation Keeps Spinning," *Globe and Mail*, June 19, 1991: C12.

12   In fact, the *Globe and Mail's* Neil Campbell wrote that Timlin had become "dreadful recently as the setup man." Neil Campbell, "What It Takes to Win a Pennant," *Globe and Mail*, October 8, 1991: D11.

13   Jerome Holtzman, "Pagliarulo Pulls His Weight … and Biggest HR," *Chicago Tribune*, October 12, 1991: A5. The *Globe and Mail* called him "one of the weaker links in the Blue Jay 'pen." Neil Campbell, *Globe and Mail*, October 12, 1991: A14.

14   Larry Millson, "Timlin Armed and Ready," *Globe and Mail*, June 13, 1992: A20.

15   Mark Newman, "What's Past Is Past," *The Sporting News*, November 2, 1992: 14.

16   Murray Chass, "Winfield and Carter: History Doesn't Repeat," *New York Times*, October 26, 1992: C1. Catcher Pat Borders agreed that they'd talked about the possibility of a bunt during a meeting on the mound. See Bill Plaschke, *Los Angeles Times*, October 25, 1992: C1. Timlin also said, "I was hoping he'd pop it up to me or it would come right to me so I wouldn't have to run over there and field it because I was afraid I was going to fall down." Neil A. Campbell and Larry Millson, "Timlin Last on Scene That Cone Helped Create," *Globe and Mail*, October 26, 1992: D5.

17   Chass. Timlin said he was one of the few pitchers who actually enjoyed pitchers' fielding practice.

18   At one point, Larry Millson wrote, "You have to wonder how many more chances Mike Timlin will get in meaningful situations." And that was early in the season. Larry Millson, "Blue Jays Bail Out Timlin," *Globe and Mail*, April 21,1994: E10.

19   Phil Rogers mentioned Timlin, Terry Mulholland, Jeff Montgomery, and a few others. "Attention, Shoppers: Stock Up on Durable Arms," *Chicago Tribune*, October 25, 1998: 135.

20   Richard Justice, "For Orioles, Opening Move Is Signing Closer Timlin," *Washington Post*, November 13, 1998: C1.

21   Justice, "Orioles' Timlin Savors Closer Role."

22   There was some suggestion that manager Ray Miller may have "misused his relievers" in 1999. See Dave Sheinin, "Comfortable and Effective? Timlin Hopes He Is Closer," *Washington Post*, February 28, 2000: C6.

23   It was thought the Orioles might have paid as much as 50 percent of the remaining money on Timlin's $16 million, four-year contract. Rick Hummel, "Jocketty Lands Bullpen Help in Trade for Orioles' Timlin," *St. Louis Post-Dispatch*, July 30, 2000: D10. It was thought Timlin's role was to set up closer Dave Veres.

24   Hummel summarized his time with St. Louis in 2000, grading him with a C+: "Timlin has well above average stuff but was less consistent than the club would have liked. He was among the most durable relievers, though, after coming from Baltimore." Rick Hummel, "Cardinals Charge into Playoffs Earns High Grades," *St. Louis Post-Dispatch*, October 22, 2000: D11.

25   He was part of a five-player swap that also involved some cash. Accompanied by Placido Polanco and Bud Smith, he went to Philadelphia for Scott Rolen, Doug Nickle, and cash.

26   Michael Silverman, "Boston Red Sox," *The Sporting News*, January 27, 2003: 57.

27   David Srinivasan, "RotoRap," *The Sporting News*, March 3, 2003: 61.

28   He was deemed "one of the most dependable arms in Boston's often-erratic bullpen." Bob Hohler, "Francona on Deck for Sox," *Boston Globe*, November 5, 2003: F56.

29   Though it was Kevin Millar who used the year's team slogan phrase "Cowboy up!" most often, it was reportedly Mike Timlin who introduced it. Nick Cafardo, "Thrills Were in Season," *Boston Globe*, October 8, 2003: 67.

30   Bob Ryan, "His Appearance May Have Provided Relief," *Boston Globe*, March 5, 2004: C6. Ryan wrote that Timlin had been "just about unhittable" in October 2003.

31   "I threw a not-so-great pitch to a really great hitter," Timlin said. He felt he'd let his teammates down, but in the end the Red Sox won. Nick Cafardo, "Pick-Me-Ups Were a Relief to Timlin," *Boston Globe*, October 9, 2004: E4.

32   John Powers, "A Clashing Combination," *Boston Globe*, October 12, 2004: C2.

33   In the six 2007 postseason games, Timlin struck out seven of the 20 batters he faced, and walked nobody. The two runs that were charged to him came in on the homer hit after he had departed.

34   Associated Press, "Veteran Bosox Pitchers Share Historic Shutout," *Globe and Mail*, May 8, 2008: S6.

RICKY TRLICEK

By David Fuller

Richard Alan Trlicek's professional baseball career began with the 1987 amateur draft when the Philadelphia Phillies, having spotted him at La Grange (Texas) High School. selected him in fourth round of the draft. The 6-foot-3, 18-year-old right-handed pitcher signed his first contract days later and started the climb from low-A ball to the major leagues where he spent parts of five seasons, including two full tours, before retiring in 1998 due to back problems.

Trlicek was born on April 26, 1969, in Houston, a fourth-generation Texan descended from Moravian immigrants (Czech Republic) who landed in Louisiana in 1872 and settled in La Grange. His father, James Charles Trlicek, owner of an HVAC company, was born in 1944. His mother, Earline Dell Wind, was born in 1945. A brother, James Earl Trlicek, was born in 1967 and a sister, Laura Kay Wolff, was born in 1971.

Trlicek (pronounced *TRIL-i-chek*) spent his first two seasons in the New York-Pennsylvania League as a

(Photo courtesy of Ricky Trlicek.)

starting pitcher, first with the short-season Utica Blue Sox and then the Batavia Clippers. After eight starts in the 1988 season for the Clippers, he finished with a 2-3 record and a 7.39 ERA. The team had tried to change his delivery and he developed a ligament strain that caused numbness in his pitching hand. He reported to spring training in 1989 but was released by the Phillies on March 23. "That was the worst moment of my baseball career and maybe my life," he told the *Toronto Star* in 1992. "The year before (1988) had been a rough year for me, and I finished with a sore arm. I threw well in spring training in 1989, but I think they had their minds made up."[1] He later learned that a typo in the Phillies media guide may also have been a reason. "I was taken in the fourth round, and they paid me $35,000 to sign," Trlicek said. "Somehow in the media guide, it was printed as 'taken in the 35th round and signed for $4,000.' So I was released. My pitching coach was furious and called it a mistake."[2] The experience stayed with him, and he rededicated himself to becoming better. "You never forget a thing like that," Trlicek said. "You take it with you for the rest of your career."[3]

Atlanta's Red Murff, the scout who signed Nolan Ryan, worked with Trlicek to get his old form back. He watched him pitch in a beer-league game and when it was over, Murff laid a contract on the hood of a car for Trlicek to sign.[4] He was sent to extended spring training in Bradenton and then to the Sumter Braves of the South Atlantic League under manager Ned Yost. He pitched in 15 games and finished with a record of 6-5 and a 2.59 ERA. His season included two starts for the Durham Bulls, then in the Class-A Carolina League. On August 28 he pitched eight innings in a regular-season game, giving up just two runs but left with the game tied. The Bulls won the game 4-2.[5] His second appearance came in a playoff game on September 6, but he lasted only 2⅓ innings and took the loss. His stint in Durham happened to coincide with the beginning of the club's rise to fame from the hit movie *Bull Durham*, released the previous year. His journey to "The Show" began in earnest during the offseason when he was traded to the Toronto Blue Jays on December 17 for popular but aging catcher Ernie Whitt, 37, the last original Blue Jay, and out-fielder-pinch-runner Kevin Batiste.

For the next three seasons, Trlicek rose through the ranks, first with the Dunedin Blue Jays of the Class-A Florida State League in 1990, where he went 5-8 with a 3.73 ERA in 26 starts with a total of 154⅓ innings, third highest on the team. He was sent to Double-A Knoxville after breaking camp in 1991and converted to a reliever. He said the team thought his ground-ball-inducing sinker and slider would be more useful in a relief role.[6] He recorded 16 saves in 41 games, with two wins and five losses and an ERA of 2.45. He missed the final month of the season with an ankle injury that required surgery and cost him a chance to play winter ball in Venezuela.[7] In 1992, Trlicek was moved up to the Triple-A Syracuse Chiefs to start the season. He pitched in 35 games, earning 10 saves with a record of 1-1 but his ERA crept up to 4.36 against Triple-A hitters.

The 1992 season, in which the Jays won their first World Series, was memorable for Trlicek for a couple of reasons, even though he wasn't a part of the post-season. In a spring-training game against the Orioles on March 24, he took over for starter David Wells with two out in the sixth. He threw one fly-ball pitch to end the inning and earned the win. He said it was his shortest game ever.[8] When final-cut day arrived, Trlicek and Pat Hentgen found they were both starting the season with the Blue Jays because three regulars were on the disabled list. That gave Trlicek the op-portunity to make his major-league debut on April 8 at Tiger Stadium.[9] He pitched two-thirds of an inning, allowing two runs, as the Blue Jays beat Detroit 10-9. Six days later, he made his second appearance, against the New York Yankees at SkyDome, pitching one shutout inning in a 12-6 win. Trlicek's first trip to the big leagues ended after just those two games and he was sent to Syracuse on April 22 for the rest of the season to make way for All-Star Dave Stieb, who was returning from back surgery. On August 12 Trlicek underwent elbow surgery for a pinched nerve and did not participate in either the playoffs or World Series. When he was sent down to Syracuse, a disappointed Trlicek vowed that he would be back, and arrived at camp for the 1993 season eager to prove he was ready to stick with the Jays. Toronto placed him on waivers, however, and the Los Angeles Dodgers claimed him on March 16.[10] It turned out to be a big break. Trlicek broke camp with the Dodgers in what was to be his first

of two full seasons in the majors. Early in spring train-ing, out of options, he had bumped rookie and future Hall of Famer Pedro Martinez back to Triple A and remained with the Dodgers. He appeared in 41 games, posting a 1-2 record with a 4.08 ERA – and received a three-day suspension for a hit-by-pitch altercation on June 10 with the Padres' Gary Sheffield, who was also suspended for three days.[11] Sheffield had taken his best home-run swing on a 3-and-0 pitch in the sixth with his team ahead 10-2. Trlicek, who responded to the swing with an inside pitch, said he wasn't trying to hit Sheffield, and Sheffield said he wasn't sure if it was deliberate, but he charged the mound anyway. It was Trlicek's first time being charged and tackled. "I guess it would happen sooner or later," he said.[12] On July 7 the Dodgers and Phillies played a 20-inning marathon that lasted 6 hours and 10 minutes. Trlicek pitched four hitless innings – the 16th through 19th – but gave up two hits and two runs run in the 20th when he had to leave the game with numbness in his pitching hand, a recurrence of the nerve problem he'd had in Toronto. The game ended in a 6-5 loss (Trlicek's) at 1:47 A.M. On September 8 Trlicek was one of seven Dodger pitchers to take the mound against Atlanta. The bright spot in the 8-2 loss to the Braves was that he collected his only major-league hit, off Tom Glavine.

Trlicek's first major-league win came the next day, on September 9 against the Florida Marlins, when he threw one inning in relief. On September 21 he pitched a shutout inning against Cincinnati to earn his first ma-jor-league save. All of these achievements in his first full season in the major leagues were not enough for him to stick with the Dodgers, who placed Trlicek on waivers during spring training the following year. He was claimed by the Boston Red Sox on April 1, 1994.

Trlicek's arrival in Boston was greeted with head-lines when, in the second game of the season, in relief of Frank Viola, he retired all five batters he faced in a 5-4 win over Detroit. He threw 21 pitches, including 15 for strikes – shutting down the same team he had faced in his major-league debut two years earlier.[13] His success proved fleeting, however, and after six games and an ERA of 17.18, he cleared waivers and was demoted to New Britain of the Double-A Eastern League in April. His woes were due to the same re-curring nerve inflammation that caused numbness in his pitching hand – a problem that he said worsened in the cold New England weather.[14] He moved up to Triple-A Pawtucket in May, was recalled to Boston in June and appeared in five more games before clearing waivers and being sent back down to New Britain as a starter. In July Trlicek cleared waivers and was sent to Pawtucket, only to be recalled on August 4.[15] He made his first major-league start on August 8, a 5-2 loss to Minnesota. When the players strike began four days later, instead of being sent down to Pawtucket for the remainder of the season so he could keep pitching (and getting paid), the Red Sox kept Trlicek and a group of other players on the major-league roster where their pay was suspended. The Red Sox released him on December 5 to make room on the 40-man roster for two Rule 5 draft picks.

In the 1992 interview with the *Toronto Star*, Trlicek said he did not want to be a player who bounced around from team to team, spending time in the minors between chances.[16] But his later career was all of that. Although he did make it back to the big leagues for parts of the next three seasons, he labored in the minors each year between opportunities with six teams. After becoming a free agent on being released by the Red Sox, he signed with the San Francisco Giants for 1995 and reported to minor-league camp in February as a nonroster invitee to avoid being a replacement player with the strike still in progress. "I'm going in under a minor-league contract," he said. "I'll have nothing to do with replacement players, or any big-league games. As of this moment, until the strike is settled, I'm a minor leaguer."[17] The strike ended on April 2, and Trlicek started the season with the Triple-A Phoenix Firebirds. He was 5-4 with a 5.29 ERA when the Giants released him on June 18, and he signed a minor-league contract with Cleveland on June 28 to play for the Double-A Canton-Akron Indians. A record of 5-3 and an ERA of 3.05 in 24 games – including a no-hitter on August 7[18] – was not enough for him to stick with Cleveland, which released him on October 16, 1995.

The next stop on Trlicek's campaign to get back to the big leagues was Detroit, which picked him up on November 30 with an invitation to spring training in 1996. By March 27, the Tigers had seen enough and released him. He hung out at his hotel room in Florida, throwing against a brick wall to keep his arm in shape. He was about ready to quit and was packing to head home to Texas when he got a call from the Mets, who signed him to play for the Triple-A Norfolk Tides.[19]

Trlicek pitched in 62 games, going 4-5 with 10 saves and an ERA of 1.87. The rebound won him a September call-up from the Mets and he appeared in five games, finishing the season with an ERA of 3.38,

but was again placed on waivers. This time it was back to the Red Sox, who picked him up on October 14.

The return to Boston started on a good note: Trlicek made the 1997 Opening Day roster and went on to appear in 18 games, going 3-4 with an ERA of 4.63. But a pitching coach had tried to teach him a split-finger pitch that may have strained the middle finger on his pitching hand. It was a decision he disagreed with as he already threw a sinker. The Red Sox sent Trlicek back to the Mets on May 12 for Toby Borland in an exchange of journeyman relievers. The return to the Mets lasted only nine games before an injury ended his season.[20] In a game at Wrigley Field on June 11, he strained the ligament in his middle finger and had to go on the disabled list. He went home on July 5 and was put on the 60-day disabled list on July 23. On October 9 he was sent outright back to Norfolk.

Trlicek re-signed with the Mets again for 1998 and returned to Norfolk, where he appeared in 19 games and finished 2-2 with a 6.08 ERA and three saves. Once again, injury sidelined him – this time it was an old back problem that flared up again and grew worse toward the end of the season. When Trlicek went home to check with his doctor, he was told his back was not going to get better, and he announced his retirement from playing at the end of the season. It took a while for him to adjust to the fact that his career was over but, "once it's gone, it's gone," he said.[21] He wrote a private memoir of his career for his family, both to catch them up on what had happened and to work out his thoughts on being out of the game.

Trlicek, then 29, turned to the oil business in 2001 and worked with his brother Jimmy, who was a land manager for an oil company until 2013. The work was hard and demanded long road trips and stressful negotiations with landowners. Jimmy gave up the work and started a sports memorabilia company in La Grange with his wife. Rick joined the company a year later and as of 2022 managed the sports-card side of the business.

Trlicek never married. He lives on an 85-acre property in La Grange that he shares with his parents and brother. In his spare time, he enjoys hunting and fishing. Although he enjoys traveling to sportsmen's camps, he said he can track deer just going out his back door or near his cabin in the Texas hill country.[22]

SOURCES

In addition to the sources cited in the Notes, the author also consulted Ancestry.com and Baseball-Reference.com.

NOTES

1   Jim Byers, "Downcast Trlicek Vows He'll Be
    Back," *Toronto Star*, April 23, 1992: C3.

2   Trlicek phone interview, April 4, 2022; *Philadelphia Phillies Media Guide
    1989*. The media guide actually says Trlicek was the Phillies' 40th pick and
    makes no mention of his signing bonus. In fact, he was the team's third pick,
    taken in the fourth round, after they traded their first-round pick for a player.

3   Trlicek interview.

4   Trlicek interview; Ed Price, "Merrill: Series for A-League Title 'A
    Natural,'" *Durham* (North Carolina) *Herald-Sun*, September 10, 1989.

5   "Bulls Box," *Raleigh* (North Carolina) *News
    and Observer*, August 29, 1989: 12.

6   Trlicek interview.

7   Alan Ryan, "Jays' Trlicek Gets Roughed Up
    Again," *Toronto Star*, March 12, 1992: D5.

8   Craig Daniels, "Pucks Fly in the Ballyard as Espo Makes His
    Pitch," *National Post* (Toronto), March 25, 1992: 35.

9   Steve McAllister, "A Brutal Day in Motown,"
    National Post, April 9, 1992: 43.

10 Jim Byers, "Trlicek Now a Dodger," *Toronto Star*, March 17, 1993: F4.

11 Mary Ann Hudson, "Dodgers Out in Left Field against
    Padres," *Los Angeles Times*, June 11, 1993: C1, C9.

12 "Dodgers Fighting Mad in Loss," *Santa Clara*
    (California) *Signal*, June 11, 1993: C4.

13 Michael Vega, "Trlicek's Debut Is a Pronounced
    Success," *Boston Globe*, April 7, 1994: 39.

14 Trlicek interview.

15 Nick Cafardo, "Red Sox Notebook," *Boston Globe*, August 5, 1994: 73.

16 Byers, "Downcast Trlicek Vows He'll Be Back."

17 Lary Stone, "Giants Don Kid Gloves to Handle 2 Camps in
    1," *San Francisco Chronicle*, February 5, 1995: D1.

18 "Phillies Lose to Indians on Trlicek's No-Hitter," *Pottsville*
    (Pennsylvania) *Republican and Herald*, August 8, 1995: 11.

19 Trlicek interview.

20 *New York Daily News*, June 14, 1997: 111.

21 Trlicek interview.

22 Trlicek interview.

DUANE WARD

By John Kennedy

Known as one of the steadiest setup and capable closers in Blue Jays history, Duane Ward was instrumental in the organization's back-to-back World Series championships, in the early 1990s. Standing at 6-feet-4 and 210 pounds, he was a powerful right-handed pitcher capable of throwing 95-mph fastballs and hard, sweeping sliders. Ward's versatility allowed him to be used differently than typical set-up pitchers in today's game. He regularly appeared in 65 to 80 games a year, often pitching multiple innings.[1]

Roy Duane Ward was born in Park View, New Mexico, on May 28, 1964, to Tommy and Evelyn Ward. Duane had an older brother, also named Tommy, and two younger brothers, Gary and Mike. All four boys played sports in school, but only Duane played professionally. Both parents worked – Tommy as an oil-field worker for Halliburton for many years and then a few other companies. Evelyn "kept busy, just

like all of us did. Over the years, she managed some stores – a Dairy Queen and a couple of restaurants."[2]

Duane showed athletic prowess at a young age, playing baseball for the Farmington High School Scorpions, known throughout New Mexico for having a well-established baseball program. On the competitive circuit, he traveled and flourished throughout the American Amateur Baseball Congress leagues and starred in the Connie Mack World Series. (His plaque hangs in the tournament's Hall of Fame at Ricketts Park in Farmington.[3]) Ward also led the Scorpions basketball team on a 26-0 run through the 1981-82 basketball season, claiming the New Mexico Activities Association Class 4A State Championship and being named to the District 1AAAA first team as a forward.[4]

In high-school baseball, Duane was primarily a pitcher, but when not pitching he filled in at other positions. On weekends, "we always played doubleheaders, back to back against, say, Albuquerque High School, and then the next day we'd travel over to Santa Fe and play a doubleheader there."[5]

Ward was selected in the first round (ninth overall) of the June 1982 amateur draft by the Atlanta Braves. Atlanta scout Bob Wadsworth had spotted and followed Ward. Wadsworth was "the one who scouted me and signed me," Ward said. "He's the one who came in and saw me and talked. He was in my living room. There's a photo of me and him in the local paper when I was signing my contract. Bob was a good man – honest and straightforward. Didn't try to sugarcoat anything. Just told me how it was. I really appreciated that."[6]

Ward was drafted just four spots after another notable pitcher, Dwight Gooden.[7] He is tied with Jim Kremmel (1971) for the second-highest draft pick of players from New Mexico, behind shortstop Alex Bregman, who was selected with the second pick in the first round of the 2015 draft.[8] There was a signing bonus, in line with other first-round bonuses of the day. Duane didn't have any agent or adviser in those days. "We didn't have that kind of help when I was coming up," he said. "I just had some local people in the area who helped me out, read the contract, stuff like that. One of the guys who helped me was a local athlete/star who turned lawyer, Tommy Roberts. I also called and talked to Terry McDermott. He was a high draft pick for the Los Angeles Dodgers [first round 1969]. I called him and just asked a few questions, which helped a little bit. It all came down to, basically, what do I want to do? But they helped as kind of a go-between. Someone to talk to. It was a lot less complicated and not as much glitz and glamour."[9]

In his 1982 rookie season, Ward split time between the Rookie-level Gulf Coast League Braves and the Anderson Braves of the low Class-A South Atlantic League, where he pitched in 13 games (starting 12) and posted a 3-5 record with a 4.80 ERA in 69⅓ innings pitched. The next season he was moved up to the Durham Bulls of the high Class-A Carolina League, for whom he posted an 11-13 record with a 4.29 ERA. In 1984 Ward was promoted to the Greenville Braves in the Double-A Southern League, where he faced a rough adjustment to higher-quality competition and posted a 4-9 record with a 4.99 ERA.

At Greenville in 1985, Ward bounced back and had a brief stay at Triple-A Richmond (International League). Between the two teams, he had an 11-11 record with a 4.46 ERA.

Ward made the big-league roster and started the 1986 season with Atlanta. He made his major-league debut on April 12, 1986, with a scoreless eighth-inning appearance during a 4-3 road loss to the Houston Astros. Ward recalled the game fondly as an opportunity to pitch against his idol, future Hall of Famer Nolan Ryan.

Of his debut game he said in 2020, "It just so happened that Rick (Mahler) and Nolan (Ryan) were going against each other. I got to see a guy I looked up to pitch live, and I'll be gosh-danged if I didn't get into that game later to pitch in the same game that Nolan Ryan did. But the special thing about it was having my mom and dad there to watch; it couldn't have been a more perfect day."[10]

Ward was 0-1 record with a 7.31 ERA in 16 innings pitched before being optioned to Richmond in early June. A month later, on July 6, the 22-year-old Ward was traded to the Toronto Blue Jays for right-handed pitcher Doyle Alexander, who was about to turn 36 and had posted back-to-back 17-win seasons for the Blue Jays in 1984 and 1985, and would eventually be dealt to the Tigers for minor-league prospect and future Hall of Famer John Smoltz.

"I always joke about it because three or four months later the Detroit Tigers traded, straight-up, John Smoltz for Alexander. So, every time I run into John I say, 'You know what, in a roundabout way, I was traded for you.'"[11]

Ward has a positive take on the trade to the American League East-contending Blue Jays.

"I think it was that (Atlanta) had to clear a roster spot at the big-league level, and I think a trade was in the making," Ward recalled. "So, they sent me down (to Richmond), and three weeks later, I think it was, I was supposed to start in Tidewater, Virginia, against the Mets. And it's a bus ride back and forth; you don't stay overnight because it's so close to Richmond. My manager, Roy Majtyka, was still in Tidewater, and I was back in Richmond, and he goes, 'I've got good news and bad news. The bad news is you're not starting tomorrow. I said, 'Well, what's going on?' And he goes, 'The good news is you just got traded to the Toronto Blue Jays for Doyle Alexander. And I'm going to tell you this: Doyle Alexander's a veteran pitcher, and for you to go straight-up in a trade, that tells me the Blue Jays think a lot of you. This is going to be a great opportunity for you."[12]

Ward switched organizations but not leagues. The Blue Jays sent him to their Syracuse Chiefs farm team. He finished the season with a brief stint with the Blue Jays, pitching in two games (starting one, in which he was the losing pitcher). His 1987 season was similar: He spent most of the season with Syracuse as a reliever, starting only three of his 46 games, and picking up 14 saves. He was called up when rosters expanded and earned a victory in relief. He had surgery in October to repair a left knee ligament tear.

At age 24, Ward's breakout year came in 1988. It was Ward's first season starting in a major-league bullpen and he rewarded the Blue Jays with highly effective pitching from the set-up position ahead of dominant closer Tom Henke.[13] He regularly finished games, pitching multiple innings well enough to allow Henke additional rest. In 64 appearances, Ward finished 32 games and recorded 15 saves. He posted a 9-3 record with a 3.30 ERA pitching 111⅔ innings. His performance ensured that the set-up position was Ward's to lose until the end of the 1992 season and Henke's departure from the Blue Jays.

Ward's 1989 season saw a slight regression on the stats sheet from 1988. In 66 appearances, he collected 15 saves, but his 12 blown saves led the league.[14] His won-lost record plummeted to 4-10 with a slight uptick in ERA to 3.77 in 114⅔ innings pitched. His strikeout-to-walk ratio, however, improved (122/58) and it was his first season of over 100 strikeouts in major-league play.

Ward also got his first taste of postseason play, appearing in two games in the American League Championship Series against the Oakland Athletics, in which he pitched ineffectively (3⅔ innings, 7.36 ERA) as the Blue Jays were eliminated in five games.

The 1990 season played similarly to the year before with a slight uptick in appearances (73) and innings pitched (127⅔) and 11 saves. The Blue Jays were unable to recapture the success of the previous season, finishing two games behind the Boston Red Sox in the AL East and missing the postseason.

The 1991 season saw Ward lead all American League pitchers with 81 appearances and a career-best 132 strikeouts in 107⅓ innings. He finished 46 games and recorded 23 saves, the most in his set-up relief role. He posted a 7-6 record with a 2.77 ERA along with the best strikeout-to-walk (4.00) and highest strikeouts-per-nine innings (11.1) rate of his career. His performance led to a ninth-place finish in the AL Cy Young Award balloting, which is highly impressive for any relief pitcher, let alone one, like Ward, in a predominantly set-up role.[15] The Blue Jays once again finished atop the AL East, and they played the Minnesota Twins in the ALCS. In two appearances, Ward went 0-1 with a 6.23 ERA in 4⅓ innings, while recording a save and six strikeouts to only one walk. The Blue Jays fell to the Twins, four victories to one.

Ward's success on the mound continued into the 1992 season. He registered a career-best 1.95 ERA in 79 appearances. He posted a 7-4 record with 103 strikeouts in 101⅓ innings of work, striking out over 100 batters for the fourth consecutive season. From 1988 through 1992, Ward was the only pitcher to have pitched more than 100 innings in relief in all five seasons. The Blue Jays, on the strength of a 96-win season, topped the AL East for the second year in a row. Ward pitched in three games in the ALCS against Oakland. His first postseason win came in Game Four after the Blue Jays rallied against Athletics closer Dennis Eckersley and won in 11 innings. Ward pitched the ninth and 10th innings, allowing one hit.

The Blue Jays won the ALCS four games to two and advanced to the World Series, taking on the Atlanta Braves. Ward pitched in four games and was the winner in two of them, giving up no runs and just one hit while striking out six batters over 3⅓ innings. Ward won Game Two by pitching a flawless eighth inning before a blown save by Braves pitcher Jeff Reardon. He won Game Three, entering after an effective eight-inning effort from starting pitcher Juan Guzmán, allowing one hit and striking out two in the ninth inning. Winning the Series in six games, the Blue Jays got their first World Series banner to hang from the rafters of SkyDome.

In the five-year period from 1988 to 1992, Ward established himself as a hard-throwing right-hander and one of the game's top set-up men, combining with closer Tom Henke to form "the most overpowering and beloved bullpen tandem in franchise history."[16] Much to the surprise of the Blue Jays organization and their fan base, Henke departed via free agency after the 1992 season, returning to the Texas Rangers, where he had started his career in 1982.[17] With Henke's departure, Ward assumed the Blue Jays closer role and posted the best season of his career.

He topped the AL (along with Kansas City Royals reliever Jeff Montgomery) with 45 saves and 70 games finished during the 1993 season, both Blue Jays single-season records that still stood as of 2022.[18] In a total of 71 appearances, he posted a 2-3 record with a 2.13 ERA, striking out 97 batters in 71⅔ innings pitched, while also posting the highest strikeouts-per-nine innings (12.2) and the lowest walks-plus-hits-per-innings pitched (1.033 WHIP) of his professional career. His performance earned Ward his first All-Star Game appearance and he finished fifth for the AL Cy Young Award and 22nd in AL MVP voting.

The Blue Jays had another 95-win season in 1993, the best in the AL East, and faced the Chicago White Sox in their third consecutive ALCS appearance. Ward pitched in four ALCS games, finishing each, and recording two saves, including one in the clinching Game Six. Against the Philadelphia Phillies in the World Series, Ward finished four games, and got two saves and the Series-clinching win in Game Six, the famous "Touch 'em all, Joe!" game, which ended on a walk-off home run by Joe Carter.

But Ward was not able to help the Blue Jays attempt the three-peat; a combination of biceps tendinitis and a torn rotator cuff forced him to miss the entire 1994 season, which was cut short by the players strike.[19] With the 1994 season officially canceled on September 14, the Blue Jays were not able to defend their World Series crown.

Ward's 1995 season began with rehab appearances, three for Dunedin of the Florida State League and six for Syracuse. Once called up, he appeared in four games for Toronto in May and June, giving up 10 runs (8 earned) in 2⅔ innings before being shut down. This stint marked the end of Ward's tenure with the Blue Jays, who allowed him to become a free agent after the season.

Ward signed with the Chicago Cubs, making total appearances for a total of seven innings pitched for Double-A Orlando and Class-A Daytona Cubs. In a full-circle moment, Ward pitched his last major-league game on June 22, 1995, against the Milwaukee Brewers, whom he had defeated for his first major-league win on September 7, 1987. He faced six batters, walking two and giving up three hits.

Myriad injuries, including the severely torn rotator cuff and bicep tendinitis, ultimately forced Ward's retirement at the age of 31. Despite having surgery to repair his rotator cuff, Ward said, "[M]y arm just never felt the same. It never came back to where it felt 100 percent. I could still throw the ball pretty well, but it wasn't … just wasn't the same Duane Ward that everybody was used to seeing."[20] In 2022 he reflected, "Just a series of recurring injuries. The arm just didn't respond the way I wanted it to. I just wasn't going to get back to where I was."[21]

In nine seasons with the Blue Jays, Ward appeared in 452 games, the second most by a Toronto pitcher, and is second all-time in both saves (121) and games finished (266) behind Tom Henke. He had a 32-37 won-loss record with a 3.28 ERA and 67 holds. He saved his best performances for when it mattered most, going 3-0, collecting two saves, with a 1.13 ERA and 13 strikeouts in eight innings in World Series appearances. Sportswriter Rob Neyer rated Ward the second-best reliever in team history.[22]

Since his retirement, Ward has become an active alumni member for the Blue Jays organization, participating in many charity efforts. He is one of the lead instructors at baseball clinics for the Toronto Blue Jays Academy and the Jays Care Foundation.[23]

As a driving force in getting the Blue Jays to hold baseball camps across the country, Ward has been eager to educate young players about the sport.[24] "I basically started up the Honda Super Camps back in 2010. We've been doing them up until 2020; they had to shut down because of COVID."[25] He was a true ambassador for the Blue Jays. "A lot of promotions there inside the Dome, and doing it all across Canada. Each summer, we'd travel to 10 different provinces. A lot of my teammates, some of the other guys, I got them involved. I got them all doing camps with us. They all like giving back to the sport that we love. Giving back to the kids of Canada."

Ward is one of five Blue Jays pitchers to appear in 80 or more games in a single season.

Ward said that if he had the entire process, highs and lows, to repeat, he unquestionably would. "If I was 100 percent healthy and not in my mid-50s," he laughed, "I'd love to be playing still today. Being around all the guys that love the game as much as you do. The thing about it is we get old, we have a few injuries, but I wouldn't trade anything about how my career went. Wish I wouldn't have gotten hurt, but I (played) to the best of my ability. And what you can do is pass those experiences on to the next generation."[26]

He has also been a regular contributor to Sportsnet, a Canadian national cable sports television station, providing his insight into the Toronto Blue Jays and current baseball topics.[27] "I did some fill-in broadcasting for a couple, three years there. I think one year I did 15 or 20 games, in the radio booth with Jerry Howarth. Giving my perspective about the team, the pitching side of it, the bullpen. I really enjoyed doing it."[28] The network constructed a Blue Jays Top 40 list and placed Ward at number 21 all-time (much to the chagrin of many analysts who believed he should have been higher).[29]

Living in Nevada, Ward has otherwise intentionally kept a very low profile, with no social media presence and wanting to "keep personal stuff personal."

Most recently, Ward was elected as part of the 2020 inductee class to the Canadian Baseball Hall of Fame alongside Jacques Doucet, Justin Morneau, and former teammate John Olerud. Reflecting on Ward's time with the Blue Jays during the Hall of Fame announcement, Olerud stated that "he was just dominant. … With 'Wardo' coming, you knew you were going to have an easy inning. There rarely was a rough inning when Wardo took the field. He just had great stuff, and the ball didn't get put in play a whole lot."[30]

In an interview after the announcement, Ward reflected on his time on the mound: "It's something that really makes you reflect back on everybody that was a part of your amateur career, of your professional career and your big-league career. … To be honored this way – at the top with the Canadian Baseball Hall of Fame – it's really something. You reflect back on almost everybody that had something to do with your success – and help you when you fail to teach you how to get out of a rut or things that come your way. But one thing you learn is that you don't do it by yourself."[31]

SOURCES

In addition to the sources cited in the Notes, the author consulted baseballalmanac.com and Baseball-Reference.com.

NOTES

1   Tom Dakers, "Top 60 All-Time Blue Jays #30 Duane Ward," *Blue Bird Banter*, February 24, 2021. https://www.bluebirdbanter.com/2021/2/24/22298673/top-60-all-time-blue-jays-30-duane-ward, accessed February 5, 2022.

2   Duane Ward interview with Bill Nowlin on May 2, 2022, hereafter cited as Ward interview.

3   Joel Priest, "Four Corners Great Duane Ward Into Canadian Hall of Fame," *Durango* (Colorado) *Herald*, June 26, 2020. https://www.durangoherald.com/articles/four-corners-great-duane-ward-into-canadian-hall-of-fame, accessed February 5, 2022.

4   Wayne Leupold, "Champions to Hit the Court Again," *Farmington* (New Mexico) *Daily Times*, March 28, 1982: 9B.

5   Ward interview.

6   Ward interview.

7   "Duane Ward," Canadian Baseball Hall of Fame, https://baseballhalloffame.ca/hall-of-famer/duane-ward/, accessed February 5, 2022.

8   Kevin Hendricks, "Bregman Can Make NM History," *Albuquerque Journal*, June 7, 2015. https://www.abqjournal.com/595581/bregman-can-make-nm-history.html.

9   Ward interview.

10 Priest, "Four Corners Great Duane Ward Into Canadian Hall of Fame."

11 Priest.

12 Priest.

13 Dakers, "Top 60 All-Time Blue Jays #30 Duane Ward."

14 *1992 Toronto Blue Jays Media Guide.*

15 Canadian Baseball Hall of Fame.

16 Dakers.

17 Canadian Baseball Hall of Fame.

18 Canadian Baseball Hall of Fame.

19 Priest.

20 "Ward Goes Into Hall with 3 Titles," *Albuquerque Journal*, February 24, 2010. https://www.abqjournal.com/231426/ward-goes-into-hall-with-3-titles.html.

21 Ward interview. In all, Ward has had two shoulder surgeries, one on his hand, and – over time – seven knee surgeries, "fixing things here and there after I got done playing."

22 Dakers.

23 Canadian Baseball Hall of Fame.

24 Leith Dunick, "Ward's Way," TBnewswatch.com, June 30, 2012. https://www.tbnewswatch.com/local-sports/wards-way-391582. Accessed February 28, 2022.

25 Ward interview. The *Toronto Star* ran a feature article in March 2012 providing the schedule for that year's camps, and said, "Duane Ward … leads the three-day camps which will include different instructors along the way. Among them: recent Hall of Fame inductee Roberto Alomar and his father Sandy, Lloyd Moseby, Jesse Barfield, Jose Cruz, Jr., and Darrin Fletcher, among others." See Brendan Kennedy, "Jays to Hold Clinics Across Canada," *Toronto Star*, March 31, 2010: U12. The 14 dates for 2012 ranged from July 2 through August 30, each camp typically for three days, with locations in Edmonton; Calgary; Kelowna, British Columbia; Vancouver; Montreal; Ottawa; London Ontario; Halifax; Charlottetown; Moncton; St. John's, Newfoundland; Saskatoon; Winnipeg; and a final weekend at Rogers Centre, Toronto.

26 Priest.

27 Dakers.

28 Ward interview.

29 "Blue Jays Top 40: How's Duane Ward Not in Your Top 10?," sportsnet.ca, August 17, 2017. https://www.sportsnet.ca/baseball/mlb/blue-jays-top-40-hows-duane-ward-not-top-10/. Accessed February 28, 2022.

30 Priest.

31 Priest.

TURNER WARD

By Warren Campbell

Turner Ward has two World Series rings from his time with the 1992 and 1993 Toronto Blue Jays. He is a member of the Mobile, Alabama, Sports Hall of Fame (2007 inductee) and is best known in baseball history for never giving up and not having taken his eye off the ball.

Turner Max Ward was born on April 11, 1965, in Orlando, Florida, to Dr. James M. and Sandra Turner Ward. His father was a longtime veterinarian in Saraland, Alabama, and he had four brothers, Wes, Jay, Wade, and Lance, and a sister, Jodi.[1] He spent a lot of time learning baseball with older brother Wes.

While playing Little League at Amelia Park, Turner would emulate his heroes like Dale Murphy. The only major-league game he went to was with his father and brothers, when Hank Aaron was closing in on Babe Ruth's career home-run record. "I was about 9 or 10 years old and had never been to a major league [game] before or since until I played in one. My dad took my brothers and I to a game in Atlanta and had us in seats in the outfield. Every swing Aaron took there were lights flashing, it was a very special moment for me. He hit one out and I like to tell people that the ball was coming right to us and that we got it, but we didn't. I didn't catch the ball but what I did catch that night was a dream to be a major leaguer. That's where it started for me."[2]

From the age of 14, he was focused on being a major leaguer. "A coach told me you if want to hit the ball farther you're going to have to get stronger. I just started training myself that way. I'd run for miles. I loved to run. It was almost like stress relief for me."[3] His parents, older brother, and coaches saw his determination and encouraged him all the way through.

Success was not guaranteed. Turner did not make the Satsuma High School freshman baseball team. "I didn't make my freshman team but it didn't discourage me. It actually turned my senses stronger to getting better. So I worked on getting better every year."[4] After graduating from high school, he was so sure he would become a major leaguer that he would sign fellow students' yearbooks with his number and draw a little baseball bat and ball.[5]

Throughout high school and as a college freshman, Turner Ward was strictly a right-handed hitter but a family member gave him advice. "My uncle Mutt spent some time in the lower minor leagues and he told me that I'll be a platoon player unless I learned to switch-hit. After my freshman year in college, I spent the winter learning to be a switch-hitter."[6]

After high school, Turner went to Faulkner State College in Bay Minette, Alabama. Thirty-seven players for the Faulkner State Sun Chiefs have gone on to professional baseball.[7] In his two years on the team, Ward broke future Boston Red Sox infielder Dave Stapleton's team records for doubles and triples in a season and batted .448. "I had a couple of pretty good seasons and some records fell but I'm sure my records have been broken since," he said.[8]

Ward then joined his brother in the outfield for the University of South Alabama Jaguars of the Sun Belt Conference, where he led the nation in outfield assists with 17. "That was something I found out about later. I had a good accurate arm and everything worked that year."[9]

In the 1986 season, Ward was spotted by Yankees scout Jack Gillis, a longtime scout for the Yankees, Rays, Rockies, and Blue Jays. (Gillis had a keen eye for talent and in 2011 was inducted into the Professional Baseball Scouts Hall of Fame.[10])

In the 18th round of the June 1986 amateur draft, the Yankees selected Ward, the third South Alabama player they chose in the draft. He was asked what it would take to sign him, and he replied, "I asked for my college to be paid for and a new car. The Yankees called my mother and then the auto dealer because she told them I was visiting my friend there. They agreed to pay for my college and a car. So I tell everybody if you need a good clean used car or a major-league contract go to Little's Auto Sales."[11]

Ward began with Oneonta of the short-season Class-A New York-Penn League. In 1987 he was promoted to Fort Lauderdale of the Class-A Florida State League. In 1988 he moved to Triple-A Columbus, where he hit .251 and stole 28 bases. In spring training of 1989, the Yankees traded outfielders Ward and Joel Skinner to Cleveland for Mel Hall. For Ward, the season started slowly after he was injured in the final spring-training game of the Indians' Triple-A affiliate in Edmonton.[12] When he returned, he hit well for Cleveland's minor-league teams in Canton/Akron in 1989 and Colorado Springs in 1990. When major-league rosters expanded in September 1990, Ward was called up by the Indians. He made his major-league debut on September 10, 1990, against the Chicago White Sox. He played right field and was 0-for-4 in a 6-2 loss. Two days later he got his first hit, off Steve Rosenberg of the White Sox, and on September 15, Ward started again, against the Kansas City Royals and went 3-for-5 in a 14-6 walkaway with a triple, a home run off Andy McGaffigan, and 6 RBIs. He finished the season hitting .348 for Cleveland in 14 games.

Ward started the 1991 season as Cleveland's starting right fielder. After playing in 40 games, he was hitting .230. On June 27 the Blue Jays were looking to shore up their pitching staff and acquired Cleveland pitching ace Tom Candiotti along with Ward for pitcher Denis Boucher and outfielders Glenallen Hill, Mark Whiten and cash.

The '91 Blue Jays were a contender and had a crowded outfield. Ward spent most of the season at Triple-A Syracuse, hitting .330, earning a September call-up during the Blue Jays' successful pennant drive. He contributed two singles in his first game, on September 2, helping the Blue Jays come from behind against the Baltimore Orioles. He ended up getting 14 plate appearances in eight games, hitting .308 for the eventual American League East champions.

The 1992 Blue Jays did not re-sign Candiotti, and other key players left the team, but they were still considered the AL East Division favorites after signing star players Jack Morris and Dave Winfield during the offseason. Ward made the Opening Day roster but played in only six games before returning to Syracuse as the Blue Jays had a strong starting outfield in Joe Carter, Candy Maldonado, and Devon White. After hitting .239 in 81 games for Syracuse, he returned in September for another successful stretch drive as the '92 Blue Jays beat out the Milwaukee Brewers by four games to win the AL East. Ward played in 18 games, had 33 plate appearances, and hit .345, filling in at all three outfield positions and pinch-hitting.

Ward did not play in the postseason. After the 1992 World Series championship, he was again ready to try to make his mark as a Blue Jays outfielder in 1993. Ward was on the major-league roster for most of the 1993 season, but the crowded outfield allowed him only limited playing time. He played in 72 games and played all three outfield positions, but batted just .192.

At the July 31 trade deadline, the Blue Jays acquired Rickey Henderson. Ward wore number 24 and Henderson was not comfortable wearing number 14. Blue Jays catcher Pat Borders acted as Ward's "agent" and helped negotiate a deal for the coveted 24. The actual terms of the transaction were never known but it has long been rumored that the transaction cost around $25,000. "I got an undisclosed amount of merchandise," Ward told the questioning media, and added, "Next thing he's going to take my locker. He already took my number and left field." Ward added said with a wide grin, "I told my wife to stay away from him."[13]

Once again, Ward didn't see any postseason action as he watched the Blue Jays win their second consecutive World Series. "No doubt that those years on the Blue Jays taught me to move to a different level. Those are some of the things that I teach now [as a hitting coach], there's a lot of frustration in this game but the battles that you can win are really in the mind. That's what I learned in Toronto, that frustration went through my whole body and I couldn't perform the way I wanted to. That time was career-changing from that point forward."[14]

After the 1993 season, the Blue Jays placed Ward on waivers and he was claimed by the Milwaukee Brewers. He spent three years with the Brewers, playing all three outfield positions. In 1994 season Ward played in what was to that point a career-high 102 games, hitting .232 with 9 homers and 45 RBIs. In 1995 and 1996, he was relegated to backup outfield duty, appearing in 44 and 43 games respectively. He hit .264 in 1995 but his average dropped to .179 in 1996. After that season he was released. In April 1997 he signed with the Pittsburgh Pirates as their fourth outfielder.

In Ward's first year with the Pirates, he began the year with Triple-A Calgary, where he batted .340 in 59 games. On July 3 he joined the Pirates and had by far his best season as a major-league batter, appearing in 71 games and batting .353 with a .420 on-base percentage and 33 RBIs.

For three seasons Ward he filled in all over the outfield and had some of his most productive seasons at the plate. On May 3, 1998, he made a catch that is long remembered. "Right from A-ball I always played as if defense should never go in a slump so if I'm not hitting well I've got to make the plays from a defensive standpoint. I told everybody in A-ball that I would run through a wall to catch a ball. I held true to my word."[15] That he did, on a fly to deep right field by Mike Piazza. Ward knew he was going to hit the wall but he was not going to let the ball fall to the ground. Instead, he went right through the wall at Three Rivers Stadium. A clip of the catch has become legendary on baseball highlight shows.[16]

Ward's 1998 season was his most active one: He played in 123 games and batted .262 with 9 home runs and a career-best 46 RBIs. Pittsburgh was a city he connected with the most. "It's a blue-collar town. I'm a guy from a small town and was most comfortable in Pittsburgh. Pittsburgh was my style of play. I wasn't an everyday guy but I was always ready to come off the bench and pinch-hit. The game kind of found me in Pittsburgh and I kind of found my game."[17]

After two strong seasons, Ward was less successful in 1999 and in mid-August, batting .209 after appearing in 49 games, Ward was released by the Pirates, A week later, he signed with the Arizona Diamondbacks. In 10 games at the end of the season, he hit .348. He appeared in just 15 major-league games in 2000, batting .173. Most of his time was spent at Triple-A Tucson, where he hit .378 in 32 games. As in many other seasons in his career, injuries played a big part in his limited appearances in 1999. "Fractures, dislocations, torn tendons; still have eight screws in my right leg. I've had surgery on my right shoulder, my left shoulder, my right knee. All of those were due to baseball injuries. There were a lot of times I was feeling like I had to reinvent myself through different ways."[18]

Released in October, Ward signed with the Philadelphia Phillies in December. He spent most of 2001 at Triple A again, with Scranton/Wilkes-Barre, with some midseason work in June and July when he hit .267 in 17 games for the Phillies.

Turner Ward was released and his 12-year major-league playing career ended. He returned to Mobile County and became a youth minister for the First Baptist Church of Satsuma. He regularly spoke about connecting his life in baseball and his religious devotion.[19] Ward began helping his father-in-law, who worked in cabinetry and refinished furniture. Ward got his builder's license and took on a bigger challenge, building homes to sell on speculation. Ward built his own home a 6,000-square-foot house.[20]

Once again, baseball returned when former teammate Doug Strange, then an assistant GM with Pittsburgh, asked Ward if he was interested in managing the Gulf Coast Rookie League team in 2006. With his family encouraging him to return to the game he managed five future major leaguers on the Gulf Coast Pirates to a third-place finish that summer.[21]

In 2007 Ward managed the State College Spikes of the New York-Penn League. In 2011 he moved on to manage the Mobile Bay Bears, the Diamondbacks Double-A affiliate. For two seasons (2011-2012) he managed the team to championships each year, was named the Southern League Manager of the Year in 2011, and later was inducted into the Mobile Sports Hall of Fame.

In 2013 he was brought on to be the assistant hitting coach with the Diamondbacks, and has since been the hitting coach with the Los Angeles Dodgers and Cincinnati Reds. For the 2022 season he was hired as the assistant hitting coach for the St. Louis Cardinals.

It was with the Dodgers that Ward was noticed nationally for his work with Yasiel Puig and Puig's celebratory kiss of Ward after every home run. "Number one, with any of these guys, I'm really trying to show how much I care – how much I love them, really," Ward said. "I wanted to hear (Puig's) story of how he came here from Cuba. I think doing that relationship early and trying to understand him more, that's only helped it grow."[22]

During the 2012 season, Ward received a life-changing call from his wife, Donna. She had been diagnosed with breast cancer. They had been together since they were teenagers and had three children together – sons Tucker and Olin, and a daughter, Kendall. Donna Ward had 14 surgeries over the next 10 years and as of 2022 was cancer-free. She was taking meticulous notes documenting her journey. In 2020 she became a public speaker and published a book, *Unexpected Hope,* that has helped others who have been on a similar journey. Together Turner and Donna created the nonprofit Hope 4110 Foundation to help women facing breast cancer and breast reconstruction.

Turner and Donna were married in 1988. "The day we got married was the day Kirk Gibson hit his homer," Ward said. "We were watching it going into our honeymoon. I always text Gibby and say, 'Happy anniversary,' because it's his anniversary too."[23]

Son Tucker, a right-handed pitcher, was selected out of Louisiana Tech University by the Diamondbacks in the 40th round of the 2015 amateur draft and spent three seasons in the Arizona organization. He is now a player agent and CEO of Ward Performance Institute.[24]

SOURCES

In addition to the sources cited in the Notes, the author consulted Baseball-Reference.com.

NOTES

1   Phone interview with Turner Ward. May 5, 2022. Hereafter Ward Phone Interview.

2   "The Interview Turner Ward," FOX 10, YouTube.com, January 23, 2014. https://www.youtube.com/watch?v=MCnRMsDC_rM

3   Ward phone interview.

4   Ward phone interview.

5   Ward phone interview.

6   Ward phone interview.

7   "Baseball Achievements of Faulkner State College of Bay Minette, Alabama," https://www.electro-mech.com/team-sports/schools-colleges-states/baseball-achievements-of-faulkner-state-college-of-bay-minette-alabama/.

8   Ward phone interview.

9   Ward phone interview.

10 "Gillis Enters Scouts Hall of Fame in Fort Myers," milb.com, March 17, 2011. https://www.milb.com/news/gcs-16996156

11 Ward phone interview.

12 Mark Spector, "Stars Have the Talent to Repeat as Champs," *Edmonton Journal,* April 8, 1989: G3.

13 Associated Press, "Rickey Has the Right Number," *Windsor* (Ontario) *Star,* August 14, 1993: B2.

14 Ward phone interview.

15 Ward phone interview.

16 "Ward Crashes Through Wall," MLB.com, May 2, 1998. https://www.mlb.com/video/ward-crashes-through-wall-c20059165.

17 Ward phone interview.

18 Ward phone interview.

19 Gannett News Service, "For First-Rate Christian Fun, Families Flock to Ballparks' *Visalia* (California) *Times-Delta,* July 22, 2005: 14.

20 Cary Osborne, "New Dodger Hitting Coach Turner Ward Knows His Lumber," dodgers.mlblogs.com, January 16, 2016. https://dodgers.mlblogs.com/new-dodger-hitting-coach-turner-ward-knows-his-lumber-efb3e9c4a546.

21 See https://www.thebaseballcube.com/content/stats/minor~2006~10224/.

22 Justin Adams, "Dodgers Hitting Coach Turner Ward Shows Care and Love for His Players by Living His Life for Jesus," sportsspectrum.com, November 1, 2017. https://sportsspectrum.com/sport/baseball/2017/11/01/dodgers-hitting-coach-turner-ward-shows-care-love-players-living-life-jesus/.

23 David Laurila, "The World Series That Participants Watched as Kids," Fangraphs.com, October 23, 2018. https://blogs.fangraphs.com/the-world-series-that-participants-watched-as-kids/.

24 Ward Performance Institute. https://www.wardinc.org/coaches-and-staff.

DAVID WEATHERS

By Adrian Fung

Right-handed pitcher David Weathers played professionally in small towns and large cities across the United States and Canada but his origins and present life are firmly rooted in southern Tennessee. He was an integral relief pitcher on the 1996 World Series champion New York Yankees and after playing for nine teams in 19 major-league seasons, Weathers retired after the 2009 campaign with 964 pitching appearances. At the time, only 16 men had pitched more regular season games in major-league history.[1]

Weathers finished his career 73-88 with a 4.25 ERA, 976 strikeouts, 75 saves, and 158 holds.

John David Weathers was born on September 25, 1969, in Lawrenceburg, Tennessee, the younger of two sons born to Thomas Rual Weathers and Gloria "Dodie" Dean Weathers (née Bennett). Weathers grew up in Five Points, Tennessee, a town of approximately 200 people, three miles north of the state's southern border with Alabama.

Gloria Weathers worked for Curtis Industries, a supplier of keys and security machinery. Thomas Weathers worked as a pipefitter. "My mother was a factory worker, and my dad was a construction worker," Weathers explained in an April 2022 interview.[2]

"He was in the Army from 1963 through 1966. When his service time was up, his regiment went to Vietnam three weeks later, but he had already gotten out. There were already soldiers over there, but he did not have to go. He was stationed in Hawaii."

Initially, David Weathers received support from only his mother to play baseball. "My mom encouraged me to play sports but my dad used to say all the time, 'Why do you want to play baseball? What are you ever going to get out of it?' My mom talked him into letting me play Little League when I was 9, and of course, 12 years after I started, I was in the big leagues. We always laughed, before he passed away, that he always said, 'What are you going to get out of baseball?' So my mom was very instrumental in getting me started."

At Loretto (Tennessee) High School, Weathers primarily pitched but also played third base and all three outfield positions. He was the Loretto Mustangs baseball team MVP in his senior year and was named All-District and All-State for three consecutive seasons. He also played basketball all four years at high school, earning All-District honors in his junior year, and was named school MVP and Associated Press All-State honorable mention in his senior year.[3]

David's brother Mike, one year older, played baseball, basketball, and football at Loretto. "My one year in junior college, we were roommates and we played together and then he played another year at University of Tennessee at Martin. He was a very good athlete, a good pitcher. Once he finished his junior year at UT-Martin, he decided to get into the work force, got married, and he's lived in Gadsden, Alabama, ever since."

After graduating from Loretto, David Weathers won the 1987 senior Babe Ruth Tennessee state

tournament and advanced to the Southeast Regionals in Cape Coral, Florida. There, he pitched a two-hit shutout with six strikeouts to lead the Lawrenceburg All-Stars to a 2-0 win over Mississippi.[4]

Later that summer, Weathers enrolled at the Moore County Campus of Motlow State Community College, a Division I junior college in Tullahoma, Tennessee. "Right after my senior year, we reported to Motlow in early August, and we had a Dodgers tryout; the Dodgers organization ran a camp at our field. There were four or five of us that they wanted to see that they had followed all through high school and when I threw that day, I threw really well, and from that day forward I knew I was going to get drafted."

Weathers struck out 67 batters to set a Motlow State Bucks single-season record.[5] The team MVP, he helped Motlow State to a 29-19 record in 1988, its best season since 1981.[6]

"One night, it was pouring rain, but our coach loved to play so we worked on our field all day. We dug holes on the infield for the water to flow into, then covered them back up. That very night, I was pitching and a Detroit Tigers scout and a Minnesota Twins scout dropped in to watch us play. That was my second start in the spring and after that start, it just exploded. Those guys turned me in to the national scouting bureau and the next time I pitched, there were probably 25 scouts there."

The Blue Jays sent scout Duane Larson, who previously recommended Kelly Gruber and David Wells to the organization, to watch Weathers pitch.

"Duane was from North Carolina, and he always had a lot of questions. He always talked to me about my mechanics and things like that," Weathers said. "My dad always said that he thought [Toronto] was going to be the team that drafted me. Duane was a great guy. He made sure that he knew where I was from. He knew I was from a small town. He knew I was from a poorer family. He made sure that once I got to the Blue Jays, he kept his word to my mom that he would take care of me. I have the utmost respect for Duane."

Toronto drafted Weathers, 6-feet-3 and 205 pounds, in the third round of the 1988 June amateur draft, 82nd overall.[7] Larson signed Weathers to his first professional contract on June 4.

Toronto assigned Weathers to short-season Class-A St. Catharines of the New York-Penn League. Weathers was one of two 18-year-old pitchers in the 12-team league and his youth betrayed him on his very first day in St. Catharines, when he met manager Eddie Dennis.

"I called him 'coach Dennis,' because that's what you said in college. My first professional day I got cussed out by our manager for calling him 'coach Dennis' [but] Eddie Dennis was one of those managers that took us young guys and absolutely helped develop us."[8]

Weathers started his professional career by winning his first two decisions. He finished the year 4-4 with a 3.02 ERA.

At Myrtle Beach of the Class-A South Atlantic League in 1989, Weathers was the ace of a club that finished in last place, going 11-13 with a 3.86 ERA, leading the league with 31 starts. He moved up another rung in 1990 when he joined the Dunedin Blue Jays of the advanced Class-A Florida State League. Once again, Weathers led the league in starts (27, tied with three other pitchers) and finished 10-7 with a 3.70 ERA.

At Knoxville of the Double-A Southern League in 1991, Weathers was 9-7 with a 2.62 ERA and 100 strikeouts in 20 starts at the end of July. His ERA and strikeouts led the Knoxville starting rotation, as did his four complete games and two shutouts. On August 1 Weathers was called up to the major leagues after the Blue Jays placed reliever Mike Timlin on the 15-day disabled list with elbow stiffness.[9]

Timlin and Weathers were A-ball pitchers one season earlier in Dunedin, and now Toronto was calling on Weathers to fill Timlin's spot.

"What is really ironic about all of that is Timlin and I were best friends and still are. We were in each other's weddings. In Orlando, [Knoxville manager] John Stearns came up to me and said, 'You're not pitching today. You're not pitching because you're going to Fenway to meet the team tomorrow in Boston.'"

When Weathers walked into Fenway Park, it was the first time in his life he had entered a major-league ballpark. "We were sitting in the bullpen and Tom Henke looked at me and said, 'Stormy, if you go in tonight, whatever you do, do not look at the Green Monster.'"

With Boston leading Toronto 5-3 in the eighth inning, Weathers, 21, the youngest player on the Toronto roster, jogged to the mound to make his major-league debut. He glanced at Fenway's 37-foot-high left-field wall, the Green Monster. "I looked right at it. I felt like I could change the numbers on the scoreboard on the wall, it was so close to me. It was so big."

Mike Greenwell, who earlier in the game had hit a go-ahead three-run home run, greeted Weathers with a double to left – off the Green Monster. After Tom Brunansky failed on a sacrifice attempt and fouled out, batterymate Pat Borders helped Weathers by throwing out Greenwell attempting to steal third. Weathers caught Ellis Burks looking at a 3-and-2 slider, to complete his first major-league inning.

When Timlin was activated from the disabled list on August 16, Toronto returned Weathers to Double A. Weathers was one of eight players recalled to Toronto when rosters expanded on September 1.[10] He earned his first major-league win on the final day of the regular season in Minnesota. After the game, Weathers and three others were added to a stand-by squad in case any postseason roster players were injured in the upcoming ALCS.[11]

Weathers, by his recollection, suffered the only major injury of his career the next season pitching for Triple-A Syracuse when he was sidelined from May 11 to July 31 with a right elbow strain. "In '92 when I strained my ligament, that was the worst injury I had and I missed two months. Other than that, 15 days here or there but nothing major."

After his arm recovered, Toronto recalled Weathers on August 20. Weathers pitched in two games for the Blue Jays, both in relief, before being sent back to Syracuse when the Blue Jays traded for starting pitcher David Cone on August 27.

Weathers was once again on standby during Toronto's postseason run, but this time he was able to keep his arm ready by pitching in the inaugural Arizona Fall League. When the Blue Jays won the World Series for the first time in franchise history, the organization gave him a championship ring and, importantly, despite only two regular-season appearances, the players voted to give Weathers 19 percent of a full World Series share, which added $22,800 to his $121,000 salary.[12]

"I was in Edmonton with the Marlins [in 1993] and [Blue Jays assistant general manager] Gord Ash gave me my ring. That's just another part of the Blue Jays where they were so classy. They flew out and gave every player their ring personally."

The Florida Marlins claimed Weathers in the autumn 1992 expansion draft. He started 1993 excellently, pitching for the Triple-A Edmonton Trappers. By mid-June he was 8-1 with a 3.59 ERA in the hitter-friendly Pacific Coast League.[13] At the end of the minor-league season, Weathers was 11-4 with a 3.83 ERA. He was called up on Labor Day, made his first

major-league start that night, and won it, pitching eight shutout innings against San Diego. Weathers finished 2-3 with a 5.12 ERA in his first taste of the National League.

In the offseason, one week before Christmas back in Tennessee, Weathers, 24, married Kelli Davis, 21, an outstanding athlete and a Loretto graduate.

In 1994 Weathers led all Florida pitchers in starts (24), wins (8), and innings pitched (135) but struggled in the strike-shortened second half of the season. At the All-Star break, he was 8-7 with a 3.86 ERA. After the break, he was 0-5 with a 12.13 ERA as opponents batted .406 against him.

Perplexed by how to optimally deploy Weathers, Florida – and later, New York, Cleveland, and Cincinnati – moved him several times between the starting rotation and the bullpen, leading to mediocre results and 3½ seasons of frustration for Weathers. From the start of 1995 with Florida until Cincinnati released him in mid-1998, he appeared in 105 games, 37 as a starter and 68 as a reliever. As a starter, he was 7-12 with a 6.08 ERA; in relief, 2-4 with a 6.14 ERA.

However, during that time, there was one spectacular six-week stretch of pitching by Weathers from mid-September to late October of 1996.

Weathers began that season as a Florida middle reliever, moved into the rotation for eight starts, then returned to the bullpen to set up closer Robb Nen. On July 31 the New York Yankees traded reliever Mark Hutton for Weathers ahead of the nonwaiver trade deadline.

Though Weathers expected to continue relieving in New York, the Yankees put the newcomer into their starting rotation out of necessity because two familiar faces from his time with Toronto, David Cone and Jimmy Key, both were recovering from shoulder surgeries. Cone had not pitched since May 2 and while Key was in the rotation, he had twice been on the disabled list earlier in 1996.

It was a disastrous move. With his arm not properly prepared for starting, Weathers allowed 10 walks, 19 hits, and 17 earned runs in four starts, leading to a demotion to Triple A. "In Columbus, I started for the most part but in the first series of the [Triple-A] playoffs, I started closing and it was just one of those times you get locked in."

Recalled to New York in mid-September, Weathers returned as a completely different hurler and the Yankees used him mostly as the seventh-inning man. He appeared in seven games, allowing one run in seven innings. On the final day of the season, Yankees manager Joe Torre told Weathers he had earned a spot on the postseason roster.

In the ALDS against Texas, Weathers was New York's bullpen ace, leading all relievers on both teams with five shutout innings. He struck out five and allowed only one single. Looking to clinch the series at Arlington in Game Four, New York trailed 4-3 in the fourth inning when Torre called Weathers into the game with two on and nobody out. Juan Gonzalez stepped to the plate, batting 7-for-14 with five home runs.

Arriving at the mound, Weathers and the infielders received one message from their manager. "Torre said, 'Let's pound the fastball in and get the double play.' I'll never forget Tino Martinez, when Joe walked off the mound, said, 'You're *not* throwing him a first-pitch fastball. He's killing us. He can't hit your slider. Throw it until he doesn't swing at it.' Sure enough, I throw a slider and he fouled it off. Then I threw two more about a foot outside and he swung at both of them."

After the huge strikeout of Gonzalez, Weathers snuffed Texas's rally by getting Will Clark to ground into an inning-ending double play. The Yankees came back to win and Weathers was credited with the series-clinching victory. Weathers blanked Baltimore in two games in the ALCS, earning a second win, then gave up his first run in October, pitching in three World Series games against Atlanta for a total of 11 nearly flawless postseason innings.

In Game Six at Yankee Stadium, New York was leading 3-1 in the sixth inning but Atlanta had a runner on third base and the potential tying run coming up to bat, NLCS MVP Javy Lopez. Torre brought in Weathers, handed him the ball and said, "It's all yours, Weatherman."[14]

"All I could think was, 'Don't give it up because if you do, you're not making it out of the Bronx tonight.'"

Working quickly, Weathers struck out Lopez on three pitches: an inside fastball, a low fastball fouled off, and the final pitch, a hard slider well outside that Lopez flailed at in vain.

"People always ask me, 'Why did he swing at that?' Well I knew I had finished him so many times inside with a fastball and in his mind he was just sitting dead-red in. Joe [Girardi] called a fastball but I chose the slider and he swung at it." Three innings later, the Yankees were World Series champions for the 23rd time.

On November 6 the Loretto Civic Center held a celebration in honor of their local world champion and the next day was declared David Weathers Day by the Lawrenceburg City Commission. After a tumultuous year, Weathers confessed that at times he doubted if his career would continue much longer and wondered if he even liked baseball anymore. Yet his wife, Kelli, who "keeps pushing me forward," and Torre had faith in him. "He said I was going to pitch in the pennant race and the playoffs. I trusted him and he brought me back up [from the minor leagues]."[15]

In one career-defining moment, coming into pitch with the World Series on the line, Weathers said, "The love for the game that had died was rekindled. I thought, 'This is what we play for.'"[16]

But just as quickly as Weathers' stock rose, it plummeted back to earth during a rocky 1997 season. Weathers came out of the bullpen in 10 games, giving up 10 runs before New York sent him back to Columbus, where he was placed in the starting rotation. He was dealt to Cleveland and continued to start at Triple-A Buffalo before his recall to the major leagues – in a relief role.

Weathers returned to the National League in 1998, signing a one-year contract with Cincinnati. Once again he was moved between the rotation and bullpen, leading to a 2-4 record and a 6.21 ERA in seven relief appearances and nine starts. It was a difficult season from the start as Weathers' father, Thomas, died unexpectedly in late April. Weathers quickly returned to Tennessee for the funeral, then two days later flew to New York and valiantly pitched eight shutout innings, striking out seven, earning the win over the Mets. "For three hours, I was able to take my mind off things. I did do it for my dad. We were real close. It was just a great feeling. But it was hard to get real emotional for a baseball game after the four days I just went through."[17]

Cincinnati waived Weathers at the beginning of the summer and Milwaukee immediately picked him up. The Brewers, strictly defining Weathers as a reliever, extracted the best results out of the right-hander. In 28 appearances, he entered games mostly in the seventh inning – the same role he flourished in during his time on the 1996 Yankees – pitching 47⅔ innings with 43 strikeouts, 3 holds and a 3.21 ERA.

"[Manager] Phil Garner was the first person who put me into a role. He said, 'You're going to pitch the seventh and eighth here,' and my career took off from that point forward. The whole time I was with the Marlins and the Yankees, those guys, they moved me back and forth so much and I never physically felt good and it's hard to compete at that level when you physically don't feel good. It was just one of those times where you have to grind through it. Fortunately for me, I got a good opportunity with the Brewers in '98 and I made the most of it."

Early in 1999, *The Sporting News* observed that the changeup Weathers rarely threw at the start of his career was now an effective weapon. "[Weathers] pounds the strike zone with a nasty late-breaking slider, a heavy sinker and a surprising changeup. In the past, Weathers was always a 'two-pitch' reliever. His changeup now gives hitters one more thing to think about. Even if he doesn't throw it for a strike all the time, it helps set up his other pitches."[18]

Now permanently a reliever, Weathers could concentrate on conditioning himself properly. "I could work out. I could get in the weight room. I could do everything that I knew for what my role was. It allowed me to stay healthier and keep my arm stronger because I knew my role. It wasn't to start. It was 100 percent to get ready that day to pitch out of the bullpen. I think that's what the hard part is between starting and relieving – going back and forth – you just can't take care of your arm. You can't take care of your body. What if I work out today and throw three innings tonight? Or what if I throw a bullpen tonight and tomorrow they say you're going to start, and they expect you to go five or six innings? Then you never know what you're going to do and you'll always have trouble preparing."

Weathers pitched the best baseball of his career the next two seasons. He set up Curtis Leskanic and Bob Wickman in 2000, leading Milwaukee relievers with 14 holds. In 2000 and 2001 combined, Weathers pitched in 121 games and posted a two-season ERA of 2.62. The Chicago Cubs also liked his .188 opponents' batting average at the 2001 trade deadline and acquired the right-hander. Weathers was a workhorse, pitching in 28 games – seven of them on zero days' rest – and recorded a 3.18 ERA in 28⅓ innings, finishing with 80 games pitched for Milwaukee and Chicago, fifth-most in the NL.

Weathers signed a three-year deal with the New York Mets before the 2002 season to be the set-up man behind closer Armando Benitez, In both 2002 and 2003, Weathers led New York relievers in games, innings pitched, holds and multi-inning appearances. Yet despite one of the highest payrolls in the major leagues, New York finished last in the NL East in both seasons.[19] In 2004, the floundering Mets began shedding salary and Weathers was on the move back to the NL Central on June 17, traded to Houston. He was less effective with the Astros, pitching 32 innings with a 4.78 ERA. He was released on September 7 and signed by a former club, the Florida Marlins, where he finished the season.

Shortly before Christmas, Weathers signed a one-year contract to pitch for another former employer, the Cincinnati Reds. He began 2005 in his usual role as a middle reliever. However, by early June, two-time All-Star closer Danny Graves faltered and was released. After Weathers and left-hander Kent Mercker alternated the eighth- and ninth-inning roles, Weathers became, for the first time in his career, a full-time closer in August. He pitched in 73 games, converting 15 of 19 save opportunities and stranding 24 of 30 inherited runners.[20]

In 2006 as the Reds' closer, Weathers stumbled, relinquishing the role to Todd Coffey and later Eddie Guardado. After Guardado required season-ending Tommy John surgery, Weathers reclaimed the closer position, finishing the year with 12 saves in 19 opportunities. Despite an up-and-down season, Cincinnati's skipper, Jerry Narron, assured Weathers he was the team's closer.

"When we went into '07, Jerry Narron and I were close and he had a lot of confidence in me. He said from day one, 'I want you to be our closer. I think you can handle it.' I loved knowing that I went out there with no net. I knew they would pitch me not like a normal closer where I'd just get my three outs. I think I led the league that year with the most four-out-plus saves but that's how I loved to pitch. For a guy that threw 90 to 92 with a breaking ball to go 33 for 40 is a pretty good year but I loved it. I loved closing."[21]

That 2007 campaign was his most notable. He pitched in 70 games, with a league-high 60 games finished and 33 saves, seventh-most in the NL. However, in the offseason, Cincinnati opted to sign hard-throwing Francisco Cordero, who had averaged 30 saves over the past six seasons with Texas and Milwaukee, to a four-year contract, moving Weathers into a set-up role. Weathers recorded a team-leading 19 holds in 2008.

Weathers started off 2009 flawlessly, pitching scoreless baseball in his first 10 appearances. Yet with the Reds headed toward a ninth consecutive losing season, Cincinnati began trading players to build for the future. As was the case 11 years before, Weathers moved from the Reds to Milwaukee at midseason. He finished with 21 holds, good for 10th in the NL, but as a team the Brewers finished well out of postseason contention.

On the second-to-last day of the season, October 3, Milwaukee played at St. Louis. Weathers came on in the bottom of the sixth inning to protect a one-run lead. He allowed a single to Mark DeRosa, then got a force out at second on a popped-up bunt by Jason LaRue that Weathers intentionally allowed to fall to the grass in an attempt to start a double play. After a pinch-hit single by David Freese put runners on the corners, Weathers ran the count to 2-and-2 on Julio Lugo. Seeking a groundball on the infield to get out of the jam, Weathers, the slider-sinker specialist, threw a fastball – his final major-league pitch. Lugo hit it sharply on the ground, right at third baseman Casey McGehee, who fielded the ball to start an inning-ending 5-4-3 double play.

The 40-year-old Weathers returned home to Tennessee after retiring but stayed involved in baseball. He created a boys travel team in his birthplace, Lawrenceburg, and in 2013 managed his squad to the district, state, and Southeast Regional championships in the Babe Ruth League 13-year-old World Series. In 2015 Lawrenceburg hosted the Babe Ruth 15-year-old World Series and Weathers' team finished as runner-up.[22]

Additionally, Weathers returned to Loretto High as an assistant baseball coach in 2013. The Mustangs appeared in four consecutive Tennessee Secondary School Athletic Association Class A state tournaments from 2016 to 2019, winning the state championship in 2017 and finishing as runner-up in 2018.[23]

Weathers' wife, Kelli, was the Loretto High Lady Mustangs' point guard for four years, then went on to a distinguished collegiate career at Belmont University in Nashville.[24] As of 2022 she was an assistant coach for the girls' high-school basketball team.

The couple's oldest child, Ryan, born in 1999, in 2022 was a left-handed pitcher in the San Diego Padres organization.[25] Daughters Karly, born in 2003, and Ally, born in 2006, were playing basketball for the Lady Mustangs. Karly, "probably the best athlete in the family," according to her father, committed to the University of Alabama women's basketball program while Ally started her basketball career as a Loretto freshman in 2021-22.[26]

Reflecting on his long career and the enduring friendships he developed from playing with over 600 different players, Weathers named pitcher Aaron Harang, his teammate for 4½ seasons in Cincinnati, as his best friend overall from the major leagues.[27] "He lives out in San Diego and my son Ryan plays for the Padres. Aaron and his wife, Jen, last year [2021],

they brought him up and fed him dinner, played golf together, so Aaron is probably my absolute best friend in the game. We talk two or three times a month to stay in contact and we get to see each other and golf together."

Weathers said the key to his durability and longevity was perseverance. "The good Lord blessed me and I'll be honest, you never think about those things until it's over with. What if I had one more year to get over 1,000 games? But that's selfish. I'll take 964."

SOURCES

In addition to the sources cited in the Notes, the author consulted Baseball-Reference.com, Retrosheet.org, SABR.org, Ancestry.com, and the following:

David Weathers National Baseball Hall of Fame file.

Mustang Yearbook. Loretto, Tennessee: Loretto High School, 1984-1987.

Player questionnaire completed for William J. Weiss. Society for American Baseball Research; San Diego, California; U.S. Baseball Questionnaires, 1945-2005; Box Number: 555697.

Sherman, Joel. *Birth of a Dynasty: Behind the Pinstripes with the 1996 Yankees* (Emmaus, Pennsylvania: Rodale Books, 2006).

NOTES

1   At the end of the 2021 season, only LaTroy Hawkins and Mariano Rivera have passed Weathers in games pitched.

2   David Weathers, telephone interview, April 15, 2022. Unless otherwise noted, all quotes are from this interview.

3   Associated Press, "A-E's Hartsell on All-State AA," *Knoxville News-Sentinel*, March 19, 1987: 27.

4   "Lawrenceburg Team Blanks Mississippi," *Nashville Tennessean*, August 12, 1987: 5-C.

5   *Toronto Blue Jays Official Guide 1992* (Toronto: Thorn Press, 1992), 122.

6   *Spring 2001 Program / Media Guide* (Lynchburg, Tennessee: Motlow State Community College, 2001), 8.

7   The lowest drafted player in 1988 to appear in at least one major-league game was the 1,390th pick overall, future Hall of Fame catcher Mike Piazza, selected by the Los Angeles Dodgers.

8   Rob Mawhood, "Former Major Leaguer Will Never Forget His St. Catharines Blue Jays Days," *Niagara Independent*, October 11, 2019. https://niagaraindependent.ca/former-major-leaguer-will-never-forget-his-st-catharines-blue-jays-days/.

9   Allan Ryan, "Dead Arm Puts Timlin on Shelf," *Toronto Star*, August 2, 1991: C3.

10   Allan Ryan, "Acker Stays, Stieb Out and Jays Call Up Eight," *Toronto Star*, September 1, 1991: G2.

11   "Myers Injured," *Toronto Star*, October 7, 1991: C2. Catcher Randy Knorr, shortstop Eddie Zosky, and outfielder Turner Ward were the other three standby squad members.

12   Marty York, "Dividing Up the World Series' Spoils," *Globe and Mail* (Toronto), October 30, 1992: C14.

13   Larry Millson, "Expansion Hasn't Rescued Ex-Jay from Farm-Team Toil," *Globe and Mail*, June 18, 1993: D10. The composite Pacific Coast League ERA from 1992 to 1994 was 4.82.

14   Nancy Brewer, "Yankees Rekindled Weathers for
      Baseball," Weathers Family File, Genealogy Collection,
      Lawrence (Tennessee) County Archives: 3.

15   Brewer.

16   Brewer.

17   Jason Diamos, "BASEBALL; Weathers Puts a Dominating Victory
      in Perspective," *New York Times*, April 26, 1998: Section 8, 3.

18   Drew Olson, "Milwaukee," *The Sporting News*, April 19, 1999: 45.

19   https://legacy.baseballprospectus.com/compensation/cots/nation-
      al-league/new-york-mets/. The Mets' 2002 Opening Day payroll was
      seventh-highest of all 30 teams. In 2003, it was second-highest.

20   Only five other NL relievers who inherited 30 or more runners
      had a better strand percentage than Weathers' 80 percent.

21   In 2007 Weathers led the NL in 4+ out saves (11). He was
      successful in 33 of 39 total save opportunities.

22   https://www.baberuthleague.org/babe-ruth-baseball-13-
      15/2015-lawrenceburg-tn/about-world-series.aspx.

23   https://tssaasports.com/school/?id=300&sportid=4.

24   "Student-Athlete Alumni Spotlight – Kelli Davis Weathers," BelmontBruins.
      com, February 8, 2016. https://belmontbruins.com/information/alumni_spot-
      light/profiles/weathers_profile. Though she graduated in 1994, winning
      National Association of Intercollegiate Athletics First Team All-America
      honors in her senior year, she still held school records, as of spring

25   At Loretto High, like his father, Ryan played basketball in addition to
      baseball. He was named Gatorade National Baseball Player of the Year in
      his senior season, 2018, when he went 11-0, striking out 148 while walk-
      ing 10 in 76 innings with a 0.09 ERA. He was selected seventh overall
      by San Diego in the amateur draft. Ryan's first major-league game was
      in the 2020 NLDS, making him the second pitcher ever to debut in the
      postseason. On Ryan's left-handedness, David Weathers said, "My wife
      is left-handed, her grandfather and my dad. We've got like six or seven
      lefties in our family. So it was not a big shock that he was left-handed."

      2022, for most points in a season (794), most three-point field goals
      in a career (415), and most three-point field goals in a season (126).

26   Logan Hanson, "Karly Weathers Builds Family Athletic Prowess,
      Wins Gatorade Tennessee POY," BVMsports.com, March 15, 2022.
      https://bvmsports.com/2022/03/15/karly-weathers-builds-family-ath-
      letic-prowess-wins-gatorade-tennessee-poy/. Karly was the 2022
      Gatorade Tennessee Girls Basketball Player of the Year and the Class
      AA Tennessee Miss Basketball in her senior year. In 2021 Karly led
      Loretto to the Class A state championship, Loretto's first girls basketball
      title in 63 years and was also named Tennessee Miss Basketball.

27   Peter Uelkes, "Seven Degrees of Separation? Analyzing MLB
      Played-With Relationships, 1930-2016," *Baseball Research
      Journal* 47 (1) (2018): 53-59. Rickey Henderson, Matt Stairs, Terry
      Mulholland, Carlos Beltran, and LaTroy Hawkins are the only other
      major leaguers to play with over 600 different teammates.

DAVID WELLS

by Norm King

You have to love a guy who takes the mound in the House That Ruth Built wearing a Cap That Ruth Wore.

David Wells did just that at Yankee Stadium on June 28, 1997, when he took the hill to pitch against Cleveland sporting his Yankee pinstripes and his Yankee cap. The problem was that it wasn't the standard-issue model his teammates were wearing; it was a cap Ruth wore in 1934 that Wells had purchased for $35,000. Yankees manager Joe Torre found out about it after the first inning and ordered Wells to remove it.

Such was the career of David Lee "Boomer" Wells, whose reverence for New York Yankees traditions contrasted with his iconoclastic attitude toward just about everything else during his 21-year major-league career with nine different teams. He retired with a career 239-157 career won-lost record (.604 winning

percentage), a 10-5 record in the playoffs, two World Series rings, and a perfect game.

Wells was born on May 20, 1963, in Torrance, California. His childhood was, to say the least, unconventional. His mother, Eugenia Ann Wells, was a biker chick with the handle Attitude Annie. Annie wasn't exactly your typical suburban soccer mom as she had five children from four different men. Wells didn't meet his father, David Pritt, until he was 22 years old.

Growing up, Wells was the only kid in the neighborhood, and possibly in the country, who could bring the Hell's Angels to his Little League games. Annie's boyfriend was Crazy Charlie Mendez, a longtime member of the San Diego chapter, and he would bring his confreres to Wells's games when he pitched. Not only that, the bikers would each give him a dollar (or 25 cents) for every batter he struck out, and $5 (or $1) every time he won.[1] And no matter how much the gang members owed him, he never worried about them welching.

"I could pull in $100 a game, and nobody dared screw around with me," said Wells. "Try, and I'd say, 'I'll get my mom's boyfriend on you.'"[2]

Charlie didn't generally abuse Wells, but he wasn't afraid to smack him if it meant teaching an important life lesson. Once, when he was 12, Wells walked into the kitchen with his fists up; Charlie greeted him with a left hook. "I said, 'What did you do that for,'" recalled Wells. "He said, 'Anytime you put your hands up, you'd better use 'em.' Other than that, he treated me like a king."[3]

Wells pitched for a very good Point Loma High School team that competed for the city championship in 1981 and 1982. If some of the stories about his high-school career are true, his coach may very well have ended up with ulcers. He once told teammates during a game that he was going to deliberately walk the bases loaded, then strike out the side on nine pitches, and proceeded to do just that. On another occasion, Wells was going for a second perfect game when the first baseman told Wells he needed one out for the gem.

Coach Steve Saracino heard the player and told him he was off the team if the batter got a hit. Well, the batter did get a hit, and Saracino followed through on his threat. The following Monday, Wells convinced his teammates to boycott practice unless the first baseman was reinstated. Saracino relented.

Wells was the starter for two championship games, losing in 1981 to Darren Balsley and Mt. Carmel High School, then coming back to beat Mt. Carmel the following year. Balsley was Wells's pitching coach during both of his stints with the San Diego Padres.

That ability to pitch in critical ballgames and being chosen for the American Baseball Coaches Association second All-American team may have encouraged the Toronto Blue Jays to pick Wells in the second round of the 1982 amateur draft. Being drafted by a team that had one of our feathered friends as a nickname didn't impress Boomer.

"I said, 'Man, if I ever sign, I'm never playing for those guys, ever,'" Wells said. "A Blue Jay? I mean, a bird? And I signed with the Blue Jays out of high school. I'm like, how cliché is that?"[4]

Wells's first stop up the minor-league ladder didn't make him very happy, either. The Jays sent him to the Medicine Hat (Alberta) Blue Jays of the rookie-level Pioneer League, where as a 19-year-old he had a moderately successful season, going 4-3 but with a 5.18 ERA. He walked 32 and struck out 53 in 64⅓ innings pitched.

Wells continued his climb through the minor-league ranks south of the 49th Parallel over the next few years as he developed his skills as a pitcher. In 1984 his ERA improved to 3.73, to go along with a 6-5 pitching record with Kinston of the Class-A Carolina League He had only 15 appearances in 1984, seven with Kinston and eight with Knoxville of the Double-A Southern League before becoming just the third pitcher in history to undergo Tommy John surgery. (The first two were Brent Strom of San Diego in 1977 and, of course, Tommy John.) The operation caused Wells to miss all of the 1985 season.

When Wells returned in 1986, he had to start again from the beginning, and advanced from Single A to Double A before landing with the Jays' Triple-A International League affiliate in Syracuse, where he spent parts of the next three seasons. He got called up to the Jays in the middle of the 1987 season and made a less than memorable major-league debut on June 30, 1987, against the New York Yankees. He gave up four earned runs in four innings of work and took the loss in a 4-0 Yankees win. Then he decided to celebrate July 4 in Kansas City by getting lit up for five earned runs in only 1⅓ innings for his second loss as the Jays got Royally routed 9-1. Wells found a plane ticket back to Syracuse in his locker after that game.

He returned as a September call-up as the Jays battled the Detroit Tigers for the East Division crown. The team used him as a reliever, and that's how he got his first major-league victory. On September 2 he came in against the California Angels with two out in the top of the eighth inning with the score tied 5-5 in Toronto's Exhibition Stadium. George Bell's two-run home run in the bottom of the inning put Toronto ahead, and Wells got the victory despite giving up an earned run in the ninth.

The Jays weren't afraid to use Wells in critical situations as the season wound down. Holding a one-game lead over Detroit going into the last weekend of the season, Toronto visited Tiger Stadium for the three-game series that would decide the division champion. In the first game, on October 2, Wells took over for Jim Clancy, who had given up four runs in two-plus innings of work. He held the Tigers scoreless the rest of the way, but the Jays still lost 4-3. Detroit ended up winning the crown.

Despite being the subject of offseason trade rumors – the Associated Press said he may have been part of a trade to the Yankees – Wells started the 1988 season in the Jays bullpen.[5] He still had his rookie status, and in a July 10 article, Associated Press sportswriter Jim Donaghy chose Wells as the midseason top rookie in the American League with a 3-5 record and four saves.[6] Any chance Donaghy ever had of being offered a job as a scout quickly went out the window as the Jays announced the next day that they had sent Wells down to Syracuse the next day. They recalled him in late August, and he pitched in four games from August 26 until the end of the season without any decisions or saves.

Wells began the 1990 season in the bullpen, but a slump by teammate John Cerutti changed the direction of Wells's career. Cerutti lost five of his first six decisions, so Jays manager Cito Gaston decided that some time in the bullpen would help him out of his funk; Gaston promoted Wells into the starting rotation on May 24 as a temporary measure. Even Wells expected to return to the bullpen. "Several times throughout June, he told reporters it was only a matter of time until he returned to the bullpen," wrote Mike DiGiovanna in the *Los Angeles Times*.[7]

Wells's assignment to the rotation turned out to be as temporary a measure as income tax. He was a starter for the rest of the season, finishing the year with an 11-6 record – his first win was in relief – with a 3.14 ERA and 189 innings pitched.

The 1991 Blue Jays began a string of three straight American League East Division titles, but for Wells the season had mixed results. On August 9 he and Gaston got into an argument on the mound after Wells had given up five runs on nine hits against the Boston Red Sox, with Wells throwing the ball away as he stormed off the mound. The two later fought under the stands.

The spat and scuffle happened during a period when Wells lost six of eight decisions between July 29 and September 8, during which his ERA rose from 2.73 to 3.75, more than one run per nine innings. Not surprisingly, Wells was relegated to the bullpen for the rest of the season.

After winning the American League East in 1985, 1989, and 1991 only to lose in the ALCS, the Blue Jays finally went all the way in 1992. They not only reached the World Series for the first time, but defeated the Atlanta Braves in six games to win it all.

For Wells, a season that culminated a championship ring got off to a lucrative start when the Jays more than doubled his salary from $800,000 to $2,063,000. That was a pretty good raise for a swingman.[8] In fact, he did so much swinging between the bullpen and the rotation that he could easily have had motion sickness. He started in his first two appearances, defeating Baltimore 3-1, and losing 1-0 to the Red Sox, which earned a ticket to the relief corps.[9] He returned to the rotation on June 24, and was inconsistent, going 5-6 between then and August 25. A 6-3 loss to the White Sox in which he gave up all six runs (three earned) convinced Gaston that Wells could better serve the team as a reliever, where he remained the rest of the season. He finished with a 7-9 record and a 5.40 ERA. He didn't play in the ALCS, which the Jays won in six games over Oakland, but he was excellent in the fall classic, appearing in four games and giving up only one hit and no runs in 4⅓ innings of relief.

After the season Wells felt that he had earned the right to be a starter. "I think I proved something not pitching for 21 days and getting into the World Series and showing I can pitch," he said.[10] Instead, the Jays gave him his unconditional release on March 30, 1993. In a 2000 *Sports Illustrated* article on Wells, former Blue Jays general manager Gord Ash explained that the team had grown tired of his inconsistency, his temper, his weight and his fondness for drinking beer – lots and lots of beer. "We did everything we could to control him," said Ash.[11]

Whatever bothered the Blue Jays didn't seem to be of concern to other teams, as Wells garnered interest from 16 other clubs within three days of his release. He signed a one-year deal with the Detroit Tigers on April 3 that included a $900,000 salary, plus $550,000 in bonus incentives. He also became a starter on a team that had the worst team ERA (4.60) in the American League in 1992.

Sparky Anderson was Detroit's manager, and besides having a penchant for removing pitchers from games early – he was nicknamed Captain Hook – he also let players be themselves, and Wells thrived without being pressured to conform. He went 11-9, although his ERA was still high at 4.19, and struck out 139 batters in 187 innings.

Those numbers proved lucrative to Wells; before the 1994 season he signed a three-year contract with Detroit worth $7.5 million. But as is so often the case, fate intervened to make management gnash its teeth over the deal. Wells went on the disabled list on April 19 to recover from having bone chips removed from his elbow. He may as well have stayed there because when he returned to the mound in June, he proceeded to lose his next three starts, and finished the strike-shortened season with a 5-7 record and a 3.96 ERA.

The 1995 season almost changed baseball history. The Tigers were going nowhere and the Yankees, in the middle of a playoff hunt, wanted Wells for their rotation, and were willing to trade a minor-league starter for him. That minor leaguer, according to Jerry Green of the *Detroit News*, was somebody named Mariano Rivera. Yankees general manager Gene Michael eventually nixed the deal after Rivera's fastball began showing improvement. Instead, the Tigers traded Wells to the eventual National League Central Division champion Cincinnati Reds on July 31 for pitchers C.J. Nitkowski and minor-leaguer Dave Tuttle. Wells had been the only bright light on a miserable Tigers pitching staff; he had a 10-3 record with a 3.04 ERA when he left Detroit, and had even pitched a third of an inning in the All-Star Game.

After he stopped pinching himself at being traded to a contender, Wells joined the Reds' rotation for the stretch run having won his last eight decisions in a row. Before his first start, against the New York Mets on August 2, Wells met with his new boss, the infamous team owner Marge Schott, who gave him some unusual encouragement.

"Reds owner Marge Schott, with her dog in tow, sought out Wells in the dugout a few minutes before the game and had an animated conversation," the newspapers reported the next day. "Schott, who is picking up the remainder of Wells' $2 million salary, patted the pitcher's belly, squeezed his elbow and waved goodbye."[12] The pep talk worked because he pitched 7⅓ innings in a 6-2 Reds victory for his ninth consecutive win.

Wells was 6-5 with Cincinnati, giving him a 16-8 record for the season, with a 3.24 ERA as Cincinnati won the NL Central division title. In his first-ever postseason start, he helped the Reds clinch the Division Series with a 10-1 win to sweep the Dodgers. In Game Three of the NLCS against the Atlanta Braves, he gave up three earned runs in six innings of a 5-2 loss. Atlanta swept Cincinnati in four straight and went on to defeat Cleveland in the World Series.

While she may have enjoyed rubbing Wells's belly, the notoriously parsimonious Schott did not want to pay the $3 million he was due for 1996 and so the Reds traded him to Baltimore for center fielder Curtis Goodwin and minor leaguer Trovin Valdez. The trade reunited Wells with Pat Gillick, his general manager in Toronto, who now held the same position with the Orioles.

Health issues hounded Wells in the spring and early in the season. He was hospitalized with a rapid heart-beat during spring training, but was released after an overnight stay. He also missed time in May with gout, returning on May 20, his birthday. His teammates welcomed him back and acknowledged his birthday by scoring 13 runs to give him his first win in five starts since April 16.

"It's a nice gift, all those runs, but you still have to go out there and do the job," Wells said. "Still, it's a great advantage when you get that type of run support."[13]

The win was a high point in an otherwise mediocre season for Wells, as he went 11-14 with a 5.14 ERA. Nonetheless, the Orioles' 88-74 record was good enough to get them the wild-card playoff spot. Wells made a huge postseason contribution. He won Game One of the ALDS against the powerhouse Cleveland Indians and went seven frames in the clincher as Baltimore won in 12 innings to pull off the upset. He also earned the only Orioles victory in the ALCS as they lost to the Yankees in five games.

Just as Victor Kiam liked Remington Razors so much that he bought the company, the Yankees went out and signed Wells, the only pitcher to beat them in the ALCS, to a three-year, $13.5 million contract on December 24, 1996. The Yankees may have regretted their decision just three weeks later when he broke his pitching hand in a fight on January 14, 1997, while he was in San Diego attending his mother's funeral. Wells ruffled the Yankees corporate feathers again when he said that he would like to wear Babe Ruth's number 3, which the Yankees had retired in 1948.

"I asked for 03 and they wouldn't do that," said the longtime admirer of the Sultan of Swat. I'm hoping Mr. (Charlie) Hayes will give up No. 33.[14] That way, I can be Babe Ruth twice over."[15]

The number issue was less serious than Wells's injury problems when spring training began. While he was still recovering from his broken hand, he had a recurrence of the gout that had bothered him the previous season. But for all the issues and headlines, Wells did produce. He went 16-10 with a 4.21 ERA and helped the Yankees win the American League wild-card playoff spot with a 96-66 record. The Yankees lost to Cleveland in the ALDS, but Wells pitched a 6-1 five-hitter at Jacobs Field to win Game Three, his only start.

Wells arrived at spring training for the 1998 season just three months shy of his 35th birthday. He strained a rib muscle early on and didn't get his first spring-training start until March 14. He proceeded to have a season for the ages, going 18-4 with a 3.49 ERA, followed by a 4-0 run in the playoffs – he was chosen MVP in the ALCS – as the Yankees won the World Series. Wells also started the All-Star Game, and just for fun, he gave himself an early birthday present by pitching a perfect game at Yankee Stadium against the Minnesota Twins on May 17. It was the first perfect game in Yankee Stadium since fellow Point Loma alumnus Don Larsen performed the feat against the Brooklyn Dodgers in Game Five of the 1956 World Series.

The circumstances surrounding his perfecto would be difficult to believe if it involved anybody but Wells. Manager Joe Torre had pulled him from a May 6 start against Texas after he gave up seven earned runs in 2⅔ innings. Torre complained that Wells was out of shape and the two, along with pitching coach Mel Stottlemyre, had a long discussion about the situation. Judging by what he wrote in his autobiography, Wells was hardly in game shape when he showed up to face Minnesota.

"In his 2003 autobiography *Perfect, I'm Not*, Wells conceded that he pitched his gem 'half-drunk, with bloodshot eyes, monster breath, and a raging, skull-rattling hangover,' having gone to bed at 5 a.m. and gotten just an hour of sleep," wrote Jay Jaffe in *Sports Illustrated*.[16]

In the Broadway musical *Damn Yankees*, the character Lola sings a song with the line, "Whatever Lola wants, Lola gets." George Steinbrenner, owner of the damn Yankees, was like Lola because he also got whatever he wanted, and after the 1998 season, he wanted Blue Jays pitcher Roger Clemens for his team, and to get him, the Yankees traded Wells back to Toronto, along with pitcher Graeme Lloyd and second baseman Homer Bush. Wells was not pleased at going back to Toronto, but Jays general manager Ash assured him that he would be treated differently this time around.

"We did everything we could to control Boomer," Ash said, referring to Wells's first stint with Toronto. "We learned the hard way: The worst way to control him is to try and control him."[17]

Hard way or not, the lesson was well learned. Boomer was allowed to be Boomer, heavy-metal music blaring in the locker room and all, and the result

David Wells was MVP of the 1998 ALCS and won another World Series ring with that year's Yankees.

was the first of two marvelous seasons. Maybe he was partying like it was 1999, since it was, because he got off to a slow start and by the end of May was 5-5 with a stratospheric 6.30 ERA. Nonetheless, the Jays inked Wells to a one-year, $11.5 million contract extension on June 20, which spurred him on to a 17-10 record with an improved 4.82 ERA; he also led the league with seven complete games.

Cue the *Twilight Zone* music at this point, because it was in the year 2000 that Wells decided to have the only 20-win season of his career when he went 20-8, with a 4.11 ERA and a league-leading nine complete games. He also started the All-Star Game – his former manager Joe Torre selected him for the honor – as the Jays were in the pennant race for the whole season before finishing with an 83-79 record, 4½ games behind the eventual world champion Yankees.

Although the Blue Jays were willing to allow Wells to be himself, they felt enough was enough in early January, 2001, when Wells accused the Blue Jays organization of not doing enough to win and said that Toronto fans were "terrible."[18] They traded him to the Chicago White Sox for four players who ended up playing a total of 65 games for Toronto. From the standpoint of number of games played, it actually turned out to be an even trade. Wells went 5-7 with a 4.47 ERA, and didn't pitch after June 28 because of back spasms. He ended up having season-ending surgery.

Just as with a great Broadway play, Wells had a New York revival when he signed for a second stint with the Yankees in 2002, because Steinbrenner wanted the now-39-year-old back in the fold. "David Wells is a winner and he belongs in pinstripes," said Steinbrenner in a statement. "People say we're going out on a limb, but we'll see. We're betting on The Boomer."[19]

It turned out to be a good bet because Steinbrenner, a breeder, knew good horseflesh. Wells not only recovered from his back injury, he won six of his first seven decisions, and went on to have a 19-7 record, leading the rotation in both victories and winning percentage (.731) as the Yankees won the American League East with a 103-58 record. The usually clutch Wells couldn't carry that regular season success into the playoffs as he got pounded in his lone start against the eventual World Series champion Anaheim Angels, who touched him for eight earned runs in 4⅔ innings in Game Four of the ALDS.

Wells was hot again in 2003, perhaps because of the hot water he found himself in prior to the season when his autobiography came out. Besides his description of his condition the day of his perfect game, he also said that a number of players were taking steroids. The resulting controversy was a pain in the Yankee brass and they fined him $100,000.

That little fracas aside, Wells was doing it again on the mound at age 40, going 15-7 with a 4.14 ERA as the Yankees went back to the World Series after a one-year drought. He defeated the Twins, 8-1, in the ALDS and Boston, 4-2, in the ALCS, but the World Series against the Florida Marlins was another matter. Wells lost Game One, 3-2, and had to leave Game Five due to tightness in his back after pitching a perfect first inning in a game the Yankees lost, 6-4.

Wells's run in the Bronx ended after New York lost the World Series, so he decided to go home, and signed as a free agent with the Padres. At first it looked as though he couldn't go home again, as he lost his first two starts, went on the disabled list due to a cut on his wrist, and by June 18 was 2-5. But damned if the old coot didn't go 10-3 the rest of the way to finish 12-8, with a not-too-shabby 3.73 ERA.

The 2004 Red Sox called themselves "idiots" for their distinctive and often offbeat personalities, so perhaps it was no surprise that they signed Wells for the 2005 season. After all, he only had to replace three-time Cy Young Award winner Pedro Martinez, who won 16 games in 2004. Wells had the wags shaking their heads again as he went 15-7 in his summer of being 42, with a 4.45 ERA that was actually below the team ERA of 4.74. The Red Sox made the playoffs again as the wild card, but even Wells couldn't prevent them from being swept by the eventual world champion Chicago White Sox. He gave up five runs, but only two earned, in 6⅔ innings of Game Two, which the White Sox won 5-4.

Age started creeping up on Wells in 2006, as he went a combined 3-5 with the Red Sox and Padres. He had one last shot in the playoffs with San Diego, and didn't pitch badly in his only start in the NLDS, giving up two runs in five innings in Game Two to the St. Louis Cardinals, but that was all the Redbirds needed for a 2-0 win as they went on to win it all. Wells had a last hurrah, of sorts, in 2007; he had a 5-8 record with a 5.54 ERA when the Padres released him on August 13. But the Los Angeles Dodgers picked him up 11 days later, and he went 4-1 with them, albeit with a 5.12 ERA. He called it a career at age 44 after the season.

Wells was able to retire financially secure after earning more than $58 million playing baseball. He returned to San Diego to live with his wife, Nina, a former runway model whom he married in 2000, and their two sons, Brandon Miles and Lars Van. He got very active in community and charitable causes, raising money for diabetes research (he was diagnosed with the disease in 2007) and helped push through a school bond to pay for major upgrades to his high school's baseball field, which now bears his name. As of 2015, he was the coach of the school's team.

"If you can give back," he said in a 2014 interview, "it's a home run."[20]

SOURCES

In addition to the sources cited in the notes, the author used the following:

Abca.org.

Bluebirdbanter.com.

Hardballtimes.com.

Herald-Zeitung (New Braunfels, Texas).

Indiana (Pennsylvania) *Gazette.*

Kokomo (Indiana) *Tribune.*

Mlbreports.com.

New York Times.

Philly.com.

Plhsalumni.org.

Razon, Max. *Born Under a Bad Sign* (Bloomington, Indiana: Xlibris, 2009).

Salina (Kansas) *Journal.*

usatoday.com

Special thanks to Tom Larwin and the members of the Ted Williams SABR chapter for their assistance.

NOTES

1 Accounts differ on the amounts. The higher numbers appear in a 1997 *Sports Illustrated* article, but Wells gave the lower numbers during a 2014 interview on the YES Network.

2 Franz Lidz, "The Unvarnished Ruth Free-Spirited Lefthander David Wells May Get Tattooed By Hitters Every Now And Then, But He's Fulfilling His Dream – Pitching For The Yankees, The Team Of His Idol, The Babe," *Sports Illustrated*, September 8, 1997.

3 Lidz.

4 YESnetwork.com interview.

5 "Cardinals talking with Horner," *Index-Journal* (Greenwood, South Carolina), January 8, 1988.

6 Donaghy's article appeared in the July 10, 1988, edition of the *Altoona Mirror.*

7 Mike DiGiovanna, "He Started a Reliever but Is Winning as a Starter," *Los Angeles Times*, July 13, 1990.

8 In baseball, a swingman is a pitcher who works as both a starter and reliever.

9 Wells went only four innings in the loss to Boston because of a 58-minute rain delay. Pat Hentgen replaced him in the fifth.

10 Steve Milton, "Toronto Blue Jays," *The Sporting News*, November 9, 1992: 46.

11   Jeff Pearlman, "Heavy Duty They said he wouldn't last, but Toronto's large-livin' lefthander, David Wells, has become baseball's most reliable pitcher – and a clubhouse wise man to boot," *Sports Illustrated*, July 10, 2000.

12   "Los Angeles Tops Colorado," *News Record* (North Hills, Pennsylvania), August 3, 1995.

13   "Orioles celebrate Wells' birthday, 13-1," *Gettysburg Times*, May 21, 1996.

14   Hayes, a Yankees teammate, gave Wells the number, and wore number 13 for the 1997 season.

15   "Wells has Ruthian request," *The Capital* (Annapolis, Maryland), February 11, 1997.

16   Jay Jaffe, "15 years ago today: David Wells' perfect game," *Sports Illustrated*, May 17, 2013. Wells later said he was misquoted.

17   Jaffe.

18   Rick Gano, "Blue Jays trade Wells to White Sox," *Daily Journal* (Ukiah, California), January 15, 2001.

19   "Slimmer Wells returns to Yankee Stadium," *Santa Cruz* (California) *Sentinel* January 11, 2002.

20   Andrea Naversen, "At Home With David & Nina Wells," *Ranch & Coast*, May 12, 2014.

DEVON WHITE

By Nick Malian

Seventy percent of the world is covered by water, the rest is covered by Devon White. Considered one of the best defensive outfielders to play the game, White was a human highlight reel who worked tirelessly to hone his craft. He was a raw athlete when he was drafted as a third baseman in the sixth round of the 1981 draft by the California Angels, but he had all the makings of becoming a big-league star. He could change the outcome of a game with a single leap and on occasion hit for power. He was pragmatic, driven, and self-aware. "I think when a ball is in the ballpark and it's not a hard line drive, I'm going to get it," he once said.[1]

Devon Markes Whyte was born on December 29, 1962, in Kingston, Jamaica. He is just one of five major-league players born in Jamaica, including future teammate Chili Davis. His family immigrated to New York when he was 9 years old. Upon his arrival, his last name was documented incorrectly as "White." In 2003 he changed it back to Whyte at the request of his three children, one of whom, Davellyn, played three seasons in the Women's National Basketball Association (WNBA) with the San Antonio Stars.

In Kingston, White played cricket and soccer. In the 1970s United States, the closest sports to cricket were stickball and baseball. White initially learned the game from his father by watching the Mets and Yankees on television,[2] but did not start playing until he was a teenager. "I was more involved with basketball," he said. "Baseball was something I played with some of my Spanish friends, just to have something to do."[3]

White excelled as a ballplayer at Park West High School in Manhattan, where he lettered all four years and hit .330 as a senior. And although basketball was his first true love, the chance of playing professional baseball was too enticing to pass up.[4] "I even had a scholarship offer to play basketball and baseball at Oklahoma State, but once I got drafted by the Angels, baseball became my favorite sport," he said.[5]

White's 1981 scouting report described him as "thin, lanky and broad across top with room to fill out … built like Rod Carew. Has all the tools, arm, speed,

quick bat and reflexes to be fine professional ballplayer. Due to range athlete may be better suited to play 2B."[6] But his first minor-league manager, Joe Maddon, quickly moved him to outfield. Maddon noted, "[He] couldn't hit a lick. Good thing we put him in the outfield and stuck with him."[7]

White was a project for the California Angels. Manager Gene Mauch recalled that the first time he saw White play in 1981, "he was the rawest professional baseball player I have ever seen. … I mean the rawest. … He could only do one thing like a big-league ballplayer, and that was run."[8]

To White's credit, he was driven to improve his hitting. Mauch noted White's commitment as the guy who asks, "What do you want me to do, how much do

All smiles for White after leaving California for greener pastures in the Great White North.

you want me to do and for how long do you want me to do it? And if I don't think I've got enough of it, I'll have some more."[9]

White's minor-league hitting instructor, Rick Down, said that White was willing to work on his craft including becoming a better bunter, studying Rod Carew, even on his own time. He said, "I don't see Devon ever being in an extensive slump, because he can put the ball down."[10]

There was a lot to be excited about White. Scouts referred to him as "Willie Wilson with power, a mirror image of Willie Davis in his prime, and a Gary Pettis with better bat control."[11] Rick Down thought White could be a 20-home run, 60-stolen-base threat. High praise for a youngster for whom baseball was his least favorite sport.[12]

The road to becoming a big-leaguer was arduous for White. Between 1981 and 1985 he played throughout the Angels farm system, with stops in Danville, Nashua, Peoria, Redwood, Midland, and eventually to Edmonton of the Triple-A Pacific Coast League.

By 1985, White flashed glimpses of greatness when he stole 59 bases in 136 games with Midland and Edmonton, leading both teams. His performance in Edmonton earned him a brief call-up to the California Angels at the end of the season. He managed just one hit in nine plate appearances and three strikeouts. In 37 innings in the outfield, he had 11 putouts and one assist and did not commit an error.

White returned to Edmonton in 1986 and led the team in stolen bases, triples, and runs. He slashed .291/.339/.479 and earned another late season call-up that made him eligible for his first postseason.[13] It was an exciting opportunity for the young ballplayer, but White was realistic about it, saying, "I'm just trying to help the club in any way I can, just trying to learn. But, yeah, you can't help but think about that (playoffs) when you're on a team like this."[14]

This was a much different experience than in 1985. "I think last year when I came up, I was more in awe of everything," White said. "This time around I'm just trying to concentrate on doing my job, to learn the fine points of the game."[15] In three games, White was a defensive substitute, pinch-runner, and defensive replacement; in Game Five he had one hit in two at-bats The Angels lost to the Boston Red Sox in the American League Championship Series, four games to three.

The next season, 1987, was White's first full season at the major-league level. He had a strong spring training, hitting .375 and leading the Angels in RBIs.

Playing primarily in right field during the regular season, White led the Angels in hits with 168, stolen bases with 32, and a 5.6 WAR. He tied Wally Joyner with 33 doubles and Jack Howell with 5 triples. White also led the team in strikeouts with 135 while walking only 39 times.

The switch-hitter finished his rookie campaign slashing .263/.306/.443, hitting 24 home runs and amassing 87 RBIs. He led American League outfielders with 424 putouts. He finished fifth in the AL Rookie of the Year voting behind Mark McGwire, Kevin Seitzer, Matt Nokes, and Mike Greenwell.

Coming off his rookie season, White was introduced to the realities of professional baseball – contract negotiations. He wanted a new contract, but the Angels were prepared to renew it as they had in previous years. White was not happy. "So far, negotiating contracts hasn't been much fun at all," he said. He had his sights on earning "somewhere between Kevin Seitzer ($175,000) and Mike Greenwell ($205,000), with some kind of incentives."[16]

The Angels were basing their contract decisions on Wally Joyner's second-season contract, which irked White. "They're comparing me with someone on my team who is not an outfielder. … If they're going to do that, I feel they should at least include some incentives."[17] White earned $185,000 in 1988 without incentives.

Before the 1988 season, Gary Pettis was traded to the Detroit Tigers, making White the full-time center fielder. In the first 29 games he hit .245 with an OBP of .312 and four stolen bases before arthroscopic shoulder surgery sidelined him for a month.[18] His absence was palpable. "With the outfield we had there for a while, the guys in the bullpen made up a little lottery to see which position would make the first error in which inning. We gave it up when Devo came back," said reliever Greg Minton. When White returned to the lineup on June 10, the Angels were in seventh place in the West. By July 22, they were 23-13, good enough for fourth place.

The 1988 season was also the first time that White led off in the majors, though it did not necessarily suit his offensive style. "I'd rather strike out on a ball in the dirt and run to first than walk. I hate to walk," he professed, not exactly the mindset of the prototypical leadoff hitter.[19]

Angels manager Cookie Rojas moved White to the leadoff position on July 7 and over the next 11 games he scored 10 runs, hit two home runs, and drove in nine runs. The Angels went 8-3 during that stretch.

And despite his opposition to the role, White would do what the team needed, commenting, "If we continue to win and I'm doing the job at leadoff, then so be it."[20] That defined White, who did what was best for his team. Although his offensive numbers declined in 1988, his defense was the best in the game, which earned him his first of seven Gold Gloves.

White began the 1989 season in contract talks again. With teammates Chili Davis and Wally Joyner receiving new and much larger contracts, White expected the same. "I think I've paid my dues," he said. "But I'm not going to cause any trouble or leave or anything like that. ... Maybe next year I can take it to them in arbitration."[21] He signed a one-year contract worth $380,000, $600,000 less than Joyner.

For the first half of the season, White slashed .259/.292/.427, hitting nine home runs and stealing 25 bases. He hit a career-high 13 triples, earning his first AL All-Star selection as a reserve center fielder behind Kirby Puckett. White also won his second Gold Glove in as many seasons.

But arguably the most memorable moment of White's 1989 season was on September 9 against the Boston Red Sox, when he put on a baserunning display for the ages and quite literally stole the game from the Red Sox.

In the bottom of the sixth inning, with Boston leading 5-3, White singled to left field, driving in Claudell Washington and closing the gap to 5-4. White then stole second. Then he stole third. And with permission from manager Doug Rader, White stole home. "He's asked to do it before, and it wasn't the appropriate time. It was appropriate tonight. ... We needed to generate some runs. We needed some excitement," Rader said.[22]

White said that he took "a big chance, stealing home with a right-handed batter at the plate. He [Johnny Ray] doesn't know what I'm doing."[23] But his decision worked in his favor because Ray blocked catcher Rich Gedman's view of the third-base line and before Gedman realized it, White was sliding into home, tying the game, 5-5. Two innings later, White added his fourth steal by taking second base, sparking an eighth-inning rally that would give the Angels an 8-5 lead and the win.[24] White finished the season with a career-high 44 stolen bases.

The 1990 season was one to forget for White. He was demoted to Edmonton in July after hitting a paltry .213 and striking out 71 times in 73 games. He earned his way back to the Angels by hitting .364/.582/1.017 with four stolen bases and four triples in 14 games. But

he could not keep up that momentum. He finished the season striking out 116 times, the third 100-strikeout performance of his career.

After the 1990 season, the writing was on the wall. With multiple public contract disputes and a demotion to Triple A, it did not appear that California had built White into its long-term plans. The Angels traded their Gold Glove outfielder to the Toronto Blue Jays along with pitchers Willie Fraser and Marcus Moore for outfielder Junior Felix, infielder Luis Sojo, and minor-league catcher Ken Rivers.

White was thrilled with the move. Reflecting on the trade, he said, "At the time, I wasn't happy anymore in California. There was a lot of misleading information out there, saying I was a bad apple and things like that ... and I don't know why that was."[25]

White's lack of production in 1990 was of no concern to Blue Jays general manager Pat Gillick. "We got him for defense. We're not worried about his hitting. We feel we have enough to carry Devon White, no matter what he hits." Three days later, the Jays acquired future Hall of Famer Roberto Alomar and Joe Carter from the San Diego Padres for Fred McGriff and fan favorite Tony Fernandez.

Moving to Canada was a revelation for White's career, both personally and professionally. He felt at home in Toronto because of the diverse Jamaican community. His fondest memories of his time in Toronto were the fans and seeing SkyDome (later renamed Rogers Centre) full every night. From 1991-93, 4 million[26] fans packed SkyDome each season, ranking first among AL teams. White is still recognized by fans when he visits Toronto.[27]

Over five seasons with the Blue Jays, he hit .270/.327/.432 with an OPS+ of 102, a significant improvement from his four years in California. His first season with Toronto was arguably the best of his career. He slashed .282/.342/.455, earned an OPS+ of 116, the highest of his career, and had 181 hits, also a career high (seven shy of Roberto Alomar's team high). He was second and third on the team with 10 triples, and 40 doubles. White also led the AL with 439 putouts. He earned his third Gold Glove.

The 1991 season was a good one for White. His daughter, Davellyn, was born in the spring and he led the Jays to first place in the AL East and ranked first among outfielders in fielding percentage. Although they lost to the Minnesota Twins 4 games to 1 in the AL Championship Series, White finished nearly atop all offensive categories for the Jays, hitting .364/.417/.409 with three stolen bases and eight hits.

Known more for his defense, White often provided timely hitting in the postseason.

The 1992 season was the apex for both White and the Blue Jays. Toronto won the AL East again and defeated the Oakland Athletics in the ALCS to earn its first berth in the World Series, against the Atlanta Braves. White continued to dazzle on defense, starting one of the greatest plays in World Series history and the hallmark play of his career.[28]

In the top of the fourth inning of Game Three, with the game scoreless, Atlanta's David Justice smacked a ball into deep center field with Terry Pendleton on first and Deion Sanders on second. White tracked the seemingly uncatchable ball, leaped, and made a backhanded grab, plucking the would-be extra-base hit out of the air, and crashed into the wall for out number one. White then quickly threw to the cutoff man, Alomar, who tossed to John Olerud at first base. Thinking it was a base hit, Pendleton passed Sanders at second base for an automatic second out. Sanders then tagged up from second and Olerud rifled it to Kelly Gruber at third, catching Sanders in a rundown. Gruber chased Sanders back to second, dived and lightly brushed a tag on Sanders' ankle, though second-base umpire Bob Davidson missed the tag by Gruber, ruling Sanders safe at second base.[29]

When asked about the play, White said, "People ask, do you wish it was a triple play? And I say no. The truth of the matter is we went on and won the World Series, so if that would have happened, everything changes, right?"[30] The Blue Jays went on to win their first World Series in six games.

In 1993 White earned his fifth Gold Glove and second All-Star appearance, as a reserve, behind Ken Griffey Jr. He also helped propel the Jays to their second consecutive World Series title. White was a standout for Toronto in the ALCS against the Chicago White Sox. In six games, he led the team with 12 hits and a .444 batting average, and finished second to Paul Molitor in on- base and slugging percentage, .464 and .667 respectively. Against the Philadelphia Phillies in the World Series, he helped beat them with his speed, legging out three doubles, a team high, and two triples in six games.

White picked up two more Gold Gloves in the 1994 and 1995 seasons. The 1995 season was White's final one with the Jays. A free agent, he signed a three-year, $9.9 million contract with the Florida Marlins.[31] Joe Carter called White's departure "by far the biggest loss. What he brings to a club as a leadoff guy and the best center fielder in baseball, you just can't replace it."[32]

Florida was a perfect location for White; he would be playing closer to Jamaica and have an opportunity to take on a leadership role with the team. "I've noticed that we have a lot of young ball players over here and I'm here to help them in every which way I can," he said.[33]

White could still fly as a 33-year-old veteran. In 1996 he led the Marlins in stolen bases with 22 and 37 doubles, which was second only to Steve Finley among National League center fielders. And his defense was still a strong asset. Joe Carter said, "I'm just thankful he's in the National League, I didn't want him running down our stuff." Blue Jays manager Cito Gaston commented, "Just when you think the ball is not going to be caught, Devon somehow kicks into a second gear and gets to the ball."[34]

In 1997 White was hampered by injury and appeared in only 74 games. He hit just .215 and stole only two bases in 16 playoff games. The highlight of his postseason came in Game Three of the Division Series against the San Francisco Giants. The Marlins were up two games to none and were looking to close out the Giants at home. After going hitless in the first two games, White hit a grand slam in the bottom of the sixth inning, giving the Marlins a 4-1 lead and eventually winning the game 6-2, sweeping the Giants.

In the World Series against the Cleveland Indians, which the Marlins won in seven games, White led the team with three doubles and 10 strikeouts.

In 1998 the Marlins brass cleaned house and sent White to the expansion Arizona Diamondbacks. The 35-year-old finished atop nearly every offensive category, including hits, home runs, and stolen bases, on a team that went 30-58 in the first half of the season. He was the inaugural Diamondbacks All-Star, the third honor of his career. White replaced Tony Gwynn in the fifth inning of the All-Star Game, and went 3-for-3 with a triple, a run, and two singles.[35] A free agent after the season, White signed a three-year, $12.4 million contract with Los Angeles Dodgers.

White's 1999 season production fell below his career average, and he was nowhere near the top of the team rankings as in prior years. He was an aging fielder who could no longer rely on speed and power to impact the game. Coming into the 2000 season, an opposing team's scout noted that "Devon White is a problem in center field. He doesn't dive for balls or come to play every day."[36]

White suffered a partial tear of his left rotator cuff diving for a ball in a game in May. He was placed on the 15-day disabled list. He played just 47 more games that season.

In the final year of his contract, White was relegated to fourth-outfielder duties, likely for a number of reasons, including injury risk, performance, and to make room for the newly acquired Tom Goodwin.[37] White was understandably unhappy and requested a trade. On February 24, 2001, he was sent to the Milwaukee Brewers for Marquis Grissom and Ruddy Lugo.[38]

The trade to Milwaukee seemed like a fresh start for the veteran. Although he would be used as a fourth outfielder, he was happy to be in Milwaukee, said Brewers general manager Dean Taylor.[39] White appeared in 126 games, starting 86 in center field and 13 in left field, and pinch-hitting 31 times. Milwaukee did not pick up his option for the following season.

After 17 seasons with six teams, three World Series championships, seven Gold Gloves, and three All-Star Game appearances, White called it quits. The switch-hitter finished his career with 1,934 hits, 208 home runs, a .263 batting average, and 346 stolen bases, and ranks 35th all-time with 4,739 putouts overall.

White was eligible for the Hall of Fame in 2007 and despite receiving seven Gold Gloves, he did not receive a single vote. He is one of only two players (Garry Maddox) to earn seven Gold Glove Awards and no Hall of Fame votes.[40] Speaking of Gold Gloves, White used the same mitt his entire career. "You take care of something, and it takes care of you," he said. "It took care of me for 17 years."[41]

White pursued coaching in retirement. Between 2008 and 2011 he was the outfield and baserunning coordinator for the Washington Nationals farm system, then moved to the Chicago White Sox as minor-league baserunning coordinator in 2011 and 2012.

But White's heart was still in Toronto. He wanted to coach in the Jays system, so he stayed close to the organization by volunteering with the Jays Care Foundation and coached at the Tournament 12 event for Top Canadian high-school prospects. Yet his efforts went unnoticed. "I did a lot for the organization as an alumni in that respect, so I was always around. I was doing it for a long time." But he felt that the general manager, Alex Anthopoulos, was dismissive of him. "Nothing against Alex, but he wasn't an alumni guy. … I spoke to him when he was an assistant GM, and the word was, if something opened up, he'd let me know. But I have to say he never responded to any of my emails."[42]

White persisted, and applied for all available opportunities. Finally, in 2017, the Jays' Triple-A affiliate, the Buffalo Bisons, named him hitting coach. "I just wanted to be in the game," he said. "When you played as many years as I did, I feel like you could take any job that's available. … I've always talked about hitting with other organizations when I was there. I helped out with the outfield and just the mental aspects of hitting and getting prepared. So, it's nothing new to me."[43] In 2018 the Bisons named White the position coach, where he has remained as of the 2022 season. In this role, White works with the Bison outfielders and teaches on base running. In 2021, the Bisons finished the season with 117 stolen bases, ranking seventh in Triple-A. When Toronto coach Mark Budzinski took a leave of absence in early July 2022 due to the tragic accidental death of his daughter Julia, the Blue Jays called up White to coach first base and the outfielders on an interim basis.

SOURCES

In addition to the sources cited in the Notes, the author consulted baseball-reference.com and mlb.com.

NOTES

1   Kristina Rutherford, "The Interview, Devon White," Sportsnet, https://www.sportsnet.ca/baseball/mlb/interview-devon-white-willie-mays-world-series-best-catch/, accessed January 17, 2022.

2   Ed Odeven, "Q&A flashback: a 1998 interview with MLB outfielder Devon White." https://edodevenreporting.com/2019/08/13/qa-flashback-a-1998-interview-with-mlb-outfielder-devon-white/ accessed January 17, 2022.

3   Mike Penner, "The Project: Devon White Was Given the Gift of Great Speed – and the Grit to Work Hard," *Los Angeles Times,* March 16, 1987.

4   Ken Rodriguez, "Sweet Homecoming," NBA.com, https://www.nba.com/spurs/features/130807_whyte, accessed January 18, 2022.

5   Gerald Scott, "Devon White Hopes for a One-Way Trip to Angels This Time," *Los Angeles Times*, September 4, 1986.

6   This report was provided to SABR by Roland Hemond, who procured it on behalf of the Scout of the Year Foundation and used it in the Diamond Mines Exhibit at the Baseball Hall of Fame in 2013.

7   Steve Wulf, "The Gnome," ESPN.com https://www.espn.com/mlb/story/_/id/9727219/a-usual-day-unusual-life-tampa-bay-rays-manager-joe-maddon. See also, Tim Hagerty, "When Joe Maddon Was a 27-Year-Old Manager," *The Sporting News*, https://www.sportingnews.com/us/mlb/news/joe-maddon-idaho-falls-angels-27-year-old-manager/1eqhcm-jomm8li1qgpx976w7mgy. Both articles accessed February 1, 2022.

8   Penner, "The Project."

9   "The Project."

10 "The Project."

11 "The Project."

12 "The Project."

13 Scott, "Devon White Hopes for a One-Way Trip to Angels This Time."

14 Scott.

15 Scott.

16 Mike Penner, "Angels: Devon White Wants Some Incentives for 1988," *Los Angeles Times*, March 5, 1988.

17 "Angels: Devon White Wants Some Incentives for 1988."

18 John Weyler, "In the Groove: Though He's a Reluctant Leadoff Hitter, White Helps Stabilize Angel Outfield and Lead Team's Resurgence," *Los Angeles Times*, July 22, 1988.

19 Penner, "White Lightning."

20 "In the Groove."

21 Mike Terry, "Davis, Joyner Happiest Campers at Angels' Spring Base," *San Bernadino Sun*, February 23, 1989.

22 Mike Penner, "White Pulls Fast One on Red Sox, 8-5," *Los Angeles Times*, September 10, 1989.

23 Penner, "White Pulls Fast One on Red Sox, 8-5."

24 Penner, "White Pulls Fast One on Red Sox, 8-5."

25 Rutherford.

26 Toronto was on pace to have just under 4 million fans in 1994 but the strike canceled their last 22 home games.

27 Amy Moritz, "Toronto Remains a Second Home to Three-Time All-Star Devon White," *Buffalo News*, August 10, 2018.

28 Morris Dalla Costa, "White's catch real Justice," *London Free Press,* February 11, 2013.

29 Rutherford.

30 Rutherford.

31 "Free Agent White Jumps to Marlins," *Los Angeles Times*, November 22, 1995.

32 Gordon Edes, "Jays' Carter Has High Praise for White," *South Florida Sun Sentinel* (Fort Lauderdale), March 11, 1996.

33 "Marlins Sign Devon White to Rich Contract," *Lakeland* (Florida) *Ledger*, November 21, 1995.

34 Edes.

35 Jim McLennan, "All-Star Diamondbacks, #1: Are We Not Men? We are Devo!" https://www.azsnakepit.com/2011/7/12/2269502/all-star-diamondbacks-devon-white, accessed February 3, 2022.

36 Ian Thomsen, "3 Los Angeles Dodgers Having Added a Touch of Green, L.A. Believes It Has Chased Away the Blues." SI Vault, March 27, 2000. https://vault.si.com/vault/2000/03/27/3-los-angeles-dodgers-having-added-a-touch-of-green-la-believes-it-has-chased-away-the-blues, accessed February 13th, 2022.

37 "Dodgers Shopping Sheffield; White Wants Out." ESPN.com, February 21, 2001. https://www.espn.com/mlb/news/2001/0219/1095073.html, accessed February 13, 2022.

38 Arnie Stapleton (Associated Press), "Dodgers Swap Devon White for Brewers' Marquis Grissom," CBC Sports, February 25, 2001. https://www.cbc.ca/sports/baseball/dodgers-swap-devon-white-for-brewers-marquis-grissom-1.257016, accessed February 13, 2022.

39 Stapleton.

40 "Devon White: Seven-time Gold Glove Winner," *Sports Illustrated*, January 6, 2017. https://www.si.com/mlb/2017/01/06/hall-fame-one-and-done-devon-white, accessed March 9, 2022.

41 Rutherford, "The Interview, Devon White."

42 John Lott, "Former Blue Jays Star Devon White Bringing Baserunning Savvy to Buffalo Coaching Gig," The Athletic, https://theathletic.com/62290/2017/05/24/former-blue-jays-star-devon-white-bringing-baserunning-savvy-to-new-coaching-gig/, accessed February 17, 2022.

43 Lott.

DAVE WINFIELD

By Doug Skipper

Imposing, confident, complex, charismatic, and controversial, Dave Winfield ranks as the greatest multisport athlete to emerge from the state of Minnesota. Drafted by five teams in five leagues in three major sports, Winfield chose baseball and compiled a first-ballot Hall of Fame career.

At 6-feet-6 and 220 pounds, the powerfully-built right-hander wielded a menacing black bat. His long, sweeping swing started with a distinctive hitch. Then, with sudden ferocity, he uncoiled and laced line drives to all parts of the park, sometimes clearing fences and walls, more often slamming into them. He ran the bases aggressively and with purpose. He was a good basestealer, but a great baserunner. He played defense with equal enthusiasm. Athletic and graceful, he gobbled up ground with long strides, sported a steady glove and boasted one of the most lethal throwing arms in the history of the game. Though he was blessed with tremendous physical ability, it was Winfield's preparation and determination, along with his ability to make adjustments at the plate and in the field that made him a player greater than his tremendous physical talent.

Winfield grew up in St. Paul and excelled in baseball and basketball at St. Paul Central High School and then at the University of Minnesota. "Winnie" averaged 9.0 points and 5.8 rebounds in 46 Gopher basketball games and posted a 19-4 record for the baseball squad. While at Minnesota, Winfield was a First Team All-America in 1973 and a two-time All-Big Ten selection in 1971 and 1973. He was 9-1 in his senior season with a 2.74 earned-run average and 109 strikeouts in 82 innings pitched. He batted .385 with 33 runs batted in 130 at-bats.

Winfield jumped straight from college to the major leagues, and compiled 3,110 hits, 465 home runs, and a .283 batting average in 22 seasons with the San Diego Padres, New York Yankees, California Angels, Toronto Blue Jays, Minnesota Twins, and Cleveland Indians. He played in 2,973 games, batted 11,003 times, collected 1,093 extra-base hits, stole 223 bases, made 5,012 putouts and 168 assists, and appeared in 12 All-Star

Games and two World Series. He was just the fifth player in the history of baseball to get 3,000 hits and 450 home runs.

But there is so much more to the man than the numbers.

There is Winfield's charity. He was the first active athlete to establish a charitable foundation. For 22 years, the David M. Winfield Foundation provided health care, holiday meals, game tickets, educational scholarships, and hope to underprivileged families. Under Winfield's leadership, the foundation developed "Turn It On," an international community action campaign to prevent substance abuse. For his charitable work, Winfield has earned the YMCA Brian Piccolo Award for Humanitarian Service, baseball's first-ever Branch Rickey Community Service Award, the

WE ARE, WE CAN, WE WILL

American League's Joe Cronin Award, the Josh Gibson Leadership Award, and Major League Baseball's Roberto Clemente Award. He was also awarded an honorary doctorate from Syracuse University[1] and recognition by Derek Jeter's Turn2 Foundation. Jeter is one of a number of players who credit Winfield's philanthropic efforts as the inspiration for their own charitable organizations.[2]

There is Winfield's business acumen. In addition to serving as president of the Winfield Foundation for years, the big slugger from St. Paul – who once played for Padres owner and McDonald's founder Ray Kroc – possessed a string of Burger Kings, art galleries, a lighting design and contracting company, and a diverse and powerful stock portfolio. He has served on the board of directors for President Bill Clinton's National Service Program, the Morehouse School of Medicine and the Century Council and on the advisory boards for the Peace Corps and MLB's Baseball Players Trust.[3] Since December 2013, he has been a special assistant to the executive director of the Major League Baseball Players Association, Tony Clark.

There is Winfield's literacy and culture. He is a prolific reader of fiction and nonfiction, collaborated on his best-selling 1988 autobiography, and outlined his plan of action to revitalize baseball in 2007 in *Dropping the Ball*. He penned *Turn It Around, There's No Place Here for Drugs*, authored *The Complete Baseball Player,* and collaborated on Frank White's *They Played for the Love of the Game: Untold Stories of Black Baseball in Minnesota*. A music lover, he served as host and narrator for the Baseball Music Project, a series of concerts that featured songs about the national pastime.

There is Winfield's race-relations leadership. As an African American youngster in St. Paul, and later as a major-league baseball player, Winfield encountered racism and battled it with dignity and determination. Granted a public forum by virtue of his occupation, Winfield has spoken and written about race relations, providing a powerful voice in the community. He helped develop the idea of the honoring former Negro League stars at MLB's 2008 draft.[5]

Winfield's guidance is not restricted to race relations. A highly respected motivational speaker with a smooth, silky voice, Winfield has addressed clubs, schools, and business about sports, education, health, fitness, teamwork, substance-abuse prevention, and youth issues.

There is also Winfield's ego. "Much of America's current self-esteem crisis could be overcome just with Winfield's excess," *Sports Illustrated* observed in 1992. "Nobody knows better than Winfield that he is handsome, buffed, richly appointed with all the options, well read, well-spoken and well paid."[6]

And then there is Winfield's pride. After eight successful seasons in San Diego, Winfield signed a contract with New York Yankees owner George Steinbrenner that made him the most highly paid player in baseball. But Steinbrenner quickly developed buyer's remorse, the two squabbled, and "The Boss" publicly declared that Winfield was not worth the money, disparaged him, and tried to trade him. "Steinbrenner, who did so much to make Winfield's life miserable in the eight-plus years he played for the Yankees, never appreciated the type of player he had," the *New York Times* observed. "All he did was look at Winfield's hitting statistics. When they lacked lusty numbers, he criticized Winfield. Unlike players and managers from other teams, Steinbrenner never understood the contributions Winfield made with his outfield defense and his base running."[7]

Eventually Steinbrenner even went so far as to pay a known gambler to discredit his star slugger. "Winfield would become the target of owner Steinbrenner's downright vicious crusade to force him out," the *New York Times* observed later. "No doubt he is having the last laugh, but there are times when Winfield sounds like someone who succeeded in spite of his father, and sometimes feels the hurt an abused child must feel all his life."[8] Stung by Steinbrenner's criticism that he was great in the regular season and awful in his first postseason, Winfield cast off the "Mr. May" label with a strong 1992 World Series performance. He earned the Babe Ruth Award as the player with the best performance in the fall classic, and placed his decade of discontent with the Yankees behind him. After Winfield revived his career in California, won a World Series in Toronto, collected his 3,000th career hit in Minnesota, and closed out his playing days in Cleveland, he and the Boss made a form of peace.[9]

In recent years, Winfield also made peace in his complicated personal life. Devoted to the mother who raised him, he reconnected with his father after her death in 1988. That same year he married, and formed a relationship with a child from a previous relationship. Later, he fathered two more children with his wife, Tonya. As a special assistant to Clark, the Players Association director, he travels the world as an ambassador for baseball, delivers motivational speeches, continues his charitable work, and spends time with his family.[10]

David Mark Winfield was born in St. Paul on October 3, 1951 – the day that Bobby Thomson hit "The Shot Heard Round the World," the pennant-winning home run for the New York Giants. David was the second son for Frank Charles Winfield, a World War II veteran and a Pullman porter on the Great Northern Railroad's flagship train, the *Empire Builder*, and Arline Vivian (Allison) Winfield, a St. Paul native. Frank, who lived in Duluth before he entered military service, met Arline through her brother. The couple divorced by the time David turned 3, and Frank eventually moved to Seattle, remarried and became a skycap for Western Airlines. Though they saw one another on occasion, David and his father remained estranged for much of their lives.[11]

Arline, who never remarried, raised David and his older brother, Stephen, in their home in a row house on Carroll Avenue, west of the Minnesota state capitol and just south of the swath that Interstate 94 now cuts through St. Paul. Arline earned a modest living at her job in the St. Paul School District's audio-visual department, and raised her sons with the assistance of her mother, Jessie Hunt Allison, who lived a block away, and an extended family of aunts, uncles, and cousins. Arline stressed the value of education to her sons, showed them educational films she borrowed from the school district, and taught them a new word every night. The family lived in a primarily African American neighborhood and worshipped at the African Methodist Episcopal St. James Church on Central Avenue, a couple of blocks north of their home.[12] "More than anything Ma and I *did*, I learned from the example she set, learned the value of education, family, work and a positive attitude," he wrote.[13]

As youngsters, Dave and Steve played baseball and hockey in St. Paul, and followed the Minnesota Twins when they moved to the Upper Midwest in 1961. Bill Petersen, a former University of Minnesota catcher, coached the pair at the Oxford Playgrounds, and the Winfield boys later led his Attucks-Brooks Post 606 baseball team to two American Legion state championships.[14]

The brothers also excelled at St. Paul Central High School. Steve lettered in baseball three times, captained the team his senior season, 1968, and was named to the school's Athletic Hall of Fame in September 2007. Younger brother Dave earned All-St. Paul and All-Minnesota honors in both baseball and basketball for the Minutemen, and was named to the Athletic Hall of Fame in 1995.

At the end of his senior year, Dave stood 6-feet-6 when on June 5, 1969, the Baltimore Orioles selected him in the 40th round of the amateur draft. He passed up that opportunity, and accepted a baseball scholarship from the University of Minnesota, where older brother Steve was already enrolled.

The scholarship covered only tuition, and as a freshman Winfield commuted 12 miles by public bus each day to attend class, play forward for the freshman basketball team and pitch for the freshman baseball squad. He went 4-0 for the Gopher frosh in the spring of 1970, then 8-0 in the Metropolitan (St. Paul) Collegiate League that summer, before he and a friend were caught snatching a pair of snow blowers from a local business. Winfield pleaded guilty to a charge of felony theft and was sentenced to three years in the St. Cloud Penitentiary, a sentence that was suspended, and years later, based on his public service and good works, expunged.[15]

Winfield made a repentant return to campus and embraced his second chance. He and Steve led a team dubbed the Soulful Strutters to the campus intramural basketball championship, and were invited to scrimmage regularly against the Gopher junior varsity.[16] After he posted an 8-3 record and a Big Ten-best 1.48 earned-run average for Dick Siebert's Minnesota varsity baseball team, Winfield pitched and played outfield for the Fairbanks Goldpanners of the Alaska Summer League, coached by college baseball legend Jim Dietz.[17]

Back on campus for his third year in the fall of 1971, Winfield worked out with the junior varsity basketball team, where he caught the eye of Gopher assistant coach Jimmy Williams. Williams invited him to try out for new head coach Bill Musselman, and Winfield earned a spot on a veteran varsity squad that included Jim Brewer, Ron Behagen, Clyde Turner, Keith Young, Bob Murphy, Bob Nix, and Corky Taylor. The veterans were slow to accept Winfield, but he won them over with his hard work, hustle, and powerful elbows.[18] "He was the best rebounder I ever saw," Musselman, who would go on to coach in the NBA and the American Basketball Association, said.[19]

"Making the team, I give up my half baseball scholarship for a full basketball scholarship," Winfield's autobiography said. "Anyway, for the first time I can go to classes, go to practices, live away from home, and not have to worry whether I'll be able to afford my meals, my books, or transportation."[20]

If life was more settled off the court, it was frantic on the hardwood, where Musselman coached his

Stuck in a 4-for-21 slump in the 1992 World Series, Winfield doubled home the tiebreaking runs in Game Six.

players to be aggressive and physical, a style Winfield embraced. "From Musselman I learned to get on that man, to get inside his jersey, his shorts, his jock. I learned first and foremost to *be* there. To get up in his face when he tried to dribble, and to stay there when he tried to shoot."[21]

On January 25, 1972, "Musselman's Musclemen" became too aggressive. Trailing late in a Big 10 show-down with Ohio State before a frenzied Williams Arena crowd, Taylor committed a hard foul on Ohio State center Luke Witte. The Gophers had been un-happy with the way Witte was throwing elbows during the game. When Taylor helped Witte up off the floor, he kneed him in the groin. Behagen who had fouled out earlier, jumped in off the bench, and stomped on Witte's head and neck. Quickly, the floor was a sea of players, fans, coaches, and officials. Winfield, who had been sitting on the sidelines, entered the fray, running across the floor to throw punches "like I was spring-loaded." Winfield later told *Sports Illustrated,* "Hey, I'm not denying I was involved. There was a fight with my team. I was swinging."[22] Though he was later blistered by media members, he escaped the pun-ishment assessed Behagen and Taylor, season-ending

suspensions. Instead, he stepped into Behagen's spot in the starting lineup. As one of the Gophers' "Iron Five," Winfield led Minnesota to its first conference championship in 35 years and an appearance in the NCAA tournament.

The baseball season went less well. In an early-sea-son game against Michigan, Winfield damaged ten-dons around his right elbow and missed the remainder of the season. Despite the injury, Dietz asked him back for the summer, and Winfield hit .315 with 15 home runs for the Goldpanners as an outfielder, and struck out 36 batters as a relief pitcher. He was named team MVP after he led Fairbanks to the ASL title.[23]

Winfield returned to campus and guided Minnesota's basketball team to a second-place Big Ten finish and a berth in the National Invitational Tournament in New York. When the Gophers were knocked out, he joined Siebert's baseball team in Texas, where he lost his season debut. After that, Winfield was magnificent. He won 13 straight, posted a 2.74 ERA, and hit .385 with 33 RBIs to earn first-team All-America honors. Appointed team captain, Winfield led Minnesota to the Big Ten title and to the College World Series in Omaha. Along the way, he pitched a nine-inning 1-0 shutout with 14 strikeouts against Oklahoma. On the tournament's final day, the Gophers lost to Arizona State, then met Southern California. Thorough eight innings, Winfield limited a Trojan team that included Roy Smalley and Fred Lynn to just one hit and struck out 15. Leading 7-0, but after nearly 140 pitches, Winfield ran out of gas and surren-dered a pair of runs in the ninth. With one out, he left the mound and moved to left field. USC rallied and won 8-7. Despite a third-place finish for the Gophers, Winfield was named the College World Series MVP.

After the season, four different teams in four leagues in three sports drafted Winfield. San Diego made him the fourth pick of the major-league baseball draft on June 5. The Atlanta Hawks picked him in the fifth round of the NBA draft, the Utah Stars drafted him in the sixth round of the American Basketball Association senior draft, and – even though he never played high-school or college football – the Minnesota Vikings selected Winfield in the 17th round of the NFL draft. Winfield, Texas Christian's Mickey McCarty, and Colorado's Dave Logan are the only players ever drafted by professional baseball, football, and basket-ball teams.

Winfield signed with San Diego for $15,000 and jumped straight to the major leagues at the age of 21. He commenced his assault on big-league pitchers with a single and a run scored in four at-bats against the Houston Astros on June 19, 1973, then collected hits in each of his next five games. Used most often in left field and against left-handers by manager Don Zimmer, the St. Paul slugger collected 39 hits, with four doubles, a triple, and three home runs, batted .277 and drove in 12 runs in his 56-game rookie campaign. He also began to buy blocks of tickets to Padres games for families who otherwise could not afford to attend.[24]

Over the next three seasons, the youngster continued to provide tickets to poor families and power and speed to the Padres lineup. Between 1974 and 1976, he slugged 64 doubles, 10 triples, and 48 homers, despite playing his home games in cavernous Jack Murphy Stadium. He stole 58 bases, with a career-high 26 in 1976. John McNamara, who replaced Zimmer at the start of the 1974 season, used Winfield in left and center, but most often penciled in the youngster into right field. Winfield remembered, "After the All-Star Break, McNamara said to me, 'Kid, I'm going to give you a chance to play every day. Play well and the job is yours.'"[25] He did, and for his efforts, the young slugger, who created a scholarship fund for minority student athletes from St. Paul that still exists, saw his pay rise to around $40,000 in 1975 and $57,000 in 1976.[26]

Winfield was unhappy with the contract the Padres offered in 1977, and elected to play out his option at a 10 percent pay cut.[27] The contract squabble pitted him against Padres general manager Buzzie Bavasi, and when it looked as though Winfield might be dealt, signs appeared in the ballpark that urged, "Keep Dave, Trade Buzzie."[28] In early July, with the two sides $100,000 apart, Winfield's friend and representative, Al Frohman, came up with an ingenious solution. Under Frohman's plan, The David M. Winfield Foundation for Underprivileged Youth, a nonprofit 501(c)(3) organization, was established. The team paid the foundation the $100,000 difference between what Winfield wanted and the Padres were willing to pay, the foundation handed it right back to the club in exchange for 100,000 game tickets at $1 apiece, and the foundation distributed the tickets to underprivileged families.[29] Everybody won. Winfield got the four-year, $1.4 million contract he wanted, the Padres sold an extra 100,000 tickets, thousands of kids got to sit in the Dave Winfield Pavilion at San Diego's Jack Murphy Stadium – and Frohman picked up a sizable commission.[30]

Winfield signed the contract in early July, in the midst of his breakout season. Just 25, he batted .275 with 25 home runs and 92 runs batted in, scored 104

times, clubbed 29 doubles and 7 triples, and was named to the National League All-Star team. Winfield made the first of his 12 consecutive appearances in the midsummer classic, smacked a double and drove in the winning runs with a single off Sparky Lyle in the NL's 7-5 victory.

The Dave Winfield Foundation drew support from a number of corporations, formed a relationship with the Scripps Foundation to provide free medical check-ups to needy families, delivered an antidrug message, and provided holiday dinners and scholarships to those who otherwise could not get them.[31]

In 1978 Winfield was named the first team captain in Padres history, was the NL Player of the Month for June, hit .300 for the first time, slugged 24 homers, 30 doubles, and 5 triples, drove in 97 runs, scored 88, and stole 21 bases. When San Diego hosted the All-Star Game, the Winfield Foundation bought its usual allotment of pavilion tickets. On local radio, the slugger from St. Paul, scheduled to play in his second All-Star Game, urged "all the kids of San Diego" to attend. When they responded by showing up in droves, Major-League Baseball opened practice sessions for the first time, starting a tradition that continues to the present day.[32] It was a highlight in a special season for San Diego. Under new manager Roger Craig, with a roster that included Winfield, Rollie Fingers, Gaylord Perry, and rookie shortstop Ozzie Smith, the Padres posted a winning record for the first time, though they finished fourth in the NL's Western Division.

A year later, San Diego slid back to 25 games under .500, though Winfield enjoyed what may have been his finest season. The 27-year-old batted .308 again, with 34 home runs, 27 doubles, 10 triples, and 15 stolen bases. Winfield drove in a career-best and NL-high 118 runs, scored 97 runs, won his first Gold Glove, and finished third in the league's Most Valuable Player Award voting behind Keith Hernandez and Willie Stargell. He drew a career-high 85 walks, and led the league in intentional passes with 24. "I became a lot more patient," Winfield said. "I learned the strike zone a lot better and I realized that sometimes it's better to take a walk than to make an out on a bad pitch."[33]

Winfield grew less patient with the Padres, and there were suggestions that he was not a team player. "If the Padres go places, I will be a main reason," he said. "But it they falter, I'll still shine."[34] With his contract set to expire at the end of the 1980 season and no extension in sight, Winfield played in all 162 games for Jerry Coleman, his sixth manager in eight years, and won another Gold Glove, but slipped to 20 home runs, 87 RBIs, 23 steals, and a .276 batting average. When the season ended, so did his tenure as a Padre. Not everyone was sad to see him go. "Dave Winfield thinks he is holier than thou," Ozzie Smith said. "He always acted as if it were his God-given right to tell other people how to do things."[35]

On December 15, 1980, Yankees owner George Steinbrenner signed Winfield to a 10-year, $23.3 million contract. Slugger Dave Winfield was leaving San Diego to play at Yankee Stadium and to become baseball's highest-paid player.

It seemed like a match made in heaven; it would begin a decade of pure hell between the two men. From the start, there were problems. Steinbrenner, who took great pride in his negotiation skills, didn't understand or didn't fully read the cost-of-living escalator clause that Frohman, a man *Sports Illustrated*'s Rick Reilly described as "a rumpled and retired New York caterer, a two-pack-a-day, fast-talking, 5 ft., 4 in., 220-pound chunk of walking cholesterol – with no experience as a sports agent," had negotiated for Winfield.[36] That clause made the contract worth $7 million more than the $16 million that Steinbrenner thought it was worth, and when alerted by a media member, the Boss was livid.[37] It was made worse when Frohman, who collected a 15 percent, $3.5 million commission on the deal, reportedly told the *New York Daily News*, "If he ever touches a hair of my boy's head ... I'll blow the lid. I've got stuff on George that if it ever came out, he would be in big trouble. It's very easy to be friends with George if you have blackmail on him."[38]

After heated exchanges, Winfield and Steinbrenner reached a compromise – an addendum to the contract that adjusted the cost-of-living increase, reportedly for $3 million to $4 million less over the life of the contract. Winfield also reached an agreement with the Padres, mediated by Commissioner Bowie Kuhn, which called for the Dave Winfield Foundation to meet a $35,000 contractual obligation to continue to buy tickets for underprivileged children to attend Padres home games. Winfield had already arranged for $3 million ($300,000 per year for 10 years) of his salary to be donated to the foundation, which funded the Dave Winfield nutrition center at Hackensack University Medical Center and collaborated with Merck Pharmaceuticals to create a bilingual substance-abuse prevention program called "Turn it Around."[39]

In his first season in pinstripes, Winfield hit .294 with 13 homers and 68 RBIs in 105 games in the strike-shortened 1981 season. He batted .350 with two doubles and a triple to lead the first-half-champion Yankees over the second-half champion Milwaukee Brewers in the AL Divisional Series. The Yankees went on to beat Oakland in the AL Championship Series, but with Reggie Jackson and Graig Nettles injured, and Winfield collecting only one hit in 22 at-bats, lost to the Los Angeles Dodgers in six games in the World Series, a loss that stuck firmly in Steinbrenner's craw. After his lone hit, a single, Winfield, perhaps in jest, asked for the ball, which made the Boss even madder.[40]

The Yankees never returned to the postseason with Winfield in the lineup, though he was one of the top players in baseball over the next seven years. He was selected to play in the All-Star Game each year, won five Gold Gloves, and drove in 744 runs. In 1982 the 30-year-old slugger clubbed 37 home runs and drove in 106 runs, batted .280, and slugged a career-best .560 for musical chairs managers Bob Lemon, Dick Howser, and Clyde King. A year later, Winfield batted .283 with 32 homers and 116 RBIs for Billy Martin, but the most notable day of his season came on August 4, 1983. Warming up in the outfield before the bottom of the fifth inning, Winfield hit and killed a seagull with a throw at Toronto's Exhibition Stadium. When he tipped his cap in a mock salute to the bird, the hometown crowd reacted by hurling obscenities and objects at him. When the game ended, Winfield was escorted to the Ontario Provincial Police station, booked on charges of cruelty to animals and forced to post a $500 bond before he was released, Martin joked, "It's the first time he's hit the cutoff man."[41] After the charges were dropped the next day, Winfield remarked to the media. "I am truly sorry that a fowl of Canada is no longer with us."[42] Although Winfield attempted to placate them,[43] Blue Jays fans booed Winfield every time he appeared in Toronto until he joined the Blue Jays in 1992.[44]

In 1984 Winfield and Yankees teammate Don Mattingly waged a dramatic and wrenching race for the AL batting title. Winfield homered 19 times, drove in 100 runs, and batted .340, but Mattingly collected four hits – and a standing ovation each time he batted – against Detroit on the season's final day to finish at .343. The two walked off the field together with clasped hands after the finale, but Winfield was clearly hurt that many of his teammates – and the Yankee ownership – had openly rooted for Mattingly, who was White, over Winfield, a Black man. "Most of their teammates were clearly pulling for Mattingly, raising questions about the possibility of race as a factor," the *New York Times* observed.[45] "I've experienced racism in my life," Winfield told sportscaster and writer Art Rust Jr. "It was all around me when I was on the Yankees and competing with Don Mattingly for the batting title. Here we both were, two guys on the same team, fighting one another for the same thing against a background of manipulative media and the perceptions of hundreds of thousands of fans that were created by that media. There was a vast difference in the amount of encouragement each of us got from the press and the public."[46] Winfield cleaned out his locker and left without speaking to the media after the final game, and some suggested he was resentful of Mattingly. "There was nothing between Donnie and I," Winfield later said. "We lived different lives. He was a young player who had a lot of support. I just know what I experienced the entire year. It was much different than my teammate did at the same time." [47]

Already strained by the Boss's buyer's remorse and his attempt to deal his big slugger to Texas in 1984, the relationship between Steinbrenner and Winfield worsened in 1985, though New York's best all-around player drove in 114 runs, batted .275, scored 105 times and clubbed 26 home runs for Yogi Berra and Martin. Late in the season, with the Yankees out of the post-season for a fourth straight year, the Boss said bitterly, "Where is Reggie Jackson? We need a Mr. October or a Mr. September. Winfield is Mr. May."[48] Winfield later told the *New York Times*, "It was irreverent, it was off-color, it was improper, it doesn't fit. I always rejected it. It doesn't apply. It was an inappropriate remark at the time. I didn't appreciate it then."[49]

Nor did he appreciate Steinbrenner's attempts – public or private – to ruin his reputation, even as he smacked 76 homers and drove in 308 runs between 1986 and 1988 for Lou Piniella and again under Martin. In 1986 Steinbrenner ordered Piniella to platoon Winfield; when he refused, the owner was livid.[50] In 1987 the Boss began to withhold payments he owed to his star slugger to be donated to the Winfield Foundation, despite three court orders to make the payments. Winfield and his new agent, Jeffrey Klein, endured lengthy, heated meetings with Steinbrenner's acerbic attorney, Roy Cohn, often on game days.[51] When Winfield sued, the Boss countersued to have Winfield removed from leadership from the foundation, suggesting that Winfield was running the foundation for personal gain and that his star slugger could not be trusted. A report in *Newsday* suggested that the foundation spent $6 for every $1 it gave away;

Steinbrenner's lawyers provided the numbers. "There is no way to fathom what was being done to me," Winfield told Reilly of *Sports Illustrated*. "It was immoral, improper and reprehensible. It was a battle for everything, your performance, your credibility. Do you know what it's like to have people fooling with your career?"[52]

Steinbrenner continued to make his managers bench Winfield or move him down in the batting order, tried to trade him to the Detroit Tigers for Kirk Gibson in 1987, and stepped up the efforts just before Winfield's 1988 autobiography, *Winfield, A Player's Life*, was published.[53] But with 10 seasons in the majors and five for the same team, Winfield could not be traded without his consent. At times, Winfield was able to joke about the situation. "These days baseball is different. You come to spring training; you get your legs ready, your arms loose, your agents ready, your lawyer lined up."[54] After setting an AL record with 29 RBIs in April 1988, he quipped, "We go on to May, and you know about me and May."[55] Whatever levity he might have felt faded away in the Fall of 1988. His mother, Arline, died of breast cancer in October; he suffered a herniated disk and endured offseason back surgery. He was forced to miss the entire 1989 season, which ended his string of 12 straight All-Star Game appearances. And when it looked as though things between him and Steinbrenner could not get worse, they did.

Back in 1981, Frohman had introduced Winfield to Howard "Howie" Spira, a gambler with alleged Mafia connections, and arranged for Winfield to make a $15,000 payment owed to Frohman instead to Spira. Five years later, Spira approached Winfield and asked for money in exchange for information that "would ruin Steinbrenner." After Winfield refused, Spira visited Steinbrenner, who was desperate for any information that would make his highly paid player look bad, and the Boss made a secret, illicit deal with the mercenary gambler. Eventually, Spira publicly accused Winfield of betting on baseball, and in the shadow of the Pete Rose investigation, the commissioner's office launched another inquisition. The investigation uncovered no evidence that Winfield had bet on baseball, but revealed that Steinbrenner had paid Spira $40,000 for his dubious information. The investigation also discovered that Steinbrenner had suggested turning over "potentially damaging" information about the Winfield Foundation to the Internal Revenue Service.[56] On June 30, 1990, Commissioner Fay Vincent ordered Steinbrenner to resign as the club's general partner and banned him from day-to-day operation of the team for life, a sanction that was lifted 2½ years later.[57] Spira was later found guilty of trying to extort an additional $70,000 from Steinbrenner, and sentenced to 30 months in prison for his role in the sordid affair.[58]

In the shadow of the inquiry, Winfield began the 1990 season in pinstripes. Angry that the Yankees left him off the All-Star ballot, he batted just .213 over 20 games with a pair of home runs and six runs batted in before the club traded him to the California Angels on May 11 for pitcher Mike Witt. Winfield argued that his contract did not allow him to be traded without his consent but accepted a negotiated deal on May 16.[59] "It's been an ordeal to a large degree," Winfield said. "Maybe things didn't work out (in New York), but I know they are going to work out in California."[60]

Although he had moved to the opposite side of the country, Winfield continued to stick in Steinbrenner's craw. On July 6 Commissioner Vincent ordered the Yankees to pay the Angels $200,000 – in addition to a $25,000 fine – for tampering with Winfield after he was traded to California.[61]

For the Angels, Winfield was brilliant. He batted .275 with 19 home runs and 72 runs batted in 112 games to earn *The Sporting News'* AL Comeback Player of the Year honors. A year later, Winfield smacked 28 more home runs and 27 doubles, and drove in 86 runs for the Angels. He homered three times on April 13 at Minnesota and on June 24, he went 5-for-5 and hit for the cycle, at 39 the oldest major-league player ever to do so. On August 14, 1991, Winfield became the 23rd player to hit 400 career home runs when he connected at his hometown ballpark, the Metrodome in Minneapolis. "Three-ninety-nine sounds like something you'd purchase at a discount store. Four hundred sounds so much better."[62] At the end of the year, he again became a free agent.

On December 19, 1991, Winfield embarked on the most successful year of his career when he signed a one-year contract with Toronto. For the 1992 AL East champs, Winfield batted .290, smacked 33 doubles and 26 homers, scored 92 runs, and drove in 108, the first 40-year-old ever to drive in 100 runs. His numbers as a designated hitter and right fielder were impressive, but it was his hard work and hustle that made him a fan favorite and earned him absolution for the seagull incident. Winfield, the Blue Jays' cleanup hitter, implored fans to be supportive of the team, and the phrase "Winfield Wants Noise" quickly appeared on T-shirts, signs, and the SkyDome scoreboard. "He is asked about his longevity," *Sports Illustrated* reported,

"and he says, 'For the last few years people have seen me and acted surprised that I'm still playing. Still playing? I'm kicking butt.'"[63]

Winfield smacked a pair of homers and a double in Toronto's four-games-to-two victory over Oakland in the AL Championship Series, then drove in three runs against Atlanta in the World Series. Two came home when he smashed a double down the third-base line in the 11th inning of the Game Six to give Toronto a 4-2 lead. When the game and the Series ended on Otis Nixon's unsuccessful bunt in the bottom half of the inning, Winfield went from "Mr. May" to "Mr. Jay." He was presented the Babe Ruth Award as the player with the best performance in the World Series. After the season, he also received the Branch Rickey Award, presented for exceptional community service.

"I've been thinking about this," Winfield told *Sports Illustrated.* "If my career had ended (before Toronto), I would not have been really happy with what baseball dealt me. I would have had no fulfillment, no sense of equity, no fairness. I feel a whole lot better now about the way things have turned out."[64]

With a World Series win under his belt, Winfield set out to accomplish another calling, playing for his hometown team. On December 17, 1992, the St. Paul native signed a free-agent contract with the Minnesota Twins. In 143 games in 1993, mostly as designated hitter, he batted .271 with 21 home runs and drove in 76 runs. On September 16, 1993, he collected his 3,000th hit, a ninth-inning single off Oakland reliever Dennis Eckersley that plated Kirby Puckett.

In 1994, at age 42, Winfield hit 10 more home runs, but the Twins fell out of contention, and on July 31, his contract was purchased by Cleveland. Two weeks later, on August 12, before Winfield ever appeared as an Indian, major-league baseball players went on strike, and after a short impasse, owners canceled the rest of the season. Winfield became a free agent in October, and Cleveland never sent a player to the Twins in the deal, but when executives of the two teams went to a dinner after the season, the Indians reportedly picked up the tab to settle the score.[65] After the season, Winfield received the Roberto Clemente Award, which annually recognizes the player who best exemplifies sportsmanship, community involvement and contribution to his team."[66]

On April 5, 1995, as baseball resumed, Winfield signed on with Cleveland. At 43, major-league baseball's oldest active player spent part of the season on the disabled list with a rotator-cuff injury, appeared in 46 games, hit the 464th and 465th home runs of his career and batted .191 for the Indians, who won their first pennant in 41 years. On September 28 he rifled a pinch-hit single to center field at the Metrodome. Two days later, he collected the 3,110th and final hit of his career, at Cleveland's Jacobs Field, and on October 1, 1995, at Cleveland, he made his final appearance in the major leagues, a pinch-hit groundout. Cleveland won the AL title, but Winfield did not appear in the postseason. After the World Series, the St. Paul slugger retired.

Winfield served as a Fox television baseball broadcaster, starting in 1996, hosted a Los Angeles morning drive time radio show, *On the Ball*, and served as a spokesman for the United Negro College Fund, the Drug Enforcement Administration, the Minnesota Board of Education, and the Discovery Channel. He also appeared in the film *The Last Home Run*, hosted the syndicated television show *Greatest Sports Legends*, and appeared on *Married with Children*, the *Drew Carey Show*, and *Arli$$*.

In 1999 *The Sporting News* ranked Winfield 94th on its list of Baseball's Greatest Players, and he was nominated for MLB's All-Century Team. In 2000 he was inducted into the San Diego Padres Hall of Fame and his number 31 was retired. Winfield had one year earlier been named to the Breitbard Hall of Fame, honoring San Diego's greatest athletes, and enshrined in the San Diego Hall of Champions.

Early in 2001, Winfield and Puckett were elected to the Baseball Hall of Fame in their first year of eligibility. Steinbrenner issued a statement that said he was delighted by Winfield's election and that he was "probably one of the greatest athletes I have ever known."[67]

Steinbrenner and Winfield had started to patch up their complicated relationship a few years earlier. "All of that never should have happened," the Boss said in early 1998. "Dave Winfield was one of the greatest athletes I've ever known. What part of it is me, I'll take the blame."[68] Just before the HOF election, the *New York Times* reported that, "Steinbrenner also acknowledged the problems the two men encountered, though he didn't say he instigated them, and said that 'today we are good friends.'"[69]

Winfield didn't go that far but said more than once that Steinbrenner had "'apologized for what he's said and what he's done."[70] The reconciliation survived yet another dustup when Steinbrenner publicly stated that Winfield's HOF bust should wear a Yankees cap, and the Boss reportedly was irked when Winfield chose

to be the first player represented with a San Diego Padres cap.[71]

On August 5, 2001, Winfield and Puckett became the seventh pair of teammates to be inducted into the Hall in the same year. Puckett recalled the time during his rookie year when Winfield had invited him to dinner, and imparted lessons about baseball and life. "From that point on, Dave Winfield was a friend of mine," Puckett said. "He's a great friend of mine. Any time I can spend in his company is special, not just when we're going into the Hall of Fame."[72]

In his induction speech, Winfield was conciliatory toward Steinbrenner.[73] The two had talked earlier, and "There were a lot of things we got out in the open," Winfield said. "He said things that made me believe he regretted what had happened."[74]

Things between the two had improved enough that on August 18, 2001, the St. Paul slugger was honored with Dave Winfield Day at Yankee Stadium. "Here's a day we thought we might not see, but it's here and it's beautiful," Winfield said.[75] The Yankees unveiled his old number 31 (though they didn't retire it), painted along the first- and third-base stands, and he was presented with keys for a sports car by his old teammate, Don Mattingly. Although Steinbrenner didn't attend, he did call Winfield, who thanked the Boss for inviting him back. "I'm not the one that's been behind trying to make a Dave Winfield Day at Yankee Stadium," Winfield told the *New York Times*. "It's been his doing. Things are certainly good now."[76]

The relationship continued to thaw. In 2008 Winfield played in the final Old Timer's Day Game at Yankee Stadium in August, and took part in the Final Game Ceremony at the Stadium in September. Earlier that summer, Winfield told *Newsday* that Steinbrenner "definitely has to be considered" for the Hall of Fame. "I might not have thought this years ago," Winfield said, "but he's had a lot to do with resurrecting the Yankees franchise and their brand and they've done really, really well during his tenure."[77] However, the Boss was not elected before he died in 2010.

Meanwhile, Winfield, who had joined the front office of the San Diego Padres as an executive vice president and senior adviser in 2001, appeared as an analyst on ESPN's *Baseball Tonight* from 2009 to 2012, and become the assistant to the executive director of the players union in 2013, continued to collect honors and accomplishments.

In 2004 ESPN named him the third best all-around athlete in the history of sport, behind only Jim Brown and Jim Thorpe.[78] He was one of the inaugural class of five players named to the College Baseball Hall of Fame in 2006, and was inducted on July 4, 2007. One year later, he was selected to the California Athletic Hall of Fame. In 2010 Winfield was named the All-Time Left Fielder the National Sports Review Poll, and named as one of 28 member of the NCAA Men's College World Series Legends Team.[79]

On July 14, 2014, Winfield was one of four St. Paul natives to throw out the first pitch for the 2014 Home Run Derby, along with Joe Mauer, Paul Molitor, and Jack Morris.

He journeyed to Cuba in March 2016 as a representative of Major League Baseball when President Barack Obama visited the island nation, participated in a press conference in Havana with Joe Torre, Derek Jeter, Jose Cardenal, and Luis Tiant, and attended an exhibition baseball game between the Tampa Bay Rays and the Cuba National Team.[80]

The 2016 All-Star Game, at San Diego's Petco Park, was dedicated to Winfield, who had represented the Padres at the San Diego's first All-Star Game at Jack Murphy Stadium in 1977.

Away from baseball, as he did with his dealings with Steinbrenner, Winfield set some of the relationships in his equally complicated personal life in order.

In 1988 he married Tonya Turner in New Orleans, seven years after they had met. Arline, battling cancer, sat in the front row. Shortly before she died in October, Winfield established contact with his daughter, Lauren Shanel Winfield, whom he fathered with Sandra Renfro, a Houston flight attendant, in 1982.[81] Renfro, who never lived with Winfield, filed a common-law marriage suit against the ballplayer in 1985, after he had supported her for several years. Renfro won a $1.6 million judgment against Winfield in 1989.[82] It was overturned in 1991, and the two reached a legal agreement in 1995 that decreed that no marriage ever existed between them. Winfield agreed to continue $3,500 monthly child-support payments,[83] and continued to be involved in Shanel's life. Winfield also reconnected with his father. Frank attended Arline's funeral, and with the encouragement of Tonya's mother, the two began to communicate more frequently.[84]

Dave and Tonya welcomed twins Arielle and David Jr. in 1995. Both enrolled at the University of Pennsylvania in 2013, where Arielle played women's volleyball and David Jr. played men's basketball.

Winfield followed his children's athletic careers, and remembered his own. "I miss going first to third in somebody's face," he told the *New York Times* just before he was inducted into the Hall of Fame in 2001.

"I miss throwing someone out from the outfield. Going from first to third, scoring from first on a double, for a big guy, those are things I really enjoyed. You can hit a ground ball right at an outfielder and if you're busting your backside from home plate, you have a chance for a double. Those are things I enjoyed. Playing defense is something you have to work on and something you have to love. When I first started, I wasn't a good defensive outfielder. I focused on it, enjoyed it, worked on things like charging the baseball. Little things that you do consistently become big things. Defense was a big part of my game."[85]

SOURCES

In addition to the sources cited in the Notes, the author also consulted a number of websites and the following books:

James, Bill. *The Bill James Historical Baseball Abstract* (New York: Villard, 1985).

Madden, Bill, and Kerin McCue. *Steinbrenner: The Last Lion of Baseball* (New York: Harper, 2010).

White, Frank, and Dave Winfield. *They Played for the Love of the Game: Untold Stories of Black Baseball in Minnesota* (St. Paul: Minnesota Historical Society Press, 2016).

Winfield, David, with Michael Levin. *Dropping the Ball, Baseball's Troubles and How We Can and Must Solve Them* (New York: Scribner, 1987).

NOTES

1   http://davewinfield.io

2   Ryan Mink, "Turn2 Foundation Celebrates 10th Anniversary; Jeter's Youth Outreach Organization Helps Kids," mlb.com, June 29, 2008.

3   http://davewinfield.io.

4   http://davewinfield.io.

5   Tim Kurkjian, "Negro League Players Will Be Recognized at Draft," ESPN.com, June 4, 2008. A group that included Winfield, Commissioner Bud Selig and MLB executive vice president Jimmie Solomon provided the idea and the inspiration for the June 5, 2008, special draft of former Negro League players. Each of the 30 major-league teams drafted one surviving Negro League player, representing all of those who were excluded from the major leagues.

6   Rick Reilly, "I Feel a Whole Lot Better Now; Dave Winfield's 20-Year Baseball Career, Often Touched by Trouble and Trauma, Has Taken a Happy Turn in Toronto," *Sports Illustrated*, June 29, 1992. Reilly's incisive interview with Winfield at a time he was a member of the Blue Jays provides a rich look into Winfield's personality, his background, and his motivations.

7   Murray Chass, "Some Slights Endure for Winfield," *New York Times*, January 18, 2001: D4.

8   Harvey Araton, "Sports of the Times; One Went; One Stayed; Both Yearn," *New York Times*, September 22, 1993: B13.

9   "Winfield Honored by Yankees," *New York Times*, August 19, 2001: D4.

10   http://davewinfield.io.

11   Dave Winfield with Tom Parker, *Winfield; A Player's Life* (New York: W.W. Norton and Company, 1988), 39-40.

12   Winfield with Parker, 40-41, and Gene Schoor, *Dave Winfield, The 23 Million Dollar Man* (New York: Stein and Day, 1982), 9-16,

both provide details about Winfield's formative years, his mother, Arline, and his close relationship with his brother Steve.

13 Winfield with Parker, 43.

14 Winfield with Parker, 35-39.

15 Winfield with Parker, 62-66.

16 Winfield with Parker, 73-75.

17 Winfield with Parker, 68-72.

18 Winfield with Parker, 77.

19 Winfield with Parker, 77.

20 Winfield with Parker, 78.

21 Winfield with Parker, 76.

22 Winfield described the incident to Reilly in the 1992 profile for *Sports Illustrated.*

23 Winfield with Parker, 83-86.

24 http://davewinfield.io.

25 Winfield with Parker, 111.

26 Schoor, 61.

27 According to Baseball-Reference.com, *The Sporting News* Salary Survey, published April 23, 1977, listed Winfield's salary at $90,000.

28 Winfield with Parker, 128-131.

29 Winfield with Parker, 130-131.

30 Reilly. Years later, according to http://davewinfield.io, Winfield learned that Blue Jays teammate David Wells had been one of the "Winfield Kids" who sat in the Winfield Pavilion.

31 Winfield's exceptional philanthropy is well known. Schoor, 57-58, 89-91, 160, and 161 provides details, as does the http://davewinfieldhof.com/winfield-foundation/ website.

32 http://davewinfield.io.

33 Phil Collier, "Hot-Hitting Winfield Shuns HR Swing," *The Sporting News,* May 5, 1979: 27.

34 Schoor.

35 Reilly.

36 Reilly.

37 The media member was the *New York Times* writer Murray Chass.

38 Reilly.

39 http://davewinfield.io.

40 Thomas Boswell, "Winfield's Single Merely a Souvenir," *Washington Post,* October 26, 1981. washingtonpost.com/archive/sports/1981/10/26/winfields-single-merely-a-souvenir/.

41 Bill Pennington, *Billy Martin: Baseball's Flawed Genius* (Wilmington, Massachusetts: Mariner Books, 2016), 393.

42 United Press International writer David Tucker reported Winfield's comment in "New York Yankees' Slugger Dave Winfield Was Arrested Thursday," https://www.upi.com/Archives/1983/08/05/New-York-Yankees-slugger-Dave-Winfield-was-arrested-Thursday/8533428904000/. The story ran in a number of newspapers.

43 Winfield with Parker, 201-203. Winfield told Parker that he donated two pieces of art to Easter Seals charity auctions he attended in Toronto the next two offseasons, worth $70,000. Despite the charity, he was heckled by arm-flapping fans on each return to Toronto prior to 1993.

44 Herschel Nissenson (Associated Press), "Winfield Arrested for Killing Seagull," *New York Daily News,* August 5, 1983: 25. See also Jane Gross, "Winfield Charges Will Be Dropped," *New York Times,* August 5, 1983: 29. Pennington, *Billy Martin: Baseball's Flawed Genius,* 393, provided comments from Martin.

45 Murray Chass, "Some Slights Endure for Winfield," *New York Times,* January 18, 2001: D4.

46 Art Rust Jr. *Get That Nigger off the Field, The Oral History of the Negro Leagues* (Los Angeles: Shadow Lawn Press, 1992), 190.

47 Chass, "Some Slights Endure for Winfield."

48 Dave Anderson, "Impatience in the Ruins," *New York Times,* September 16, 1985: C3. Murray Chass, "On Baseball; Familiar Problem for Piniella," *New York Times,* December 15, 1985: S7; "Murray Chass: "On Baseball: Sorry, Harvey," *New York Times,* July 19, 2008: 14. Steinbrenner entered the Yankee Stadium press box during the late innings of the September 15, 1985, game and addressed his comments to the media. Anderson reported Steinbrenner's outburst in the next day's *New York Times.* He was one of several to report the incident. In a 2008 column, Chass, who covered the Yankees for the *New York Times* from 1970 to 1986, disputed a claim that Steinbrenner called Winfield "Mr. May" much earlier, after Winfield's struggles in the 1981 World Series.

49 Chass, "Some Slights Endure for Winfield."

50 Bill Madden and Moss Klein, *Damned Yankees: Chaos, Confusion, and Craziness in the Steinbrenner Era* (Chicago: Triumph Books, 2012) (reprint). Steinbrenner denied he ordered Piniella to platoon Winfield, but that he might do so. Ross Newhan, "Baseball: Drug Deaths Don't Change the Real Issue," *Los Angeles Times,* July 13, 1986: Sports 3.

51 Reilly.

52 Reilly.

53 E.M. Swift, "Yanked About by the Boss; Bringing Their Feud to a Head, George Steinbrenner Sought to Discredit, to Humiliate and Unload Dave Winfield," *Sports Illustrated,* April 11, 1988; and Michael Martinez, "Baseball; Dark Cloud Obscures Winfield," *New York Times,* May 1, 1988: S1.

54 Murray Chass, "Winfield Is Hoping Yanks Will Focus on Play, Not Feuds," *New York Times,* February 27, 1983: S3.

55 Michael Martinez, "Baseball; Winfield Ties R.B.I. Mark as Yankees Roll," *New York Times,* May 1, 1988: S2. Winfield broke the AL record and tied the major-league record held by Ron Cey of the Dodgers and Dale Murphy of the Braves. Martinez wrote that Winfield would reportedly be a part of a three-way trade between the Yankees, Toronto, and Houston later that week.

56 David E. Pitt, "Baseball: Steinbrenner Had Ex-I.R.S. Man Check Winfield," *New York Times,* August 26, 1990: A2.

57 Kevin McCoy and Richard T. Pienciak, "Gone! The Boss Gets the Thumb: Loses Control of Yankees, *New York Daily News,* July 31, 1990: 1, 4-5. Vincent lifted the ban on March 1, 1993. Mark Hermann, "His Yankee Years: The Life and Career of George Steinbrenner," *Newsday,* July 14, 2010: W8.

58 Bill Brubaker, "Steinbrenner, Winfield and Friend a Tangled Web," *Washington Post,* March 30, 1990: S1; David E. Pitt, "Baseball; Steinbrenner Had Ex-I.R.S. Man Check Winfield."

59 Robert McG. Thomas Jr. "Winfield Approves Trade to the Angels," *New York Times,* May 17, 1990: B13.

60 Helene Elliott, "Winfield Reaches Settlement, Ready to Join the Angels: Baseball: He Gets Contract Extension for One Year, Plus Two Option Years. Package is Worth as Much as $9.1 Million," *Los Angeles Times,* May 17, 1990. C1.

61 "Yanks Must Pay $225,000 for Winfield Tampering," *New York Times,* July 6, 1990: A17. *The Times* reported that "Winfield challenged the trade and threatened to take the case to arbitration. Steinbrenner met with Winfield on May 14 and said the outfielder would still have a place on the Yankees if he won in arbitration. Winfield then agreed to go to the Angels and accepted

a three-year, $9 million contract extension." Baseball Commissioner Fay Vincent explained: "Mr. Steinbrenner's statement that Mr. Winfield would be welcomed back to the Yankees if he won the arbitration and should play on a full time basis was clearly improper. It follows therefore, that Mr. Steinbrenner's improper statements harmed the Angels' bargaining position."

62   Robyn Norwood, "No Place Like This for Winfield's 400th: Angels; He Becomes 23rd Player to Reach Home Run Milestone, Doing It in the Area Where He Grew Up," *Los Angeles Times*, August 15, 1991: C1.

63   Reilly.

64   Reilly.

65   The Associated Press story that appeared in the *New York Times* on September 1, 1994, under the headline "Baseball; It's a Deal: Indians Grab Winfield" said that the Indians had obtained Winfield for a player to be named later. According to Tom Keegan in "Owners Try on Global Thinking Cap," *Baltimore Sun*, September 11, 1994, if the season did not resume, Indians general manager John Hart had agreed to pay the Twins $100 and take Minnesota's Andy MacPhail out to dinner. MacPhail had already left the Twins to join the Chicago Cubs at that point. Several sources claim that Indians team personnel treated Twins team personnel to dinner after the season to settle the score.

66   "Robert Clemente Award – About the Award," mlb.com._https://www.mlb.com/community/roberto-clemente-award._

67   Chass, "Some Slights Endure for Winfield."

68   Murray Chass, "Baseball; Mr. Break-It and Mr. Fix-It," *New York Times*, January 4, 1998: 1.

69   Chass, "Some Slights Endure for Winfield."

70   Tyler Kepner, "Winfield Recalls Reconciliation with Steinbrenner," *New York Times*, July 13, 2010: S1.

71   Murray Chass, "Winfield Chooses Padres Over Yanks," *New York Times*, April 14, 2001: D1; Harvey Araton, "Sports of the Times: Winfield and Steinbrenner and Reconciling the Past," *New York Times*, July 18, 2008: S1.

72   Puckett's comments were included in an Associated Press story that appeared in several newspapers, including the *Arizona Daily Sun* (Flagstaff), which headlined it, "Hall Open Doors to Puckett, Winfield," on January 16, 2001.

73   Jayson Stark, "Détente? Winfield Gives Thanks to the Boss," ESPN.com, Monday, August 6, 2001.

74   Araton, "Sports of the Times: Winfield and Steinbrenner and Reconciling the Past."

75   "Winfield Honored by Yankees," *New York Times*, August 19, 2001: 83.

76   "Winfield Honored by Yankees."

77   Jim Baumbach, "Even Winfield Believes in Boss," *Newsday*, July 26, 2008, S1.

78   Jeff Merron, "The Best All-Around Athletes," ESPN.com, April 26, 2004.

79   https://www.ncaa.com/news/baseball/article/2019-06-10/we-picked-all-time-college-world-series-starting-lineup.

80   "Taking the Field in Cuba: MLB, Obama Visit the Island," *Boston Globe*, March 22, 2016: D4; "Why Derek Jeter Agreed to Accept Spotlight of Cuba Trip," *New York Post*, March 21, 2016; "Rays Win as Presidents Watch: Visit First by a Major-League Team Since 1999," *Orlando Sentinel*, March 23, 2016: C3; Joe Giglio, "Derek Jeter, Dave Winfield greet President Obama in Cuba at MLB," NJ.com Advanced Media, March 22, 2016, Derek Jeter, Dave Winfield greet President Obama in Cuba at MLB exhibition (VIDEO) – nj.com, accessed February 16, 2022.

81   Reilly.

82   "Sidelines: Winfield Loses Palimony Suit," *Los Angeles Times*, March 22, 1990: S10.

83   United Press International, "Winfield Ends 10-Year Legal Battle," November 7, 1995, Winfield ends 10-year legal battle – UPI Archives, accessed February 17, 2022; George Flynn, "Winfield's 10-year Legal Slump Ends/Woman, Baseball Star Agree to Forgo Retrial," *Houston Chronicle*, November 7, 1995: A13.

84   Reilly.

85   Murray Chass, "Some Slights Endure for Winfield."

EDDIE ZOSKY

By Paul Sinclair

The Toronto Blue Jays' "former shortstop of the future," Eddie Zosky, a first-round draft choice, selected 19th overall in 1989, played in 44 major-league games for four teams over five seasons and hit .160.[1]

His baseball "future" came up very short. Is his story a tragedy in which a collegiate star, named All-American by *The Sporting News* and *Baseball America*, is brought down in his professional career by some ordinary human flaw? Or is it a treatise on the uncertainties of talent evaluation and development in professional baseball? Perhaps his story is a quest in which an elusive goal consistently remains out of reach. Maybe his story, like the Robert Frost poem *The Road Not Taken*, is an assessment of choices along his life's path.

No, Eddie Zosky's story is an adventure – an excellent adventure in amateur baseball and 12 years of professional baseball.

Edward James Zosky was born on February 10, 1968, in Whittier, California, 12 miles southwest of Los Angeles in the largest walnut-growing area in the United States.

Zosky was born to Ed and Yvonne Zosky. Ed, a factory manager in Whittier, influenced Eddie's love of baseball and developed his talent for the sport by spending hours hitting grounders to his son. His mother's heritage would give Eddie the distinction of being in the select group of Jewish major-league baseball players.

Eddie attended St. Paul High School, a private Catholic high school located in Sante Fe Springs, a neighboring city to Whittier. He starred on the St. Paul baseball team and attracted both college baseball recruiters and professional scouts.

The June 1986 amateur draft was held shortly after he graduated from high school. Selected by the New York Mets in the fifth round, the 18-year-old Zosky faced Robert Frost's poetic dilemma: commencing his professional career or remaining an amateur and attending Fresno State University.

Not signing professionally with the New York Mets organization was Zosky's *Road Not Taken*. Instead, he elected to further develop his skills and attended Fresno State, playing shortstop for the Bulldogs under the tutelage of legendary head coach Bob Bennett.[2]

In 1987 as a 19-year-old freshman, Zosky hit .292 and evidenced good hitting discipline and power with an on-base percentage of .328 and slugging average of .389. He earned second-team All-Conference honors.[3]

Zosky's 1988 sophomore season was exceptional. He hit .320 with an on-base percentage of .338 and slugging average of .500. However, he showed little patience at the plate, walking only eight times in 306 at-bats. Defensively, Zosky's fielding percentage of .928 suggested that his fielding needed further development and refinement.

Zosky helped the Bulldogs to a regular-season record of 51-9, highlighted by a 32-game winning

Eddie Zosky - 1989 first round draft pick.

streak that ended with his absence from the lineup due to mononucleosis. Zosky recovered in time for the playoffs and helped the Bulldogs win the Pacific Coast Athletic Association championship. In the postseason, he was an All-Conference selection to the first team All-Big West and, the National Honors first team for the All-West Region.[4]

After the playoffs, Zosky received an invitation to try out for the US Olympic baseball team. To this point, his natural talent meant that the game had always come easy. The Olympic tryouts were different; he was behind other players offensively and lacked the versatility to play anywhere but shortstop.[5] When the final roster cuts were made in August, Zosky's name was not on the team list.

Zosky returned to Fresno State for his junior year in 1989 and took his performance to an even higher level. Leading the team with 101 hits, he batted .370 while significantly improving both his plate discipline (on-base percentage of .421) and power (slugging average of .516). He was an All-American selection, first team for the American Baseball Coaches Association, *Baseball America*, and *The Sporting News*. He was again named to the National Honors first team All-West Region and the All-Conference first team for the All-Big West.[6]

Zosky's back-to-back stellar collegiate seasons made him a top professional prospect.

On June 5, 1989, with the 19th selection of the draft, the Blue Jays chose Zosky.

His professional career began on June 28, 1989, when the 21-year-old Zosky signed with the Blue Jays for a bonus of $175,000. It was anticipated that he would start his professional career at the A level with the Dunedin Blue Jays of the Florida State League.[7] Given his outstanding collegiate statistics and his first-round selection, expectations were high. The short-stop talent pool within the Blue Jays organization was strong at the major-league and Triple-A levels but weak at Double A and A. Tony Fernandez, 27 years old and in his seventh major-league season, was entrenched as the starter in Toronto and was supported by Manny Lee, a 24-year-old who could also play second and third. At Triple A, the Syracuse Chiefs' starting shortstop was Luis Sojo, a solid hitter and fielder who projected to be of major-league caliber. Light hitting and error-prone fielding characterized the starters in the lower farm system at Knoxville (Double A) and Dunedin (A). Anemic batting averages (sub-.200) and too many errors curtailed the advancement

potential for Knoxville's shortstops, Jose Diaz and Jerry Schunk, and Dunedin's shortstop, Jimy Kelly.

The lack of depth in the Blue Jays' low minor-league system presented the road on which Zosky's professional baseball journey commenced. The original plan to start at Dunedin was upgraded. This time Zosky's *Road Not Taken* was Dunedin, where he would have been tutored by Bob Bailor, Dunedin's manager and a former Blue Jays infielder and outfielder. Instead, the Blue Jays, pressed to fill an immediate organizational need, decided that Zosky would start at Double A with the Knoxville Blue Jays of the Southern League.

In his professional debut with Knoxville, on July 3, 1989, Zosky had a single and an RBI. The initial adjustment from college to Double A was difficult. He did not get his average over .200 until late August. Highlighted by an eight-game hitting streak to finish his first season, he compiled a batting average of .221, on-base percentage of .256, and slugging average of .303. His plate discipline still needed improvement with only 10 walks in 208 at-bats.

Transitioning to professional baseball involved many adjustments: being away from his native California; using wooden bats instead of the aluminum bats used in college; and hitting against older, more experienced, higher-caliber pitching. The Blue Jays continued to assess his potential as high, minimizing his initial struggles at Knoxville.

Zosky returned to Knoxville in 1990 for what was expected to be a year of significant development. He played well and improved his batting average (.271), on-base percentage (.316), and slugging average (.367). Defensively, there was room for improvement: He made 31 errors for a fielding percentage of .941. After the season Zosky was named the third-best prospect in the Southern League and *Baseball America* named him the 22nd best prospect in professional baseball. Ranked behind Zosky were future Hall of Famers Jeff Bagwell (32nd), Chipper Jones (49th), and Jim Thome (93rd).[8]

The opportunity to be the Blue Jays' starting shortstop opened in December 1990 when Toronto made a franchise-changing trade. Tony Fernandez, the starting shortstop for six years, and first baseman Fred McGriff were sent to the San Diego Padres for second baseman Roberto Alomar and outfielder Joe Carter.

Barring a further trade or free-agent signing, the starting shortstop role for 1991 was now a competition between Zosky and the 25-year-old Lee. Alomar's arrival forced Manny Lee to transition from second base back to shortstop.

Zosky acknowledged that the Fernandez trade was "a big plus for me" and that "it could mean that I'm a step closer to 'The Show.'"[9] Regarded as the "heir apparent to the shortstop job for the Jays," Zosky, a non-roster invitee to spring training 1991, said, "[N]ow I have to go to spring training and prove myself."[10]

Playing 19 spring-training games, Zosky struggled at the plate and in the field. He collected 7 hits in 32 at-bats, mostly as a late-inning replacement. Defensively, he committed six errors. He admitted that he felt the pressure from being on the cusp of getting a spot on the Blue Jays' 25-man roster. Under pressure to perform well, his fielding technique suffered as his strong arm was wild and his footwork needed further refinement.[11]

Zosky's performance that spring confirmed that he was not ready for the major leagues. On the eve of the 1991 season, his road diverted to Syracuse; he was assigned to the Chiefs.

Syracuse Chiefs manager Bob Bailor was charged with developing Zosky's fielding.[12] Focusing on footwork and throwing, Zosky's defensive improvement was slow, with 18 errors in the first half of the season. Feeling more comfortable and relaxed in the second half, he improved remarkably, committing only six errors to lead the International League in fielding percentage (.961). Playing 119 games for Syracuse, he had a solid season offensively, hitting .264 with an on-base percentage of .315, and slugging average of .350, culminating in Zosky's being named to the 1991 International League all-star team. When September 1 arrived and the major-league rosters were expanded, Zosky was called up.

The media coverage after his major-league debut was full of hyperbole when in the fourth inning of the September 2 game against the Baltimore Orioles, he replaced the starting shortstop, Manny Lee, who was suffering from dizziness and a stiff neck. In Zosky's first at-bat in the big leagues, he singled to left field. He finished the game batting 1.000 (1-for-1) and was removed in the sixth inning.

Reporting on Zosky's debut, the *Toronto Star*'s Dave Perkins queried, "Eddie Zosky takes his first major league swing, gets his first major league hit and all a guy can think is this: Did Manuel Lee just become Manuel Pipp?"[13] Could Zosky substituting for the injured Lee really be equated to Lou Gehrig taking the unfortunate Wally Pipp's position on the 1925 New York Yankees? Comparing Zosky's debut to Gehrig's was beyond ridiculous, but one can't help but wonder how such hyperbole played out in the mind of that 23-year-old shortstop who had two innings of major-league experience.

Zosky had a hitless streak of 14 at-bats with seven strikeouts over the next eight games. On September 14, starting for the once-again-injured Lee, Zosky collected his first major-league extra-base hit, a triple. In the third inning, hitting against Oakland starter Bob Welch, his bloop single bounced over right fielder Jose Canseco and rolled to the wall. His bid for an inside-the-park home run failed on a perfect Oakland relay that nailed him by a stride at the plate. The next inning, he singled for his first two big-league RBIs.

Zosky finished his 1991 season having played 18 games for the Blue Jays, who won the American League East title. He posted a batting average of .148 with no home runs and two RBIs. His fielding was flawless with no errors in 38 chances. Lacking plate discipline, he failed to walk in 28 plate appearances. He was left off the postseason roster; the Blue Jays lost the American League pennant to the eventual world champion Minnesota Twins.

As the 1992 season approached, expectations for Zosky remained high, though there was evidence that perceptions of his potential were shifting downward. Listed in the top prospects for 1992 by *Baseball America*, he slipped to the 82nd spot. *Baseball America*'s list of the top 20 preseason rookies included Zosky in the 11th spot. Their list of top 10 Blue Jays prospects had Zosky sixth but behind shortstop Alex Gonzalez, the Blue Jays' 1991 13th-round pick, who was ranked second in the organization. In its commentary, *Baseball America* noted Zosky's strengths: his work ethic, range, and strong arm, but also noted that he needed more patience at the plate, suggesting that a higher on-base percentage was a prerequisite to advance to the major leagues.[14]

The starting shortstop role was a competition between the incumbent Manny Lee, Zosky, and spring training nonroster invitee Alfredo Griffin. Lee had hit only .234 with 107 strikeouts during the previous season, and his hold on the position was shaky. Zosky was viewed as the heir-apparent to be the starter. Having missed out on the pennant in 1991, the Blue Jays were focused on immediate performance, not potential.

Zosky's second spring training competing against Lee for the starting shortstop role did not go well. A batting average of .163 in 23 preseason games and poor fielding destined him to start the season at Syracuse.

Lee was named the starter, and the backup spot went to Griffin. Bad habits, particularly fielding, resurfaced and self-doubt and lack of confidence compounded Zosky's struggle to play well.[15]

Zosky remained at Syracuse for the entire 1992 minor-league season. In a disappointing year offensively, he finished with a batting average of .231 and walked only 19 times in 373 plate appearances.

For the second consecutive year, the September roster additions included Zosky being promoted to the Blue Jays. He played in eight games, appearing seven times as a late-inning replacement. In his lone start, on September 14, exactly one year after his notable 1991 game against Oakland, Zosky went 1-for-3, highlighted by a triple off Cleveland starter Jose Mesa. He finished September with two hits in seven at-bats for a batting average of .286.

As a September call-up, he was again not eligible for the Blue Jays' postseason roster. The Blue Jays went on to win their first World Series in a thrilling six-game series over the Atlanta Braves.

After the season, Manny Lee became a free agent and signed with the Texas Rangers. Now that Zosky's main competitor had moved on, general manager Pat Gillick declared that the organization felt Zosky could do the job and he would be the starting shortstop for the 1993 season.[16] Gillick's decision softened after Zosky suffered an elbow injury while playing in the 1992 Arizona Fall League. Diagnosed with a stress fracture of a bone spur in his right elbow, Zosky curtailed throwing activities and rested.

The road to Toronto seemed imminent but there remained competitors to encounter and obstacles to overcome.

By the start of spring training, Zosky's anointing as the starting shortstop had been rescinded. His chances of making the team were now reported to be no better than 50/50.[17] The Blue Jays ventured into the free-agent market and added depth to their shortstop position by signing Dick Schofield, a light-hitting infielder who played mostly with the New York Mets in 1992. They also re-signed Alfredo Griffin and traded for former Blue Jay Luis Sojo.

Within a few months, Zosky's burden of expectation had shifted from the pressure of having a starting role to the pressure that the window was closing on his opportunity to play regularly in the big leagues.

In mid-March, his right-elbow bone spurs necessitated surgery and he was placed on the 15-day disabled list. His recovery from surgery kept him off the playing field until late July. In a five-game

rehabilitation sojourn with the Hagerstown Suns of the Double-A South Atlantic League, he struggled in his short stint with two singles in 20 at-bats. For the remainder of the season, Zosky returned to Syracuse. His offensive slump continued. Overall for the 1993 season, at Hagerstown and Syracuse combined, his batting average, on-base percentage, and OPS were an anemic .195, .234, and .239 respectively, in 126 plate appearances.

During the 1994 offseason, Zosky was dethroned as the Blue Jays' "shortstop of the future"; that label passed to Alex Gonzalez. Dick Schofield was projected to be the starting shortstop for the Blue Jays as spring training for the 1994 season got underway. Looking to be on the Blue Jays' Opening Day roster, Zosky was aiming for a utility role behind Schofield. Zosky had a good spring training, highlighted by a walk-off three-run home run, but was assigned to Syracuse.

Zosky's potential to be a major leaguer rose with his strong 1994 season, highlighted by a 16-game hitting streak and a solid .264 batting average. Defensively, he enhanced his versatility, playing at second base (41 games) more times than his customary shortstop position (34 games). His power improved with a slugging average of .412. However, his performance in 1994 was clouded by an anemic on-base percentage of .264 as he walked only nine times in 306 plate appearances.

Despite his best season so far, there would not be a September promotion to Toronto. On August 12, the 1994 major-league season was curtailed by a players strike.

Toronto's legendary GM Gillick retired after the 1994 season and Gord Ash was promoted to be the new general manager. Ash's first trade sent Zosky to the Florida Marlins for Scotty Pace, a left-handed pitcher whose career consisted of 395 innings in the minor leagues.

Zosky made the Marlins' Opening Day roster. The strike that curtailed the 1994 season meant that until May 15, major-league rosters were increased to 28 players from the usual 25. Starting at shortstop on April 29 against the San Francisco Giants, he appeared in his first major-league game since October 1992 and went 1-for-3 with a single. As a late-inning defensive replacement, he played five more games for the Marlins, going hitless in two at-bats.

When the Marlins reduced their major-league roster to 25 players, Zosky was sent to their Triple-A affiliate, the Charlotte Knights of the International League. He hit .247 and continued to struggle at getting on base, walking only seven times in 312 at-bats. After the season he was granted free agency.

Zosky's career path would now lead to new organizations. No longer the "shortstop of the future" but now an itinerant minor-league player, he was playing the game he loved while holding on to the hope of securing a position on a major-league roster.

After each of the 1996 to 2000 seasons, Zosky was granted free agency. During those offseasons, he signed a minor-league contract with an invitation to spring training with four different organizations: Baltimore (1996), San Francisco (1997), Milwaukee (1998 and 1999), and Pittsburgh (2000).

During each spring training, he was ultimately sent to the minor-league camp and assigned to that organization's Triple-A affiliate. Zosky spent the entire 1996 season with the Rochester Red Wings of the International League and the entire 1997 season with the Phoenix Firebirds in the Pacific Coast League. Continuing to redefine himself as a utility infielder, with the Firebirds he had more appearances at third base (42) than at shortstop (30). At Phoenix, he had a career year offensively with his best in batting average (.278), home runs (9), RBIs (45), on-base percentage (.323), and slugging average (.465).

Zosky spent the entire 1998 season with the Louisville Redbirds. Seeking a major-league spot as a utility infielder, he spent time at shortstop, second base, and third base. He returned to Louisville (now called the RiverBats) for the 1999 season. He was having a great season when he was called up to Milwaukee on August 1. After pinch-hitting in the sixth inning, he played the remainder of the game at second base and went 1-for-2. His stay in Milwaukee was short-lived; he was sent back to Louisville on August 5. When major-league rosters expanded in September, Zosky was again promoted to Milwaukee, where he played six more games but went hitless in four at-bats. Overall, for the Brewers that season, he played in eight games and had one single in seven at-bats.

At Louisville in 1999, Zosky had the best season of his career. Playing in 116 games, he exceeded his career highs in batting average (.294), home runs (12), RBIs (47), and on-base percentage (.333).

In 2000 he had a short stint in the Pirates organization, playing for the rookie-level Gulf Coast League Pirates (eight games) and the Triple-A Nashville Sounds (53 games). In late August Zosky was traded to the Houston Astros and assigned to the Triple-A New Orleans Zephyrs, where he played in 11 games and had nine singles in 33 at-bats. The Astros promoted

him to the major leagues as part of their September roster expansion. Playing sparingly, he appeared in four games and went hitless in four at-bats.

On October 14, 2000, the Associated Press reported that Zosky had cleared waivers and again become a free agent.

This time, his path led home to California. His journey as an amateur and professional baseball player had ended.

A search of publicly available social media indicates that Zosky has settled with his family in Fresno, California, where he has worked as a sales rep for a commercial and residential plumbing supply company for the past 11 years.

Zosky's mother's Jewish lineage qualified him to be on the roster of players in the Jewish Baseball Museum.[18]

In 1995 Zosky was inducted into the Fresno State Bulldogs Hall of Fame.[19]

In the 1990s, Zosky appeared in 328 games for the Syracuse Chiefs, more than any other player that decade. His best memories were not of a particular season, game, hit, or play.[20] Instead, there were fun, unique moments. There was the brawl in Columbus when the teams left the field and dugouts to join a fight in the clubhouse between Turner Ward and the Columbus pitcher; and there was the night at a sold-out game when the trees just beyond the center-field fence caught fire from an ill-fated postgame fireworks show.

Zosky's most memorable moment occurred during the 1992 season.[21] The first game of a doubleheader went into extra innings, forcing the second game to start around midnight. Syracuse third baseman Ed Sprague pulled a veteran move, not wanting to be out there all night and, in his first at-bat, was ejected for arguing a called strike. Reaching the Chiefs' clubhouse, Sprague found the costume for the Chiefs mascot (Scooch), put it on, and went into the stands where, to the amusement of his teammates, he mocked the umpires.

Four major-league teams, 10 minor-league teams, 1,100 games played, and 3,720 at-bats limit the fullness of Eddie Zosky's 12-year journey in professional baseball. His story is indeed an adventure: a tale of talent and shortcomings, key happenings, and noteworthy achievements. It is a baseball adventure story of one player's grasping for, and repeatedly missing, the brass ring of a starting role on any major-league team. Indeed, Eddie Zosky's baseball career story must be looked upon as an adventure, with moments of struggle, moments of adversity, and fleeting moments of greatness. So many roads, so many miles, and such an adventure.

SOURCES

In addition to the sources cited in the Notes, the author consulted Baseball-Reference.com; thebaseballcube.com; clippings from Zosky's file at the National Baseball Hall of Fame Library in Cooperstown, New York; the *Toronto Star* archives; newspaperarchive.com for articles from the *Syracuse Herald Journal*, the *Syracuse Post-Standard*, and the *Orange County Register* (Anaheim, California); PaperofRecord.com for *The Sporting News;* and linkedin.com.

NOTES

1   The phrase appears in Allan Ryan, "Zosky Could See It Coming," *Toronto Star*, April 1, 1991: C4.

2   Bob Bennett was the head coach of the Fresno State Bulldogs from 1970 to 2002. He was *The Sporting News* NCAA Coach of the Year in 1988 and 14-time winner of the Conference Coach of the Year. With 1,300 wins he is 11th in NCAA Division I wins (minimum 10 years as a Division I coach). He helped develop many major leaguers, including Terry Pendleton, Dick Ruthven, Dan Gladden, Tom Goodwin, Steve Hosey, Jeff Weaver, and Dennis Springer.

3   Travis Blanshan and Matt Burkholder, *2019 Fresno State Baseball Fact Book* (Fresno, California: Fresno State Athletic Communications office, 2019), 61-64.

4   *2019 Fresno State Baseball Fact Book.*

5   Chuck Abair, "One-Dimensional Players Could Feel Marquess' Knife," *Orange County Register*, June 17, 1988: C16.

6   *2019 Fresno State Baseball Fact Book.*

7   Neil MacCarl, "Jays Draft Pick Helps Sick Kids," *Toronto Star*, June 30, 1989: D2.

8   jewishbaseballmuseum.com, http://jewishbaseballmuseum.com/player/edward-eddie-zosky/?msclkid=dfa17a65af6611ec82523f186b00158b.

9   Norman DaCosta, Mary Ormsby, and Tom Slater, "Trade Winds Ruffle Some Jays," *Toronto Star*, December 6, 1990: D4.

10   "Trade Winds Ruffle Some Jays."

11   Rosie DiManno, "Zosky's Armed for Another Shot at the Jays Starting Shortstop Job," *Toronto Star*, February 27, 1992: D3.

12   Jacque Thomas, "Chiefs Zosky Here to Polish Tools," *Syracuse Herald-Journal*, July 8, 1991: E6.

13   Dave Perkins, "Cast of Thousands Take Top Billing," *Toronto Star*, September 3, 1991: C3.

14   "Top 10 Prospects AL East," *Baseball America*, January 25-February 9, 1992: 15.

15   Matt Michael, "Zosky: Hope, Hype and Hops," *Syracuse Post-Standard*, April 8, 1992: D4.

16   Jim Byers, "Jays Give Zosky Second Chance to Prove He's Everyday Shortstop," *Toronto Star*, December 22, 1992: D5.

17   Rosie DiManno, "Zosky Knows His Time Is Running Out," *Toronto Star*, February 25, 1993: H3.

18   jewishbaseballmuseum.com.

19   *2019 Fresno State Baseball Fact Book.*

20   Matt Michael, "RiverBats Zosky Recalls Earlier Days," *Syracuse Herald American*, June 27, 1999: C9.

21   "RiverBats Zosky Recalls Earlier Days."

BALLPARK

SKYDOME

By Allen Tait

The term "nova" is a good metaphor for describing the story of SkyDome. The stadium burst on the scene in 1989 and shone brightly as a state-of-the-art multi-use stadium. It was the first stadium with a fully retractable roof, the first that helped attract 4 million fans in a season for baseball and the first stadium to host a World Series game that was not played on US soil. However, by 1993 the stadium began to lose its luster due to a combination of construction debt for original construction "add-ons" plus a "multi-use" seating design that did not always provide the best sight lines for the primary stadium function of baseball. Despite these challenges, SkyDome remained in use and in late 2021, plans for additional stadium upgrades were announced.

THE VISION

The vision of a domed ballpark for Toronto predates the city obtaining a franchise. Paul Godfrey, first elected as an alderman in 1968, attended the 1969 baseball winter meetings and asked Commissioner Bowie Kuhn for a franchise. The response: "Let me tell you the way we do it in major-league baseball. First, you build a stadium. And then we consider if we want to give you a baseball team."[1]

In 1973 Godfrey had been reelected to the Metropolitan Toronto Council and was selected as chair by his fellow peers. Godfrey promised to deliver a baseball franchise, domed stadium, and conference center.[2] Obtaining financing to construct a new domed stadium did not seem feasible so the focus was on renovating the existing Exhibition Stadium, which was then being used by the Toronto Argonauts of the Canadian Football League and hosted rock concerts.

Exhibition Stadium was intended to be a temporary facility until a domed stadium could be built. The stadium had adequate capacity: 38,522 (1977); 43,737 (1978).[3] Seating, however, could be uncomfortable. Only the outfield bleachers had a roof. Ten sections along the first-base/right-field line were aluminum benches.

Weather was always a concern for early- and late-season games at Exhibition Stadium. Concerns were greater as the prospect of the Jays playing in the postseason became legitimate with the team showing true progress starting in 1982. While summers are pleasant in Toronto, average highs between 72 and 82 degrees Fahrenheit from June through September, the average lows and highs for April (38-53), May (51-68), and October (46-59) made for some unpleasant conditions at times. The discomfort level was magnified by the lack of cover for fans excluding the bleachers and, particularly in the spring, the warmer southerly winds were cooled by Lake Ontario, which was immediately

A view of the SkyDome and neighboring CN Tower, looking north-east towards downtown Toronto and beyond.

south of the stadium. The phrase "cooler by the lake" is used with some frequency in spring weather forecasts for Toronto.

THE CONSTRUCTION

Official progress for construction of a domed stadium began in 1983 when Ontario Premier William Davis proposed the construction of a $150 million (CDN) domed stadium supported by all three levels of government (federal, provincial, municipal).[4] As for location, after an eight-month study a location was originally recommended at Downsview Park. The park is approximately 11 miles from downtown Toronto and was adjacent to the federally owned Downsview Airport, an air-force base, not a civilian airport. The location was accessible by highway and public transit. However, the federal government was not interested in having a stadium in the vicinity of its federal asset.[5] The Canadian National Railway offered an undeveloped railyard land by the CN Tower and the site was selected in January 1985. This location was also attractive by being downtown and within easy walking distance of Union Station, a major transportation hub for the Toronto subway system as well as the primary commuter and intercity railway terminal for Toronto.

The federal government was also not interested in providing financing, thus necessitating a public/private partnership with a sharing of profit and risk. An August 1983 feasibility study stated, "Our analysis indicates that private financing is not a viable method for the domed stadium. The main reason is projected net operating revenues are insufficient to generate positive cash flows (after debt service)."[6] A 25-member corporate consortium was organized with each corporate partner to contribute $5 million each in exchange for exclusive promotion or concession rights at the stadium.[7]

The next task was selection of an architect. The selection of the contract of architect Rod Robbie (six employees, zero experience in building skyscrapers, shopping malls, or convention centers) in conjunction with Canadian structural engineer Michael Allen to design the retractable roof was met with skepticism.[8]

The construction contract was awarded to EllisDon for an original lump sum price of $184.2 million. During construction, the scope was expanded to include a hotel, health club, restaurants, "Skybox" luxury suites, and a Jumbotron scoreboard, causing the budget to increase to $527 million.[9]

From a technology perspective, the skeptics were wrong. The roof did work on day one and continues to work to this day. The roof is 339,343 square feet in area, weighs 11,000 tonnes[10] with a maximum height of 282 feet. The roof is comprised of four panels. Panel four is stationary; panels two and three slide along horizontal rails and panel one slides in a circular motion to tuck under panels two and three.[11] The roof can open/close in about 20 minutes. Subsequent to SkyDome, other stadiums with retractable roofs have been built in Phoenix (1998), Seattle (1999), Milwaukee (2001), Houston (2002), Miami (2012), and Arlington, Texas (2020).

Budget management for construction of SkyDome was not a success story. The corporate consortium financing construction expanded the contract scope as noted above to increase the potential revenue stream. Hence the SkyDome design evolved from a baseball stadium to a multipurpose facility including baseball. It was billed as "The World's Greatest Entertainment Center."[12] The final construction cost for the SkyDome, including interest charges, is estimated at $650 million.[13]

SkyDome comprises five decks; however, in terms of seating capacity, SkyDome was 19th in seating capacity in comparison to the 26 stadiums in use at the time it opened.[14] Regular tickets for fans were available in tiers 1 and 5 and part of tier 2. Ticket prices in 1990 were $15 for all tier-1 seats between the foul poles and all outfield tier-2 seats. Outfield tier-1 seats were $12. Tier-5 tickets were $12, $9, or $4 depending on location.[15] Tier-2 also included 5,800 SkyClub seats roughly foul line to foul line, costing $2,000 to $4,000 for the season. Tiers 3 and 4 were the location of 161 SkyBox luxury suites costing $150,000 to $225,000 per season.[16]

SkyDome was scheduled to open for the start of the 1989 season, but labor strikes delayed the opening.[17] It opened for baseball on Monday, June 5, 1989.[18] A detailed write-up of the first game, can be found on the SABR website, Games Project section.[19] However, the first event, an opening gala on Saturday, June 3, left some patrons unhappy with their first SkyDome experience.[20] The 90-minute program for the opening ceremonies gala, hosted by Canadian celebrities Alan Thicke (*Growing Pains*) and Andrea Martin (*SCTV*) were themed around the retractable roof. Tickets were priced from $57 to $252, or $5,000 for a 12-seat SkyBox.[21] The roof was closed at the start of the gala and there were thunderstorms in the area. The gala finale was to include an opening of the dome and a decision was made to do so despite the weather, soaking the 45,000 spectators and entertainers. Upset attendees were offered free dry cleaning and 6,000 took up the offer.[22]

THE GLORY YEARS 1989-1993

Baseball fans were enthusiastic about SkyDome. Despite playing the first 26 games at Exhibition Stadium that season, the Blue Jays still led the major leagues in attendance by selling out 50 of 54 home dates and drawing 3,375,883 fans.[23] Support carried over as the Blue Jays set a new major-league attendance record on September 17, 1990, and in 1991 became the first club to draw over 4,000,000 fans.

The Blue Jays again drew over 4,000,000 fans in the World Series championship years of 1992 and 1993. The team led the American League in attendance for six consecutive seasons (1989-1994). Toronto led major-league baseball in attendance from 1989 to 1992 before being passed by the expansion Colorado Rockies in 1993 and 1994 who played at Mile High Stadium with capacity in the range of 76,000.[24]

SkyDome was very busy during this era. In addition to hosting Blue Jays fans, other events held included being home to the Canadian Football League Toronto Argonauts, hosting the 1989 and 1992 Canadian Football League Championship Game (Grey Cup), an NBA exhibition game, lacrosse, tennis, cricket, ice-skating shows, *Wrestlemania VI*, Supercross, concerts, trade shows, the opera *Aida*, and a stage production of *Les Misérables*.[25]

FINANCIAL PRESSURES

Despite strong attendance for the Blue Jays and the many other events being held at the SkyDome, the stadium was losing money. Cash flow by 1993 was insufficient to service the outstanding stadium debt and interest payments were not being made. Hence the outstanding debt on the stadium had climbed to $400 million. A recalculation of cash-flow budgets indicated that the SkyDome had to be open for events 600 days per year to cover costs and generate a small profit.[26]

Although the original agreement was for a sharing of profit and risk between the corporate consortium and the provincial government, the government ended up protecting the consortium members from the overrun losses and this led to a $300 million write-off being incurred by the provincial government.[27]

In 1993 the provincial government sold the SkyDome to a private company for $150 million. Despite the sale price at around the original stadium budget, finances did not improve. In 1998 the owners filed for bankruptcy indicating they were losing $3 million per year and owed millions in back property taxes.[28] In 1999, SkyDome was sold under supervision of a bankruptcy court for $80 million to Sportsco International Limited Partnership. In 2004 the current Blue Jays ownership purchased the $650 million stadium for $25 million and renamed the facility the Rogers Centre.[29]

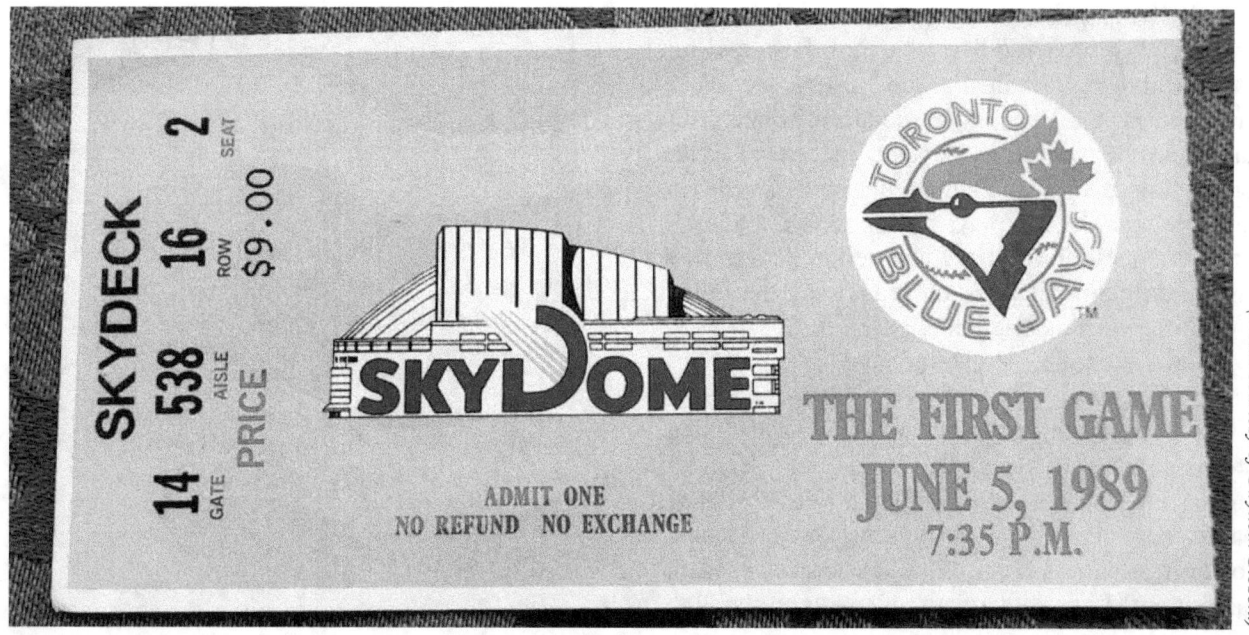

(Photo courtesy of Gwyneth Gibson.)

ROGERS CENTRE ERA

SkyDome continues to operate today, although additional investment has been needed. In 2013 then Blue Jays president Paul Beeston noted that it required $250 million of renovations and upgrades to remain comparable to contemporary baseball standards.[30]

Significant upgrades included replacement of the sliding pits with a full dirt infield in 2016;[31] a rebuild of the retractable roof operating system that extended into the 2016 season;[32] and, new AstroTurf installed for the 2021 season.[33]

A few other notable events at SkyDome:

- It served as home to the Canadian Football League Toronto Argonauts for 27 seasons (1989-2015).
- It served as the original home to the National Basketball Association Toronto Raptors from November 1995-February 1999.
- Occasional rain delays occurred when the roof did not close in time at the onset of sudden rain.
- On three occasions, fans either assumed or forgot their hotel rooms facing the playing field were not one-way glass and provided "X-rated" entertainment to fans in the stands.[34]
- Two 30-pound roof tiles fell during a game on June 22, 1995, injuring seven fans.[35]
- A game on April 12, 2001, was postponed when two of the three roof panels collided, sending roof siding and insulation debris into left field during Kansas City Royals batting practice; no one was injured.[36]

In 2020 the future of SkyDome was in doubt. The Blue Jays had proposed that it be torn down and replaced with a new stadium at the existing site. After further study, the Blue Jays announced in late 2021 that SkyDome would be renovated instead.[37] The reconstruction plan would have required five years to complete with the Blue Jays having to find a temporary home park during the construction period. The renovation plan will focus on renovating the lower bowl of the existing stadium.

Upon reflection, SkyDome may not have received a balanced review of its accomplishments. It is very easy to criticize the cost overrun and falling into bankruptcy 10 years after it was built. Being a circular multipurpose stadium, sight lines for some seats were not considered ideal for watching baseball. However, as current (2022) Blue Jays President Mark Shapiro noted in an interview reflecting on the 30th anniversary of SkyDome, the stadium was a state-of-the-art multi-use facility when it opened in 1989. It had the largest Jumbotron of its era. However, it opened at the end of the multi-use stadium era.[38]

The legacy of SkyDome includes the accomplishments that it hosted the first World Series game not on US soil, hosted back-to-back World Series titles for the Blue Jays, and was the first stadium to draw 4,000,000 fans in a single season. The financial challenges should not distract from the proud legacy of the stadium.

SOURCES

In addition to the sources cited in the Notes, the author consulted the Baseball-Reference.com website.

NOTES

1   Stephen Brunt, *Diamond Dreams: 20 Years of Blue Jays Baseball* (Toronto: Viking, 1996), 17.

2   Brunt, 17.

3   Philip J. Lowry, *Green Cathedrals 5th Edition* (Phoenix: Society for American Baseball Research, 2019), 289.

4   Brunt, 150. All dollar figures cited are in Canadian dollars.

5   Brunt, 150.

6   Brunt, 150.

7   Brunt, 151.

8   John Mays, "Designed SkyDome as 'a pleasure palace for the people,'" *Globe and Mail* (Toronto), January 6, 2012.

9   Lindsay Cole, "Raising the Roof: Toronto's Rogers Centre Remains a Marvel," EllisDon.com, July 4, 2017. https://www.ellisdon.com/news/raising-the-roof-torontos-rogers-centre-remains-a-marvel/, accessed January 9, 2022.

10   A tonne, or metric ton, is 2,205 pounds.

11   Cole.

12   Ira Rosen, *Blue Skies Green Fields* (New York: Clarkson Potter, 2001), 170.

13   Mays,

14   "Ballpark Ballistics," *Blue Jays Scorebook* 14 (1990), 34.

15   *Blue Jays Scorebook*, 137.

16   "Countdown to SkyDome," *Blue Jays Scorebook* 12 (1988), 298.

17   *Blue Jays Scorebook, Collector's Edition* (1989), 136.

18   Lowry, 290.

19   Adrian Fung, "June 5, 1989: Blue Jays Play First Game in SkyDome," SABR Games Project. sabr.org. https://sabr.org/gamesproj/game/june-5-1989-blue-jays-play-first-game-in-skydome/. Accessed January 9, 2022.

20   https://www.theweathernetwork.com/ca/news/article/this-day-in-weather-history-june-3-1989-skydome-gala, last accessed December 27, 2021.

21   *Blue Jays Scorebook, Collector's Edition* (1989), 136.

22   *Blue Jays Scorebook* 14 (1990), 106.

23   *Blue Jays Scorebook* 14 (1990), 38.

24   Lowry, 112.

25   *Blue Jays Scorebook* 14 (1990), 110-120.

26   *CBC Archives*, February 9, 2011.

27   Brunt, 151.

28   *CBC Archives*, November 26, 1998.

29   Marcus Gee, "SkyDome's Legacy: Not with My Money,
      Never Again," *Globe and Mail*, June 3, 2009.

30   Eric Enders, *Ballparks Then and Now* (San
      Diego: Thunder Bay Press, 2015), 154.

31   Brendan Kennedy, "Blue Jays Debut Rogers Centre All-
      Dirt Infield on Friday," *Toronto Star*, April 7, 2016.

32   Cole.

33   Shi Davidi, "Blue Jays Getting New Astroturf Field Amid Hopes
      for Full Season in Toronto," SportsNet.ca, December 11, 2020.
      https://www.sportsnet.ca/mlb/blue-jays-getting-new-astroturf-field-
      amid-hopes-full-season, last accessed December 27, 2021.

34   Lowry, 290.

35   Lowry, 291.

36   Lowry, 291.

37   Mark Zwolinski, "Renovation Planned for Rogers
      Centre," *Toronto Star*, December 24, 2021: S5.

38   Ian Hunter, "Mark Shapiro Says Something Big Is Brewing with Rogers
      Centre Renovations," BlueJaysNation.com, July 13, 2019. https://
      bluejaysnation.com/2019/07/13/mark-shapiro-something-big-brew-
      ing-rogers-centre-renovations/ accessed January 16, 2022.

GENERAL MANAGER

PAT GILLICK

By Dan Levitt and Mark Armour

Pat Gillick served four different stints as a general manager, and during each his task was different. That he succeeded at all four marks Gillick among the very best in the history of the game. In Toronto, he built an expansion team into one of baseball's best organizations (winning 86 or more games for 11 straight seasons), culminating in five division titles and two World Series championships. In Baltimore, he worked for an impatient owner who wanted his team to compete right away – Gillick delivered two consecutive ALCS appearances, the Orioles' only postseasons between 1983 and 2012. In Seattle, he was tasked with trading one of the game's best players and then watching another superstar leave as a free agent a year later. Despite this, his Mariners teams won over 90 games all four of his years at the helm and an all-time record 116 in 2001. At his final stop, in Philadelphia, he took over a good team that had not been able to get over the hump and into the playoffs. Gillick's Phillies made the postseason in his second year and then won the World Series in 2008, the team's first in 28 years. A few days later, he retired to an advisory role.

Gillick's approach was to make sure he had great scouts and then to widen his talent search to nontraditional avenues. As he put it: "One needs to fish in many waters." In Toronto, Gillick and his longtime friend Epy Guerrero were at the forefront of creating an identifiable presence in the Dominican Republic. He also looked for underappreciated opportunities with multisport athletes. His success in the mostly ignored Rule 5 draft of veteran minor leaguers was legendary; no one else approached his success. His skill forced teams to be much smarter about protecting their players from this draft. Moreover, Gillick used free agency to perfection in Baltimore and Seattle – in both places he quickly reloaded franchises with mostly barren minor-league systems. With the latter organization, he also signed the first hitter from Japan to star in the major leagues, Ichiro Suzuki, along with a first-rate reliever, Kaz Sasaki.

Lawrence Patrick David Gillick was born to George Lawrence "Larry" Gillick and Thelma (Daniels) Gillick on August 22, 1937, in Chico, California. His mother, a minor silent-movie screen actress, and his father, a pitcher for several seasons in the Pacific Coast League who later became the sheriff of Butte County, California, separated when he was a baby. Gillick and his mother moved into her parents' home in Van Nuys, California, where he was mainly raised by his maternal grandparents.

Gillick's grandfather sent him to Ridgewood Military Academy in Woodland Hills, where he excelled in both baseball and football. On the gridiron, Gillick played center and snapped the ball to quarterback Bobby Beathard, later to gain fame as general manager of the NFL's Washington football team during their Super Bowl years in the 1980s. He graduated at 16 and enrolled at LA Valley Junior College,

Pat Gillick, Toronto's Hall of Fame GM, built the franchise's two World Series champions.

later transferring to USC under legendary coach Rod Dedeaux. In Gillick's 1958 senior season, the Trojans, featuring future big-league stars Don Buford and Ron Fairly, won the College World Series. Dedeaux later related that Gillick "remembered everything I told him."[1] Over the years his incredible memory and recall became a recurring theme in his colleagues' descriptions of him. Some bestowed on him the nickname "wolley segap," which is "yellow pages" spelled backward.[2]

Gillick graduated from USC with a business degree, but the left-handed hurler wanted to try professional baseball first, pitching semiprofessionally in Canada, before signing with the Baltimore Orioles organization in 1959. He topped out at Triple A, and after the 1963 season, having just turned 26, Gillick returned to school, possibly to become a high-school coach. Eddie Robinson, the farm director of the Houston Colt .45s, intervened, however. Robinson, who had known Gillick from his time in the Orioles organization, offered him a job as his assistant in Houston.

As the southernmost team in the majors, Houston had already developed a Latin American presence, and Gillick, moved into a scouting role, spent much of his time combing the area for ballplayers. In the fall of 1967 Gillick was in the Dominican Republic when part-time scout Epy Guerrero introduced him to 16-year-old César Cedeño, whom they quickly signed. Gillick and the Astros later hired Guerrero as a full-time scout, and the two worked together for the next 28 years in three different organizations.

In August 1974 Tal Smith, with whom Gillick had worked in Houston, brought Gillick to the Yankees as coordinator of player development and scouting. Two years later, Toronto team president and top baseball operations executive Peter Bavasi, who was building out a front office for his expansion franchise, hired Gillick as head of player personnel and his second in command. In the expansion draft the Blue Jays emphasized younger pitchers (nine of their first 14 selections) while also mixing in a few well-known veterans. They drafted two players, pitcher Jim Clancy and catcher Ernie Whitt, who would become All-Stars and play prominent roles on the franchise's first division winner many years later.

Surprisingly, the Blue Jays also drafted Rico Carty, an aging slugger with bad knees, from the Cleveland Indians. "What do we need Carty for?" Bavasi asked Gillick before they made the pick. "Rico was Mr. Wahoo," Gillick told him. After a blank stare from Bavasi, Gillick continued. "The Indians Man of the

Year. Let's take him. In Cleveland the writers and fans will kill the team if they lose Carty. Then they'll have to trade and get Rico back." Sure enough, in trading Carty back to Cleveland he extracted young catcher Rick Cerone, who played another 16 years in the big leagues.[3]

To fill their organization, Bavasi and Gillick cast a wide net for players. "There are five or six rivers flowing into one river – fish in all of them," Gillick said, describing his philosophy in finding players.[4] One river involved trading with other major-league teams, and Gillick was always on the lookout for unappreciated young talent. Two of his early deals landed shortstop Alfredo Griffin and second baseman Damaso Garcia. Griffin won the 1979 Rookie of the Year Award, and the two made up the Blue Jays' double-play combination for several years.

Gillick once again teamed with Epy Guerrero. In 1977, using borrowed money, Guerrero spent $9,000 on 18 acres and some cinder-block buildings outside of Santo Domingo. He built a ballpark and created a rudimentary baseball school for youngsters. Several years later the Blue Jays began to fund the operation, expand it, and run it year-round.[5] Guerrero helped the Blue Jays sign several top Dominican players, enrich the organizational environment for Latin players, and identify worthwhile trade and draft targets. Other organizations soon followed, but Toronto established a prominent presence in the country, one that provided an advantage for a decade or more.

In the fall of 1977, Gillick exploited a little-used "river" when he selected first baseman Willie Upshaw, whom he and Guerrero knew from the Yankees organization, in the Rule 5 draft. Over the years Gillick mastered the Rule 5 draft to uncover several valuable contributors, including George Bell, Manny Lee, Jim Gott, and Kelly Gruber. Gillick was also willing to take risks with multisport athletes, accommodating them in ways other teams might not have. In 1977 Gillick drafted multisport prep star Danny Ainge in the 15th round. Two years later Toronto drafted prep quarterback and baseball catcher Jay Schroeder in the first round, paying a $100,000 bonus and allowing him to play college football at UCLA.

Despite their poor showing on the field in 1977, this first season was widely viewed as a triumph for baseball in Toronto. The Blue Jays' attendance of 1.7 million surpassed expectations and ranked fourth in the American League. For his success, the Toronto and Montreal baseball writers named Bavasi baseball's Man of the Year in Canada.[6] In recognition of the team's success, the board promoted Bavasi to president and Gillick to VP of baseball operations, effectively making him GM.

While Toronto was fielding poor teams at the major-league level, Gillick was expending his energies creating the team he hoped would someday contend. In Toronto's first amateur draft in 1977, he selected Illinois prep outfielder Jesse Barfield. The next year he nabbed high-school first baseman Lloyd Moseby, whom Toronto converted into an outfielder, and Dave Stieb, who had starred at Southern Illinois. Stieb hoped to play the outfield, but after Gillick met his asking price, he agreed to switch to the mound.[7]

Gillick gained additional control over baseball operations when Bavasi was forced out after the disappointing 1981 season. Feeling the team should be ready to take a step toward contention, Gillick hired manager Bobby Cox, who had managed in the Yankees system while Gillick was there and had just been released as manager by the Braves.

Gillick continued to promote his prospects and make trades to solidify the positions not sufficiently addressed by the farm system. He traded veteran first baseman John Mayberry to the Yankees to open a spot for Upshaw, while Cox gave starting jobs to Barfield (right field) and Moseby (center field). Gillick also acquired two valuable platoon players: third baseman Rance Mulliniks and catcher Buck Martinez (obtained during the 1981 season). With his remarkably young team ready to break through, after the season Gillick acquired two older players – Cliff Johnson and Jorge Orta – to platoon at designated hitter.

Gillick also traded for 30-year-old speedster Dave Collins to play left field, a trade he later labeled one of his favorites, not because of Collins, but for the additional prospect he coaxed out of the Yankees. Gillick initially negotiated with Bill Bergesch, the latest general manager in the Yankees' ever-changing and chaotic front office. The Yankees desperately sought Toronto's relief ace Dale Murray, and after several rounds of negotiations, Gillick agreed to take outfielder Dave Collins and pitcher Mike Morgan in exchange. But like any savvy trader, he wanted an additional prospect, particularly one with power. Gillick and his scouts liked 18-year-old first baseman Fred McGriff, still in Rookie ball, but didn't mention him right away for fear the Yankees would ask for more. Instead Gillick mentioned Dan Pasqua and Don Mattingly, two prospects he knew the Yankees didn't want to surrender. Finally, George Steinbrenner stepped in and called Gillick, telling him that he would

have to take McGriff as the third player in the deal or there wouldn't be one. Gillick coyly said that he needed to check with his scouts and would call back in 15 minutes. When he did so, he got the player he wanted.[8]

In 1983 the Blue Jays won 89 games with a deep and strong club, winning 89 games the next season as well. In 1985 the Blue Jays broke through with a 99-62 record to win the highly competitive AL East and the franchise's first division title. To bolster the bullpen, Gillick again took advantage of an unconventional source. For a few years in the 1980s, teams that lost a free agent (as the Blue Jays had lost Cliff Johnson) could select from a pool of players made available by teams that signed free agents. As compensation for losing Johnson, the Jays had selected Tom Henke, a young, hard-throwing relief pitcher who had yet to break through with the Rangers. Promoted late in the season, Henke ended the year with 13 saves, blowing just one, and an ERA of 2.03. In the 1985 American League Championship Series against Kansas City, the first year the Series expanded from best of five to best of seven, Toronto won three of the first four games. Then the offense went cold, and Kansas City prevailed in seven games.

After the season, Bobby Cox jumped to the Braves, and Gillick promoted third-base coach Jimy Williams, a natural choice. Otherwise Gillick returned almost the same team that fell one game short of the World Series. Over the next three years the Blue Jays won between 86 and 96 games, but never enough to win the division. During this period Gillick earned the moniker "Stand Pat" for his perceived reluctance to make trades or sign free agents to shake up his club. In fact, he did not make a single trade in 1988. Gillick was substantively inactive again before the 1989 season, but with the team at 9-16 on April 30, he finally made a deal, sending Barfield to the Yankees for left-handed pitcher Al Leiter.

Shortly thereafter, Gillick sacked Williams and promoted batting coach Cito Gaston. The team responded with a 77-49 record after the change, enough to win the division by two games. More significantly for the long-term future of the club, on June 5 the Blue Jays opened SkyDome (now Rogers Centre), the start of what was to become a baseball stadium boom in North America. Helped immeasurably by their new ballpark, over the next five years Toronto consistently ranked among baseball's top three teams in attendance.

Gillick remained creative and aggressive in landing future stars. In the 1989 amateur draft he selected

Washington State pitcher-first baseman John Olerud in the third round. As a sophomore in 1988, Olerud was named *Baseball America's* college player of the year. Before his junior season, however, Olerud underwent surgery for a brain aneurism, putting his future in doubt. Olerud played that spring but told scouts he would return to college for his senior season. Gillick selected him anyway, visiting him nine times before Olerud finally signed a contract. Along with a $300,000 bonus, Gillick agreed to start him in the major leagues.

For nine seasons, from 1983 to 1991, the Blue Jays had been remarkably consistent, winning at least 86 games every season and capturing three division titles. Gillick had integrated a number of young stars in this period, one or two at a time, while continuing to win. Eight years into the run of solid seasons, the team could still boast a core of players not yet past their prime: Bell, shortstop Tony Fernandez, Henke, McGriff, reliever Duane Ward, Olerud, lefty David Wells, and catcher Pat Borders. Now 54, Gillick had been running the Blue Jays front office for 14 years and had experienced some health issues. He told ownership he intended to retire in three years, imposing a personal deadline as well a franchise-based one on winning the division again.[9] Toronto became much more active on the trade and free-agent fronts.

Early in the 1990 winter meetings, Gillick traded outfielder Junior Felix to the Angels for 28-year-old Devon White, one of baseball's best defensive center fielders (a deal that also included several less notable players). Three days later, he made much larger headlines when he swapped McGriff and Fernandez, two of his best players, to San Diego for second baseman Roberto Alomar and left fielder Joe Carter. McGriff and Fernandez would be missed, but the 31-year-old Carter was a valuable run-producer and Alomar, the best player in the deal, was a great offensive and defensive player and still only 23. Olerud took over at first base and replaced McGriff's production, while Manny Lee shifted from second to shortstop to complete the infield.

In the 1991-92 offseason, Gillick made his first significant foray into the free-agent market, by signing 37-year-old Twins pitcher Jack Morris, a five-time All-Star fresh off a 10-inning shutout to win Game Seven of the World Series, and aging Angels slugger Dave Winfield. To reinforce their rotation for the 1992 stretch run, Gillick acquired free-agent-to-be David Cone for three players. Gillick later reflected on the trade: "One of the guys [we gave up] probably is a marginal Hall of Famer, Jeff Kent. We thought about it and said, 'David Cone is a guy we think can get us over the hump,' and at the same time a deal like that kind of deflates your competition."[10] The 1992 Blue Jays won 96 games and their fourth division title, before finally breaking through in the ALCS, then beating the Atlanta Braves in six games to give Canada its first-ever World Series championship.

Gillick's strategy of signing or dealing for short-term solutions worked because he had a young core to build around and the money to find new solutions when the old ones left or declined. After the 1992 season, Gillick was faced with just this problem when seven key Blue Jays became free agents: Jimmy Key, Cone, Henke, Winfield, Carter, Lee, and left fielder Candy Maldonado. Of the seven, Gillick re-signed only Carter.

Though he had entered the free-agent market a year earlier, Gillick did not compete for the best mid-career players because he would not offer contracts longer than three years. He had hoped to re-sign Key, but the pitcher inked a four-year deal with the Yankees. Cone took three years from the Royals but received a $9 million signing bonus that Gillick would not match.[11] Instead Gillick signed short-term players in their mid-30s, landing veterans Dave Stewart to bolster the pitching staff and Paul Molitor to replace Winfield at DH. The team also had a couple of prospects ready for regular roles: starting pitcher Pat Hentgen and third baseman Ed Sprague. The Toronto core, however, had gotten older.

Toronto's reliance on veteran players can be seen in the team's increasing payroll. After ranking 19th in 1991, the team jumped to the game's highest payroll in 1992, further increasing payroll the next year.[12] To Gillick's credit, the money was well spent; he and his scouts correctly identified veterans – particularly Winfield, Morris, Molitor, Stewart, and Carter – who still offered valuable production. In 1993 Gillick landed outfielder Rickey Henderson at midseason to solidify the outfield and leadoff spot of an already formidable team. The Blue Jays finished 95-67 to win the division easily, and then dispatched the White Sox and Phillies to capture their second world championship. Gillick reconfirmed after the World Series that 1994 would be his last season in Toronto.

After the 1995 season, Gillick joined the Orioles, a team managed by his friend Davey Johnson. Owner Peter Angelos offered a three-year contract for $2.4 million, one of the highest packages ever for a general manager. Moreover, Angelos promised Gillick complete freedom to run the baseball side of the organization. "He has all the leeway a general manager should have and probably more. I don't tell the GM who to get, or the manager who to play, he knows that."[13] Not everyone was convinced. "It's silly to believe that Angelos will simply sit back and watch Gillick run the operations without a few suggestions here and there," wrote sportswriter Bob Nightengale.[14] Angelos was also willing to spend money to build out a winning team.

The challenge ahead of Gillick was similar to that of his final years in Toronto: get into the playoffs by building on the team's revenue advantage and solid talent base. Like in his later stops, Gillick did not bring an entourage with him; he evaluated the front-office staff just as he did his players and came to recognize that many were sound baseball men.

Gillick inherited a team with several excellent players, including first baseman Rafael Palmeiro, shortstop Cal Ripken Jr., catcher Chris Hoiles, outfielders Bobby Bonilla and Brady Anderson, and pitchers Mike Mussina and Scott Erickson. The team's two biggest major-league deficiencies were at second and third base and the balance of its pitching staff, without much potential help from a farm system ranked 24th of 28 teams by *Baseball America*.

Gillick filled many of these holes quickly and effectively, while still holding to the three-year contract limit he had used in Toronto. He signed free agents Robbie Alomar, his old Toronto standout, to play second, and Milwaukee veteran B.J. Surhoff to play third. To shore up the bullpen, he signed Randy Myers, and Roger McDowell.[15] Finally, to make up for the loss of departing free-agent hurler Kevin Brown, Gillick traded young outfielder Curtis Goodwin to the Reds for David Wells, another ex-Blue Jay.

Although many of these moves worked out quite well, the Orioles were playing just .500 ball in late July 1996, and Gillick wanted to cash in a couple of his veterans for younger players. Angelos stepped in and vetoed a couple of trades, telling Gillick it was not a baseball decision but one that concerned his relationship with the city and the fans. Angelos's meddling clearly stung, but Gillick pivoted, now looking to bolster the club for the stretch run. Accordingly, he traded pitcher Kent Mercker to the Indians for aging but still effective DH Eddie Murray, and acquired slugging third baseman Todd Zeile, allowing Surhoff to fill a hole in left field. Gillick's biggest frustration was that he couldn't land a front-line starter.

Even without an additional ace, the team rebounded over the last two months of the season to finish 88-74, four games behind the Yankees but good enough to earn the AL's wild card. The Orioles overcame a mediocre rotation by slugging a then-record 257 home runs. They defeated defending AL champion Cleveland to reach their first league championship series in 14 years, before falling to the Yankees.

The Orioles were a good team, though every key regular other than Alomar and outfielder Jeff Hammonds was over 30. Gillick wanted to pursue younger players, but Angelos insisted that they not sacrifice the talent on the present team. The Orioles lost both Bonilla and Wells to free agency after the season, and Gillick responded by signing another of his old Toronto favorites, Jimmy Key, to replace Wells, and veteran Eric Davis to replace Bonilla. He also signed shortstop Mike Bordick, paving the path for Johnson to move Ripken to third base.[16] Gillick's moves generally played out well in 1997. The Orioles finished 98-64, the American League's best record. The team dispatched Seattle in the Division Series before falling to Cleveland in six games in the LCS.

Gillick also was caught between his owner and manager, who had been sparring for two years. Gillick reportedly brokered a truce, but an incensed Angelos accepted Johnson's resignation when he threatened to quit without an extension.[17] Angelos named pitching coach Ray Miller the new manager, and Gillick, finding himself as somewhat of a bystander in baseball matters, likely had no interest in staying beyond the remaining year of his own deal.

With his aging team, Gillick once again went back to the free-agent well for 1998, but this time his signings were over-the-hill veterans who did not produce. Thirty-year-old Roberto Alomar was the youngest player of the 11 Orioles who received 200 at-bats. The team fell to 79-83 in 1998 with the highest payroll in baseball, and after the season Gillick resigned. In his three years with the Orioles, he had performed the job he had been hired to do. Angelos wanted to postpone a rebuild so that his team could win, and Gillick put together a team that played in two consecutive Championship Series, their first postseason appearances since 1983.

Gillick spent the 1999 season outside of major-league baseball, enjoying what he called a "sabbatical."[18] But another team soon came calling. In Seattle, the Mariners had recently opened Safeco Field and wanted a proven GM to give the city a winning ballclub. Gillick accepted the GM job and was given an expanded budget to restock with free agents.

One of Gillick's first chores, though, was to address the situation with his franchise's all-time greatest player. In November 1999 Ken Griffey Jr. told Gillick and owner Howard Lincoln that he planned to leave as a free agent after the 2000 season and asked to be traded. Wanting to avoid potential disruption from a disgruntled superstar, the Mariners reluctantly agreed. As a so-called 10/5 player (a 10-year veteran, including five with his current team), Griffey had the right to approve any trade. When Griffey gave Gillick a list of only four teams to which he was willing to be dealt, the outfielder greatly hampered Gillick's leverage. He ended up trading Griffey to his hometown Reds for center fielder Mike Cameron, pitcher Brett Tomko, and two minor leaguers. Of the four, only Cameron, who turned in four excellent seasons in Seattle, proved a valuable addition.

In Seattle Gillick fished a new river, signing Japanese relief pitcher Kaz Sasaki in December 1999. A few days later, he secured one of baseball's best left-handed relievers, Arthur Rhodes, with a four-year deal, one of the few times he inked a contract longer than three years.[19] Gillick bolstered his starting staff by adding free agent Aaron Sele. Turning to the offense, Gillick landed one of his favorites, first baseman John Olerud. He also signed infielder-outfielder Mark McLemore, a veteran with much-needed on-base skills. Finally, the club signed utility outfielder Stan Javier to bolster the bench. The team rebounded to 91 wins and returned to the playoffs, where they beat the White Sox in the Division Series before losing the ALCS to the Yankees.

Gillick's second offseason in Seattle might have been even more dramatic than his first. The overriding story, once again, was the disposition of a Mariners superstar, this time free-agent shortstop Alex Rodriguez. Though the Mariners hoped to keep him, the Texas Rangers landed Rodriguez with a 10-year, $252 million contract, well beyond the terms of any previous baseball contract. Meanwhile, Gillick turned back to Japan, signing Ichiro Suzuki, major-league baseball's first Japanese position player. In December Gillick reinforced his bullpen by signing skilled setup man Jeff Nelson and improved the infield by inking veteran second baseman Bret Boone. The Mariners exploded out of the gate in 2001 and finished with 116 wins, setting the AL single-season wins record and tying the 1906 Chicago Cubs' major-league record. In the playoffs, the Mariners squeaked by the Indians three games

to two in the Division Series, before falling once again to the Yankees in the ALCS, a disappointing end to a historic season.

The 2001 Mariners dramatically highlight how free agency could be used as a tool for assembling a team. Of their 18 most significant players, only Edgar Martinez and Bret Boone (who was traded away and later re-signed as a free agent) were products of the Mariners farm system. Just seven of these players were on the roster during the 1999 season. Gillick signed nine free agents during the two subsequent offseasons. Several other players were acquired as an indirect result of free agency, in the forced trades of Randy Johnson and Griffey.

One of the pitfalls of this approach is that free-market players are generally nearing or past age 30, since they must have accrued six years of service time. For that reason, they often need to be replaced quickly, requiring either a productive farm system or continually guessing correctly in a risky marketplace. Gillick lost his magic touch during the 2001-02 offseason. He acquired three players to shore up his three weakest offensive positions, but none of them made an impact. Even with an aging squad and a less than stellar offseason, the Mariners were 60-36 on July 18 with a four-game lead in the division. But in the end the Mariners fell back to 93 wins and a third-place finish. Gillick still believed he could deliver a title to Seattle and re-upped with the team for one more year at the helm. The team again won 93 games but fell short of the playoffs.

Though Gillick hoped to rebuild the farm system during his years in Seattle, that goal was secondary to delivering a title. He was hampered by the loss of draft choices from his free-agent signings, another pitfall of relying heavily on free agency during an era with an onerous draft-choice penalty for signing free agents. In fact, the Mariners had only one first-round draft choice during his four years at the helm and failed to sign him (John Mayberry Jr.). Gillick's scouts remained active internationally, and the team landed four impact players (career WAR over 10) for the minor-league system during Gillick's tenure.

In November 2005 Phillies President Dave Montgomery turned to Gillick to reprise his success in Baltimore and Seattle: get a team with a new stadium and high expectations deep into the playoffs. The Phillies possessed several young stars who had recently graduated from the team's farm system, most notably slugging first baseman Ryan Howard, second baseman Chase Utley, shortstop Jimmy Rollins, left fielder Pat Burrell, and pitcher Brett Myers. "My challenge," Gillick said, "is to try and coax five more wins out of this team and get us into the playoffs. Once you get into the playoffs, anything can happen."[20] Gillick often reacquired players he had on previous clubs, and that offseason his two most productive signings were Arthur Rhodes and Ryan Franklin, players he had at earlier stops.

The 2006 season started disappointingly. Despite the call-up of future ace Cole Hamels in May, the team was below .500 in July, and Gillick looked to shake up the team. At the trading deadline he swapped star right fielder Bobby Abreu along with pitcher Cory Lidle to the New York Yankees for four players, none of whom ever panned out. But Gillick felt dealing Abreu opened up some payroll flexibility and transformed the team's leadership.[21] Several weeks later he swapped a couple of nondescript minor leaguers for another old favorite, veteran hurler Jamie Moyer. Mainly because the team began playing up to its talent level, the Phillies rebounded over the second half to win 85 games.

After the season Gillick used some of the money freed up from the Abreu trade to sign several free agents, most of whom performed below expectations. In his most successful move, Gillick signed free-agent outfielder Jayson Werth, who had been injured for a year and a half. The team rebounded from its disappointing 2006 season due mainly to the development of its young position players. It was enough to win 89 games and, thanks to a collapse by the New York Mets in late September, the NL East title.

After the Phillies were swept in the Division Series, Gillick went back to work. He traded a package of players to Houston for closer Brad Lidge, allowing the Phillies to return Myers to the starting rotation. Lidge responded with a historic season, saving 41 games in 41 save opportunities with an ERA of 1.95. The team also benefited from several lesser moves. Free agent signing J.C. Romero proved a reliable lefty specialist out of the bullpen. Another free agent, third baseman Pedro Feliz, wasn't great but a marked improvement over the 2007 hot-corner contingent. At midseason Gillick acquired pitcher Joe Blanton, who provided solid rotation depth down the stretch and in the playoffs.

The 2008 squad won 92 games, just three more than it had in 2007. But it was enough: The team won 13 of its last 16 to capture the division by three games. In the postseason, the Phillies won each series, losing only one game in each round, beating the Brewers, the Dodgers, and ultimately the Tampa Bay Rays in the World Series.

With his three-year contract up after 2008 and his third world championship, Gillick decided it was time to retire. He was 71 years old and had succeeded with a fourth organization, fully validating his credentials as a master team builder. Gillick's extraordinary success as an executive can be credited in part to his adventurousness, to his willingness to discover new ways of finding players. His exploitation of the Rule 5 draft remains unprecedented, and likely led to teams being much more careful about whom they left unprotected. His inroads into the Dominican Republic in the 1980s changed the game, as one look at the All-Star rosters and league leaderboards can attest. His acquisition of Japanese stars in Seattle, especially Ichiro Suzuki, ended any misconceptions Americans might have had about the talent there.

Over Gillick's outstanding career as a baseball executive, a career that would be recognized in 2011 by induction into the Hall of Fame, he built one World Series champion from the ground up while at his other three stops he overcame a different challenge: taking talented but flawed teams deep into the playoffs. Both undertakings required him to call on many of the same qualities: managing people, judging talent, and expanding his "many rivers" philosophy in finding players.

NOTES

1   Frank Fitzpatrick, "The Education of Pat Gillick," *Philadelphia Inquirer*, July 22, 2011: C1, C5.

2   Philippe van Rjndt and Patrick Blednick, *Fungo Blues: An Uncontrolled Look at the Toronto Blue Jays* (Toronto: Seal, 1985), 196.

3   Terry Pluto, *The Curse of Rocky Colavito: A Loving Look at a Thirty-Year Slump* (New York: Fireside, 1995), 262.

4   Pat Gillick, interview with Levitt, October 2, 2012.

5   William Plummer, "Baseball Scout Epy Guerrero Looks for Rough Diamonds Amid Hunger and Poverty," *People*, April 10, 1989; Jim Sandoval, "Epy Guerrero: Super Scout," in Jim Sandoval and Bill Nowlin, eds., *Can He Play? A Look at Baseball Scouts and Their Profession* (Phoenix: SABR, 2011), 103.

6   *The Sporting News*, undated article in Peter Bavasi's Hall of Fame file.

7   Dave Stieb with Kevin Boland, *Tomorrow I'll Be Perfect* (Toronto: Doubleday, 1986), 27-32.

8   Gillick, interview.

9   Stephen Brunt, *Diamond Dreams: 20 Years of Blue Jays Baseball* (Toronto: McClelland and Stewart, 1987), 291-292.

10   Frank Fitzpatrick, "Before Hall, Gillick Talks of Phils," *Philadelphia Inquirer*, July 16, 2011: E4.

11   Tim Kurkjian, "The Blue Days," *Sports Illustrated*, July 11, 1994: 54-59.

12   Salary data from baseball-reference.com.

13   Bob Nightengale, "With Gillick at the Top, the Orioles Will
Be, Too," *The Sporting News*, December 11, 1995: 54.

14   Nightengale.

15   John Eisenberg, *From 33rd Street to Camden Yards: An Oral History of
the Baltimore Orioles* (New York: Contemporary Books, 2001), 455.

16   Gillick interview; Eisenberg, *From 33rd Street to Camden Yards*, 465-466.

17   *The Sporting News*, November 10, 1997: 38; Eisenberg,
From 33rd Street to Camden Yards, 473-477.

18   Joe Strauss, "Murray, O's Chat," *Baltimore Sun*, October 26, 1999: D1, D4.

19   Jon Wells, *Shipwrecked: A Peoples' History of the Seattle
Mariners* (Kenmore, Washington: Epicenter, 2012), 141.

20   Zack Zolecki, "Complex Challenges Already Awaiting Phils' General
Manager," *Philadelphia Inquirer*, November 3, 2005: E1, E10.

21   Pat Hagen, "In Gillick, Phils Made Hall of a Choice,"
Philadelphia Daily News, July 22, 2011: 80, 82.

MANAGER

CITO GASTON

By Alfonso L Tusa C

Clarence "Cito" Gaston was a National League out-fielder from 1967 to 1978. At his best, he was an All-Star in 1970. He also made a vivid impression on the fans in Venezuela, where he won two batting titles in winter ball. However, Gaston attained much greater fame and respect as a manager. He became the first Black skipper to lead his team to the playoffs and then to win a World Series. His Toronto Blue Jays won back-to-back championships in 1992 and 1993. "Cerebral, dignified, and tolerant" describe this imposing man's best qualities as a leader.[1]

Clarence Edwin Gaston was born in San Antonio, Texas, on March 17, 1944.[2] His parents were Sammy Gaston and Gertrude Coley.[3] Gaston spent his early years in the small city of Seguin, Texas, about 36 miles northeast of San Antonio, and at least one story states that he was born there rather than in San Antonio, his generally accepted birthplace.[4] Clarence had five sisters. Cito's friend of nearly five decades, Johnny Cardona Sr., said that Gertrude was remarried, to a man named Collins, when her son was young. Cardona recalled that Sammy moved to Oklahoma.

It's quite possible that Gaston inherited some of his ability. Negro Leagues legend Ted "Double Duty" Radcliffe, from Mobile, Alabama, which has a long record as a hotbed of Black baseball talent, said in his biography:

"You know who else lived in our neighborhood? Cito Gaston's daddy. We used to call him 'Big Boy' 'cause he was a big heavyset fella — he could hit!"[5]

Radcliffe's collaborator, author Kyle McNary, states in another of his books that Gaston's father was a Negro Leaguer.[6] However, references for the "major" Negro Leagues do not show either a Gaston or a Collins who fits the bill. Whichever man it might have been, his experience may have come in a local circuit, the South Texas Negro League.

Cito was raised by a truck driver. Gertrude was a homemaker and at times a waitress. A San Antonio sports scribe wrote, "Religion was a big part of the Gaston family's life. His grandfather was a Baptist minister and the Gastons often attended church twice on Sundays."[7]

Young Clarence had ambitions of being either a truck driver, a singer, or a major-league baseball player.[8] Said another San Antonio sportswriter, "Some remember Gaston as a backyard preacher, the kid who always took the pulpit when the neighborhood children would gather to play church. Others remember him as a garbage man, who would trade his work gloves for a baseball."[9]

At some point in his teens, Gaston acquired his nickname from a neighborhood friend in San Antonio. In a May 2002 online chat with Toronto fans, he said it came when he was 14, but earlier stories suggest

that it was a few years later as he began to play amateur ball. At any rate, the man responsible was Carlos Thompson, who later became a police detective in San Antonio. He thought Gaston resembled a Mexican wrestler whose stage name was Cito.[10]

Gaston grew up in both San Antonio and Corpus Christi. He attended Wheatley High School in San Antonio for a year.[11] After that he went to both Holy Cross High in San Antonio and Solomon-Coles High in Corpus Christi, and sources are split as to where he actually graduated.[12] However, it is clear that he was a three-sport star: baseball, basketball, and football. At Solomon-Coles, he was a pitcher. After graduating, "he returned to San Antonio, married and went to work on the midnight-to-dawn shift parking cars at a downtown garage."[13]

In 1961 the young man joined the Cardona Welders baseball team in San Antonio. Local businessman Johnny Cardona Sr. sponsored this amateur squad from 1954 to 1984. "There were some Anglos, a couple of black guys, and the rest were Mexican," said Cardona. Among other opponents, the Welders faced South Texas Negro League teams such as the San Antonio Black Sox, from the East Side, the city's traditionally African-American area. "When he first played for us, he was barefooted," Cardona told Richard Oliver of the *San Antonio Express-News* in 2006. "He showed up and nobody paid much attention to him. He went up there and hit the ball all the way out there in deep center field. I bought him his first pair of spikes, and the rest is history."[14]

More recently Cardona said, "The deal was, you bring your spikes and glove, we furnish the uniform and everything else. But Cito didn't have the spikes. I told him I'm gonna make an exception, I'm gonna call the sporting goods store. The owner, Rudy, he said, 'Since when in the hell are you buying the guys spikes?' I said, 'Just this one, Rudy — don't tell anyone else!'"

Gaston worked for the San Antonio sanitation department in 1963. "I don't regret that nine months," Gaston told a sportswriter. "The work puts muscle on you."[15]

The Milwaukee Braves signed Gaston as an amateur free agent on March 22, 1964. George Vecsey of the *New York Times* told the story in 1989, as did Richard Oliver. Scouting legend Al LaMacchia, then with the Braves, stopped by Olmos Field in San Antonio to watch a Welders game. LaMacchia — later Cito's colleague for many years in Toronto — recalled, "Great build on him, wiry and strong. First thing he

did was to chase a ball in deep center field, so I knew he could catch. Then he fired a strike so I knew he could throw. Then he beat out a groundball, so I knew he could run. And then he hit a home run, so I knew he had power." The stories went on to recount how LaMacchia beat out Houston scout Andy Andrews; the bottom line was that Gertrude said, "Sign the contract, Clarence."[16]

The young outfielder made his pro debut in 1964 with the Binghamton Triplets of the New York-Penn League (Class A), playing 11 games there before being sent to the Greenville Braves in the Class-A Western Carolinas League, where he batted .230 in 49 games. In 1965, with the West Palm Beach Braves of the Class-A Florida State League, Gaston suffered growing pains: .188 with 9 RBIs in 70 games. He was still bothered by a cracked shinbone that had gone undiagnosed during the 1964 season.[17]

In 1966 Gaston joined the Batavia Trojans in the Class-A New York-Pennsylvania League and enjoyed much better success, leading the league in homers (28) and RBIs (104) while batting .330. He was selected to the league's all-star team and was voted the league's player with the brightest professional future.[18] At the end of the season he played four games for the Austin Braves of the Double-A Texas League.

Back with Austin in 1967 after a stint in the Arizona Instructional League, Gaston had a good year (.305-10-70) with some standout moments. On June 12 he ended a scoreless pitching duel between Wally Wolf (El Paso) and Joe Cisterna (Austin) with a bases-loaded single in the ninth inning. On August 28 Gaston smacked a solo homer over the right-field wall to break a 2-2 tie with Amarillo. That earned him a cup of coffee with the Atlanta Braves in September. He pinch-ran for Tito Francona in his debut on September 14, flied out in his first, at-bat off Chicago's Rich Nye, two days later, and tripled off Nelson Briles on September 24 for his first big-league hit. In nine games, he went 3 for 25 (.120). The young man got a special mentor as roommate: Hank Aaron, whom he credited with teaching him "how to be a man; how to stand on my own."[19]

After that performance Gaston headed south to play with Cardenales de Lara of the Venezuelan Winter League in the 1967-68 season. Perhaps he had difficulty adjusting to the city of Barquisimeto, or was homesick, or the league was beyond his capabilities. He played in just 31 games, with a modest batting line of .254-0-3. The Cardenales released him. In the mid-1980s, Gaston returned to the Cardenales as a batting instructor. He declared to journalist Rodolfo Mauriello that Lara's management didn't give him the chance to recover back in '67-68.

Gaston started the 1968 spring with the Richmond Braves in the Triple-A International League. After 21 games (.239-2-8), he was sent down to Double-A Shreveport in the Texas League (.279-6-57 in 96 games).

That winter Cito's career took a great step forward thanks to Rodolfo Mauriello. Then general manager of another Venezuelan team, Navegantes del Magallanes, Mauriello offered Gaston a contract. Gaston replied that he'd had a hard time with Lara the previous season. Mauriello told him not to worry about that because he now had one more year of experience.

With Magallanes Gaston led the league in hitting (.383) and RBIs (64). His 11 home runs ranked second behind Brant Alyea's 17. In Venezuela many people still remember a weekend "a la Gaston." On December 8, 1968, the Navigators played the Caracas Lions. Cito won an exciting 13-inning game with a homer to the center-field bleachers. The next day, Magallanes played the La Guaira Sharks starting at 11 A.M. Again the game went to extra innings, as Gaston tied it with a bad-hop single over the head of his future teammate in San Diego, Enzo Hernández. He then won it in the 11th with a single to center.

The league's talent level was high, as evidenced by the long roll call of major leaguers who took part in those two games alone. Rollie Fingers, Mike Epstein, Bo Belinsky, Walt Hriniak, and Pat Kelly were some of the Americans, while the homegrown stars included César Tovar and Vic Davalillo.

The duo of Gaston and Kelly had special significance in Venezuela. According to a historian of Latin American baseball, "[They] became the first members of the Poder Negro — Black Power — era of the Magallanes team: African American import players who hit for power. Venezuelan sportswriters coined the term 'Poder Negro' after the incident at the Mexico City Olympics in 1968 when Tommie Smith and John Carlos raised black-gloved fists."[20] Carlos Tovar Bracho, a Venezuelan sportscaster, described Gaston and Kelly as a Black version of Batman and Robin.

Gaston was taken by the San Diego Padres from Atlanta in the 1968 expansion draft, their last of 30 picks. In the spring of 1969, *Sports Illustrated* noted, "Their most exciting player may be a rookie named Clarence Gaston, a centerfielder with speed and power."[21] In his first complete major-league season, Gaston played in 129 games. However, in 391 at-bats, he hit just .230 with 2 home runs and 28 RBIs. The

rookie was a very free swinger, especially for that era, striking out 117 times.

Gaston returned to Venezuela in October to play with Magallanes in the winter of 1969-70, but had to leave the team on December 20 because of a knee injury. However, he had enough at-bats (161 in 43 games) to win his second Venezuelan batting title, with an average of .360. His 8 doubles, 3 triples, and 7 home runs made him the leader in slugging at .578.

In 1970 Gaston enjoyed easily his best big-league season with the Padres. He played for the National League in the All-Star Game, going 0-for-2 with a walk. In 146 games, he hit 29 homers, drove in 93 runs, and batted .318. In addition to Hank Aaron, Gaston credited several men for his emergence. Richie Allen provided moral support, Billy Williams advised him to switch to a lighter bat, and San Diego batting coach Bob Skinner bolstered his confidence and adjusted his swing. Finally, Padres manager Preston Gómez stuck with him through nagging injuries and bad times during his rookie year.[22] Much of the success came from within, though — Cito had learned about pitchers and learned how to relax.[23]

Gaston returned to play 35 games with Magallanes in the winter of 1970-71, but did not approach his former peaks (.260-3-27). Then he did not sustain his fine form with the Padres in 1971. He played in 141 games, but slumped badly to .228 in 518 at-bats. His power numbers declined to 17 homers (including two solo shots on May 4 in a 3-2 win over Atlanta) and 61 RBIs. Another notable moment came on June 16, as he got the only hit off Bill Stoneman at Montreal's Jarry Park. Stoneman told *Baseball Digest* in 2005 that he regarded this outing as "The Game I'll Never Forget" — even over his two no-hitters.[24]

In 1970 Cito had shown at least some patience at the plate, walking a career-high 41 times to go with 142 K's. In '71, however, he drew just 24 passes and whiffed 121 times. On August 10 San Diego obtained speedy center fielder Johnny Jeter from Pittsburgh, viewing Gaston in turn as trade bait. However, the Padres wound up not dealing Gaston away that winter, which he again spent with Magallanes (.299-1-16 in 25 games).

During the spring of 1972, Jeter became the starter in center, and Gaston shifted to right. He would remain a corner outfielder for the rest of his career, seldom playing in center again. In 111 games, while his batting average picked up to .269, he dropped off further to 7 homers and 44 RBIs in 379 at-bats. One of those homers, off hard-throwing Don Gullett, provided

Toronto manager Cito Gaston in conversation with umpire in Atlanta during 1992 World Series.

the game's only run as San Diego beat Cincinnati on September 15.

Johnny Jeter was a bust, and the Padres traded him to the Chicago White Sox. However, the team's first-round draft pick in the 1971 secondary-phase draft, Johnny Grubb, was ready to take over center field in 1973. Gaston — who, as his 1973 baseball card noted, had "been plagued by injuries the past two seasons" — remained in right. He enjoyed a fairly decent season (.250-16-57 in 133 games).

The Padres made some more moves that winter. They picked up veteran first baseman Willie McCovey from the Giants and added Bobby Tolan from the Reds, who got most of the time in right. More than anything, though, Dave Winfield blossomed as the full-time left fielder. Gaston became the fourth out-fielder (.213-6-33 in 106 games).

That November, San Diego dealt Gaston back to the Atlanta organization for reliever Danny Frisella. In 1975 he played in 64 games for the Braves (.241-6-15). Then, in the winter of 1975-76, at age 31, he reappeared in Venezuela to play with Magallanes. It was a successful winter (.296-5-31 in 60 games).

Gaston remained with Atlanta in 1976. He remained a reserve, although he felt he was still capable of making a greater contribution.[25] In 134 at-bats (69

games), he posted his best average in years (.291) to go with 4 home runs and 25 RBIs. On August 3, in a rare start at first base, he hit two homers and drove in five runs (a career high) off San Diego's Rich Folkers. It was the second time he'd connected twice in a game.

The 1976-1977 season was Gaston's last in Venezuela. With La Guaira, he appeared in 56 games (.262-4-38). He was taken as a reinforcement player by Magallanes to play in the 1977 Caribbean Series. Gaston joined a lineup that already had Dave Parker and Mitchell Page, the latest members of the Poder Negro tradition. He batted .300 with 4 RBIs in the Series (won by the Dominican team, the Licey Tigres). Gaston's career totals in Venezuela (seven seasons) were 31 homers, 207 RBIs, and a .307 batting average.

Gaston remained with the Braves in 1977 (.271-3-21 in 56 games) and most of 1978 (.229-1-9 in 60 games). On September 22, 1978, the Pittsburgh Pirates purchased his contract. With the Pirates at the tail end of that season, he was 1-for-2 in two games — which turned out to be his last in the majors. On October 11, Pittsburgh declined to offer Gaston a contract for the 1979 season.

Gaston decided to play for the Santo Domingo Azucareros in the short-lived Inter-American League, which featured many veteran big leaguers hanging on. Before the league folded in June, he played in 40 games (.324-1-14 in 148 at-bats). Then he left for the Mexican League to play for the León Bravos. There he appeared in 24 games (.337-1-8). In 1980 he returned to León and played in 48 games (.238-4-27). Gaston then retired as a player.

In 1981 Hank Aaron helped his friend find a spot with the Braves as their minor-league hitting instructor. "I had finished playing and Hank got me back in baseball," Gaston said. "He called me a couple times and asked me to come back as a coach. I said no. The third time he called, I said yes."[26]

The following year, 1982, Bobby Cox became manager of the Toronto Blue Jays after Ted Turner fired him in Atlanta, and took Gaston along as his batting coach. As the sixth-year expansion club matured into a winner, Gaston helped develop the likes of George Bell, Jesse Barfield, Lloyd Moseby, and Willie Upshaw. "He made a huge impression on journalists and baseball people as the rock of the clubhouse during two jittery pennant races in 1985 and 1987," the New York Times's George Vecsey wrote.[27]

Jimy Williams was fired on May 15, 1989, and Gaston stepped in as interim manager — the fourth Black man to manage in the majors. The organization had actually been considering him for a greater role for some time:

"Two springs ago, in the roiling wake of The Campanis Affair, Blue Jays General Manager Pat Gillick approached [Cito Gaston] and asked if he would be interested in managing," wrote a Los Angeles Times sportswriter. "Not the Blue Jays quite yet, but winter ball. It would be an apprenticeship, servicing both the Jays' belief that Gaston might make a useful manager someday amid baseball's fresh demand for minority candidates. No matter, Cito Gaston wasn't hot on the idea. His father was ill, his second marriage (with two children added to his own two) was just getting its sea legs and life as a coach wasn't at all intolerable. So he said no."[28]

Gillick was hoping to hire Lou Piniella but was unable to do so. After encouragement from his players and Sparky Anderson, Gaston took the job full-time. Toronto was 12-24 when he took over but went 77-49 the rest of the way, winning the AL's Eastern Division (but then losing in the playoffs to Oakland). George Vecsey's article from the end of the season that year contained some other intriguing quotes:

"I never thought I'd be a manager. But once it happened it's pretty much what I expected. The worst part is the questions from the press. When the games

start I relax." With regard to being a Black manager, he commented, "I don't get too emotional about it. To me, it doesn't matter what color you are. I only think about it when you guys bring it up."[29]

The Jays finished second in the AL East behind Boston in 1990. They recaptured the division in 1991, but lost the pennant to Minnesota. The next year, though, in late August David Cone joined a strong talent base including Joe Carter and Roberto Alomar. Toronto was prepared to move to a higher level. Their field leader was feeling better too. George Vecsey noted, "Gaston showed courage by coming back from back surgery after 1991, showing more energy and less pain. He rarely complained or lost his temper, becoming ever more of a yup-and-nope guy." That same article compared him to "strong and silent" types such as Gil Hodges and movie star Gary Cooper.[30]

The Blue Jays beat Oakland in the AL playoffs in 1992 and then won their first World Series on October 24 by defeating the Atlanta Braves in six games. The winning run in Game Six, an exciting 4-3, 11-inning affair, was driven in by Dave Winfield. The veteran was then in his 19th season, 18 years after his emergence in San Diego prompted Gaston's trade.

George Vecsey observed, "Gaston has been skewered by a few critics in Toronto, which is normal in these critical times. 'I don't know, I don't feel any animosity in my heart toward the media,' Gaston said. … He admitted he had been hurt by inscrutable managers when he was a decent outfielder in the '70s, and he has tried to be open with his players. 'In this game, you meet good people and you meet bad people,' Gaston said. 'I guess I learned that everybody has feelings.'"[31]

In 1993 Gaston and the Blue Jays again won the World Series. Joe Carter's memorable home run lifted the Jays over the Philadelphia Phillies in Game Six. He became the first manager to win two consecutive Series since Sparky Anderson did it with the Cincinnati Reds in 1975-1976.

Gaston continued managing Toronto until the 1997 season was almost finished. But he never had another winning record — he came under fire for not developing good relationships with younger players like John Olerud and Shawn Green, and he lost support in the press. His none-too-subtle hints that racism was a factor did not help his cause. (He followed with a qualified apology.)[32]

Gaston's total record as manager when he lost his job was 683-636. In July 1999 he became the fourth of nine men on the Blue Jays Level of Excellence, and his two World Series titles gained him entry into the Canadian Baseball Hall of Fame in 2002.

Gaston returned to the Jays as hitting coach for the 2000 and 2001 seasons. Yet while other teams had considered making him their manager, for over a decade he never landed another top job. Blue Jays President and CEO Paul Godfrey called it "the one big mystery in baseball, why this elegant, decent man had never been offered another job in baseball."[33] After the 1999 season, Gaston interviewed with the Indians and Brewers; the Angels were also interested, but he withdrew from consideration for family reasons.[34] He came closest in November 2003, when the White Sox chose Ozzie Guillén.

In recent years, Gaston has served, along with former Blue Jays pitcher Pat Hentgen, as a club ambassador and special assistant to Godfrey. He also made occasional appearances at spring training in Dunedin, Florida, as a guest coach. As of 2018 Gaston lived in nearby Oldsmar with his third wife, Linda, whom he married in 2003.[35] Gaston thought the baseball life was why his first marriage, to Lena Green, ended in divorce.[36] That union produced two daughters, Rochelle and Shawn. In the late '80s, Gaston married a Canadian woman named Denise; that marriage lasted into the early 2000s.

Gaston was inducted into the San Antonio Sports Hall of Fame in 2006. He appeared to be peacefully retired, golfing and traveling the world. According to a Toronto sportswriter, "He eventually started to turn down clubs that wanted him to interview for vacant jobs." The suspicion lurked that he was being used as a token candidate.[37] But life changed for Gaston on June 20, 2008.

Amid a slump that saw the team win just four out of 17 games, Blue Jays general manager J.P. Ricciardi fired manager John Gibbons. "We know we've got a better team than this," Ricciardi said. "Right now, we just needed something to spark us, and I think Cito is the right guy for that." He cited Gaston's experience, respect, and credibility. Gaston observed that he didn't know the hitters as well as he did the last time Toronto called on him — but overall, he said, "I don't think the game has changed."[38] The Jays responded with a 51-37 record after Gaston's return, and late in the 2008 season Toronto gave him a two-year contract extension. In October 2009, he announced that his last season would be the upcoming one. After the 2010 season Gaston retired, left the dugout, and took a front-office consultant's post. He worked through 2015, and then retired from that position as well.

Perhaps his fondest memory? "The 1989 team was one of the most fun teams that I have ever managed," Gaston said. "I took over from Jimy and we came back to win the division. That was a team that could manufacture runs anytime we wanted to. All of the teams that I've had, you have to adapt as a manager and go from there."[39]

Perhaps the best expression of Gaston's even-keeled approach to baseball and life goes back to his earliest days as manager. As he told George Vecsey in 1989, "I don't mind if the guys laugh after we lose. They've got to get themselves ready for the next day. The same when we win. Enjoy it, but you can't take it with you. You've got to start again tomorrow."[40]

SOURCES

In addition to the sources cited in the Notes, the author also consulted Venezuelan newspapers and magazines *El Nacional, El Universal, Meridiano,* and *Sport Gráfico,* as well as baseball-reference.com, baseballlibrary.com, and retrosheet.org.

Gutierrez, Daniel, Efraim Alvarez, and Daniel Gutierrez. *La Enciclopedia del Béisbol en Venezuela. Tomo II* (Caracas, Venezuela: Fondo Editorial Cárdenas Lares, 1997).

Additional research by Rory Costello and Maxwell Kates. Thanks to Johnny Cardona Sr. for his memories.

NOTES

1   George Vecsey, "One Baseball Man Who Got His Chance," *New York Times,* September 24, 1989.

2   *2010 Toronto Blue Jays Media Guide.*

3   Harold Scherwitz, "S.A.'s 'Cito' Gaston Hopes to Make San Diego a Winner," *San Antonio Light,* January 17, 1971: 5-D.

4   "Braves Think They've Got Star in San Antonio's Cito Gaston," *San Antonio Light,* October 2, 1966: 62.

5   Kyle McNary, *Ted "Double Duty" Radcliffe: 36 Years of Pitching & Catching in Baseball's Negro Leagues* (Minneapolis: McNary Publishing, 1994).

6   Kyle McNary, *Black Baseball: A History of African-Americans & The National Game* (New York: Sterling Publishing Company, Inc., 2006), 68.

7   Tim Griffin, "Cito Gaston: Laid-back Perfection," *San Antonio Express-News,* March 20, 1994: 1C.

8   Walter Leavy, "Cito Gaston: On Top of the Baseball World," *Ebony,* May 1, 1994.

9   Harry Page, "From Sandlot, to SkyDome: Gaston's Family, Friends Will Watch Series Closely," *San Antonio Express-News,* October 17, 1992: 14D.

10   Various citations, including Scherwitz; Gib Twyman, "Gaston Makes Another Name for Himself: Champ," *Kansas City Star,* October 26, 1992: C2; John Matthew IV, "Fans Chat with Cito Gaston," mlb.com, May 7, 2002. See also Richard Oliver, "Long Journey Home," *San Antonio Express-News,* February 12, 2006: 1C. To confuse matters further, at least two stories suggest that the nickname arose in Venezuelan winter ball. See Page, "From Sandlot, to SkyDome"; Frank Hyland, "Next Black Manager? Cito Gaston," *Atlanta Journal-Constitution,* June 5, 1988: D-24.

11   Page, "From Sandlot, to SkyDome."

12 Harry Page, "Gaston Graduated from Coles," *San Antonio Express-News*, October 25, 1992.

13 "Braves Think They've Got Star in San Antonio's Cito Gaston."

14 Richard Oliver, "Long Journey Home."

15 "Braves Think They've Got Star in San Antonio's Cito Gaston."

16 See both George Vecsey and Richard Oliver.

17 "Braves Think They've Got Star in San Antonio's Cito Gaston"; Scherwitz.

18 "Braves Think They've Got Star in San Antonio's Cito Gaston."

19 Walter Leavy.

20 Milton H. Jamail, *Venezuelan Bust, Baseball Boom: Andres Reiner and Scouting on the New Frontier* (Lincoln: University of Nebraska Press, 2008), 27.

21 William, Leggett, Mark Mulvoy, Peter Carry, and Roy Blount, "Old Saws Over a New Mays," *Sports Illustrated*, April 14, 1969.

22 Paul Cour, "Gaston Credits Tutors for His Swatting Rise," *The Sporting News*, March 27, 1971: 42.

23 "Gaston Concentrates on Pitchers' Styles," *San Antonio Light*, August 5, 1970: 50.

24 Al Doyle, "Bill Stoneman: The Game I'll Never Forget," *Baseball Digest*, June 1, 2005.

25 Wayne Minshew, "Braves' Gaston Eager to Shed Pinch-Hitter Tag," *The Sporting News*, August 28, 1976: 11.

26 Murray Chass, "Blue Jays Utilize a Strength Within," *New York Times*, June 6, 1989.

27 George Vecsey, "One Baseball Man Who Got His Chance."

28 Tim Layden, "Cito Gaston Is Getting Job Done as Toronto Manager," *Los Angeles Times*, June 18, 1989: 4.

29 George Vecsey, "One Baseball Man Who Got His Chance."

30 George Vecsey, "Cito Gaston Is a Baseball Man Who Finally Got His Chance," *New York Times*, October 26, 1992.

31 Vecsey, "Cito Gaston Is a Baseball Man Who Finally Got His Chance."

32 John Harper, "Jays' Gaston Stirs Racism Flap," *New York Daily News*, April 18, 1997; "Toronto's Gaston Apologizes," *New York Times*, April 18, 1997.

33 Dave Feschuk, "A Triumphant Renaissance for Cito Gaston," *Toronto Star*, September 27, 2008.

34 Teddy Greenstein, "Williams, Gaston Reportedly Discuss White Sox Vacancy," *Chicago Tribune*, October 1, 2003.

35 Dave Feschuk.

36 "Blue Jays Fire Williams, Look for a Manager," *Los Angeles Times*, May 16, 1989.

37 Allan Ryan, "Gaston Still Questions Past Rejections," *Toronto Star*, June 22, 2008.

38 Jordan Bastian, "Gibbons Out; Gaston Returns to Jays," toronto.bluejays.mlb.com, June 20, 2008.

39 Murray McCormick, "Cito Gaston Left His Mark on Baseball and Blue Jays," *Regina Leader-Post*, April 21, 2017. https://leaderpost.com/baseball/cito-gaston-left-his-mark-on-baseball-and-blue-jays.

40 Vecsey, "One Baseball Man Who Got His Chance."

COACHING STAFF

BOB BAILOR

By Rory Costello

A shortstop by trade, Bob Bailor could also play the outfield quite well. In fact, he played every position but first base and catcher during his 11 big-league seasons. Bob Murphy, the late New York Mets radio announcer, said, "He's not a heavy hitter, but he is a tough competitor." Like Rex Hudler and Joe McEwing in more recent years, Bailor was a throwback type, a gritty, hustling blue-collar player. He chewed tobacco and loved hunting and fishing. His all-out style led to injuries – but it endeared him to several managers. "I had to work to be average," he said in 1988. "I don't think I was overly talented. I worked hard, and it's probably why I hung on as long as I did. The ability to play all those positions helped too."[1]

At bat, Bailor choked up and held his hands slightly apart like Ty Cobb. He hit just nine home runs in 954 games, but his career average was .264 and he was a tough man to strike out, fanning in only five percent of his plate appearances in the majors. He liked to swing at the first pitch, though, so he also walked just six percent of the time. This and a suspect shoulder (not to mention the team's tremendous depth) were among the reasons the Baltimore Orioles left him exposed in the 1976 expansion draft.[2] The first original Blue Jay was a fan favorite in Toronto, managed in their minor-league system, and became first-base coach on the back-to-back World Series champions of 1992-93.

Robert Michael Bailor was born on July 10, 1951, in Connellsville, Pennsylvania. This small town is in Fayette County, amid the Appalachian Mountains, a little less than 60 miles southeast of Pittsburgh. At one time, in the early twentieth century, Connellsville boasted wealth from coal and coke, but after the boom ended it wasn't easy to make ends meet there. In 1977 Canadian columnist Earl McRae wrote a vivid feature about Bailor and his roots. Bob's father, Robert Joseph Bailor, made his living as an engineer for the Chesapeake & Ohio Railroad, hauling coal, iron ore, and limestone. He was a third-generation railroad man whose grandfather had come from Poland; the family name was originally Bialkowski. McRae wrote, "It's a fact and a proud one that most of the men in town,

like Bob Bailor's father, wear blue shirts and carry lunch pails. Most of their women, like Bob Bailor's mother Agnes [née Bunch], wear aprons and carry pots and pans."[3]

Bob was one of six children. He had three younger brothers (James, William, and David) plus two sisters (Christine and Mary Beth).[4]

"There were plenty of opportunities to fish and hunt around Connellsville," Bailor told Jim Kaplan of *Sports Illustrated* in 1978. "I started doing both when I was five. The legal hunting age is 12 in Pennsylvania, but I cut it a few years."[5] Yet he started playing baseball even earlier. As his father told Earl McRae, "When

Bob Bailor, Toronto's first pick in the 1976 expansion draft, was first-base coach for the 1992 championship team.

Bob was hardly able to walk, he wanted me to go out in the snow and play catch with him."[6]

As one might expect, Bailor (whose childhood nickname was "Buzz") was a Pittsburgh Pirates fan as a boy. His favorite player was Roberto Clemente. In August 1963, Connellsville won the Pennsylvania state Little League title. In the final game against Levittown, Bob scored the game's only run.[7] "After we won the state championship, we played in the Eastern Regionals in New York," he said in 2010. "We went on a plane, and we saw a Pirate game at the Polo Grounds." He recalled correctly that it was the last season for the old stadium, and that the home team was one of his future clubs, the Mets.[8]

Oddly enough, Bailor did not play high school baseball. In part because of the area's chilly spring weather, Connellsville High did not have a team, and neither did the school he wound up attending, Geibel Catholic High, also in Connellsville. Like his father, Bob was short and wiry. Nonetheless, he played halfback on a town football team and was a good basketball player, too. At least as late as 2016 (the last public mention available), he still held Geibel's school record for most points in a game (47).[9]

Tom Sankovich, who started the Connellsville High baseball program in 1971, said, "There was so much talent, probably the most talent that Connellsville had in baseball was between 1960 and 1970 and none of those kids played high school baseball because Connellsville didn't field a high school team." He added, "There was a great baseball tradition in Connellsville because of the American Legion team and Little League baseball. The Little League had a bunch of old-time guys coaching that had no kids playing and they coached the kids to play the right way. They were teaching them fundamentals and they had great discipline."[10]

"The American Legion competition was real good," said Bailor in 2010. "That was the only baseball going at that time in that area. A couple of years we went to the Legion state championship and got close, but could never get over the hump."[11] One of his teammates was Bob Galasso, who pitched in the majors in 1977, 1979, and 1981. Another was a slugging first baseman named Jim Braxton, who became best known as O.J. Simpson's blocking back with the Buffalo Bills in the NFL.

After graduating, Bailor considered going to Gannon College in Erie, Pennsylvania, as a basketball player.[12] He wound up enrolling in California State College – not any of the campuses in the Golden State's system, but rather the school in California, Pennsylvania, near Pittsburgh. One reason he went to college was to escape going to Vietnam, because he had a low draft number.[13]

In August 1969, however, the Baltimore Orioles signed Bailor as a free agent. "I think I probably only weighed 140 pounds back then," he explained. "I never got drafted – there were a couple of other guys on our Legion team that got drafted. Herman Welsh was the Legion coach and he probably played a big role in me getting signed. A scout for the Orioles, Jocko Collins, offered me a contract."[14] Collins, who also signed Bob Galasso for the Orioles that year, was able to get Bailor a modest $1,500 bonus. The teenager bought himself a 1964 Plymouth Valiant.[15]

In the summer of 1970, Bailor reported to his first minor-league club: Bluefield, West Virginia in the Appalachian Rookie League. It was about 250 miles straight down Interstate 79 from Connellsville. In 46 games he batted .273 with no homers and eight RBIs. He also pitched in one game, allowing eight earned runs in just one inning.

From 1971 through 1973, Bailor made steady progress through the lower levels of Baltimore's chain. In 1971 he won the batting title in the Class-A Northern League, hitting .340 with two homers and 50 RBIs in just 68 games for the Aberdeen Pheasants. In 1972, he was a California League All-Star with Lodi (.290-2-34 and a league-leading 63 steals in 129 games). In 1973, moving up to Double-A Asheville, he was a Southern League All-Star. He hit .293-0-29 in 115 games and was chosen as the league's best hustler.[16] He made it up to Triple-A Rochester for 17 games at the end of that season. In November 1973, the *Baltimore Sun* highlighted him as one of the organization's 12 standout prospects.[17]

When that story came out, Bailor was getting his first experience of baseball overseas, as he went to play with Magallanes of the Venezuelan Winter League. It was a successful time, as he batted .318 in 54 games. On a sad note, though, Bailor watched on New Year's Day 1974 as his roommate, pitcher Mark Weems, went for a swim but was swept out to sea and drowned. For three days, Bailor, pitcher Don Hood, and Ray Miller (then a player-coach for Rochester) searched for the body so they could send it back to the Weems family for burial. "It made me realize how fragile life really is," Bailor told Earl McRae.[18]

Bailor's progress stalled at Rochester in 1974. He played in just 96 games and batted only .230-1-25. "Due to injuries and the play of [Tim] Nordbrook,

Bailor was installed in center field upon his return."[19] He returned to Magallanes that winter, batting .267-0-12 in 60 games. In spring training 1975, he battled for a roster spot in Baltimore with Doug DeCinces. DeCinces stayed, playing all four infield positions that year, while Bailor went back to Rochester. Baltimore skipper Earl Weaver said, "His ticket to the major leagues is his wheels."

"We were kind of backed up when I started progressing through the farm system," Bailor said in 2010. "I played the infield—all the infield positions—but they had Brooks Robinson and Mark Belanger and Bobby Grich, so Earl Weaver asked me to go out in the outfield and they had Don Buford, Paul Blair and all these Gold Glove outfielders, so it was tough. But you just had to keep grinding and try to make a name for yourself."[20] In addition to Belanger, a perennial Gold Glover, and Nordbrook, the Orioles had another major-league shortstop in their very deep system then, Kiko Garcia.

Bailor added that the veteran O's "were all real good with the young guys. There was none of that looking over your shoulder – they went out of their way to help you. To this day Brooks Robinson is probably the best guy I ever played with as far as personality and helping and doing all the right things."[21]

At Rochester in 1975, Bailor hit .293-5-39 in 129 games, although he missed some time with a leg that became infected after a severe bruise.[22] He was an International League All-Star, ranking among the circuit's leaders in hits (147), triples (6), and stolen bases (21). The Orioles called him up in September. He got into five games and went 1-for-7.

That winter, he was enjoying the hunting at home when he got a call on New Year's Day 1976 to replace Yankees second baseman Willie Randolph with Magallanes. Bailor played in just six games, as he developed a sore shoulder from playing second, an unfamiliar position, after rushing back into action. Despite his inflamed rotator cuff, he made Baltimore's Opening Day roster, but he got into only one game in April. "[He was] unable to play the field. . .Frustrated by doctors' inability to fix his throwing arm, Bailor requested to come down to Rochester, where he could at least DH. He joined the club in early June but had to wait for a roster spot to open."[23]

Once he finally returned to action, Bailor hit .311-1-12 in 36 games for the Red Wings. The Orioles recalled him in September, and after pinch-running seven times, he went 2-for-6 as the DH in the last game of the season. A little over a month later, on November 5, the Toronto Blue Jays made him their first pick in the 1976 expansion draft. Toronto general manager Peter Bavasi called him, "the best shortstop available" and added, "We've checked him out thoroughly and the shoulder's fine."

"It was a big break," Bailor recalled in 2010. "When the expansion draft came, it worked out perfect for me—granted we didn't have good teams in Toronto early, but it gave me some exposure as far as other ball teams."[24] He also liked all the opportunities to fish and hunt in Ontario and elsewhere in Canada.

Bailor's 1977 rookie season was his best in the majors. He played 122 games, mainly at shortstop and in center field, although he missed a month with torn knee ligaments. The injury came as he stole third base at Anaheim Stadium on August 21; he was carried off on a stretcher. In 1988, Bailor recalled that the doctors told him he could continue his career until the knee gave out. He said, "I'm surprised it lasted as long as it did."[25]

Bailor finished the season hitting .310, best among all big-league rookies that year and still a record for expansion teams. That July, he said, "When I was leading the league for a while earlier in the season, I cut the averages out of the paper because I figured I'd never be ahead of Rod Carew again."[26] His five homers accounted for more than half his career total in the majors. The first of them came on April 16 at old Comiskey Park off Steve Stone of the Chicago White Sox. He struck out just 26 times (while drawing only 17 walks). Dennis Leonard of the Kansas City Royals said, "I struck him out five times on really tough pitches, sliders that were low and away. He rarely goes after a bad pitch. He's an intelligent hitter, a good, scrappy player."[27] The Toronto baseball writers named him the Blue Jays' player of the year.

In 1978 Bailor posted a .264-1-52 batting line in a career-high 154 games and 676 plate appearances. He was playing primarily right field, because Toronto installed Luis Gómez at short, but also saw much action at third base and in center. The next year, however, still playing mainly right field, he slumped to .229-1-38 in 130 games. By that time, young Alfredo Griffin was Toronto's shortstop.

Things weren't much better for Bailor in 1980 (.236-1-16 in 116 games). He missed nearly a month in June and July after suffering a broken wrist while hit by a pitch in an exhibition game against Toronto's top farm club, Syracuse. That August, Bailor made three relief pitching appearances for the Jays, all in games where they were trailing by several runs. The first two

WE ARE, WE CAN, WE WILL

outings were scoreless, but he failed to retire a batter in the last and wound up with a 7.71 ERA.

In 2010, Bailor said, "I think the big reason Toronto took me in the expansion draft was because I could play everywhere. I started out playing shortstop with them, but then when they started building the foundation and getting new players – well, then I'd move somewhere else – third base and second, centerfield, all over the place. Well, finally they got good and they traded me."[28] (It actually wasn't until 1983 that the Jays broke above .500, though.)

On December 12, 1980, the New York Mets obtained Bailor for pitcher Roy Lee Jackson. "It was kind of a shock to me," he said in 2010. "I lived in Manhattan and going there as a visiting player – you knew you were going to leave in three days, but coming from Connellsville and then living in New York City was kind of a shock."[29]

In his three seasons with the Mets, Bailor played mostly shortstop and second base, but he also filled in at third base and occasionally in the outfield. He missed the first three weeks of the 1981 season with a rib cage injury. During the remainder of that strike-interrupted season, he saw limited action (.284-0-8 in just 51 games and 95 plate appearances). However, he was an "irregular regular" in both 1982 (.277-0-31 in 110 games) and 1983 (.250-1-30 in 118 games). Bailor came up with a number of key late-inning plays while he was a Met. One memorable performance came at Riverfront Stadium in Cincinnati on August 23, 1981. He knocked in the winning run with a sacrifice fly in the 10th inning, then after moving to left field, ended the game with a leaping, over-the shoulder catch of George Foster's long drive.

George Bamberger, who managed the Mets in 1982, loved Bailor. That August Bamberger said, "Who on this club could be having a better year than him? I'd have to say he's the most valuable player on the club at this moment. He's just done so much.... He can do so many things." Teammate Hubie Brooks, then a second-year player, said of his fellow infielder, "A lot of times when I'm not sure of something, I go to him." Bailor's versatility and "heady game" also won him praise from rival managers such as Pittsburgh's Chuck Tanner.[30]

Bailor told a self-deprecating anecdote about the anonymity of his time in New York. He kept two back covers from the *New York Post*. The first came after the highly popular Rusty Staub delivered another pinch-hit. The headline read, "Rusty does it again!"

Later, when Bailor had a key hit of his own in extra innings, the *Post* proclaimed, "Miracle at Shea!"[31]

Those were dark years for the Mets. Starting in 1983, however – especially with the midseason arrival of Keith Hernandez – one could sense that the club's fortunes were ascending. On December 8, 1983, Mets general manager Frank Cashen made one of his best rebuilding trades. He sent Bailor and lefty reliever Carlos Diaz (who was coming off a very effective season) to the Los Angeles Dodgers. In return, the Mets got another middle infielder named Ross Jones – but the key to the transaction was young pitcher Sid Fernandez. It is interesting to observe that Davey Johnson, whom the Mets had named their manager that October, wasn't crazy about the deal at first. In his book *Bats*, Johnson said, "[Cashen] traded two guys I could have used. . .for a pitcher who wasn't ready to play regularly in the spring. In the end it turned out for the best, but in the short run, it handicapped me."[32]

In 2010 Bailor joked, "I went from New York City to LA – I felt like Jed Clampett going out there. [Tom] Lasorda was good to play for – he let you do your own thing and had a lot of enthusiasm and kept you pumped up all the time."[33] Not long after the trade, Bailor remarked that he didn't like to be called a utilityman. "That makes it sound like I change light bulbs for a living," he said.[34] He had a chance to win the starting shortstop job for the Dodgers, but in spring training 1984, he dislocated his left shoulder diving for a ground ball. He did not come back until early May, went on the DL again in August, and got into just 65 games overall (.275-0-8).

Davey Johnson and Frank Cashen still liked Bailor. In *Bats*, a chronicle of the 1985 season, Johnson wrote that Cashen got excited because Dodgers GM Al Campanis had said that he was willing to make a deal. Johnson said, "Bailor would be the perfect right-handed bat. What do they want for him?" The asking price was a top prospect, though, and it turned the Mets off from dealing with Campanis.[35] In 1985, Bailor started the season on the DL again and landed there once more in June. He went .246-0-7 in 74 games, but he finally got a taste of the postseason as Los Angeles lost the NL Championship Series to the St. Louis Cardinals. He appeared in two games and was hitless in his only plate appearance.

As Bailor was fighting for a job in spring training 1986, his wife, Jamie, delivered their first child, Robert Michael Jr. There was talk that he would be traded to Philadelphia, and Bob said, "It couldn't have come at a worse time."[36] However, the Dodgers made him one of their final two cuts. Toronto then immediately approached him to be a player-coach for Syracuse. However, "Bailor rejected the offer because he wanted to spend time with his baby son and was comfortable with the knowledge that the Dodgers still owed him about $400,000 for 1986. Jays' personnel director Gordon Ash explained, 'Bob's a good baseball man and we've told him he could have a good future in our organization in some capacity.'"[37]

Bailor had begun thinking like a manager as he sat on the bench alongside Tommy Lasorda and helped Dodgers third-base coach Joey Amalfitano.[38] In 1987 he rejoined the Blue Jays organization, managing the Dunedin club in the Florida State League. "There he displayed the grasp of strategy, the leadership skills and the flair for teaching [Blue Jays executive Paul] Beeston had recognized so long before."[39]

He then spent four seasons as Syracuse's skipper. The Chiefs finished first in the International League in 1989 but lost the Governor's Cup playoff finals to the Richmond Braves. Of greater interest that year, though, was how close Bailor came to being manager of the big club. After Jimy Williams was fired in May, the *Buffalo News* wrote, "The Toronto Blue Jays' brass is said to be divided evenly between interim manager Cito Gaston and Syracuse manager Bob Bailor as the permanent replacement."[40] When Gaston's interim tag was removed, though, it came as a relief to Bailor because the speculation had ended.[41]

Toronto finally did bring the first Blue Jay back to the big leagues in November 1991, naming him first-base coach. When the club won the World Series for the first time in 1992, he said, "I've gone from walking in snow to walking in champagne," (a reference to Toronto's first game ever, played with snow on the Exhibition Stadium field).[42] That winter, the press called him a dark-horse candidate for the opening with the Texas Rangers, but that job went instead to Kevin Kennedy.

In subsequent years, the Toronto press noted that the Blue Jays had groomed Bailor as Gaston's eventual successor. He served as first-base coach through 1995; in June of that year, he was still described as a "manager-in-waiting."[43] The Blue Jays sacked all of Gaston's coaches after the season, though, and did not offer Bailor another job in the organization. He was still without a job in baseball in early 1996. He soon retired and didn't look back.

Bob and Jamie Bailor moved to Palm Harbor, Florida, near Tampa, where Bob continues to enjoy fishing and hunting. For several years in the '80s

and '90s, he and his brother Jim were commercial hunting guides in Colorado during the offseason. He maintained a house in Connellsville, where he lived throughout his playing career. In 2010 he said, "If it were up to me I would probably be in Connellsville fulltime." He also had a hunting cabin in Somerset County, Pennsylvania, which borders Fayette County on the east. When Fayette County inducted him as part of the second class in its Sports Hall of Fame that year, Bailor said, "It's a big thing for me. Being from there and growing up there and playing a lot of sports, this means a lot to me."[44]

Connellsville has continued to honor Bailor, as seen in April 2016, when he was on hand for the Opening Day of the Little League in which he had once starred.[45] Bailor was described as "still the same hometown guy."[46] The Connellsville Little League Board named the local field after him. He remarked, "I'm living proof a dream can come true."[47]

SOURCES

In addition to the sources cited in the Notes, the author consulted www.baseball-reference.com, www.retrosheet.org, www.findagrave.com, www.checkoutmycards.com, www.pelotabinaria.com.ve (Venezuelan statistics), and www.ultimatemets.com.

NOTES

1   Valerie Vecchio, "Bailor of Connellsville," *Syracuse Post-Standard*, February 5, 1988: B1.

2   Joseph G. Preston, *Major League Baseball in the 1970s* (Jefferson, North Carolina: McFarland & Co., 2004), 223.

3   Earl McRae, "Goodbye Connellsville," in McRae, *Requiem for Reggie, and Other Great Sports Stories* (Toronto, Ontario: Chimo Publishing, 1977). Available online at http://news.google.com/newspapers?id=hJAjAAAAIBAJ&sjid=fKEFAAAAIBA-J&pg=3786,3023995&dq=bailor+connellsville&hl=en

4   James Bailor obituary, June 12, 2012, legacy.com (https://www.legacy.com/us/obituaries/triblive-penn-hills/name/james-bailor-obituary?pid=176594157)

5   Jim Kaplan, "I'll Tell You What–This Guy Can Hit," *Sports Illustrated*, May 22, 1978.

6   McRae, "Goodbye Connellsville."

7   Associated Press, "Connellsville Cops State Title," August 11, 1963.

8   Jason Black, "Hall of Fame induction thrills Bailor." *Connellsville* (Pennsylvania) *Daily Courier*, June 23, 2010. On a side note, the team that defeated Connellsville in the regional final, Stratford, Connecticut, was national runner-up that year.

9   Jim Downey, "Connellsville Little League honors Bob Bailor," *Uniontown* (Pennsylvania) *Herald-Standard*, April 10, 2016.

10   George Von Benko, "Chemistry carried 1989 Connellsville baseball team," *Uniontown Herald-Standard*, April 5, 2011.

11   George Von Benko, "Bob Bailor: from Legion to Big Leagues," *Uniontown* (Pennsylvania) *Herald Standard*, June 24, 2010. This article formed the basis for Bailor's page on the Fayette County Sports Hall of Fame website (http://www.fayettecountysportshalloffame.com/2010/bailor.html)

WE ARE, WE CAN, WE WILL

12 Herschel Nissenson, Associated Press, "Bailor Is Written-In Candidate,"
," *Evening Standard* (Uniontown, Pennsylvania), July 1, 1977: 3.

13 McRae, "Goodbye Connellsville."

14 Von Benko, "Bob Bailor: from Legion to Big Leagues."

15 Bill Heufelder, "No Blue With Jays," *Pittsburgh Press*, June 29, 1977.

16 Associated Press, "Two Named Loop's Best," August 22, 1973.

17 Lou Hatter, "12 Oriole farm prospects stand out,"
Baltimore Sun, November 14, 1973: C3.

18 McRae, "Goodbye Connellsville."

19 Brian Bennett, *On a Silver Diamond: The Story of Rochester
Community Baseball from 1956-1996* (Scottsville, New
York: Triphammer Publishing, 1997), chapter 4.

20 Von Benko, "Bob Bailor: from Legion to Big Leagues."

21 Von Benko, "Bob Bailor: from Legion to Big Leagues."

22 Von Benko, "Bob Bailor: from Legion to Big Leagues."

23 Bennett, *On a Silver Diamond*, chapter 4.

24 Von Benko, "Bob Bailor: from Legion to Big Leagues."

25 Vecchio, "Bailor of Connellsville."

26 "League Top Hitter Needs Fans Votes."

27 Kaplan, "I'll Tell You What–This Guy Can Hit."

28 Von Benko, "Bob Bailor: from Legion to Big Leagues."

29 Von Benko, "Bob Bailor: from Legion to Big Leagues."

30 Steve Halvonik, "Mets' Best Player? Versatile Bob
Bailor," *Pittsburgh Press*, August 9, 1982: C-5.

31 Vecchio, "Bailor of Connellsville." Bob Elliott, "Bailor
doesn't hate Jays," *Toronto Sun*, June 30, 2010.

32 Davey Johnson and Peter Golenbock. *Bats*
(New York: G.P. Putnam, 1986), 37.

33 Von Benko, "Bob Bailor: from Legion to Big Leagues."

34 Gordon Edes, "Bailor May Become Dodger Shortstop, Campanis
Says," *Los Angeles Times*, December 17, 1983: OC-C1.

35 Johnson, *Bats*, 143.

36 "Proud Papa Has a New Worry," *Daily News of Los Angeles*, March 26, 1986.

37 "Jays sign Bailor to one-year deal," *Globe and
Mail* (Toronto), October 10, 1986.

38 Vecchio, "Bailor of Connellsville."

39 Jim Proudfoot, "Bailor surprised to be a Jay again,"
Toronto Star, March 11, 1992: C4.

40 Larry Felser, "Successor to Williams Divides Blue
Jay Brass," *Buffalo News*, May 15, 1989.

41 Neil MacCarl, "Gaston gets praise from losers in race
for job with Jays," *Toronto Star*, June 1, 1989.

42 Jim Henneman, "Jays' Bailor sees the best and worst of
times," *Baltimore Sun*, October 26, 1992: 3C.

43 Steve Milton, "Gaston hangs tough at Jays helm,"
Spectator (Hamilton, Ontario), June 28, 1995.

44 Black, "Hall of Fame induction thrills Bailor."

45 Downey, "Connellsville Little League honors Bob Bailor."

46 Jim Downey, "Bailor still the same hometown guy,"
Uniontown Herald-Standard, April 12, 2016.

47 "Class Notes," Geibel Family Newsletter, Fall 2016 (https://www.gei-
belcatholic.org/alumni/Documents/2016%20Fall%20Newsletter.pdf).

GALEN CISCO

By Les Masterson

Though Galen Cisco pitched in nearly 200 games over his seven-year major-league career, his athletic accomplishments were much more substantial and longer-lasting than that: He played in a Rose Bowl game as a young man, and was still helping major-league pitchers four decades later.

Galen Bernard Cisco was born on March 7, 1936, to Beryl and Esther Cisco in St. Marys, Ohio, a town of about 8,000 near the Indiana border, halfway between Dayton, Ohio, and Fort Wayne, Indiana. The Ciscos owned a farm, and Galen and his three brothers and one sister spent hours working in the family business. "We kind of had a really great family life," Cisco recalled. "We were brought up on the farm. ... Everyone had their chore and we all did the things that we needed to do growing up on the farm."[1]

When young Galen wasn't taking care of livestock, he squeezed in time playing sports, namely football and baseball. At Memorial High School in St. Marys, he played both sports. His football coach was Jack Bickel, who had been a running back at Miami (Ohio) University for Woody Hayes. Cisco recalled that many of the plays in the Memorial playbook were the same ones Hayes later ran at Ohio State.

Like most young Buckeyes, Cisco dreamed of playing for The Ohio State University. After graduating from high school in 1954, he enrolled at Ohio State with a major in education. Freshmen were not allowed to play on varsity teams in that era, so the pride of St. Marys spent a year practicing with the varsity. Once Cisco got the chance to play, he excelled in both sports. He sported a 12-2 collegiate pitching record and was named a third-team All-American in 1956. But he gained greater acclaim in football, as a running back and linebacker.

In his senior year Ohio State went to the Rose Bowl on New Year's Day 1958. Before a big game, many athletes focus strictly on the showdown, but that wasn't true for Cisco. Preparing for the biggest (and final) gridiron game of his college career, he made a life-changing decision. Coach Hayes told his players that anyone who was married could bring their wives

free to Pasadena to attend the Rose Bowl game. Cisco was engaged to his longtime girlfriend, Martha. With this Rose Bowl-colored carrot dangling over their heads, Galen and Martha decided there was no reason to wait until after the football season to tie the knot. "She married me and got a free trip to the Rose Bowl," Cisco recalled.

The 8-1 Buckeyes were a 21-point favorite over 7-3 Oregon, Cisco recounted, but the Ohio State offense just couldn't get started that day. Oregon gained more yards and collected more first downs than the favorites. Ohio State still prevailed, 10-7, thanks to a 34-yard field goal by Don Sutherin in the fourth quarter.

While some players suffered under Hayes' rough nature, Cisco enjoyed playing for him. "He was a very, very fundamentally-minded coach. He didn't get too fancy. He didn't pass a lot. He seemed to think that if

you take a few plays and play them better than anyone else, you're going to be successful," said Cisco. "He was a no-nonsense guy. He probably was one of the most prepared people I have ever been around."

Cisco's collegiate career was coming to an end in 1958, but he didn't need any help choosing which sport to pursue. He recalled that a few professional football teams called Hayes about the two-way star, but were told he was interested in throwing baseballs – not throwing tackles. "The closer I got to the latter years in college, I thought baseball would have more longevity than football. I had an opportunity to sign so I did," said Cisco.

Signed in 1958 by Red Sox scout Denny Galehouse, Cisco wasted no time hurling the horsehide in the minors. He pitched in 32 games for Corning of the Class-D New York-Pennsylvania League and Raleigh of the Class-B Carolina League that summer, with a composite record of 6-12.

Since he still was two quarters short of receiving his bachelor's degree, Cisco spent the 1958-59 off-season back in Columbus to finish his schooling, and Hayes hired him as the backfield coach for the fresh-man football team. He stayed in that position for four offseasons, coaching future NFL stars Paul Warfield and Matt Snell, among others.

While teaching young running backs how to find holes each autumn, Cisco spent his springs and sum-mers becoming a more accomplished pitcher. Along with brief 1959 stops in Raleigh and Allentown (Eastern), he won 15 games with a Midwest League-leading 2.23 ERA for Waterloo. The next year he fin-ished 3-7, but with a fine 2.93 ERA, for Minneapolis in the American Association, and joined the Seattle Rainiers of the Pacific Coast League in 1961.

Along with teammates Dick Radatz and Don Schwall, Cisco pitched for manager Johnny Pesky in Seattle. In his nine games with the Rainiers that year, Cisco finished 6-1, compiled a 1.54 ERA, and completed five of his starts. Cisco was clearly ready for the call, and he quickly followed his teammate Schwall to Boston.

The Red Sox team Cisco joined had suffered through a decade of mediocrity, and in 1961 Ted Williams no longer patrolled left field for the team. If fans hadn't attended games at the ballpark with the great Williams in the lineup, they surely stayed away from a team made up of unproven players like Carl Yastrzemski. "The product we put on the field was not that great," said Cisco. "It was a tough place to play. The writers there were tough."

Cisco's first game was a Fenway Park start on June 11, and he allowed five hits and five runs in 2⅓ innings against the Minnesota Twins. Six days later he won a start against the Washington Senators, but by mid-July he was out of the rotation. Cisco struggled with the second-division team (2-4, 6.71), but the Red Sox were excited about the future of their rotation with Schwall, Tracy Stallard, Bill Monbouquette, and Cisco. His former manager, Pesky, predicted that Cisco was "an-other Schwall," who won the Rookie of the Year in 1961.[2]

Schwall himself said that the Galen Cisco who pitched in Boston was not the same guy who was his teammate in the minors. "When he came up here, he got off to a bad start. Then he began to press. He wasn't pitching normally and as a result he didn't look like the pitcher he was when I was with him in Minneapolis and Seattle," Schwall told *The Sporting News* after the 1961 season.[3]

But Cisco showed great improvement in spring training before the 1962 season. In 28 innings he al-lowed only three earned runs for an 0.86 ERA, while scattering 23 hits. Shortly before Opening Day, Red Sox manager Pinky Higgins told the press, "Nobody can believe Cisco is the same guy who was with us for the last half of 1961."[4]

But Cisco's 1962 season with the Red Sox mirrored his struggles of the previous year. On July 27 Higgins even left him on the mound to allow 16 hits and 13 runs against the Senators, finally taking him out of the game in the sixth inning. Two relief appearances later, the Red Sox placed Cisco on waivers, and he was claimed by the New York Mets.

The right-handed pitcher went from a mediocre team to one of the worst in the history of baseball. "We had guys who couldn't hit the ball and didn't catch it," Cisco recalled. Cisco now played for Casey Stengel, a learning experience for the young pitcher. After splitting two decisions in September 1962, Cisco was 7-15, 4.34, in 51 games in 1963.

While in New York, "Ohio State" (Stengel's name for Cisco) started and relieved. Despite the team's fu-tility, he was able to discuss the art of pitching with teammates Roger Craig, Al Jackson, Don Rowe, Bob Miller, and Larry Bearnarth, all of whom later became pitching coaches in the major leagues. "I think every-body used to talk more [then] about the game than they did later. I'm talking about in the 1990s on. I think they talked about the game much more then," said Cisco.

While the team did not perform well, Cisco was likely the best pitcher on the 1964 Mets' staff. Pitching in the new Shea Stadium, the right-hander finished with a 3.62 ERA while going 6-19 for the still-hapless team. In that season Cisco's pitching forced a future Hall of Famer to try a new pitch.

Cisco came in in the 14th inning of the second game of a doubleheader against the San Francisco and proceeded to shut down the Giants. His mound opponent late in the game was Gaylord Perry, who was struggling to stay in the major leagues, but who would ultimately win 314 games and a plaque in Cooperstown. Perry was called into the game in the 13th inning, and he later acknowledged throwing his first spitball in this game. Cisco and Perry traded scoreless innings until Jimmy Davenport tripled in the winning run for the Giants in the 23rd inning.

Undeterred, Cisco came back in his next start and four-hit the world champion Los Angeles Dodgers, 8-0, in front of 55,000 fans at Shea. Cisco's performances made an impression on his manager. During the 1964 season, Stengel acknowledged that the Mets had debated in the spring whether to even keep Cisco on the roster. "Then he got a little bit better and a little bit better and a little bit better. Now he's about as good as anyone we have," Stengel told *The Sporting News*.[5]

The Cisco followed this fine season by limping to a 4-8 record and a 4.49 ERA in 1965. After the season, Cisco was sent to the minors, finishing his four-year Mets career with an 18-43 record and 4.04 ERA.

After starting the 1966 season with the Mets' Triple-A Jacksonville affiliate, in June Cisco was sold back to the Red Sox, and he finished the season with their Toronto club. Dick Williams, the Toronto manager, knew Cisco was only about 60 days of service time away from his pension, and wanted to help the soft-spoken Ohioan. For the season, Cisco finished 11-6 in 157 innings in his two International League stops.

Williams, who was named manager of the 1967 Red Sox, told Cisco he would try to get him his pension. "He told me if he had a chance he would give me a look or maybe bring me up even for two years the last 30 days when teams could expand the club," Cisco recalled. If he'd been hurting the team, Williams would have sent him down, but Williams stuck to his word in 1967 and gave him a shot. Cisco started the year with the Red Sox as a reliever. Looking back 40 years later, Cisco said the team didn't seem special at the start.

"I think we thought we had a pretty good club. What it boiled down to was what kind of pitching staff you had," said Cisco. "I don't think anybody expected us to do anything like (the 1967 Red Sox eventually) did." Cisco was used mostly in mop-up work. He pitched in 11 games and threw 22⅓ innings for the Impossible Dream team. But shortly after the All-Star break, the Red Sox saw an opportunity to improve their bench by picking up Norm Siebern, and sent Cisco to the minors to free up the roster spot.

A number of players chafed under the pressure of playing for Dick Williams, but not Cisco. "I learned a lot of baseball as a player from Dick," he said. "He was a no-nonsense guy. You didn't have to wonder what he was thinking about." In this regard, Cisco added, Williams was much like Woody Hayes. "He was honest with me always. I got along with him just fine."

For the remainder of the 1967 season, Cisco pitched for Pittsfield (0.82 ERA in 11 innings) and Toronto (2.08 ERA in 65 innings). He enjoyed a renaissance in 1968 for Louisville, the Red Sox' new International League affiliate. He led the league with a 2.21 ERA while winning 11 games for the Colonels, at one point throwing 22 consecutive scoreless innings.

After the season, Cisco was sold to the expansion Kansas City Royals, who would begin play the following spring. Unlike the Mets in 1962, though, the Royals were more mediocre than atrocious. "The Royals I think had a little bit better draft. The way the draft was set up I think the Royals had a little bit better advantage than the Mets," Cisco said, comparing the two expansion clubs.

Despite struggling with Omaha in the early season (5.00 ERA in 10 games), Cisco was called up by Kansas City in June and the Buckeye finished the season in the Royals' bullpen. Cisco finished with a 3.63 ERA, in what would be the last 22⅓ innings of his major-league playing career. He was 33 years old.

The following year Omaha hired Cisco as a player-coach. The plan was to work as the pitching coach, but to take to the mound if there were injuries or if the team was in dire need of an arm. He threw 76 innings and finished his final year as a player with a 2.49 ERA. Cisco also won his final six decisions, the longest winning streak in his pro career.

Just 35 years old, Cisco became the pitching coach for Bob Lemon in Kansas City in 1971. During his tenure with the Royals, he worked with such top-notch starters as Dennis Leonard, Steve Busby, and Paul Splittorff. All three credited Cisco for their successes. "I had been dropping too much on my slider and Galen got on me about throwing more over the top," Busby told *The Sporting News* in 1973, after the publication named him the American League Rookie Pitcher of the Year and a year before he won 20 games with the Royals. "I guess I was doing the same thing with my fastball. I know I felt better and threw better when I went back to the old way."[6]

Mound ace Leonard told *The Sporting News* in 1976, "When I struggled last season, Galen worked with me. He told me I was dropping down too much and everything I was throwing was flattening out. He worked with me for hours and hours."[7]

When Splittorff contemplated quitting in the minors, Cisco talked him out of it.

"I told him you're left-handed and your time will come when you're going to get a shot at the big leagues. You have spent three full years playing this game and you should give it one or two more years before retiring," Cisco told the young pitcher, who won 166 games in 15 major-league seasons.

Cisco was the pitching coach for the Royals' division championship teams in 1976-1978 before being let go when Whitey Herzog was fired after the 1979 season. The experienced pitching coach quickly found work; his old friend Dick Williams hired him to lead the pitchers in Montreal.

A few years later Cisco worked with Williams in San Diego. In 1987 the Toronto Blue Jays hired Cisco as their pitching coach, and within four years his staff included Jimmy Key, Dave Stieb, Todd Stottlemyre, and David Wells. Wells, not known for his love of management, appreciated Cisco's assistance. "Galen Cisco helped me a lot. He would help me correct little things if he saw me doing something wrong, and we would talk pitching," Wells said in 1990.[8]

Cisco led the Jays' pitchers during their world championship years of 1992-1993, the first team to win back-to-back World Series in 15 years. In addition to Key, Stieb, Stottlemyre, and Wells, pitchers who threw for him during those two years included Jack Morris, David Cone, Dave Stewart, Tom Henke, Duane Ward, and Mike Timlin. "I have to give (Pat) Gillick a lot of credit, and the scouting department," Cisco said. "After the first (championship), most teams would have stayed pretty much pat, but they brought in two or three key players. ... Without those players, I wonder if we would have won it back to back."

Toronto did not re-sign Cisco after the 1995 season, but the year wasn't all bad for the Ohio State graduate. He was inducted into OSU's Varsity Hall of Fame.

Two years later, Cisco accepted his final major-league job – pitching coach of the Philadelphia

Phillies under new manager Terry Francona, who later led the Red Sox to their first World Series championship in 86 years in 2004. After being let go by the Phillies, Cisco worked in the Blue Jays' minor-league system before retiring after 45 years in pro baseball.

Looking back on his successful career as a pitching coach, Cisco said he didn't have one favorite hurler. "I think that two starters had as good stuff as anybody: One was Dave Stieb and one was Steve Rogers," he said. The smartest pitcher? Busby. "He studied (hitters') weaknesses and was a student of pitching. If this guy stayed healthy, he would have been something," Cisco said of his former pupil, whose career was cut short by injuries.

Cisco pointed to Willie Blair as a pitcher of borderline talent stuck in Toronto's Triple-A farm club who really worked hard on his game. Blair won 60 games in the major leagues, including 16 for Detroit in 1997. "I don't know if I had a lot to do with it or not, but he went on and had some pretty good years," said Cisco modestly.

In 2006 he was enjoying retirement in Celina, Ohio, only a few miles from his hometown of St. Marys. St. Marys inaugurated the Galen Cisco Award to the Little League MVP. The award has been given since 1965 and was won by Galen's nephew, Ty, in 1980. The Cisco baseball legacy carried on. His sons, Galen Jr. and Jeff, both played minor-league ball, and his grandson, Mike Cisco, was a pitcher at South Carolina in 2006.

SOURCES

In addition to the sources cited in the Notes, the author also consulted:

Cataneo, David. *Casey Stengel: Baseball's "Old Professor"* (Nashville: Cumberland House, 2003).

Koppett, Leonard. *The New York Mets: The Whole Story* (New York: Macmillan, 1974).

Perry, Gaylord, and Bob Sudyk, *Me and the Spitter* (New York: Signet Books, 1974).

Editors of Total Baseball. *Total Mets* (Kingston, New York: Total Sports, 2000).

ohiostatebuckeyes.cstv.com/ (Ohio State University Athletic Department website).

ridertown.com (virtual St. Marys Ohio website).

NOTES

1   Author interview with Galen Cisco, April 25, 2006. Unless otherwise indicated, all quotations from Cisco come from this interview.

2   Hy Hurwitz, "Hub Hose Peg Kid Mound Comers to Pace '62 Climb," *The Sporting News*, January 24, 1962: 21.

3   Hy Hurwitz, "Schwall and Schilling Speed Big Rebuilding Program by Red Sox," *The Sporting News*, November 29, 1961: 45.

4   Hy Hurwitz, "Cisco Kid Rides to Rescue – Fills Bill on
     Hub Hill," *The Sporting News*, April 18, 1962: 24.

5   Barney Kremenko, "Cisco Kid Rides to Rescue; Hero of Met
     Mound Corps," *The Sporting News*, June 20, 1964: 18.

6   Sid Bordman, "Steve's Buzz Bomb Act Captures Tigers
     Again," *The Sporting News*, May 12, 1973: 12.

7   Sid Bordman, "'I Plan to Win 20,' Says Royals' Ace
     Leonard," *The Sporting News*, July 31, 1976: 13.

8   Neil McCarl, "In Role As Starter, All Is Well for
     Wells," *The Sporting News*, July 20, 1990: 9.

RICH HACKER

By David Vincent, with Sam Gazdziak

Rich Hacker worked in professional baseball for many years as a player, coach, manager, and scout. He had a brief stint in the majors as a shortstop for the Montreal Expos in 1971 but is best known as a coach for the St. Louis Cardinals and Toronto Blue Jays in the 1980s and '90s.

Richard Warren Hacker was born in Belleville, in southern Illinois, not far from St. Louis, on October 6, 1947, the first of three children of Paul Emil George Hacker and Dorothy Deane Ablett Hacker.

His sister Ruth Ann was born in 1950, and the third child, Jeanne Louise, was born in 1955. Paul's younger brother, Warren Hacker, pitched in the major leagues for the Chicago Cubs (1948-56), Cincinnati Reds (1957), Philadelphia Phillies (1957-58), and Chicago White Sox (1961).

Paul Hacker, the oldest of 11 children, attended school until the eighth grade, then stopped to work as an unpaid laborer on his parents' farm in Marissa, Illinois, a tiny village approximately 30 miles southeast of Belleville. Paul Hacker enlisted in the United States Marine Corps in World War II serving from 1943 to 1946 at the rank of MC Cpl. In civilian life, he worked as a molder for Autocrat Stove Foundry in New Athens, Illinois.

Paul Hacker and Dorothy Ablett, a native of West Frankfort, Illinois, were married in Belleville in 1946 then settled in New Athens. Dorothy Hacker worked for 26 years as a teller for New Athens State Bank and United Illinois Bank and also managed the New Athens Senior Center thrift store. She was prolific in her community service in New Athens. She was a charter member of the town's Historical Society and also served as a treasurer, choir member and soloist in the United Methodist Church while volunteering at the Senior Center.

Both Mr. and Mrs. Hacker were active in the New Athens Veterans of Foreign Wars organization.

Rich Hacker grew up in New Athens, attending school there. He played in the New Athens Khoury League (their version of Little League) from 1953 through 1960. He played baseball and basketball at New Athens High School from 1962 through 1965 and played American Legion ball in 1964. Hacker was part of a basketball team that went 26-2 in 1965 and won the Cahokia Conference title, even though the school had just 60 boys in its student body. Hacker averaged 14 points and 7 assists while hitting 54 percent of his field goals and 75 percent of his free throws.[1] New Athens High has one other major-league alumnus: Whitey Herzog.

The St. Louis Cardinals selected Hacker in June 1965 in the first-ever amateur draft held by major-league baseball. Hacker was selected in the 39th round, the 699th overall pick. Instead of signing with the Cardinals, he chose to go to college, attending Southern Illinois University in Carbondale. He played freshman basketball and one season of baseball (1967), playing for former major leaguer Joe Lutz. Hacker led the baseball team in hits (35) and doubles (6) and was named MVP of the Saluki Nine that played in the NCAA tournament.[2]

After his sophomore year in college, Hacker was picked by the New York Mets in the June 1967 draft in the eighth round, the 154th overall pick. He signed with the Mets, having been scouted by Charley Frey for the New Yorkers.

The Mets assigned the 6-foot-tall, 180-pound, right-handed Hacker to their short-season Northern League team in Mankato, Minnesota, where he led all league shortstops in fielding percentage while playing in 49 games of the 70-game season. The squad was managed by Buddy Peterson, who had played 13 major-league games at shortstop for the Chicago White Sox and Baltimore Orioles in the middle 1950s.

Hacker was promoted to Visalia in the California League for the 1968 season, and he played there for 1 1/2 seasons. In 1968 Hacker played 76 games for the last-place team and hit .224. The first home run of his professional career was a grand slam that broke a 3-3 tie and sparked an 11-8 Visalia win.[3] Among Hacker's teammates that season were future major leaguers Ken Singleton and Jerry Morales. Hacker started the 1969 season in Visalia but was promoted to Memphis of the Double-A Texas League in midseason. The team, featuring such players as Jim Bibby, won the East Division of the league. Hacker played in 27 games for Visalia and 34 for Memphis that season.

Hacker started the 1970 season with Memphis but went on the disabled list on May 2 after injuring his left knee on a ground ball up the middle. He turned to run toward the path of the ball and twisted his left knee, injuring the medial meniscus in the leg. He did not have surgery but was finished for the season. Hacker wore a brace and then strengthened the knee through therapy during the offseason. The injury canceled a promising season for Hacker as he had collected 14 hits in only 43 at-bats before getting hurt. He never ran as well again after the injury.

Hacker arrived at the Mets' spring training camp in 1971 with hopes of advancing higher in the minors. "I don't know that I'm ready for Triple A ball yet or not but I feel I've got a good chance of making it at Tidewater," he said.[4] He did make it to Triple A, but it was with a different team. Near the end of spring training, Hacker and outfielder Ron Swoboda were traded to the Montreal Expos for outfielder Don Hahn on March 31, 1971.

Hacker was assigned to Winnipeg of the Triple-A International League that season. He played 98 games for the Whips and was the primary shortstop on the squad, playing 94 games at the position. One other infielder on the squad was future major-league manager Jimy Williams. Hacker's typical strong fielding and weak hitting continued in his new organization, as he hit .236 for the season with Winnipeg but had the highest OPS (on-base average plus slugging average) of his career that season at .620.

Expos shortstop Bobby Wine was hurt in mid-June after punching a water cooler and breaking a bone in his wrist.[5] Hacker was called up to the Expos to replace him and made his major-league debut on July 2 by playing a doubleheader against the Philadelphia Phillies at Jarry Park in Montreal. In the first game, Hacker hit eighth and went 0-for-3 against Rick Wise, who threw a complete game while being charged with the loss. Hacker struck out in his first at-bat and later lined out and grounded out.

In the second game of the twin bill, Hacker again played shortstop and batted eighth. After striking out in the second inning, he doubled to right field off Woodie Fryman and drove in a game-tying run for his first major-league run batted in. In the two games that day, Hacker collected two putouts and 10 assists and participated in one double play.

"I didn't even know the kid's name," Fryman said about Hacker's hit after the game. "I tried to jam him with a fastball, and he got the bat on it somehow."[6]

The next day Hacker again started against the Phillies and collected his second hit, a single to left field in the seventh inning off Bucky Brandon. On July 4 Hacker played in the finale of the series, again batting eighth. In the eighth inning, he walked with two out and scored his first big-league run two batters later, on a single to left by Ron Hunt.

Hacker traveled with the Expos to New York to play the Mets at Shea Stadium. He started both games of a doubleheader on July 5, going 0-for-6 with four strikeouts. He was removed from the second game in the middle of the fifth inning as part of a double switch. Bobby Wine returned to the lineup on July 6 and, with no reason to keep Hacker in the big leagues, he returned to Winnipeg to resume his minor-league career. To this point, Hacker had been a right-handed batter, but the Expos told him to learn how to hit left-handed to become more valuable to the team. He had collected two hits in 19 at-bats with the big-league team and walked only once, so it was thought that adding a switch-hitting capability might improve his offense.

The Expos recalled Hacker, now a switch-hitter, to the big leagues in September and he played on September 3 and 4 in Pittsburgh, entering both games as a late-inning replacement at shortstop. On September 6 he played the ninth inning against the Mets in Montreal. He had no plate appearances in those three games.

Hacker did not play again until September 21, when he started the first game of a doubleheader against the Phillies in Montreal. He went 0-for-2 with a walk before being removed for pinch-hitter John Bateman in the ninth inning with the team trailing 5-4. Hacker started the next day against the Phillies and collected his third major-league hit, a single to left off Rick Wise that drove in Ron Fairly from third. On September 23 he started against Philadelphia and was 0-for-2 before Fairly pinch-hit for him in the sixth inning.

The Expos traveled to St. Louis, in Hacker's home territory, to play a series against the Cardinals. He played in all three games, starting two, and collected his last big-league hit. On September 24 Expos manager Gene Mauch inserted Hacker into the lineup as part of a double switch in the ninth inning after the Expos had tied the game in the top of the frame. Hacker grounded out in the 10th inning and the Cardinals won the contest in the bottom of the inning on a grand slam by Joe Hague.

The next day Hacker started the game, walked in the fifth, and scored on a Stan Swanson pinch-hit home run off Jerry Reuss. Jim Fairey batted for Hacker in the sixth inning. In the last game of the series, on Sunday, September 26, Hacker started at shortstop and singled to left field to start the top of the ninth inning off Redbird hurler Dennis Higgins. In the fifth inning, Hacker made his only major-league error, on a groundball by Milt Ramirez, who eventually scored an unearned run on a single by Joe Torre. Hacker's miscue was one of four errors in the contest by the hapless Expos, who lost, 7-1.

The Expos finished the season with three games at home against the Cubs from September 28 through 30. Hacker played once that weekend, entering the game on the 29th in the top of the ninth as a defensive replacement. He struck out in the bottom of the frame in his last big-league plate appearance.

In December 1971 Hacker married Kathryn Louise Hunter, two years his junior, whom he had met in 1968 in California while playing for Visalia. She was living with her sister and working a summer job in the San Francisco Bay area. A mutual friend, a serviceman stationed at Treasure Island, a Navy base in San Francisco Bay, asked to go to Visalia to see Rich. The two men had played ball against each other in school. Rich and Kathryn reconnected two years later when she was attending Southern Illinois University and rooming with Rich's cousin.

Hacker's 1972 season got off to a scary start when he was hurt in an auto accident in Florida during spring training. He was driving to camp on February 29, 1972, when he stopped for a school bus ahead of him. A Greyhound bus, driving too close behind him, slammed into the back of his car. He walked away with nothing more than muscular soreness, but it was one more injury that showed him down when he needed a good spring to return to the majors.[7]

Hacker played two more seasons, 1972 and '73, with the Expos' Triple-A team in the International League. The club, now in Hampton, Virginia, was called the Peninsula Whips. Hacker played 209 games for Peninsula in those two seasons before ending his playing career (except for a brief encore in 1979).

In his brief major-league career Hacker collected four hits, including one double, in 33 at-bats for a .121 batting average. He walked three times while striking out in 12 plate appearances. His short career did not leave him disappointed or bitter about baseball. "My biggest thrill in the major leagues was just getting there," Hacker later said.[8]

For the next two seasons, Hacker was out of baseball. He worked as a purchasing agent for Allied Chemical and hated it.[9] When the plant closed, he went back to school at Southern Illinois University. Then, during the 1975 Christmas season, he was named the baseball coach at Southeastern Illinois College, a community college in Harrisburg, Illinois. Hacker coached there for three seasons (1976-78), and the school won a state championship in 1977. That club lost in a regional tournament and did not progress to the national tournament.

During the summers of 1977 and 1978, Hacker coached in the Alaskan Summer League. He worked with Mark Newman, who at the time was the pitching coach at Southern Illinois University in Carbondale and in 2010 was senior vice president of baseball operations for the New York Yankees. The Kenai Peninsula Oilers team that Hacker coached won the National Baseball Conference title in Wichita, Kansas, in 1977.

Rich and Kathryn celebrated the birth of their first child, Roger, in September 1977 while living in Harrisburg. Roger later worked for a few years in the public relations department of the Chicago Bears (NFL) before returning home to St. Louis.

In 1979 Rich was hired as a scout by the San Diego Padres. He spent some time in Houston scouting pitcher Mark Thurmond and signed him for the Padres. Thurmond had an eight-year major-league career, much of it as a reliever. Glenn Ezell, the manager of the Amarillo Gold Sox in the Texas League, suffered a heart attack in 1979, so the Pads sent Hacker there to help out as a coach. While there, he played six games – four at second base and two at third base. He collected two hits in 14 at-bats and walked twice. This was Hacker's last appearance as a professional player.

"This is not the kind of summer I'd envisioned," he said of his journey from player to college coach to scout to coach to player. "I'm down here staying at a Quality Inn with no transportation. I've got a boy 21 months old and a wife and I won't be home until September."[10]

Including that brief appearance in 1979, Hacker played all or parts of eight seasons in the minor leagues with a career .227 batting average. He appeared in 512 games, collecting 353 hits in 1,558 at-bats. Those hits included 36 doubles, 12 triples, and 5 homers. Although he was a shortstop he also played second base and third base and even caught a few games for Peninsula in 1973.

Hacker continued to scout for the Padres in 1980. In 1981 he was hired by the Toronto Blue Jays to scout. He also coached the Blue Jays' Gulf Coast League team in Bradenton, Florida, that summer. The league was made up mainly of teenagers from the Caribbean and was intended as a first experience in the United States for these young players. In June of that year, the Hackers celebrated the birth of their second son, Scott.

Hacker's hometown team, the St. Louis Cardinals, hired him as a minor-league manager in 1982. He was assigned to the Johnson City (Tennessee) Cardinals of the Rookie-level Appalachian League. The squad, which featured future major leaguers Vince Coleman, Mike Hartley, Stan Javier, and Terry Pendleton, finished with a 32-35 record, first in the Southern Division. Kevin Maris, son of Roger Maris, also played for Hacker for part of the campaign.

Hacker returned to Johnson City for the 1983 season to lead a team that saw 34 different players on the roster, none of whom ever played a major-league game. Hacker was the lone coach on the staff that summer for a team that finished with a 30-42 record, good for sixth place in the seven-team league. In September 1983, the Hackers welcomed their third

child into the family with the birth of Kathryn Ann, who is known as Katy.

Hacker was sent to Erie, Pennsylvania, for the 1984 season to manage the Cardinals' short-season A team in the New York-Penn League. This squad finished with a 43-31 record with three future big leaguers on the roster: Lance Johnson, Greg Mathews, and Craig Wilson.

In 1985 Hacker returned to Johnson City for his third campaign in the Appalachian League. This team finished the season in second place with a 39-29 record with four future major leaguers on the roster: Alex Cole, Tim Jones, Joe Magrane, and Steve Peters.

Hacker received his call to the majors for the second time in 1986, as he was named the first-base coach for St. Louis. This was the first of five years in which he was a member of Whitey Herzog's coaching staff in the Gateway City. The two had a shared history of being from New Athens, and Hacker could recall the excitement in the neighborhood when the major leaguer came back to town with bats and balls for the kids. Herzog flatly denied that the New Athens connection had anything to do with the spot on his coaching staff.

"I'll tell you one thing, I wouldn't have made a guy coach just because he comes from New Athens. Otherwise, I'd have brought the bartender in here. He was better to me than anyone else.

"Rich Hacker has a hell of a future in baseball. He was a smart player, a smart minor-league manager and a smart scout. Since I've had him in here, the players like him and respect him, and he's worked hard," Herzog said.[11]

This team compiled a 79-82 record and finished third in the National League East Division. In 1987 the Cardinals won 95 games to finish first in the division and beat the San Francisco Giants in the League Championship Series, thus earning Hacker his first trip to the World Series. The Minnesota Twins beat the Cardinals in seven games.

In 1988 Hacker returned to the first-base coaching box for the Cardinals, who could not repeat their performance of 1987, as they finished in fifth place in their division with a 76-86 record. Manager Herzog picked Hacker as a coach for the National League All-Star team, and thus appeared in the game played in Cincinnati.

After Nick Leyva, the Cardinals' third-base coach, was named the manager of the Philadelphia Phillies for the 1989 season, Hacker was switched by the Redbirds from first-base coach to third-base coach, a job he held for two seasons. The 1989 team won 86 games but finished third in the division behind the Chicago Cubs and New York Mets, while the 1990 squad won only 70 games and finished last. Herzog quit as the manager after 80 games in 1990. At the end of the season new skipper Joe Torre hired his own coaches for 1991 and Hacker was dropped. He was hired by the Toronto Blue Jays as their third-base coach in 1991 and the Jays won the American League East Division title but lost in the Championship Series to the Minnesota Twins, four games to one.

On September 7, 1992, the Jays lost a 12-inning contest in Kansas City, 5-4, but the big news that day for the Hacker clan was that Rich was ejected from a game for the only time in his major-league career. He objected to the strike zone as called by umpire Greg Kosc, and the arbiter excused Hacker for the rest of the contest.

In 1992 the Blue Jays won five more games than in the previous season to finish with a 96-66 record and repeat as division champs. They beat the Oakland Athletics in the League Championship Series and went on to play the Atlanta Braves in the World Series. The Jays beat the Braves in six games, thus earning Hacker his first World Series championship ring.

Hacker returned as third-base coach with the world champions in 1993, but this season was to prove a difficult one for the Hacker family. Toronto finished the first half on July 11 with a 49-40 record to lead their division. Manager Cito Gaston, as the skipper of the previous year's American League World Series team, managed the AL squad in the All-Star Game on July 13 and took his coaches with him to the game in Baltimore. However, Hacker decided to skip the exhibition and go home for the three-day break.

After flying to St. Louis, he was driving home in a borrowed van when he encountered two vehicles drag-racing across the Martin Luther King Bridge. One of the vehicles struck Hacker's vehicle head-on and he suffered a fractured right ankle and severe head injuries. Taken to the intensive-care unit at St. Louis University Hospital; Hacker was in a coma for a few days but eventually regained consciousness. When he woke, the last thing he remembered was taking his family to a science center in Baltimore. He had no memory of his accident, his job, or even the fact that he had spent most of his life in baseball. By bits and pieces his life gradually came back to him, and

he went through therapy at a rehabilitation center in St. Louis to put back his past. He even saw what was left of the van he was driving to try and remember anything further about the accident. "I don't see how anybody could have lived through that. I know how lucky I was," he said.[12]

The Blue Jays, who won the AL East again in 1993, invited Hacker to Toronto to throw out the ceremonial first pitch for a game during the World Series. The Jays won their second consecutive World Series title that season when Joe Carter hit a Series-ending home run in Game Six with Hacker on the bench instead of at his usual spot in the third-base coaching box. He didn't mind. "I've always been upbeat. There's nothing to be sorry about," he said.[13]

Hacker was replaced as the third-base coach for 1994 by Nick Leyva, who had been fired by the Phillies in 1991 and joined the Blue Jays. Leyva had filled in for Hacker during the second half of the 1993 season. Hacker was still a member of the coaching staff but held other off-field responsibilities due to the lingering effects of his injuries. His main task was to create hitting charts for opposing teams during games. In 1995 he was not rehired by Toronto. The next year Hacker rejoined the Padres as an area scout, a position he held until he retired at the end of 2003. He was responsible for scouting amateur players in the Northeastern states from New Jersey to Maine during this time.

In 2001, Hacker was elected to the Midwest Professional Baseball Scouts Association Hall of Fame for his long service to the profession. In 2005 he was elected to the Southeastern Illinois College Hall of Fame for his coaching accomplishments there in the 1970s.[14]

After his retirement from scouting, Hacker spent time enjoying his family and living in his hometown of Belleville, Illinois. He was also an avid bow hunter.

After battling leukemia for 15 months, Rich Hacker died on April 22, 2020, in Fairview Heights, Illinois.[15] He is buried in Oak Ridge Cemetery in New Athens.

SOURCES

David Vincent conducted multiple interviews with Rich Hacker over the years 1982-2010. He relied on Retrosheet.org for information obtainable from game logs and regarding trades, Baseball-Reference.com for minor-league statistics, additionally consulting the Southern Illinois College website.

Parts of this biography originally appeared in Rich Hacker's obituary on RIP Baseball (see Notes), written by Sam Gazdziak. Thanks to Adrian Fung for Hacker family history research.

NOTES

1   Bob Posen, "All-East Team is short, sweet," *St. Louis Post-Dispatch*, March 25, 1965: 70.

2   "Pavesich top hitter for Salukis," *Southern Illinoisan* (Carbondale), June 11, 1967: 10.

3   "Reno grabs third spot," *Times-Standard* (Eureka, California), July 11, 1968: 20.

4   Larry Odell, "Triple-A for Rich Hacker?" *Southern Illinoisan* (Carbondale), March 26, 1971: 12.

5   "Expos reactivate Wine," (Paterson, New Jersey) *News*, July 6, 1971: 15.

6   Dan Rosenburg, "McGinn stops Phillies but win streak is short-lived," *Montreal Star*, July 3, 1971: 32.

7   Ian MacDonald, "Expos' Hacker hurt in car crash," *Gazette* (Montreal), March 1, 1972: 11.

8   Norm Sanders, "Hacker keeps eye on budding Birds," *Belleville News-Democrat* (Belleville, Illinois), May 7, 1985: D2.

9   Rich Hacker interview with David Vincent, date unknown.

10   Dave Distel, "It's life on the farm for Padre minor leaguers," *Los Angeles Times*, August 10, 1979: 14.

11   Kevin Horrigan. "New Athens to St. Louis, the long way," *St. Louis Post-Dispatch*, March 13, 1986: 1D.

12   Brian Schmitz. "Hacker best Jays' comeback story," *Akron Beacon-Journal*, October 26, 1993: B3.

13   Schmitz.

14   "Hacker, Wahlig earn nice honor," *Belleville News-Democrat* (Belleville, Illinois), February 23, 2005: D2.

15   Sam Gazdziak. "Obituary: Rich Hacker (1947-2020)," RIP Baseball. https://ripbaseball.com/2020/04/27/obituary-rich-hacker-1947-2020/. Access November 25, 2021. It is reported that multiple newspapers stated his surname was pronounced HOCK-er and not HACK-er.

LARRY HISLE

By David E. Skelton

Consider the two nearly identical rookie seasons below:

	AB	R	H	2B	3B	HR	**RBI**	**AVG**
Player #1	464	59	127	22	5	20	68	.274
Player #2	482	75	128	23	5	20	56	.266

These highly acclaimed prospects started 18 years apart. Both were center fielders, blessed with power and speed. Player #1 was the runaway choice for National League Rookie of the Year and had one of the greatest careers in major-league history. Player #2 finished a distant fourth in the N.L. Rookie of the Year voting, suffered a "sophomore jinx" that nearly ended his career, rebounded with some excellent seasons, but was derailed by injury. Though they were playing for

different teams, Player #1 offered batting tips to Player #2 at one point during the latter's rookie season.[1] Player #1 is Hall of Famer Willie Mays – Player #2 is Larry Hisle.[2]

Hisle, an Ohio native, grew up playing sports alongside fellow major-league star Al Oliver. He was also a fine basketball player but passed up a possible NBA career to sign with the Philadelphia Phillies in 1965. His most productive seasons came more than a decade later for the Minnesota Twins and Milwaukee Brewers. He made two All-Star appearances and received Most Valuable Player consideration in two of his 14 major-league seasons. Yet, in the course of attaining this success, his career encountered various detours.

Larry Eugene Hisle (pronounced HY-sul) was born on May 5, 1947, in Portsmouth, Ohio. This municipality along the northern banks of the Ohio River has been home to other baseball notables such as Branch Rickey and Al Bridwell. Gene Tenace, who grew up and went to high school in nearby Lucasville, played American Legion ball in Portsmouth with Hisle and Oliver. Hisle's life echoes the nineteenth century rags-to-riches stories of Horatio Alger. After a childhood of want and pain, Hisle's determination and continued hard work eventually made him wealthy – though family and friendship were what made him happiest.

After baseball, Hisle's message of endurance has resonated. His memory of personal hardship and generous spirit have motivated him to help numerous children in need. This calls baseball's foremost legend to mind: Babe Ruth.

Larry Hisle was the only child of Hubert and Claudine Hisle. Claudine, a big baseball fan, named her son after Lawrence Eugene "Larry" Doby, the African-American baseball star who made his debut with the Cleveland Indians just two months later.[3] Alas, Larry lost both parents at an early age. When he was just 10 years old, his father suffered a devastating brain hemorrhage – "Jupiter" Hisle never again recognized his son (he eventually died in 1962).[4] Single mother Claudine struggled to keep basic utilities running. "We were on welfare and things were tough," Larry recalled in 1978. "We used to get checks around the fourth of each month and around the last week of the month things became extremely difficult."[5] Yet even though they were poor, Hisle called himself "the happiest kid on the planet" thanks to his mother. However, several months after her husband was stricken, Claudine Hisle died from a kidney infection – it was even more poignant because she hadn't been able to afford earlier treatment.[6]

Hisle lived for several years with his mother's sister and then was adopted by Orville Ferguson, a successful construction contractor, and his wife Kathleen. The foster parents "treated me better than any son could be treated."[7] Yet his mother had a lasting impact, instilling "a will to settle for nothing less than the absolute best that life had to offer."[8] Hisle channeled his grief by throwing himself into sports with a self-imposed goal of making his beloved mother proud. "I lived in a housing project adjacent to a park and I'd go out there every morning and practice," Hisle said. "When I'd begin to get tired and think of going home, I would ask myself, 'What would my mother do if she were in my shoes?' She would do her absolute best to be the best she could be. I'd stay out there and work harder."[9]

The hard work paid off handsomely; Hisle became a high school All-American in both baseball and basketball. He was also an honor student. Before long, colleges were furiously bidding for his talents, with some notable recruiters. NBA superstar Oscar Robertson called on behalf of the University of Cincinnati.[10] Hisle visited Ohio State University many times, meeting with the state's Governor, Jim Rhodes, plus Buckeye basketball greats John Havlicek and Jerry Lucas.[11]

Hisle signed a letter of intent with Ohio State – but the Phillies, led by scout Tony Lucadello, had also been pursuing him weekly. Lucadello later described what impressed him while scouting Hisle in an American Legion tournament game. "Portsmouth was playing in Athens on the diamond of Ohio University. . .Larry put three home runs out of the park, one to left that bounced off the gymnasium, one to center and a third to right. . .Larry's awesome display of power was like nothing I had ever witnessed."[12]

Lucadello – joined by Phillies owner Bob Carpenter, general manager John Quinn, and farm director Paul Owens – convinced Hisle that baseball was the way to go. A hefty signing bonus, reportedly in the $40,000-$60,000 range, got the young man

to sign with the Phillies in August 1965.[13] He had been chosen in the second round (38th pick overall) in the major leagues' first-ever amateur draft. Hisle attended Ohio State that fall (he eventually continued his education there during the baseball off-seasons) but was ineligible to play basketball.

By the following summer, the 19-year-old found himself nearly 1,000 miles away from home playing for the Huron (South Dakota) Phillies in the Northern League (short-season Class A). The schedule was short – 70 games – and curtailed even more by the discovery of Hisle's previously unknown spinal defect (which kept him out of military service). Still, a .433 batting average and .667 slugging percentage in 60 at-bats showed the Phillies why the large signing bonus was warranted.

Hisle started the following spring with the Tidewater (Virginia) Tides of the Carolina League (Class A). He got off to a strong start, with two home runs and four RBIs on April 19, and made the league's All-Star Game. He "topped the East [squad's] win with three straight hits and two RBIs before being lifted."[14] By season's end, Hisle ranked among the league leaders in every offensive category (including .302-23-78 in the major three). He fell just short of winning the Most Valuable Player award in what was reported to be the closest voting in the league's 22-year history to that point. The winner was his future teammate with both the Phillies and Brewers, Don Money (then a shortstop).

On December 15, 1967, the Phillies traded Jim Bunning, their mound ace and future Hall of Famer, to the Pittsburgh Pirates for a package of youngsters that included Money. Hisle and Money were considered key components in the parent team's future, even though they had played fewer than 500 pro games between them, and none above Single-A ball. The prospects, both just 20 years old, appeared destined for further minor-league development – but instead they both made the Phillies' starting lineup on Opening Day 1968. A strong spring, combined with nagging injuries to the Phillies' veteran shortstop and center fielder, contributed to this startling maneuver. Yet as manager Gene Mauch said, "I've got to see what [Hisle and Money] can do...They're exceptional young men, and exceptional young men do exceptional things."[15]

Hisle started three times, pinch-hit once, and appeared in three more games as a late-inning defensive replacement. He was 4-for-11 (.364) in his limited duty. Both he and Money were optioned to the team's Triple-A affiliate in San Diego in late April, and both continued to do well, finishing 1968 with identical .303 batting averages. Hisle's season ended in July, however, after he was diagnosed with hepatitis.

Meanwhile, the Phillies plummeted to a distant seventh-place finish, and the club evaluated its older veterans amid rebuilding. As part of this process, they left Tony González, their starting center fielder for most of the 1960s, unprotected in the expansion draft. The San Diego Padres claimed González, and the door was fully open for Hisle to step into the center-field position.

Hisle was again in the Opening Day lineup when the Phillies opened their 1969 season in Chicago. He hit just .159 in April, though that included his first big-league homer. It came on April 21 at Shea Stadium off Gary Gentry of the Mets. Hisle got his first four-hit game in the majors on May 2 and another on May 18. He continued to heat up as the summer went on and finished the season batting .266, with 20 homers (second on the team behind Dick Allen) and 56 RBIs. It would likely have been more except for a thumb injury – later determined to be a hairline fracture – that limited Hisle to 23 at-bats after September 1. Had he sustained his output over the full year, Hisle would likely have placed higher in the Rookie of the Year voting, or won outright. As consolation, he was eventually selected to the Topps Rookie All-Star Team, along with teammate Don Money and childhood competitor Al Oliver.

The Phillies opened 1970 with a largely new cast. Gone were such long-time notables as Allen, Johnny Callison, and Cookie Rojas. Rookies Larry Bowa and Denny Doyle came in, along with manager Frank Lucchesi, finally getting his shot in the majors. For the second straight season, the Phillies avoided a last-place finish in the NL East division only thanks to the Montreal Expos, the league's other expansion team. Hisle fared even worse than his team. He had a good spring and a strong start, but then went into a severe and extended slump. He was below the Mendoza Line for nearly half his season, and strikeouts – a concern dating back to his minor-league days – were again a problem (more than one in every three at-bats). A flurry in late September lifted him over .200, but by that point Hisle was a platoon player. He appeared in only 126 games with 405 at-bats overall. He was deemed vulnerable to high, inside fastballs, and Lucchesi offered that in "some way, we've got to get Larry started [again]."[16]

Intense training in the Florida Instructional League was the perceived solution, and Hisle responded positively. The Phillies were confident that the slugger who had displayed such early promise would return. Indeed, when the Pittsburgh Pirates dangled former batting champ Matty Alou in trade for a package that included Hisle, the Phillies declined. Unfortunately, management's confidence did not extend past spring training. The Phillies again platooned Hisle, starting him only against lefty pitchers. A mere 14 at-bats in April further indicated the team's lost confidence; in early June, they optioned Hisle to Triple-A Eugene. He did well there and was recalled in September, but finished the year at just .197-0-3 in 36 games.

Less than a month later, Hisle's ties to the Phillies were severed. He was traded even-up to the Los Angeles Dodgers for first baseman Tommy Hutton. The deal required the approval of Bob Carpenter – showing that certain circles of the organization still held Hisle in high regard. Yet the trade also re-opened an ugly, lingering side of the Philadelphia franchise: its race relations.

Over the years, Hisle had been variously described in the oft-critical Philadelphia press as "polite [and] soft-spoken,"[17] "modest [and] unassuming,"[18] and "mild-mannered."[19] So when this genuinely nice, honest athlete opened up about his perception of the Phillies' negative treatment of African-American players, his opinions made news. Long-respected columnist Allen Lewis latched on and issued a withering appraisal of both the checkered history – the Phils were the last National League team to employ an African-American player – and the problems the club had in retaining once-budding stars such as Richie Allen, Grant Jackson, and Johnny Briggs. Uncited, but certainly relevant, was the team's lack of patience with African-Canadian Ferguson Jenkins, who became a Hall of Famer with the Chicago Cubs. Bob Carpenter admitted, "Our track record hasn't been good," and club officials stated their commitment toward resolving the situation.[20]

Hisle was moving on to the team renowned for breaking the color barrier with Jackie Robinson – but he never played a big-league game in Dodger blue. Los Angeles was on the verge of becoming one of the most successful teams of the decade. A lot of young talent was on the way up, especially in the infield – but in 1972 the starting outfielders were all veterans: Willie Davis in center, flanked by Manny Mota and Frank Robinson. Bill Buckner and Willie Crawford were their backups. Hisle could not break through and was assigned to Triple-A Albuquerque. There he mounted the comeback that defined the rest of his professional career. His numbers – .325-23-91 – ranked him with teammate Ron Cey, Gary Matthews, and Mike Schmidt among the Pacific Coast League's leaders. It was reported that "Hisle [was] probably the most scouted player in the Pacific Coast League… [with] no fewer than nine major league scouts watching him nightly."[21]

The Dodgers shipped him to St. Louis for two minor-league hurlers. Yet just over a month later, the Cardinals flipped Hisle to Minnesota for veteran reliever Wayne Granger.

In Hisle, the Twins were perceived to be filling various needs going into the 1973 season – greater defensive range in the outfield, plus a combination of speed and power from the leadoff position. Aside from his continued propensity to strike out, Hisle filled those needs well over a very successful five-year run with the Twins. As it developed, though, he seldom led off after 1973.

There were a couple of interesting side notes to the 1973 season. After a freak accident, Hisle became the Twins' designated hitter in the opening game of spring training – the first big-league DH ever, albeit in exhibition play. He made the new rule look good – though baseball purists will never agree – by hitting two home runs (including a grand slam) while driving in seven runs. Also, the Twins had an odd number of African-American players, so Hisle had a White roommate on the road. It's amusing in retrospect, but this was called "one of the most progressive moves in the franchise's history."[22]

Hisle took a modest step up in 1974, lifting his basic batting line from .272-15-74 to .286-19-79. His OPS rose from .773 to .818. His club did not improve quite so much, though; the Twins finished 82-80, one game better than the prior season.

Minnesota had not been truly competitive since winning the AL West in 1970, but Hisle – now batting in the middle of the lineup – was a big contributor to a team that hoped to be on the rise. "I was having the best season of my career," he said that October.[23] He may have had additional incentive because he was not listed on the computerized All-Star ballots.

Unfortunately, a bone spur in his elbow (and subsequent surgery) limited Hisle to just 35 at-bats after June 17. In his absence, the team fell below .500 and finished 20 1/2 games behind the division champion Oakland Athletics. Manager Frank Quilici was fired, and Hisle was reunited with his first major-league skipper, Gene Mauch.

Shortly after taking the helm, Mauch expressed a need to improve the Twins' defense and run production.[24] The club did score slightly more in 1976, leading the AL in runs with a small-ball approach that emphasized sacrifice bunts and stolen bases. Unfortunately, they were also third in the AL in runs allowed, fueled by a league-leading 172 errors. Still, by closing the season with a 21-8 run, the Twins finished third in the division, just five games behind Kansas City.

Hisle's season mirrored the team's offense. He led the Twins in RBIs with 96, while hitting 14 homers and batting .272. On June 4, he became the third player in Twins' history to hit for the cycle. Yet he also laid down 11 sacrifice bunts and stole 31 bases, both career highs.[25] Speed had always been part of Hisle's arsenal, but Mauch gave him the green light. For example, on June 30, Hisle stole four bases against the Royals, a team record that he still held alone as of 2012. Small ball seemed to agree with Hisle – but he would come to flourish as a power hitter.

The Twins spent much of 1977 in first place but collapsed down the stretch (something Mauch could remember most painfully from his 1964 Phillies). Their distant fourth-place finish disappointed fans, team, and Hisle himself, despite his personal success. Hisle started strongly and stayed consistent –his batting average never dipped below .290 after May 13. He finished at .302– the only time he hit .300 over a full season in the majors – and led the AL with 119 RBIs. His 28 home runs also placed him among the league's top 10. He made the American League All-Star squad for the first time and got some votes for Most Valuable Player.

His performance also came against a backdrop of long and sometimes bitter contract negotiations. The tone was actually set after Hisle won in arbitration before the 1974 season. In response, Twins owner Calvin Griffith –a noted tightwad – allegedly said that "he would get back the money…even if [the team] had to trade" Hisle.[26] The Twins submitted a two-year pact before the 1977 season, but Hisle discovered that the amount "wasn't [nearly] as flattering" as the period.[27] Considering that other star outfielders such as Reggie Jackson, Joe Rudi, and Gary Matthews had signed attractive free-agent deals, Hisle contemplated playing out his contract and exploring the market himself.

Negotiations continued throughout the 1977 season, and despite hopeful indications of closure, terms could not be reached. Time ran out and Hisle became a free agent. He was courted aggressively by numerous clubs

– including the Texas Rangers, whose owner was fined on charges of tampering. Hisle eventually signed with the Milwaukee Brewers for a structured six-year contract exceeding $3 million, a vast increase over the reported $47,200 he'd earned the year before.

The Brewers (formerly the Seattle Pilots) had never finished above .500 in nine seasons. The perceived route to success was free agency. The club had already made a splash by signing Oakland's slugging third baseman Sal Bando a year earlier. The lineup also included Cecil Cooper, future Hall of Famers Robin Yount and Paul Molitor, and Hisle's former teammate Don Money. The team looked like a contender in the AL East.

Hisle immediately contributed to this powerful squad – he became the AL's first Player of the Week in 1978 and was second runner-up for Player of the Month for April. Though he missed the second half of May, Hisle returned and had his strongest season overall. He hit .290, with a personal best of 34 homers (second in the league behind Jim Rice) and 115 RBIs (third after Rice and Rusty Staub). His OPS of .906 was a career high. Milwaukee won 93 games, but still finished third, behind the New York Yankees – the eventual world champions – and Boston. Yet Hisle's efforts were recognized; he became an AL All-Star for the second time, and he finished third in the MVP voting behind Rice and Ron Guidry. The Milwaukee chapter of the Baseball Writers' Association of America named him team MVP. Hisle was still just 31, and a league MVP award seemed within his grasp.

Yet after an excellent start in 1979 – .341, 3 home runs, and 10 RBIs in 10 games – Hisle suffered a devastating injury in a game at Baltimore on April 20. That summer he said, "I was playing left field. . . and had six balls hit out to me. . . I had to make hard throws on all six of them, and on the last one, I felt something snap in my shoulder."[28] The diagnosis was a torn rotator cuff – the severity was the fourth degree out of five.[29]

Determined to play through the pain, Hisle served as Milwaukee's designated hitter over the next two weeks, but he eventually was forced to yield and went on the disabled list. An exercise program to strengthen the shoulder – in lieu of surgery – took longer than expected, and Hisle did not make another appearance until early September. Even then, he was limited to eight at-bats before he was shut down.

Hisle continued his hard exercise over the off-season – he was reluctant to undergo surgery, in part because he saw that other victims of rotator-cuff tears weren't the same after their operations. He pointed to pitchers Don Gullett and Wayne Garland, as well as fellow outfielder Hal McRae.[30]

On Opening Day 1980, he was back in uniform and ready to play. Milwaukee used him strictly as a DH, bringing him along slowly to avoid aggravating the injury. He hit two homers on May 17 – the last of eight times he achieved this feat – but two days later, he hurt the shoulder again while sliding into second base. Initially, it was thought that rest would suffice, but subsequent tests "revealed another tear in the rotator cuff. . .[and] surgery was performed by Dr. Frank Jobe," innovator of the Tommy John procedure.[31]

A second, related procedure – the removal of a bone spur from Hisle's right shoulder – was required in July 1981. Along with the players' strike, that limited Hisle to just 87 at-bats for the season. He doggedly pursued his comeback against long odds – he later said, "[It] took more guts, work and determination than everything else I accomplished in life," ranking it right along with overcoming the death of his mother.[32] However, he fared no better in 1982. He made a total of just nine appearances and 31 at-bats before another disabled list assignment. His last of 166 major-league homers came as a pinch-hitter off Kansas City's Paul Splittorff on May 3 – his final game in the majors was just three days later.

Hisle still held out hope of coming back that fall, but he said that the variety of surgical procedures – five areas of his shoulder had been worked on – and rehabilitation had damaged the shoulder enough. "The team doctor [Paul Jacobs] said any part of the body can take only so much."[33] He announced his retirement that off-season. The same report stated that he would "become a special instructor in the Brewers' minor league system and a scout. . .work[ing] with the Brewers' Class A and rookie league teams."[34]

Over the next 15-plus years, Hisle served in a similar capacity with his first pro organization, the Phillies. He also had brief coaching stints in the minors with the Houston Astros (1989), Toronto Blue Jays (1990-91), and the Brewers again (1997). From 1992 through 1995, Hisle was with the Blue Jays' parent team as batting coach. He won a strong review after the 1992 season, the first of back-to-back World Series championships for Toronto. "The team's improved hitting. . .benefited from Hisle's emphasis on patience and discipline."[35] In 1993 a trio of Blue Jays – John Olerud, old teammate Paul Molitor, and Roberto Alomar – finished one-two-three in the American League batting race. That feat had been accomplished only once before, by three Phillies players exactly 100 years earlier.

Hisle and his wife, the former Sheila Sanford, were married on September 28, 1970. She was a secretary for a law firm that handled some Phillies affairs. They had one child, a son named Larry Jr.[36] The Hisles had always extended themselves in charitable efforts throughout his baseball career. But after he retired to his home outside Milwaukee, this endeavor went into overdrive. The man once dubbed the "honorary captain of the major league Nice Guy Team"[37] demonstrated an even deeper meaning of nice-guy.

Rather than plush, multi-million-dollar stadiums and the adulation of thousands of sports fans, Hisle sought out community group homes, detention centers, and public schools. He assisted youngsters of little means, with the profound appreciation of social workers, teachers and judges. In addition to his status as the Brewers' Manager of Youth Outreach, he has joined forces with his son, Larry Jr., a strong basketball player who also performed in independent baseball leagues from 1995 through 1997. Larry Jr. founded Directors of Continuing Services, a firm that provides psychological, educational and mentoring services to children and families. His father, the orphan who had once longed for such assistance, stepped into a mentoring role himself. He has often taken on round-the-clock responsibilities to help those most at risk.

"I'm only doing something for these kids that should be done for every kid in the country," says the ever-humble ex-athlete renowned for never turning down a request for help. His expressed goal is to "manufacture dreams" for those that "society has written off," and in this capacity, Hisle has been described as "one of the best things happening in Milwaukee."[38]

This man with the infectious smile had never been forgotten in his native Portsmouth either. Around 2,000 of his hometown fans celebrated "Larry Hisle Day" at Cincinnati's old Crosley Field in August 1969.[39] Portsmouth held another such day in October 1977, dedicating a city park in Hisle's name. The affection ran both ways, as a Twins teammate, the late Lyman Bostock, remembered. "When I met this fellow, all he would do is talk about Portsmouth."[40]

People readily respond to Hisle in the most positive ways, as these descriptions demonstrate:

"The kind of player kids should look up to…without a doubt, one of the nicest men I've ever known." – George Bamberger, former Brewers manager[41]

"A wonderful human being…he is one of the nicest human beings I've ever met in my life."

– Bud Selig, former Brewers owner/Commissioner of Major League Baseball[42]

"No matter what good things have been written about him, he's even better…one of the nicest ballplayers ever to come in here."[43]– Jim Ksicinski, former Milwaukee clubhouse attendant.

ACKNOWLEDGMENTS

Thanks for assistance from Jan Larson, Jim Baker, Rory Costello, and the unknown sportswriter who originally came up with the Mays/Hisle comparison that I never forgot.

SOURCES

In addition to the sources cited in the Notes, the author consulted baseballlibrary. com, baseball-reference.com, www.retrosheet.org, mlb.com and Adam McCalvy, "Where have you gone, Larry Hisle?" MLB.com, June 12, 2002 (http://mlb.mlb. com/news/article.jsp?ymd=20020612&content_id=51295&vkey=news_mil&fext=. jsp&c_id=mil)

Aaron Gleeman, "Top 40 Minnesota Twins: # 27 Larry Hisle," December 28, 2010, http://aarongleeman.com/2010/12/28/top-40-minnesota-twins-27-larry-hisle/

NOTES

1   Associated Press, May 19, 1969. The San Francisco Giants visited Connie Mack Stadium in Philadelphia for a weekend series.

2   Associated Press, "Larry Hisle Strives for Improvement Over 1969 Despite Good Statistics," March 7, 1970. This may not be the exact story that the author remembers, but it is very similar.

3   Jael Ealey Richardson, *The Stone Thrower* (Markham, Ontario: Thomas Allen Publishers, 2012), This book is by the daughter of Chuck Ealey, a former pro football player in Canada who was a close friend of Larry Hisle's as they grew up in Portsmouth.

4   Richardson, *The Stone Thrower*; for Hubert Hisle's death record, see ancestry.com.

5   Lou Chapman, "Welfare to Well Off Is Story of Hisle's Life," *Milwaukee Sentinel*, March 1, 1978: Part 2, Page 2

6   Gary D'Amato, "Ex-Brewer Hisle goes to bat for troubled youth," *Milwaukee Journal-Sentinel*, November 8, 2011. http://www.jsonline.com/sports/brewers/hisle-goes-to-bat-for-troubled-youth-nr2vf38-133507288.html

7   D'Amato, "Ex-Brewer Hisle goes to bat for troubled youth."

8   Richardson, *The Stone Thrower*

9   D'Amato, "Ex-Brewer Hisle goes to bat for troubled youth."

10   Allen Lewis, "Hisle Looks Like Money In Bank," *The Sporting News*, April 13, 1968: 21.

11   Lee Caryer, "The Buckeye Who Never Played A Game," Bucknuts. com website, December 27, 2010 (http://ohiostate.247sports.com/Article/OSU-Hoops-Becomes-Black-and-White-35287)

12   David V. Hanneman, *Diamonds in the Rough: The Legend and Legacy of Tony Lucadello* (Austin, Texas: Eakin Press, 1990). Quoted in Steve Triplett, "Lucadello Book 'Real Diamond,'" *Portsmouth Times*, February 26, 1990: 11.

13   Lewis, "Hisle Looks Like Money In Bank."

14   Tom Northington, "Slugger Walton Hero of Carolina All-Star Game," *The Sporting News*, July 29, 1967: 39.

15   Allen Lewis, "Frosh Hisle, Money Spring Surprises – Earn Phillies Jobs," *The Sporting News,* April 20, 1968: 24.

16   Allen Lewis, "Phils Sink Outfield Bundle on Gamble," *The Sporting News,* October 31, 1970: 48.

17   Allen Lewis, "Phils Figure on Hisle in Center, Despite Mini-Mini Experience," *The Sporting News,* November 9, 1968: 52.

18   Allen Lewis, "Hisle Severe Self-Critic…But Phils Say He's Great," *The Sporting News,* April 5, 1969: 20.

19   Allen Lewis, "Phils Attack Old Problem: Handling of Negro Players," *The Sporting News,* November 20, 1971: 48.

20   Lewis, "Phils Attack Old Problem: Handling of Negro Players."

21   "Pacific Coast League," *The Sporting News,* July 8, 1972: 32.

22   Bob Fowler, "Possum, Bam-Bam Strike Terror for Twins," *The Sporting News,* April 21, 1973: 19.

23   Bob Fowler, "Twins' Fortunes Faded Following Hisle's Injury," *The Sporting News,* October 4, 1975: 19.

24   Bob Fowler, "A New Twist for the Twins: Mauch Will Stress Defense," *The Sporting News,* January 31, 1976: 35.

25   Both Hisle and Rod Carew had 30-plus stolen bases, the only time in Twins history (through 2012) that two players achieved that threshold in the same season. Indeed, only six other Twins players have ever had 30 or more steals in a season.

26   Bob Fowler, "Consultation With Rowe Bolsters Brye," *The Sporting News,* July 27, 1974: 28.

27   Bob Fowler, "Twins' Low-Ball Pay Pitch Jolts Hisle," *The Sporting News,* January 15, 1977: 31.

28   "Portsmouth native roots for team," *Pomeroy* (Ohio) *Daily Sentinel,* July 19, 1979: 4

29   Don Willman, "Hisle Faces Probable End of Career," *Portsmouth Times,* September 10, 1982: 10.

30   Bob Wolf, "Hisle getting himself armed for 1980," *Milwaukee Journal,* February 15, 1980: Part 2, page 1.

31   "Brewers' Larry Hisle Undergoes Surgery," *The Sporting News,* August 2, 1980: 12.

32   Willman, "Hisle Faces Probable End of Career"; D'Amato, "Ex-Brewer Hisle goes to bat for troubled youth."

33   Willman, "Hisle Faces Probable End of Career."

34   Tom Flaherty, "Good Health Meant Success for Money," *The Sporting News,* January 24, 1983: 47.

35   Neil MacCarl, "Toronto Blue Jays," *The Sporting News,* October 5, 1992: 23.

36   "Sheila Hisle Enjoys Pro Baseball Life," *Portsmouth Times,* October 27, 1977. Online obituary of Sheila Sanford's mother, Dorothy (http://www.krausefuneralhome.com/obituary.php?id=2631)

37   Mike Gonring, "Hisle a Brewer Money Player in All Respects," *The Sporting News,* July 29, 1978: 16.

38   D'Amato, "Ex-Brewer Hisle goes to bat for troubled youth."

39   Don Lundy, "Portsmouth Area Fans Treat Hisle to Big Day," *Portsmouth Times,* August 11, 1969: 1.

40   Dan Montgomery, "Area Pays Tribute to Larry Hisle," *Portsmouth Times,* October 28, 1977: 1, 6.

41   D'Amato, "Ex-Brewer Hisle goes to bat for troubled youth."

42   D'Amato, "Ex-Brewer Hisle goes to bat for troubled youth."

43   Mike Gonring, "Realtor Clubhouse King to Brewer Visitors," *The Sporting News,* June 30, 1979: 18.

JOHN SULLIVAN

By Bob Hurte

John Sullivan probably caught 10,000 to 100,000 baseballs during his professional baseball career, but none more significant than the last one he caught in the Toronto Blue Jays' bullpen on October 23, 1993.

It was Game Six of the 1993 World Series; the ninth inning. Sullivan, the Blue Jays bullpen coach from 1982 through 1993, was warming up a pitcher in Toronto's bullpen. Philadelphia Phillies pitcher Mitch "Wild Thing" Williams stood on the mound to face Joe Carter. After four pitches, the count was 2-and-2. The fifth pitch never made it to Darren Daulton's glove. Instead, a thunderous crack from Carter's bat echoed throughout the ballpark, sending the ball deep to left field and bouncing off of the back wall of the Blue Jays' bullpen until it ended up in Sullivan's catcher's mitt.

For only the second time in baseball history, a home run ended a World Series.

Sullivan said, "I stashed it in my locker because I wanted Joe (Carter) to have it, and then he could decide what to do with it! Once things died down in the clubhouse, I called Joe over and told him I had something for him. When I gave him the ball, he was all smiles."[1]

Sully, as he was called, confided to this author that Joe wanted to give the ball to his father.[2]

John Sullivan's professional baseball career spanned 35 years; he spent 14 seasons as a catcher, including 116 games in parts of five seasons with the Tigers, Mets, and Phillies.

On January 3, 1941, John Peter Sullivan was born to Jack and Helen Sullivan in Somerville, New Jersey; they divorced when he was young. John split time between his father and grandmother and his mother. Growing up, John loved to play baseball. He played Little League and Babe Ruth League around Peapack Gladstone, New Jersey. At 15, he played in the Morris/Somerset County men's league.

At Bernardsville High School, John was talented enough to play football, basketball, and baseball. He made All-County one year in basketball, and All-State several times in baseball.[3]

After graduating from Bernardsville High School in 1958, Sullivan was signed by Irving "Rabbit" Jacobson, an area scout for the Detroit Tigers. Since he was just 17 years old, the Tigers instructed him to stay home and play in the leagues around home, but also remember that he was under contract.[4]

In 1959, Sullivan, having turned 18, was assigned to the Erie Sailors of the Class-D New York-Penn League. He showed some power, hitting 13 home runs and batting .322 in 110 games. He was selected as the catcher for the league's all-star team. Over five seasons Sullivan also made stops in Durham, Birmingham, Knoxville, and Syracuse, before making his major-league debut with the Tigers on September 20, 1963, against the Chicago White Sox at Tiger Stadium. In that game, he caught Mickey Lolich. The Tigers lost, 2-0. At the plate, Sullivan struck out

against Eddie Fisher in his first at-bat and walked in his two other plate appearances.

What did it feel like to finally put on a major-league uniform? Sullivan replied, "It was great! When you think about it, it was something you wanted to do your whole life. I was very fortunate to do it."[5]

Sullivan played in two April 1964 games for the Tigers, but spent most of the season with Syracuse of the Triple-A International League.

The Tigers felt no urgency to make deals with other teams to plug holes on the ballclub. Instead, they expected to fill those holes with players from Syracuse. They were confident that Chiefs players like Willie Horton, Jim Northrup, Bill Roman, Ray Oyler, Bruce Brubaker, and John Sullivan could fill such voids.[6] Sullivan's own confidence was boosted that winter when he hit a home run off major-league pitcher Juan Pizarro in the Puerto Rico winter league, especially since he was competing for the number-two catching job behind Bill Freehan.[7]

Because Freehan was injured, Sullivan was the Opening Day catcher for the Tigers in 1965, catching Lolich. He went 2-for-4. His first big-league hit was an eighth-inning home run off Wes Stock of the Kansas City Athletics. He added a single the next inning.[8] The Tigers won, 6-2.

Freehan returned shortly afterward, and remained as the number-one catcher until 1976. At first, Sullivan was regarded as the number-two catcher behind Freehan, but after playing in 11 games over the first month, he was sent down to Syracuse. He hit a couple of homers for the Chiefs, and was recalled by the Tigers on June 29. That night in Baltimore, he hit his second (and final) major-league home run, off Milt Pappas of the Baltimore Orioles in a 5-2 Tigers loss.

Sullivan played in 34 games with 86 at-bats during the 1965 season. He batted .267 with two home runs and had 11 runs batted in, which proved to be the best offensive performance of his major-league career.

Sullivan spent the entire 1966 season in the minors. This was surprising since in February of that year, the media expected the Tigers to carry three catchers, with McFarlane and Sullivan as backups behind Bill Freehan. Sullivan was assigned to Syracuse but never played there; instead he ended up playing for the Vancouver Mounties of the PCL (Kansas City Athletics).

After the 1966 season, Sullivan was picked by the Mets in the Rule 5 draft.

Bing Devine, the Mets' general manager, said, "We invited three catchers strictly for the workouts.

They are there to provide us with more manpower. But Jerry Grote, Greg Goossen, Johnny Stephenson, and John Sullivan are the only ones who will play in the games."[9]

Sullivan was known as a defensive receiver and served as the primary backup for Grote, playing in 65 games for the 1967 Mets, with 147 at-bats. He caught a pitching staff that included Jack Fisher, Don Cardwell, Bob Shaw, Bob Hendley, and rookie Tom Seaver.

It was Sullivan's only full season behind the plate in the major leagues. He batted .218, with no home runs, but with 5 doubles and 6 RBIs.

(Sullivan did hit a homer against the San Francisco Giants in an exhibition game known as the Mayor's Trophy Game, which raised money for New York City sandlot baseball programs.)[10]

When the Mets embarked on West Coast trip in late July, Sullivan got five of his runs batted in for the season. He enjoyed two different multi-hit games during the trip.

The Mets brought up Duffy Dyer in 1968, while also acquiring catcher J.C. Martin, essentially ending Sullivan's time with the Mets. He was traded to the Philadelphia Phillies for a player to be named later (Billy Sorrell). Sullivan started the season with the San Diego Padres of the PCL. He was called up late in the season, playing in 12 games, batting .222 with one RBI. That proved to be Sullivan's last season as a major-league player.

Sullivan went to spring training in 1969, feeling good about his chances of catching on, since the Phillies had traded Clay Dalrymple to the Baltimore Orioles, opening the door to a catching competition. More than half of the players on the Phillies' roster were rookies, but only a few of them had a better chance than the 28-year-old Sullivan. He was the only experienced catcher aside from Mike Ryan on the roster.[11] However, Sullivan was hampered by recent foot surgery that affected his conditioning. "The toes on my right foot started bothering me late last season," when he was with San Diego, he said. "I felt like a knife was jabbing into me when I put any pressure on my toes. I guess this came about from all the foul tips that had hit me there, but it sure hurt."[12] He went to a doctor, decided against the surgery, got some pills, and was informed that he would need to live with it.

Sullivan was traded with Anthony Giresi, a minor leaguer, to the Baltimore Orioles for Vic Roznovksy and spent the 1969 season playing for the Rochester Red Wings, batting .253 while driving in 44 runs.

Playing with the Red Wings afforded Sullivan an opportunity to find his future home. It was located a little over 50 miles south, in Dansville, New York, the hometown of his wife, Betty, where they still lived in 2022. Sullivan enjoyed the friendliness of the town. When his playing career ended in 1972, the Sullivans made the town their permanent home. John spent his fall and winters there, and his springs and summers away coaching and managing.

The Kansas City Royals organization purchased Sullivan's contract on April 13, 1970. He played for their Triple-A team in Omaha in 1970 and 1971, before finishing his career with the Royals' Jacksonville Suns farm team in the Double-A Southern League in 1972.

Sullivan then embarked on a minor-league managing career in which he built a cumulative record of 434-288, winning four league championships in six seasons, reaching the finals but falling short in 1977. He summed up those years: "Mainly, we had good players. You can't win without the players. It was fun."[13]

Sullivan's first stop was managing the Kingsport Royals of the Rookie League in 1973. They won the league championship with a 53-17 record. In 1974 he moved up to the Waterloo Royals of the Class-A Midwest League. They won the league championship in 1975.

Sullivan moved up to Triple A at Omaha in 1977; his squad won their division but lost in the league championship. One of Sullivan's bright stars was Clint Hurdle, who had also played for John at Waterloo the year before. He said, "We thought Clint would play at Class AA this year. But he earned a shot to be here. He had a heckuva spring with the big club (Royals) and kept hitting when he came to us."[14] The Royals were in last place on July 8, 10 games behind the Indianapolis Indians but tied with them in August with the help of a 19-4 record.

Hurdle won the Rookie of the Year Award for the Omaha Royals of the American Association in 1977.

In 1978 all four teams in the American Association's West Division finished under .500. Omaha, at 66-69, led the division and wound up defeating the East Division leading Indianapolis Indians for the league championship.

Sullivan was promoted to Kansas City as a coach under Whitey Herzog in 1979. The Royals dropped Charlie Lau as the team's batting instructor and both Sullivan and Chuck Hiller assumed that role. Herzog had a difference of opinion with Lau's hitting philosophy. General manager Joe Burke described Sullivan as "very qualified."[15]

Sullivan contributed to the Royals organization in many ways. Dan Quisenberry credited his former manager at Waterloo for converting him into a relief pitcher. He became a reliever after making his minor-league debut with the Waterloo Royals as a starter. That was his last professional start. He said, "I started that first game for Sully. It was a seven-inning game, the first of a doubleheader, and I won 4-1. After that game Sully told me he was going to use me out of the bullpen, and that's where I've been ever since."[16]

Manager Herzog was free with his criticism of the front office and was fired after the 1979 season. His coaching staff was also told that they were free to seek other employment.

Less than a month later, Atlanta Braves manager Bobby Cox hired Sullivan as the team's bullpen coach for 1980 and filled the void created by Alex Grammas's departure.[17]

Bullpen coaches usually do not get a chance to make many suggestions other than reporting whether a relief pitcher is ready to come into a game. During the 1980 season, Sullivan, the former major-league catcher, suggested that backup catcher Biff Pocoroba break his habit of throwing across his body. He had him pitch batting practice while he was on the disabled list. Sullivan was also helpful with Braves catcher Bruce Benedict.

The Braves finished the 1980 season with an 81-80 record. The strike-shortened season of 1981 did Cox in; he was fired by owner Ted Turner after the season. Cox was quickly hired by the Toronto Blue Jays for the 1982 season; he brought Sullivan along as bullpen coach as part of a Toronto staff that also consisted of Cito Gaston (batting instructor), Jimy Williams, and Al Widmar. Both Gaston and Williams later became Blue Jays managers.

With Cox at the helm, the Blue Jays improved in each of his four years there. The team finished sixth the first season, fourth the second, second in his third season, and first in 1985. Toronto lost the 1985 ALCS to the Royals. Cox returned to Atlanta as general manager in 1986, moving back into the dugout in 1990, where he remained until his retirement in 2010.

For Sullivan, a baseball lifer (35 years in professional baseball), it was many years before he was able to reach out and grab the brass ring. That time came when the Blue Jays beat the Atlanta Braves in the 1992 World Series.

It was hard for him to hold his emotions in. Ace reliever Duane Ward recounted the time: "There were tears in his eyes; I'll never forget his words. 'Son, I've been waiting 34 years for this moment. You can't believe how good I feel.'" Ward added, "I felt so good for him."[18]

Sullivan decided that 1993 would be his last year in professional baseball. He had become weary of travel and stymied by arthritic joints.

What a way to end a baseball career. At precisely 11:36 P.M. in SkyDome in Toronto, the greatest home run in Toronto Blue Jays' history was hit. It was the 90th World Series, the first to begin and end on Canadian soil, and it ended in dramatic fashion. The Blue Jays were on their way with a three-games-to-one series lead, until they dropped Game Five in Philadelphia when Curt Schilling threw a five-hit shutout.

In the sixth game, Toronto saw a four-run lead evaporate when the Phillies scored five times in the seventh inning. The powerhouse part of the Blue Jays lineup was due up in the ninth. Going into the bottom of the ninth, the Phillies were up by one, 6-5. Pitcher Mitch Williams walked Rickey Henderson on four straight pitches and Devon White flied out deep to left-center. That brought up Paul Molitor, who singled to center, putting Henderson at second. On a 2-and-2 pitch, Joe Carter became the second person after Bill Mazeroski in 1960 to hit a walk-off home run to win a World Series.

Reflecting on the victory, Sullivan said, "There was a lot of pressure on us in '92. It was all about business. In '93, we had the experience of the postseason play and winning the World Series under our belts. We were so relaxed. We enjoyed what we had accomplished in 1992 and all the of pressure was off us in '93."[19]

Then the pitch came that Carter struck for his historical blow. Carter said, "I have to make sure I hit the ball. Don't worry about yanking it. Just see the ball and put the ball in play somewhere. If I could do cartwheels; I would have done cartwheels as I rounded the bases. That's how happy I felt."[20]

Fifty-two thousand delirious fans rocked SkyDome.

Sullivan told the author, "I was warming up a pitcher, and I saw the ball go over my head, hit the back wall and came back to me. I shoved it in my jacket pocket. Everyone took off running. Some of us were running faster than others."[21]

That game was the last of Sullivan's 35-year professional baseball career. He was asked to come back the following season to unveil the 1993 World Series banner.

Shortly after his retirement, Sullivan volunteered to help coach the Dansville High School baseball team. Apparently, he could not get the game out of his blood. Nearly 30 years later, he admits that he still enjoys baseball's chess-move challenges as a former catcher, coach, and manager. He loves to watch games on television, and then try to decipher what will happen next.

"It's funny, I'll say something to my wife about how so-and-so is probably going to throw such-and-such a pitch and then the announcers will say the same thing, and she'll start laughing. I can't help it, but I guess I enjoy managing the games from my living room."[22]

Reflecting on having batted against Hall of Famers Phil Niekro, Bob Gibson, Ferguson Jenkins, Jim Bunning, Catfish Hunter, Gaylord Perry, and Jim Palmer during his 116-game major-league career Sullivan said, "Every day was a thrill for me, just to be there and a part of it."[23]

SOURCES

In addition to the sources cited in the Notes, the author consulted Baseball-Reference.

NOTES

1   Scott Pitoniak, "Former Blue Jays Bullpen Catcher Made Catch of Lifetime," *Sports Collectors Digest*, December 12, 2016.

2   John Sullivan, telephone interview with author, December 23, 2021.

3   Sullivan interview.

4   Sullivan interview.

5   Sullivan interview.

6   Watson Spoelstra, "Tigers Trapped as Traders Count on Boys from Syracuse," *The Sporting News*, December 19, 1964: 10.

7   "Northrup's Noisy Bat Could Crash Tiger Picket Line," *The Sporting News*, January 23, 1965: 10.

8   "John Sullivan: New Jersey Born Mets Reserve Catcher (1967)," www.centerfieldmaz.com, January 3, 2021.

9   Barney Kremenko, "Films to Help Mets Iron Out Batting Flaws," *The Sporting News*, February 25, 1967: 19.

10 Initially the game pitted the New York Giants against the New York Yankees. In 1951 the Brooklyn Dodgers became the Yankees' new opponent. Afterward the two National League teams (Giants and Dodgers) traded years. The game had proved itself to be financially successful; bringing in $2 million over the course of a 19-year run. The fans loved it. They saw it as a chance to claim unofficial city bragging rights. The Mets on July 12, 1967 won the 1967 game, 4-0. Sullivan hit his home run as a pinch-hitter.

11 Allen Lewis, "Sullivan Out to Win Phil Catching Job," *The Sporting News*, March 16, 1969: 16.

12 Lewis.

13 Sullivan interview.

14   "Hasbach and Hurdle Shine," *The Sporting News*, May 7, 1977: 28.

15   "Royals Retain Herzog, Drop Lau as Coach," *The Sporting News*, November 4, 1978: 46.

16   "Submarine Hurler Tosses Royals a Life Raft," *The Sporting News*, August 11, 1979: 10.

17   "Woy Silent and Braves Edgy," *The Sporting News*, November 3, 1979: 59.

18   "Dansville's Sullivan Had a Hand in World Series Drama 20 Years Ago," *Rochester Business Journal,* October 25, 2013.

19   "1993 Toronto Blue Jays," *Ontario Sports Hall of Fame*, October 23, 1993.

20   *Ontario Sports Hall of Fame.*

21   Sullivan interview.

22   "Dansville's Sullivan Had a Hand in World Series Drama 20 Years Ago."

23   Sullivan interview.

GENE TENACE

By Joseph Wancho

The Cincinnati Reds did not seem a bit concerned about their opponent from the junior circuit. The Big Red Machine were the bullies on the beach, waiting to kick sand in the face of their rival, the Oakland Athletics. Pete Rose viewed the coming 1972 World Series as anticlimactic. "The real World Series was between the Reds and Pirates," said Rose of the Reds' opposition in the NLCS.[1] Cincinnati skipper Sparky Anderson chimed in, "If I said the American League was as good as the National League, I'd be lying."[2]

The Athletics franchise was appearing in the Series for the first time in 41 years. Slugger Reggie Jackson was sidelined with a hamstring injury, and the Reds were overwhelming favorites.

Catcher Gene Tenace was penciled into the seventh spot in the batting order in Game One at Cincinnati's Riverfront Stadium. Tenace, despite having got just one hit in the League Championship Series against

Detroit, felt that he was seeing the ball very well. "The balls that I was hitting were right on the nose, but right at somebody," he recalled.[3]

Tenace may have been on to something with his analysis. After a walk to George Hendrick in the third inning, Tenace sent a Gary Nolan pitch into the left-field bleachers for a 2-0 Oakland lead. In the fifth inning he homered again off Nolan, giving the visitors a 3-2 advantage. That was the final score.

Tenace became the first major leaguer to homer in his first two at-bats in the World Series. "I never hit two home runs in one game before," he exclaimed. "The first one was on a fastball out over the plate. The second was on a hanging curve."[4]

He was not finished, as he added round-trippers in Games Four and Five. He had hit only five home runs in the regular season, and had four in the Series. The four home runs tied a major-league mark for home runs in a World Series. After number four, the scoreboard at the Oakland Coliseum delivered this message to Tenace, and the 49,000-plus fans: The mark equaled those of Babe Ruth, Duke Snider, Lou Gehrig, and Hank Bauer. "I don't belong with those guys," Tenace remembered thinking to himself.[5]

Cincinnati catcher Johnny Bench credited Tenace with taking advantage of mistakes. "Any time a batter hits a home run, he hits a pitcher's mistake — and I see a lot of that behind the plate," Bench said. "Tenace hit a curveball that hung and a couple of sliders that didn't slide. But Gene knew what to do when he got those mistakes, and that's what counts."[6]

Tenace, who batted .348 in the Series and knocked in nine runs, was named the Series' Most Valuable Player, an honor that earned him a sports car from *Sport* magazine. Tenace brushed off the honors, claiming that there were 25 heroes on the team, not just one. Always humble and reserved, he was happy to be a face in the crowd.

Fury Gene Tenace was born on October 10, 1946, in Russellton, Pennsylvania, the second of three children born to Fiore and Ethel Tenace. He had an older sister, Nadine, and a younger sister, Serena Kay, who was killed in an auto accident at the age of 21. His original name was Fiore Gino Tennaci. But his maternal grandfather, who had emigrated from Italy, wanted to Americanize the family name. It was also his grandfather who gave the youngster the nickname "Steamboat," because of his block-like build.

Gene's father dropped out of school at the age of 16 and joined the Merchant Marine. He enlisted in the Navy when World War II began and also served in the Korean War. After he was discharged, Tenace moved his family to Lucasville, Ohio, where he found work as a laborer, and then as a union truck driver.

Fiore Tenace put tremendous pressure on young Gene to become a ballplayer. Fiore had played semi-pro ball around the Ohio-Pennsylvania border area. Ethel Tenace recalled her husband berating the youngster in front of others. "'Didn't I always tell you to swing at a third strike? How come you didn't swing?' his father used to scream. Gene, he didn't say anything except, 'I don't know.' If Gene would ever attack back at his father he probably would've got a slap across the mouth. His father used to say, 'No kid who lives under my roof is goin' to sass me. If he's going to be a ballplayer, he'll do as I say.'"[7]

Because of this treatment, young Gene suffered from ulcers. He couldn't play baseball for a year, and was restricted to a special diet. When he recovered enough to return to the diamond, he asked his father not to come to his games because it made him too nervous.

Tenace eventually grew into a fine ballplayer at Valley Local High in Lucasville. He was a two-sport star, excelling in football and baseball, earning all-state honors while playing shortstop. He also played on an American Legion team that featured future major-league stars Al Oliver and Larry Hisle, both of nearby Portsmouth, Ohio. "We could put some runs on the board, but we just didn't have the pitching to get past the state playoffs," recalled Tenace.[8]

After graduating from high school in 1965, Tenace was drafted by the Kansas City Athletics in the 20th round of the June amateur draft. He puttered around the Athletics organization as a utility player. Once, while with Peninsula of the Carolina League, Tenace played all nine positions in one game as part of a promotion. "I pitched the first inning and got out of it, though I nearly got the third baseman killed," he remembered. "I caught the second inning, then moved around the horn each inning and ended up in right field. It was fun till I got to the outfield. There was no action there."[9]

In 1969 Tenace was promoted to Birmingham of the Double-A Southern League. Manager Gus Niarhos, known for his skill at developing young receivers, went to work on his newest pupil. "I'd call Tenace an adequate catcher now," said Niarhos near the beginning of the season. "His arm is good. The biggest thing is getting him to relax. When he does, and if he keeps hitting, he'll be up there. That could be next year — that's how much I think of his chances. Tenace wants to know. He asks, too. He's a good student."[10] Tenace showed that his progress was ahead of the timetable Niarhos had set, when he was promoted to Oakland after backup catcher Jim Pagliaroni was sold to Seattle and Dave Duncan was called into military service. Tenace made his big-league debut on May 29, 1969. Tenace played in five games as a backup for Phil Roof. His first major-league hit was a single off Cleveland's Luis Tiant on May 30. His second was a solo home run off Detroit pitcher Earl Wilson on June 6.

The A's acquired catcher Larry Haney from Seattle on June 14, and returned Tenace to Birmingham. He had a solid year there, batting .319 with 20 homers, and 74 RBIs. Behind the plate, he fielded a respectable .988 with 46 assists in 80 games. He capped off his season when he was recalled to the varsity after the Southern League season. Tenace was dispatched to Iowa of the Triple-A American Association to begin the 1970 campaign. He flourished again, and was recalled to the Athletics for the last two months of the season. Gene saw more action, hitting .305 in 105 at-bats. (He did not come near .300 again in his career.)

In 1971 the Athletics' third season in the Bay Area after relocating from Kansas City, the team broke through to end Minnesota's hold on the American League's Western Division. Other than pitcher Vida Blue, the A's star players had all begun their careers in Kansas City. Now Charlie Finley's team was about to get a taste of the postseason.

Tenace was Dave Duncan's backup at catcher. Manager Dick Williams favored Duncan, who was a better defensive player, possessed a stronger arm, and had the intangibles such as success in handling the pitching staff. But Baltimore swept the A's in the League Championship Series, claiming the American League pennant for the third straight year.

If their quick exit from the playoffs taught the A's anything, it was that they needed to bolster their pitching staff. After the season the A's traded promising outfielder Rick Monday to the Chicago Cubs for pitcher Ken Holtzman. With Blue and Catfish Hunter, the Oakland rotation was suddenly a force. But their offense, outside of Reggie Jackson and Joe Rudi, was anemic at times. Their pitching staff was the cornerstone that Oakland rode to three straight world championships, beginning in 1972.

Dick Williams realized that his team needed an infusion of offense. Tenace provided a bit more than Duncan. "He wasn't doing it with the bat," Williams said of Duncan. "It began to affect his catching."[11] Williams then went against his normal thinking of playing the better defensive player, and inserted Tenace in the lineup for the last two months of the season. Oakland was in a fight with the White Sox all season, outlasting them by 5½ games. The League Championship Series against the Tigers went the full five games, and Tenace knocked in outfielder George Hendrick with the go-ahead run in the fourth inning of Game Five. The 2-1 win was Blue Moon Odom's second victory of the series. Tenace's game-winning blow was his only hit in 17 at-bats, but a key one nonetheless.

The World Series was a tightly matched battle between Oakland and Cincinnati, with six of the seven games being decided by a single run. Oakland prevailed in seven games, starting a dynasty such as the Bay Area had never seen before.

An interesting story developed before Game Six, as the Series moved back to Cincinnati. A woman waited in line to purchase standing-room tickets. She overheard a man remark, "If Gene Tenace hits a home run today, he won't walk out of the ballpark."[12] The woman alerted police, and Finley and Williams requested extra security. They decided not to tell Tenace of the threat until after the game. The man, who carried a loaded gun and a bottle of whiskey, was arrested during the game.

The next year Dave Duncan was a holdout as spring training commenced. Tenace took over the catcher duties. As late March approached, Duncan was still unsigned. Rather than deal with the contract issue, Finley traded Duncan and George Hendrick to Cleveland for catcher Ray Fosse and infielder Jack Heidemann. Fosse, an excellent fielder (Gold Gloves in 1970 and 1971) but lacking on offense, became the starting catcher. But the Athletics were anxious to keep Tenace and his bat in the lineup. They asked Mike Hegan, who was a defensive specialist at first base, to tutor Tenace on the finer points of becoming a first sacker. "All the time Mike was doing this," said Tenace, "he was pushing himself further and further away from the job. He knew it and I knew it, but he

still kept helping me."[13] Hegan was sold to the Yankees during the season.

Besides starting at first base, Tenace sometimes filled in for Fosse, who was often injured. He hit 24 home runs. In 1973, the first of four straight seasons in which he smacked at least 20 homers. Despite mediocre batting averages Tenace proved to be a valuable offensive commodity. In 1974 he batted only .211 but led the league in walks (110). He was the starting first baseman for the American League in the 1975 All-Star Game.

The Athletics were a strong team, dominating the American League's West Division. They dispatched Baltimore two years in a row in the ALCS, and topped the New York Mets in the 1973 World Series and the Los Angeles Dodgers in 1974 to win three straight world championships.

The major-league owners locked the players out of spring-training in 1976 until a new contract could be reached. The gates were finally opened in mid-March, and Finley sent out the obligatory contracts, cutting each player's salary by 20 percent. Sensing that free agency was imminent, Finley dealt Holtzman and Jackson to Baltimore a few days before the season began. Thus began the fire sale as the trade deadline approached in June. Finley offered all of his starters to all interested parties for the right price. The players were willing to play out the year, hoping to cash in at the end of the season when free agency was granted. Finley's attempts to sell or trade his stars were doused by Commissioner Bowie Kuhn.

The players were correct in their assumption that the moolah would be coming their way. Tenace, who made a salary of $40,800 in 1976, signed a six-year contract with San Diego for a total of $1.85 million. Rollie Fingers joined Tenace in the Padres' fold.

Despite owner Ray Kroc's attempt to bolster the Padres, they were not a competitive team. The Dodgers, Astros, and Reds fought it out at the top of the Western Division. Each team had its way with the weaker Padres. San Diego signed Tenace to be the starting catcher, even though his skills may have been better suited for first base. As it turned out, he split time between the two positions. His power numbers tailed off; he reached 20 home runs only once in his four years at San Diego. Kroc was dissatisfied with his free-agent acquisition. "Tenace kept saying if he played every day he'd improve. Well he's been in there every day and he hasn't done a damn thing," the owner said. "All he wants to do is walk. Well, we can't win games waiting for walks. He's being paid to hit and he can't hit. Nobody in either league wants him and we're paying a premium price."[14] For his part, Tenace did not respond negatively to Kroc's criticism; he acknowledged that he was not playing well and said Kroc's tirade was intended to stir up the Padres.

On December 10, 1980, Tenace was part of an 11-player deal, going with Fingers, pitcher Bob Shirley, and catcher Bob Geren to St. Louis. The principal player among seven Cardinals going to San Diego was catcher Terry Kennedy. During the 1981 season Tenace went back and forth between first base and catcher, backing up Darrell Porter and Keith Hernandez.

In 1982 Tenace broke a bone in his right thumb in spring training. Later in the year, he broke a bone in his right hand diving into third base. Despite these setbacks, Tenace played a key role among the reserves, always encouraging them. "Gene Tenace keeps my head above water," said outfielder Tito Landrum. "If I start having a letdown, he comes over and kicks my rear end. Literally. He pulls no punches. He lets you know."[15] Tenace preached to the bench players to always be ready because they never knew when they would be called upon to enter a game.

The Cardinals won the 1982 World Series, topping Milwaukee in seven games. Tenace, who had hit his 200th career home run during the season, went hitless in six at-bats with one walk in the Series.

Tenace became a free agent after the season and signed with Pittsburgh. He played sparingly (78 plate appearances) and quit as a player after the season. He retired with a .241 batting average, 201 home runs, and 674 RBIs. He had a respectable fielding percentage of .986 as a catcher, and .993 as a first baseman. Tenace served as a minor-league instructor for the Boston Red Sox and also coached in the majors, primarily with Toronto. He was the bench coach on Cito Gaston's staff that won back-to-back world championships in 1992 and 1993.

Tenace retired from baseball after the 2009 season. As of 2022, he and his wife, Linda, lived in Redmond, Oregon. They have two daughters.

The 1972 World Series was not all rosy for Gene Tenace. The Reds swiped 12 bases in the Series, taking advantage of Oakland pitchers' inability to hold baserunners. Tenace did not have the strongest of throwing arms, which did not aid the cause. Asked after the A's victory in Game Seven if he thought he might be elected the MVP of the Series, Tenace responded, "What the hell, even if I do, the Reds'll steal it from me."[16]

SOURCES

In addition to the sources cited in the Notes, the author also consulted baseball-almanac.com, baseball-reference.com, retrosheet.org, sabr.org, and Green, G. Michael, and Roger D. Launius, *Charlie Finley* (New York: Walker Publishing Company, 2010).

NOTES

1   Bruce Markusen, *A Baseball Dynasty: Charlie Finley's Swingin A's* (Haworth, New Jersey: St. Johann Press, 2002), 143.

2   Markusen, 143.

3   Markusen, 144.

4   Markusen, 144.

5   Markusen, 158.

6   Bob Addie, "Addie's Atoms," *The Sporting News*, November 11, 1972: 14.

7   Ira Berkow, *Beyond the Dream: Occasional Heroes of Sports* (Lincoln, Nebraska: Bison Books, 1974), 6-9.

8   Interview, *Sport* magazine, September 1979. Information obtained from a summary sheet created by *Sport* which is found in Tenace's player file at the National Baseball Hall of Fame.

9   Interview, *Sport* magazine, September 1979.

10   Alf Van Hoose, "Quick Bat, Shift to Backstop Propel Tenace Toward Top," *The Sporting News*, May 31, 1969: 41.

11   Ron Bergman, "If A's trade Catcher, It'll Probably Be Duncan," *The Sporting News*, November 11, 1972: 36.

12   Markusen, 162.

13   Markusen, 181.

14   Phil Collier, "Man Upstairs Gives Word to Padres: 'Yccch'," *The Sporting News*, July 1, 1978: 23.

15   "Cards Can Count on Husting Tenace," *The Sporting News*, August 9, 1982: 14.

16   Al Hirschberg, *Sport*, October 1973. From *Sport* summary sheet in Tenace Hall of Fame player file.

THE BROADCASTERS

TOM CHEEK

By Joseph Thompson

Baseball on the radio is an important part of the lives of countless people. The radio play-by-play announcer serves as the narrator of the game. The personal connections developed between fans and their favorite announcers can last for decades. The radio talent becomes the "voice of baseball" and the inside, personal connection that fans have with their favorite teams.

Tom Cheek was the voice of baseball and the narrator of summer for Blue Jays fans throughout Canada and beyond for almost three decades. Starting with the team's first regular-season game on April 7, 1977, he shared the game with fans from February through October. He shared some of his favorite baseball moments and told stories about the people he knew and met. He shared his raw emotion when something good or bad happened during a game. He shared all that he knew about the game he loved so much. He shared it until a brain tumor made it impossible for him to continue in 2004. And then the sharing was gone.

When Cheek's voice disappeared from the airwaves, it shook the very foundations of Blue Jays nation. Club President Paul Godfrey said as much in 2005: "When Tom suddenly stopped, it was like the whole organization stopped. That's how much he means to the club."[1] It was as if a close friend had been taken away very suddenly, never to be heard from again. "I can't tell you anyone who more epitomizes the heart and soul of the Toronto Blue Jays than Tom Cheek," said Godfrey. "His voice has touched millions of fans over the years."[2]

Thomas Fred Cheek was born on June 13, 1939, in Pensacola, Florida. His father, also named Tom, served as a World War II fighter pilot in the Battle of Midway in 1942. Following in his father's footsteps, Cheek himself joined the military and served in the US Air Force from 1957 to 1960. While he was in the service he met broadcaster Red Barber.[3] He met his future wife, Shirley, a native of Hemmingford, Quebec, while stationed in Plattsburgh, New York. They married in 1959 and soon had three children, Lisa, Jeffrey, and Tom.

Cheek knew from a young age that he wanted to be in broadcasting. After his discharge he went to school at SUNY Plattsburgh and then the Cambridge School of Broadcasting in Boston. He began his career in broadcasting as a disc jockey in Plattsburgh. His next job was in Burlington, Vermont, where he worked as a corporate sales manager and as sports director for a group of three radio stations including WBMT, which carried Montreal Expos baseball. He also called University of Vermont sports and was almost hired to take over as the full-time play-by-play announcer for the expansion Atlanta Hawks of the National Basketball Association.[4]

While in Burlington, Cheek found occasional work as a fill-in broadcaster for the Expos, Cheek said in an 1985 interview that broadcasting games for the Expos put him on the path to become the future Toronto Blue Jays radio play-by-play announcer. He

made the 99-mile trip to broadcast games usually on Wednesdays in 1974 through 1976.[5] His work with the Expos did not go unnoticed. According to John Lott, "His work convinced Len Bramson, a Toronto broadcast executive who was developing a coast-to-coast radio network for the expansion Blue Jays, to make Cheek the lead man in the radio booth."[6]

The expansion Toronto Blue Jays announced in December 1976 that Tom Cheek would become the play-by-play announcer for the new club. Hewpex Sports Enterprises announced that the radio broadcast borders for the new club would cover a 14-city area across the province of Ontario with the possibility of adding more stations before the club began spring training for its first season. The network would extend to "Kingston in the East to Sarnia in the West, in Tiger Territory, and Timmins in the North,"[7] With a 14-city network in place, and a radio announcer ready to go, all that was left for Tom Cheek to fulfill a lifelong dream was call his first game with his new club.

On a snowy April 7, 1977, with the temperature right around freezing, Bill Singer threw out the first pitch for the expansion Blue Jays against the Chicago White Sox at Exhibition Stadium. Upward of 44,649 fans including a young Wayne Gretzky, packed the ballpark to see Toronto's first major-league baseball game. Trailing 2-0 in the first inning, Doug Ault hit the first home run in franchise history, which started the team's comeback that day. The Blue Jays rallied and won, 9-5. Cheek said the win that day ranked as his top Blue Jays memory.[8] There would not be much more for Cheek to cheer for the rest of the season or for a few years to come. The Blue Jays finished their inaugural season with a 54-107 record, 45½ games behind the New York Yankees. For the first six years of its existence, the team did not have a winning record. That started to change in the mid-1980s.

Fans tuning in to hear Cheek's baritone voice over the years also heard the voices of his radio partners. From 1977 through 1980 former major-league pitcher Early Wynn called games alongside Cheek. Jerry Howarth replaced Wynn in 1981.

Cheek and Howarth constituted the play-by-play tandem of Blue Jays baseball for over two decades. The partnership covered the evolution of the franchise from an American League East bottom feeder to its rise to prominence starting in the 1980s, and then to its rise to the top of the baseball world with back-to-back World Series titles in 1992 and 1993. The duo stayed together for the duration of Cheek's career.[9]

From the start, Cheek remained a constant in the radio booth, never missing a game until 2004. The Blue Jays' fortunes started to turn in the mid-1980s and into the 1990s, and they won their first division title in 1985. A year before his death, Cheek recalled how he felt when that happened: "When George Bell dropped to his knees on the turf at Exhibition Stadium in 1985 as the Blue Jays won their first division title, I started thinking about all the guys who'd contributed over the years to get them there – and I choked up," said Cheek. "You could hear the catch in my throat. I promised I'd never do anything like that again."[10]

The Blue Jays were not yet in a position to go far in the playoffs. They lost the American League Championship Series to the Royals in 1985, the Athletics in 1989, and the Twins in 1991. They finally captured the pennant in 1992, becoming Canada's first team to make it to the World Series. Members of the press seemed to be relieved by the club's first pennant. "The next step for the Blue Jays, who have been carrying enough guilt for an entire country because of their three previous playoff failures, is the World Series, in which they will take on the Atlanta Braves beginning Saturday in Atlanta."[11]

The Blue Jays beat the Atlanta Braves in six games to become the first team outside of the United States to win the championship. The Series was noteworthy when it came to Cheek and the broadcast. During Game Two of the series, the US Marine Corps accidentally displayed the Canadian flag upside down during the national anthem. This outraged Blue Jays fans but did not seem to bother pinch-hitter Ed Sprague, who hit a game-winning home run off Jeff Reardon, at the time baseball's saves leader. The round-tripper was the first pinch-hit home run for the Blue Jays all season. And probably more prophetic than odd, before Sprague hit the home run, Cheek commented on the air, "Watch him hit a homer."[12]

In Game Six, Cheek and Howarth went outside their normal broadcasting rotation once the Blue Jays took the lead in the top of the 11th inning. Normally, Cheek would call the first two innings of a game then turn the play-by-play over to Howarth for the next two innings and they would continue this pattern for the remainder of a game. Howarth called the top of the 11th as usual but after the mid-inning commercial break, Howarth turned the broadcasting call over to Cheek for the bottom of the inning. Howarth, in a grand gesture, was hoping to have Cheek call the Jays' first-ever World Series win. With two outs in the 11th, Cheek made the call that gladdened Blue Jays fans:

"Timlin to the belt. ... Pitch on the way. ... There's a bunted ball, first-base side. ... Timlin to Carter and the Blue Jays win it! The Blue Jays win it! The Blue Jays are World Series champions!" As fans across Canada began to celebrate, Cheek went on: "The Blue Jays have won the World Series so Canada, let it all out, it's party time! It was a long time coming but it's here."[13] Canadians across the nation celebrated alongside Cheek well into the night.[14]

The Blue Jays won the pennant again in 1993, and one of the most dramatic endings to a World Series occurred in Game Six. With Toronto leading three victories to two, the Philadelphia Phillies led 6-5 going into the bottom of the ninth inning. Phillies closer Mitch "Wild Thing" Williams was on the mound hoping to send the World Series to a decisive Game Seven. The Blue Jays' Rickey Henderson started the inning with a walk. Devon White flied out to deep left field. Paul Molitor singled. With two on and the count 2-and-2, Joe Carter cemented his legacy as a Blue Jays legend by driving Williams's next pitch over the left-field wall to win the Series in a walk-off. Fans over the years have pointed to Cheek's call of Carter's home run as perhaps his best-known call. Cheek reflected on the call at spring training camp in Florida in 2005. "I was looking for something to say, and Joe gave it to me because he was jumping up and down. I was merely mentioning to him through the airwaves that you've got to touch all the bases." Those listening heard that call live with the type of raw emotion that often engulfs someone who has seen something almost magical. "Touch 'em all Joe, you'll never hit a bigger home run in your life!"[15] It has become one of the most famous lines in baseball broadcasting history.

Over the seasons Cheek acquired a unique insider's view of the club that very few in the organization had achieved. So he decided to share some of his knowledge about the team and in 1993 he and co-author Howard Berger released *Road to Glory: Sixteen Years of Blue Jays Fever*, which chronicled the first 16 years of Blue Jays baseball. Jim Proudfoot of the *Toronto Star* opined that "Cheek, who's witnessed every inning the team has played, is perceived as the ultimate insider," and added, "His viewpoint was bound to be uniquely revealing."[16] Cheek wrote of why Peter Bavasi abandoned the club presidency in 1981 and why Tony Fernandez, in Cheek's view, abandoned the team in 1987. Baseball fans loved the book and made it a best-seller. Bookstores all across Canada had a hard time keeping the book on their shelves.[17]

After the dramatic World Series win in 1993, the Blue Jays began to slide. For the rest of Cheek's time with the team, it didn't finish any higher in the standings than third.

On Thursday, June 3, 2004, the Blue Jays lost to the Oakland Athletics, 2-1, in 11 innings but the game itself took a back seat to what happened in the Blue Jays radio booth that night. Cheek's father, Tom Sr., had suffered a fatal heart attack the previous night and so Tom rushed home to be with his family. After 4,306 regular-season games and 41 postseason contests without missing a broadcast, Cheek was not in the booth that night. Howarth handled the game with color commentary for a few innings provided by injured Jays outfielder Frank Catalanotto. Howarth took a moment to reflect on the now-broken broadcasting streak of his longtime partner. "Having sat here for 23 years, it's incredible because of all of the factors that go into broadcasting a game," Howarth said. "It's a testament to his professionalism, to his commitment to fans. It takes a lot to keep a streak like that alive. There are several factors, like health, graduation, funerals, that can intrude."[18] Blue Jays President Paul Godfrey weighed in: "A feat of this magnitude does not occur without a great deal of sacrifice and perseverance from the Cheek family. Tom's dedication and contributions to the Toronto Blue Jays organization are immeasurable."[19] Former major-league pitcher Tom Candiotti compared Cheek's streak to that of another baseball ironman, Cal Ripken Jr. So did former Blue Jays general manager Pat Gillick, who said, "He was sort of like Cal Ripken, in that you knew he was going to show up every day, you knew he was going to be there with the same pride, the same dedication to excellence. You could always count on Tom to bring his very best every day."[20] Cheek accepted the kind words but would not accept the comparison of his streak with Ripken's. "There will only ever be one streak in baseball," Cheek said. "That would be the one that Cal Ripken put together. He was out on the field doing it every night while I was just up there watching."[21] Cheek returned to the booth soon after the funeral and tried to get back to doing what he loved. His return did not last long. Cheek soon found himself in the biggest battle for his own life.

Cheek felt ill a week after returning to the booth. Tests at a Toronto hospital indicated a brain tumor. On June 13, his 65th birthday, Cheek underwent surgery to remove the tumor. "Everyone at the Toronto Blue Jays wishes Tom a speedy recovery," club President Paul Godfrey said. "Our thoughts are with the entire Cheek family, and we hope to see Tom back in the broadcast booth very soon."[22] And Cheek returned to broadcasting six weeks later despite chemotherapy treatments that impaired his short-term memory. On July 23, 2004, he called two innings of the Blue Jays game against the Tampa Bay Devil Rays.[23] Cheek was able to return and broadcast home games on a limited basis while undergoing treatments, but he was replaced by guest announcers when the team was on the road. His popularity with the fans never wavered during his absence. Thousands sent him best wishes and wished the longtime broadcaster a speedy recovery.

The Blue Jays invited Cheek for an on-field presentation at SkyDome on August 29, 2004. Mike Wilner served as one of the replacements for Cheek as he recovered from surgery. Cheek and Wilner sat in the dugout looking out onto the field and talking before the ceremony. Cheek soon noticed that a portion of the 400 level was covered with a blue tarp. "It was amazing to see the look of recognition, and then of genuine embarrassment move across his face," Wilner remembered. "He kept saying 'You have GOT to be kidding me,' because he honestly didn't believe that just showing up to work every day deserved such major praise."[24]

An emotional crowd of 44,072 was there to honor Cheek. The Blue Jays had played the Yankees that weekend and had not performed well so the team and its fans were eager to have something to cheer about. Cheek sat with his wife and watched as the Blue Jays removed the blue tarp to officially add him as the newest member of the team's Level of Excellence. Geoff Baker of the *Toronto Star* described the scene: "They sat through a video montage on the SkyDome's JumboTron, one that replayed Cheek's greatest calls, including Toronto's first division title clinch in 1985, Dave Stieb's no-hitter in 1990, and Joe Carter's decisive home run in the 1993 World Series. Eyes throughout the stadium turned moist as photos from Cheek's younger days flashed on the screen, accompanied by the strains of Frank Sinatra's "It Was a Very Good Year."[25] Cheek made his way to the podium and addressed the crowd. After making a crack about the Yankees, he addressed his medical condition. "I've been fighting a situation now for over a month, almost two months now," he said. "We're doing the best we can to stay ahead of it. A brain tumor. We're dealing with it."[26] Even Yankees radio announcer John Sterling had to take a moment to compose himself. Cheek, the consummate professional, went back to the Blue Jays

radio booth after the ceremony to take his place and get ready for the game.

Tom's wife, Shirley, told a reporter almost a decade later how that day changed his life. Cheek had told her that he had never imagined the connection he had forged with the fans and how important that connection was to them. "I never could really get the point until somebody said, and a lot of others followed, 'Since I was a little kid, you've been giving the sound of summer.'"[27] It finally clicked for him. "He had so many people that would say he was the voice of summer," she said. "'I listen to you on the lake. I listen to you on the tractor out in Saskatoon, or, you know, wherever. But I think it really hit home when he saw that his name was going up on the wall and how much he had meant to the fans listening on radio."[28]

Cheek wanted to bounce back and try to return to the booth for good in 2005. He was nominated for the National Baseball Hall of Fame Ford C. Frick Award for the first time before the 2005 season. He was honored to be nominated and even though he didn't win it (San Diego Padres announcer Jerry Coleman did), he looked forward to getting back into the booth to call Blue Jays games in the coming season. "I can't wait to get out here and get back on the field and get back in the booth," he said.[29] Early in spring training, Rogers Media announced that Cheek would be back in the booth for Opening Day with Jerry Howarth. But Cheek suffered a setback when in March an MRI revealed that the cancer had returned and another tumor had formed. Rogers Media canceled his return pending the results of his surgery. Cheek, determined to beat the odds and do his job, made one more appearance in the radio booth for the Blue Jays on Opening Day. "The last time Cheek was in the booth was Opening Day 2005," Mike Wilner wrote, "when he joined Howarth and Warren Sawkiw at Tropicana Field in St. Petersburg, Florida, close to his home in Oldsmar, and Jerry insisted he get on the mic and call a few pitches. Reluctantly he agreed, and took over as Orlando Hudson came to the plate in the top of the third. Hudson homered, and so did Vernon Wells behind him, and that was enough for Cheek."[30] Cheek's career as a broadcaster essentially ended that day.

On October 14, 2005, with his wife; his three children, Jeff, Lisa, and Tom; and his seven grandchildren present, Cheek died at the age of 66 at his Florida home. "It's difficult to put into words the overwhelming sense of grief and loss shared today by the Blue Jays family, the city of Toronto, the extended community of Major League Baseball and its many fans,"

Blue Jays President Paul Godfrey said. "He was a great goodwill ambassador for baseball in Canada."[31]

Cheek did not believe that he deserved a lot of praise for just showing up to work every day. He seemed genuinely embarrassed that the Blue Jays added him to their Level of Excellence in 2004. Despite his resistance, others sought to reward Cheek for his efforts in promoting baseball. The Canadian Baseball Hall of Fame honored Cheek with the Jack Graney Award for his contributions to baseball in Canada in 2001. The Canadian Sports Hall of Fame established an annual Tom Cheek Media Leadership Award, with Cheek being honored with the first award in 2005. The award was established to recognize media members who help promote Canadian sports "in an extraordinary and enduring way." A website was created that sold wristbands to help fund cancer research. The year after Cheek died, the Blue Jays wore a white circular badge with the letters "TC" and a microphone in black on their left sleeve.[32] And in 2013 Cheek was honored with the Ford C. Frick Award and earned enshrinement into the National Baseball Hall of Fame in Cooperstown.

Baseball over the radio serves as the preferred way of catching baseball games for countless numbers of baseball fans all over the world. Even though television broadcasts have long replaced the radio as the most used communication device for watching baseball, there are still many who will turn their television volume down and listen to their favorite radio announcer call the game. The best of the baseball radio talent through the years: Mel Allen, Vin Scully, Gene Elston, and Ernie Harwell have become the voice of baseball for many. "Tom Cheek was the voice of summer for generations of baseball fans in Canada and beyond," said Hall of Fame President Jeff Idelson in a press release announcing the Ford C. Frick Award for Cheek. "He helped a nation understand the elements of the game and swoon for the summer excitement that the expansion franchise brought a hockey-crazed nation starting in the late 1970s."[33]

Tom Cheek "was more than just a broadcaster," said Len Bramson, the one-time talent-hunting guru who lured him to Toronto from Vermont hoping he'd establish an identity for the newly awarded Jays franchise. "He was big, had the voice. He was cordial with everybody, he could talk to anybody. In front of a crowd, he was outstanding. He did it with no notes. He just loved to talk about baseball."[34] Baseball fans all over Canada and beyond loved to hear him talk about baseball.

SOURCES

In addition to the sources cited in the Notes, the author consulted Baseball-Reference.com.

NOTES

1   Shi Davidi, "Cheek Up for Honour," *Toronto Star*, February 22, 2005: E06.

2   Davidi.

3   Tom Cheek, *Road to Glory* (Toronto: Warwick Publishing, 1993), 7-30.

4   Cheek, *Road to Glory*; Canadian Press, "Tom Cheek, Voice of Toronto Blue Jays, Dies." http://www.americanssportscastersonline.com/tomcheekmemoriam.html.

5   Home Town Cable Network, "Toronto Broadcaster Tom Cheek – 1985," YouTube, October 3, 2016. https://youtu.be/htUotdoaavA.

6   John Lott, "Voice of Summer; Tom Cheek, Who Brought His 'Folksy, Intimate' Style to Jays Broadcasts For 27½ Years, Is Finally Headed to Cooperstown," *National Post*, Toronto, December 6, 2012: B5.

7   Neil MacCarl, "Blue Jays Polish Skills in Winter Loops," *The Sporting News*, December 18, 1976: 54.

8   Sam Jarden, "April 7, 1977: Blue Jays Play Their First Ever Game," *The Sporting News*, April 7, 2020. https://www.sportingnews.com/ca/mlb/news/april-7-1977-toronto-blue-jays-play-their-first-ever-game/17if403ul-mlq418soqp71hx20t. "Tom Cheek, Voice of Toronto Blue Jays, Dies." http://www.americansportscastersonline.com/tomcheekmemoriam.html.

9   CatchTheTaste, "1991: Behind the Scenes with Tom Cheek and Jerry Howarth," YouTube, July 6, 2019. https://youtu.be/ILDzMImogvc.

10   "2013 Ford C. Frick Award Winner Tom Cheek," National Baseball Hall of Fame and Museum, https://baseball-hall.org/discover-more/awards/frick/tom-cheek.

11   David Bush, "O, Canada! A's Fall, 9-2, Blue Jays win A.L. pennant, finally reach their 1st World Series," *San Francisco Chronicle*, October 15, 1992: C1.

12   "Jays: Memories of '92 and '93 Series," *Toronto Star*, August 11, 2018: S4.

13   Eye Flow, "Toronto Blue Jays World Series 1992 Tom Cheek," YouTube, October 21, 2014. https://youtu.be/xODky9oDqMI.

14   Canadian Press and Herald Staff, "Blue Jays Fever: Canada Gets World Series," *Calgary Herald*, October 15, 1992: A1.

15   Jeremy Sandler, "Blue Jays Broadcaster Misses Out on Hall of Fame Award," *National Post*, February 23, 2005: B10.

16   Jim Proudfoot, "Cheek's Book on Blue Jays a Treasure Hunt," *Toronto Star*, July 6, 1993: D4.

17   Proudfoot.

18   Geoff Baker, "Sadly, Cheek Finally Misses a Jays Game," *Toronto Star*, June 4, 2004: C04.

19   Geoff Baker, "Sadly, Cheek Finally Misses a Jays Game."

20   Geoff Baker, "Tom Cheek: Ironman of the Airwaves," *Kitchener-Waterloo* (Ontario) *Record*, October 11, 2005: D2.

21   Geoff Baker, "Blue Jays Honor Emotional Cheek," *Toronto Star*, August 30, 2004: E07.

22   "Jays Announce Cheek Has Brain Tumor Removed," *Detroit Free Press*, June 15, 2004: 8E.

23   "Touching All the Bases," *Seattle Post-Intelligencer*, July 24, 2004.

24   Mike Wilner, "Wilner on Jays: Remembering the Great Tom Cheek," Sportsnet Canada, July 3, 2013, https://www.sportsnet.ca/baseball/mlb/wilner-on-jays-remembering-the-great-tom-cheek/.

25 Geoff Baker, "Blue Jays Honor Emotional Cheek."

26 Geoff Baker, "Blue Jays Honor Emotional Cheek."

27 John Lott, "Voice of Summer; Tom Cheek, Who Brought His 'Folksy, Intimate' Style to Jays Broadcasts For 27½ Years, Is Finally Headed to Cooperstown."

28 Lott.

29 Jeremy Sandler, "Blue Jays Broadcaster Misses Out on Hall of Fame Award," *National Post,* February 23, 2005: B10.

30 Mike Wilner, "Memories of Cheek, Who Touched So Many Lives," *Toronto Star,* March 20, 2021: S1.

31 Associated Press, "Tom Cheek, 66; Announcer Called Blue Jay Games for 27½ Seasons," *Los Angeles Times,* October 11, 2005, https://www.latimes.com/archives/la-xpm-2005-oct-11-me-cheek11-story.html; CBC Sports, "Tom Cheek, Longtime Voice of Blue Jays, Dead," October 9, 2005, https://www.cbc.ca/sports/tom-cheek-longtime-voice-of-blue-jays-dead-1.528332.

32 "Voice of the Blue Jays Tom Cheek Dies," *Pittsburgh Tribune Review,* October 9, 2005.

33 "Tom Cheek: Late Blue Jays Announcer Wins Top Hall of Fame honor," *Sherman Report,* December 5, 2012. http://www.shermanreport.com/tom-cheek-late-blue-jays-announcer-wins-top-hall-fame-honor/.

34 Geoff Baker, "Tom Cheek: Ironman of the Airwaves," *Kitchener-Waterloo Record.*

DON CHEVRIER

By Joe Marren

Don Chevrier was there from the beginning, a 9-5 win against the Chicago White Sox that began as a snowy Thursday on April 7, 1977, at Exhibition Stadium.

And he was there for the next 20 years, too. He would have stayed even longer but the broadcasting contracts were moved as deftly as Roberto Alomar could turn a double play and, voila, "Chevy" was gone.

"I have some other opportunities [in baseball] and I guess I'd better pursue them," he told a reporter from the *Globe and Mail* in 1992. "I would have loved to stay with the Blue Jays, but it's not possible. The package has been diluted and I can't build around 30 games as my main base of income."[1]

What happened is that Chevrier did continue broadcasting some Jays games on CTV each season until 1997. Here's how that happened: Baton Broadcasting Inc. held the telecast rights for Jays games and worked primarily with CTV. In 1992, Baton negotiated a new contract to broadcast at least 60 games per year for five years for $60 million.[2] At the time it cost about $48,000 per game to produce a Jays telecast and speculation was that Baton wanted to cut about $3,000 per game from that figure. One of the ways it did that was by letting producer Tom McKee go as others took pay cuts. In another belt-tightening move, Baton then resold the rights for some games in that five-year period to CTV and CBC.[3] Then, in 1997, Baton, the Jays and CTV failed to reach an agreement.[4]

"I never imagined 25 or 30 games not being done," Chevrier said at the time. "I'm out a lot of money and have no means of recovering it. [Calling Jays games] was the centerpiece of my work. If I'd seen it coming, I would have diligently pursued other avenues in the offseason. I'm very disappointed."[5]

It was late March 1997 when Chevrier lamented his financial plight, a time when other baseball broadcasting jobs were filled.

"I'm sorry Don feels that way, but you can't make those arrangements unless they're predicated on a justifiable business case," said Tom Curzon, Baton's director of communications at the time.[6]

But here's how the Chevrier story begins. Donald Barry (sometimes spelled Barrie on some government forms) Chevrier was born in Toronto on December 29, 1937, but the family moved to Edmonton when he was 6. His father, Romain, was born in Winnipeg and is listed as an insurance salesman when he moved to the United States in 1928. His mother, Orva Heal, was born in Saskatchewan and listed her occupation as stenographer on a government form when she briefly moved to the United States in 1928. That seems to have set a pattern for the pair as they moved between the two countries. Both listed their residence

Don Chevrier was the Jays' first TV broadcaster, calling all or parts of 20 seasons from 1977 to 1996.

as Detroit when they married in that city on May 16, 1929. Romain was 23 and Orva 24.

In 1953, when he was 16, he began a career in sports reporting/broadcasting that lasted in one form or another right up until his death in Palm Harbor, Florida, near Tampa, on December 17, 2007.

The late singer Robert Goulet, who worked in radio in Edmonton as a teenager at the time, gave Chevrier his first broadcasting job at radio station CKUA (Edmonton), where Chevrier covered high-school sports.[7] Chevrier also worked with Goulet on a children's drama program that year.[8]

From there it was on to CJCA to do daily sports reports. An ad in the *Edmonton Journal* on November 25, 1955, asked listeners to tune in to *Teen Sport Review* at 5:05 P.M. on CJCA. By age 20 Chevrier was announcing Edmonton Eskimos home games. Sticking with football, he did play-by-play for CFL teams when he moved to CFRA in Ottawa and then CJAD in Montreal. He called his first Grey Cup game for CBC/CTV in 1969 and then again from 1971 to 1980. In recognition of all that, he was posthumously inducted into the Canadian Football Hall of Fame in November 2016.[9]

In 1966 Chevrier joined CBC in Toronto, working first in radio and then television. Then, in the 1980s and '90s, he was working at CTV. He also covered the Olympics for the CBC, ABC, and NBC television and radio networks handling everything from curling to synchronized swimming. The Olympics portion of his résumé began with him covering team handball and boxing at the Summer Games in 1976; hockey during the Winter Games in 1980 (including the US-Soviet game for ABC Radio); badminton, table tennis, and synchronized swimming in the 2004 Summer Games; and curling at the Winter Games in 2002 and 2006

"Synchronized swimming – he'd never done that in his life," said Don Duguid, who worked alongside Chevrier on Olympic curling broadcasts for NBC. "We had a lot of fun with that. ... I said, 'What do you know about swimming?' he said, 'It's just one hand in front of the other.'"[10]

He called the 1980 Winter Olympics hockey game between the Soviets and the US men's teams for ABC radio. Even after he was supposedly retired in Florida, he still wanted to keep announcing by trying to land a job with the expansion Tampa Bay Lightning of the NHL. That didn't pan out but he did hook up with the Ottawa Senators and broadcast games from the 1992-93 through 1997-98 seasons for CHRO-TV.[11] If there

was a regret, Chevrier said, it was that he never got to broadcast a "Hockey Night in Canada" game.[12]

Given all that – his résumé included broadcasting 21 different sports[13] – his career basically could be centered on three main themes Blue Jays: curling, and the Olympics. His obituary in the *Toronto Star* noted, "If there was a sport Don Chevrier couldn't call, it was probably only because he hadn't been asked."[14] His success derived from thinking of what the viewer needed to know. Rick Brace, who was president of CBC when Chevrier died in 2007, said about his colleague: "He kind of brought us into the age of the viewer demanding more information and more insight, and not just straight commentary. Don pioneered that."[15]

Let us look at some of the accomplishments on Chevrier's résumé:

- He won an Association of Canadian Television and Radio Artists ("Nellie") award in 1975 as Canada's best sportscaster.

- He won the Canadian Sports Media Achievement Award and was inducted into the Canadian Media Hall of Fame in October 2004.

- And, as mentioned earlier, he was inducted into the Canadian Football Hall of Fame in November 2016.

- Away from the world of sports, his voice was also used in a 1988 episode of the TV show *The Twilight Zone* and in the 2005 movie *Brokeback Mountain*.

Hockey broadcaster and former NHL goalie Greg Millen summed up Chevrier's impact: "He will go down as one of those Canadian icons in broadcasting."[16]

Clearly, Chevrier had a long and varied résumé, but he is clearly best remembered as being the voice of the Jays (And in the World Series of 1992 he worked alongside color commentator Tommy Hutton and field reporter Ken Daniels.) The fictional Terence Mann tells Ray Kinsella in the 1989 movie *Field of Dreams* that "People will come, Ray. ... The one constant through all the years, Ray, has been baseball." And so it was with Chevrier, the one constant through all the boxing, curling, Olympic, and all the other broadcasts was baseball, and it was largely defined by the Blue Jays.

Just before that snowy first game in Exhibition Stadium in 1977, Chevrier had already been on the air for an hour doing the pregame show. Then the snow cleared and the game was on. For three hours he called the balls and strikes, the innings and outs, and the *sturm und drang* of a typical early-season game. It's 5:18 in the afternoon and the game is already an official W for the hometown good guys, the postgame show is wrapped up … and then they realize they have to fill the time for the next 12 minutes until 5:30. Chevrier handled it with seeming ease because he was ready for emergencies.

"In broadcasting, preparation is everything," he told a reporter a few days after the game.[17]

"You just can't go in and fake it," he told another reporter. "Baseball, for example, is a game where you can get caught very easily if you don't prepare lots of material in advance."[18]

What also helps is a deep knowledge of the game and its personalities. When told Chicago White Sox owner Bill Veeck would be a guest during part of a game, Chevrier had precious little time to prepare. But he hit a metaphorical home run with the interview.

"Afterward, Veeck told me how impressed he was with how much Don knew about baseball," said producer Ralph Mellanby.[19]

Preparation is important, but a sense of self-effacing humor and comedic timing also helps from time to time when needed. Chevrier wouldn't hesitate to tell stories about those "oops!" moments that are inevitable in any live production. Like this one: Once, during a game against the Boston Red Sox, his color commentator, Tony Kubek, said that relief pitcher Greg Harris was ambidextrous. Chevrier replied that that "would be a manager's dream come true because it would save him having to go to the bullpen again because Greg Harris, being ambidextrous, could relieve himself on the mound." As Chevrier told it, there was 15 seconds of silence before he spoke again. Whether the quip was a mistake or intentional isn't the point, but know this: Chevrier was a storyteller nonpareil.[20]

When the Jays won the World Series in 1992 the humor was more confident and intentional, but in those early years it had to be more pronounced to keep the customers satisfied.

Paul Godfrey, who was Jays president from September 2000 to September 2008, said Chevrier was essential during the team's early, struggling years because his broadcasts at least made the games sound interesting.

"When the team loses 100 games in its first year, the TV broadcast has to make sure the fans keep coming back, even though they were outclassed by most of the opposition," Godfrey told a reporter.[21]

Chevrier endured, along with the fans, and saw the team's glory years when the Jays won back-to-back World Series titles in 1992 and 1993. Chevrier was living in Florida when he died at age 69.

"I knew the voice before I knew the person," Gord Ash, former Jays general manager, told a reporter. "The voice was so dramatic and authoritative and you just felt whatever he was trying to convey, no matter what sport he was doing at the time. It sent a powerful message.

"You don't see that much anymore, there's such specialty now. You don't see a guy cross over as much as he did."[22]

NOTES

1   Neil Campbell, "Chevrier Quitting as Jay Announcer," *Globe and Mail* (Toronto), October 14, 1992: C7.

2   Unless noted otherwise, all financial transactions are in Canadian dollars.

3   James Christie and John Partridge, "Jays' Broadcaster from Early Days Out in Squeeze Play," *Globe and Mail*, March 17, 1992: D18.

4   However, CBC picked up 35 games on weekends and TSN had 80 games on Mondays, Tuesdays, and Thursdays. "MAKING THE PITCH: CTV Ends 15 Years of Covering the Blue Jays, but CBC and TSN Have Picked Up the Ball," *Globe and Mail*, April 5, 1997: F19.

5   William Houston, "Truth & Rumours: William Houston's World of Sport – Chevrier Slams Baton," *Globe and Mail*, March 18, 1997: D13.

6   Houston.

7   Goulet was born in Lawrence, Massachusetts, in 1933. His mother, Jeannette, moved the family to Edmonton after the death of her husband in 1949.

8   John Krobank, "'Voice of God' Broadcaster Returns to His Maker," *Edmonton Journal*, December 24, 2007: B-7.

9   "Don Chevrier, Class of 2016," at https://cfhof.ca/members/don-chevrier/.

10 Peter James, *CanWest News Service* at https://www.cfl.ca/2007/12/19/don_chevrier_remembered/.

11 F.F. Langan, "He Was the Voice of the Blue Jays and 'a Producer's Dream'," *Globe and Mail*, December 20, 2007: S-8.

12 Langan.

13 "First Blue Jays broadcaster Chevrier found dead at 69," *ESPN.com*, December 18, 2007, at https://www.espn.com/espn/print?id=3160666

14 Chris Zelkovich, "Mellow tones silenced," *Toronto Star*, December 19, 2007: S4.

15 William Houston, "'Voice of God' silenced," *Globe and Mail*, December 19, 2007: S1.

16 "Legendary sports broadcaster Don Chevrier passes away," *CBC Sports* at https://www.cbc.ca/sports/legendary-sports-broadcaster-don-chevrier-passes-away-1.664796

17 Bryan Johnson, "The golden throat of the Blue Jays," *Globe and Mail*, April 9, 1977: 28.

18 "Chevrier career spans 22 years," *Winnipeg Free Press*, October 15, 1977.

19 Zelkovich. Also in that same article American sportscaster Howard Cosell, who broadcast boxing with Chevrier, rhetorically asked, "Are all Canadian sportscasters as good as Don Chevrier?"

20 Zelkovich. Also, "Call him Hopeful Harry," *Toronto Star*, October 15, 2004: C9. There is a discrepancy in the anecdote. The Zelkovich story has Harris playing for the Red Sox, the earlier anonymous story says Harris was playing for the Texas Rangers. What is known is that Harris pitched for the Rangers from 1985-87, and for the Red Sox from 1989-93 and for part of 1994.

21 Langan.

22 *ESPN.com*.

JERRY HOWARTH

By Allen Tait

Jerry Howarth is the longest-tenured Blue Jay broadcaster to date, having covered the team for more than 36 years. Following brief stints of three games in 1980 and 20 games in 1981, Howarth became a full-time radio voice with the Blue Jays from April 9, 1982, to October 1, 2017.[1] Anyone who has heard Howarth broadcast will remember his trademark home-run call (insert your favorite field): *"Fly ball to left, deep, yes sir, there she goes."*

Howarth was born in York, Pennsylvania, on March 12, 1946. A month later his father, a mechanical engineer, relocated the family to the San Francisco Bay Area to pursue a business opportunity.[2] A year and a half later, Jerry and his parents, June and Jerry, welcomed sister Anita to the family.[3]

Howarth recalled in his memoir that he responded to a challenging childhood home life by making positive convictions to guide his life:

> I would lie awake in bed at night, listening to the uproar in the house and telling myself that I would avoid conflict at all costs the rest of my life. That I would not drink. That I would learn to walk away.[4]

Sports was an important part of Howarth's school life. He played one season as backup quarterback for his Novato High School junior-varsity football team. In his freshman year, he also played guard on the basketball team. However, baseball was his primary sport; he played four years for his high-school team as a third baseman-center fielder while batting leadoff. He also played for a semipro team in the summer and a winter league team in nearby Fairfax, California.[5]

Upon graduation from high school in 1964, Howarth received career advice from his father, who explained that he could be drafted and sent to Vietnam right out of high school. However, if he chose to pursue postsecondary education, he would receive a draft deferment.[6]

Howarth enrolled at Santa Clara University, initially with a major in accounting. He tried out for the Santa Clara Broncos baseball team in his freshman

year. Santa Clara had a strong team at that time. As recently as 1962, it had been in the College World Series finals, losing 5-4 to the University of Michigan on a wild pitch in the 15th inning.[7] Howarth's stint with the Broncos was short: He was cut after the first game.[8] Howarth shifted his extracurricular activities to working at the campus newspaper covering sports and for one year working at the campus radio station, KSCU.[9]

In his third year, Howarth decided accounting was not for him and changed his major to economics. He graduated from Santa Clara in 1968 with a bachelor's degree in commerce, majoring in economics with a minor in philosophy.[10]

While enrolled at Santa Clara University, Howarth spent four years in the ROTC (Reserve Officers' Training Corps), through which students receive military officers' commissions after graduation. One of the undergraduate training programs was held at Fort

Lewis, Washington, where Howarth earned one of six Distinguished Military Student Awards.[11] The award allowed Howarth to choose the Adjutant General's Corps as his branch.

After graduating, Howarth went to Fort Benjamin Harrison in Indianapolis for three months of officer training.[12] Upon completion of his training, Howarth was sent to Frankfurt, Germany, in the fall of 1968 to serve for two years.[13] In his memoir he recalled the tension among the North Atlantic Treaty Organization (NATO) members at the time after the Soviet Union invaded Czechoslovakia on August 20, 1968.

Howarth returned to the United States in August 1970, retired from active duty and enrolled in law school at the University of California at Hastings in San Francisco.[14] In early 1971, two significant events occurred. Jerry met Mary McMorrow, whom he married later in 1971,[15] and he withdrew from law school to pursue a career in sports as a fundraiser for the Santa Clara University Bronco Bench Foundation.[16]

Howarth, who was interested in sports broadcasting, had been told he did not have a major-league voice.[17] His response was to buy a tape recorder and practice broadcasting while watching football and basketball games. Two years later, although he had started taking his tapes to radio stations, no openings were available.[18] Howarth added baseball to his practice list and was hired by the Pacific Coast League Tacoma Twins to be their broadcaster for the 1974 season.[19]

Howarth was the Tacoma broadcaster for two seasons and in the summer of 1975 had a meeting that influenced his play-by-play style from that day forward. He recalled the meeting in his memoir:

Tacoma was in Phoenix to play the Giants. Beside the open broadcast booth sat a couple, Ginny and John Redfield. Ginny was the ballpark organist and was blind. Ginny asked if she could sit next to me to hear the play-by-play and I agreed. I wanted Ginny to see the movement of the ball off the bat. Those calls for Ginny are still my calls today for everyone else.[20]

At the end of the 1975 season, Howarth successfully applied for a position as assistant general manager and radio broadcaster for the Pacific Coast League Salt Lake City Gulls.[21] During their time in Salt Lake City, the Howarth family grew with the adoption of week-old Benjamin George, born October 3, 1976, and week-old Joseph Michael, born June 26, 1978.[22]

The end of the 1978 season represented five years of broadcasting Triple-A baseball for Howarth. Jerry decided to expand his résumé and was hired as the assistant general manager and broadcaster for the Utah Pros of the newly formed Western Basketball Association.[23] The team folded after one year when the New Orleans Jazz of the National Basketball Association relocated to Salt Lake City as the Utah Jazz. Howarth was then hired to work in economic development for the Salt Lake City Chamber of Commerce.[24] Six months later, after receiving advice that the longer one stayed out of sports, the more difficult it would be to return, Howarth hired on as group sales director for the Jazz, for the 1979-80 season.[25] After the season he worked as a sports reporter for KWMS Radio.[26]

Howarth first thought about a major-league baseball broadcasting career with the 1976 announcement that the major leagues were expanding to Seattle and Toronto. Having broadcast in Tacoma, he was interested in the Seattle job but was unsuccessful. As he recalled in his memoir:

Mary suggested I apply to the other team. I said no and Mary repeated the suggestion more earnestly. I asked for the atlas, as I did not know where Toronto was. Mary, being from Kalamazoo, Michigan, and quite familiar with Toronto, found that amusing. From the index, I saw a listing that read "Toronto, Ont., Canada." I did not know what Ont. stood for and after looking at the distance from Salt Lake City and being a different country, I said I would not apply. Mary persuaded me to apply for the job and I did. A few months later I received a response from the HEWPEX Sports Network telling me they had hired Tom Cheek and Early Wynn, but that I should keep in touch.[27]

The HEWPEX Sports Network (HSN) contacted Howarth in June 1980 and offered him an opportunity to work with play-by-play radio announcer Tom Cheek on a weekend series in Detroit. The regular analyst, Early Wynn, was away participating at an old timers game at Dodger Stadium.[28] Howarth recalled the experience of broadcasting his first major-league game:

I was in awe of Tiger Stadium and being on the field in one of baseball's oldest ballparks. As I looked around at the completely enclosed stadium, I also noticed that the upper deck was right over the lower stands in one of the most intimate ballparks ever for the fans to sit and enjoy the games. Then when I went upstairs to the radio booth, I was completely surprised to see our booth almost directly over home plate, too. That was later backed up when from the booth I could hear conversations down at home plate when voices were raised by players arguing with the home plate umpires. I was never that close to the plate in a radio booth ever again. The booth had net coverings over the front because of hard hit foul balls coming straight back from that too nearby plate but I had the security people take my half down because I did not want to call a game in that unique radio booth setting looking through a net. Tom covered his side as did the Tigers radio broadcasters in theirs but not stubborn me. I did that all the years we were at Tiger Stadium until they moved to Comerica Park in April 2000."[29]

After those three games, HSN told Howarth that he would be hired to replace Early Wynn at the end of the season. However, a week before that 1980 season ended, HSN advised Howarth that out of sentiment and consideration of Wynn's Hall of Fame career, he would stay for one more season. Howarth was offered a 40-game schedule to broadcast games throughout the 1981 season. (Because of the two-month midseason strike, the 40-game schedule became 20.)[30] After the 1981 season, Wynn joined the Chicago White Sox radio broadcast team and the Blue Jays hired Howarth to replace him as analyst.[31]

Howarth was assigned the role of analyst despite not having played professional baseball. He notes in his book that at that time most radio broadcast teams were two play-by-play announcers.[32] Today, most major-league radio teams consist of a play-by-play announcer and a former player as the analyst.

Howarth believed his pairing with Cheek made an effective broadcast team, in part because of their contrast in styles.[33] He recalled Cheek as a Blue Jays fan who could reflect the ups and downs of the team with his voice, and the fans loved him.[34] Howarth focused on the game and strove for objectivity. He believed objectivity was a product of preparation and the ability to deliver constructive criticism. "There is a good way to be constructively critical of a player when you are up in the booth," he wrote. "Pretend the player is right beside you as you say it."[35]

Over a 36-year broadcasting career, Howarth had many career experiences. The 1992 season was a highlight. The Blue Jays, after losing the 1991 ALCS to the Minnesota Twins, had strengthened the team by acquiring Dave Winfield and Jack Morris. Howarth recalled having a sense of optimism about the 1992 season heading into spring training. This optimism was reinforced when a Blue Jays pitcher told him, "On day one, Jack Morris showed up in the clubhouse at the crack of dawn before anyone else. We all knew immediately that he meant business. He was here to do one thing; to win another World Series. It was an early wake up call for all of us."[36]

During the season, Howarth wrote, he could see that the 1992 Blue Jays were an outstanding team. When the Milwaukee Brewers challenged the Blue Jays starting in late August, Howarth felt that because every game down that last five-week stretch was so important it would make the Blue Jays that much better and stronger mentally to compete in the playoffs. In essence, September was like October and the experience proved to be a huge advantage for the Blue Jays.[37]

Howarth had 10 years of major-league broadcasting experience, including four League Championship Series (1985, 1989, 1991, and 1992), before he had the opportunity to call World Series games. As to whether broadcasting World Series games for the first time was different, he wrote:

For me, the World Series broadcasts were only different from this standpoint: because the crowds and crowd noise for each and every game was so loud and fun to listen to, it made all those games that much more enjoyable to be a part of including when there were big plays made by either team that allowed me then to purposely stop talking on the air after my call to let that crowd noise come into the microphone for our listeners to enjoy as much as I did. At times, I waited up to 40 and 45 seconds without saying a word for our audience to fully feel like they were at that game, too. My dad told me when I began my radio career in the AAA in Tacoma, Washington, "Jerry, broadcast every game as if it were a major league game" and I did that for my dad with my preparation for each game from day one right to my very last broadcast in the 2016 playoffs against Cleveland.[38]

After the 1992 World Series, Howarth got a letter from a member of a First Nations Community in Northern Ontario. The letter had an impact on how Howarth called games for the rest of his career.[39] The letter-writer's "polite request" described how the terms "Indians," "Braves," "pow-wows on the mound," and Cleveland's red-faced Chief Wahoo were so offensive. Howarth wrote back, promised to not use the terms any more and kept his word for the rest of his career.[40]

The Blue Jays won the World Series again in 1993, when Joe Carter hit a walk-off Series-ending home run for only the second time in major-league history. The first time was 1960 when Bill Mazeroski hit a home run in the bottom of the ninth inning in Game Seven as the Pittsburgh Pirates defeated the New York Yankees. Among teammates waiting at home plate for Mazeroski to celebrate was Pirates shortstop Dick Schofield. Thirty-three years later, celebrating at home plate with Joe was Blue Jays shortstop Dick Schofield Jr.[41] "What are the odds? That's why baseball is such a fascinating game."[42]

April 21, 1994, was an important day for the Howarth family. On that day, Jerry, his wife, Mary, and their two children, Ben and Joe, were sworn in as Canadian citizens.[43]

Howarth's broadcasting career expanded to include some limited television work in 2000 and 2001. Sportsnet, covering Blue Jays games on TV, had asked him to fill in for a couple of games during the 2000 regular season when none of the regular analysts were available. The network was pleased with his work and he was signed to work 20 TV games in the 2001 season. Howarth broadcast all the other games in the 2001 schedule on the radio with Cheek. After the season, Sportsnet advised Howarth that the number of TV broadcasts would expand to 140 and they were going to hire former Blue Jays pitcher John Cerutti as analyst. Howarth enjoyed his TV experience but "was also very happy to remain on the radio side where I was most comfortable."[44]

In 2003 Howarth and Cheek received the Sports Media Canada Award for Achievement in Broadcasting.[45]

The radio broadcast team continued to work together until Cheek was affected by illness. Howarth recalled that in 2004 Cheek began making serious mistakes in the play-by-play culminating in an incident in which he gave the score mentioning a team Toronto was not playing.[46] The next night, medical assistance was called as Cheek was unable to write his opening comments beyond "Live! From the Rogers Centre."[47] Cheek was diagnosed with a malignant brain tumor and died on October 9, 2005.

Howarth assumed the play-by-play duties and handled them for the balance of his broadcasting career. Told to choose his on-air partner, he elected to work in 2004 with nine different minor-league broadcasters whom he had mentored when their team played the Blue Jays.[48]

For the balance of Howarth's career, he worked with a variety of former players as his broadcast partner and analyst:

2005-2006	Warren Sawkiw[49]
2007-2012	Alan Ashby[50]
2013	Jack Morris[51]
2014-2017	Joe Siddall[52]

In 2012 Howarth received the Jack Graney Award for lifetime achievement from the Canadian Baseball Hall of Fame.[53] In 2016 he again received the Sports Media Canada award, this time as an individual.[54]

In the latter stages of Howarth's career, he did battle some health challenges. In November 2016 he required prostate cancer surgery,[55] after which he came back to broadcast for the 2017 season. On February 13, 2018, Howarth announced his retirement after deciding he no longer had the voice or the stamina to meet the level he had set for himself.[56]

In early 2022 Howarth was enjoying his retirement with Mary, his wife of 50 years. The couple enjoyed spending quiet time together as well as with their sons' families including three grandchildren. Playing duplicate bridge was also a favorite activity as well as following the Blue Jays as a fan. "I have been blessed with my life and I know it," he wrote in his memoir.[57]

In 2021 Howarth was honored by the City of Toronto with a street named Jerry Howarth Drive in Etobicoke, an area of Toronto where he and Mary live.[58]

ACKNOWLEDGMENT

Special thanks to Jerry Howarth, who provided biographical notes in personal correspondence with the author in January 2022.

SOURCES

In addition to the sources cited in the Notes, the author consulted the Baseball-Reference.com website.

NOTES

1   Jerry Howarth, *Hello Friends! Stories from My Life and Blue Jays Baseball* (Toronto: ECW Press, 2019), ix.

2   Howarth, 1.

3   Jerry Howarth, Biographical notes.

4   Howarth, 9.

5   Jerry Howarth, Biographical notes.

6   Howarth, 8.

7   Ryan Ford, 'Michigan Baseball's history at the College World Series," NCAA.com, June 22, 2019. https://www.ncaa.com/news/baseball/article/2019-06-22/michigan-baseballs-history-college-world-series, last referenced January 7, 2022.

8   Howarth, 13.

9   Howarth, 13.

10   Howarth, 10.

11   Howarth, 18.

12   Howarth, 18.

13   Howarth, 19.

14   Howarth, 20.

15   Howarth, 25.

16   Howarth, 26.

17   Howarth, 27.

18   Howarth, 29.

19   Howarth, 30.

20   Howarth, 37.

21   Howarth, 39.

22   Howarth, 40.

23   Howarth, 43.

24   Howarth, 47.

25   Howarth, 48.

26   Howarth, 49.

27   Howarth, 42.

28   Howarth, 51.

29   Jerry Howarth, Biographical notes.

30   Jerry Howarth, Biographical notes.

31   Howarth, 53.

32   Jerry Howarth, Biographical notes.

33   Howarth, 87.

34   Jerry Howarth, Biographical notes.

35   Howarth, 288.

36   Howarth, 144.

37   Jerry Howarth, Biographical notes.

38   Jerry Howarth, Biographical notes.

39   Howarth, 180.

40   Jerry Howarth, Biographical notes.

41   Howarth, 165.

42   Jerry Howarth, Biographical notes.

43   Howarth, 202.

44   Jerry Howarth, Biographical notes.

45   Sportsnet staff, "Blue Jays Broadcaster Jerry Howarth Retires After 36 Seasons," sportsnet.ca, February 13, 2018. https://www.sportsnet.ca/baseball/mlb/blue-jays-broadcaster-jerry-howarth-retires-36-seasons/, last referenced February 1, 2022.

46   Howarth, 246.

47   Howarth, 246.

48   Howarth, 246.

49   Howarth, 254.

50   Howarth, 254.

51   Howarth, 284.

52   Howarth, 283.

53   "Blue Jays Broadcaster Jerry Howarth Retires After 36 Seasons."

54   "Blue Jays Broadcaster Jerry Howarth Retires After 36 Seasons."

55   Howarth, 287.

56   Howarth, 323.

57   Jerry Howarth, Biographical notes.

58   Mark Zwolinski, "Jerry Howarth Drive Hits Close to Home for the Former Voice of the Blue Jays," *Toronto Star*, November 20, 2021.

BUCK MARTINEZ

By Curt Smith

Some baseball players evoke a position. Recall catcher Mickey Cochrane. Others define managing: Connie Mack comes to mind. Many broadcast as a color analyst or play-by-play man, like Bob Uecker and Bob Costas. Few have performed *all* of the above at one time or another as well as the Blue Jays' John Albert "Buck" Martinez, for whom the 2021 season marked his 53rd big-league year.

Before Buck became a Canadian fixture, his youth had a distinctly American lilt. According to Martinez, mother Shirley once served in the Women's Army Corps and made the cover of *Stars and Stripes* newspaper.[1] On December 7, 1941, his father John, a miner, was at Pearl Harbor in the midst of building a huge underground storage area to house fuel for the US Navy. Completing it, he enlisted in the Army in 1942.[2]

Buck was born on November 7, 1948, in Redding, California. He still has a picture of himself, at age 3, in a baseball uniform, near the site where his dad later built a diamond in their back yard. Martinez was in grammar school before learning that his real name was *John,* the sobriquet *Buck* hailing his Native

Buck Martinez: A Blue Jay on and above the field.

American heritage as an enrolled member of Northern California's Karuk Tribe.[3] By 10, the family in South Sacramento, he played on Parkway Little League and Southgate Babe Ruth teams, enamored of the pastime from the start.[4]

At nearby Elk Grove, Martinez was a three-year All-Conference choice, batting .512 as a senior. In 1966, the 5-foot-10, 190-pound right-handed catcher graduated from high school. Not immediately drafted by a big-league team, he got an associate of arts degree at Sacramento City College and studied at Sacramento State University. Meanwhile, Buck was signed by the Phillies as a 1967 amateur free agent, taken by the Astros in the December 1968 Rule 5 draft, and dealt later that month to Kansas City.[5]

The 1969 Royals began as an American League expansion team, Martinez debuting in the major leagues that June 18 at 20. Through 1977, his last year in Kansas City, Buck socked 13 homers, knocked in 104 runs, and averaged .222, including .333 in the then-best-of-five 1976 League Championship Series. By then, Martinez had met his future wife, Arlene, in San Juan, Puerto Rico in 1971 – Buck there for winter baseball; she, an American Airlines attendant, on vacation.[6]

"We had dinner, exchanged phone numbers, but then sort of lost touch for a few years," said Buck.[7] In 1974 they met again, began dating, and wed on July 14, 1975. In 1977, son Casey was born, later becoming a 47th-round pick by Toronto in the 2000 first-year player draft. A catcher like his father, he reached the Blue Jays' Triple-A Syracuse affiliate by 2001, his four-year playing career ending in the Phillies system in 2003.

Daily, baseball teaches humility. For Buck, November 1976 taught life's fragility. Arlene told him she was expecting their first child on the same day Martinez was shot in the left eye while hunting. After nine hours of surgery for a detached retina, his vision devolved from 20/15 to 20/250. "I went from play-off catcher to fourth-string catcher," he said, drolly, though the incident was no laughing matter. Martinez "needed to wear a contact lens in his left eye from then on," read the *Karuk Newsletter*.[8]

As a catcher, Buck upheld several long-held beliefs. One was the position's perceived weak-hitting bent. Thrice traded, Joe Garagiola, a .257 hitter from 1946 to '54, played for half of the then-eight National League clubs.[9] "I thought I was modeling uniforms," he joked.[10] Martinez may have felt that, too. On December 8, 1977, the Royals shipped him to St. Louis, which that day sent Buck to Milwaukee. On May 10, 1981, he was dealt again – to Toronto, for which he hit a career .222 but forged a single-year fielding percentage as high as .995.

Buck also affirmed catching's need to hang tough, "knocked out two or three times in collisions at home plate," he told CBS Sports.[11] In his first big-league start, Martinez collided with and tagged out the Twins' Bob Allison at the plate. "I threw the ball to third base, and I collapsed and I was unconscious. The trainers came out and gave me smelling salts, and I actually hit my first major-league home run in the next half-inning."[12]

At this point, Toronto still lacked a big-league franchise, Canada's largest city awarded an AL expansion team in March 1976.[13] "A nationwide contest chose the name Blue Jays. Fans came to our games from every province," Martinez said. "And we were aware of what we represented to the country."[14] The team's tricolor insignia fluttered in every province, even in the Montreal Expos' Quebec.

The Blue Jays' April 7, 1977, first opener remains parts fact and fable. Snow fell. "On the shores of Lake Ontario," Buck said, "people sat on aluminum chairs, the wind in force [wind-chill hit 10 degrees Fahrenheit]. Fans bundled up all year. So *Canadian!*"[15] The Jays beat Chicago, 9-5, before an overflow 44,649 in a 43,737-seat baseball capacity site. Doug Ault homered twice, becoming the club's first legend.[16]

In 1977 Buck's first visit to Toronto with the Royals, he saw how Exhibition Stadium resembled a "long, college football-style facility … converted for baseball use." Seats behind the plate and down each line "were really glorified bleachers." A left- to left-center-field football grandstand boasted the joint's "only covered seats."[17] In right field, a chain-link fence separated the outfield and vast "dead area," said Martinez. Behind it loomed a scoreboard, "far away from everything in the opposite end zone."[18]

Built on the Canadian National Exhibition's 350-acre fairgrounds, the makeshift *faux* grass park (née CNE Stadium) flanked "landscaped gardens, an amusement park, restaurants and concert facilities."[19] Frisbees and picnicking lent a down-home feel. A block away Lake Ontario brandished boats – and seagulls. Dave Winfield's 1983 warm-up throw accidentally killed one, prompting the Yankees outfielder's arrest.[20]

The first-year team drew 1,701,052, but lost 107 games. Between halves of the seventh inning, Exhibition crowds stood and stretched, yet invariably clapped softly – said Martinez, "the quietest in the league."[21] Once his wife, sitting with other Blue Jays wives, stood and implored spectators, "Come on, holler!"[22] To Martinez, noting how the park didn't sell beer, the stillness contrasted with his prior club in Milwaukee, where beer was appetizer, main course, and dessert.

"At first there was little reason to listen [or attend]," conceded 1977-2004 radio voice Tom Cheek, "except for the sheer novelty of big-league ball."[23] Blue Jays wireless/TV forged another. From birth, much of Canada has been isolated. The Jays wove a thread. Former Mets and Orioles Voice Gary Thorne once recalled how "Somewhere in a small town in the country [Canada or America], when you talked about the team, the broadcaster pictured the game for them night after night"[24] – mic men like Cheek their link to the club.

Other links became Tom's 1977-81 and 1981-2005 partners Early Wynn and Jerry Howarth, respectively – and eventually Martinez. As a player, Buck had aired 1982 World Series, LCS, and All-Star Game color commentary on the Telemedia Radio Network across Canada, Cheek on play-by-play.[25] Martinez also frequently appeared on Canada's The Sports Network (TSN) television. "Up 'til about then I hadn't really thought of retiring or announcing," Buck said. He might not have, if not for a play that begs credulity, even now.[26]

Martinez's second career unfolded from a July 9, 1985, match in Seattle's Kingdome. Buck started in his frequent role as a reserve or platoon catcher to Ernie Whitt, as he had to the Royals' Darrell Porter and Brewers' Ted Simmons, said SABR's David Firstman.[27] In the third inning, a *Ripley's Believe It or Not!* moment occurred that led Jays vice president Bobby Mattick, a 1938-40 Cubs and 1941-42 Reds infielder, to hail "the greatest baseball play I'd ever seen."[28]

The Mariners' Phil Bradley led off by singling. With one out, pitcher Tom Filer balked him to second base. Gorman Thomas then singled to right field, Jesse Barfield – to Firstman, "possessor of one of the finest outfield arms in history" – charging the ball and "uncork[ing] a laser toward the plate."[29] The throw, slightly up the third-base line, arrived as Bradley crashed into Martinez and knocked him on his back in the right-hand batter's box. Somehow, he held the ball for the out, but Buck's spikes caught in the ground and "two bones came dislocated out of the ankle socket and in fact, I broke the fibula – the small leg bone – up to my knee," he told the Canadian Broadcasting Corporation's *Midday*.[30]

At first Martinez thought that his leg was asleep. "There was no pain involved, but I couldn't move my leg. I couldn't rely on it at all to prop me up or move about anymore. It was dead."[31] As play continued, Buck, sitting but unable to stand, saw Thomas running between second and third base and threw toward third baseman Garth Iorg, the toss sailing into left field. Picking it up, George Bell fired to the plate. Martinez nabbed the ball as the 210-pound Thomas plowed homeward, tried to score standing up, but instead felt the prostrate Buck's tag to complete a surreal 9-2-7-2 double play.

Out for the season, Martinez missed the Jays' LCS loss to Kansas City, his mental pain as bad as physical, but wrote a book, *From Worst to First: The Toronto Blue Jays in 1985*.[32] After Buck's collision, wrote ESPN senior writer Tim Kurkjian, "he endured five months of 50 hours a week rehab just so he could play one more year for the Blue Jays at age 37."[33] In 1986 he hit .181 in 81 games, penned his second tome, *The Last Out: The Toronto Blue Jays in 1986,* and that December called its title "my last out as a player, the way it looks right now."[34]

In 1981-86, Martinez had graced up to 102 games (1984), hit as many as 10 homers (1982 and 1983), batted as high as .253 (1983), and made only two errors in each of 1981, 1984, 1985, and 1986. Buck's career featured 1,049 games, 58 homers, 321 RBIs, a .225 batting average – his offensive peak the early 1980s – and a .984 fielding percentage. Torn, wanting to play again, Martinez thought he could. Blue Jays President Paul Beeston didn't, thinking the injury had dimmed Buck's skill. They met prior to the 1987 season, Beeston asking, "Albert, you want to do TV?" as a Jays "colour commentator" on TSN.[35]

Buck's wife, his agent and future actress, suggested he try, saying, "You can't play anymore. This is a great opportunity."[36] Direct, she was correct. Martinez signed with TSN, utilizing, as Kurkjian wrote, what a makeup woman termed his "great [facial] base" and "a marvelous tone."[37] Buck began a new life by practicing

his delivery on the roof of the Jays' then-spring training park, Grant Field, in Dunedin, Florida. On the first-day ride home, he heard the tape and thought, "This is awful. I'm rotten."[38] Jerry Howarth added, "[Buck] always wanted to get better," amenable to criticism.[39]

Initially, Arlene told him, "You're trying to be [actor] Ted Knight," the formalized comic character Ted Baxter on TV's *The Mary Tyler Moore Show.* "Just be yourself."[40] She also persuaded him to take speech and acting classes. Ida Weedle, a speech pathologist, "got me [Buck] to start finishing my words."[41] Martinez's 1987-89 partner was play-by-play's Fergie Olver,[42] an ex-minor league and semipro Western Baseball League outfielder turned co-host of a CTV Television children's show, *Just Like Mom,* with then-wife Catherine Swing. Steadily improving, Buck never looked back.

On May 28, 1989, the Blue Jays bade Exhibition adieu: Toronto 7, White Sox 5. In 1963 John F. Kennedy recalled how as a boy the Irish writer Frank O'Connor and his friends would come to an arched wall while exploring the countryside. If it seemed too high or hard to hurdle, they removed their caps, flung them over the wall, and had to follow.[43] Domed stadiums kept out bad weather. Yet fans wanted to feel the sun and breeze. SkyDome became a solution, its first game June 5: the world's only stadium with a fully retractable roof,[44] which flung caps over the future, making baseball follow.

The 50,016-seat, five-tiered orb housed the 1991-92-93 AL East and 1992-93 World Series titlist. Its new digs helped lure a 1993 still-league record (as of 2022) 4,057,947 gate, averaging 50,098 per date. At SkyDome, Jim Hughson became TSN's Blue Jays play-by-play man in 1990, replacing Olver. He and Buck teamed through 1994, the British Columbia native calling each 1991-93 Jays division-clinching title.[45] (In 1995-2001, Toronto-born Dan Shulman succeeded him.) Martinez added 1994-95's ABC/NBC *The Baseball Network* – and 1992-2000's and 2002-05's ESPN, its coverage of Cal Ripken Jr.'s record-breaking 2,131st straight game taking a 1995 Sports Emmy Award.[46]

In early 2000 ESPN enlarged Martinez's portfolio by hiring him for *Baseball Tonight*. "His first appearance looked like it could have been his 500th, it was that seamless," wrote Tim Kurkjian. Buck wasn't pleased with his preparation, thinking, "That won't happen again." It didn't. "One night," Tim noted, "he did a Blue Jays game on TSN, but because the game ran late, he missed his flight to Connecticut for a *Sunday Baseball Today* show."[47] Martinez drove 500 miles from Toronto to ESPN's Bristol, Connecticut, home, "using his cell phone for script updates and arriving 10 minutes before airtime." Buck minimized the effort, saying, "It was my job."[48]

That year attendance fell to 1,819,919,[49] helping induce another Martinez career – his November 3 hiring to replace Jim Fregosi as 2001 Jays skipper despite a lack of even coaching experience. Buck's sole managerial stint had been with "Martinez's Marauders" at the 1995-96 Blue Jays' Fantasy Camp. Former Padres and Astros skipper Preston Gomez told him, "Remember, the ball looks really small up in the booth. But down on the field, the ball is really big."[50] The populace cheered. Drivers left their cabs in the middle of the street to thank him. Martinez recalled season-ticket holders saying they hadn't been "so excited in five years."[51]

After Buck's signing, Kurkjian observed that "even as a player, [Martinez] was the guy from whom many of the Blue Jays players sought advice and went to," not "some self-infatuated gasbag who believes the team revolves around him."[52] GM Gord Ash said, "Sports is a people business. It's a business of communication and Buck is an excellent communicator."[53] He wrote letters to 32 players, telling them "he thought they could make up the five games that kept them from the [2000] playoffs."[54] Martinez phoned several personally, also speaking with big-league players-turned-managers Cookie Rojas, Don Zimmer, and, most famously, Joe Torre.[55]

Sadly, the 2001 Jays finished 80-82, had a home game postponed by metal siding and insulation falling from the roof,[56] and braved an adverse currency exchange rate: revenue in Canadian dollars, salaries in more costly US dollars. On June 3, 2002, the 20-33 Jays ditched Buck for minor-league skipper Carlos Tosca. "I don't know if [he] even knows what his philosophy or style is because he hasn't had a lot of time to manage," said new GM J.P. Ricciardi. "It's not so much the wins, the losses at this point, it's more the leadership."[57] Of Martinez he told CBC: "He's a class act. He handled this in a very professional manner."[58] Said Buck: "Gord Ash had been fired after my first season, never a good sign. I made mistakes, but … it made possible all that's happened since."[59]

Martinez managed Team USA in the 2006 inaugural World Baseball Classic, airing the next WBC tournaments in 2009, 2013, and 2017.[60] In 2003-09, Buck did Baltimore Orioles color with play-by-play's

Jim Hunter, then Gary Thorne, on TV's Mid-Atlantic Sports Network (MASN), taking a second Emmy for Best Analyst, Regional Sports Network.[61] He added TBS's 2008-09 postseason and *Sunday Afternoon Baseball* color with Chip Caray – and co-hosted 2005-09 XM Radio's *Baseball This Morning*; in 2009 substituted for the ill Jerry Remy on the Red Sox' New England Sports Network (NESN); and did the 2016-20 World Series and All-Star Game for MLB International.

In 2010, returning to the Jays, Martinez did play-by-play for 110 games on Canada's Rogers Sportsnet cable TV network, replacing Jamie Campbell,[62] and was hired to host the new pregame *Blue Jays Central*.[63] "I think it's a different challenge for me," Buck said. "Obviously, it's a different role but because I've been blessed with so many play-by-play partners – Tom Cheek, [previously noted] Jim Hughson, and Dan Shulman and the guys at ESPN – I think I can take something from all of them."[64]

By now, Jays radio/TV headliners largely differed from a decade earlier. In 2001 Cheek received the Canadian Baseball Hall of Fame's Jack Graney Award, named for the first Canadian major-league voice.[65] Tom broadcast 4,306 consecutive games, the streak ending with his father's death in 2004. Ten days later, he braved brain tumor surgery on his 65th birthday.[66] Cancer returned that offseason, demanding further treatment. On Opening Day 2005, Cheek aired an inning in person on the wireless at Tampa Bay, near his Florida home.

A nation grieved Tom's October 9 death at 66, ending the beloved "Tom and Jerry [Howarth] Show." In 2013 he posthumously became the 37th annual recipient of the National Baseball Hall of Fame and Museum's Ford C. Frick Award for "broadcast excellence."[67] Martinez recalled, "He was the voice and face of the Blue Jays."[68] Cheek often said, "Give me music with a message."[69] His message – inspiring other Toronto mic men – was that knowing baseball's heart could make its music soar.

Shulman, for instance, the first Canadian named National Sportscaster of the Year by the National Association of Sportscasters and Sportswriters and a 2020 Graney Award recipient, buoyed 2002-17 ESPN TV and 2016- Sportsnet Jays play-by-play with Buck.[70] In 1993 another contemporary, Pat Tabler, joined TSN's *Baseball Tonight* after a 12-year playing career.[71] Hired by Sportsnet in 2005, a decade later he inked an extension with Martinez through 2019 – "our soundtrack to a season of strikeouts, stolen bases, and home runs," said network vice president Rob Corte.[72]

Increasingly, their club bounced between poles. In 2003 Roy Halladay's 22-7 holiday earned a Cy Young Award. The '04-05ers then flunked .500. In 2005 SkyDome was renamed the Rogers Centre after its purchase by Jays owner Rogers Communications. Next season five Blue Jays made the All-Star team – the most since 1993. In 2008 nostalgia bloomed, 1989-1997 skipper Cito Gaston rehired to manage. Halladay won his 129th Jays game, behind only another big-game pitcher Dave Stieb's 175.

On October 3, 2009, Ricciardi was ditched for assistant general manager Alex Anthopoulos, Toronto having missed the playoffs in J.P.'s eight years as GM.[73] Next season the Blue Jays hit a franchise-high 257 home runs: Like 2000, seven smacked 20 or more, José Bautista (54) the 26th player with 50 or more.[74] "I was marking my scoreboard when suddenly I looked up to see the ball clearing the fence," said a surprised Martinez. "All I could say was, 'Fifty!'"[75] Halladay moved to Philadelphia, retiring in 2013 after signing a ceremonial one-day Toronto pact.[76]

At his 2015-19 Sportsnet signing, Buck evoked 2010: "[Then] I stepped into the unknown as the play-by-play guy but now, looking ahead for the next five years, I couldn't be happier." Reader critique included "Buck is a boring parrot" to "He's [equal to] Vin Scully."[77] Ending North America's longest active professional sports playoff drought, the '15 Jays took the AL East and erased Texas's 2-0 best-of-five Division Series lead on Bautista's last-game three-run homer succeeded by an "epic bat flip"[78] – to some, violating an unwritten code against disparaging the other team.[79]

In the melee's wake, benches twice cleared and garbage littered the Rogers Centre field. Toronto next advanced to the LCS, Game Six drawing Sportsnet's then-all-time largest audience – 5.12 million viewers for Kansas City's Game Six-clinching triumph.[80] On May 15, 2016, a pitch by the Rangers' Matt Bush hit José to repay his prior year bat flip. In turn, the Jays' slugger illegally slid into infielder Rougned Odor, who slugged Bautista in the jaw to start the first of two more brawls.[81]

On October 4 Toronto met Baltimore in the league's wild-card game. An average audience of 4.02 million viewers eyed Sportsnet's most-watched 2016 telecast, Edwin Encarnacion's three-run 11th-inning homer sealing a 5-2 Jays triumph.[82] Implausibly, almost as many Canadians as Americans watched, despite the huge disparity in population: an estimated 36,379,574 in Canada vs. the United States' 324,738,713.[83] Toronto again beat Texas in the Division Series before losing the LCS to Cleveland.

Thirty years earlier Martinez had released *The Last Out: The Toronto Blue Jays in 1986*. In 2016 he issued his third book, *Change Up: How to Make the Great Game of Baseball Even Better*.[84] "Current players make much more money than he did behind the plate," said CBC Sports, "but [Buck] thinks they're the ones missing out" – in part because money "has displaced team unity as the heart of baseball – and the spirit of the game has suffered as a result." How to revive it? Martinez had a thought.

"The money being made today is great," he began.[85] In his first year in Kansas City, Buck had made $10,000. In 2021, said Statista, the big leagues' *average* yearly wage was $4.17 *million*.[86] "I don't begrudge the players, most of 'em now a mini-corporation," Martinez said. "It's just that when you get more financially secure, you get more independent – it's a natural progression. That's why guys today miss a lot of what we had."[87]

Playing, he said, "we lived in the same spring training complex, had barbecues on the beach, most of us with only one car, so we car-pooled to the park. Our wives baby-sat for each other's kids. We looked after each other." Come April, "we lived in the same apartment complex – a place near Exhibition Stadium named the Palace Pier." Friendship fueled success "because you don't want to let your friends down."[88] Today, money made that feeling hard.

To Martinez, former Yankees captain Derek Jeter showed how money did not negate the reason "we played the game. Derek was in love with baseball, demanding respect from players *for* it."[89] After teammate Robinson Cano "had a great game," he sat reading a paper at his locker while giving an interview. Jeter told him, "We don't treat people like that in this clubhouse." Cano never read papers again, talking to a reporter.[90]

"Whenever I'd see Derek, he was messing with the guys, a great sense of humor,"[91] Buck continued. Chemistry was key – in or beneath the booth. He and Pat Tabler met at 3:30 before a night game "to talk about what we wanted to note," letting "one [broadcaster] know where the other was going before he said a word." It helped them accent how one player's strengths could enhance another's, "showing your audience in advance what they are."[92]

In 2017 polarity continued. Steve Pearce belted grand slams three days apart. Halladay was killed in a plane crash. Next season Tampa Bay bench coach Charlie Montoyo became the Blue Jays skipper. In 2019 several second-generation players made the team: Bo Bichette (his father, Dante), Cavan Biggio (Craig), and Vladimir Guerrero Jr. (Sr.)[93] A year later Halladay made Cooperstown. The Covid-19 virus forced the Jays to move most SkyDome games to Triple-A outlet Buffalo's home ballpark, Sahlen Field.

In 2020 Martinez was named president of a group founded in 1986 by former big-league players, especially 1991 Frick honoree Joe Garagiola: the Baseball Assistance Team.[94] At BAT's birth, the average major-league salary was $412,520.[95] "One pitcher didn't have the money to bury an 11-year-old son. A former Dodger had to consider a raffle to afford an amputated leg," Joe said. "There was no pension then to help."[96] BAT paid bills, bought insurance, preserved dignity: for Buck, a natural evolution.

In 2021 the Karuk Tribe descendant also went to bat for the Indigenous people "[who] did many great things that still aren't recognized as part of the overall culture of Native Americans," said Buck. He voiced video biographies for *The Indigenous Sports Heroes Education Experience,* a "multi-platform, web-based book, curriculum and celebration of 14 Indigenous Hall of Famers" from Colette Bourgonje and Bill Isaacs to Chief Wilton Littlechild and Bryan Trottier, available to teachers and students from kindergarten to grade 12.[97]

That July 30, the Jays returned to Rogers Centre from Covid-19-dictated games in Dunedin and Buffalo. Robbie Ray became their fourth Cy Young Award pitcher, joining Pat Hentgen, Stieb, and Halladay. Toronto's power was as potent: eight homers in a game and a team and big-league season record 262. In 2021, Guerrero clubbed 48 to lead a franchise-tying seven Jays who for a third time hit 20 or more. Others: Marcus Semien, Teoscar Hernandez, Bichette, George Springer, Randal Grichuk, and Lourdes Gurriel Jr.[98]

Each Blue Jay helped fashion a 91-71 record, one game behind the Red Sox and Yankees in a wild last-week AL wild-card race. Since 1977 interest in the club has rarely failed, as John F. Kennedy said, to "throw [its] cap over" Exhibition Stadium's and Rogers Centre's "wall."[99] A reason is the man who as of 2021 had spent 17 years playing, two managing, and 34 in the booth.

Early in 2022, Buck was diagnosed with cancer, leaving the Blue Jays broadcast booth. "I'm grateful for a tremendous medical team, who has given me great optimism that I will come through this with flying colours,"[100] Martinez said, hoping to rejoin Sportsnet later in the year. Until then, Buck would be "watching from the sidelines."

He returned to the Sportsnet booth in Toronto on July 26, broadcasting that night's game with Dan Shulman. Likely, he took solace from past experience, where good fortune had followed bad. After all, the 1985 collision that broke a small leg bone may have been the best break of Buck Martinez's career.

SOURCES

I wish to thank the sources cited under "Interviews by author," notably Buck Martinez. Grateful appreciation is made to reprint all play-by-play and color radio text courtesy of The Miley Collection. In addition to the sources cited in the Notes, most especially the Society for American Baseball Research, the author consulted Baseball-Reference.com and Retrosheet.org websites, box scores, player, season, and team pages, batting and pitching logs, and other relevant material to this history. FanGraphs.com provided statistical information. Beyond the sources cited in the Notes, the author consulted:

BOOKS

Elliott, Bob. *If These Walls Could Talk: Toronto Blue Jays: Stories from the Toronto Blue Jays Dugout, Locker Room, and Press Box* (Chicago: Triumph Books, 2020).

Martinez, Buck. *From Worst to First: The Toronto Blue Jays in 1985* (Toronto: Fitzhenry and Whiteside, 1985).

Martinez. *The Last Out: The Toronto Blue Jays in 1986* (Toronto: Fitzhenry and Whiteside, 1986).

Martinez, with Dan Robson. *Change Up: How to Make the Great Game of Baseball Even Better* (Toronto: HarperCollins, 2016).

O'Connell, Kevin, and Josh Pahigian. *The Ultimate Baseball Trip: A Fan's Guide to Major League Stadiums* (Guilford, Connecticut: Lyons Press, 2012).

Public Papers of the Presidents of the United States: John F. Kennedy 1963 (Washington, D.C.: Office of Federal Register, National Archives and Records Administration, 1964).

Shea, Stuart. Gary Gillette (ed.) *Calling the Game: Baseball Broadcasting from 1920 to the Present* (Phoenix: Society for American Baseball Research, 2015).

Ward, Geoffrey C. *Baseball: An Illustrated History* (New York: Alfred A. Knopf, 1994).

NEWSPAPERS

The *Globe and Mail* (Toronto), *Toronto Star,* and *Toronto Sun* have been primary sources of information about Buck Martinez and his playing, managing, and broadcasting career. Other key sources include the *Baltimore Sun, Kansas City Star,* and *USA Today.*

Interviews by author

Tom Cheek, 1994 and 2002.

Joe Garagiola, 1993.

Jerry Howarth, 2009.

Tim Kurkjian, 2010.

Buck Martinez, 2022.

Dan Shulman, 2009.

Gary Thorne, 2010.

NOTES

1   Buck Martinez interview, January 2022.

2   Martinez interview, 2022.

3   Martinez interview.

4   *Karuk Newsletter*, Spring 2017, 18. https://www.karuk.us/images/docs/newsletters/2017_Spring_Newsletter.pdf.

5   Martinez interview.

6   https://dodoodad.com/buck-martinez/.

7   Martinez interview.

8   *Karuk Newsletter*, Spring 2017, 18.

9   Warren Corbett, "Joe Garagiola," SABR BioProject. https://sabr.org/bioproj/person/joe-garagiola/.

10 Warren Corbett, "Joe Garagiola."

11 R.J. Anderson, "Buck Martinez, Who Says He Was 'Knocked Out' Many Times, Still Opposes Posey Rule," CBS Sports.com, September 28, 2017. https://www.cbssports.com/mlb/news/buck-martinez-who-says-he-was-knocked-out-many-times-still-opposes-posey-rule/.

12 Anderson.

13 https://www.thecanadianencyclopedia.ca/en/article/toronto-blue-jays.

14 Martinez interview.

15 Martinez interview.

16 Ron Smith, *The Ballpark Book: A Journey Through the Fields of Baseball Magic* (St. Louis: The Sporting News, 2000), 294.

17 *The Ballpark Book*, 294.

18 Martinez interview.

19 *The Ballpark Book*, 294.

20 *The Ballpark Book*, 293.

21 Martinez interview.

22 Martinez interview.

23 Tom Cheek interview, 1994.

24 Gary Thorne interview, 2010.

25 Martinez interview.

26 Martinez interview.

27 David Firstman, "July 9, 1985: Catcher Buck Martinez Tags Out Two Baserunners on Same Play," SABR Games Project. https://sabr.org/gamesproj/game/july-9-1985-catcher-buck-martinez-tags-out-two-baserunners-on-same-play/.

28 Tim Kurkjian, "Buck Martinez Is About to Take On a Brand-New Role – One He's Been Rehearsing For His Whole Life," ESPN.com. https://www.espn.com/espn/magazine/archives/news/story?page=magazine-20010122-article38.

29 David Firstman.

30 "Buck Martinez's Broken Leg and His Journey into Broadcasting," CBC Archives, January 6, 2019. https://www.cbc.ca/archives/buck-martinez-s-broken-leg-and-his-journey-into-broadcasting-1.4963392.

31 "Buck Martinez's Broken Leg and His Journey into Broadcasting."

32 https://www.goodreads.com/book/show/3746572-from-worst-to-first.

33 Kurkjian.

34 "Buck Martinez's Broken Leg and His Journey into Broadcasting."

35 Martinez interview.

36 Martinez interview.

37 Kurkjian.

38 Kurkjian.

39 Kurkjian.

40 Martinez interview.

41 Martinez interview.

42 https://www.liquisearch.com/buck_martinez/broadcasting.

43 https://www.markholan.org/archives/2810.

44 www.pbs.org/wgbh/buildingbig/wonder/structure/sky.html.

45 https://icehockey.fandom.com/wiki/Jim_Hughson.

46 "Blue Jays Broadcasters." https://www.mlb.com/bluejays/team/broadcasters.

47 Kurkjian.

48 Kurkjian.

49 https://www.baseball-almanac.com/teams/toroatte.shtml#:~:text=Toronto%20Blue%20Jays%20Attendance%201977%20-%202020%20,%20A.L.%20Average%20%203%20more%20rows%20?msclkid=4da140dea57111ec8dac2f9a5f96cbd7.

50 Kurkjian.

51 Martinez interview.

52 Kurkjian.

53 Kurkjian.

54 Kurkjian. The deficit was actually 4½ games in 2000.

55 Kurkjian.

56 "SkyDome Roof Shreds," CBC Sports, April 12, 2001. https://www.cbc.ca/sports/baseball/skydome-roof-shreds-1.277009.

57 Associated Press, "Martinez Fired During Second Season with Jays," ESPN, June 4, 2002. https://a.espncdn.com/mlb/news/2002/0603/1390123.html.

58 "Blue Jays Fire Buck Martinez," CBC Sports, June 4, 2002. https://www.cbc.ca/sports/baseball/blue-jays-fire-buck-martinez-1.349252.

59 Martinez interview.

60 "Blue Jays Broadcasters,"

61 "Blue Jays Broadcasters."

62 Chris Zelkovich, "Sportsnet Hits a Homer in Landing Martinez," *Toronto Star*, December 11, 2009. https://www.thestar.com/sports/baseball/2009/12/11/zelkovich_sportsnet_hits_a_homer_in_landing_martinez.html.

63 https://www.imdb.com/title/tt4368002/characters/nm7061962.

64 Chris Zelkovich, "Buck Martinez Returns as Blue Jays TV Announcer," *Toronto Star*, December 10, 2009. https://www.thestar.com/sports/baseball/2009/12/10/buck_martinez_returns_as_blue_jays_tv_announcer.html.

65 "Tom Cheek," Canadian Baseball Hall of Fame. https://baseballhalloffame.ca/hall-of-famer/tom-cheek/.

66 "Tom Cheek."

67 "Tom Cheek."

68 Martinez interview.

69 Cheek interview, 1994.

70 "Blue Jays Broadcasters."

71 "Blue Jays Broadcasters."

72 Sportsnet staff, "Sportsnet Locks Up Blue Jays Broadcast Duo," Sportsnet.ca, September 25, 2014. https://www.sportsnet.ca/baseball/mlb/martinez-tabler-to-return-for-five-more-years/.

73 Associated Press, "Blue Jays Fire GM Ricciardi," ESPN.com, October 3, 2009. https://www.espn.com/mlb/news/story?id=4528183.

74 "Jose Bautista Becomes First Player Since 2007 to Hit 50 Home Runs in One Season," NESN.com, September 23, 2010. https://nesn.com/2010/09/jose-bautista-becomes-first-player-since-2007-to-hit-50-home-runs-in-one-season/.

75 Martinez interview.

76 Matt Snyder, "Roy Halladay Retires as a Blue Jay," CBSports.com, December 9, 2013. https://www.cbssports.com/mlb/news/roy-halladay-retires-as-a-blue-jay/.

77 "Sportsnet Locks Up Blue Jays Broadcast Duo."

78 Howie Kussoy, "Jose Bautista's Epic Bat Flip Is Quite Polarizing," *New York Post*, October 15, 2015. https://nypost.com/2015/10/15/jose-bautistas-epic-bat-flip-is-quite-polarizing/.

79 Kussoy.

80 Sportsnet, "5.12 Million Viewers Watch Blue Jays vs. Kansas City ALCS Game 6 on Sportsnet; Delivers Most-Watched Broadcast in Network History," newswire.ca, October 26, 2015. https://www.newswire.ca/news-releases/512-million-viewers-watch-blue-jays-vs-kansas-city-alcs-game-6-on-sportsnet-delivers-most-watched-broadcast-in-network-history-537260561.html.

81 SI Wire, "Watch: Blue Jays, Rangers Brawl after Takeout Slide," www.si.com. May 15, 2016. https://www.si.com/mlb/2016/05/15/watch-blue-jays-rangers-brawl-after-takeout-slide.

82 Ian Campbell, "Sportsnet reporting big ratings win with Blue Jays wild card game." Calgary CityNews, October 5, 2016. "https://calgary.citynews.ca/2016/10/05/sportsnet-reporting-big-ratings-win-blue-jays-wild-card-game/"

83 Andrew Buckholtz, "Almost as Many Canadians as Americans Watched Jays-O's Despite Population Difference," AwfulAnnouncing.com, October 5, 2016. https://awfulannouncing.com/2016/almost-as-many-canadians-as-americans-watched-jays-os-despite-population-difference.html#.

84 CBC Radio, "Why Buck Martinez Feels Bad for Today's Baseball Players," cbc.ca, March 22, 2016. https://www.cbc.ca/radio/q/schedule-for-tuesday-march-22-2016-1.3501928/why-buck-martinez-feels-bad-for-today-s-baseball-players-1.3501932.

85 Martinez interview.

86 https://www.statista.com/statistics/236213/mean-salary-of-players-in-majpr-league-baseball/#.

87 Martinez interview.

88 Martinez interview.

89 Martinez interview.

90 Martinez interview.

91 Martinez interview.

92 Martinez interview.

93 Joon Lee, "Why Vladimir Guerrero Jr., Bo Bichette and Cavan Biggio Are Ready for the Next Step," ESPN.com, February 25, 2020. https://www.espn.com/mlb/story/_/id/28711372/why-vladimir-guerrero-jr-bo-bichette-cavan-biggio-ready-next-step.

94 Associated Press, "Joe Garagiola, Ex-Player Turned Glib Broadcaster, Dies at 90," Newschannel 5 Nashville, March 23, 2016. https://www.newschannel5.com/news/national/joe-garagiola-ex-player-turned-glib-broadcaster-dies-at-90#.

95 Edmund P. Edmonds, "MLB Minimum and Average Salaries, 1967-2012," Notre Dame Law School, February 2, 2012. https://scholarship.law.nd.edu/cgi/viewcontent.cgi?article=1000&context=baseball_salaries.

96 Joe Garagiola interview, 1993.

97 David Giddens, CBC Sports, "Indigenous Sports Heroes in the Classroom," cbc.ca, August 9, 2021. https://www.cbc.ca/sportslongform/entry/indigenous-sports-heroes-heading-to-the-classroom.

98 Laura Armstrong, "A Look at Blue Jays Season, by the Numbers, Will Make Fans Wonder Why the Team Didn't Make the MLB Playoffs," *Toronto Star*, October 4, 2021. https://www.thestar.com/sports/bluejays/2021/10/04/a-look-at-blue-jays-season-by-the-numbers-will-just-make-fans-wonder-why-the-team-didnt-make-the-mlb-playoffs.html#.

99 Mark Holan, "Remember J.F.K. – 3 – Caps Over Walls," n.d. https://www.markholan.org/archives/2810.

100 https://www.aol.com/mlb-broadcaster-stepping-away-following-165556490.html.

POSTLUDE

EPILOGUE

BLUE JAYS PLAY CAPITAL CITY DOUBLEHEADER DECEMBER 16, 1992: W ORLD SERIES CHAMPIONS FETED AT WHITE HOUSE AND RIDEAU HALL

By Mark Davis

Many Blue Jays fans will forever remember the television play-by-play call after the final out of the 1992 World Series: "For the first time in history, the World Championship banner will fly north of the border. The Toronto Blue Jays are baseball's best in 1992."[1] In defeating the Atlanta Braves and becoming the first Canada- (and non-American) based team to win the World Series, the Blue Jays not only made baseball headlines, they also added a new chapter to America's and Canada's political histories.

The day after the win, manager Cito Gaston received the customary congratulatory phone call from President George H.W. Bush, along with an invitation for his team to attend a celebratory reception at the White House.[2] For the first time in World Series history, the winning manager received a second congratulatory message from another world leader, the prime minister of Canada, Brian Mulroney.[3] This message was followed by an invitation from Ray Hnatyshyn, the governor general of Canada (the Queen's representative), to a reception in the team's honor at his official residence at Rideau Hall in the Canadian capital, Ottawa.[4]

(Photo courtesy of Library and Archives Canada.)

Governor General Ray Hnatyshyn greets Roberto Alomar as Paul Beeston looks on during a reception honoring the World Series Champion Toronto Blue Jays at Rideau Hall in Ottawa on December 16, 1992.

WE ARE, WE CAN, WE WILL

(Photo courtesy of Library and Archives Canada.)

Ottawa: The Governor General chats with Juan Guzman and American League President, Dr. Bobby Brown, during the Rideau Hall reception.

Perhaps it was fitting that the Blue Jays were hosted by President Bush and Prime Minister Mulroney on the same day, December 16, 1992. The two leaders enjoyed a close relationship during President Bush's term in office and achieved many accomplishments, most notably the signing of the North American Free Trade Agreement (NAFTA).[5] Bush and Mulroney also shared a common interest in major-league baseball. During his time as prime minister, Mulroney invited Bush to Toronto's SkyDome twice for baseball-related events: The pair threw out the ceremonial first pitch for the Blue Jays' home opener against the Texas Rangers in 1990, and Bush was Mulroney's guest at the 1991 All-Star Game.[6]

It is perhaps also ironic that although Bush and Mulroney enjoyed many successes, they also suffered similar career-ending electoral defeats around the same time as the Blue Jays' historic win. On November 3, 1992, Bush lost his race for reelection to Bill Clinton.[7] Earlier, on October 26, Canadians voted a resounding "No" in a national referendum on constitutional reform. Mulroney's popularity, already at historic lows, plummeted even further in light of this defeat, which led him to announce his intention to resign from office in February 1993.[8]

Members of the World Series champions assembled at the Capital Hilton Hotel in Washington on the afternoon of December 15. There were 21 players, including Jack Morris, Joe Carter, and Mike Timlin. Representing the coaching staff were Cito Gaston and first-base coach Bob Bailor, who was the first Blue Jay selected in the 1976 major-league expansion draft. Also present were Blue Jays President Paul Beeston and general manager Pat Gillick. The group also featured several recently departed and longtime Blue Jays including Kelly Gruber, who had been traded to the California Angels, and Dave Stieb, who had signed as a free agent with the Chicago White Sox. Notable players absent included World Series MVP Pat Borders, who was unable to attend due to the imminent birth of his second child,[9] and Dave Winfield, who declined the invitation after failing to negotiate a two-year contract extension with the club.[10] That evening, the Canadian ambassador to the United States hosted the team at a reception in their honor at the Canadian embassy on Pennsylvania Avenue, a few blocks from the US Capitol.[11]

The next morning the Blue Jays arrived at the White House for a public reception with President Bush in the Old Executive Building. Representing Major League Baseball were American League President Bobby Brown, Deputy Commissioner Steve Greenberg, and umpires Mike Reilly and Joe West. Also in attendance were four national Little League championship teams, including the 6-12-year-old division champions from Lexington, Kentucky, who surprised the press pool by claiming they were more excited to meet the Blue Jays than the president. "We just like baseball better," one boy explained.[12]

The president began his remarks by poking fun at his government's NAFTA negotiators, quipping, "Our free trade agreement with Canada did not mean that the United States would trade away the world's championship."[13] Bush commended the Atlanta Braves and the Blue Jays for a hard-fought World Series, saying they "staged a fall classic that even Ripley wouldn't believe."[14] He congratulated the Blue Jays on their accomplishment, saying that although he had rooted for the Braves, he was proud of Cito Gaston and his team. "By winning Canada's first World Series … you did it with class … and class, of course, has marked the entire Blue Jays history. In 16 years, you've gone from the doghouse to the penthouse."[15] Acknowledging that the reception was "about as much fun as I've had since the election," Bush concluded his remarks by presenting Gaston with a baseball card from his playing days at Yale University, noting, "This is a rookie ballplayer who needs a job."[16] Before Bush departed, Beeston and Carter presented the president with a customized white home jersey.[17]

After the White House visit, the Blue Jays flew north to Ottawa. Upon arrival, the team briefly chatted and signed autographs for a small group of fans at the airport before proceeding to Rideau Hall. Governor General Ray Hnatyshyn led the welcoming delegation that also included the prime minister and two Canadian Supreme Court justices.[18] In addition to the team, the official guest list also included patients and staff from the local children's hospital, members of a local Little League team, and students from a local high school who earned their invitation by collecting the most items for the Ottawa food bank.[19]

Hnatyshyn began by welcoming "Canada's team" to Ottawa. He referred to the Blue Jays as "the greatest group ever to come out on a baseball field," and shared his belief that the team's success would inspire more Canadian youth to pursue professional baseball.[20] Hnatyshyn also made reference to Mulroney's low popularity among Canadians, claiming that unlike Mulroney, he was an appointed official and thus had a "no-cut contract."[21] The prime minister commented that "the Blue Jays have finished off what the Expos began," a reference to the major leagues' Canadian debut in Montreal in 1969.[22] Mulroney also quipped that he would likely soon be available to be drafted, should the Blue Jays be interested.[23] The team each

(Photo courtesy of the George H.W. Bush Presidential Library and Museum.)

Washington: President George H.W. Bush delivers opening remarks at a White House reception for the World Series Champion Toronto Blue Jays on December 16, 1992.

(Photo courtesy of the George H.W. Bush Presidential Library and Museum.)

Washington: Paul Beeston and Joe Carter present the President with his customized Blue Jays jersey at the conclusion of the White House reception.

presented Hnatyshyn and Mulroney customized white home jerseys, both bearing the number 1.[24]

While the Blue Jays' World Series victory no doubt helped to promote baseball in Canada, it could also be argued that their whirlwind celebration on December 16, 1992, helped to recognize major-league baseball as a truly international league. As an article in the *Chicago Tribune* noted the day after the Blue Jays became champions, "Finally, the World in baseball's Series is more than a meaningless adjective."[25]

NOTES

1   MLB Vault, "1992 World Series, Game 6: Blue Jays @ Braves," https://www.youtube.com/watch?v=IKwinmoAR2w (accessed February 14, 2022).

2   Canadian Press, "Series Notes: On to White House," *Ottawa Citizen*, October 26, 1992: C2.

3   Nicolaas van Rijn, "Jubilant Jay Fans Pack Yonge St. in Delirium of Joy," *Toronto Star*, October 25, 1992: A1.

4   "Series Champs to Visit Ottawa," *Ottawa Citizen*, December 15, 1992: C1.

5   Laura Macdonald, "Canada and NAFTA," https://www.thecanadianencyclopedia.ca/en/article/north-american-free-trade-agreement-nafta (accessed February 7, 2022).

6   Stephen Dame, "First Base Among Equals: Prime Ministers and Canada's National Game," *Baseball Research Journal* 49, no. 1 (2020), 57-61.

7   Michael Levy, "United States Presidential Election of 1992," https://www.britannica.com/event/United-States-presidential-election-of-1992 (accessed February 7, 2022).

8   Norman Hillmer, "Brian Mulroney," https://www.thecanadianencyclopedia.ca/en/article/brian-mulroney (accessed February 7, 2022).

9   George H.W. Bush, "Public Papers: Remarks Honoring the World Series Champion Toronto Blue Jays," https://bush41library.tamu.edu/archives/public-papers/5119 (accessed February 7, 2022).

10 Associated Press, "Blue Jays Land Stewart," *Ottawa Citizen*, December 9, 1992: E1.

11 Jim Byers, "Gruber Won't Retaliate Against Critical Ex-Mates," *Ottawa Citizen*, December 16, 1992: D2.

12 Mary Ann Roser, "Blue Jays Bigger Hit Than Bush with Bambinos," *Lexington* (Kentucky) *Herald-Leader*, December 17, 1992: 27.

13 Bush.

14 Bush.

15 Bush.

16 Bush.

17 "Mulroney, Bush Say They're Ready to Play Ball as the Popular Blue Jays Meet the Leaders," *Edmonton Journal*, December 17, 1992: 2.

18 Jeffrey Simpson, "Some Jays Finally Visit Bush, Mulroney/Winfield, Key, Cone, Henke Among No-Shows as 21 Players from World Series Team Make Trip," *Globe and Mail* (Toronto), December 17, 1992: C8.

19 *Ottawa Citizen.*

20 Simpson.

21 *Edmonton Journal.*

22 Ken Warren, "PM Delivers Blue Jays," *Ottawa Citizen*, December 17: D1.

23 *Edmonton Journal.*

24 *Edmonton Journal.*

25 "What They Said About Jays Win," *Toronto Star*, October 26, 1992: D4.

QUEST FOR A REPEAT IN 1993

By Allen Tait

FINANCIAL CONSIDERATIONS

History clearly showed the quest to repeat as World Series champions is not easily achieved. Through 1992, the last team to win back-to-back World Series titles had been the 1977-78 New York Yankees. A repeat would require a critical assessment of the current roster to project what changes would be required to maintain a contending team within the salary budget approved by ownership. This evaluation was complicated by the fact that several key Toronto Blue Jays players were eligible for free agency after the 1992 season.

Further, despite the huge boost to attendance with the 1989 in-season move to SkyDome, the salary budget remained a pressure. A significant factor in the budget pressure was that while ticket sales and Canadian broadcast revenue were received in Canadian dollars, major expenses such as player salaries and travel expenses were paid in US dollars. On December 31, 1992, the US-Canadian dollar exchange rate was $0.791.[1]

The Blue Jays' profit, despite not making the World Series, had risen from $10 million CDN in 1989 to $14 million CDN in 1990 to $17.5 million CDN in 1991.[2] When considering the financial investment required to improve the team for 1992, management calculated that the achievement of maximum attendance (i.e., sell out every game) would lead to an attendance increase of only 74,000 over 1991.[3] Management had made the investment for 1992, won the World Series, and made a small profit that was attributed to the $2 million CDN generated by the playoff run.[4]

With total 1992 attendance at 4,028,318 and a maximum attendance for 81 sellouts at 4,091,796 (50,516 tickets x 81 regular-season home games), the maximum potential attendance increase was 63,478. Blue Jays management accepted these capacity limitations and decided to increase their payroll in 1993; they were the top spenders in baseball. As a result, the Jays calculated that they broke even for the year, thanks to the playoff revenue, although Labatt Breweries, the club's majority owner, realized profit through increased beer sales and broadcasting revenues.[5]

ROSTER ADJUSTMENTS

Work on addressing the list of pending Blue Jays free agents began early in the 1992 postseason period. Of the core 14 players from the 1992 World Series (nine hitters, four starters, and the closer), seven were free agents at the end of the season: shortstop Manny Lee, left fielder Candy Maldonado, right fielder Joe Carter, designated hitter Dave Winfield, starting pitchers David Cone and Jimmy Key, and closer Tom Henke.

Of those seven, only Carter was re-signed, joining 1992 returnees catcher Pat Borders, first baseman John Olerud, second baseman Roberto Alomar, and center fielder Devon White in the projected 1993 starting lineup.

Paul Molitor was signed as a free agent, leaving the Milwaukee Brewers. His primary role in 1993 would be designated hitter to replace Dave Winfield, who signed with the Minnesota Twins. Toronto initially planned to utilize Derek Bell to be the starter in left field in place of Candy Maldonado, who had signed with the Chicago Cubs.[6] However, that plan was abandoned as Bell and a minor-league player, Stoney Briggs, were dealt to the San Diego Padres on March 30, 1993, for outfielder Darrin Jackson.

The left side of the infield was uncertain. Ed Sprague was tabbed to replace Kelly Gruber (traded to the California Angels for Luis Sojo) at third base, and the starting shortstop position was an open competition to replace Manny Lee, who had signed with the Texas Rangers.

Toronto signed Dave Stewart, leaving the Oakland Athletics, to address a gap in the projected starting rotation. Free agents David Cone had signed with the Kansas City Royals and Jimmy Key had signed with the New York Yankees. Cone and Key had started five of the 12 postseason games played by Toronto in their successful 1992 postseason. Stewart joined a projected starting rotation that included returning starters Jack Morris, Juan Guzman, and Todd Stottlemyre.

Toronto closer Tom Henke had signed with the Texas Rangers, leaving an opening in the bullpen. Henke had accounted for five of the six saves awarded to Toronto relievers in the 1992 postseason. Duane Ward, who had saved 12 games for Toronto in 1992 during the regular season, was promoted to the closer role for 1993.

THE SEASON

The Blue Jays did not get off to a strong start in 1993. On May 13 they were in fourth place in the American League East with a 17-17 record. On that day, starting shortstop Dick Schofield, who had signed with the club on January 15, 1993, suffered a broken arm.[7] Toronto searched for a replacement starting shortstop and on June 11 sent Darrin Jackson to the New York Mets in exchange for Tony Fernandez. Fernandez was well known to Blue Jays fans: His major-league career began in Toronto as a 21-year-old rookie in 1983. Fernandez was the Blue Jays' starting shortstop from 1985 until he and Fred McGriff were traded to the San Diego Padres after the 1990 season for Joe Carter and Roberto Alomar.

Despite stabilization at the shortstop position, the Blue Jays, with a 49-40 record, had a slight half-game lead over the Detroit Tigers at the All-Star break. With the New York Yankees (one game back), Baltimore Orioles (1½ games back), and Boston Red Sox (three games back), a tight second-half pennant race appeared to be in the offing.

The Blue Jays were not struggling offensively. The top five hitters in the order were referred to as WAMCO (Devon White, Roberto Alomar, Paul Molitor, Joe Carter, John Olerud).[8] The starting pitching had been below expectations, due in part to veteran Jack Morris being in decline and three starters going on the disabled list. (Juan Guzman and Pat Hentgen were the exceptions).[9]

At the July 31 trade deadline, the Blue Jays were tied for first at 60-45 with the Yankees, and the Red Sox were only 1½ games back. Toronto traded pitcher Steve Karsay and a player to be named later (outfielder José Herrera) to the Oakland Athletics for outfielder Rickey Henderson.

The acquisition of Henderson to play left field was a bit of a surprise. In the days prior to the trade, it had been reported that Toronto was concerned about the uncertainty in left field as well as inconsistency in the starting rotation.[10] General manager Pat Gillick, in discussing the trade with the media, described the transaction as "Plan 1A."[11] Gillick added that acquisition of a pitcher would have been preferred but described Henderson as a "catalyst."[12]

The acquisition of Henderson led to a change in the WAMCO portion of the batting order. Henderson was inserted in the leadoff spot, White moved to second, with Alomar batting third; Molitor sixth against right-handers; and Molitor batting third and Alomar sixth against left-handers.[13]

The pennant race continued and on September 9, the Blue Jays were tied for first with the Yankees at 78-63, with the Orioles a half-game back at 77-63. Toronto then went on a 13-2 streak, pulling away from the Yankees (7-9) and Orioles (5-11) over the same period. Toronto clinched the division title on September 27. The season ended with the Blue Jays at 95-67, seven games ahead of the second-place Yankees.

The Blue Jays were led by starters Juan Guzman (14-3) and Pat Hentgen (19-9) with closer Duane Ward picking up 45 saves. The other three starters (Todd Stottlemyre, Dave Stewart, and Jack Morris) were a combined 30-32.

On offense, WAMCO lived up to their name with the following batting average/home run/RBI slash lines:

Devon White	.273/15/52
Roberto Alomar	.326/17/93
Paul Molitor	.332/22/111
Joe Carter	.254/33/121
John Olerud	.363/24/107

Rickey Henderson in 44 games was .215/4/12.

The American League Championship Series matched Toronto against the 94-68 Chicago White Sox. On paper, the series appeared to be a battle between the Blue Jays offense against the White Sox pitching. The White Sox were led by a starting trio of Jack McDowell (22-10), Alex Fernandez (18-9), and Wilson Alvarez (15-8). The number four and five starters were a combined 15-10. The closer was Roberto Hernandez with 38 saves. On offense, the key hitters were first baseman Frank Thomas .317/41/128 and third baseman Robin Ventura .262/22/94.

The ALCS opened in Chicago with Guzman besting McDowell in Game One with a 7-3 victory. The

Blue Jays chose 36-year-old Dave Stewart to start Game Two against Fernandez. Although Stewart (12-8) was fifth in games started during the regular season, due in part to a stint on the disabled list, the Blue Jays relied on Stewart's postseason experience. Stewart at the time was a lifetime 8-5 in postseason appearances with the 1981 Los Angeles Dodgers and 1988, 1989, 1990, and 1992 Oakland Athletics. Further, Stewart had been named World Series MVP in 1989 and ALCS MVP in 1990.

In contrast, the number-two regular-season starter, 24-year-old Pat Hentgen, was in his third season. Hentgen had only 57 2/3 innings of major-league experience prior to the start of the 1993 season and did not pitch in the 1992 postseason for Toronto. The Blue Jays' faith in Stewart was rewarded as he defeated the White Sox' Fernandez in Game Two with a 3-1 victory, a save going to Ward.

With the Blue Jays returning to Toronto for the next three games, Blue Jays fans were hoping for a quick end to the series. However, the White Sox rebounded with victories in Games Three and Four by scores of 6-1 and 7-4 respectively.

With the series tied 2-2, Game Five was a rematch of Game One starters Guzman and McDowell. Guzman got his second win of the series with a 5-3 victory, the first win by a home team in the series. The ALCS shifted back to Chicago for Game Six and Toronto advanced to the World Series with a 6-3 victory. Stewart picked up his second win of the series over Fernandez with Ward picking up his second save. Stewart was named the ALCS MVP.

The World Series matched Toronto against the Philadelphia Phillies. The Phillies were led by catcher Darren Daulton (.257/24/105), third baseman Dave Hollins (.273/18/93), and first baseman John Kruk (.316/14/85). The Phillies had a balanced five-man rotation (69-40) comprised of Curt Schilling (16-7), Danny Jackson (12-11), Tommy Greene (16-4), Terry Mulholland (12-9), and Ben Rivera (13-9). Closer Mitch Williams had 43 saves.

The World Series opened at SkyDome with the Blue Jays winning Game One, 8-5. Al Leiter got the win in relief, Duane Ward picking up a save with Curt Schilling taking the loss. Philadelphia rebounded in Game Two with Terry Mulholland defeating Dave Stewart in a 6-4 win.

The Series moved to Philadelphia and Pat Hentgen defeated Danny Jackson 10-3 in Game Three. In a wild nine-inning Game Four, the Blue Jays outlasted the Phillies 15-14. Tony Castillo got the win over Mitch

Williams with Duane Ward picking up the save. Curt Schilling kept the Phillies' hopes alive, defeating Juan Guzman 2-0 in Game Five. This was the only game in the Series where the winning team scored fewer than six runs.

Returning home to Toronto with a 3-2 Series lead, Game Six found the Blue Jays trailing 6-5 heading into the bottom of the ninth.[14] Phillies closer Mitch Williams was brought in. Leadoff hitter Rickey Henderson walked. Devon White was retired on a fly out. Paul Molitor singled. With Alfredo Griffin on deck, having pinch-run for Olerud earlier in the game, Joe Carter hit a walk-off three-run homer for an 8-6 Blue Jays victory and back-to-back World Series titles for Toronto.

In summation, this was not a pitchers' World Series. The Phillies had a Series team ERA of 7.39, the Blue Jays, 5.77. Paul Molitor was named World Series MVP, hitting .458 and driving in seven runs. However, the winning home run by Carter is arguably the most remembered play in the Series, including the call by Blue Jays play-by-play announcer, the late Tom Cheek: "Touch 'em all, Joe. You'll never hit a bigger home run in your life."[15]

SOURCES

In addition to the sources cited in the notes, the author consulted the Baseball-Reference.com website.

NOTES

1   https://freecurrencyrates.com/en/exchange-rate-history/CAD-USD/1992/cbr. Last referenced December 31, 2021.

2   Steven Brunt, *Diamond Dreams: 20 Years of Blue Jays Baseball* (Toronto: Viking, 1996), 234.

3   Brunt, 235.

4   Brunt, 258.

5   Brunt, 283.

6   Brunt, 261.

7   Brunt, 265.

8   Brunt, 267.

9   Brunt, 269.

10   Steve Milton, "AL East Report Toronto Blue Jays," *The Sporting News*, August 2, 1993: 29.

11   Mark Newman, "One Week, One Race," *The Sporting News*, August 9, 1993: 13.

12   Newman.

13   Steve Milton, "AL East Report Toronto Blue Jays," *The Sporting News*, August 16, 1993: 28.

14   Brunt, 281.

15   https://baseballhalloffame.ca//hall-of-famer/tom-cheek/, last referenced January 16, 2022.

SELECTED GAMES

BLUE JAYS NEWCOMERS DELIVER ON OPENING DAY

APRIL 6, 1992:
TORONTO BLUE JAYS 4, DETROIT TIGERS 2,
AT TIGER STADIUM, DETROIT

By Brian M. Frank

The Blue Jays finished the 1991 season by losing in the American League Championship Series to the Minnesota Twins four games to one. Falling just shy of the World Series was becoming an all-too-familiar feeling for the team and its fans. The Blue Jays had winning records in nine consecutive seasons, but it was the third time in seven years that the team had lost in the ALCS.

Blue Jays general manager Pat Gillick went to work in the offseason to try to push the team over the top. He signed World Series hero Jack Morris to lead Toronto's rotation. Morris seemed like a prime candidate to help lead the team to playoff success. Not only had he beaten the Jays twice in the 1991 ALCS, but he was also the hero of the most recent World Series, going 2-0 with a 1.17 ERA in three starts – including an epic Game Seven, in which he pitched a 10-inning shutout in the Twins' 1-0 win over the Braves.

Also coming to Toronto was free agent Dave Winfield. The 40-year-old was signed to help strengthen the Blue Jays at the designated-hitter position. Toronto's designated hitters had finished dead last in both home runs (5) and RBIs (57) in 1991. Winfield, who banged out 28 home runs and had 86 RBIs for the Angels in 1991, seemed all but certain to improve Toronto's run production, as well as provide veteran leadership.

When Morris took the mound on Opening Day in Detroit, he broke a tie with Robin Roberts and Tom Seaver, starting his 13th consecutive Opening Day – 11 of which had come while pitching for the Tigers.

Morris faced Bill Gullickson, who was making his first Opening Day start in his 11-season major-league career. Gullickson was coming off a tremendous season for the Tigers, having gone 20-9 with a 3.90 ERA in 1991.

Tigers fans – many of whom were still in a sour mood because longtime radio announcer Ernie Harwell was let go by the organization in the offseason – did not give Morris a warm welcome. The former Tigers ace was booed loudly during player introductions. Many fans were still upset that the Minnesota native had spurned the Tigers as a member of the 1990 free-agent class to sign with his hometown Twins, only to leave after a season in Minneapolis to sign with Toronto.

There had been some question as to whether Winfield would be in the Blue Jays lineup after he missed the last 10 games of spring training with a sore left hamstring. Not only was Toronto's new slugger in the lineup, but he made his presence felt early.

Toronto scored a run in the first inning. Roberto Alomar doubled with one out and moved to second on Joe Carter's fly to center field. That brought Winfield to the plate for his first at-bat as a Blue Jay. He poked the ball into right field to bring Alomar home with the first run of the season.

Morris worked himself into a jam in the second inning when he walked Cecil Fielder and gave up a single to Mickey Tettleton. He struck out Tony Phillips and Rob Deer before allowing an infield single to Travis Fryman to load the bases for Milt Cuyler. The last time Morris faced Cuyler – in a game at Tiger Stadium when Morris was on the Twins – the Tigers outfielder hit a grand slam. This time, Morris got the upper hand, by striking out Cuyler to end the inning.

"I was more comfortable than last year," Morris explained. "I was pressing too much last year. It's different now. I'm with a new team. I came over here to just do my best every time out and whatever happens, happens."[1]

The game got a little bizarre in the fourth inning while Blue Jays catcher Pat Borders was batting with two outs and the bases empty. An exotic dancer from Windsor, Ontario, ran onto the field and tried to kiss the startled Borders.

"It scared me," Borders said. "I was concentrating on the pitch. She came up from the backside, and I didn't see her. I was scared to death. … I turned with the bat and almost hit her. She's lucky she didn't get hit. I really jerked the bat around."[2]

Borders was able to fend off her advances before the security crew caught her as she scampered toward center field.[3] Despite his shock, or maybe because of it, four pitches later Borders lined a pitch deep over the right-field wall to give Toronto a 2-0 lead.

"I don't know," Borders said. "It really got my adrenaline going after that. She might have helped me actually."[4]

After striking out the side in the fourth inning, Morris walked Fryman to lead off the fifth. The next batter, Cuyler, ripped a ball up the middle that second baseman Alomar made a diving stop on and fired to first to nail the speedy Tigers outfielder. With Fryman at second base, Dan Gladden blooped a sinking liner into shallow left-center field that looked as though it would bring home the Tigers' first run, but center fielder Devon White made a diving catch for the inning's second out. Lou Whitaker ended the inning by flying out to White for the first routine out of the inning.

"That wasn't bad, the defense today, was it?" Morris said after the game.[5]

Toronto added to its lead in the sixth inning when John Olerud stroked a solo home run off Gullickson into the upper deck in right field. The Blue Jays scored another in the eighth on an RBI single by Derek Bell off reliever Mark Leiter.

Morris took a 4-0 lead into the ninth inning, looking to provide his new team with something he'd become known for – throwing a complete game. He'd allowed only three hits through the first eight innings, two of which were of the infield variety.

However, Fielder led off the bottom of the ninth with a deep drive into the upper deck in right-center field to ruin Morris's bid for a shutout.

"Cecil got what people came to see," Morris said. "I could have pitched him smarter. So what, I had some runs to play with."[6]

Fielder's blast brought manager Cito Gaston out to the mound for a visit with Morris, with both Tom Henke and Duane Ward ready in the bullpen.

"If I get to the ninth, then there's only one job to do, and that's finish the ballgame," Morris declared after the game. "If you're going to bail, bail in the fifth."[7]

"He's the only guy on this team that would have stayed in," Gaston said. "I just wanted to see if he was tired and let him know he'd thrown 120 pitches."[8]

After Gaston's mound visit, Morris retired the next two batters. However, Deer, who'd struck out looking in his three previous at-bats, deposited a ball into the upper deck in left field to cut Toronto's lead to 4-2.

Morris finally induced Fryman to ground out to third to finish the game on his 144th pitch of the afternoon. The win gave Morris a victory over every existing American League team.

"No extra incentive because of the Tigers," he said. "It feels like a long time ago and, I suppose, that helped me. There's a lot of new faces over there."[9]

Winfield finished the game 3-for-4 with an RBI. His third single of the day was the 2,700th hit of his career.

"Yeah, 3-for-4, I'm real happy about that," he said. "I've played so well against Toronto all my career, I'm just glad I started out doing something for 'em."[10]

"They're not weak in that (the DH) spot anymore," the slugger added.[11]

Winfield was also impressed with his new team's other new acquisition: "That was something to watch. I know Jack's not going to go 145 pitches all the time, because that takes it out of you, but he was pumped and I think he wanted to put a few things in our guys' minds. That this is what he's all about."[12]

The Blue Jays and their fans had high hopes heading into the season. The Opening Day performance of their two big free-agent signings only heightened expectations.

"Winning the whole thing, that's the motivation for me, and coming here … well this team's close," Winfield said. "I got a gut feeling."[13]

SOURCES

In addition to the sources cited in the Notes, the author consulted Baseball-Reference.com and Retrosheet.org.

NOTES

1 Dave Perkins, "Jack Morris Gets Out of Trouble with the Fortitude of a Champion," *Toronto Star*, April 7, 1992: B3.

2 Curt Sylvester, "Devine Intervention Precedes Borders' HR," *Detroit Free Press*, April 7, 1992: 6C.

3 Sylvester.

4 Sylvester.

5 Neil A. Campbell, "Morris Goes Distance in Grand Opener," *Globe and Mail* (Toronto), April 7, 1992: E12.

6 Perkins.

7 Campbell.

8 Charlie Vincent, "Fans Can Boo Morris, But It's Time to Cheer a Great Career," *Detroit Free Press*, April 7, 1992: 7C.

9 Allan Ryan, "Jack-Pot," *Toronto Star*, April 7, 1992: B3.

10 Allan Ryan, "Ailing Winfield Picture of Health on Opening Day," *Toronto Star*, April 7, 1992: B3.

11 Campbell.

12 Ryan, "Jack-Pot": B1.

13 Allan Ryan, "Ailing Winfield Picture of Health on Opening Day."

LINTON PROVIDES TIMELY LIFT IN FIRST MAJOR-LEAGUE START

AUGUST 13, 1992:
TORONTO BLUE JAYS 4, BALTIMORE ORIOLES 2,
AT SKYDOME, TORONTO

By Joel Rippel

The Toronto Blue Jays went into the finale of their four-game series with the Baltimore Orioles clinging to their hold on first place in the AL East Division standings.

The Blue Jays, who had held a five-game advantage over the second-place Orioles on July 23 and led them by 4½ games on August 2, had lost five of six games – including two of the first three games in the series – to see the Orioles pull within one game of first place.

A loss to the Orioles in the Thursday matinee would knock the Blue Jays out of sole possession of first place for the first time since June 20 and leave the teams tied for the division lead with 47 games to play.

Adding to the urgency for the Blue Jays were injuries to starting pitchers Juan Guzman (shoulder) and Dave Stieb (elbow), who were on the disabled list.

Prior to the series, one newspaper, the *Globe & Mail,* alluded to the Blue Jays' pitching issues: "The upstart O's are only two games behind the Jays, and the pitching matchups unquestionably favour the visitors at the SkyDome. But the Jays' pitching would match up unfavourably against the Toledo Mud Hens these days."[1]

Before their series against the Orioles, the Blue Jays had lost three of four games in Detroit while giving up 35 runs.

Blue Jays manager Cito Gaston designated rookie Doug Linton, who had made three relief appearances since being recalled by the Blue Jays on August 1, to start the crucial game.

A preview of the series finale pointed out the challenge facing Linton: "Doug Linton will try to do today what Jack Morris could not do on Tuesday and what Jimmy Key failed to do last night. He will try to beat the Baltimore Orioles."[2]

Linton, who was 12-9 with a 3.38 ERA in 23 starts for Triple-A Syracuse at the time of his recall and was Syracuse's Pitcher of the Month for July, appeared ready for the challenge. In his first three appearances for the Blue Jays, Linton, who was 27, had a 1.80 ERA in 10 innings. He struck out 10 and in one stretch retired 16 consecutive hitters.

After the Orioles' 11-4 victory over the Blue Jays in the third game of the series, Linton put his first major-league start into perspective. "Granted they're right on our heels. But (Thursday's) game isn't the end of the season," he said. "I mean, we've got 40 or some games left."[3]

Asked by reporters if he was nervous, Linton told them to go to the Orioles clubhouse and ask their scheduled starter, rookie pitcher Arthur Rhodes, whether he had "any butterflies." Linton added, "Hey, those guys are the ones who are a game back."[4]

With 50,405 fans on hand, Linton retired leadoff hitter Brady Anderson on a groundout.

Mike Devereaux, who was 3-for-5 with two doubles and five RBIs in the Orioles' 11-4 victory the previous night, singled to left to bring Cal Ripken to the plate.

Ripken, who hadn't hit a home run in 45 games – the longest stretch of his career since his rookie season in 1982, flied out to center. Devereaux was caught stealing to end the inning.

With two outs in the bottom of the first, Joe Carter hit his 26th home run of the season off Rhodes for the Blue Jays' first run.

The Orioles immediately tied the game when Glenn Davis led off the second inning with his 10th home run of the season. Linton walked the next hitter, Randy Milligan, – but regrouped to retire the next three hitters.

The Blue Jays regained the lead in the bottom of the second when Kelly Gruber led off with a triple. After Derek Bell flied out to center, Gruber scored on a single by rookie catcher Randy Knorr.

The score remained 2-1 for the next four innings, as Linton pitched four hitless innings and Rhodes allowed just one baserunner (a walk).

Linton retired 15 consecutive hitters before Ripken doubled to left to lead off the seventh. After advancing to third when Davis grounded out to Carter at first base, Ripken tied the score on Milligan's sacrifice fly to center.

Linton retired the Orioles in order in the eighth, and the Blue Jays took the lead in the bottom of the inning.

Devon White led off with a single to left and scored the go-ahead run on a double by Roberto Alomar. Todd Frohwirth relieved Rhodes and Carter's sacrifice moved Alomar to third. After Dave Winfield walked, Alomar scored on a single by Candy Maldonado. Frohwirth struck out Gruber and Bell to end the inning.

Blue Jays closer Tom Henke retired Anderson, Devereaux, and Ripken in order in the ninth to seal the victory and earn his 21st save of the season.

In eight innings, Linton had allowed two runs and three hits and walked just one. He faced just 27 batters. In the Jays' 10 games before Linton's start, the starting rotation had an ERA of 9.49. Linton's effort was just the fourth in 12 games in which a Blue Jays starter went at least seven innings.

Gaston praised Linton for his performance. "We were hoping he could get by for maybe six innings," the manager said. "He gave us a lot more than we expected and at a time we needed it the most."[5]

Henke concurred, saying, "You just don't expect that out of a young guy. He picks up the whole staff with this one, and considering how the last two went, we got to feel we won the series even though it was a tie."[6]

Linton gave his teammates the credit for the victory. "It's a great feeling," he said, "but if we don't score two runs in the eighth, I wouldn't be talking about my first win."[7]

Gaston also mentioned the significance of the victory, "You go from tied for first (had Baltimore grabbed a third straight) to two games up. … Well, right, it's pretty important. It was such a lift for all of us."[8]

One newspaper account said the Jays "rebounded to claim their biggest win of the season so far."[9]

The Orioles and Blue Jays played a three-game series in September. The Blue Jays won two of the games to finish the season with an 8-5 season advantage over Baltimore. Since Linton's win over Baltimore six weeks before, the Orioles had slumped, posting an 18-19 record to fall into third place in the division. Meanwhile, Toronto went 23-16, strengthening its lead atop the AL East, on track for a second straight division title.

SOURCES

In addition to the sources cited in the Notes, the author consulted Baseball-Reference.com, Newspapers.com, and Retrosheet.org.

NOTES

1 Marty York, "Jays Do Little Against Tigers to Change Sparky's Mind," *Globe and Mail* (Toronto), August 10, 1992: D2.

2 Neil A. Campbell, "Linton's Task to Hold Top Spot," *Globe and Mail*, August 13, 1992: C8.

3 Campbell.

4 Campbell.

5 Allan Ryan, "Rookie Rescue," *Toronto Star*, August 14, 1992: D1.

6 Ryan.

7 Associated Press, "Blue Jays Rookie Brings Down Orioles, 4-2," *Los Angeles Times*, August 14, 1992: C6.

8 Ryan.

9 Ryan. This game had the highest Championship Leverage Index (cLi) value of any 1992 regular-season Blue Jays game as computed by Baseball-Reference.com. According to Baseball-Reference, "cLi measures the importance of a game to a team's chances of winning the World Series." https://www.baseball-reference.com/about/wpa.shtml.

AN INSIGNIFICANT GAME OF SIGNIFICANCE

SEPTEMBER 6, 1992:
TORONTO BLUE JAYS 4, MINNESOTA TWINS 2,
AT SKYDOME, TORONTO

By F. Timothy Deeth

They say that hindsight is 20/20.

This can be particularly true in baseball, as in other sports, where both the media and fans love to look back on games or seasons, and second-guess or debate plays, strategies, and outcomes. Sometimes, this hindsight will recognize a significance that was not apparent at the time.

Take for example, the game between the Blue Jays and the visiting Minnesota Twins on Sunday, September 6, 1992. Entering the game, the Jays were leading the American League East by a very slim one-half game. They were finishing a three-game series against the Twins and had won the first two games, 16-5 and 7-3. They had been playing well, having won seven of their previous 10 games; however, the second-place Baltimore Orioles were on a roll of their own. They had won seven in a row and nine of their previous 10 games, and had cut into the Blue Jays' lead.

That Sunday marked the opening of the NFL season, and the US Open Tennis tournament was in full swing, but an overcast, 75-degree afternoon attracted a capacity crowd of 50,421 fans to Toronto's SkyDome to see the series finale. The open-roof game also provided an overhead air show, courtesy of the Canadian National Exhibition, which was just about to finish its annual season, about a mile down the road.

In 1992 the Minnesota lineup featured stars like Kirby Puckett (hitting .328 with an OPS of .868), Shane Mack (.326, .878), Chuck Knoblauch (.305, .752), Kent Hrbek (.244, .768), and Brian Harper (.301, .734). The defending World Series champion Twins were in second place in the American League West,

4½ games behind the Oakland Athletics but, having won six of their last 10, they had been gaining ground on the A's, who had lost 7 of 10.

To be sure, this was an important game for both teams, but the real importance of that game for the Blue Jays would not be known until season's end.

Todd Stottlemyre started for the Jays while Mike Trombley, a rookie, was making his second start ever for the Twins. The Blue Jays' starting lineup was missing center fielder Devon White, who was nursing a sore thigh, and his regular backup, Derek Bell who was out with neck pain. Turner Ward started the game in center field. The Jays' regular catcher, Pat Borders, was given the day off, and Ed Sprague was behind the plate. Sprague had spent most of the season with Triple-A Syracuse, but since his call-up had caught Stottlemyre's previous two starts – both wins.

Stottlemyre made quick work of the Twins in the first inning, retiring all three batters he faced on 14 pitches, while Trombley retired the Jays in order as well, needing only 11 pitches.

The second inning proved more troublesome for the Jays starter. After he got Hrbek to line out to Roberto Alomar at second base, Stottlemyre's first pitch to Mack was drilled into center field for a single, and Harper, on a 2-and-2 count, hit a home run to deep left field, giving Minnesota a 2-0 lead.

Dave Winfield hit a leadoff double in the bottom of the second inning, but the Jays couldn't get him beyond third base.

Both pitchers then seemed to find their groove, and while each team managed to scatter a few hits along with a couple of walks, only one runner from either team made it as far as third base until the Blue Jays came to bat in the bottom of the seventh inning.

John Olerud led off the Jays half of the seventh by hitting a 0-and-1 pitch to deep left-center for a double. Candy Maldonado then walked on a 3-and-2 count. Turner Ward struck out, but the next batter, Sprague, smashed Trombley's 100th pitch (on a 0-and-1 count) into the deep left-field seats, and the Jays were suddenly up 3-2. Trombley was allowed to remain in the game for one more pitch (which Alfredo Griffin deposited into right field for a double), then was replaced by Tom Edens.

"It just kind of rolled up there," Trombley said, referring to the hanging slider Sprague hit over the fence. "It wasn't a very good pitch. I'd like to have it back. I was pleased with the way I threw the ball during the game, but I still have to make a good pitch there."[1]

His batterymate, Harper, said, "They scored four runs in an inning in all three of these games. And we couldn't get a big inning of our own. It gets kind of frustrating."[2]

Minnesota skipper Tom Kelly echoed Harper's frustration. "It's been a different guy for them every game. Did anyone think Sprague was going to hit a home run? If so, raise your hand. I certainly didn't."[3]

Edens was greeted by Alomar, who singled to right field, scoring Griffin. Further damage was averted when Edens picked off Alomar trying to steal second and, after walking Kelly Gruber, coaxed Joe Carter into grounding into a force out at second.

Stottlemyre came out to start the eighth inning for the Jays, but got into trouble by walking Knoblauch. After striking out Scott Leius, he gave up a single to Puckett, putting runners on first and second with one out. With Hrbek and Mack due up next, the Jays' closer, Tom Henke, was brought in to relieve Stottlemyre, to try to get the final five outs. While Henke was the Blue Jays' closer in 1992, it was somewhat unusual for him to be called upon to go more than one inning. In fact, for the season, Henke appeared in 57 games but pitched fewer than 56 innings.

After giving up a first-pitch single to Hrbek, Henke got Mack to ground into an inning-ending double play, Alomar to Griffin to Olerud. On that play, the Blue Jays apparently caught a break.

TV video replay of that play showed that Mack beat the throw to first. (In 1992, in-game appeals were not allowed, so umpire Ken Kaiser's out call at first stood.) After the game, Henke said, "You gotta have a break once in a while."[4]

In the ninth Henke set down the Twins in order on two groundouts and a pop fly. The Twins didn't get the ball out of the infield and Henke had his 25th save.

Sprague's three-run homer – his first home run since August 9, 1991 – had been the big hit. He contributed more than that, though, said starter Stottlemyre: "He's had just as much to do with my last three wins as I have. Sprague's been catching me like a veteran. I don't lose anything when he's behind the plate."[5]

A tidy 4-2 Blue Jays win was completed in a compact 2 hours and 38 minutes.

Shortly after the Blue Jays' victory, the California Angels, sitting in fifth place in the American League West, took on the Orioles in Anaheim. Behind the pitching of future Hall of Famer Bert Blyleven and two relievers, the Angels beat the Orioles 5-2 in 2 hours and 16 minutes, a time unheard of by today's standards. (By comparison, the length of an average major-league baseball game in 2021 was 3 hours, 10 minutes, and 7 seconds.[6])

The Blue Jays' win, coupled with the Orioles' loss, moved Toronto 1½ games ahead of the Orioles in the American League East. The third-place Milwaukee Brewers also lost, moving them 5½ games back of the Jays.

From September 7 to the end of the season, the Jays went 17-8, finishing at 96-66, 30 games over .500 and four games ahead of second-place Milwaukee. The Brewers finished very strongly, going 19-7 after September 6 to finish at 92-70. Meanwhile the Orioles, who had closed the gap to a half-game before the games on September 6, finished the balance of the season going 12-14 to finish a distant third at 89-73, seven games behind the Blue Jays.

AUTHOR'S NOTE

On a personal note, this author was at the September 6 game between the Blue Jays and the Twins. As I normally do, I scored that game and still have my handmade scorecard, to which I referred for the purpose of writing this article. I always try to make notes of anything noteworthy about any games – whether it be a spectacular play in the field, a disputed call, or anything to tweak my recollection of the game itself. Apart from noting that Stottlemyre's first pitch to Knoblauch was a called ball, and Trombley's first pitch to Alomar was grounded to Gene Larkin, I made no other notes on this game. Neither team made an error, each team hit a home run, and the Jays outhit the Twins 8-7. The Twins hit into two double plays, and the Jays were caught stealing twice. In the end, the

WE ARE, WE CAN, WE WILL

Jays came back from a two-run deficit, scoring four in the seventh inning to win 4-2. There was nothing particularly remarkable about this game at all; however, that Sunday afternoon game was a significant moment in the season for the Jays.

What wasn't known to me or any of the other 50,420 in attendance that afternoon, was that that day was the last time during the 1992 season that any team would be as close as a half-game behind the Blue Jays in the American League East standings. From the perspective of today, September 6 was a key turning point in the 1992 season.

As they say, hindsight is 20/20.

SOURCES

In addition to the sources cited in the Notes, the author consulted Baseball-Reference.com and Retrosheet.org.

https://www.baseball-reference.com/boxes/TOR/TOR199209060.shtml

https://www.retrosheet.org/boxesetc/1992/B09060TOR1992.htm

NOTES

1   Jeff Lenihan, "Again, Twins Can't Beat Blue Jays' Big Inning," *Minneapolis Star Tribune*, September 7, 1992: 1C.

2   Lenihan.

3   Lenihan.

4   Tom Slater, "Powerful Battery Gives Jays Boost," *Toronto Star*, September 7, 1992: D1.

5   Associated Press, "Blue Jays Escape Minnesota, 4-2," *Corpus Christi Caller-Times,* September 7, 1992: D6.

6   Associated Press, "Average Time of Nine-Inning Games Sets MLB Record Despite Efforts to Improve Pace of Play," ESPN.com, October 3, 2021. https://www.espn.com/mlb/story/_/id/32335481/average-nine-inning-games-sets-mlb-record-efforts-improve-pace-play. Accessed March 12, 2022.

JAYS CLAIM SECOND CONSECUTIVE AL EAST TITLE WITH VICTORY OVER ARCHRIVAL TIGERS

OCTOBER 3, 1992:
TORONTO BLUE JAYS 3, DETROIT TIGERS 1, AT SKYDOME, TORONTO

By Frederick C. Bush

A crowd of 50,412 rabid fans packed Toronto's SkyDome on Saturday, October 3, 1992, in the hope of watching the hometown nine clinch the American League East title for the second consecutive year and the third time in four seasons. However, by the time the game against the division archrival Detroit Tigers began, the division crown already belonged to the Blue Jays as the second-place Milwaukee Brewers had been eliminated via a loss to the Oakland A's earlier that afternoon. Nonetheless, the Jays players wanted a victory for themselves and their fans. After Toronto had indeed triumphed, 13-game winner Jimmy Key noted, "It's more fun this way. I didn't want Milwaukee to lose it. I wanted us to win it."[1]

Key, a nine-year veteran who had spent his entire career with the Jays, knew what this game and this season meant to a Toronto franchise that had the "chokers" label applied to it due to its inglorious postseason history and an ignominious fade down the stretch that cost it a division title in 1987. He had been a member of the 99-win squad that had squandered a 3-games-to-1 ALCS lead to the Kansas City Royals in 1985, which was the closest Toronto had come to the World Series; the 1989 and 1991 teams both had lost in five games to Oakland and Minnesota respectively.

General manager Pat Gillick had set about to obtain the missing pieces that might finally get the Jays over the hump to the World Series. On December 18, 1991, he signed Jack Morris, that season's World Series MVP, who had pitched an epic 10-inning shutout victory for the Minnesota Twins in Game Seven. Morris had also won a title with the Tigers in 1984 and owned a 7-1 postseason record, including a 4-0 ledger in the two World Series. The 37-year-old righty logged 240⅔ innings for Toronto in 1992 and won 21 games, which tied him for the AL lead with the Texas Rangers' Kevin Brown.

The very next day, Gillick signed Dave Winfield to be Toronto's designated hitter. The free-agent slugger was coming off a subpar season – by his Hall of Fame standards – for the California Angels in which he had batted .262 with a .326 on-base percentage and 86 RBIs. Winfield rewarded Gillick's confidence in him with a .290 BA, .377 OBP, and 108 RBIs that netted him the Designated Hitter of the Year award and a fifth-place finish in the AL MVP vote.

Gillick still had work to do, though, as the season began to take its toll on Toronto's pitching staff. In early August, longtime ace Dave Stieb suffered a season-ending injury. Second-year starter Juan Guzmán, who had won 11 of his first 12 decisions and was 11-2 with an AL-leading 2.11 ERA at the All-Star break, also spent most of that month on the disabled list.[2] On August 27 Gillick traded rookie third baseman Jeff Kent and minor-league outfielder Ryan Thompson to the New York Mets for David Cone, who was 13-7 with a 2.88 ERA and was tied with Tom Glavine for the NL lead in shutouts with five. Cone pitched to an even better 2.55 ERA in eight appearances (seven starts) for Toronto, though he was saddled with a hard-luck 4-3 record for his efforts.

Cone was a great insurance policy and Morris provided hard-nosed veteran leadership, but it was Guzmán – who had come off the DL on August 30 – who took the mound for the Jays to try to tame the Tigers and claim the division with a victory rather than back into the postseason via Milwaukee's loss. Guzmán was fired up and firing on all cylinders as he pitched four perfect innings, striking out seven batters, before allowing Detroit's first baserunner, in the top of the fifth.

The Blue Jays offense struck quickly in the bottom of the first inning against Detroit starter Dave Haas. Devon White stroked a leadoff single past the reach of Tigers shortstop Travis Fryman. After Roberto Alomar lined out, Joe Carter launched a homer that gave Toronto a 2-0 advantage. Haas set Winfield down on strikes and retired John Olerud on a comebacker to the mound, but the Jays already had all the runs they needed on this day.

Haas allowed two Toronto baserunners in the second and one in the third, but the Jays were unable to push additional men across the plate. All was quiet until the top of the fifth when Guzmán's shot at a perfect game ended as he surrendered walks to the first two batters, Cecil Fielder and Mickey Tettleton. After Rob Deer struck out swinging, Scott Livingstone hit a grounder that forced Tettleton at second but enabled Fielder to advance to third. Guzmán then got Dan Gladden to swing at strike three for Detroit's final out of the inning. Eight of the nine Tigers batters Guzmán struck out went down flailing at his offerings, prompting the Jays righty to exclaim after the game, "I've prayed for this day. I haven't pitched like this since before [he was injured]."[3]

In the bottom of the fifth, Haas ran into trouble when he walked Manny Lee and White dropped a bunt down the third-base line that resulted in a base hit. Alomar followed with a sacrifice that advanced both runners. Tigers skipper Sparky Anderson had Haas issue a free pass to Carter to load the bases. Winfield hit a grounder to Fryman that forced Carter at second, but Lee scored Toronto's third run of the game. After Haas issued his second unintentional walk of the inning, to Olerud, Anderson sent Mark Leiter to the hill in relief. Leiter kept the Jays from putting up a

crooked number in the inning by striking out Candy Maldonado.

Guzmán lost his no-hitter in the top of the sixth when designated hitter Mark Carreon led off the frame with a solid single into right field. It was the only hit Guzmán allowed this day, and he retired the next three batters in order. In fact, Guzmán allowed only one additional baserunner in his final two innings of work – Carreon, who drew a two-out walk in the top of the eighth.

The Jays tried to manufacture an insurance run in the bottom of the seventh. Alomar worked a leadoff walk and stole second. After Leiter retired Carter on a fly ball to left field, he was replaced by lefty Mike Muñoz. With Winfield batting, Alomar stole third. Muñoz was ordered to walk Winfield, and he then induced an inning-ending double-play grounder off the bat of Olerud.

Although Guzmán had shown no signs of tiring and pitch counts were still a thing of the future – Guzmán had thrown 117 pitches, 77 of which were strikes – Toronto manager Cito Gaston opted to bring in closer Tom Henke for the ninth inning. It turned out to be a good thing that the Jays were no longer in a must-win situation as the ghost of shortcomings past attempted to haunt Henke and the Jays once more.

After Lou Whitaker hit a weak groundout to Olerud at first base, Fryman and Fielder banged out back-to-back singles; Skeeter Barnes ran for Fielder. When one of Henke's pitches got past catcher Pat Borders, who was charged with a passed ball, the Tigers had two runners in scoring position. Henke dug his hole deeper by walking Tettleton unintentionally to load the bases. After Deer popped out, Henke forced in a run with another base on balls, this time to Livingstone. Gaston replaced Henke with Duane Ward, who induced a pop fly from Gladden on his second pitch to end the game as a 3-1 victory.

Winfield, one of Toronto's key offseason acquisitions, had been in the visiting dugout as a member of the Angels when the Jays had clinched the AL East title in 1991.[4] This time around, he was able to celebrate being part of a division champion on his 41st birthday. The crowd helped him to celebrate by singing "Happy Birthday" which Winfield said was "really nice, it was great" as he had never had 50,000-plus people serenade him with birthday wishes before.[5]

Henke, who had almost allowed the Tigers to rain on Toronto's championship and Winfield's birthday celebrations, summed up the Jays' new attitude after the game:

"People have labelled us chokers and I know [Milwaukee manager Phil] Garner said a couple of times 'We'll get them, we know their reputation,' and this and that," Henke said. "Hey, we stayed focused and won the games. We didn't count on anybody else to help us out, we went out and did it ourselves. Now we need to win eight more games."[6]

The Blue Jays did exactly that, defeating Oakland in the ALCS and the Atlanta Braves in the World Series – both in six games – to become World Series champions for the first time in franchise history.

SOURCES

The author consulted baseball-reference.com and retrosheet.org for the box score and play-by-play of the game as well as player statistics, awards, and transactions.

NOTES

1   Larry Millson, "Half a Pennant Old Hat for Veterans/ Players Who Have Been There Want to Progress to Champs," *Globe and Mail* (Toronto), October 5, 1992: D2.

2   Malcolm Allen, "Juan Guzmán," SABR Baseball Biography Project, https://sabr.org/bioproj/person/juan-guzman/, accessed March 18, 2022.

3   Tom Gage, "Jays Down Tigers to Wrap Up East," *Detroit Free Press*, October 4, 1992: 5E.

4   Neil A. Campbell, "Players Leave the Noisy Celebrations for the Real Pennant," *Globe and Mail*, October 3, 1992: A22.

5   Millson, "Half a Pennant Old Hat for Veterans."

6   Millson.

ALOMAR, BLUE JAYS EMERGE OUT OF SHADOWS IN ALCS GAME FOUR

OCTOBER 11, 1992:
TORONTO BLUE JAYS 7, OAKLAND A'S 6 (11 INNINGS),
AT OAKLAND-ALAMEDA COLISEUM, OAKLAND
(GAME FOUR OF THE AMERICAN LEAGUE
CHAMPIONSHIP SERIES)

By Adrian Fung

When Blue Jays second baseman Roberto Alomar stepped into the late-afternoon shadows at home plate in the top of the ninth inning, a figurative darkness overshadowed Toronto as well. Needing two runs to tie the game, time was running out for the Blue Jays to rally. Toronto trailed 6-4 in Game Four of the 1992 American League Championship Series and was three outs away from a loss that would even their series against the Athletics at two games apiece.

Alomar dug in against Dennis Eckersley.

All-Star vs. All-Star.

Best vs. best.

It was the apical moment of the Toronto-Oakland rivalry that had simmered over the past few years. Since 1985, both clubs had won their respective division four times. Yet in the postseason, the Blue Jays always fizzled while Oakland sizzled. The Athletics added three pennants and the 1989 World Series title after easily pushing aside the Blue Jays in a five-game ALCS that ended tersely. In the ninth inning of the final game, Toronto manager Cito Gaston asked the umpires to check if Eckersley was scuffing baseballs. An insulted Eckersley shouted profanities at an irate Gaston who fired right back at the Oakland closer after the game.[1]

In Game Four of the 1992 ALCS Oakland jumped out to a 6-1 lead, and the Toronto bats looked lifeless entering the eighth inning. However, Alomar led off with a double, chasing Oakland starter Bob Welch and ushering in reliever Jeff Parrett. Alomar promptly stole third and scored on a Joe Carter single. After Dave Winfield singled Carter to third, Oakland manager Tony LaRussa had seen enough. With the potential tying run on deck, he signaled for Eckersley from the bullpen.

The Oakland-born Eckersley, 37, was a six-time All-Star, widely acknowledged as the best closer in the game. He started 1992 with 36 straight saves en route to a major league-leading 51.[2] Since 1988, Eckersley was simply dominant. No reliever in either league recorded more saves (220), had a lower WHIP (walks plus hits per innings pitched) ratio (0.792), or had a strikeout-to-walk ratio (9.95) that was even half as good as his mark.[3] His 10 career LCS saves were already a record that would not be broken until 2009.[4]

But on this afternoon, Toronto was not interested in history, only in stringing together hits to climb back into the game. The next two Toronto hitters – John Olerud and Candy Maldonado – attacked early, each jumping on Eckersley's first pitch for run-scoring singles, cutting the Athletics lead to 6–4, putting the tying runs on first and second. However, Eckersley coolly retired the next three batters, ending the inning with a strikeout of pinch-hitter Ed Sprague. Following the strikeout, Eckersley pumped his fist, and then yelled and pointed at the Toronto dugout. Immediately, the Blue Jays bench rose up indignantly. "It was a little gesture and the guys responded. We got very, uh, vocal. It's a good thing the TV cameras weren't in the dugout," said Winfield.[5] "He should know to let sleeping dogs lie. You don't wake 'em up. It's a cardinal sin in baseball," added Toronto starter Jack Morris.[6]

Eckersley later downplayed his actions. "Aw hell, I was just excited. I mean, things were starting to slip away and I thought that strikeout of Sprague was the ballgame. Sometimes I do crazy stuff, but I didn't mean to show those guys up. It was just a reaction to the moment."[7]

In the ninth, as darkness enveloped the home-plate dirt, leadoff hitter Devon White lined a single to left field, then raced all the way to third when Rickey Henderson misplayed the ball. Up stepped Alomar, representing the tying run.

Alomar, 24, was already a three-time All-Star and two-time Gold Glove Award winner. The Toronto second baseman was considered one of the best young all-around, five-tool players in baseball. Alomar had already generated 23.3 wins above replacement (WAR) in his first five seasons. Only four other second basemen before him had accumulated more than 23.3 WAR over the first five seasons of their respective careers, and he was the first to do so since Jackie Robinson 41 years ago.[8]

Carter had given Alomar some simple advice moments before in the on-deck circle: "Look for a strike … hit the ball hard and try to keep the inning going."[9] With the count 2-2, Eckersley fired. Alomar swung, immediately dropped his bat and thrust both arms upward in triumph as he slowly trotted up the first-base line, out of the darkness at home plate and into the sunshine of the basepath, knowing his line drive would clear the right-field wall. When the ball landed, just to the left of a policeman standing on a stairway beyond the fence, Alomar continued to slowly circle the bases. The entire Toronto bench rose up, shouting, gesturing, and staring out at the stunned Eckersley.

"Eck stuck it in our faces and we kicked his ass," a fired-up Morris thundered, after the game. "We're happy as hell about it. I used to do a lot of gesturing and stuff like Eck does … and I realized I had to change. You just don't go around trying to show teams up – it may finally have come back to hurt him today."[10]

For the tying run, Alomar emphatically jumped on home plate with both feet. It was his fourth hit and fifth consecutive time reaching base on the day. The Blue Jays had finally broken through. On one swing of Alomar's bat, the constant disappointment of postseasons past seemed to melt away. His game-tying home run was not only the biggest clutch hit in Blue Jays history, but it lifted the franchise to uncharted territory: Never before had a Toronto player come through under intense playoff pressure as Alomar had, rejuvenating his team when all hope looked lost.

"This was the greatest game of my career, and that home run was the best thing that ever happened in my life," gushed Alomar. "As soon as I made contact, I knew it was out of there. As I was rounding the bases, I was thinking, 'Yeah, that ball is gone, gone, GONE!'" Analyzing the at-bat, Alomar continued, "That's not the Eckersley I've come to know. He wasn't throwing the good slider he usually does – it was flat and his fastball wasn't moving that much. On the home run, I was hoping he'd come inside and he did."[11]

A somber Eckersley was matter-of-fact about what transpired. "Hey, it's Toronto's day. They hit the f--- out of me … I just couldn't stop the bleeding. That's as hard as I've gotten hit since I can remember. Failure of this magnitude is tough to handle. I wanted to throw it down and away but I threw it high and he hit the s--- out of it. What can I say? It's going to be tough to sleep tonight."[12]

The remainder of the game was similarly pressure-packed. Toronto nearly took the lead after Alomar's home run by loading the bases, but reliever Jim Corsi retired Pat Borders on a groundout to end the inning. For Eckersley, it was his final postseason appearance in an Oakland uniform.

In the last of the ninth, the Athletics were 90 feet from winning the game, but with one out, fireballer Duane Ward got Terry Steinbach to hit a grounder to second. Alomar came up throwing to the plate to gun down pinch-runner Eric Fox, and one pitch later, Carney Lansford grounded into a fielder's choice to send the game to extra innings.

Finally, in the top of the 11th, Toronto took the lead. Derek Bell worked a nine-pitch leadoff walk, and moved to third on the next pitch when Maldonado, again attacking early, punched a single to right field. With one out, Borders lined to left, deep enough so that Bell could tag and score. In the bottom of the inning, Toronto closer Tom Henke threw just 13 pitches to lock down the most improbable victory in Blue Jays history, and ending the longest game in ALCS history at that time (4 hours and 25 minutes).[13]

The Blue Jays became the first team in postseason history to come back and win after trailing by at least five runs after seven innings.[14]

Somehow, Toronto had the 7-6 victory, a 3-1 ALCS lead, and the psychological edge of knowing it could beat the best, Eckersley, the winner of both the 1992 Cy Young and Most Valuable Player Awards. The game was a gilded building block in Toronto's path to eventually winning its first World Series two weeks later in Atlanta. It would not have been possible, however, had Alomar not struck the biggest blow, helping Toronto emerge from the shadows of another possible ALCS defeat and ultimately triumph.

SOURCES

In addition to the sources cited in the Notes, the author consulted the following:

https://www.baseball-reference.com/boxes/OAK/OAK199210110.shtml

https://www.retrosheet.org/boxesetc/1992/B10110OAK1992.htm

NOTES

1   Dave Perkins, "'I Don't Cheat,' Eck Rasps at Cito," *Toronto Star*, October 9, 1989: D1.

2   Craig Barbarino, "1992 Year in Review," *Official Major League Baseball Program – World Series* (1992): 29.

3   http://bbref.com/pi/shareit/sX3xf

4   http://www.baseball-reference.com/postseason/LCS_pitching.shtml

5   Rosie DiManno, *Glory Jays: Canada's World Series Champions* (Champaign, Illinois: Sagamore Publishing, 1993), 252–253.

6   DiManno.

7   Tom Cheek and Howard Berger, *Road to Glory: An Insider's Look at 16 Years of Blue Jay Baseball* (Toronto: Warwick Publishing, 1993), 299.

8   http://bbref.com/pi/shareit/P4eOo

9   Dave Perkins, "Alomar's Heroic Homer A Shot Heard Around Blue Jays' World," *Toronto Star*, October 12, 1992: D2.

10   Cheek and Berger, 299-300.

11   Cheek and Berger, 300.

12   Cheek and Berger, 300.

13   "Extra-Inning Affair Marks Longest Game in AL Playoff History," *Toronto Star*, October 12, 1992: D5.

14   Jack Curry, "The Playoffs: Who's Sorry Now? The A's, Not Jays," *New York Times*, October 12, 1992: C4.

BLUE JAYS ADVANCE TO CANADA'S FIRST WORLD SERIES

OCTOBER 14, 1992:
TORONTO BLUE JAYS 9, OAKLAND ATHLETICS 2,
AT SKYDOME, TORONTO
(GAME SIX OF THE AMERICAN LEAGUE
CHAMPIONSHIP SERIES)

By Brian M. Frank

The Blue Jays entered Game Six of the 1992 ALCS just one win away from winning their first-ever playoff series and advancing to the first World Series in Canadian history. The team had 10 consecutive winning seasons, winning the American League East in 1985, 1989, and 1991, but had always fallen short in the playoffs. One more win over the Oakland Athletics would help overcome a history of playoff disappointments.

Toronto failed to close out the series in Game Five in Oakland. The A's chased starter David Cone from the game after just four innings in a 6-2 Oakland win. With back-to-back shaky starts from Jack Morris and Cone, Blue Jays manager Cito Gaston had come under some criticism for deciding to go with a three-man rotation for the series and relegating Jimmy Key to the bullpen. After the Blue Jays' loss in Game Five, Gaston was asked about his decision to use only three starters in the series. "I don't know," he responded. "I wish I knew. It could be a mistake, or it might not be. I can't answer that one."[1]

Juan Guzmán, who'd been outstanding in the regular season, going 16-5 with a 2.64 ERA in 28 starts, was Toronto's Game Six starter. He had a solid start in the Blue Jays' 7-5 Game Three victory, allowing two runs over six innings on seven hits and three walks. The 25-year-old right-hander was unfazed by the fact

that he'd be starting on just three days' rest. "For me, it's no problem," he said. "I always have my good stuff. I could pitch on two days' rest."[2]

Oakland countered with Mike Moore. He'd given up three runs in seven innings in Oakland's Game Two loss. However, the 32-year-old veteran had a career postseason record of 4-1 with a 1.88 ERA heading into Game Six.

The Blue Jays were fortunate to have leadoff hitter and defensive outfielder extraordinaire Devon White in the lineup. The day before, he'd been involved in an auto accident when a car being test-driven lost control, hit a pole, and ended up in a ditch – but the speedy center fielder escaped unharmed.

After Guzmán retired the A's in order in the first inning, White hit what looked like a routine fly ball to shallow left field to lead off the bottom of the inning. However, left fielder Rickey Henderson closed his glove too early, the ball bounced off it, and White raced into second base.

Moore struck out Roberto Alomar, but Joe Carter, who was just 4-for-21 in the series with one RBI so far, drove a ball over the wall in center field to give the Blue Jays the early lead.

"I told the guys as soon as I got to the park, 'C'mon, hop on,'" the ever-confident Carter said. "I'd been riding their backs through this thing; it was time they got on mine. I stole it from Puck (Kirby Puckett) from Game Six of the World Series last year."[3]

Alomar singled to lead off the third inning and extend his hitting streak in ALCS games to 11. Carter struck out, but Alomar stole second in the process. Dave Winfield was walked intentionally to bring up the more inexperienced John Olerud. The sweet-swinging first baseman answered the call by hitting an 0-and-1 pitch into the right-field corner for a ground-rule double to bring home Alomar. Candy Maldonado then drilled a three-run home run over the right-center-field wall, giving Toronto a 6-0 lead.

Meanwhile, Guzmán was proving he could indeed pitch on short rest. He didn't allow a hit until Terry Steinbach led off the fifth with a single. Oakland finally scored in the sixth inning, when Mark McGwire singled home Ruben Sierra. Guzmán ended up allowing a lone run on five hits and two walks while striking out eight on 118 pitches over seven stellar innings. "I had great stuff today," he proclaimed. "Maybe my best slider of the whole year."[4]

The fans at SkyDome were in a celebratory mood throughout the game, with the Blue Jays in control from the early going. Fans chanted, "We want Eck! We want Eck!" and a drawn-out "Rickey, Rickey!" to needle closer Dennis Eckersley and Henderson, two players who'd tormented the Jays over the years – Eckersley with his fist pumps, Henderson with his "styling," and both with their level of play.[5]

"That's the way it's always been with me," Henderson said. "I guess they love me or hate me. They don't want me to beat up on their Blue Jays."[6]

The A's cut into the lead in the eighth inning when Steinbach singled home Harold Baines against reliever Duane Ward. However, in the bottom of the inning, Toronto increased its lead to 9-2 on a sacrifice fly by White and an RBI single by Alomar.

Tom Henke walked Walt Weiss to start the ninth, before striking out pinch-hitter Randy Ready and getting pinch-hitter Jamie Quirk to fly out for the second out. After Carney Lansford drew a walk, Sierra hit a high fly ball to left field that Maldonado squeezed for the final out – and the Blue Jays were finally headed to the World Series.

Blue Jays players felt redemption after the team's playoff losses in previous years, even though many of the players weren't on the earlier teams. "Throw it all out, 1985, '87, '89, '91, throw all those things out," Carter said. "All those people who wrote we were chokers, it'll be fun to watch them eat their words."[7]

Alomar was named the Championship Series MVP after going 11-for-26 (.423) with 2 home runs and 4 RBIs. He also went 5-for-5 on stolen-base attempts, had a .464 OBP, and slugged .692 in the series. "Everybody said we'd choke in the end," he said. "We didn't. The monkey, we can take it off our back."[8]

Players were aware of the historic nature of their victory and took pride in the fact that they were bringing Canada its first-ever World Series.

"We're keenly aware that we don't represent just a city. We represent an entire country," said Winfield. "Every team has its territory of course – maybe a state or a region – hey, but we've got all of Canada."[9]

"This is big," echoed Carter. "We understand it's very big. It's something that has avoided Canadians for a long time. And now they can be well represented in a World Series. People will get a chance to see what a first-class country Canada is and what a first-class city Toronto is. These are great fans here in Toronto. They totally fill the SkyDome for every game and the best way we can repay them is to bring home a World Series."[10]

As fans across Canada celebrated, 51,335 fans filed out of SkyDome, and thousands of exuberant Torontonians filled Yonge Street to celebrate the long-awaited victory.

Despite the relief that winning a playoff series finally provided, Alomar made clear that the Blue Jays were not satisfied with winning just one series.

"I want to enjoy this a little bit," he said as the Blue Jays waited to see whether the Atlanta Braves or Pittsburgh Pirates would prevail that evening in Game Seven of the NLCS. "This is fun, everybody's having a good time. But I want to win the World Series."[11]

SOURCES

In addition to the sources cited in the Notes, the author consulted Baseball-Reference.com and Retrosheet.org.

NOTES

1   Bob Valli, "Will Pitching Strategy Kill the Jays?," *Oakland Tribune*, October 13, 1992: C1.

2   Helene Elliott, "Jays Gambling that Guzman Will Be Sharp," *Oakland Tribune*, October 14, 1992: C2.

3   Allan Ryan, "Carter Gets World Serie-ous: 'The Timing Was Pretty Good,'" *Toronto Star*, October 15, 1992: B3.

4   Tom Sandir, "Juan-derful World!," *Toronto Star*, October 15, 1992: B1.

5   Alomar had hit a dramatic two-run home run off Eckersley in the ninth inning of Game Four to tie the score at 6-6. Toronto eventually won the game 7-6 in 11 innings.

6   Ray Ratto, "A's Provide Fodder for Celebration," *San Francisco Examiner*, October 15, 1992: E4.

7   Joan Ryan, "Long Losing Trail Finally Ends at Gaston's Doorstep," *San Francisco Examiner*, October 15, 1992: E5. In 1987 the Blue Jays lost their final seven games to blow a 3½-game lead with a week to play in the season.

8   Sandir, "Juan-derful World!"

9   Jim Proudfoot, "Patriotic Pride Blooms for Canada's Blue Jays," *Toronto Star*, October 15, 1992: B2.

10 Proudfoot.

11 Monte Poole, "World Series-Bound, They're 'Blew Jays' No More," *Oakland Tribune*, October 15, 1992: D3.

SPRAGUE'S BLOW SQUARES SERIES AFTER CANADIAN FLAG SNAFU

OCTOBER 18, 1992:
TORONTO BLUE JAYS 5, ATLANTA BRAVES 4,
AT ATLANTA-FULTON COUNTY STADIUM, ATLANTA
(GAME TWO OF THE 1992 W ORLD SERIES)

By Mark S. Sternman

Politics and sports collided uneasily before Game Two of the 1992 World Series when a member of the U.S. Marine Corps color guard displayed the Canadian flag upside down; although "American [meaning U.S.] viewers didn't see the gaffe … it was included on the feed … to Canada."[1]

The *Globe & Mail*'s Stephen Brunt had an understandably snarky reaction: "Designed as it is, with a great big maple leaf in the centre … most sentient beings probably could have figured [the correct way to carry the flag]. (Note to the U.S. Joint Chiefs of Staff: The stem goes at the bottom.)"[2]

The *Toronto Sun*'s Christie Blatchford had a much more forgiving take, wondering at Canadians who "were outraged. … You think the wicked Yanks … did it on purpose? Good Lord, this city is trying so hard to prove itself a worthy host for the 1996 Olympics, they are running scoreboard messages in Spanish and French just to accustom the populace to foreign tongues."[3]

After Atlanta's 3-1 Game One win, the Jays in Game Two achieved divine retribution on the diamond.

Two hard-throwing righties dominated the first part of the game. John Smoltz of the Braves retired the first eight Blue Jays, fanning five. After a one-two-three first, David Cone of the Blue Jays struggled in the second. He walked leadoff batter David Justice. With one out, Justice started a stolen-base parade against Cone, "a pitcher notoriously poor at holding runners,"[4]

by swiping second. Jeff Blauser grounded to Manny Lee at short. Justice reached third on Lee's throwing error. With Damon Berryhill up, Blauser stole second. Justice had not sought to advance but scored on a wild pitch on the steal with Blauser taking third. Berryhill walked but Mark Lemke hit into a double play to keep the Atlanta lead at 1-0.

Surprisingly and portentously, Cone got the first hit by the Jays with a single in the third. Neither team scored although the Braves again threatened thanks to a prime-time (football) player. "I'm going to play Deion [Sanders] instead of (Ron) Gant in left field," Atlanta manager Bobby Cox told reporters before the game. "Deion hit … Cone really well during the spring and he hit him pretty well during the season."[5] Sanders would prove productive at the plate; in the third, he walked with two outs and went to third on an infield single by Terry Pendleton. But Justice flied out to right to strand the runners.

Matching Atlanta's aggressiveness, Toronto almost tied the game in its third but to no avail, according to home-plate umpire Mike Reilly.[6] Roberto Alomar drew a leadoff walk, went to second on a wild pitch, and moved to third on a grounder. With two outs and John Olerud up, a Smoltz pitch eluded Berryhill, but the backstop, in Reilly's judgment, threw out Alomar "despite [Smoltz's] arriving at home plate with enough time to cook breakfast prior to the tag being made[.]"[7] "I thought he was safe," said Toronto manager Cito

Gaston. "You all had [television] monitors, you all saw [the replay]."[8]

The Braves added a second run in the bottom of the inning. Sid Bream drew a leadoff walk and went to third on Blauser's single. With one out, Lemke singled to score Bream and move Blauser to third. But Cone kept the deficit at two runs by getting another DP, this time off the bat of Smoltz.

Smoltz seemed in control. In the fifth inning he had a 2-0 lead with two outs and none on facing Pat Borders. Smoltz walked Borders and gave up a single to Lee. Pitcher Cone was up next. On the one hand, Smoltz had to respect Cone for his earlier single. On the other, he had to feel confident that the AL pitcher would not do so a second straight time, particularly when Smoltz would bear down with the tying runs on base. Shockingly, Smoltz gave up another hit to Cone, an RBI single scoring Borders. When cutoff man Bream made a throwing error, Cone and Lee advanced to second and third. "I feel good about doing something good tonight – and it wasn't on the mound," said Cone after the game.[9] The error proved critical: An infield hit by Devon White tied the score.

The adventures in hitting and baserunning may have weakened Cone. With one out in the Braves' half of the inning, Sanders singled, stole second, and took third on Borders' bad throw to second. Cone walked Pendleton and gave up an RBI single to Justice, with Pendleton moving to third. Southpaw David Wells replaced Cone and Brian Hunter batted for Bream. Hunter's sacrifice fly restored the Atlanta margin to two at 4-2.

With one out in the Blue Jays' seventh, Borders doubled. With two outs, he moved to third on a wild pitch. Smoltz escaped further trouble by striking out Candy Maldonado, batting for Wells.

Todd Stottlemyre had a one-two-three seventh. Smoltz finally sagged in the eighth. With one out, Alomar doubled. Joe Carter singled him to third and Dave Winfield singled him home to make the score 4-3. With the tying run on third, Cox first turned to Mike Stanton, who got Olerud to pop to third baseman Pendleton, and then to Jeff Reardon, familiar to Canadian baseball fans from his dominating days in Montreal. Reardon struck out Kelly Gruber looking on a pitch one Toronto writer said seemed "clearly inside."[10] The Braves needed three more outs to take a 2-0 Series lead.

Duane Ward replaced Stottlemyre in the eighth and like his predecessor retired all three batters.

Reardon returned for the ninth, which started well for Atlanta as Borders lined out. Derek Bell batted for Lee and walked. "You can't be walking a guy in that spot," said Reardon. "That's what lost the game, you could argue."[11]

Gaston needed another substitute with the pitcher due. "Given that Reardon is a right-hander, many expected veteran Rance Mulliniks to be sent to the plate," one writer observed. "'It was [Ed] Sprague all the way,' Gaston said."[12] Sprague hit for Ward. Bell represented the tying run, and Sprague the go-ahead run. "I knew I hit it good," Sprague said. "I looked up and it was in the lights and then I threw my hands up in the air"[13] to celebrate his homer that put the Jays up 5-4. Said Reardon: "I made a pitch to Sprague that was low. Usually I get hitters on a high fastball. It didn't happen tonight."[14] He retired the next two batters to keep the deficit at one run.

Tom Henke replaced Ward on the mound in the bottom of the ninth and retired Lemke. Lonnie Smith hit for Reardon, and Henke hit him. Gant ran for Smith. With two outs, Gant stole second, and Henke walked Sanders. With the tying and go-ahead runners on, Henke sealed the first World Series win by a Canadian team, getting Pendleton to foul out to Gruber, who "did the tomahawk chop" after making the catch. "'We won one,' said Gruber. 'I really like the Braves' song. It's a sedate song. It relaxes you and then it puts you on the warpath at the same time.'"[15]

The flag from Canada may have flown upside down, but Toronto could fly home with heads held high after squaring the World Series.

SOURCES

In addition to the Sources cited in the Notes, the author consulted the Baseball-Reference.com website for pertinent material and the box score noted below.

https://www.baseball-reference.com/boxes/ATL/ATL199210180.shtml

NOTES

1   Glenn Sheely, "Inverted Flag Angers Canadians," *Atlanta Constitution*, October 19, 1992: 31. Like many U.S. residents, Sheely used the word "American" as a synonym for the United States of America. "The inverted maple leaf confirmed Canada's worst suspicions, that Yanks don't know much about geography, or national flags, for that matter, and are particularly numb regarding Canada," wrote George Vecsey in "Some Hits and Runs, But Short on Sleep," *New York Times*, October 19, 1992: C9.

2   Stephen Brunt, "Marines Wave Red Flag at Canada – Upside Down," *Globe & Mail*, October 19, 1992.

3   Excerpt from Christie Blatchford of the *Toronto Sun* as reprinted in the *Atlanta Constitution*, October 19, 1992: 32.

4   Al Strachan, "The Manager," *Globe & Mail*, October 19, 1992.

5   Neil A. Campbell, "Sanders Gets Nod from Cox," *Globe & Mail*, October 19, 1992.

6   Canadian sports fans might more fondly recall another Mike Reilly, namely, the star Canadian Football League quarterback.

7   Kirk Makin, "1992 World Series/A Fan's View with Kirk Makin," *Globe & Mail*, October 19, 1992.

8   Larry Whiteside, "Fresh Start for Sanders in Left," *Boston Globe*, October 19, 1992: 44.

9   Claire Smith, "Cone Does His Best Work with Bat," *New York Times*, October 19, 1992: C9.

10   Rosie DiManno, "Jays Tie It in a Pinch," *Toronto Star*, October 19, 1992: A1.

11   Joe Sexton, "A Fast Pitch That Fell a Few Feet Too Short," *New York Times*, October 19, 1992: C9.

12   Neil A. Campbell, "Jays Swing Series Momentum Their Way," *Globe & Mail*, October 19, 1992.

13   Marty York, "Reardon Is Pure Relief for Jays," *Globe & Mail*, October 19, 1992.

14   Larry Whiteside, "Blue Jays Stun Reardon, Braves," *Boston Globe*, October 19, 1992: 44.

15   "Glavine Appears OK for Game 4," *Boston Globe*, October 20, 1992: 80. Gruber would likely not have made this insensitive gesture and comment a few decades later given the increased sensitivity to the racist treatment of indigenous people in both Canada and the United States.

JAYS WIN FIRST WORLD SERIES GAME IN CANADA

OCTOBER 20, 1992:
TORONTO BLUE JAYS 3, ATLANTA 2,
AT SKYDOME, TORONTO
(GAME THREE OF THE 1992 W ORLD SERIES)

By Tim Hannan

The Toronto Blue Jays scored three runs in their last two innings to beat the Atlanta Braves 5-4 in Game Two of the 1992 World Series and tie the Series at one victory each after the first two games in Atlanta. This victory was another part of the team's 1992 season story: teamwork at the right times resulting in wins.

The Blue Jays had won their fans' hearts as well as those of the whole Canadian nation as they won the American League Championship Series in impressive fashion. The club had failed to win a pennant in three postseason series (1985, 1989, 1991), with a post-season record since 1985 of five wins and 12 losses. Having reached the World Series – the first in their 16-year franchise history – offered a level of competition on the international stage comparable to the 1972 Canadian-Russian hockey series.

Which Toronto club would show up at SkyDome? Could Atlanta recover from its Game Two loss? The Blue Jays' pitching and defense had earned their tie despite starting position players having a combined batting average of .151 in the first two games. Atlanta played well at times but its pitching and defense faltered at other times.

Game Three was the first World Series game to be played outside the United States. An enthusiastic sellout crowd of 51,813 and a CBS television audience watched this historic game.

In the pregame ceremonies, some controversies from the previous game were resolved without incident. The US Marine Corps Color Guard had inadvertently displayed the Canadian flag upside down before Game Two. And Canadian singer Tom Cochrane sang lyrics from an earlier version of the Canadian national anthem than the one which had been officially designated as such in 1980. The Canadian flag was properly displayed by the Color Guard and singer Anne Murray sang the anthem's correct (1980) version prior to this game.[1]

Game Three began as a pitchers' duel between Blue Jays starter Juan Guzmán and Braves starter Steve Avery. Neither team scored in the first three innings.[2]

In the fourth inning, Atlanta threatened to score the game's first run. Deion Sanders led off with an infield single and moved to second base on Terry Pendleton's single to right-center field. Then fans saw one of the greatest catches in World Series history on the next play and a near triple play.[3]

David Justice hit a high fly ball off Guzmán toward deep center field, where Blue Jays center fielder Devon White made a spectacular backhanded catch as he crashed into the wall just to the left of the 400-foot sign. This play robbed Justice of an extra-base hit and was reminiscent of Willie Mays' catch of Vic Wertz's fly ball in the 1954 World Series.[4]

As the play developed, Sanders stood on the base-path between second and third base watching the ball's flight while Pendleton, who had started to run when the ball was hit, passed Sanders between second and third base. Both runners began to retreat back to their original bases when the ball was caught. Meanwhile, White threw the ball to second baseman Roberto Alomar, who was in shallow center field. Then Alomar threw to first baseman John Olerud in an attempt to double up Pendleton. But Pendleton was already automatically out for passing Sanders. Olerud saw that Sanders had started running toward third and threw the ball to third baseman Kelly Gruber to try to put Sanders out. Gruber began to chase the runner back toward second base and tagged Sanders on his right heel before Sanders could slide back into the base. However, second-base umpire Bob Davidson called Sanders safe and it appeared that he did not see the tag. His call denied the Blue Jays a rare World Series triple play.[5]

The third baseman tried to appeal his case to the umpire. "Are you crazy?" said Gruber. Davidson's response stunned Gruber, "Kelly, you might have, but I saw daylight."[6] Television replays and media photographs indicated that Gruber had tagged out Sanders. After the game, Davidson admitted in an interview that he had made the wrong call. "When I first called the play, I thought I was 100 percent right," Davidson, a National League umpire, said. "It was right there. It was right in front of me. Then I saw the replays and the picture and I thought I probably missed the play. But that's baseball, and I have to turn the page and go on today. No one feels worse about it than I do. I don't like to miss plays. Gruber told me right away that he had gotten his heel. He was professional about it, though, and it was no big deal. I thought I was correct at first. But then I saw the pictures, and I had to admit that I probably missed it."[7]

It was ruled a double play. With Sanders standing on second base with two outs, Guzmán struck out Lonnie Smith to end the inning and the Braves' scoring threat.

With one out in the Blue Jays' fourth, Joe Carter hit a solo home run over the left-field fence to give Toronto a 1-0 lead – the first World Series home run hit outside the United States. Avery retired the next two Toronto batters to end the inning.

Atlanta rallied to tie the score at 1-1 with some good hitting off Guzmán in the sixth inning. Sanders hit a one-out double to right field and moved to third on Pendleton's single to deep shortstop. Justice's single to right field scored Sanders and moved Pendleton to second base. But Guzmán then retired the side on a fly out and a groundout.

Atlanta took a 2-1 lead in the eighth inning. Otis Nixon, leading off, reached first base on Gruber's error and stole second. Sanders popped out, but Pendleton's groundout sent Nixon to third. Justice was intentionally walked. Nixon scored on Lonnie Smith's single to left field, but Justice was thrown out at third base, retiring the Braves.

The Blue Jays quickly forged another tie when Gruber led off the bottom of the eighth inning by hitting an Avery 3-and-2 pitch over the left-field fence to square the game at 2-2. The SkyDome crowd roared their approval as the ball disappeared into the crowd. The next three Jays batters were quickly retired by Avery to end the inning.

In the ninth, both managers used late-inning strategies and the fans saw the first World Series managerial ejection since 1985.

When the Braves came to bat, Toronto manager Cito Gaston replaced Guzmán with Duane Ward, who allowed Sid Bream's leadoff single to right-center field. Brian Hunter, an excellent baserunner, replaced Bream at first. Hunter attempted to steal second on Ward's 2-and-2 pitch to Jeff Blauser. As Blauser appeared to check his swing, Blue Jays catcher Pat Borders threw to shortstop Manuel Lee, who tagged out Hunter.

Borders argued to home-plate umpire Joe West that Blauser had swung on the pitch for a third strike. West asked first-base umpire Dan Morrison for a decision on the pitch; Morrison said that Blauser had swung for a third strike, and it was a double play.

Braves manager Bobby Cox, upset with the ruling, angrily tossed a batting helmet from the dugout onto the field, and was ejected by West with the SkyDome crowd's approval.[8] Ward struck out Damon Berryhill to end the Braves' inning.

Braves third-base coach Jimy Williams, who had taken over managerial duties, Williams allowed Avery to start the ninth inning, but when he gave up a single to Alomar, Williams replaced him with Mark Wohlers. Alomar stole second base on Wohlers' 2-and-0 pitch to Carter, then was walked intentionally.

Dave Winfield laid down a surprise sacrifice bunt to advance both runners. Williams replaced Wohlers, calling on Mike Stanton to face Olerud.

Once Stanton was announced, Gaston sent up pinch-hitter Ed Sprague, whose home run had won Game Two. Stanton walked Sprague intentionally, loading the bases with one out.

Williams summoned the inning's third relief pitcher, Jeff Reardon, to face Candy Maldonado. On a two-strike count, Maldonado drove the ball over Nixon's head in center field and Alomar scored the game-winning run. He did the "Tomahawk Chop" as he ran home from third base.

The Jays had won their second consecutive game over the Braves with a 3-2 walk-off win in the bottom of the ninth inning. SkyDome fans celebrated in the stands while the Blue Jays celebrated on the field.

In a postgame interview, Gruber said, "We've been known as the 'Comeback Jays' and that's an attitude that I am proud of."[9]

The Braves' loss meant that each of their last four World Series defeats the decisive scores came in the final inning, and that their last three World Series road defeats were walk-offs.

Toronto took a two-games-to-one Series lead with two more games to be played at SkyDome. The Blue Jays' 3-2 walk-off win was the first Series victory for a major-league ball club outside the United States.

SOURCES

In addition to the sources cited in the Notes, the author consulted Baseball-Reference.com, Retrosheet.org, SABR.org, and a number of other sources, including the following:

https://www.baseball-reference.com/boxes/TOR/TOR199210200.shtml

https://www.retrosheet.org/boxesetc/1992/B10200TOR1992.htm

NOTES

1   The original Canadian anthem was written in 1880 which was 13 years after the Canadian Constitution was written. For 100 years, there were various anthem versions used by the Canadian people. In 1980, the Canadian Parliament passed the National Anthem Act which designated "O Canada" as Canada's national anthem, with the lyrics as sung by Anne Murray.

2   Atlanta's Avery and Toronto's Guzmán each gave up one hit and struck out three batters over the first three innings.

3   The near triple play would have been the second triple play executed in World Series history (1903-2021). In Game Five of the 1920 World Series, Cleveland Indians second baseman Bill Wambsganss made an unassisted triple play against the Brooklyn Robins. SABR Triple Play Database (https://sabr.org/tripleplays). Also, see YouTube video clip for Devon White's catch. (https://www.youtube.com/watch?v=GYA61SGGjbw).

4   New York Giants center fielder Willie Mays, with his back facing home plate, made a spectacular overhead catch of a fly ball by the Cleveland Indians' Vic Wertz in deep center field at the New York Giants' Polo Grounds in Game One of the 1954 World Series. Associated Press, "White's Catch Ranks Among All-Time Best," *Ocala* (Florida) *Star Banner*, October 22, 1992: 2.

5   Mike Lopresti, "Oh, Candy: O Canada," *Rochester* (New York) *Democrat & Chronicle*, October 21, 1992: 1D.

6   Callum Hughson, "Profiling Former Blue Jays Third Baseman Kelly Gruber," mopupduty.com. (January 17, 2020 Interview), retrieved March 25, 2022. https://mopupduty.com/toronto-blue-jays-third-baseman-kelly-gruber-011720/ Gruber was stunned by the umpire's response to his appeal and was expecting an argument to ensue.

7   On Davidson's admission of his missed call after viewing the television replays, see Mark Maske, "Umpire Admits His Mistake," *Washington Post*, October 22, 1992. Retrieved March 25, 2022. https://www.washingtonpost.com/archive/sports/1992/10/22/umpire-admits-his-error/350344e6-607a-48d0-b884-eb00d9ccb411/.

8   St. Louis Cardinals manager Whitey Herzog was ejected for arguing an umpire's balls/strikes call in Game Seven of the 1985 World Series against the Kansas City Royals.

9   Tom Slater, "Right Side Up!," *Toronto Star*, October 21, 1992: D1.

KEY LOCKS THE DOOR, BLUE JAYS ONE WIN AWAY FROM CHAMPIONSHIP

OCTOBER 21, 1992:
TORONTO BLUE JAYS 2, ATLANTA BRAVES 1,
AT SKYDOME, TORONTO
(GAME FOUR OF THE 1992 W ORLD SERIES)

By David Matchett

On Wednesday evening, October 21, 1992, Torontonians could have gone to see Tom Selleck in *Mr. Baseball*, attended the Toronto Ski Show or hung out with Keith Richards at the Squeeze Club, but over 52,000 opted to spend the cool, wet night inside SkyDome watching Game Four of the World Series between the Blue Jays and the Atlanta Braves. The previous night's walk-off victory had given the Jays a two-games-to-one Series lead and the crowd was eager to see them move one step closer to the championship.

Toronto manager Cito Gaston had been relying on a three-man pitching rotation in the postseason but he decided to go with Jimmy Key, considered the team's fourth-best starter that year.[1] Rosie DiManno wrote, "Gaston had a change of heart ... figuring that Key's off-speed, left-handed stuff would be a good weapon to offset the big Atlanta bats."[2] Key was rested, having pitched only five innings over the previous 22 days, but he commented that "the club knows I'm not as effective a pitcher when I do have a long layoff."[3] Atlanta's ongoing batting slump, however, eased the pressure on Key. After three games the Braves were hitting a collective .196/.306/.239 against Toronto and, making matters worse for them, manager Bobby Cox loaded his lineup with right-handed batters to face Key. This left the team's two hottest hitters, left-handers Deion Sanders and Sid Bream, on the bench. Key's counterpart was Tom Glavine, who had tossed

a complete-game four-hitter to beat the Jays in the Series opener.

After Winona Judd and Michelle Wright belted out the national anthems, Atlanta's leadoff hitter, Otis Nixon, belted Key's fourth offering for a single. Nixon was a speedster and the Jays were having trouble with the running game.[4] Dave Perkins wrote, "The large stolen-base totals against the Jays ... were not the fault of [catcher Pat Borders's] throwing so much as they were a staff-wide weakness at holding runners close."[5] But the Braves hadn't seen Key. Key's last pickoff was in 1990, but after a strike to Jeff Blauser, he launched "a whippet throw that caught Nixon by a foot."[6] Blauser followed that with a single to center, then stole his way into scoring position. Terry Pendleton hit the next pitch on the nose, but right at shortstop Manuel Lee. The inning ended with a groundout but three of the four batters had made solid contact and concerns about Key's rustiness seemed to have had some merit.

A single, two groundouts, and a steal put Roberto Alomar at third base in the bottom of the first but Dave Winfield was retired to end the inning. Key and Glavine settled in and each retired the side in order in the second. Key repeated the feat in the top of the third but Toronto broke through in the bottom of the inning when Borders hit a 1-and-1 pitch over the left-field fence. "It was off a changeup," Borders said, "over the plate and thigh high. I was trying to hit it up the middle but I got good wood on it and it really carried."[7] Glavine was a bit shaky after that, giving up a one-out double and a walk, but Joe Carter's line shot was snagged by shortstop Blauser, who flipped the ball to second baseman Mark Lemke to catch Devon White off base and kill the rally.

Key set the Braves down in order on seven pitches in the fourth and the Jays started the bottom of the frame with a walk and a single, but Glavine got out of trouble with a fly ball and a double play. Both pitchers had one-two-three fifth innings and Key got the first two batters of the sixth before Nixon ended a string of 16 consecutive outs with a line-drive single. It was for naught, however, as Blauser grounded out. The Jays rallied again when a walk and a single put runners on the corners with two out in the bottom of the sixth, but the threat ended when Candy Maldonado was called out on a 1-and-2 pitch that missed the plate by several inches.[8]

Key was winning the pitching battle and Glavine was showing his frustration. Steve Hummer commented, "Coming off the field … Glavine showed uncommon fire as he strode toward his bench. Loudly he told them to get it going. He was a man who had charged into one too many fights on his own; and now he was demanding support."[9] He didn't get it in the seventh as Key shut the Braves down with only eight pitches to extend his streak to 20 of 21 batters retired since the first inning.

After the seventh-inning stretch, Kelly Gruber drew a leadoff walk and Lee's one-out grounder moved him to second. White followed with a groundball between third and short and the aggressive Gruber headed for home. Left fielder Ron Gant's throw was cut off and White was caught in a rundown but Gruber scored before the out was registered. Gruber didn't know that the throw wasn't coming home and he knocked his chin while sliding headfirst. "I saw the ball was coming right at the plate," on-deck hitter Alomar explained, "so I told Kelly to slide. It was going to be real close, until they cut the throw."[10] Gruber, obviously shaken up, added, "I don't remember running the bases or even getting on, I just saw stars."[11]

Now trailing 2-0 the Braves were down to their last six outs. In the eighth Gant hit a leadoff double, just the team's third extra-base hit of the Series,[12] and Brian Hunter followed with a perfectly placed bunt single to put runners at the corners with nobody out. Damon Berryhill then surprised everyone by bunting at Key's first pitch, but he popped it up for an easy out. Cox wasn't happy: "[W]e were stealing. I don't know what went through Damon's mind."[13] Berryhill added, "I didn't believe there was one (steal) on. … I was bunting on my own, I didn't see a sign."[14]

Next up was Lemke, whose sharp grounder was deflected by Key. Gruber raced by, made a barehanded grab, and retired Lemke at first as Gant scored. Gruber said, "It was do or die. I knew I had to field it barehanded. It took a good hop for me … and I was going to the base where I had to throw."[15] The play was all the more remarkable since Gruber was still groggy from his slide a few minutes earlier. "I just saw it in there," Gruber later declared as he pointed to the video room, "I didn't know a thing about it until I saw it on TV."[16]

There were now two out but the tying run was on second and the switch-hitting Nixon was due up. He was weaker from the left side so Gaston removed Key in favor of right-hander Duane Ward.[17] Key tipped his cap to a standing ovation and, as Rosie DiManno wrote, "Everyone in the park knew that this may very well have been the last they saw of Key doing his stuff … in a Blue Jay uniform. He would be a free agent at the end of the year and his five-hit, one-run performance was his swan song."[18]

Jays relievers hadn't blown a save since July 24[19] and the streak looked to be intact when Ward struck Nixon out, but the ball eluded Borders and the Braves' hopes were still alive as Nixon reached first and Hunter moved to third. Nixon immediately stole second and suddenly the go-ahead run was in scoring position. The next batter was the right-handed-hitting Blauser, who was a meek 2-for-14 to this point in the Series.[20] Lefty hitters Sanders and Bream were sitting on the bench with a combined Series OPS of 1.112, but with left-hander David Wells warming up to face a pinch-hitter, Cox decided to stick with Blauser.[21] The batter repaid his manager's faith by scalding a ball down the first-base line but John Olerud was in perfect position to field the grounder and end the inning.[22] "Blauser hit a bullet," said Cox. "I still haven't figured out why Olerud was just two, three feet off the line."[23]

That would prove to be Atlanta's last gasp. Glavine set the Jays down in order in the bottom of the eighth and Toronto closer Tom Henke finished the game with a clean ninth. At just 2 hours and 21 minutes it was "the fastest Series game in seven years."[24] No World Series contest has been played in less time in the three decades since. The Jays were now one win away from their first championship with hopes of wrapping it up at home the next day.

SOURCES

All statistics and play-by-play information for this game were found at Baseball-Reference.com, https://www.baseball-reference.com/boxes/TOR/TOR199210210.shtml, accessed February 7, 2022.

All game logs and season and career statistics for individual players were found at their respective Baseball-Reference pages.

The full CBS broadcast of the game, with all advertisements deleted, can be found on YouTube at https://www.youtube.com/watch?v=HiYVHqTQctU

NOTES

1   Dan Diamond and Associates, *Toronto Blue Jays Official 25th Anniversary Commemorative Book* (Toronto: Dan Diamond and Associates, Inc., 2001), 116. "Jimmy Key is the winningest left-handed pitcher in Blue Jays history, but he was not at his best in 1992. … [H]e had been relegated to number-four starter. …"

2   Rosie DiManno, *Glory Jays, Canada's World Series Champions* (Toronto: Sagamore Publishing, 1993), 276.

3   Tom Slater, "Key's Masterful Outing Might Be Last as a Jay," *Toronto Star*, October 22, 1992: C3. Key made six starts in September, all of which lasted at least six innings, the last of them on September 29. Key started Toronto's last game of the season, on October 4, but left after pitching two innings. His only previous appearance in the 1992 postseason was three innings of relief on October 12 in Game Five of the ALCS. Other than these October 4 and 12 appearances, this start was Key's first outing in 22 days.

4   From 1988 through 1997 Nixon averaged 50 stolen bases per season, including 41 in 1992. He finished no worse than seventh in stolen bases in his league in each of those years. His 620 career steals place him 16th on the all-time list.

5   Dave Perkins, "O Canada!," in Major League Baseball Properties Inc., Jon Rochmis, ed., *A Series for the World* (San Francisco: Woodford Press, 1992), 80.

6   DiManno, 276.

7   Jim Proudfoot, "Blue Jays Going to Bat for Larry Hisle," *Toronto Star*, October 22, 1992: C4. This was Borders' first home run of 1992 off a left-handed pitcher. He had hit 13 home runs in the regular season and all of them were off right-handers. That season was uncharacteristic for Borders; in his career of 3,499 plate appearances, he hit a home run every 52.3 plate appearances off right-handed pitchers and one every 48.4 plate appearances off lefties.

8   Prentis Rogers, "Analysts Zero In on Ump's Strike Zone," *Atlanta Constitution*, October 22, 1992: E13.

9   Steve Hummer, "Braves Don't Really Need Miracles to Carry Them Home – Just Some Hits," *Atlanta Constitution*, October 22, 1992: E1.

10 Tom Slater, "Gruber's a Knockout in Game 4 Win," *Toronto Star*, October 22, 1992: C3.

11 DiManno, 277.

12 Damon Berryhill had hit a home run in Game One and Deion Sanders doubled in Game Three.

13 DiManno, 276-7.

14 Dave Perkins, "Are Cox's Braves Simply Unlucky? Uh, Not Exactly," *Toronto Star*, October 22, 1992: C2. Perkins also noted, "Since homering in Game 1, Berryhill had had 10 at-bats and struck out in seven of them." Berryhill had 1,284 plate appearances from 1987 through 1992 with only seven sacrifices: three in 1988 and four in 1989. His most recent successful bunt had been on July 19, 1989, but he would later have one in Game Six of this series.

15 "The Inside Pitch," *Toronto Star*, October 22, 1992: C2.

16 DiManno, 277.

17 Over his full career Nixon's OPS was .663 versus right-handed pitchers and .647 versus left-handers, but in 1992 it was .620 versus righties and .812 against lefties.

18 DiManno, 278.

19 The Toronto relief corps had 10 blown saves in 1992, four by Duane Ward, three by Tom Henke, two by David Wells, and one by Pat Hentgen. Three of these were in April (19, 20, and 30), two were in May (16 and 20), two in June (2 and 28) and three in July (9, 24, and 24). Henke and Ward each had a blown save in a loss at Oakland on July 24: Ward allowed the tying run to score in the seventh inning in relief of starter David Wells, Toronto retook the lead in the top of the ninth inning and Henke allowed two runs in the bottom of the inning to lose the game.

20 Blauser had a single in 11 at-bats in the first three games of the series and was 1-for-3 to this point in Game Four. His slump extended back to the second game of the NLCS: After hitting a second-inning triple he had three hits in his last 20 at-bats of that series for an overall streak of five singles in his previous 34 at-bats, with four walks and nine strikeouts in that period.

21 Tommy Hutton, "Key Set the Tone by Nailing Nixon Right Off the Bat," *Toronto Star*, October 22, 1992: C4. "Cox had Deion Sanders and Sid Bream on the bench. And there's no way Blue Jays manager Cito Gaston is going to go to left-hander David Wells in the bullpen, even though both Sanders and Bream are left-handed hitters. With the way Ward was throwing, that would have been unlikely. So if you're the Braves, you're assured of the matchup you want with a right-handed pitcher against a left-handed batter."

22 I.J. Rosenberg, "Braves: Face 3-1 Deficit After 2-1 Loss," *Atlanta Constitution*, October 22, 1992: E9. "Blauser sliced a ball down the first-base line, but John Olerud went down on one knee to get it and ran to first to retire Blauser and end the inning."

23 Dave Perkins, "Are Cox's Braves Simply Unlucky? Uh, Not Exactly," *Toronto Star*, October 22, 1992: C2. Olerud's positioning on the play can be seen on YouTube at 1:55:37: he is to the second-base side of the first-base sliding pit, more than 15 feet off the line.

24 Brad Henderson and Gerry Hall, eds., *On Top of the World, The Toronto Star's Tribute to the '92 Blue Jays* (Toronto: Doubleday Canada Limited, 1992), 86. Game Four of the 1985 World Series lasted 2:19 and no other subsequent World Series game had lasted less than 2½ hours until this one.

JAYS BECOME FIRST CANADIAN TEAM TO WIN WORLD SERIES

OCTOBER 24, 1992:
TORONTO BLUE JAYS 4, ATLANTA BRAVES 3 (11 INNINGS),
AT ATLANTA-FULTON COUNTY STADIUM, ATLANTA
(GAME SIX OF THE 1992 W ORLD SERIES)

By Adrian Fung

After the Atlanta Braves staved off elimination with a win in Toronto two nights earlier, Game Six of the 1992 World Series once again began with the historic possibility of the Toronto Blue Jays becoming the first non-US and first Canadian-based team ever to win the fall classic.

In Toronto's first at-bat, Devon White singled, stole second, and later scored on a sacrifice fly by Joe Carter to open the scoring. Atlanta tied the game in the third when Deion Sanders doubled, stole third, and scored on Terry Pendleton's fly out.

Leading off the fourth inning, left fielder Candy Maldonado made it 2-1 for Toronto by belting a Steve Avery fastball over the left-field wall. Atlanta mounted a scoring threat in the fifth when Toronto starter David Cone labored through a 26-pitch inning. He gave up a walk, two-out single, and stolen base to put runners on second and third but the veteran right-hander got out of the jam by recording a fourth straight inning-ending strikeout.

Pitchers on both sides frustrated batters all night. Atlanta ended up leaving 10 runners on base; Toronto, which put at least one runner on in each inning, stranded 13.

In the bottom of the ninth, with the score 2-1, veteran Toronto closer Tom Henke came on to get the biggest three outs of his career. Toronto's all-time saves leader was riding a 14⅔-inning scoreless streak in postseason play and had already preserved Toronto's wins in Games Two and Four.

But Atlanta rallied. Jeff Blauser reached second on a single and a sacrifice by Damon Berryhill. Lonnie Smith walked, bringing Francisco Cabrera off the bench for his first appearance of the World Series. Ten days earlier, Cabrera had hit a walk-off two-run single in Game Seven of the NLCS, giving Atlanta the National League pennant over Pittsburgh. Now he found himself in almost the identical situation: elimination game, bottom of the ninth, down by a run, the tying and winning runs on base. Cabrera cracked a liner to left field. Maldonado misjudged the ball for a split-second but stepped back, leaped up, and caught it.

One out to go …

Henke slipped two breaking balls by Otis Nixon to get ahead, 0-and-2. *One strike* to go … but Nixon slapped Henke's next offering through the left side to score Blauser with the tying run. Smith and Nixon advanced an extra base on Maldonado's wild throw home. With the winning run at third, Henke composed himself and got Ron Gant to fly out to deep center, sending Game Six into extra innings.

After an uneventful 10th inning, White was hit by a pitch with one out in the top of the 11th from left-hander Charlie Leibrandt, pitching his second relief inning. Roberto Alomar lined a changeup on one hop to center field, moving White to second. Despite Toronto's top right-handed run producers due up and right-handed closer Jeff Reardon warming up in the bullpen, Atlanta manager Bobby Cox elected to stick with Leibrandt. Reardon had been ineffective in two earlier Series appearances, giving up the game-winning RBIs each time.

Leibrandt got Carter to pop out to center, bringing cleanup batter Dave Winfield, 41, to the plate. Including a dismal performance in the 1981 fall classic, the veteran of 19 major-league seasons was now mired in a career 5-for-43 World Series slump with no extra-base hits and just two RBIs. Cox weighed the slump versus Winfield's four career home runs against Leibrandt and stuck with his southpaw.

Could Winfield shed the "Mr. May" label bestowed on him by Yankees owner George Steinbrenner?[1]

Winfield pulled a 3-and-2 changeup down the left-field line for a double. White and Alomar, both running on the pitch, scored easily as Gant, chasing the ball, stumbled briefly on the warning track.

"I didn't do a whole lot, but I did it at the right time. This is the best team I ever played on," a relieved Winfield reflected after the game. "I'll tell you, I'm the oldest man in this room, the longest waiting for a world championship, but also the happiest man here."[2]

Winfield's perfectly timed clutch hit gave Toronto a 4-2 lead. Cox would be second-guessed again as Leibrandt was saddled with the ignominy of giving up another devastating extra-inning World Series hit to a right-handed batter. Exactly 52 weeks earlier, he had served up Kirby Puckett's Game Six-winning home run in Minnesota.

Yet the Braves did not concede meekly. Blauser – as he had done in the ninth inning – led off the bottom of the 11th with a single. Berryhill grounded Jimmy Key's next pitch on the infield, a sure double play, but the ball hopped unexpectedly off shortstop Alfredo Griffin's glove, putting runners on the corners. Pitcher John Smoltz entered the game as a pinch-runner for Berryhill, representing the tying run. Rafael Belliard sacrificed Smoltz to second.

Like Cox, Toronto manager Cito Gaston stuck with his left-hander, Key, despite right-handed pinch-hitter Brian Hunter coming up. Hunter grounded out to first base, scoring Blauser and trimming Toronto's lead to 4-3 as Smoltz reached third.

Nixon marched to the plate with two out, looking to rescue his club again. Gaston walked to the mound and years later recalled that Key was honest about the situation. "You know what, Cito? I haven't had a lot of luck with this guy," Key acknowledged.[3] Gaston summoned young righty Mike Timlin into the game.

As the speedy Nixon dug in, Gaston and several infielders warned Timlin that Nixon might bunt. "Cito told me about it and [Toronto catcher] Pat Borders told

me about it and then [Kelly] Gruber mentioned it," Timlin said. "And then Joe Carter, who was at first, he comes over and says, 'You've got to help me out on the bunt a little bit.'"[4] Nixon fouled off the first pitch. Then, as if on cue, he bunted the ball between the mound and first base. Fully prepared, Timlin fielded it cleanly and lobbed the ball to Carter, nipping Nixon by a half-step for the final out. "I dreamt and dreamt of this day, this situation. I always wanted to be in it. Tonight I came through, just like I always came through in my dreams," Timlin remarked.[5]

At 12:50 A.M. Sunday, the Toronto Blue Jays had finally won the World Series and a championship pennant would be raised outside the United States for the first time ever. Borders was named MVP of the Series after leading his club in batting (.450) and all batters in hits (9) and slugging (.750). "It's unbelievable. I never even thought I'd make it to the major leagues, let alone be an MVP in a World Series," said Borders.[6]

The calm, understated Gaston was the first Black manager to win the World Series and he gave credit to his players at the championship parade in Toronto the next day. "From Day One in Detroit, if you could have seen their faces, how determined they were, you'd know this was going to happen. I'm so proud of you guys, you're the greatest. Let's do it again."[7]

Gaston, in turn, received praise from team members. "He's doing a great job," said All-Star second baseman Alomar. "He's man-to-man, not the kind of guy who likes to show people up. A lot of players respect that."[8] The franchise's chairman of the board, Peter Widdrington, agreed. "This is a great personal triumph for Cito. I think he was absolutely the right guy at the right time for the right team. ... He's as tough as nails. He commands a great deal of respect without asking for it. He's completely supportive of his playing personnel and he's a first-rate guy."[9]

Tributes for the Blue Jays came from around the world, and even from out of this world. President George H.W. Bush, entering the last days of the 1992 election campaign, made a congratulatory phone call to Gaston from Air Force One, declaring, "America is proud of you."[10] Steve MacLean, Canada's third astronaut, crowed from the space shuttle *Columbia*, "I've always said from the beginning that the Jays would win in six."[11]

The Blue Jays World Series victory occurred at just the right time. Canada seemed to be coming apart from high unemployment, economic recession, and the quagmire of divisive constitutional amendments that were to be voted on in a national referendum taking place the same day as the World Series parade. The significance of Toronto's championship win was succinctly summed up by Canadian Prime Minister Brian Mulroney in his congratulatory memo to the ballclub.

"This triumph is a dream come true for Blue Jay players and fans and the culmination of many years of planning and effort by the coaching staff and management," the prime minister said. "As the first Canadian team ever to win the series, yours is an historic victory, one which will live forever in Canadian sports history. For all the fans who have supported your club right from that first game on a snowy April day in 1977, this is a sweet moment indeed. You have united a nation behind you, capturing the imagination of Canadians from coast to coast."[12]

SOURCES

Besides the sources cited in the Notes, the author also consulted the following:

Cheek, Tom, and Howard Berger. *Road to Glory: An Insider's Look at 16 Years of Blue Jay Baseball* (Toronto: Warwick Publishing, 1993).

DiManno, Rosie. *Glory Jays: Canada's World Series Champions* (Champaign, Illinois: Sagamore Publishing, 1993).

Kinsella, W.P., Furman Bisher, Dave Perkins, and Stephen Green. *A Series for the World: Baseball's First International Fall Classic* (San Francisco: Woodford Publishing, 1992).

World Series Game Six: Toronto Blue Jays at Atlanta Braves, CBS Television (Buffalo, New York: WIVB, October 24, 1992).

NOTES

1 Murray Chass, "Baseball; Winfield Convinces His Chief Doubter," *New York Times*, October 6, 1985: S3.

2 Allan Ryan, "WORLD BEATERS! Jays Best in Baseball After Nail Biting, 11-Inning Victory," *Toronto Star*, October 25, 1992: E1.

3 http://sportsnet.ca/baseball/mlb/blue-jays-oral-history-memories-of-92-world-series/.

4 Robert MacLeod, "Timlin Still Has Fond Memories of Championship Year With Jays," *Globe and Mail* (Toronto), September 7, 2007: S6.

5 Dave Perkins, "Timlin's 'Dream' of Victory Realized," *Toronto Star*, October 25, 1992: E4.

6 Marty York, "It Doesn't Get Any Better Than This," *Globe and Mail*, October 26, 1992: D1.

7 Jack Lakey, "250,000 Jays Fans Line Streets," *Toronto Star*, October 27, 1992: A4.

8 Larry Millson, "Cito Gaston Proves That His Way Is the Winning Way," *Globe and Mail*, October 26, 1992: D2.

9 Millson.

10 Neil A. Campbell, "Top of the World," *Globe and Mail*, October 26, 1992: D1.

11 Nicolaas van Rijn, "Raves Pour in for Cito's Jays," *Toronto Star*, October 26, 1992: A4.

12 Caroline Mallan, "Half a Million Jubilant Jays Fans Pack Downtown," *Toronto Star*, October 25, 1992: A1.

CONTRIBUTORS

Sean Addis lives outside of Ottawa, Ontario, and just recently completed his MBA. He was a high-school teacher, worked in sport media and now is in his third career as a marketing director for a youth baseball organization. Sean wrote for Baseball Prospectus Toronto and joined SABR in 2020.

Malcolm Allen lives with his wife, Sara, and daughters, Ruth and Martina, in Brooklyn, New York. He manages a warehouse for Crossfire Sound Productions. Originally from Baltimore, he had a good seat on June 5, 1992, when Cal Ripken's two-out single off Duane Ward in the bottom of the eighth drove home Brady Anderson with the only run in the first-ever 1-0 game played at Camden Yards.

Mark Armour is the founder and former chairman of SABR's Baseball Biography Project, the founder of SABR's Baseball Cards Committee, and the author or co-author of eight baseball books. His latest, *Intentional Balk: Baseball's Thin Line Between Innovation and Cheating* (with Dan Levitt), will be published in the summer of 2022. He writes from his home in Oregon's Willamette Valley.

Richard Bogovich's new book in 2022 is *Frank Grant: The Life of a Black Baseball Pioneer*. For McFarland & Co. he'd previously written *Kid Nichols: A Biography of the Hall of Fame Pitcher* and *The Who: A Who's Who*. He has contributed to such SABR books as *When the Monarchs Reigned: Kansas City's 1942 Negro League Champions* and *The Newark Eagles Take Flight: The Story of the 1946 Negro League Champions*. He works for the Wendland Utz law firm in Rochester, Minnesota.

Thomas J. Brown Jr. is a lifelong Mets fan who became a Durham Bulls fan after moving to North Carolina in the early 1980s. He was a national board-certified high-school science teacher for 34 years before retiring in 2016. Tom taught science to ELL students in the last eight years of his career and still mentors many of them. He has been a member of SABR since 1995, when he learned about the organization during a visit to Cooperstown on his honeymoon. Tom became active in SABR after his retirement, writing biographies and game stories, mostly about the New York Mets. He loves to travel with his wife, always visiting major-league and minor-league ballparks whenever possible. Tom also loves to cook and writes about the diverse recipes that he makes on his blog, Cooking and My Family.

Frederick C. "Rick" Bush joined SABR in March 2014. Since that time, he has written articles for more than two dozen SABR books as well as for the Biography and Games Project websites. Rick also has co-edited five SABR books about the Negro Leagues with Bill Nowlin: *Bittersweet Goodbye* (2017), *The Newark Eagles Take Flight* (2019), *Pride of Smoketown* (2020), *When the Monarchs Reigned* (2021), and *The First Negro League Champion* (2022). He remembers coming across his first Toronto Blue Jays baseball card during his age-10 season in 1977, and the team's inaugural-season cap is still his favorite to this day. Rick lives with his wife, Michelle, their three sons – Michael, Andrew, and Daniel – and their border collie, Bailey, in the greater Houston area, and he teaches English at Wharton County Junior College's satellite campus in Sugar Land, the home of the Astros' Triple-A affiliate.

Warren Campbell is a Toronto-based entertainment industry executive. For 30 years he's avoided being on a stage and spends his free time searching through old publications for curious baseball stories. He still has dreams of owning an independent baseball team.

Alan Cohen has been a SABR member since 2010, and he serves as vice president-treasurer of the Connecticut Smoky Joe Wood Chapter. He heads the fact-checking committee for the SABR BioProject and is a datacaster (MiLB First Pitch stringer) for the Hartford Yard Goats, the Double-A affiliate of the Colorado Rockies. His biographies, game stories, and essays have appeared in more than 60 SABR publications. Since his first *Baseball Research Journal* article appeared in 2013, Alan has continued to expand his research into the Hearst Sandlot Classic (1946-1965) from which 87 players advanced to the major leagues. He has four children and nine grandchildren and resides in Connecticut with wife Frances, their cats, Morty, Ava, and Zoe, and their dog Buddy.

Rory Costello got involved in this project because he admired Bob Bailor as a player. Rory lives in Brooklyn, New York, with his wife, Noriko, and son, Kai, who was too small to be ready for a trip to a ballgame in Toronto when the family was there.

Joe Cox has written or contributed to 11 sports books. His most recent solo effort, *A Fine Team Man: Jackie Robinson and the Lives He Changed* was published by Lyons Press in 2019. Joe is an attorney and writer who lives near Bowling Green, Kentucky, with his family. A longtime Cubs fan, he's had to adjust to success in rooting for the Class-A Bowling Green Hot Rods.

Born and raised in Newfoundland, **Mark Davis** developed a youthful passion for baseball and the Toronto Blue Jays that continues to this day. A life-long learner, he holds undergraduate and master's degrees in economics, as well as a PhD in public policy. Mark is a published academic author and relatively new SABR member. He enjoys researching baseball history and recently gave a presentation on the connection between Freemasonry and baseball at his local Masonic lodge. He currently resides in Ottawa with his wife, Melissa, and their young daughter, Felicity.

F. Timothy Deeth was born and raised in Toronto and continues to reside there with his wife of 46 years. An avid baseball fan, Tim has traveled all over North America and has watched baseball games at more than 75 major- or minor-league ballparks. A graduate of Osgoode Hall Law School, Tim has practised law in the Province of Ontario since 1975. This is his first contribution to a SABR publication.

Brian Frank is passionate about documenting the history of major- and minor-league baseball. He is the creator of the website The Herd Chronicles (www.herdchronicles.com), which is dedicated to preserving the history of the Buffalo Bisons and professional baseball in Buffalo. His articles can also be read on the official website of the Bisons. He was an assistant editor of the book *The Seasons of Buffalo Baseball, 1857-2020*, and he's a frequent contributor to SABR publications. Brian and his wife, Jenny, enjoy traveling around the country in their camper to major- and minor-league ballparks and taking an annual trip to Europe. Brian was a history major at Canisius College, where he earned a bachelor of arts. He also received a juris doctor from the University at Buffalo School of Law.

David Fuller is a former newspaper editor and now writes historical articles for various organizations. He is a graduate of York University in Toronto, where he majored in Victorian history. He also studies and writes about Canada's military in the First World War. He has been involved in amateur baseball for many years as a parent, coach, and umpire, and is currently a vice president of the Toronto Baseball Association.

For the centenary of the Ontario Baseball Association, he wrote a short biography of W.J. Smith, Ontario's "Mr. Baseball," the founder of the TBA in 1913 and OBA in 1918.

Adrian Fung lives and works in Toronto. He joined SABR (Hanlan's Point Chapter – Toronto) in 2014 and has contributed several stories to the SABR Games Project, mostly about memorable games in Blue Jays history. Adrian attended the 2019 SABR Black Sox Scandal Centennial Symposium in Chicago and survived the Friday night deluge that washed away the scheduled doubleheader at Guaranteed Rate Field. In January 2020, at a Hanlan's Point Chapter meeting, he presented cases for how the 1919 Reds could have won a "clean" World Series and how Buck Weaver was unfairly treated.

J.P. Garrett is a native Hoosier and marketing/communications executive who writes extensively about sports in general and baseball in particular.

Sam Gazdziak has been a trade journalist for 20 years and writes about music and baseball whenever he can. In 2018 he decided to combine his two loves of baseball and cemetery exploration into the website RIP Baseball, which features stories about the baseball graves he's found. He's visited more than 500 graves in more than 20 states so far and has almost been locked in cemeteries twice. He also writes obituaries for recently deceased ballplayers, and other interesting bits of baseball history that he comes across. Sam lives in the Atlanta area but was born in Chicago and remains a diehard Cubs fan. For more information visit ripbaseball.com.

Tim Hannan is a retired swim coach and paramedic who resides in Farmington, New York. He is a long-term SABR member who was a contributor to *The SABR Baseball List and Record Book*. Tim has been a Jays fan since he watched Toronto's first franchise (home) game on a cold and snowy day in April 1977 at Exhibition Stadium

Tom Hawthorn is a longtime newspaper and magazine writer. He is the author of *The Year Canadians Lost Their Minds and Found Their Country: The Centennial of 1967*, *UVic Athletics: A Century of Excellence: The McKinnon Years*, and *Deadlines*. He has served on the selection committees of two sports halls of fame and has been made an honorary member of Havana's Peña Deportivo for his writing on Cuban baseball. Born in Winnipeg and raised in Montreal and Toronto, he lives in Victoria, British Columbia, where he is a speechwriter for Premier John Horgan. Bats: Right. Throws: Up.

Paul Hofmann has been a SABR member since 2002. He has contributed to more than 25 SABR publications. Paul currently teaches in the College of Management at National Changhua University of Education in Taiwan. A native of Detroit, Paul is an avid baseball-card collector and lifelong Tigers fan. He currently resides in Folsom, California.

Bob Hurte lives in Stewartsville, New Jersey. He works at Catholic Charities as a family specialist. Bob is interested in ballparks, the Pittsburgh Pirates, the Brooklyn Dodgers, and the Negro Leagues, and has been a SABR member since 1998. He is a longtime member of BioProject, and has written more than 20 bios. He co-wrote with Dr. Dale Caldwell *Intelligent Influence in Baseball: Amazing Stories of Influence, Success and Failure* (2022). Bob met John Sullivan (Blue Jays bullpen coach) when he was 10 years old at a local American Legion hall.

Chris Jones is an attorney at Phelps Dunbar, where he practices in the area of commercial litigation, with a focus on property rights, eminent domain, real estate disputes, and contract disputes. He is a lifelong baseball fan and a member of SABR since 2015. The highlight of his playing days was being drafted by the Toronto Blue Jays in the 2001 amateur draft, though writing for this book is the closest he has come to actually contributing to the team. He resides in the Dallas/Fort Worth area with his wife and four children.

John Kennedy is a market research and user experience consultant based in London, Ontario, where he is also a PhD candidate at Western University. His passion for baseball research truly blossomed during his history-degree thesis project, which focused on the transition from wooden to steel ballparks in the Progressive Era and their effect on local communities.

Norm King (1957-2018) of Ottawa, Ontario, joined SABR in 2010 and became a prolific contributor to the SABR BioProject and Games Project until his untimely death from a rare form of bile duct cancer in 2018. He was the lead editor and author of *Au jeu/Play Ball: The 50 Greatest Games in the History of the Montreal Expos*, published in 2016, and wrote chapters for a number of other SABR books, including *Thar's Joy in Braveland: The 1957 Milwaukee Braves; Winning on the North Side: The 1929 Chicago Cubs*; and *A Pennant for the Twin Cities: The 1965 Minnesota Twins*. He was an active member of SABR's Quebec Chapter and a friendly face at the SABR national convention each year.

Tara Krieger didn't grow up a Blue Jays fan, but one of the first baseball games she watched on TV was when they lost the 1991 ALCS to Minnesota. After witnessing that agony of defeat, she couldn't help but root for them in the World Series the following year. She has previously been on staff as a sportswriter at *Newsday* and as an editorial producer for MLB Advanced Media. She currently works as an attorney for the City of New York and has been a member of SABR since 2005.

Justin Krueger is an assistant professor of social studies education at Delta State University in Cleveland, Mississippi. The university is the home of the Fighting Okra, "Queen of Basketball" Lucy Harris, and coaching great and Boston Red Sox Hall of Famer Dave "Boo" Ferriss.

Bob LeMoine is a high-school librarian and adjunct professor at White Mountains Community College and Emporia State University. He lives in New Hampshire and has contributed to several SABR projects. Bob is the author of the forthcoming book *When the Babe Went Back to Boston: Babe Ruth, Judge Fuchs, and the Hapless 1935 Braves* (McFarland & Co., 2022).

Len Levin is a longtime newspaper editor in New England, now retired. He lives in Providence with his wife, Linda, and an overachieving orange cat. He now (Len, not the cat) is the grammarian for the Rhode Island Supreme Court and edits its decisions. He also copyedits many SABR books, including this one. He is just down the interstate from Fenway Park, where he has spent many happy hours.

Dan Levitt is the author of several award-winning baseball books and numerous essays. He is the treasurer of SABR and co-chair of SABR's Business of Baseball committee. Dan is a recipient of the Bob Davids Award and the Chadwick Award. His most recent book is *Intentional Balk: Baseball's Thin Line Between Innovation and Cheating* (coauthored with Mark Armour), released in the summer of 2022.

Nick Malian lives with his wife and daughter in LaSalle, Ontario, where he was born and raised. Growing up in a border city, he idolized Detroit Tigers greats Cecil Fielder and Alan Trammell. As an impressionable 12-year-old, though, his allegiance shifted to the New York Yankees after their 1996 World Series victory; Nick still attempts the "Derek Jeter jump-throw" (with limited success) at his weekly softball games. Nick is a pharmacist by day and amateur home-chef by night.

Joe Marren was born, bred (and buttered) in Buffalo, New York, and has divided his loyalties between the New York Yankees and Toronto Blue Jays. (Something he hopes never to be called to account for because no fan can serve two American League teams.) He is a professor in the Communication Department at SUNY Buffalo State College, where he has been teaching journalism theory and application courses for the past 25 years. He also teaches religious studies classes in the Philosophy Department at Buffalo State. As such, his philosophy about baseball is "Spahn and Sain and pray for rain." Marren was also a newspaper journalist for 18 years at community dailies in Western New York, including a stint as a sports reporter and editor, as well as a stringer for the Associated Press helping to cover Buffalo Bills home games. When he retires he hopes to spend his days ushering in the sun at spring-training games in Florida.

Les Masterson is a deputy editor at *Forbes Advisor* and has contributed to multiple SABR books. He has won numerous awards for his newspaper writing and editing from the New England Press Association and Massachusetts Press Association. He was also a rarity – a New York Mets fan who was born and raised in the shadows of Boston.

David Matchett grew up in Lachine, Quebec, and had his sixth birthday a month before the Montreal Expos played their first game. He earned a degree in finance and later moved to Toronto to pursue his career, arriving the same day the Blue Jays acquired Dave Winfield for their World Series run in 1992. David first discovered SABR when he bought a few back issues of the *Baseball Research Journal* on his initial trip to Cooperstown in 1981, and he has been a member for over 25 years. He is a certified financial planner and he lives in downtown Toronto, a 15-minute walk from Rogers Centre. When he isn't watching a game or doing research, he enjoys travel, movies, and taking in all of Toronto's cultural activities with his friends.

Bill Nowlin, a Boston native, has been fortunate to be able to visit more than 100 countries – and Canada was the first. His father took him to Montreal for his first airplane ride at about age 12. Decades later, he returned to watch the Expos host the Red Sox. As one of the founders of Rounder Records, he helped encourage Mark Wilson to produce more than 25 albums of Cape Breton fiddle music; Rounder later released several albums by the band Rush, thanks to aficionado John Virant (and SABR member Donna Halper, a former deejay who launched the band's US career). Bill has been on SABR's board of directors since 2004 and has helped edit somewhere around 50 SABR books.

Carl Riechers retired from United Parcel Service in 2012 after 35 years of service. With more free time, he became a SABR member that same year. Born and raised in the suburbs of St. Louis, he became a big fan of the Cardinals. He and his wife, Janet, have three children and he is the proud grandpa of two.

Joel Rippel, a Minnesota native and graduate of the University of Minnesota, is the author or coauthor of 11 books on Minnesota sports history and has contributed as a writer to several books published by SABR.

Harry Schoger is a Hoosier transplanted to the Canton, Ohio, region of the Buckeye Nation. He graduated from Indiana University with a BA in economics and history, little of which he used during a 33-year career in information technology management. While retired, he put his passion for history in gear by writing and lecturing on the Lewis and Clark Expedition and the US Civil War. He joined SABR to sustain his longtime love of baseball history, particularly of the span from 1900 to 1970. He has written several pieces for SABR over the past five years.

Paul Sinclair retired after a 38-year career as an investment professional for a leading Canadian life insurance company. A graduate of the University of Toronto, he is a lifelong Toronto resident, baseball player, and fan. As a player he tried out for both the Montreal Expos and Toronto Blue Jays. Highlights of his lifelong fandom include watching spring training with the Detroit Tigers in the mid-'70s, enduring the snow and cold of the first Blue Jays game ever, and throwing out the first pitch at a Blue Jays game in August 2015.

Steve Sisto is a lifelong New York Mets fan who has written several SABR biographies for Mets players of the late 1990s and early 2000s that he grew up watching. In addition to his work with BioProject, he is also co-chair of the Origins Research Committee. He and his father are nearly halfway complete in their goal to see a game in every major-league ballpark. A native of Brooklyn, New York, Steve currently lives in Framingham, Massachusetts, with his fiancée, Caroline, and their dog, Monty.

Tim Sitar is a social studies assessment developer living in Fairfax, Virginia. In past years, he covered prep and local sports for two daily newspapers and contributed to several prep and soccer sites. His baseball interests include the Pacific Coast League and researching the history of semipro and minor-league baseball in his native Monterey County, California. Tim and his wife, Katie, have two sons, Rhett and Arlo.

David E. Skelton developed a passion for baseball early on when the lights from Philadelphia's Connie

WE ARE, WE CAN, WE WILL

Mack Stadium shone through his bedroom window. Long removed from Philly, he now resides with his family in central Texas but remains passionate about the sport that evokes many of his earliest childhood memories. Employed for over 30 years in the oil and gas industry, he became a SABR member in early 2012 after a chance – and most fortunate – holiday encounter with a Rogers Hornsby Chapter member. He has written dozens of biographies for BioProject.

Doug Skipper has contributed to a number of SABR publications, presented research at national and regional conventions, and written more than a dozen player, manager, and game profiles for SABR's BioProject. A SABR member since 1982, he served as president of the Halsey Hall (Minneapolis-St. Paul) Chapter in 2014-2015, is a member of the Deadball Era Committee and chairs the Lawrence Ritter Award Committee. He is interested in the history of Connie Mack's Philadelphia Athletics, the Boston Red Sox, the Minnesota Twins, and old ballparks. A market research consultant residing in Apple Valley, Minnesota, Doug is also a veteran of father-daughter dancing. Doug and his wife, Kathy, have two daughters, MacKenzie and Shannon.

Curt Smith has followed the Blue Jays since their birth by radio across Lake Ontario from his native New York. His 18 books include *Voices of the Game,* described in 2021 by *Esquire* magazine as among "the 100 Best Baseball Books Ever Written," and the current *Memories from the Microphone.* He is a former speechwriter for President George H.W. Bush, past host or keynote at the Cooperstown Symposium on Baseball and American Culture, the Great Fenway Writers Series, and Smithsonian Institution, and senior lecturer of English at the University of Rochester.

A full-fledged Canadaphile, **Mark S. Sternman** attended his first baseball game in Toronto on Canada Day 2016 and saw a spectacular 19-inning marathon that he later recapped for the SABR Games Project. His ideal vacation day includes a walk around Toronto listening to his favorite CBC podcasts (*The House* and *Power and Politics*), a visit to the High Park Zoo to hang with his favorite capybaras (Bonnie and Clyde), and pit stops at his favorite eateries (Steam Whistle Biergarten and Seven Lives Tacos y Mariscos).

Allen Tait has been a SABR member since 1976. A retired fraud investigator, he is chapter leader for the Hanlan's Point (Toronto) chapter and a member of numerous SABR Research Committees.

Dr. Joseph Thompson (B.A., M.A., PhD, University of Houston) is a professor of international business and American history at the University of Houston. He is currently the Houston SABR chapter president and its social media director. He has co-authored several books including *Mexican American Baseball in Houston and Southeast Texas* and *Houston Baseball, The Early Years.* He has also contributed several articles to different SABR publications including *Time for Expansion Baseball* and *Dome Sweet Dome.* He is a US Air Force Desert Storm veteran. He currently spends what little off time he has with his family, reading, playing with his two dogs, and playing catch with his grandson.

Stew Thornley has been a SABR member since 1979. He has long been active in the Halsey Hall Chapter (Minneapolis-St. Paul) and is a past vice president of SABR. Since 2007 he has been an official scorer for Major League Baseball and is a member of the Official Scoring Advisory Committee.

Alfonso Tusa is a writer who was born in Cumaná, Venezuela. At the moment he keeps writing about baseball, sports, gastronomy, nostalgia, and movies from Los Teques, Venezuela. Author of *Una Temporada Mágica* (A Magical Season), *El Látigo del Beisbol: Una Biografía de Isaías Látigo Chávez* (The Whip of Baseball: A Biography of Isaías Látigo Chávez), *Pensando en ti Venezuela: Una Biografía de Dámaso Blanco* (Thinking About You Venezuela: A Damaso Blanco Biography), *Voces de Beisbol y Ecología* (Voices of Baseball and Ecology), *Un Barco en Santa Inés* (A Vessel at Santa Inés), and *Una Docena de Cuentos de Beisbol* (A Dozen Baseball Stories). He has contributed to websites, books, and newspapers. He tries to share as many moments as he can with his teenage boy, Miguel.

Eric Vickrey is a physician assistant who works in emergency medicine. A native of Illinois and lifelong fan of the St. Louis Cardinals, he now calls the Pacific Northwest home. He and his wife, Gina, have adopted the Mariners along with a dog and two cats. He has authored more than two dozen SABR bios.

The late **David Vincent** had a remarkably varied career in baseball. He was a SABR Board member, an official scorer for minor- and major-league teams and a founding board member of Retrosheet, for which he served as secretary for 20 years. He was closely associated with major-league umpires and compiled many reports for the men in blue.

Joseph Wancho resides in Brooklyn Ohio. As a member of SABR, he has contributed to 35 of the organization's publications.

Bob Webster grew up in northwestern Indiana and has been a Cubs fan since 1963. After relocating to Portland, Oregon, in 1980, Bob spends his time working on baseball research and writing and is a contributor to quite a few SABR projects. He worked as a stats stringer on the MLB Gameday app for three years and is a member of the Pacific Northwest Chapter of SABR and is on the board of directors of the Old-Timers Baseball Association of Portland.

SABR Books on the Negro Leagues and Black Baseball

From Rube to Robinson: SABR's Best Articles on Black Baseball

From Rube to Robinson brings together the best Negro League baseball scholarship that the Society of American Baseball Research (SABR) has ever produced, culled from its journals, Biography Project, and award-winning essays. The book includes a star-studded list of scholars and historians, from the late Jerry Malloy and Jules Tygiel, to award winners Larry Lester, Geri Strecker, and Jeremy Beer, and a host of other talented writers. The essays cover topics ranging over nearly a century, from 1866 and the earliest known Black baseball championship, to 1962 and the end of the Negro American League.

Edited by John Graf; Associate Editors Duke Goldman and Larry Lester
$24.95 paperback (ISBN 978-1-970159-41-7)
$9.99 ebook (ISBN 978-1-970159-40-0)
8.5"X11", 220 pages

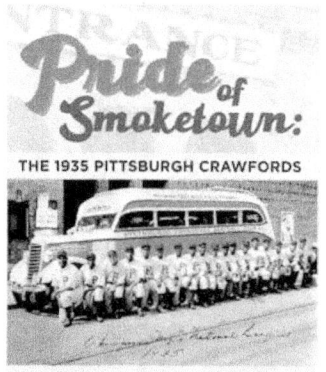

Pride of Smoketown: The 1935 Pittsburgh Crawfords

The 1935 Pittsburgh Crawfords team, one of the dominant teams in Negro League history, is often compared to the legendary 1927 "Murderer's Row" New York Yankees. The squad from "Smoketown"—a nickname that the *Pittsburgh Courier* often applied to the metropolis better-known as "Steel City"—boasted four Hall-of-Fame players in outfielder James "Cool Papa" Bell, first baseman/manager Oscar Charleston, catcher Josh Gibson, and third baseman William "Judy" Johnson. This volume contains exhaustively-researched articles about the players, front office personnel, Greenlee Field, and the exciting games and history of the team that were written and edited by 25 SABR members. The inclusion of historical photos about every subject in the book helps to shine a spotlight on the 1935 Pittsburgh Crawfords, who truly were the Pride of Smoketown.

Edited by Frederick C. Bush and Bill Nowlin
$29.95 paperback (ISBN 978-1-970159-25-7)
$9.99 ebook (ISBN 978-1-970159-24-0)
8.5"X11", 340 pages, over 60 photos

The Newark Eagles Take Flight: The Story of the 1946 Negro League Champions

The Newark Eagles won only one Negro National League pennant during the franchise's 15-year tenure in the Garden State, but the 1946 squad that ran away with the NNL and then triumphed over the Kansas City Monarchs in a seven-game World Series was a team for the ages. The returning WWII veterans composed a veritable "Who's Who in the Negro Leagues" and included Leon Day, Larry Doby, Monte Irvin, and Max Manning, as well as numerous role players. Four of the Eagles' stars—Day, Doby, Irvin, and player/manager Raleigh "Biz" Mackey, as well as co-owner Effa Manley—have been enshrined in the National Baseball Hall of Fame in Cooperstown. In addition to biographies of the players, co-owners, and P.A. announcer, there are also articles about Newark's Ruppert Stadium, Leon Day's Opening Day no-hitter, a sensational midseason game, the season's two East-West All-Star Games, and the 1946 Negro League World Series between the Eagles and the renowned Kansas City Monarchs.

Edited by Frederick C. Bush and Bill Nowlin
$24.95 paperback (ISBN 978-1-970159-07-3)
$9.99 ebook (ISBN 978-1-970159-06-6)
8.5"X11", 228 pages, over 60 photos

Bittersweet Goodbye: The Black Barons, The Grays, and the 1948 Negro League World Series

This book was inspired by the last Negro League World Series ever played and presents biographies of the players on the two contending teams in 1948—the Birmingham Black Barons and the Homestead Grays—as well as the managers, the owners, and articles on the ballparks the teams called home. Also included are articles that recap the season's two East-West All-Star Games, the Negro National League and Negro American League playoff series, and the World Series itself. Additional context is provided in essays about the effects of baseball's integration on the Negro Leagues, the exodus of Negro League players to Canada, and the signing away of top Negro League players, specifically Willie Mays. Many of the players' lives and careers have been presented to a much greater extent than previously possible.

Edited by Frederick C. Bush and Bill Nowlin
$21.95 paperback (ISBN 978-1-943816-55-2)
$9.99 ebook (ISBN 978-1-943816-54-5)
8.5"X11", 442 pages, over 100 photos and images

Friends of SABR

You can become a Friend of SABR by giving as little as $10 per month or by making a one-time gift of $1,000 or more. When you do so, you will be inducted into a community of passionate baseball fans dedicated to supporting SABR's work.

Friends of SABR receive the following benefits:
- ✓ Annual Friends of SABR Commemorative Lapel Pin
- ✓ Recognition in This Week in SABR, SABR.org, and the SABR Annual Report
- ✓ Access to the SABR Annual Convention VIP donor event
- ✓ Invitations to exclusive Friends of SABR events

SABR On-Deck Circle - $10/month, $30/month, $50/month
Get in the SABR On-Deck Circle, and help SABR become the essential community for the world of baseball. Your support will build capacity around all things SABR, including publications, website content, podcast development, and community growth.

A monthly gift is deducted from your bank account or charged to a credit card until you tell us to stop. No more email, mail, or phone reminders.

  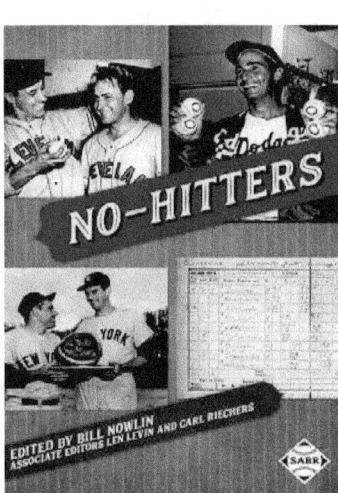

Join the SABR On-Deck Circle

Payment Info: _____Visa _____Mastercard

Name on Card: _____

Card #: _____

Exp. Date: _____ Security Code: _____

Signature: _____

- ○ $10/month
- ○ $30/month
- ○ $50/month
- ○ Other amount _____

Go to sabr.org/donate to make your gift online

Society for American Baseball Research

Cronkite School at ASU
555 N. Central Ave. #416, Phoenix, AZ 85004
602.496.1460 (phone)
SABR.org

Become a SABR member today!

If you're interested in baseball — writing about it, reading about it, talking about it — there's a place for you in the Society for American Baseball Research.

SABR memberships are available on annual, multi-year, or monthly subscription basis. Annual and monthly subscription memberships auto-renew for your convenience. Young Professional memberships are for ages 30 and under. Senior memberships are for ages 65 and older. Student memberships are available to currently enrolled middle/high school or full-time college/university students. Monthly subscription members receive SABR publications electronically and are eligible for SABR event discounts after 12 months.

Here's a list of some of the key benefits you'll receive as a SABR member:

* Receive two editions (spring and fall) of the *Baseball Research Journal*, our flagship publication
* Receive expanded e-book edition of *The National Pastime*, our annual convention journal
* 8-10 new e-books published by the SABR Digital Library, all FREE to members
* "This Week in SABR" e-newsletter, sent to members every Friday
* Join dozens of research committees, from Statistical Analysis to Women in Baseball.
* Join one of 70+ regional chapters in the U.S., Canada, Latin America, and abroad
* Participate in online discussion groups
* Ask and answer baseball research questions on the SABR-L e-mail listserv
* Complete archives of *The Sporting News* dating back to 1886 and other research resources
* Promote your research in "This Week in SABR"
* Diamond Dollars Case Competition
* Yoseloff Scholarships

* Discounts on SABR national conferences, including the SABR National Convention, the SABR Analytics Conference, Jerry Malloy Negro League Conference, Frederick Ivor-Campbell 19th Century Conference, and the Arizona Fall League Experience
* Publish your research in peer-reviewed SABR journals
* Collaborate with SABR researchers and experts
* Contribute to Baseball Biography Project or the SABR Games Project
* List your new book in the SABR Bookshelf
* Lead a SABR research committee or chapter
* Networking opportunities at SABR Analytics Conference
* Meet baseball authors and historians at SABR events and chapter meetings
* 50% discounts on paperback versions of SABR e-books
* Discounts with other partners in the baseball community
* SABR research awards

We hope you'll join the most passionate international community of baseball fans at SABR! Check us out online at SABR.org/join.

✂

SABR MEMBERSHIP FORM

	Standard	Senior	Young Pro.	Student
Annual:	❏ $65	❏ $45	❏ $45	❏ $25
3 Year:	❏ $175	❏ $129	❏ $129	
5 Year:	❏ $249			
Monthly:	❏ $6.95	❏ $4.95	❏ $4.95	

(International members wishing to be mailed the Baseball Research Journal should add $10/yr for Canada/Mexico or $19/yr for overseas locations.)

Participate in Our Donor Program!

Support the preservation of baseball research. Designate your gift toward:
❏ General Fund   ❏ Endowment Fund   ❏ Research Resources   ❏_____
❏ I want to maximize the impact of my gift; do not send any donor premiums
❏ I would like this gift to remain anonymous.

Note: Any donation not designated will be placed in the General Fund.
SABR is a 501 (c) (3) not-for-profit organization & donations are tax-deductible to the extent allowed by law.

Name _____

E-mail* _____

Address _____

City _____ ST_____ ZIP_____

Phone _____ Birthday _____

* Your e-mail address on file ensures you will receive the most recent SABR news.

Dues $_____

Donation $_____

Amount Enclosed $_____

Do you work for a matching grant corporation? Call (602) 496-1460 for details.

If you wish to pay by credit card, please contact the SABR office at (602) 496-1460 or sign up securely online at SABR.org/join. We accept Visa, Mastercard & Discover.

Do you wish to receive the *Baseball Research Journal* electronically? ❏ Yes   ❏ No
Our e-books are available in PDF, Kindle, or EPUB (iBooks, iPad, Nook) formats.

Mail to: SABR, Cronkite School at ASU, 555 N. Central Ave. #416, Phoenix, AZ 85004

10/19